D0866209

Harvard Historical Studies, 119

Published under the auspices
of the Department of History
from the income of the
Paul Revere Frothingham Bequest
Robert Louis Stroock Fund
Henry Warren Torrey Fund

The Peace Progressives and American Foreign Relations

ROBERT DAVID JOHNSON

HARVARD UNIVERSITY PRESS

Cambridge, Massachusetts
London, England
1995

This book is printed on acid-free paper, and its binding materials
have been chosen for strength and durability.

Library of Congress Cataloging-in-Publication Data
Johnson, Robert David, 1967–
    The peace progressives and American foreign relations / Robert David Johnson.
      p. cm. — (Harvard historical studies; v. 119)
    Includes bibliographical references and index.
    ISBN 0-674-65917-1
    1. United States—Foreign relations—1913–1921. 2. United States—Foreign
relations—1921–1923. 3. United States—Foreign relations—1923–1929. 4. United
States—Foreign relations—1929–1933. 5. Progressivism (United States
politics). 6. United States—Politics and government—1901–1953.
I. Title. II. Series.
E744.J658 1995
327.73—dc20   94-25609
               CIP

Acknowledgments

Throughout the writing of this work, Akira Iriye has served as my personal and intellectual mentor, providing me with guidance and assistance whenever they were needed. Ernest May took the time to read several drafts and forced me to explore questions that I would otherwise have avoided. This book never would have been written without the aid of Thomas Schwartz, who introduced me to the field of U.S. foreign relations. In its later stages the manuscript benefited greatly from the perceptive comments of Alan Brinkley and John Milton Cooper, Jr. I am very grateful to George Eliades and Drew Erdmann, both of whom read several drafts and never seemed to tire of speaking about the peace progressives. At Harvard University Press, Elizabeth Suttell's patience and helpfulness eased my task in completing the book, and Ann Hawthorne's editing substantially improved the final result. Finally, for helping in other ways during this project, I thank Jean B. Emerson, Ralph Worden, Ann Hunter, Diane M. Stevenson, H. G. Brady, Rob Silver, Lee Cheng, Je Lee, and especially John Morris.

Generous financial assistance from the Charles Warren Center at Harvard University, the Harvard University History Department, and the Minnesota State Historical Society helped fund my research. A grant from the John Kittredge (Anson) Fund helped free my time to work on the book.

This book is dedicated to my father, J. Robert Johnson, who encouraged me to study history; my mother, Susan McNamara Johnson, who stimulated my interest in dissent; and my sister, Kathleen, who bolstered my morale throughout this project.

Contents

Illustrations

Introduction

On July 6, 1911, Senator Asle Gronna (R–North Dakota) rose to speak against President William Howard Taft's proposed treaty for tariff reciprocity with Canada. Son of Norwegian immigrants, the man dismissed by one conservative North Dakotan as "that prune peddler from Nelson County" had arrived in the Senate in 1910, with a reputation as a quiet progressive. Described by his later opponent Henry Cabot Lodge (R–Massachusetts) as "simply dull," Gronna was at his least exciting when making long Senate speeches such as the one he made against the reciprocity treaty. Viewing it as his duty to inform the Senate on the plight of the average North Dakota farmer, he droned on endlessly; this speech touched mostly on the dangers that lower agricultural tariffs for Canadian goods posed to American farmers. Gronna also feared that reciprocity would act as a "cloak to hide the adoption of a new economic and industrial policy" that would rob agriculture of its dignity and expose the United States to the dangers of industrialization. Finally, he launched a savage attack against Taft, charging that "if this invasion of the prerogatives of the Senate is countenanced . . . some President whose penchant will be the extension of territorial dominion instead of the surrendering of the farmers' markets" would make use of it to mischievous ends. Despite the rhetoric, neither Gronna nor any of the other opponents of the treaty succeeded in blocking its Senate approval.[1]

Nearly eighteen years later, on February 22, 1929, an "obviously startled" Naval Committee chair Frederick Hale (R–Maine) informed the Senate that its passage of a rider amendment authored by C. C. Dill (D–Washington) to cut off funding for the occupation of Nicaragua by the American Marines had endangered the 1929 Navy bill. The Washington senator, an ideological descendant of Gronna but an adherent to a much broader foreign policy vision, had justified his move by noting that with the completion of the American-sponsored 1928 presidential election, no possible rationale any longer existed for keeping the Marines in the country. According to Dill, the only American lives remaining in danger were those of "the American Marines themselves who were sent there." Conservatives struggled to refute Dill's reasoning; Hiram Bingham (R–Connecticut) said that the occupation should continue because the Nicaraguan government needed the Marines to stay in power, while William Cabell Bruce (D–Maryland), somewhat confusedly, wondered what kind of logic would call for the Marines to withdraw, seeing that they had accomplished their mission. Administration forces regrouped, however; opposition senators such as South Carolina's Cole Blease and Ellison Smith were persuaded to change their votes after the Navy threatened to cancel a $350,000 appropriation for improving Charleston harbor, and enough conservatives absent for the Friday vote appeared for an unusual Saturday session. The Senate as a whole then reversed itself and rejected the Dill Amendment by a tally of 48–32, but, as the New York *World* commented, "the moral effect of the original gesture" remained, although the final Marine would not depart until 1932. The initial Dill Amendment vote marked the first occasion in American history on which a branch of Congress had cut off funding for an overseas military conflict still in progress.[2]

The vote on the Dill Amendment capped off a brilliant two-year run by a group of dissenting senators, the peace progressives, that had solidified their position as the leading spokesmen of 1920s foreign policy liberalism in the United States. In 1927 the threat of a peace progressive filibuster had led the Coolidge administration to slash its desired naval budget; at the same time, under the leadership of William Borah (R–Idaho) and working in tandem with the organized peace movement, the dissenters had pushed through the Senate a resolution demanding that the administration arbitrate its differences with Mexico. The next year featured the initial fight against the Nicaraguan occupation as well as the negotiations for the Kellogg-Briand Pact to outlaw war, the best example of the moralist foreign policy that the dissenters had championed throughout the decade. Finally, in early 1929, in addition to the Dill Amendment success, the peace progressives again had cooperated with peace activists in a furious campaign against the Coolidge administration's bill to authorize the construction of fifteen cruisers for the Navy, filling the Senate chamber with some of the most powerful antimilitarist rhetoric in this century. These battles cemented the alliance between the peace progressives and the public foreign policy left.

This study is the first to examine the foreign policy perspectives of the peace progressives during the 1920s. Although the term has appeared occasionally in the historiography of congressional dissent, it generally has referred to a faction of Midwestern progressives whose domestic agenda led it to make keeping the United States at peace its chief foreign policy priority.[3] I employ the term much more broadly, arguing that the peace progressives hoped to achieve a more peaceful world order through an active American foreign policy along reformist lines. Their instrument for this reform was a well-developed anti-imperialism that in the 1920s expanded considerably beyond their domestic program. In this sense, peace progressivism became fundamentally a foreign policy vision that usually led the senators to oppose political commitments involving the Western European states. Such arrangements, however, were not central to their agenda. Rather, they wanted the United States to employ a variety of economic, moral, and diplomatic tactics on behalf of weaker states and peoples to help create what they hoped would be a more stable and peaceful international order. This work traces the evolution of this dissenting outlook through three eras: from the early 1910s until the League of Nations fight, when the peace progressives were still only groping toward a unified ideology; from mid-1919 through the early years of the Great Depression, when they united behind the anti-imperialism that they first had articulated during the League of Nations debate; and from 1931 through 1935, when a combination of economic, political, and international factors led the group to shed its anti-imperialism and adopt the foreign policy positions detailed by Wayne Cole in his works on the subject.[4]

During their period of greatest influence—1919 through 1930[5]—the peace progressives acted as a well-organized congressional bloc articulating a consistent anti-imperialist vision, which they applied to all areas of the world. (They viewed the tariff and immigration as domestic concerns solely.) The peace progressives advocated this anti-imperialism not simply for moral reasons,[6] but for strategic and economic reasons as well. In short, they developed a quite consistent foreign policy critique.

Daniel Patrick Moynihan has observed that "the neglect of congressional history is something of a scandal of American scholarship."[7] After all, the Constitution grants the U.S. Congress a potentially huge amount of power over foreign policy, and although the executive quite quickly came to dominate the nation's international affairs, the 1920s is one period of American international history in which the Congress, particularly the Senate,[8] played a significant role in diplomatic events. Obviously any analysis of the inter-American policy pursued by Frank Kellogg cannot begin without an intensive examination of the Senate; as David Pletcher has observed, "no generalizations on American opinion of Caribbean policy are completely valid unless they take anti-imperialist views into consideration fully, not just in passing."[9] In addition, although writers such as Michael Hogan and Melvyn Leffler have offered a penetrating view of the European policies pursued by the decade's leaders,[10] the peace progressives offered an alternative to corporatism that combined anti-imperialism, economic diplomacy, and antimilitarism to produce a dissenting position that in its consistency and originality, if not its practicality, rivaled that put forth by the business internationalists. Any study of thought on the American role in post–World War I Europe therefore needs to take the peace progressive perspective into account.

The peace progressives also deserve a prominent place in the study of American liberal thought on the non-European world. Although recent studies have cited Woodrow Wilson as the first American political figure to grapple with this issue,[11] in fact Wilson and the peace progressives approached it simultaneously. True, they developed quite different approaches concerning the American role toward weaker states. Wilson believed that the United States needed to guide formerly colonial peoples toward democracy, to "teach them to elect good men"; a key innovation in this regard was the mandate system, which he viewed as a compromise between colonialism and independence. The peace progressives rejected this approach, preferring instead to see the United States side with nationalist elements in the underdeveloped world; they argued that a world of nationalistic, autonomous states would produce a peaceful world order, in both strategic and economic terms. They disagreed with Wilson that an American-style democracy necessarily represented the proper form of government for the nations of Latin America or East Asia, contending that the United States should demand only a regime that served the interests of the common people. Like more mainstream figures both then and later, the peace progressives devoted considerable attention to issues such as the role played by American foreign investments in underdeveloped countries, whether the United States should intervene in the internal affairs of other nations to aid reformist forces, and how the United States should protect the internationally recognized rights of American citizens in foreign countries while avoiding military intervention in weaker states. As a result of divisions within the Democratic party during the 1920s, the peace progressives became the first left-wing American political group to give sustained attention to many of these questions, and their responses to these problems illustrated both the range and limitations of American liberal thought on the underdeveloped world. This split in American liberalism about how the United States should treat weaker states recurred often in the next half-century, most notably in the 1940s when the Roosevelt administration debated how literally to apply the principles of the Atlantic Charter, in the 1950s when the Democrats struggled for alternatives to Dwight Eisenhower's Middle Eastern and East Asian policies, and in the 1960s when a liberal rift occurred first over whether to oppose and then over how strongly to oppose the Vietnam War. As the first manifestation of this dual liberal mindset, the battle between the Wilsonians and the peace progressives needs more attention than it has received, and it deserves recognition as a two-sided debate, not merely as the story of congressional radicals reacting to Wilsonian initiatives.

By treating the peace progressive ideology of the 1920s as distinct, this book proposes a reevaluation of the role of the peace progressives in the history of American thought about foreign relations. From the Revolutionary era on, politicians of various persuasions, including Benjamin Franklin, Tom Paine, Thomas Jefferson, the Anti-Federalists, William Jennings Bryan, Albert Gallatin, Daniel Webster, and a host of congressional dissenters, had searched for alternative conceptions of power that would allow the United States to achieve the foreign policy goals that they desired without transforming the nation into a militarized state that practiced the traditional power politics of eighteenth- and nineteenth-century Europe. In this quest, certain themes—a concentration on commercial or ideological definitions of power, antimilitarism, a suspicion of the formal diplomatic practices of the time, and an anti-imperialist sentiment—consistently reappeared. These themes formed part of the framework of the peace progressive dissent as well, but the senators employed the themes differently from any major group that preceded them. By placing a far greater stress on anti-imperialism than any of their intellectual predecessors, the peace progressives, especially in the 1920s, articulated a foreign policy ideology that was striking at the very least for its originality. The framework of the peace progressive dissent remained relevant for later dissenters even though the 1930s discredited many of the senators' specific ideas. It is no coincidence that a figure such as Ernest Gruening, who as a senator from Alaska in 1964 cast one of the two votes against the Tonkin Gulf Resolution, matured as a dissenter during the 1920s as an intellectual ally of the peace progressives. Gruening in particular forms a bridge between the dissenting movements of the 1920s and 1960s, but as the Vietnam War progressed other senators opposed to that conflict also returned to ideas resembling those of the peace progressives.[12]

Finally, this work also addresses a larger question inherent in the study of peace history itself. Lawrence Wittner's 1987 essay on the subject properly celebrates the attention that peace history has received since 1965,[13] enlarging our understanding of how the United States peace movement thought about international affairs. Yet this surge of interest in peace history too often has been confined largely to studies of peace movements and internationalists themselves, and has not extended to the role played by congressional peace activists.[14] Events of the 1920s demonstrate the danger of this approach. Not only did much of the decade's peace ideology originate with the peace progressives, but the intellectual exchange between the peace movement and the peace progressives made the program of the decade's peace movement far more potent politically. The next logical step is to branch out into more intensive studies of the political wing of the movement, as Charles DeBenedetti has done in his recent work on the antiwar movement of the 1960s.[15]

Unlike the case of many groups in Congress, some of the foreign policy positions of the senators who formed the peace progressive bloc have received scholarly attention. Historians have focused primarily on two schools of inquiry. The first has attempted to explain what "motivated" the senators (almost always referred to as isolationists) to adopt the foreign policy positions that they did. Historians led by Ray Allen Billington have advanced variations on a thesis suggesting that a combination of regional and ethnic factors, particularly the insularity of the Upper Midwest and the large number of German-Americans and Scandinavian-Americans present in the states represented by most of the isolationists, accounted for their opposition to many of the internationalist policies before 1940.[16] In a careful study, Robert Wilkins has disputed the thesis, using North Dakota as an example of how "nonethnic" factors such as beliefs rising from the senators' domestic policy views accounted for their foreign policy positions; while others, such as William Carleton, have offered partisanship as a possible explanation for the group's behavior.[17] Historians who have attempted wider studies of the isolationist movement also have addressed this issue; Selig Adler explicitly terms the 1920s dissenting movement pro-German, while Wayne Cole has argued that agrarianism, not ethnicity, bound the group together.[18]

The following chapters do not concentrate on this question, largely because I think that it addresses the wrong issue. Obviously, political elements peculiar to their states allowed the peace progressives to be elected to the Senate in the first place, and the foreign policy views of the senators were not divorced from their sectional, ethnic, or domestic environment. But asking what "motivated" the Senate dissenters implies that somehow factors not concerned with international relations—the ethnic compositions of their constituencies, their domestic ideology, regionalism—predetermined their foreign policy positions. Quite simply, this was not the case; the peace progressives thought far more deeply about foreign policy issues than did any other group in Congress during the 1920s. As Adler points out, the peace progressives often adopted pro-German foreign policy positions, but during the 1920s these views fitted into their global program for reforming international affairs; certainly their pro-Nicaraguan, pro-Chinese, or pro-Egyptian positions, which sprang from similar ideological beliefs, cannot be described as ethnically or politically motivated. Also, the ethnicity/regionalism arguments fail to explain why the Middle West in that period produced senators with a wide array of foreign policy perspectives apart from those of the peace progressives, such as the nationalism of Medill McCormick in Illinois, the Republican-oriented internationalism of Irvine Lenroot in Wisconsin, and the Democratic conservatism of Dan Steck in Iowa. Nor do the regional arguments explain the similarity in positions between the peace progressives and the decade's peace movement, very few members of which came from the states represented by the peace progressives. Finally, although the domestic positions of the peace progressives may have shaped their foreign policy outlook in the 1910s, in the 1920s, as LeRoy Ashby has established, their domestic consensus collapsed, a victim of ideological disunity over how much power to confer on the national government.[19] By the 1920s, foreign policy formed the bond that joined the movement together, and the foreign policy positions taken by the senators stood on their own, not merely existing as an outgrowth of the group's domestic agenda.

The second line of inquiry has centered on identifying the beliefs held by these dissenters. William Appleman Williams portrayed them flatteringly in his *Tragedy of American Diplomacy;* Barton Bernstein and Franklin Leib picked up this theme in a 1967 article on progressivism and foreign policy. Both of these works and similar accounts have focused on peace progressive opinions on the underdeveloped world, suggesting that the peace progressives selflessly desired the United States to play a moral role in the world.[20] Not surprisingly, this glorification of the peace progressive and isolationist position produced a counterreaction. The opponents built upon the work of Selig Adler, who in a virtual polemic against the dissenters portrayed them as nineteenth-century nationalists unable to adjust to the modern world, and John Chalmers Vinson, who in three carefully researched monographs argued that isolationism motivated Senate opponents of the League of Nations and Washington Treaties. The counterreaction culminated in Robert James Maddox's *William E. Borah and American Foreign Policy,* which contended that despite apparent shifts in their foreign policy recommendations the dissenting senators maintained an isolationist perspective throughout their Senate careers. Maddox explained any changes of opinion by hypothesizing that Borah, Dill, and their colleagues advanced positive solutions that they knew mainstream figures would not adopt, solely to avoid being portrayed as obstructionists.[21]

These competing arguments vastly oversimplify the peace progressive foreign policy ideology. Both examine peace progressive attitudes toward selected areas of the world, Latin America and Africa for the Williams group, Europe for the followers of Maddox. Both groups thus ignore the fact that the dissenters had a world vision, not opinions on various regions that existed in isolation from each other. Moreover, the Williams group observes the peace progressives largely in economic terms, while Maddox and his followers adopt a power-oriented approach that concentrates on peace progressive opinions on issues such as treaties, diplomatic recognition issues, and American ties to European political organizations.[22] Both schools thus fail to acknowledge that the peace progressives engaged in primarily a cultural and ideological critique of American foreign relations.

The peace progressive John Blaine (R–Wisconsin) elucidated the essence of this critique in a particularly stirring fashion during a two-day Senate speech in February 1928. Terming the U.S. occupation of Nicaragua a "compromise with evil," Blaine contended that a foreign policy that relied on military force failed to serve American strategic, economic, or moral interests. He argued that the country's "tremendous influence and power for world peace demand strict adherence to the doctrine of inherent fairness and justice." Therefore, the United States could tolerate "no encroachment upon the rights of small nations and the equality of nations guaranteed by the conscience of international morality and rectitude" without weakening its own stance internationally. The Wisconsin senator justified this ideologically oriented definition of power by appealing to American traditions. Blaine, like the peace progressive movement as a whole, believed that "the destiny of America" in world affairs "was to be one of peace, one of justice, one of equity," based upon the sentiment "that the strong, whether an individual or a nation, has no right to beat down the weak."[23] The peace progressive attempt to implement this anti-imperialist vision formed the dominant theme of the senators' response to international affairs in the twenty years after the start of World War I.

1

Patterns of Dissent

In their foreign policy dissent, the peace progressives contributed to a long tradition of American thought about alternatives to the established patterns of international relations. By the 1920s, several sets of ideas about foreign affairs had become embedded in the American political consciousness. Although no strict chronological or intellectual evolution in these ideas occurred—each generation and in many cases different factions within each generation applied the heritage differently—common themes did emerge in two general areas that the peace progressives would explore as well. As early as the Revolution, the American colonists expressed a sense of discomfort with traditional international power politics and began to conceptualize alternative means that would permit the new nation to achieve its foreign policy aims without becoming a militarized state. With the Declaration of Independence and rhetorical suggestions that the United States could serve as a model to oppressed peoples everywhere, the founding generation also bequeathed a legacy of anti-imperialism to which later American reformers would return. The dissent of the peace progressives cannot be understood apart from this intellectual background.

To a certain extent, the American decision to break from England in the first place reflected a different view of foreign affairs from that common in Europe at the time. In *Common Sense*, published in 1776, Tom Paine articulated a vision of commercial internationalism as the proper foreign policy for the colonists to pursue. Paine contended that an independent America could achieve a commercially oriented foreign policy more easily, in part because of its geographic isolation from the centers of world power and in part because of the desirability of its commerce for all the major powers of Europe. He added that "America's plan is commerce, and that, well attended to, will secure us the peace and friendship of all Europe." Throughout the Revolution, Paine's ideological successors continued his search for alternative conceptions to international relations. Although substantially different interpretations exist regarding the nature of the foreign policy ideas held by the founders, most participants in the historiographic debate agree that the diplomatic agents of the government under the Articles of Confederation had little use for the military-oriented power politics of the day. Felix Gilbert suggested that the Model Treaty of 1778, which sought to obtain military and diplomatic assistance from France in exchange for commercial concessions, represented a step in the American redefinition of alliance from power-political to commercial terms. Gilbert also contended that the revolutionaries believed that similar diplomatic arrangements would eliminate political issues from international diplomatic discourse, focus these exchanges on commercial matters, and then orient commercial relations in such a liberal fashion that no cause for international conflict could continue to exist. James Hutson has taken issue with this interpretation, pointing out that the Revolutionary leaders were comfortable working within the existing parameters of the international situation. He has instead contended that the colonists sought to maximize the American advantage within that system by employing different means of power. This pattern began in the colonial era with the writings of Benjamin Franklin, who opined that the commercial benefits that the colonies offered to the British Empire made them far more valuable to London than any traditional military measure of power would suggest. Hutson has suggested that the Model Treaty constituted an attempt by the revolutionaries to use the balance of power system for their own advantage, and that the founders desired a modest military establishment to deter a foreign attack. Reginald Stuart has added a slightly different interpretation to this argument with his observation of the attraction of limited war theory among the Revolutionary generation. Despite the differences among Gilbert, Hutson, and Stuart, all contend that the founders did not see the United States functioning as simply another power within the established confines of the European-oriented system of power politics.[1]

An innovative attempt to find an alternative to traditional power politics came after the election of Thomas Jefferson in 1800. Jefferson made his boldest attempt to articulate a different definition of American power in 1807, when he called for an embargo on all U.S. trade with Europe to protest the anticommercial policies of the warring British and French empires. He had raised this idea as early as 1801 in a letter to the Quaker senator George Logan: the United States could use "the means of peaceable coercion" to ensure freedom of the seas, since American commerce was "so valuable" to the nations of Europe "that they will be glad to purchase it when the only price we ask is to do us justice." Efforts to use American commerce as a foreign policy tool began as early as the 1770s, when the colonies had experimented with the nonimportation acts, and a similar mindset had motivated the proposals of James Madison during the 1790s to use discriminatory tariffs to obtain foreign policy concessions from England. After the Declaration of Independence, however, all these proposals had been defeated, and Jefferson's experiment fared little better; widely unpopular at home and ineffectual in securing the broader foreign policy goals expected of it, the embargo was repealed in stages beginning in 1809.[2]

In addition, as Drew McCoy has observed, Jeffersonian foreign policy, designed to inaugurate a peaceful, agrarian-oriented republic, tied the United States to a series of risky overseas maneuvers that, in its quest for empire, built upon some of the conceptions of power first articulated by Franklin in the 1750s and 1760s. The importance of foreign commerce for the prosperity of American agriculture formed one of the key reasons that Madison decided for war with England in 1812 after the embargo experiment had failed. In addition, the desire to prevent American society from becoming prematurely "old" and urbanized necessitated what Jefferson called an "empire of liberty," under which the United States would expand across the continent (and perhaps also to the north and south). This ideology led the President to accept the Louisiana Purchase of 1803, which more than doubled the land mass of the United States but also was an acquisition of dubious constitutionality that had the equally unappealing side effect of extending United States rule over Louisiana's sizable French population without its consent. In addition, this ideology produced both the aggressive Jefferson and Madison policies toward the Spanish Floridas, which Americans feared Spain could cede to a stronger power, and Jefferson's occasional statements in favor of annexation of Spanish Cuba to the United States, a policy that contradicted the President's writings dating from the Revolution on behalf of liberty. The foreign policies of Jefferson and Madison illustrated the way in which these rather vague sentiments about alternative conceptions of power dating from the Revolutionary era could produce quite different approaches to international affairs.[3]

Merrill Peterson has observed the sustained hold of the Jeffersonian image over the American political psyche, but the vagueness of many of Jefferson's statements and policies allowed advocates of radically different policies to claim him as their inspiration. In the 1840s, for example, supporters of the annexation of Texas and war with Mexico used what Thomas Hietala has called neo-Jeffersonian arguments to gain public support for their policies, which at least through 1847 the vast majority of congressional members of Jefferson's old Democratic party backed enthusiastically. And both sides in the debate over the acquisition of the Philippines in 1899 and 1900 claimed to be pursuing Jeffersonian policy. Jefferson did bequeath a less ambivalent legacy on some issues; his long-standing hostility to the Navy remained a dominant position of Democrats for virtually all of the nineteenth century, and although no later President attempted to replicate his policies of commercial coercion, the United States before 1900 did demonstrate a rather consistent skittishness about increasing its military establishment or involving itself extensively in international power politics. These Jeffersonian themes were shared by a wide array of Americans who sought to reform international relations.[4]

Other figures from the Revolutionary era applied these sentiments differently. The Anti-Federalists, who opposed adoption of the 1787 Constitution, put forward a foreign policy ideology that stressed anti-militarism and the power of American ideas. The Anti-Federalists preferred a limited role for the government in international affairs, since the well-being of society depended on domestic prosperity, not the "most brilliant martial achievements." New York's "Brutus" accused his foes of relying too much upon the European model in constructing the American national government, dangerous since the European governments were almost "all framed, and administered with a view to arms, and war." He argued that instead "we ought to furnish the world with an example of a great people, who in their civil institutions hold chiefly in view, the attainment of virtue, and happiness among ourselves." The Anti-Federalists conceded that the country might need a stronger national government if military power dominated international relations, but "fortunately" commerce could serve as the "principle to substitute in the room of power." In any case, they preferred to rely on the "spirit and special exertions" of the people to guard against foreign foes, mentioning the Swiss ability to overcome the ambitions of its neighboring monarchs without relying upon its military as a possible model. Finally, opponents of the Constitution criticized the document for allowing the government to establish one of the chief tools of traditional power politics, a standing army. "Brutus" termed an army "abhorrent to the spirit of a free republic" and stated that he could support only a defensive war, while Virginia's "Impartial Examiner" noted that standing armies, "besides being useless, as having no object of employment . . . are inconvenient and expensive." George Mason, an Anti-Federalist who attended the Constitutional Convention, devoted the most attention to this issue, proposing a number of unsuccessful amendments to limit the power of the national army and to strengthen the militia, the "real and natural strength" of the people. Norman Graebner contends that isolationism formed the central component of the Anti-Federalist conception of international affairs, but the Constitution's opponents also contributed to the debate about alternative conceptions of American power that dated from Franklin and Paine.[5]

Another outlook based largely on these Revolutionary sentiments came in what Henry Adams described as the most complete exposition of Republican foreign policy aims articulated during the 1790s.[6] Albert Gallatin, then a congressman from Pennsylvania and a leader of the Republican contingent in the House of Representatives, in 1798 commanded a Republican attempt to limit the number of U.S. ministers accredited to European capitals. A suspicion of conventional diplomatic contact with Europe had existed as early as 1783, when the future Anti-Federalist Elbridge Gerry announced his fear that sending diplomatic agents abroad could lead to the "inconveniences" of "being entangled with European politics, of being the puppets of European Statesmen, of being gradually divested of our virtuous republican principles, of being a divided, influenced and dissipated people." Gallatin built upon this theme, arguing that since the primary purpose of American foreign policy was commercial, consuls could handle most necessary overseas diplomatic actions. If the United States could "obtain from all nations such general alterations in the law of nations as would secure" the broader foreign policy goals of the country, then perhaps increasing the number of ministers would be merited, but, as things had developed since the Revolution, he doubted "whether we have derived any commercial advantage from the commercial treaties we have heretofore made." At the same time, these treaties "have been attended with political consequences fatal to our tranquillity." More generally, Gallatin called for limiting formal American diplomatic contact as a way of making a firm statement to Europe "that we wish not to mix in their political sphere of action," since "we have no interest whatever in that balance, and by us it should be altogether forgotten and rejected." Gallatin's speech reflected an increasing tendency to distance the United States from European affairs altogether; as the congressman noted, "the glimmerings of liberty, which for a moment shone in Europe," had passed, and little indication existed that they would reappear again any time soon. To this dissent Gallatin and his Jeffersonian allies added a sharp opposition to any expansion of the national military establishment, particularly the Navy, which they argued would threaten the survival of republican institutions domestically and tempt the country to pursue an overly aggressive foreign policy.[7]

These intellectual currents yielded even more radical perspectives on international affairs. During his presidency, Jefferson himself found his foreign policy under attack from a small group of congressional extremists, the Old Republicans. These dissenters used arguments prominent among both Anti-Federalists and Adams-era Republicans to criticize the foreign policies pursued by both Jefferson and Madison, ending with opposition to Madison's request for authorization of war against England in 1812. John Randolph, the Virginia congressman who served as the faction's political leader, called the war "not of defence, but of conquest, aggrandizement, and ambition," and instead supported a policy of letting trade shift for itself on the open seas. Richard Stanford, in what Randolph described as "an old fashioned & most admirable discourse," followed up on these arguments in a much more comprehensive speech a few days later. The North Carolina congressman, worrying that the "spirit of conquest and dominion" would not subside even when the war ended, added that the United States, as a peace-loving nation, could not jump into war every time it felt its honor slighted. He also asked his colleagues to remember that offensive wars, as the producers of large standing armies, "had always proved the bane of free Governments." Stanford concluded with the argument that the United States, as the only major power still at peace, would lose its moral influence by entering the war. This final point demonstrated the way in which themes common in Revolutionary and Anti-Federalist thought continued to appear. With only a handful of adherents and beset both by internal divisions and an intensely partisan approach to foreign affairs, the Old Republicans failed to persuade a majority of their Jeffersonian colleagues to repudiate the foreign policies of either Jefferson or Madison. Nonetheless, their opposition to increased military appropriations and their fight, on ideological grounds, against American participation in the War of 1812 indicated the way in which the hostility to power politics could sustain a quite radical critique of American foreign relations.[8]

Subsequent nineteenth-century dissenters returned to this antimilitarist perspective. In the 1840s congressional critics fretted about the reliance on the military in President James Polk's foreign policy. One such figure was New Hampshire's John Hale, who attracted national attention when, shortly after his arrival in the Senate, he became the only member of the body to oppose a resolution of thanks to Mexican War generals Zachary Taylor and Winfield Scott. Throughout the 1850s, Hale continued his fight as a member of the Senate Naval Affairs Committee, where he questioned the necessity of a large navy, arguing that naval officers, with their "enormous allowances," remained on the government payroll forever, either doing nothing or going on "needless" missions like that of Commodore Perry to Japan. When pressed, the senator stated that he harbored no hostility toward the Navy "except to say that I think it is, in a great measure, entirely useless." Although Hale was more outspoken on this issue than most of his colleagues, other dissenting senators were thinking along the same lines. Indeed, Massachusetts' Charles Sumner, probably the most famous of the group, launched his public career with an 1845 oration which articulated the thesis that "IN OUR AGE THERE CAN BE NO PEACE THAT IS NOT HONORABLE: THERE CAN BE NO WAR THAT IS NOT DISHONORABLE." Sumner viewed "the costly *preparations* for war, in time of peace," as the chief cause of international conflict, and he pronounced the United States as guilty on this score as the nations of Europe. As an alternative, he argued that the true basis of foreign policy should lie not in military affairs but in a search for "moral elevation, enlightened and decorated by the intellect of men." Like other American reformers, Sumner sought to place more emphasis on the power of ideals to achieve American foreign policy goals.[9]

A desire to move beyond the accepted norms of traditional power politics, often accompanied by a suspicion of developing a large military and a powerful diplomatic corps, permeated the American political culture from Revolutionary times through the progressive era. Figures such as Theodore Roosevelt and James Polk, who employed more power-political conceptions in framing the foreign policies of their presidencies, stood out precisely because they departed from these sentiments. The peace progressives took a similar path in their critique of interwar American foreign relations.

In 1907 the German theorist Otto Hintze wrote that "the fight for great-power status is the true essence of the imperialist movement in the modern world."[10] Given this linkage, it is perhaps not surprising that the Revolutionary era also featured a lively anti-imperialist current. The Declaration of Independence, with its assertion of the equality of all men, was among the most forthright American anti-imperialist statements ever produced. As Peggy Liss has noted, the ideological underpinnings of the colonies' bid for independence were not confined to North America; the commercially oriented ideas associated with the Enlightenment had spread through a network of trade and ideas to the Spanish and Portuguese colonies to the south as the eighteenth century progressed. Much of this rhetoric was contradicted when the United States met with outright hostility the first anti-imperial revolution that it faced, the 1791 revolt of former slaves led by Toussaint L'Ouverture in Haiti. The administration of George Washington funneled funds to the white French planters, and Americans from all regions worried that Haitian independence could undermine the racial system in the United States.[10] Meanwhile, strategic concerns in the Caribbean further tempered the American anti-imperialist vision; Jefferson himself expressed a desire to see Cuba ultimately annexed to the Union, a goal that most American policymakers of the period shared. Nonetheless, the sentiment remained powerful enough, when the areas in revolt were perceived as less threatening to United States interests than Haiti or Cuba, to produce congressional bids to fashion anti-imperialism as one of the key foreign policy ideologies of the country.[11]

Henry Clay's unsuccessful attempts during the 1810s and early 1820s to wrest control of Latin American policy from the administration of James Monroe by sponsoring congressional resolutions urging U.S. diplomatic recognition of several of the South American states fitted this pattern. Looking to position the United States "on the side of liberty and the happiness of a large portion of the human family," Clay denied that U.S. recognition of the Spanish American republics would provoke a war with Spain. Although he believed that the political turbulence in Spain associated with the Napoleonic wars had resulted in Spain's forfeiting its legal right to continue its autocratic rule over the colonies, he preferred to take a "broader and bolder position" on the matter than resting his case on international law. Citing Emre de Vattel as his authority, Clay contended "that an oppressed people were authorized, wherever they could, to rise and break their fetters," and that the United States, unless it wanted to "pass sentence of condemnation upon the founders of our liberty," needed to provide support to such a move. To soothe his opponents, Clay linked his plea to the traditional hostility to balance of power politics. The Kentucky representative reasoned that an independent Spanish America would be "guided by an American policy," under which "they would obey the laws of the system of the New World . . . in contradistinction to that of Europe." He went on to observe that "without the influence of that vortex in Europe, the balance of power between its several parts . . . America is sufficiently remote to contemplate the new wars which are to afflict that quarter of the globe, as a calm, if not a cold and indifferent, spectator." Clay also promised that his policy would serve the commercial interests of the United States by opening up new and lucrative markets.[12]

Clay confined his anti-imperialist appeal to the Western Hemisphere, but an even broader definition of anti-imperialism came during congressional debate over Massachusetts Representative Daniel Webster's resolution expressing American sympathy with the Greek revolution in 1824. In defense of his proposal, Webster contended for confirming the American commitment to the "general tendency . . . which may be said to characterize the present age": that "the men of this age will not be satisfied even with kind masters." Webster feared that under the Holy Alliance "every sovereign in Europe may go to war to repress an example" of freedom, setting up an international system with the "radical defect" of dividing civilization by allowing "it to go on in all other matters, but not in principles of Government and civil liberty." To counter this trend, the congressman called for the

United States to act "on principle." He denied charges of his opponents that he wanted to involve the United States in a military conflict in Europe, noting that such "reasoning mistakes the age. Formerly, indeed, there was no making an impression on a nation but by bayonets ... but the age has undergone a change: there is a force in public opinion which, in the long run, will outweigh all the physical force that can be brought to oppose it." In such a world order, the United States could play a prominent role on behalf of freedom and liberty without entangling itself militarily or diplomatically in European matters. This line of thinking tied Webster into an intellectual current shared by many since the Revolutionary era. From outside Congress, Edward Everett, editor of the *North American Review* and future Secretary of State, welcomed the Greek appeal to the United States for aid as an illustration of "the great and glorious part, which this country is to act, in the political regeneration of the world." He added that private material aid to the Greeks in combination with governmental expressions of sympathy "will teach those who are now toiling and bleeding for freedom, that we prize the blessing too highly, not to aid them in attaining it."[13]

The Clay and Webster resolutions precipitated a series of fierce congressional debates which ultimately produced a consensus that in general a policy of unconditional U.S. aid for colonial revolutions did not serve the national interest. South Carolina Representative Joel Poinsett (himself prone to interventionism on behalf of U.S. ideals during his days as a diplomat in Spanish America) agreed with Webster that "our sympathies are always with the oppressed," but he maintained that keeping the United States at peace had to be the chief priority of Congress. New York's Silas Wood summed up the position of the House majority that voted down Webster's resolution when he commented that the United States had no authority to embark upon diplomatic crusades, military "wars of ambition, or to propagate the principles of religion or liberty by the sword." Wood here built upon an earlier theme articulated by Albert Gallatin, who had remarked in the 1790s that while the United States always had to lament the fate of "independent nations blotted from the map of the world," it should avoid a forceful policy on their behalf, since in the end "their destiny does not affect us in the least." Congressional majorities opposed Clay's resolutions on behalf of Spanish American independence using similar arguments, while John Quincy Adams, then Secretary of State, cautioned of the "inevitable tendency of a direct interference in foreign wars, even wars for freedom, to change the very foundations of our own government from *liberty* to *power*."[14]

But fear of international involvement alone did not cause the failure of the Clay and Webster resolutions. As Piero Gleijeses has observed, by the mid-1820s congressional majorities had dismissed the assumption that American ideals dictated an anti-imperialist policy, and had begun applying the "lessons" learned from Cuban and Haitian policy to the issue of anti-imperialism as a whole. The United States actively opposed a joint Colombian-Mexican scheme to liberate Cuba during the mid-1820s, with one congressman remarking that "there is a point, beyond which, even parental bounty and natural affection cease to impose an obligation. That point has been attained with the States of Spanish America." Debate over U.S. participation in the Panama Congress of 1826 revealed just how limited this sympathy had become. Supporters and opponents of U.S. participation in the Congress (with only one exception in the Senate and a handful in the House) agreed that the United States should oppose Cuban independence and do everything in its power to prevent Latin American diplomatic recognition of Haiti, two items on the agenda of the Congress. Louisiana Senator Josiah Johnston called for U.S. attendance so as to "menace" Colombia and Mexico "if necessary, against a step so dangerous to us, and perhaps fatal to them"; likewise, he wanted to express "to the South American States, the unalterable opinion entertained here in regard to intercourse" with Haiti. Georgia Senator John Berrien, who opposed U.S. participation in the Panama Congress, emphatically remarked that Cuba "*is a question which we cannot safely commit to negotiation,*" and added that any diplomatic contact with Haiti "would be productive of the most awful calamity—would introduce a moral contagion, compared with which, physical pestilence, in the utmost degree of its horrors, would be light and insignificant." Only a few voices echoed the anti-imperialism of the debates over the Clay and Webster resolutions a few years earlier. Martin Van Buren, then a New York senator, noted that Cuban policies placed the United States in an "embarrassing" position, since "we affect to glory in the success of the principles upon which the Revolution of Spanish America is founded—but still consent to become the advocates of a peace which will condemn Cuba and Porto Rico to the yoke of Spain." Van Buren went no further than this, however, and simply maintained that since continued Spanish control of Cuba served the national interest, the United States should have "simply and plainly informed" the South Americans "that we would not suffer the occupation of the Island of Cuba by any other power except Spain, cost what it might." His colleague in the New York delegation, Representative Wood, chided opponents of the Panama Congress for expressing fear that it could revolutionize international statecraft. In the firmest link to the now repudiated anti-imperialism, he urged that the United States not only attend but actively participate, since "are not the principles of the South American states conformable to ours? Is it unworthy of us to join with the group of Republics and band against the tyranny of the world?" The Speaker of the House ruled Wood out of order "on the ground that his remarks were taking too wide a range." The ruling symbolized the growing perception that an anti-imperialist foreign policy would not serve the American national interest.[15]

American anti-imperialism revived in a different context in the late 1830s, when abolitionists began petitioning the House of Representatives on behalf of diplomatic recognition of Haiti. That anti-imperialism had emerged as the foreign policy counterpart to abolitionism became apparent in debate over the Polk administration's decision to go to war with Mexico. From outside Congress, the pacifist and radical abolitionist William Lloyd Garrison believed that the conflict represented "a distinct, all-crushing pro-slavery movement," opposition to which activists should consider "the chief anti-slavery work which they are . . . called upon to do." Within the House, all fourteen opponents of the declaration of war represented solidly antislavery districts and employed arguments honed in their domestic crusades against the influence of slave power. The chief ideologue of the group, Ohio Representative Joshua Giddings, termed the war a "magnificent scheme of extending the slave power" so that slave states could maintain their majority in the Senate, while Charles Hudson of Massachusetts fretted that victory in such a war "would eventuate in the destruction of our free institutions at home." Polk's decision to employ the military to achieve his objectives also allowed the group to tap into the American tradition of antimilitarism. For instance, Massachusetts Representative George Ashmun echoed Jeffersonian fears when he remarked that the meager opposition to the war served as a "portentous omen of the early and premature decay into which our institutions are fast falling." Though unsuccessful, the Mexican War dissent did illustrate the degree to which anti-imperialism had become linked with a radical domestic ideology.[16]

This pattern continued throughout the 1850s as the anti-imperialist

debate shifted to the Senate with John Hale's faction, the Free Soil
Whigs, combatting the aggressive Latin American policies of both the
Franklin Pierce and James Buchanan administrations. In 1853 Hale
lashed out against executive statements concerning alleged Mexican
maltreatment of American concessionaires in the Tehuantepec region
(a possible spot for a transisthmian canal), contending that the concessionaires had no right to "plead alien privileges, nor any other privileges, except those which have been granted to them by the laws of the
country." The senator felt that Mexico, as a weaker nation, deserved
"magnanimity," since the United States needed to heed "forces more
formidable than armies," such as enlightened world public opinion.
The Free Soil Whigs later opposed Buchanan's request for congressional authorization to adjust American differences with Paraguay in
1858 (an American vessel, the *Water Witch*, had taken fire in the Parna
River), again invoking antimilitarist notions. Vermont's Jacob Collamer
charged that the President sought the unconstitutional power "to commence war at his discretion." The senator elaborated on his viewpoint
during the 1859 debate over Buchanan's request for a $30 million ap-
propriation with which to begin negotiations with Spain for the purchase of Cuba. Given Spain's repeated assertions that it would not sell
the island, Collamer charged that the administration actually wanted
to "find fault with the people they are about to rob of this possession"
as a way to rally support for a war of conquest. The bill amounted to
a predated declaration of war, "a most extraordinary stretch of the claim
of power in the hands of the Executive." It thus represented the "first
incipient stage" of a Southern plan to conquer for slave territory all of
Mexico and Central America. Collamer added that a good case existed
against the intervention quite apart from the slavery angle, noting that
the Southerners incorrectly assumed that "because we like our form of
popular government that, therefore, [the Cubans] would desire it." He
concluded that nations which coveted their neighbor's territories, such
as the United States, were "likely to be . . . unacceptable neighbors in
the family of nations." The American minister in Madrid, William
Preston, complained that the Senate opposition had stiffened Spanish
resolve against selling Cuba.[17]

The onset of the Civil War changed the context of both the foreign
and domestic policy debates, removing the slavery issue, the group's
binding argument against expansion. In addition, the replacing of the
despised Pierce and Buchanan administrations with Lincoln and the

Republicans eliminated the partisan aspect of the group's critique of foreign affairs. Some, such as Hale, retained the faith, but most chose to follow the administration's foreign and military policies, making Hale's isolation so complete that by 1864 one Republican senator joked that his colleague's "long habit of continued denunciation against the Administration or the party in power for fifteen or twenty years in succession has had some effect on the habits of his mind, both in thought and in action."[18]

Familiar themes resurfaced when Charles Sumner, who had retained his prestige after the Civil War through his position as chair of the Senate Foreign Relations Committee, revived the ideology in his opposition to President Ulysses Grant's scheme to annex the Dominican Republic. The Massachusetts senator alleged that Grant wished to bypass congressional power by initiating a policy that represented a "new stage in a measure of violence" justified by nothing "except what is found in the law of force." While conceding that annexation would drain the public treasury and would admit people impossible to assimilate into the Union, Sumner concentrated his fire on the twin issues of American aggression and the danger to Haiti. He charged that the American Navy had oppressed "a sister republic too weak to resist" when it had pressured the Port-au-Prince regime not to pursue claims against the Dominican government. The senator saw this as particularly heinous since Haiti stood as a "republic seeking to follow our great example." He added that he desired to preserve Haitian and Dominican independence in order to make the countries "a successful example of self-government for the redemption of the [African] race."[19]

Debate over Grant's scheme revealed new themes in the dissenting anti-imperialist ideology. Racism had served as a deterrent against expansion even in the 1850s; Ohio Free Soiler Benjamin Wade dismissed Buchanan's scheme to acquire Cuba as a "nigger bill" to add 750,000 "niggers" to the United States. This perspective became far more prevalent beginning in the 1870s, as evidenced by the unity achieved by the Senate's eleven Democrats, already strong administration opponents on domestic issues, in opposition to annexation. Thomas Bayard (D–Delaware) reasoned that embarking "upon the vast and trackless sea of imperialism," in addition to threatening republican institutions at home, would incorporate into the United States "part of an island now held by a semi-barbarous race, the descendants of African slaves," whose political institutions "are mere mockeries, bloody travesties of political government." Bayard added that "the fiat of nature has declared that we are unable to elevate such a race as inhabit that island to the level of our own," and that therefore the United States would be dragged down to the level of the Dominican Republic's "amiable and lovely population of black cut-throats." Nonetheless, alongside this racism stood appeals to traditional American idealism: Allen Thurman (D–Ohio) called the proposal "the greatest subject that has been before the American people since the Constitution has been formed," passage of which would trigger "a policy of unlimited colonial acquisition." Republicans other than Sumner who opposed the President combined idealist and racist themes. Carl Schurz (R–Missouri) pointed to Germany as an example of a country that had benefited from commercial rather than imperial expansion, and he saw the American destiny as avoiding seduction "by the deceptive allurements of tropical splendor," lest the country engage in "starting and carrying on a rapacious tyranny." At the same time, however, Schurz also made extended remarks on the inability of the tropics to support a people interested in achieving liberty, a point echoed by his Vermont colleague Justin Morrill; administration supporter Oliver Morton (R–Indiana) gleefully interrupted Schurz's longest address several times to point out that many of Schurz's arguments earlier had been used to justify slavery. Outside the Senate, Schurz's perspective was more common than Sumner's. E. L. Godkin, editor of *The Nation*, called on the Senate to reject the treaty, since if it did not "new reasons for annexation will every day make their appearance." He also admitted that he did not want "ignorant Catholic Spanish negroes" joined to the Union as part of a "policy of absorbing semi-civilized Catholic states."[20]

The debate over Dominican annexation established a framework for anti-imperialism that continued for the next quarter-century. Although the more radical anti-imperialism associated with the Free Soil Whigs remained, strands of racism and domestic conservatism associated with the Senate Democrats became more prominent in the foreign policy outlooks of the opponents of expansion. The issue also transformed the Democrats into opponents of Caribbean Basin expansionism, making anti-imperialism bipartisan and bringing the issue closer to the political mainstream than at any time since the 1820s. Unlike that period, however, Gilded Age anti-imperialism had a more inward orientation. Grover Cleveland, in opposing Republican plans for U.S. assumption of a protectorate over Nicaragua, announced that such a policy contradicted "the tenets of a line of precedents from Washington's day, which proscribe entangling alliances with foreign states"; Bayard, who moved from the Senate to become Cleveland's first Secretary of State, announced that "the policy of the United States, declared and pursued for more than a century, discountenances and in practice forbids distant colonial acquisitions." Such statements drew praise from Carl Schurz, who had prodded Cleveland before his inauguration to make a statement promising to avoid entangling alliances and to maintain "the Monroe Doctrine without any desire of territorial aggrandizement." Although the anti-imperialists of the era were not as united on the issue of commercial expansion (Schurz, for example, championed it), most nonetheless questioned the means pursued by the era's Republican administrations, particularly the G.O.P. tactics of negotiating commercial reciprocity treaties with less powerful states. Cleveland repeatedly criticized such proposals both in and out of the White House, while Justin Morrill feared that reciprocity treaties with Central American nations could "make future acquisitions of territory inevitable, giving us more of the Latin race than the stomach of Uncle Sam can safely bear."[21]

Dissent during the eighteenth and nineteenth centuries provided a foreign policy framework to which the peace progressives returned in the 1910s and especially the 1920s. Early reformers of various sorts searched for alternatives to the traditional conceptions of power common in the European-dominated international system of their eras. By the Civil War, they had proposed a variety of solutions, including Paine's commercial internationalism, the stress on the power of the American example in "Brutus," Jefferson's empire of liberty, and the extreme antimilitarism of Hale and Sumner. Ironically, the concern with overseas military involvement and diplomatic aggressiveness prevalent in many of these critiques helped cool the American ardor for the anti-imperialist outlook that came to be associated with the peace progressives, and by the 1820s both the executive and legislative branches had beaten back attempts to make anti-imperialism a key facet of the nation's foreign policy. Nevertheless, anti-imperialism maintained its place in the American political consciousness, reappearing often in various contexts throughout the nineteenth century. Except for a brief period during the 1850s, however, these two broad patterns of thought—anti-imperialism and the search for alternative conceptions of power—did not intersect. The peace progressives differed from their earlier counterparts in the way in which they paired anti-imperialism with hostility to traditional power politics, positioning the ideology as the answer in the perennial American quest for an alternative approach to international relations.

This process began when the Gilded Age anti-imperialist ideology went into decline, starting with the aggressive diplomatic policies of William McKinley and continuing through the Roosevelt and Taft presidencies. The Gilded Age anti-imperialist coalition made its final stand in opposition to McKinley's decision to annex the Philippines in 1899. The President's most numerous foes in Congress, the Senate Democrats, continued to base their opposition on the principles established during their fight against the Dominican annexation scheme and solidified during the first Cleveland presidency. They followed the rhetorical lead of Georgia Senator Augustus Bacon, who, like earlier congressional dissenters, warned that expansion contradicted republican principles. He noted that the United States, as the only major power in the world that recognized (rhetorically at least) the right to self-government, could not in good faith withhold that right from others without lessening its moral influence in the world; he also feared that annexation would inaugurate a dangerous period of American imperialism, which would require "the necessity of cruelty" for enforcement, like England with its "Hindoos." Finally, expanding on the Cleveland/Bayard perspective, Bacon cautioned that possession of the Philippines would nullify both the Monroe Doctrine and Washington's Farewell Address, invite European meddling in the Western Hemisphere, and possibly involve the United States in a major international conflict in the Pacific.[22] Like their predecessors in the 1870s and 1880s, the Senate Democrats added less altruistic appeals. Jefferson Caffery (D–Louisiana) opposed acquisition of the Philippines out of fear that annexation could permit Filipino sugar to enter the United States duty-free, undercutting the price of Louisiana sugar. Caffery's South Carolina colleague Ben Tillman dismissed the Filipinos as "not ready for liberty as we understand it," a fact known by those experienced with the "colored race." Finally, virtually all Democratic opponents of McKinley's policy pointed to the expansion of executive power inherent in the President's plan, implying, as had Bayard and Thurman a quarter-century earlier, that the President in turn could use this increased power for domestic purposes contrary to the interests of the South.[23]

As in the Gilded Age, reform-minded Republicans joined the Democrats in opposing American expansionism. Schurz, long since exiled from the Senate, maintained his earlier perspective, terming the Filipino population a "large mass of more or less barbarous Asiatics" whose presence in the Union could lead to nonwhite members of Congress and presidential electors. He added the more idealistic argument that adopting an imperialist policy would relegate the Declaration of Independence to "a mere glittering generality and antiquated rubbish," rejecting the country's long-established principles in exchange for a doctrine which held that "the strong must not be too squeamish about the rights of the weak." E. L. Godkin agreed with Schurz on all counts, noting that "unquestionably, our present Constitution was not intended for a conquering nation with several different classes of citizens," particularly given that many of these citizens would be members of "alien, inferior, mongrel races." He termed McKinley's suppression of Emilio Aguinaldo's Filipino nationalist forces "the most savage [conflict] which was ever known in the history of our republic," a "shameless abandonment of the noble faith under which we have lived for a century." The Anti-Imperialist League, founded by aging Northeastern Republicans who shared the ideological perspective of Schurz and Godkin, became the most powerful public organization opposed to McKinley, organizing public rallies and publishing literature against the administration's policies.[24]

Senate support for this position came from a small clique of Northeastern Republicans led by Massachusetts Senator George Frisbie Hoar, a onetime Sumner protégé. Hoar (ironically a caustic critic in the 1880s of the Republican reformers with whom he now was allied) cautioned that a democracy "cannot rule over vassal states or subject peoples without bringing in the elements of death into its own constitution," since the McKinley policy declared "in effect that these ten million people have in our judgment no constitutional rights, no right to liberty, no right even to be heard in the determination of their own self-government." The Massachusetts senator, who also termed imperialism contrary to the principles of the Constitution, managed to carry only one Republican colleague, Eugene Hale of Maine, with him in opposition to the annexation. Soon the ideology with which he and the Anti-Imperialist League were associated went into decline. Hoar himself died in 1904, and several other Republican anti-imperialists passed away in the first decade of the 1900s; those that did not tended to retire from active participation in politics. In one of his more candid remarks, Hoar admitted that "I appeal from the Present, bloated with material prosperity, drunk with the lust of empire, to another and better age. I appeal from the Present to the Past." Unfortunately for the opponents to annexation of the Philippines, such an appeal was unlikely to win adherents in the optimistic Progressive Era.[25]

This left the Senate Democrats to carry on in opposition to the foreign policies of McKinley's successor, Theodore Roosevelt, which they criticized from an exceedingly narrow perspective based almost entirely on constitutional grounds. Bacon reflected the Democratic tone in a long speech that attacked administration supporters for "magnifying the powers of the President and minimizing the powers of the Senate." He contended that in the framers' vision "Congress and not the President is supreme under the Constitution in the control of our foreign affairs." The Georgia senator's address, delivered in opposition to Roosevelt's plan to establish an American customs receivership over the Dominican Republic, could have been uttered by virtually any Southern Democrat on any foreign policy issue of the day. Roosevelt understood as much, remarking that one leading Democrat "told me that he had taken it for granted that I would have to take some such action as that proposed, and believed it necessary. I understand, however, that this was merely his unofficial position, and that officially he is going to condemn our action as realizing his worst forebodings."[26]

The one exception to this pattern during Roosevelt's two terms in office—and the only Senate Democratic challenge to the actual policies pursued by the Roosevelt administration in foreign affairs—came when Maryland's Isidor Rayner joined Bacon in opposing the Dominican treaty. Rayner did not deny the constitutional premise of his fellow Democrats' critique, noting that no clause in the Constitution empowered the United States to act as receiver for another government. He focused, however, on what he viewed as more important issues, such as the belief that the Monroe Doctrine did not authorize the United States to set up protectorates in Latin America. The senator added that this new policy, as "strictly a financial doctrine," would benefit only the "syndicate of relentless mercenaries and money lenders," since they would manipulate the President into intervening so that they would not have to follow local law. Instead, he called for an end to use of the Doctrine "as an instrument of terror and oppression" to the South and denied that "we are trustees under God of the civilization of the world"; he preferred that the United States not become a world power if one of the prerequisites for such status was participation in European-style imperialism. Rayner's argument stood out in its willingness to move beyond a narrow constitutional opposition to Roosevelt's diplomacy.[27]

By refusing to take the political risk in criticizing Roosevelt directly, the Senate Democrats failed to present an alternative policy, and forfeited the agenda to administration supporters who could (and occasionally did) make the case that the opposition sympathized with the President's policies if not his methods.[28] This caution, however, did not apply to the Democratic party nationally, which, under the leadership of William Jennings Bryan, began to interpret foreign affairs through the lens of a populist domestic ideology, producing a view of many foreign policy issues not dissimilar to that offered by Rayner in his criticism of the Dominican protectorate scheme. In the process, Bryan and his followers began to articulate a more radical version of anti-imperialism, foreshadowing the rise of a much more powerful dissenting ideology, peace progressivism, fifteen years later.

The first sign of this development came in debate over acquisition of the Philippines. In the Senate, a small band of Populists, led on foreign policy issues by South Dakota's Richard Pettigrew, predicted that expansion would trigger the rise of "a despotism where the will of one man can march armies, declare war, and act with great rapidity." Pettigrew also dismissed the argument that the United States needed the Philippines to expand its overseas markets, cautioning his countrymen against following the British example, asking them to look at the examples of Ireland, India, Egypt, and the natives of New Zealand, where British conduct had produced some of the "blackest pages in the history of the world." He concluded with an unusually vigorous defense of the Filipinos, charging that the administration had brushed aside "innumerable efforts" by Aguinaldo to achieve peace so that it could extend a military regime "over that government of a sister republic, founded upon a constitution similar to ours." By 1901 the senator was charging the administration with "crushing out . . . a better government for those people than we can ever institute in our place," saying that if he were a Filipino he "would fight until [he] was gray . . . against this unholy and infamous aggression." Outside the Senate, Tom Watson, the Populist nominee for Vice President in the 1896 election, offered a more sophisticated approach based on the teachings of populism. Watson had exhibited little desire for the United States to enter the war in Cuba, fearing (correctly, as it turned out) that intervention could sidetrack domestic reform efforts. He noted that the "national bankers . . . the privileged classes . . . [and] politicians" would benefit from the war, with the people getting no more than "the fighting and the taxes." More broadly, he worried that going to war, even for noble purposes, eventually would make the United States oppressors like the Spanish, since "republics cannot go into the conquering business and remain republics."[29]

Pettigrew's radical rhetoric did little to persuade his Senate colleagues, and Watson's political power was waning, not increasing, by 1899. Yet the populist alternative that they forwarded was picked up by the Democratic presidential nominee in the 1896, 1900, and 1908 presidential contests, William Jennings Bryan. Arguing that imperialism "finds its inspiration in dollars, not in duty," Bryan maintained that the government should not "burden our people with increased taxes in order to give a few speculators an opportunity for exploitation"; like Watson, he feared that "while the American people are endeavoring to extend an unsolicited sovereignty over remote peoples, foreign financiers will be able to complete the conquest of our own country." The Commoner specifically linked his domestic and international crusades, promising not to concede any aspect of the nation's policies to the "gold standard financiers," since "we can not make peace with them on one thing without weakening our fight against other things." Somewhat like Pettigrew, Bryan moved beyond these points to question whether the United States in particular should practice a policy of imperialism. He argued that subjecting a people by force against their will would run counter to the pattern of the last hundred years, when the United States "has been the most potent influence in the world," since "the growth of the principle of self-government, planted on American soil[, has been] the overshadowing political fact of the nineteenth century." Finally, the Democratic standard-bearer attacked the policy of imperialism itself, contending that it inevitably promoted militarism; he also noted that "history has thus far failed to furnish a single example of a nation selfish enough to desire a colony and yet unselfish enough to govern it wisely at long range." He never carried his arguments to their logical extreme, though, advocating an American protectorate for the Philippines as the best long-term policy and supporting the retention of a coaling station in the islands to improve prospects of East Asian trade. Nonetheless, as Kendrick Clements has observed, Bryan, although he lost his 1900 rematch with McKinley, won the intellectual battle on imperialism with the President, defining it in such odious terms as to discredit it as an official policy.[30]

Bryan always expressed a degree of ambivalence about adopting anti-imperialism as his dominant foreign policy ideology; as LeRoy Ashby has observed, Bryan's approach to imperialism "carried within it contradictory messages." He did make a passionate case against U.S. colonization of the Philippines, and he also criticized British imperialism in South Africa and India, questioned the great power intervention to suppress the Boxer Rebellion in China, and advocated a far more consistent and idealistic approach against Roosevelt's actions in Panama than did his party colleagues in the Senate. On the other hand, his support for a protectorate for the Philippines revealed a greater willingness to compromise than many later anti-imperialists would demonstrate. Bryan also did not uniformly oppose the idea of the United States holding colonies, backing the acquisition of Puerto Rico, for example. He termed the island "the key to the East Coast of South America," "the very base needed for the extension of our trade with, and our influence over," the region. Also, befitting his missionary nature, Bryan did not question American cultural imperialism, supporting the efforts of legitimate American businessmen, missionaries, and teachers to export the country's economic and political systems, culture, and values to Latin America. (These beliefs, in part, foreshadowed his support for American intervention to "uplift" Caribbean states during his tenure as Secretary of State.) He parted company with the administrations of both Roosevelt and Taft in maintaining that the United States should refrain from using force in its diplomacy toward less developed areas. Bryan also bitterly attacked Taft's "Dollar Diplomacy" policies in Central America and East Asia for extending the power of the business interests that he opposed on the domestic scene. Through such criticisms Bryan's dissent revealed how domestic reformism, as it had during the 1840s and again during the Gilded Age, could trigger an anti-imperialist perspective in international affairs.[31]

Bryan and his followers also were unabashed admirers of Jefferson, whom Bryan described as "the greatest statesman our country produced." Not surprisingly, then, Bryan revived his mentor's search for countering the predominance of force in international affairs, looking to his domestic ideology to provide him with a program. His most innovative peace plan derived from arbitration, which he had championed for the settling of domestic labor disputes. The Nebraskan based his plan on investigation rather than on compulsory arbitration, hoping that in this way he could get around the nationalistic sentiments that had felled treaties of compulsory arbitration in the past. He never explained, however, how investigation of international disputes alone would bring peace, nor did his "cooling-off" treaties provide sufficient guarantees that parties to a dispute would allow the time sufficient for investigation to overcome its other obstacles and possibly succeed. Despite its technical weaknesses, Bryan's plan fitted into the American heritage of searching for alternatives to the use of force in international relations. Moreover, like post-Jeffersonian dissenters, Bryan coupled his peace proposals with support for disarmament efforts. He ridiculed Roosevelt as a "human arsenal, a dreadnought wrought in flesh and blood," and consistently opposed the President's efforts to expand the size of the Navy. As early as 1892, Bryan had cautioned against putting "our safety in a great navy" or a "great standing army," recommending instead that the United States rely on "happy and contented citizens" as its best means of defense. This type of rhetoric prefigured the anti-militarist positions that he would adopt after resigning as Secretary of State in 1915.[32]

By the end of Taft's term, Bryan had become the unquestioned leader of the Democratic party on foreign policy issues. The Senate Democrats had treated Taft and his Secretary of State, Philander Knox, with far less deference than that granted Roosevelt, but in the process had exposed quite severe ideological divisions. These internal differences, coupled with the deaths of the two intellectual leaders of the group, Bacon and Rayner, all but eliminated the faction as an independent force in the enunciation of the Democratic position on international affairs. Both Bacon and Rayner criticized what they viewed as the overly aggressive manner in which Taft handled the events of the Mexican revolution. Bacon defended the "God-given . . . natural right of any people to attempt to throw off a government if they find that government burdensome and tyrannical," while Rayner went further, denying the relevance of the Monroe Doctrine to the crisis (some Republicans argued that Japan might use the domestic crisis in Mexico to gain access to a Mexican naval base). The Maryland senator admitted that the Mexican turbulence affected property held by American investors in Mexico, but he contended that the duty of the United States to protect its citizens under international law could go no further than diplomatic demarches. Rayner also dismissed the danger—"presently or remotely"—of an American-Japanese war over Mexico, praising the Japanese as "a marvelous and courageous race." This prompted a response from Bacon, who asserted that the United States had a right to intervene if Mexican actions "are found to be inimical to our peace and our safety," although he did not specify whether he considered a private Japanese lease of land inimical to American interests. Meanwhile, William Stone of Missouri, the third-ranking Democrat on the Foreign Relations Committee, disagreed with both of his colleagues and called for military intervention in Mexico to protect American lives and property, since "we cannot remain passive and inactive and permit disorder . . . to the peril of the lives, liberty, and property of American citizens lawfully resident in that republic."[33] This pattern of Senate Democratic aggressiveness and factionalism carried over into their critiques of Taft's European and military policies.[34] Bryan, using his alliance with House Democrats and his increasing support among Jeffersonians in the Senate, maneuvered to fill this ideological void opened by his more conservative opponents. Shortly, though, he too would be challenged by a Democratic voice far more powerful than his.

Bryan's foreign policy innovations were the last before the arrival of the peace progressives onto the national scene in the middle of the Taft administration. The Commoner's originality came in his application of strands of his domestic populist inclinations to foreign affairs, but the intellectual tradition to which he contributed dated from the Revolutionary era. Like Paine, the Anti-Federalists, Jefferson, and others, Bryan searched for alternative approaches for the American conduct of international relations. Somewhat unlike these earlier figures, he entertained the prospect, particularly in his 1900 presidential campaign but also in his critique of Taft's diplomacy, of making anti-imperialism the vehicle with which to satisfy this quest. In the end, however, he shied away from this possibility, and never embraced anti-imperialism in its entirety, as the Free Soil Whigs before him had declined to do in the late 1850s and early 1860s. After a period of division, the peace progressives would select a different route.

2

The Emergence of the
Peace Progressives

The peace progressives emerged from this varied intellectual and political milieu. Much like Bryan, their initial foreign policy perspectives derived from their domestic dissent, particularly during the Taft administration, which, in language that increasingly resembled Bryan's, they attacked as dominated by business interests. Like Bryan, too, they offered some probing insights into the nature of American foreign relations, which established them as the principal left-wing opposition group in Congress by 1917. They could not advance beyond that point, however, in the years before American entry into World War I. Woodrow Wilson had come to the presidency in 1913 expecting to concentrate on domestic affairs, but crises in Mexico and Europe caused the President to take American foreign policy in radically new directions. The peace progressives could not obstruct the President in the process. From 1914 through 1917, for the first time, they began giving sustained attention to international affairs, and in the process the outlines of the foreign policy ideology that they would articulate in the 1920s began to form. Nonetheless, they failed in these years either to construct a coherent alternative foreign policy or to impede Wilson seriously in his conduct of international affairs. When coupled with the gradual eclipse of Bryan's power in the Democratic party, this failure allowed Wilson to assume the role of spokesman of the American left on foreign policy matters.

Some signs of renewed Republican dissent appeared as early as 1908, when Moses Clapp (R–Minnesota) joined Democrats in their questioning of Theodore Roosevelt's naval policy. A fairly loyal follower of Roosevelt during the latter's two terms, Clapp's domestic agenda led him to believe that the United States should intensify its efforts for international peace. He thus argued that the United States needed to take the lead in promoting world disarmament; since it could not disband its navy, it at least "can be the first nation . . . to put a stop to the useless building of navies beyond reason." Dismissing arguments that American trade demanded a large navy, the senator contended that history had discredited "the policy of forcing trade at the mouth of the gun or in the presence of hostile fleets." (Bryan had been making similar arguments since 1899.) Clapp expanded his "mission of peace" during the next few years. Borrowing from earlier antimilitarist rhetoric, Clapp feared the Navy as "a menace to the peace of the Republic," leading Americans into the "dangerous realm of the aggressive"; he rebuked administration officials, who contended that the United States had to keep up with the naval increases of foreign powers, for being in "overawe" of monarchical governments. Finally, the Minnesota senator dismissed Japan as a threat, praising Japanese "expansion" and "development" and contending that a conflict would result only if "we bully Japan into war."[1]

For the most part, however, the senators who became Taft's Republican critics either had supported the foreign policies of the President's two predecessors or had given no sustained thought at all to international affairs. Those that had supported the international policies of McKinley and Roosevelt generally had done so because they perceived such a task as the best way of achieving their overarching goal of domestic reform. The most obvious example was Wisconsin's Robert La Follette, who in 1900 was making his third bid for governor of Wisconsin; conservative opposition had sidetracked his two previous campaigns in the Republican primary. For the 1900 contest, as part of a self-conscious attempt to reach out to standpat forces in the state, La Follette delivered a number of speeches praising McKinley's Philippines policy, about which he privately admitted he knew very little. La Follette parroted the administration line, arguing that without American troops, "the government of the Philippines would speedily lapse into anarchy," producing foreign intervention. He quickly moved on from there to how the policy would benefit the United States, contending that imperialism would allow the country to tap into the "great market" of East Asia and also to fulfill the traditional "policy of this government," which, from the Revolutionary era, "has been to expand." La Follette was not the only Republican reformer who looked to use compromises on foreign policy as a way of either furthering his career or aiding the cause of domestic reform. In Idaho, William Borah used expansionism as a way of proving his mettle to regular Republicans suspicious of his bolt to the Silver Republican cause in 1896, using a whirlwind tour of the state on behalf of Roosevelt's reelection in 1904 to provide a particularly vigorous defense of the assertive aspects of the President's foreign policies. George Norris (R–Nebraska) later recalled that although he had "some doubts" about Roosevelt's foreign policy, he had not raised them in Congress at the time, because the President advocated "so many reforms . . . American life needed badly," and, despite Norris' qualifier, there was little indication that either he or any other peace progressives found anything particularly distasteful about Roosevelt's foreign policy before Clapp's dissent in 1908. Clapp himself joined La Follette and Borah in support of Roosevelt's plan for a customs receivership over the Dominican Republic, while future peace progressive Joseph Bristow (R–Kansas) served as one of the President's chief officials in the Panama Canal Zone, and Asle Gronna praised American colonial policy in the Philippines. In addition, most of the future peace progressives in the years before 1910 backed commercial expansion and a larger merchant marine. The peace progressives fitted into a general pattern of progressive support for imperialism before 1908, but, unlike figures such as Albert Beveridge (R–Indiana), they came to the positions they did because they devoted little attention to foreign policy matters and found in their mostly positive view of Roosevelt's domestic performance little reason to join Democrats in a critique of the President's foreign policies.[2]

These patterns did not continue to hold during the Taft years, as the senators quickly became estranged from a President they saw as dominated by the conservative, Eastern, probusiness wing of the party. The dispute began when Taft sided with probusiness forces in the Payne-Aldrich Tariff of 1909, which vastly increased the tariff on manufactured goods. Although they lost the fight, the split between the Senate insurgents and the regulars was irrevocable, and in the next year the dissenters again attacked administration financial policy, which Bristow charged was designed to give "J. P. Morgan and Co. and a few of their financial associates control of the currency." They also joined with Democrats in beating back Taft's 1910 railroad bill, described by La Follette as "the rankest, boldest betrayal of public interest ever proposed in any legislative body," thus establishing a pattern of cooperation that continued for the next two years. To explain Taft's policies, they hypothesized that the President had fallen under the influence of the trusts. By 1911 Bristow was arguing that most of Taft's cabinet was beholden to Wall Street, prompting Clapp to remark that "there is no likelihood that we can ever stand for any legislation which they will frame." This sense of alienation peaked in early 1912, when La Follette challenged Taft for the Republican presidential nomination, making economic issues the central focus of his candidacy. By 1912 the insurgent Republicans were sounding very much like Bryanite Democrats, and, as David Sarasohn has observed, a type of informal alliance came into being between the two groups.[3]

The sense of personal rapport that had led the peace progressives to support Roosevelt's foreign policy obviously did not exist with regard to Taft, and in any case the emerging antibusiness domestic ideology of the senators led them to take a closer look at international affairs. As they did so, they became convinced that Taft was operating under the same probusiness principles overseas as on the domestic front. Bristow dismissed Philander Knox as "the minister of the steel trust and the Pennsylvania railroad," and joined in a peace progressive revolt against the administration's Latin American policies, marking a complete reversal from the dissenters' praises of imperialism during the Roosevelt era. William Borah (joined by a unanimous Democratic contingent) provided the critical Foreign Relations Committee vote against Knox's treaty with Nicaragua, which would have established a United States customs receivership over the Central American nation and given Washington extensive formal political control over Nicaraguan affairs. La Follette and John Downey Works (R–California) more actively opposed Taft's policy. In March 1911 the Wisconsin senator accused Taft of moving the Army to the border to "stamp out the Mexican insurrection against the dictatorship, and if necessary . . . to intervene" as part of a plot to assist the "MORGAN banks to float loans, secured by the government army and navy." La Follette worried about the military's assisting "a gigantic Wall Street gamble," one of the many "interesting and instructive" comparisons between American policy in Mexico and the English protectorate in Egypt. He criticized the Secretary's proposed Honduran treaty (modeled on his aborted treaty with Nicaragua) on similar grounds and called for Knox to submit the treaty to an open session of the Senate. A bewildered Knox privately wrote that the dissenters had based their position on "a complete misunderstanding of the realities of the situation, and an idea probably that Wall Street is using the Department, instead of the realization that the Department is seeking to make American capital an instrumentality of American diplomacy." In any case, La Follette was not persuaded, and he launched a similar campaign against a 1911 proposal by the administration to sell American warships to Argentina.[4] Works, as California's junior senator, concentrated on the issue closest to home, articulating a forceful case against intervention though barraged with letters from Californians with property holdings in Mexico urging action. Works did not deny the duty of the State Department to offer protection to American nationals in Mexico, but he argued against any type of intervention, describing the choices as "the loss of a few American lives or their property against the loss of a great many more lives, running up into the thousands, by attempting in any forcible way to protect those who are there." The California senator also urged Knox to frustrate the interests of American business by working against future American concessionaires trying to gain rights in Mexico.[5]

Even had the new, populistic domestic ideology of the peace progressives not stimulated an interest in foreign affairs, it is doubtful that they could have remained entirely ignorant of international matters after 1909, since from 1911 through 1914 a number of foreign policy issues arose that the senators perceived as threatening to their domestic agenda. Debate on these matters led the peace progressives to turn their attention more fully to the outside world. Taft's 1911 treaty for reciprocal trade with Canada, which prompted a series of lengthy addresses by virtually all the peace progressives then in the Senate, represented the first of these measures. The Senate dissenters unanimously opposed the treaty, which they contended would destroy the well-being of farmers in the Midwestern and Western states whose agricultural goods competed with those of the Canadian plains provinces. Albert Cummins (R–Iowa) said that because of this threat the United States needed to deal with Canada "upon an entirely different basis" from that used for dealings with other nations; Borah agreed, reasoning that the administration had sponsored the proposal to "place an additional embarrassment, an additional hardship upon the American farmer." In more nationalistic tones, La Follette charged that reciprocity "takes from the American farmer something of great value, which is given to the Canadian farmer, and to the millers, packers, and other big interests." Such a policy, according to the peace progressives, could threaten the fabric of the nation. Borah, noting that "the first symptoms of an approaching aristocracy is an attempt to discriminate against or a contemptuous neglect of the agricultural interests," placed reciprocity in this category, as did Gronna, who, in words that could have been uttered by Jefferson, observed that "thoughtful men have long seen the danger lying in the overemphasis of manufacturing and commerce, resulting in our becoming more and more a nation of city-dwellers." In addition to this clash of visions of political economy, the debate between the peace progressives and Taft was intensely personal. Gronna charged that the President's ideal Congress would "be ignored and coerced whenever he deems it expedient," while Cummins denied that the President even possessed the authority to negotiate the treaty. Taft returned the fire, recalling peace progressive criticisms, made during the Payne-Aldrich debate, that high tariffs always injured the consumer. The President chortled that now "it is pretty hard for these valiant defenders of God's patient poor to step safely along the edge of such a narrow fence." The peace progressives failed to secure the votes necessary to block Taft's proposal, in part because of the parochial nature of their appeal, which even they seemed to recognize on occasion. Clapp insisted that despite pressure, "congressmen and senators should have the right to defend the interests of the people" whom they represented on foreign policy matters, while Gronna recalled "a time when a man having in mind the interests of those who till the soil of this country was in no danger of being accused of narrowness." Such an era, in any case, had passed by 1911.[6]

Although Canadian reciprocity was an issue unusually threatening to the perceived interests of their constituents, it was not the only foreign policy matter on which the dissenters' domestic and foreign interests seemed to converge. In 1912 George Norris (R–Nebraska), then still in the House of Representatives, introduced a bill to give the Justice Department the power to break a scheme to corner the world coffee market attempted by the Brazilian state government of São Paulo. The congressman declared that "we ought to be just as careful to protect our citizens against monopoly if the promoters of such monopoly are sovereign states as though the affairs were accomplished by our citizens alone." Norris continued this battle once he advanced to the Senate in 1913, blasting the Brazilian scheme as "one of the most obnoxious, gigantic, conscienceless and corrupt combinations that has ever bid defiance to our anti-trust laws." As Joseph Smith has noted, Norris did not harbor any specific antagonism toward Brazil, but merely viewed his measure as one of a series designed to weaken the power of the "trusts" that he and the other peace progressives believed had come to dominate the American economy.[7]

This line of thought peaked in 1914 debate over Woodrow Wilson's proposal, under British pressure, to eliminate the exemption enjoyed by American ships from Panama Canal tolls. The peace progressives argued that such a measure, while perhaps soothing relations with England, would devastate the economic interests of their constituents, reliant as they were on foreign commerce to transport their surplus agricultural goods. Borah noted that the railroad interests had opposed toll exemption from the beginning, because, through the lowering of costs to transport agricultural goods by sea, a system had developed for farmers in which the railroad and shipping "interests must bid against one another for the carrying of your grain, your live stock, and your merchandise." Clapp agreed that once the Senate recognized "that the underlying spirit that is demanding this repeal consists of the railroad interests of the country," it would begin approaching the matter in a different light. James Vardaman (D–Mississippi), who devoted a lengthy address to attacking Wilson for abandoning the pledges made in the 1912 Democratic platform, also ridiculed the President's proposed substitute for the toll exemption, a plan, initially forwarded by former Secretary of State and present New York Senator Elihu Root, for government subsidies of American vessels that used the canal. Vardaman contended that the idea would place the government in the hands "of the Shipping Trust," and he lambasted Wilson for relying on the policy suggestions of Root, "that astute, resourceful, untiring lawyer whose professional career is distinguished by his successful defense of predatory interests and 'the malefactors of great wealth,' this erudite, radical exponent of the Hamiltonian theory of government." Bristow said that despite the threat of poor relations with England, he could not even favor "arbitration of a question that is of such vital concern to the domestic interests of the people of the United States," while Borah wondered when "we have come to the conclusion that it is a part of national honor to resolve all doubts against our interests." Even the few peace progressives who supported the repeal, led by George Norris, used economic arguments to justify their position, contending that the exemption had not given the Midwest the economic benefits that its adherents had promised.[8]

The dissent of the peace progressives, amounting to little more than a projection of their domestic beliefs onto the international arena, did not reach a particularly sophisticated level in the years before 1914. Rarely did they propose workable alternative policies, and the far more numerous Democrats continued to carry the principal burden of dissent during the Taft administration. In comparison with Bryan and his followers, or even with the Southern Democrats, both of whom had engaged in a far broader critique of American foreign relations for more than a decade, the peace progressives offered a weak dissent, and did not contribute any particularly new perspectives to the dissenting arsenal. A tendency to approach foreign policy matters solely from the standpoint of their domestic concerns stood as the chief characteristic of the peace progressive perspective on international affairs before 1914. While their opposition to Taft's Mexican and Nicaraguan policies put them in favor of a more peaceful U.S. foreign policy, their reciprocity and toll exemption positions, if adopted, would have had the effect of increasing tensions between the United States and various foreign powers. In 1914 they offered little challenge to Bryan as the unquestioned leader of the American left on foreign policy matters, and also showed little promise of emerging as rivals to Woodrow Wilson on international affairs either.

The years 1914–1917 altered this situation in two ways. First, in 1913 Wilson appointed Bryan as his Secretary of State, transforming the longtime critic into a maker of policy, a transition that Bryan did not handle particularly well. Bryan's major initiative was his "cooling-off" treaties, which seemed considerably less practical after the outbreak of World War I; even one of Bryan's Senate supporters, Henry Ashurst (D–Arizona), observed that the only person in Washington who believed that the treaties would prevent war was Bryan himself. Elsewhere in the world, Bryan had difficulty even translating his ideas into practicable policies. Initially in Latin America, Bryan thought that the replacement of Dollar Diplomacy with something more moral would be straightforward enough, but he quickly fell into the Roosevelt/Taft pattern of recommending interventions to prevent future interventions. In both Haiti and the Dominican Republic, despite his antimilitarist background, the Secretary recommended forcible American measures to combat "pernicious revolutionary activity," while with Nicaragua he negotiated a treaty which so violated Nicaraguan sovereignty that even partisan Democratic senators rebelled against its measures. In both Europe and East Asia, Bryan strove to avoid U.S. involvement in the international conflicts that had erupted in 1914, but he never came up with a consistent program that realized his ideological objectives. He finally resigned as Secretary of State in 1915 over a dispute with Wilson about the stiff wording of a protest note sent to Germany following the sinking of the *Lusitania*. Now clearly out of step with the political mainstream, he was something of a political liability, at least in the short term. Even one of his congressional sympathizers, North Carolina Representative Robert Page, remarked that "no American with red blood in his veins can subscribe to the ideas of Mr. Bryan at this time."[9]

Bryan's decline should not be overestimated. As early as 1908, one Bryanite had commented that "we are in good shape in the House," and this situation persisted through the mid-1910s. Bryan sympathizers in the House were particularly active in fighting against wartime proposals to increase the nation's military spending. In February 1915 Democrats accounted for 139 of the 155 representatives who favored an amendment to reduce funds for new battleship construction, while the next year, over two-thirds of the 51 representatives who opposed the expanded 1916 naval appropriation bill came from the Bryan wing of the Democratic party. Two Bryanite congressmen, Claude Kitchin (D–North Carolina) and Warren Worth Bailey (D–Pennsylvania), proved effective and quite influential foes of many of Wilson's foreign policies. Meanwhile, Bryan himself grew noticeably more comfortable following his resignation. For instance, he engaged in a public debate with Taft, now head of the League to Enforce Peace (LEP), an organization founded to support American membership after the war in an international organization endowed with collective security powers, dismissing the LEP plan as a scheme to "make ourselves partners with other nations in the waging of war." Instead, he promised to lead the fight against either entering the war or committing to a forceful policy after its conclusion. The former Secretary also urged the United States to postpone the settlement of its disputes with Germany until after the war had concluded as a way of lessening the passions that might trigger a more forceful American policy.[10]

Yet Bryan's political strength, concentrated in the Democratic party and particularly in the House of Representatives, weakened noticeably in 1916. Wilson's emergence as a figure determined to articulate his own foreign policy and to remake the Democratic party in his image threatened Bryan's primacy as party spokesman on foreign affairs. Furthermore, Democratic occupancy of the White House lessened the partisan motivations that in part had contributed to the impressive Democratic unity on most foreign policy issues during the Taft years. In addition, the House proved particularly vulnerable to Wilson's decision to exercise his political power on behalf of his foreign policy, as finally occurred in early 1916 after the introduction of a resolution by Democratic Representative Jeff McLemore of Texas to sacrifice American neutral rights as a way of lessening the possibility of coming into conflict with Germany. If passed, the resolution would have given Congress something akin to a coordinate voice over the making of foreign policy, and initial reports indicated that nearly two-thirds of the Democratic members of the House favored the proposal. A massive lobbying campaign by Wilson reversed the tide, and the McLemore Resolution and the accompanying Gore Resolution (in the Senate) were overwhelmingly defeated. In the process, Wilson had asserted his power over the Democratic party on matters of foreign affairs. More important, Wilson's willingness to use the power of his office made it extremely unlikely that the House, over which the leadership exerted far greater control and dissent had a more difficult time establishing an effective voice, would play an independent role on foreign policy at any point in the near future. Given that Bryan's strength was concentrated in the House, this outcome had particularly serious consequences for him.[11]

A few Bryanites in the Senate rebelled against these developments and gradually broke with the administration entirely on foreign policy matters, joining the peace progressives. Though different in background and temperament, the five Southern peace progressives shared two characteristics: a domestic background in either populism or Bryanite Democratic activity in the 1890s and an either personal or political break with Wilson. Their nominal leader was James Clarke (D–Arkansas), who served as president *pro tempore* of the Senate until his death in 1916. A former Free Silver governor, Clarke began showing a greater affinity for the dissenting position as Wilson departed from the traditional Bryan moorings. Georgia's Thomas Hardwick, a Bryanite member of the House during the 1900s, who did not firmly join the peace progressive ranks until after the outbreak of World War I, oc-

casionally joined Clarke. A more radical wing of Southern peace progressives looked to James Vardaman (D–Mississippi), a self-described
"Jeffersonian Democrat" who while governor of Mississippi had
pushed through a broad reform program that also incorporated a virulent racism rivaling that of any other Southern state. Vardaman carried
his mixture of radicalism and racism to his foreign policy. Less racist,
though for a time no less radical, was Clarke's successor from Arkansas,
William Kirby, who had challenged Clarke for his Senate seat with the
argument that Clarke was too conservative. The blind senator Thomas
Gore (D–Oklahoma), one of Mississippi's most effective Populist ora-
tors during the 1890s, fell somewhere between these two groups. A
strong admirer of La Follette and a bitter opponent of Taft (who later
dismissed him as "that blind fraud from Oklahoma"), Gore's foreign
policy stances, like Clarke's, bore a good deal of similarity to those of
Bryan during the 1900s. These defections allowed for the (brief, as it
turned out) creation of a bipartisan peace progressive coalition.[12]

The insurgent Republicans in turn broke into two loose foreign
policy coalitions, determined largely by the degree of their alienation
from the domestic agenda of the mainstream G.O.P. The more radical
faction, the Middle Border progressives, included many of the best-
known names of the Progressive Era: La Follette, Norris, Gronna,
Clapp, Bristow, and William Kenyon (R–Iowa). On most issues they
gained cooperation from the slightly more conservative Works and
Harry Lane (D–Oregon). Their complaints about American foreign
policy centered upon the alleged influence held by Eastern business
interests over foreign policy matters, sometimes producing quite rigidly
ideological stances that seemed far removed from reality. During the
war era, La Follette charged that a "world-wide organization . . . [is]
stimulating and fomenting discord in order that it may make profit out
of the furnishing of munitions of war"; Kenyon heard the "jingle of
the bloody dollar" in cries for American intervention in the war. The
faction's desire to preserve an earlier view of democratic government
enhanced their suspicion of an active, promilitary foreign policy. The
Middle Border progressive goal to involve the people more directly in
government manifested itself in their backing of a national advisory
referendum before a declaration of war; it more commonly appeared
in their hostility to increasing the power of the executive over foreign
affairs. At the same time, no group in the pre-1917 Senate, including
Wilsonian Democrats, were as consistent in the call for American entry

into a postwar international organization as the Middle Border progressives. The idealism of the group worked both ways, and at no time during the course of the war did they support an outright isolationist (or internationalist) position. Like the Southern peace progressives, those of the Middle Border were influenced by many of the same factors that shaped Bryan's foreign policy perspective, but, remaining in opposition for the duration of the war, they succeeded in allowing their ideology to develop free from partisan or personal constraints for the entire 1910s.[13]

A second group of ex-insurgents, concentrated more in the Western states, had a somewhat different outlook on foreign policy matters, in large part because they were less influenced by the populism associated with the Middle Border group. Consequently, they were more likely to entertain some of the other differing strains associated with progressivism and foreign policy, particularly the nationalist perspective most fully developed by former senator Albert Beveridge (R–Indiana). Also, the faction, which included several who aspired to the Republican presidential nomination in 1916, allowed partisan political considerations to influence their foreign policy positions to a far greater degree than did the peace progressives from either the Middle Border or the South. This group included Borah, Albert Cummins, Hiram Johnson (R–California), and Wesley Jones (R–Washington).[14]

Despite their differences, the peace progressives shared three traits that distinguished them from the Senate of the era. First of all, by 1914 they were the Senate faction least likely to support a forceful American foreign policy toward East Asia and particularly Latin America, largely because of the conviction, developed during the Taft years, that such a policy served the interests of their domestic economic foes. An anti-militarism of the type demonstrated by Clapp as early as 1908 reinforced this belief. Second, as Bryan had done fifteen years before, their anti-imperialism made them more likely to oppose increased defense expenditures, as did the admiration that most of them felt for Jeffersonianism. Finally, the Jeffersonian outlook that they had demonstrated in foreign policy matters before the outbreak of the world war (especially during the Canadian reciprocity debate) made them suspicious of American involvement in power politics and subsequently of U.S. participation in the European conflict. From 1914 through 1917 the peace progressives (as Bryan had done during his tenure as Secretary of State) struggled to translate these three sentiments into a coherent alternative to Wilson's foreign policy. In this they failed, in part because they tended to focus more on domestic affairs through early 1917, and in part because of the complexity of the issues associated with World War I. Nonetheless, these years marked the beginning of an emergence of a foreign policy ideology far more sophisticated than any previously articulated by the dissenting senators.

Wilson inherited a confused Mexican policy from Taft. In early 1913, a combination of counterrevolutionaries under Felix Díaz and remnants of the federal army under Victoriano Huerta overthrew the revolutionary regime of Francisco Madero. In large part as a result of the machinations of Taft's ambassador in Mexico City, Henry Lane Wilson, Huerta assumed the presidency, whereupon he promptly ordered the assassination of Madero and his vice president, Pino Suárez. Back in Washington, Taft and Knox denied any complicity in the assassination, and then withheld recognition from the new regime in the hope of extracting concessions from Huerta. The nonrecognition policy remained in place as Wilson entered the White House. In a famous address in Mobile, the new President seemed to imply a change in direction from Taft's policy, expressing sympathy for Latin American efforts to curb the power of foreign capitalists, and promised never to seek any Latin American territory by conquest. Despite such pronouncements, the administration's Mexican policy quickly became decidedly more interventionist than Wilson's rhetoric suggested, as the President's desire to drive Huerta from power created controversy on both sides of the border.[15]

The peace progressives struggled to come up with a consistent Mexican agenda. On the one hand, Joseph Bristow agreed "from the beginning" with Wilson's attempt "to restore order without armed intervention," although he urged that the "Mexican people should be permitted to fight out their own domestic troubles the same as we did from 1861 to 1865." To solve the situation, Bristow recommended recognizing the Constitutionalists under Venustiano Carranza and supplying them with arms, both out of a policy of "fairness" and as the best way to avoid American intervention. Wesley Jones agreed that the United States should not intervene to protect American nationals in danger in Mexico, since this could create a dangerous precedent. On the other hand, some peace progressives questioned the wisdom of Wilson's policy. They argued that the President should concentrate on the protection of Americans in Mexico. Works wanted a "firm hand" to uphold the "sacred right" of protection, a goal that nonrecognition, which left "us with no one to negotiate or deal with, no one upon whom we could call for the protection of our citizens or their property," could not fulfill. Borah concurred, although both senators rejected American intervention as a solution. The peace progressives presented a fairly solid anti-interventionist front before April 1914, but they failed to agree upon the details of a positive American policy toward Mexico.[16]

Meanwhile, a frustrated Wilson decided to increase the pressure militarily. After a series of complicated maneuvers, he ordered American Marines landed to occupy Veracruz after Huerta refused a twenty-one-gun salute to the American flag. Expecting to trigger a general uprising on behalf of the Constitutionalists, Wilson saw that part of his policy backfire when Carranza publicly opposed the American action. Meanwhile, the domestic side of Wilson's plan went awry when the resolution submitted by the administration authorizing the operation failed to reach the Senate until after American troops had already landed. Once the military operation had commenced, the peace progressives (and some Democrats) had the unenviable choice of holding to their principles or backing American troops in the field.[17]

The Middle Border progressives, led by Bristow and George Norris, provided the most powerful opposition to the President's resolution. Norris criticized the timing of the Veracruz bill, arguing that the Senate needed to "be allowed here to exercise our discretion and our judgment" without the White House's impugning the patriotism of the opposition. He defended Wilson's policy of not recognizing Huerta, who the senator charged had obtained office by treason, butchery, and murder; but the Nebraskan urged conciliation, fearing that the "evil effects" of the resolution "will go on long after those who have caused it have passed away." Bristow echoed such sentiments in two longer and more hostile addresses expressing surprise that an administration supposedly devoted to peace "should be so hasty to plunge the country into war upon the first occasion that seemed to favor it." He was seconded in his dissent by Works, who introduced a resolution forgiving Mexico for the Tampico affair, noting that "it requires more courage sometimes to withhold the hand than to strike." Works, like Bristow, worried about the international ramifications of war, asking "what . . . we mean when we declare for universal peace, when at the very first instant . . . we are ready to go to war." Realistically sensing that they

could not defeat the resolution, the dissenters united around an unsuccessful La Follette amendment disclaiming any intention to annex Mexican territory.[18]

Faced with the prospect of voting up or down on the resolution, a
majority of the peace progressives waffled and voted yes. Borah, who
privately lamented that protecting American citizens "was an easy and
simple matter" before the United States entered the business of "cen-
soring the internal affairs" of neighboring republics, feared that the
resolution could lead to a permanent American occupation of Mexico.
Nevertheless, he argued that Congress should "recognize the fact that
we are at war" and pass the resolution. An even more reluctant approval
came from Clapp, who termed the resolution "without any warrant or
justification" and predicted that it would result in American lives' being
"sacrificed to maintain peace and order in a conflict between bandits
down in Mexico." Even so, he felt compelled to support the troops in
the field, although he urged his colleagues to use the affair as an example of the need to "deprive the President of the sinews of war."
Other peace progressives, such as Jones and Gore, backed the President
somewhat more enthusiastically. Of the dissenters, only Bristow,
Gronna, La Follette, Norris, and Works wound up opposing the resolution; Borah, Clapp, Cummins, Jones, Kenyon, and Lane backed
both the La Follette and administration measures.[19]

After Veracruz, domestic considerations obstructed the creation of a
unified peace progressive position on Mexico. One group looked to
expand on the economics-based anti-imperialist position first articulated during the Taft years. Though conceding that American property
had been destroyed in Mexico, La Follette argued that the corporations
wanted to exploit the issue to produce a "military despotism" of the
Díaz or Huerta type, since the only risk that Latin American investments entailed was the political instability of the native governments.
La Follette called thoughts of a war with Mexico "criminal," and in
July 1916 he introduced an amendment that battleships "shall not be
used for financial adventurers who go into the weaker countries of this
hemisphere and exploit them," hoping that corporations, once denied
this protection, would invest their surplus capital in the "farmer, small
merchant, or small enterprise" at home. The amendment drew only
eight votes, but all seven peace progressives present voted yes. By
adopting this viewpoint on Latin American affairs, the peace progressives had begun to move beyond the Bryan position, which had stressed

that the United States acted as a benevolent protector for the Latin American nations and had maintained that U.S. investment in less developed areas benefited them by allowing for the possibility of economic uplift. Given this distinction, the La Follette program had some similarities to the anti-imperialism articulated by the peace progressives during the 1920s. Still, his positions continued to exist more as the outgrowth of domestic ideas than as the result of any sustained attention to foreign affairs.[20]

At the same time, another domestic motivation tugged some peace progressives in a very different direction, constructing a Mexican policy based largely on the exigencies of partisan domestic politics. Reversing his earlier position, Works argued that Mexico had sacrificed its sovereignty by refusing to protect foreign citizens. Therefore, in January 1916 he introduced a resolution authorizing war with Mexico, both as a way to address his policy concerns and more importantly as a way to remove the key decisions from the "trickster" and "deceiver" Wilson. The *New York Times* spoke for the Washington community when it called Works the "last man expected" to take such a stance given his previous peace-oriented foreign policy. Cummins, meanwhile, offered a full-fledged defense of the Roosevelt Corollary, Theodore Roosevelt's dictum that the Monroe Doctrine gave the United States the right to intervene to impose political stability on the nations of the Caribbean Basin to forestall action by European governments, contending that "if we do not permit European nations to enlarge their sovereign influence on the American continents, and to protect their business affairs lawfully existing in the Southern republics, we must undertake that duty for ourselves." The Iowa senator also dismissed the Wilson policy as a "stupid blunder from start to finish," although he did not offer specifics as to Wilson's errors beyond disputing the attempt to "force an election and a stable Government in Mexico." Borah expanded on his earlier theme that the United States possessed enough power to remake Mexican politics or to protect American citizens in Mexico but not to do both. He now argued that owing to Wilson's "procrastinating, uncertain, and timid policy" dating from Veracruz, the United States had become so involved in Mexican affairs that withdrawing "in chagrin, leaving chaos and murder and bloodshed" appeared the only alternative to some kind of American intervention, but beyond demands for "decisive action" and constant criticisms of Wilsonian diplomacy he did not articulate an alternative policy. Finally, in May 1916 Jones asserted that since "we will have to intervene, and . . . the sooner the better," a 500,000-man American force should be assembled to "establish a Government there that would soon gather to itself the element which surely desires peace." The Democratic peace progressives, meanwhile, did not care enough about Mexican policy to challenge their President on an issue on which he had risked so much of his prestige. The dissenting senators thus shared only an approach to the matter derived primarily from domestic concerns.[21]

The peace progressive critique of Wilsonian diplomacy in Central America, particularly in Nicaragua, offered a better indication of the ideology's ultimate course, and unity here was easier to obtain because the dissenters' domestic ideological and partisan motivations suggested similar responses to the issue. Wilson and Bryan, after criticizing Dollar Diplomacy as immoral during the 1912 campaign, decided to expand upon it with the Bryan-Chamorro Treaty, in which Nicaragua offered the United States the right to construct a canal and the United States promised to assume a protectorate over the country. Norris and Borah now led the opposition. The Nebraska senator, extending the economic argument apparent in his Mexican critique by contending that the Conservative regime of Adolfo Díaz did not represent "more than ten per cent of the people of Nicaragua," speculated that the "real object" of the treaty was to find an "excuse" to funnel $3 million to Wall Street bankers (through granting the Nicaraguan government the money in exchange for rights to a canal across the Nicaraguan isthmus). Borah agreed, but broadened his critique by using Nicaragua as an example of how policymakers had interpreted the Monroe Doctrine incorrectly so as to give the United States the right "to go in and censor the internal conditions" of Central American states. He argued that John Quincy Adams and Thomas Jefferson, who he believed really had authored the doctrine, had never intended it to "be turned by us into an instrumentality of imperial aggression." Borah acknowledged that the governments of the Central American states appeared inefficient to Americans, but "in their own way they are self-governing people" and as such deserved the rights of self-government. The peace progressive fury contributed to Bryan's decision to resubmit the treaty without the protectorate provision. When it became clear that Bryan's move had succeeded in getting the votes of enough wavering Democrats to secure passage, the peace progressives changed tactics and began urging consideration in open session, where they hoped to embarrass enough senators into deserting Wilson. In this they failed, but nonetheless the dissenters showed impressive unity on the final treaty vote, with all twelve peace progressives (neither Gore nor Hardwick stated his view) opposing the treaty out of a total of only nineteen.[22]

Despite the unity, hints remained that the chief disagreement of the peace progressives concerned Wilson's tactics rather than his long-term goals. Norris wrote that it "might" be acceptable—although he refused to concede the point—for the United States "to establish a stable government and prevent revolutions to which . . . [Nicaragua] has been much subjected in the past," but if Washington were to follow such a course, it should occur in the open, and "we ought to put honest men in charge of the Government" rather than tools of Wall Street. More broadly, La Follette praised the decision of Secretary of the Treasury William Gibbs McAdoo to call a Western Hemisphere trade conference, hoping that it would cause "our brothers" to realize that large financial interests did not really represent the American people. In almost Wilsonian terms, La Follette noted that "above all else" he desired to promote democracy in the region out of not "merely an altruistic desire" for Latin Americans but to achieve the twin aims of creating a community of interest in the hemisphere and to "extend our commercial relations" with Latin American regimes. That the peace progressives saw no contradictions between such statements and their opposition to Wilson's overall Caribbean policies indicated the softness of their ideology. By 1916 they had begun their journey to anti-imperialism, but they had not yet reached the ultimate destination.[23]

Their responses to issues concerning the Philippines underscored that the peace progressives had not yet coalesced behind an anti-imperialist position. Every Democratic platform since 1900 had included a plank calling for Filipino independence. Wilson attempted to deliver on this promise, introducing a vaguely worded bill to grant eventual independence, which generally drew peace progressive support. The most powerful peace progressive argument for independence came from James Vardaman, who, after dismissing the Filipinos as a "mongrel race," denied that there was ever "the slightest element of altruism in our policy toward" the Philippines, characterizing the occupation as "very, very tyrannous, bloody, and arbitrary." Vardaman also contended that the United States needed to grant independence as quickly as possible, since "the speculator, the financial buccaneer, the commercial bandit" would use any delay to entrench themselves in the islands and make independence when it came a hollow gesture. The Mississippi senator denied that the United States or any other country could teach self-government, and reasoned that anyway the Filipino revolutionaries had already demonstrated their ability to govern themselves despite the fact that the revolutionaries "almost universally come from the class of people who Senators maintain upon this floor are incapable of self-government." A proposal that all underdeveloped nations receive their independence and then be aided as necessary by the great powers represented the extreme of Vardaman's concession to the ideals of colonialism. Clapp added that democracy might not be the type of government most applicable to Asians, and he resurrected the traditional argument that continued holding of a colony could menace "the upbuilding of American ideals." The Clapp and Vardaman points represented suggestions that the group was thinking along lines quite different from those of both Wilson and Bryan, foreshadowing a schism that would become far more apparent during the League of Nations fight. This faction united around an unsuccessful Norris amendment forfeiting an American right to military bases in an independent Philippines.[24]

Several other peace progressives backed independence with considerably less enthusiasm. In a long, rambling speech Borah argued that good reasons existed for retaining the islands, notably a threat from Japan and the American mission to civilize the Filipinos, but announced that he would support independence, since it would take the United States at least five hundred years and perhaps longer to teach the Filipinos, as non-Anglo-Saxon peoples, the intricacies of self-government. Privately the senator worried that without independence "an inferior class of people" eventually could become admitted as a state, marking "the beginning of the end of the kind of Republic the fathers made." William Kenyon expressed similar views. He openly sympathized with the Filipino revolutionaries of the 1890s but, despite supporting independence, alleged that "no nation ever undertook a more splendid mission for humanity" than had the United States when it colonized the Philippines. A somewhat different position was offered by James Clarke, who introduced an important amendment to replace the administration's vague language with a commitment to independence in two to four years. (Clarke's amendment, which permitted the retention of naval bases and coaling stations on the islands and called for either an international conference to neutralize the Philippines or a unilateral five-year American guarantee of their integrity, was more moderate than that introduced by Norris.) Clarke also allowed that "we ought to protect the Philippines as far as we can so long as we stay there and protect our own rights."[25]

A few peace progressives used points such as those raised by Borah and Kenyon to oppose independence outright. Gronna argued that Filipino illiteracy indicated that the islands were "unfit for self-government," and that such a condition would produce either oligarchy or political instability of the Mexican variety. He urged retention until the United States could uplift Filipino society further, although he urged a complete break if independence was granted and thus supported the Norris Amendment. Cummins cautioned that the moral obligations of the United States dictated further reform, and that American economic interests suggested the United States should retain at least a coaling station and the means with which to defend it. Jones speculated that Wilson's liberal colonial policy could lead to a renewal of the insurgency, since "theories are alright probably in the school room . . . but in dealing with the peoples of the Islands . . . they will not be much regarded."[26]

Their differences on the Philippines reflected a more general peace progressive indecision on what role the United States should play in underdeveloped areas. Throughout the 1910s, they tended to formulate their responses to East Asian or Latin American issues by relying on ideological perspectives that they had developed solely for domestic use, as seen in Vardaman's positions on the Philippines or the Latin American proposals of various peace progressives, although by 1916 some indication existed that a few of them had begun to move beyond this rather narrow framework. In addition, the senators generally remained reactive, commenting on Mexican, Nicaraguan, or Filipino policy when others raised the issue, but rarely initiating the discussion themselves. When the problem was not raised—as occurred with Wilson's occupations of Haiti and the Dominican Republic, which the American press barely mentioned[27]—the peace progressives did not attack the policy either. Signs of an emerging anti-imperialist critique of American foreign policy existed, but as of 1917 the critique remained tentative.

Whereas the dissenters had the advantage of having considered some of the associated issues associated with Wilson's policy toward East Asia and Latin America before 1914, up to that time they had given very little thought to European matters. In dealing with the issues raised by the war, they fell back on two principles long associated with the American left: antimilitarism and a search for alternatives to traditional power politics. This agenda at the very least offered them some ideological allies, since Bryan and his followers used similar principles in formulating their responses to the war. Unfortunately for the dissenters, translating these principles into actual policy options proved next to impossible, and as late as 1917 they had failed to come up with a unified and consistent alternative to Wilson's European measures. Given the paucity of their numbers, only by obtaining such unity could they have hoped to influence the policy pursued by the executive branch.

The peace progressives realized more fully the first of their principles, antimilitarism. Building upon positions initially advanced by Bryan and his followers, one faction of the dissenters added an economic argument to the traditional antimilitarist fare, producing a quite consistent record of opposition to increased funding for the Army and support for higher taxes on munitions makers. Kenyon announced that he would oppose any preparedness measure carried out through private contracts, and introduced a resolution in late 1915 calling for all revenues for extraordinary defense expenditures to come from taxes on munitions makers, since up to then "the profit of the few has imperiled many." A fear of militarism, along traditional dissenting lines, reinforced these sentiments. Works, who opposed all military training because of "the probability that young men may become attached to the idea of militarism and with a desire to enter into actual warfare," dismissed large military expenditures (always using the term "Standing Army" when referring to land defenses) as a "menace to liberty and inconsistent with the free institutions of this country." He denounced the theory that "the one and only means against attack is men with arms in their hands," and called instead for preparedness for peace based on the principles of "honesty, justice, unselfishness, and love of all mankind."[28]

Under La Follette's lead, the economic antimilitarists repeated his contention that all modern wars had grown out of governments' use of their military and naval power to enforce the shaky claims of private interests (the Wisconsin senator did not specify how this held for European war), and argued that therefore the various Wilsonian preparedness schemes fitted "into the commercial, industrial, and imperialistic schemes of the great financial masters of this country." La Follette noted with interest that preparedness advocates desired a large navy but not more forts because the navy could be used to "back up foreign loans." Vardaman used arguments reminiscent of earlier dissenters to warn that "republican institutions have not in the past nor will they in the future live very long if they must be upheld and defended by a hired professional army." Rather than dealing with the alleged dangers posed by Germany, Vardaman sought an antidote to the "militarist germ that seems to be poisoning the blood of the American people" and allowing the state to be turned over to "commercial pirates," while Gronna termed it "little less than criminal to ask the young men of our country to spend the very best days of their lives in idleness in the barracks of a Standing Army." As alternatives to increased preparedness, Lane recommended "popularizing the Army" by improving working conditions for the soldiers and advocated government manufacture of all munitions of war; while both Works and Vardaman, showing how antimilitarism could lead to an internationalist outlook, urged Wilson to redirect the effort expended on preparedness toward a search for an international court to end to war, where the "rule of reason rather than arbitrament of the sword" would govern. Norris expanded on this perspective, noting that the preservation of American neutrality would prove to the world that a government could maintain national security without resorting to violence. "At a time when the principal nations of Europe are exerting themselves in an effort to exterminate each other," the Nebraska senator could "see no good reason why we should grow excited and squander our efforts and money in building up a fighting machine all out of proportion with our needs for defensive purposes." The peace progressives justified these positions by dismissing the German threat. Gronna claimed that a German victory would pose no threat to American interests, while Clapp felt that the war probably would end in peaceful political revolutions in most European countries that would make the world a safer place. Works saw the United States as having no stake in the European outcome, since the war amounted to a conflict of "kings against kings, empire against empire." By the end of 1916, therefore, this faction had succeeded in fusing the nineteenth-century tradition of American antimilitarism with the more radical intellectual currents of the Progressive Era.[29]

An equally sizable group of dissenters disputed La Follette's economic arguments against increased military expenditures, and did not share his confidence in either the weakness of the German threat or the contemporary value of traditional dissenting arguments. Although they retained most of the traditional antimilitarist perspective, they also indicated a desire to deal with preparedness issues more flexibly. In 1915 even Kenyon cautioned that "we have got to realize as a practical people that if a foreign fleet on conquest bent is approaching our shores we cannot go out and read them the Lord's Prayer or the Ten Commandments, or invite them to a Chautauqua lecture to solve the difficulty." The group's solution to Kenyon's concerns was what Jones termed "reasonable and adequate naval and military preparations for defense," to include "special inducements" to facilitate the construction of submarines and light cruisers and increased funding for the National Guard. Borah agreed, although he was rather vague on what kind of naval increase he wanted (calling for a "strong, efficient Navy," not an "extraordinary navy," but "one of sufficiently commanding influence" to ensure peace for the United States). He added that it "will be some time after this war before we are in immediate danger." The peace progressive who devoted the most time to this issue was Albert Cummins, who hoped to use his program against Wilson in the 1916 presidential campaign. His naval statements paralleled Borah's, except that the Iowan worried that too hasty a naval expansion could lead to American participation in a "mad competition" for naval arms. To temper any call for a drastic naval increase, he proposed the federalization of the National Guard, which could accomplish preparedness "without greatly increasing our present expenditures for the army and navy." He tied his ideas to a hope that the United States would never have to use the arms, since the end of the war could result in an exhausted Europe that would support American-sponsored arbitration treaties leading to gradual disarmament.[30]

Throughout 1916 this faction continued to struggle with the preparedness issue. Although Kenyon agreed with La Follette that some Army officers appeared "determined to force the Nation" into adopting conscription by manipulating the hysteria created by preparedness propaganda, he remained genuinely frightened of the prospect of a foreign invasion, and so he tempered his antimilitarist leanings to back some preparedness bills, notably the naval increase of 1916. Cummins, meanwhile, now argued a plan for a National Guard section for the general staff; he also called for the United States "to go quietly, firmly forward" in creating the strongest navy in the world. At the same time, however, the senator advocated moderation, opining that "preparedness is no solution for the world's troubles," and so, despite his previous calls for the world's strongest navy, in 1916 he introduced an amendment to reduce the number of battleships and cruisers authorized by the Navy bill.[31] Jones occupied a position considerably more extreme than that of Cummins, calling for "a strong Navy to insure peaceful respect for our just rights," including a more equitable distribution of the fleet between the Atlantic and Pacific coasts, since Japan and not Germany posed the greater threat to the United States. He maintained, however, that "the greatest military preparation that we can make is to prepare for the commercial contests that are to come after this war closes." Jones also privately admitted that his June 1916 call for a 500,000-man volunteer force to occupy Mexico (which he felt that 50,000 men could handle easily) flowed in part from a desire "to meet the fears" of those who wanted conscription to deal with European events; it seemed to him that the tensions with Mexico "would be ample excuse for our calling out 500,000 volunteers instead of trying to impose a large standing army upon our people for the future." Borah took the most extreme position of the peace progressives on the issue. Reminding his colleagues of previous republics—Greece, Venice, the Netherlands—that had lost power because of their military weakness, he worried that the traditional republican fear of militarism could force the United States to delay until things were too late. He called for an aggressive maintenance of American neutral rights, even at the cost of war with Germany, since peace ought not to "be purchased at the price of the dignity and the security of American citizens." At the same time, the senator held that land preparedness "must in some way be adjusted to democratic ideals and conceptions," although he never succeeded in finding a solution that suited his tastes. He also differed strongly with Cummins on increased funding for the National Guard, which he believed had no usefulness in conflict, "as disclosed particularly by the Mexican fiasco"; therefore, it "would be nothing less than slaughter, cold, deliberate slaughter," to send it to the front in wartime. The Idaho senator instead backed vastly increased naval spending (not on a delayed program as Cummins wanted) and voluntary military training, to make "our young men more familiar with the discipline and physical efficiency" of Army life.[32]

The peace progressives failed to present a unified position on preparedness issues. The dilemma faced by the senators who failed to follow the La Follette lead highlighted the common view (eventually shared by many of its former Democratic adherents as well) that traditional antimilitarism alone could not suffice as a policy alternative in the modern era. At the same time, however, the peace progressives did succeed in clinging to their antimilitarism even under the most trying of circumstances, in contrast to Wilson, who inched toward support of increasingly greater preparedness measures as the war progressed. Even Borah, the peace progressive most inclined to support increased defense expenditures, never felt comfortable with his position, making his transition to the antimilitarism of peace progressivism during the 1920s that much easier. The peace progressive inability either to produce an alternative defense policy as a whole or to link their antimilitarism with other facets of their ideology showed that on this issue they still had progress to make. This development would have to wait for the 1920s.

The peace progressives' attempt to fulfill their second broad goal, keeping the United States disentangled from traditional power politics, proved substantially more difficult. At least until 1917 they tended to respond ad hoc to crises raised during the war by the complicated problems related to the rights of neutral states. Their approach to these issues illustrated the enduring dilemma that had faced American reformers since the Revolutionary era. A bare majority of the dissenters argued that the United States should pursue an activist foreign policy, seeking to reform traditional international relations through innovative, nonmilitary uses of American power. On the other hand, a more politically influential minority recommended a policy of unilaterally maintaining American sovereign rights, avoiding substantial overseas commitments, and concentrating on preserving republican institutions at home. During the war era, the peace progressives did not reach a consensus on such matters, bequeathing a legacy of division and doubt in their reaction to the series of events leading up to American entry into the war in April 1917.

The peace progressives cheered Wilson's August 1914 recommendation for complete American neutrality after the outbreak of the European war. Their thoughts on the war had progressed no further when a German submarine sank the *Lusitania*, with 128 American citizens among the dead. Wilson responded with two stiff notes to Germany, the second of which caused Bryan's resignation. The peace progressives reacted to the incident with confusion. Gronna termed the sinking a just cause for war and urged the President to "take a positive stand and make some specific demand and stand by it," while Bristow described the sinking as "more infamous than piracy and should be so treated by the Governments of all civilized nations." While the other dissenters did not go that far, Borah predicted that the United States would be "far more likely to keep out of war in the long run by a bold, determined policy of protection to American citizens," although he declined to urge intervention. Norris backed Wilson's response, noting that since the incident "cannot be justified under any possible view of the situation," the United States should threaten to break diplomatic relations (but not go to war) if the Germans did not promise to cease similar actions in the future. At the same time, two other peace progressives adopted an extreme stance in Germany's favor. Vardaman excused Germany as "only guilty of retaliation for the damage to her own commerce by England," and described German conduct as "not half so reprehensible and offensive" as the British placing of Southern cotton on the contraband list, a "contemptuous violation of international law." Works believed that ultimately "we are ourselves responsible for the destruction of these innocent people" by allowing passenger travel on a ship loaded with munitions of war. While agreeing that the German action was unjustifiable, he reasoned that "many extenuating circumstances" militated against a policy of harshness toward Germany and instead suggested a firmer policy toward England, which had denied Germany access to American raw materials. La Follette merely praised Bryan as one of the nation's great foreign ministers and said that he hoped the President would keep the country out the war. The wide array of peace progressive responses to the issue confirmed that few of the dissenters had paid much attention to European affairs between 1914 and the spring of 1915. They returned their focus to domestic affairs after the war scare with Germany passed.[33]

Such a situation could not continue forever, and international events soon forced the peace progressives to consider how the United States should deal with neutrality-related issues. A slight majority of them came to favor working to reform the international system, even as the war was progressing, as the best way of avoiding U.S. military intervention in the conflict.[34] Works's concern that the shipping of arms to only one side "in effect makes us a party to the conflict that is going on in Europe" reflected a broader peace progressive interest in the issue. La Follette asked how long the United States could remain neutral while it supplied the Allies with both munitions and money. Meanwhile, early in 1916 Kenyon presented a petition signed by more than a million people calling for an arms embargo, an idea that also appealed because it fitted into their economic-based interpretations of foreign affairs and provided a way to strike back at "the great corporations that are making enormous sums of money out of the trade." This economic tact influenced several other peace progressives, notably Jones, and the fact that the policy would hurt England attracted the strongly anti-British Vardaman. Nonetheless, the peace progressives never united behind the embargo. Borah opposed the matter out of hand as an infringement upon American sovereignty, while Norris argued that an embargo would breach neutrality by violating the international law that existed at the start of the war. Norris' opposition doomed any chance that the proposal had of attracting enough Senate support to embarrass the President, and although the pro-embargo senators continued to press the issue publicly, they never forced a Senate vote.[35]

Norris' objection raised a more general point concerning the role of international law in the thinking of the peace progressives, and discarding a reliance on what they saw as an international law corrupted by the needs of the European powers became another peace progressive goal. Before World War I, appeals to law had represented a critical portion of the progressive plan for peace.[36] With the outbreak of war, the peace progressives (though not more mainstream progressives) began to doubt the efficacy of this traditional approach. Works took the most extreme position. Contending that since "international law, in time of war, is no better than so much blank paper," he reasoned that only through a "regeneration of mankind" with the reform of individuals—not by laws—could the world achieve peace. La Follette declined to go that far, but he did acknowledge that since international law had been shattered by both sides in the European conflict, the United States had to look for some other way to achieve peace. Clarke agreed that international law was no longer sufficient and cryptically called for Congress to supplement it. Despite remaining somewhat tentative, these offerings represented the first indications of an important rethinking of the progressive ideal for world peace to which the peace progressives would return in the 1920s.[37]

Logically, however, a commitment to international law could also lead to calls for the unilateral sacrificing of American rights as the safest way to assure peace, and most of the other peace progressives (excepting Borah and Cummins) accepted this position. This became evident when Gore introduced his resolution to prohibit the issuance of American passports for travel on belligerent ships, to withdraw protection from American citizens who traveled on such ships, to prevent vessels of nations at war from entering American ports if they transported American citizens, and to prohibit American and other neutral vessels from transporting American citizens if the ships contained contraband of war. The Oklahoma senator justified his resolution with the comment that an American citizen "has the legal right, not the moral right, to run the risk of involving this Nation in war," a position that drew enthusiastic support from most peace progressives. Jones, who noted that "this is not the time to be technical or 'finnical' about our rights," termed any American who traveled on a belligerent vessel as "utterly lacking in patriotism and wholly regardless of the rights of humanity." Likewise, Clapp viewed the legal right to travel on a belligerent vessel as the outmoded vestige of a bygone age. Unity eluded the group when Borah argued that passage of the resolution would remove the United States from the ranks of the great powers and possibly injure American commerce for years to come, and warned that Wilson could not continue his "milk and water" policy of allowing Germany to "ravage and outrage American citizens."[38]

Ironically, Wilson's tactics in suppressing the Gore-McLemore Resolution earned as much comment from the peace progressives as had the resolution itself, revealing the group's narrow conception of executive authority over foreign affairs. Clarke reasoned that the Senate had an "affirmative duty" to face international questions, while La Follette, increasingly suspicious of the President, termed Wilson's conduct "not only unusual but unprecedented," based apparently on a belief that "the Executive should be left free to pursue any foreign policy whatever the issue." Even Borah, who opposed the principle behind Gore's resolution, voted with the peace progressive majority as a way of condemning Wilson's "very discreditable methods." In addition to arousing Wilson's fury, the peace progressives also attracted the attention of the New York Times, which accused them of paving the way for a "cowardly surrender" by trying to "filch" the executive of its powers, all at the behest of the German government.[39]

When the peace progressives attempted to translate these sentiments into concrete policy options, however, they failed, as occurred most

notably with their sporadic attempts to adopt a national war referendum, an idea seized upon in 1916 by antipreparedness groups as a
way to delay American entry into the war. A war referendum provided
Clapp with the answer to his 1914 quest to deprive the President of the
"sinews of war." Accordingly, he introduced a bill for it in mid-1916,
contending that it would balance the proven danger of the President's
use of his powers as commander-in-chief to precipitate a war. La
Follette concurred, hoping that "democratic control of foreign policies," by giving the people "a deciding voice in the declaration of war,"
would form the basis for permanent world peace. Finally, Norris and
Gronna teamed to introduce a war referendum bill of their own. They
freely admitted their intention to strip from the President the exclusive
power of "the handling of diplomatic relations with foreign governments" and instead compel Wilson to "report to Congress all the facts
and all the evidence before he takes any serious step that may lead either
to the severance of diplomatic relations or to a declaration of war" and
then ask the Congress for its recommendations. Norris also wanted the
President to refrain from using his influence on congressional votes
relating to foreign policy.[40]

Despite this impressive array of rhetoric the peace progressives again
failed to unite or to bring any of the referenda proposals to the floor
for a vote. Borah said that he sympathized with the ideas of his colleagues but doubted that "we can have anything like an authentic expression of public opinion upon an abstract question" like war and
peace. Borah's critique struck at the heart of the war referendum idea.
Moreover, this indecision over how much to weaken the President's
authority appeared in the positions of other peace progressives; even
Norris conceded, in almost an afterthought, that Wilson, "of course,
has jurisdiction over matters pertaining to our relations with foreign
countries." The most extraordinary statement on executive authority
came from the usually temperate Kenyon, who speculated in early 1916
that it might be better "if Congress didn't have to convene," since there
were "always a few indelicate members who will make the wrong sort
of speeches"; instead, "it is better for the president to handle the [for-
eign policy] alone and not with the worry and responsibility of a congress upon his hands." Undoubtedly some of these feelings flowed from
the peace progressive belief that Wilson had prevented a more interventionist Congress from pushing the country into war from the outset
of the conflict. The sympathy of many of the senators with Wilson's

domestic agenda, in combination with some residual remembrances of the use that Theodore Roosevelt had made of a strong presidency to achieve needed domestic reforms, also made the senators less likely to make a virulent anti-executive power position the heart of their ideology. Despite their disagreements with his foreign policy, all the Democratic peace progressives supported Wilson's reelection bid in 1916, while La Follette, Norris, and Gronna provided at least covert support, and the others did little to aid the cause of G.O.P. nominee Charles Evans Hughes. The most intense peace progressive support for the war referendum idea came in early 1917, when the group appeared increasingly desperate for a way to avoid war and had soured entirely on Wilsonian diplomacy.[41]

Given that stripping the executive of his powers did not seem practical, at least in the short run, the peace progressives had no choice but to return to more internationally oriented policies in their attempt to keep the United States out of the conflict. In mid-1915 Gronna, building on an earlier idea forwarded by Works, called for economic retaliation against belligerents who restricted American commerce (obviously England in this instance) as a prelude to the United States' acting as a mediator in the war. Meanwhile, Works advocated, as an alternative to an arms embargo, U.S. interposition "by peaceful means [to] bring about a settlement to the whole problem." Several other peace progressives, though not yet prepared to go as far as Works, backed American mediation of the European conflict; the first such proposal came from Kenyon, who called in December 1914 for a twenty-day Christmas truce to "stimulate reflection" and perhaps lead the Europeans to appeal to an outside power for assistance. La Follette brought these ideas together in February 1915, when he called for a conference of neutrals, patterned on the ABC mediation of the Mexican-American dispute, to resolve the European crisis. The conference would oversee the ending of the war and then proceed to nationalize all munitions factories, prohibit all arms exports, and ultimately establish an international tribunal whose decrees would "be enforced by the enlightened judgment of the world," perhaps eventually leading to a worldwide federation of neutral nations. He wavered, however, on the question of investing the tribunal with military power. Wilson, who did not rule out the possibility of American mediation, was cool to the idea, while European sources termed the idea "premature" and wondered "which organizations or which personalities" had stimulated La

Follette to act. In the face of this opposition, the idea floundered, although La Follette did not until mid-1916 discard hope that Wilson would change his mind.[42]

Once it became clear that Wilson would not accept a neutral conference, the La Follette faction moved on to an even broader perspective. Norris noted that every country possessed a domestic legal system, but in international affairs violated "the principle of the law which they compel their subjects to obey"; he recommended extending the law to international disputes, but he had had in mind something substantively different from the traditional court of arbitration or the reliance on international law preached by more mainstream progressives. Norris wanted "some international agreement between civilized nations of the world" to maintain peace, including an international navy for enforcement. To prove his seriousness, he proposed an amendment to the 1916 Navy bill calling for Wilson to hand over part of the American Navy to such an international force. La Follette added support for a postwar "international federation ... which shall ensure equity and justice among nations and free humanity from the fear and horrors of war," and he reversed his 1915 position by calling for an "adequate" international navy and army to back up the federation. Works reiterated his support for commercial coercion or a trade embargo directed against an aggressor state and backed what he called a council of conciliation after the war.[43]

La Follette, Norris, and Works never convinced all of their dissenting colleagues that committing the nation to overturning the established international order would work. Consequently, a sizable minority opposed such efforts. Borah, Cummins, and Jones headed this group, arguing that the United States should distance itself from international affairs to the extent possible, even if this meant adopting a more nationalistic foreign policy. The trio joined with their more optimistic colleagues only in opposing the plans of Taft's League to Enforce Peace. Works pointedly declined a March 1916 invitation to join the California chapter of the LEP, arguing that the League had proved its lack of interest in genuine peace by opposing an arms embargo and that any peace-oriented organization should not try to "compel a nation to keep the peace by force." Borah cautioned that the "perfectly vicious" League "would at no distant date bring us into actual conflict with European countries and invite European countries to take part in American affairs." He questioned whether the United States ever could solve the "boils and dissensions of Europe," and expressed verbal support only for the United States' exertion of its influence as a "moral mediator." Although Cummins went slightly further, arguing for an active American world role in what he called the worldwide educational movement for peace based on arbitration, he did not think that the LEP would advance this aim.[44]

The conflict between those peace progressives who wanted to reform the international system and those who wanted to shield the nation from it became obvious to all when the dissenters responded to Wilson's "Peace without Victory" speech. The address called for a peace based upon the principles of equality among all nations, the right of peoples under alien domination to govern themselves, disarmament, and freedom of the seas. Wilson also indicated his support for American participation in some sort of postwar League of Nations. Borah predicted that Wilson's plan could yield a possible League attack on the United States if Washington declined to submit questions of immigration, citizenship, or "territorial propinquity" to the League, and instead produced a resolution calling for the Senate to reaffirm its support for the traditional policies associated with the Farewell Address. Hiram Johnson, recently elected from California to take the place of the retiring Works, even opposed an active U.S. role in the peace proceedings for fear of becoming too closely tied to British diplomacy, while Cummins described the League idea as a "new and supreme government which is to command our resources in both blood and treasure." On the other hand, Clapp compared the speech to the Gettysburg Address, and Vardaman predicted that it could produce a turning point in the history of modern international relations.[45]

The peace progressives had begun this period torn in a number of different directions with the *Lusitania* crisis, and they ended it in a similar fashion. They agreed that the United States should do all that it could to avoid involvement in the European war, that the Senate should attempt to formulate a liberal response consistent with American ideals to the issues raised by the war, and that the continued existence of the European balance of power system threatened those ideals. Beginning in 1919, the group would unify around the argument that anti-imperialism would satisfy these conflicting demands. In 1917, however, although they agreed on the proper ends of American policy, they had yet to decide on the proper means needed to achieve their common goals.

The division of the peace progressives on war-related issues prevented them from playing anything but a fragmented role in the events
that culminated in American participation in the European war.[46] The
confusion reached its height during consideration of the armed ship
bill, introduced by Wilson as the congressional session neared expira-
tion to authorize the arming of American merchant ships for defensive
purposes. Seeing that they lacked the votes to defeat the proposal, the
peace progressives, under the leadership of La Follette and Norris, decided to filibuster. In a stirring address, Vardaman described the battle
as one between the partisan patriot and the "shrewd manipulator of
governmental functions for personal profit," and he doubted that war
would come if the administration would place a higher value on "human
life than commercial conquest." Unlike Vardaman, Lane did not worry
about the grant of power to Wilson personally, but was concerned
about the precedent that such a grant could create, and he feared that
the bill would lead Americans to "hunting to make enemies." Clapp,
who had finished third in a four-way 1916 G.O.P. primary, lamented
that his final Senate address would describe the country as "thoroughly
today in the hands of commercialism." He called for either preserving
the "sacred" principles of the Constitution by upholding congressional
power or enacting a war referendum to return to the democratic spirit
of the Constitution, and he further questioned the advisability of going
to war on the basis of abstract and changeable principles of international
law. In the most important address, Norris called the bill an "illegal
amendment" to the Constitution resulting in the Senate's "surrendering our authority"; to drive his point home, he quoted passages on
the need for a strong congressional role in foreign affairs from Wilson's
Congressional Government. Like Works and Vardaman, the Nebraska
senator questioned the degree to which Germany was more guilty than
England of violating American rights. Parliamentary maneuvering by
the Democrats denied La Follette, who had planned to close out the
filibuster, a chance to make his address, but the session adjourned with
the filibuster successful in preventing enactment of the armed ship
bill.[47]

Cummins, Kenyon, and Jones also opposed the bill, but for very
different reasons from those of the La Follette group. Cummins favored
giving "our merchant ships the right to arm and defend themselves,"
provided that they did not carry munitions to the European Allies, and
not through a method that would "confer upon the president unlimited

authority." By mid-March he publicly acknowledged the possibility that Wilson's path had been the correct one, although he found himself "beset with many doubts and in the midst of great perplexity." Kenyon did not speak during Senate debate on the measure, but shortly afterward he supported giving "the president the power to arm ships if they are not munition ships but not to give him unlimited power." He declined to be more specific, although La Follette reported privately that Kenyon "manifestly disapproved of what we were doing." Jones backed the principles of the bill even more strongly than Cummins, but like the Iowa senator worried about its constitutional ramifications, while Borah did not speak during debate and intimated that he backed the bill. In the end, the success of the filibuster proved an extremely costly victory. Wilson proceeded to arm the ships anyway under the authority of an 1819 statute, and denounced the filibusterers as a "little group of willful men"; the *Atlanta Journal* spoke for the national press when it charged that the Senate had been "disgraced and degraded by cowardly treason in its very midst" headed by the "asinine" Vardaman and the "odious" La Follette.[48]

The group fractured further when Wilson came to Congress a month later with the inevitable declaration of war. With Clapp and Works gone from the Senate and Kirby and Kenyon politically cowed by the fierce reaction to the filibuster, only five peace progressives opposed the war resolution. Pronouncing himself "opposed to war in any form," Gronna called for a referendum before the final vote, noting that the United States previously had criticized "European monarchies for forcing their subjects into war against their will"; Vardaman agreed that the war vote put "the Republic on trial" by subjecting democratic principles to the "acid test." La Follette denounced the "new spirit of intolerance . . . that challenges the right of any man to utter his independent judgment" on vital questions. Forecasting a dissent to come, the senator suggested that Wilson make American support of the Allies conditional on Britain's granting independence to Ireland, India, and Egypt. For an alternative to war, he returned to the Jeffersonian solution of a commercial embargo. Norris touched on identical themes in more spectacular prose, charging that "we are going to war upon the command of gold" and possibly sacrificing millions of American lives so that the rich "may coin their life blood into money"; he cautioned that the United States was entering the war "all because we went to preserve the commercial right of American citizens to deliver munitions of war to belligerent nations." At the end of his speech, Democratic senators Ollie James of Kentucky and John Sharp Williams of Mississippi hinted that Norris had committed treason.[49]

Several peace progressives, however, sided with the President. Hiram Johnson, reasoning that "democracy, to survive, must be ever ready to protect its own," enthusiastically backed a war for national honor, since "ours is the heritage of democracy triumphant, and our destiny must be the ultimate destiny of world democracy." Borah less excitedly endorsed the war, making it clear that he desired only to defend American rights. Cummins distanced himself somewhat from his previous antiwar position and rejoiced that unlike the case of the armed ship bill, Congress had asserted its constitutional function, but he cryptically commented that "there is another, a better, and a more effective course than the declaration of war." Kenyon joined ranks in the spirit of "100 per cent Americanism," although privately he provided Norris with information allegedly proving Wall Street's desire for war. Like Kenyon, Kirby voted for the declaration but privately questioned the wisdom of Wilson's policy. The Arkansas senator, alleging that the "eastern papers yonder" had "lashed" popular sentiment into a "fury," leading the United States to adopt "this same militarism which we have denounced and decried," announced his support for the resolution with the comment that he would have opposed it if it had had a realistic chance of being beaten. Kirby's vote marked the beginning of a remarkable political odyssey that by 1920 would see him as the Senate's most resolute defender of Wilson's foreign policy. In the process, he lost most of his original political support without gaining the trust of Arkansas Wilsonians, and was crushed in a 1920 bid for renomination.[50]

The war vote represented a curious reversal for the peace progressives. Many of their number who in 1915 and 1916 had advocated an active American foreign policy to reform the international order now argued that the nation should shield itself from the dangers of power politics, even to the extent of adopting an arms embargo. On the other hand, many who in 1915 and 1916 had opposed the efforts of these reformers now supported, albeit reluctantly, American entry into the war. Nonetheless, the goals throughout remained the same—as did the indecision about how best to achieve them.

The war threatened the survival of peace progressivism as an ideology, especially since several of the senators did not feel committed enough to their foreign policy beliefs to take the political risk of voting against the declaration in the Senate. By 1917, though, the peace progressives had achieved some successes. The La Follette group, in somewhat simplistic fashion, had begun to explore the links between American economic and military expansion in the underdeveloped world, while reviving the tradition of dissenters' hostility to large military budgets. Led by Works, the majority of the peace progressives also had eroded the progressive consensus that international law paved the road for peace, embracing instead a more radical position that international law could succeed only with a peace-based reform of the major governments of the world. The group had confronted the difficult issues associated with whether the United States should seek to change or shield itself from international power politics, and although they failed to resolve this dilemma, their tackling the question revealed a willingness to move beyond the narrow parochialism typified by the Canadian reciprocity and Panama Canal toll exemption debates. In addition, the peace progressives had endured while their former ideological allies on the left, the Bryanites, noticeably declined in power and influence, a process completed when Bryan began championing the war effort despite the obvious contradiction between this position and many of his previously stated ideals. Although the dissenting senators failed to keep the United States out of the European war and had also proved unable to realize their policies in secondary foreign policy arenas, ranging from Mexico to the Philippines to military policy, by 1917 they exhibited signs of agreement on what should constitute the broad goals for American foreign policy. Ironically, the prosecution of the war that most of them had opposed ultimately unified the peace progressive movement under an anti-imperialist banner. This development in turn paved the way for the formation in the 1920s of the most powerful left-wing dissenting ideology that Congress has ever produced.

3

Alternative to Wilsonianism

The peace progressives did not know what policy Wilson had in mind with the arrival of war. Two days after the war declaration, Borah introduced a resolution to reaffirm the traditional attachment to non-entanglement dating from the Farewell Address and the Monroe Doctrine; he argued that keeping trade routes open should constitute the top American priority, which would not require "entering at once into the European war." He also urged Wilson to press for the right to ship "innocent" products to neutral nations regardless of British opposition. Kenyon and Gore believed that the United States should contribute money and munitions to the war effort but not send men, since the sentiments of the American people remained for peace. Johnson added that "out of the war there must come some positive benefits to democracy." Other peace progressives did not share the California senator's optimism, and most seemed to believe, as Wilson himself had supposed, that the war would retard the reformist domestic program.[1]

By the end of 1919, however, this tentativeness in the peace progressive position had vanished. The process occurred in two stages. The first, which unfolded during the war itself, featured the fusing of domestic and international issues, eliminating the concentration on domestic affairs that had plagued the peace progressives before 1917. Then in the aftermath of the conflict, the peace progressives coalesced around an anti-imperialist ideology that attacked Wilsonianism from the left. The two sides sparred over Wilson's decision to send American troops to Russia, and the President and his left-wing foes articulated radically different visions of the postwar order during debate over American membership in the League of Nations. The League battle, in particular the two sides' contrasting interpretations of Article XI of the Covenant, first illustrated what became the two significant approaches of the twentieth-century American left to international affairs. Wilson did not lose the League of Nations fight because he failed to persuade the peace progressives to support his program (although their defection had high political costs for him), but after 1919 the President's foreign policy ideology had a strong left-wing rival that challenged Wilson's liberal credentials.

The scope of the administration's wartime program stunned even the most pessimistic of the peace progressives. By the end of 1917 Congress had passed and the President had signed into law bills providing for conscription, censorship, and a new wartime financial system. Through the Committee for Public Information, the government had established a vast propaganda network. In addition, the onset of war unleashed a stream of patriotic hysteria that came to equate dissent with treason; the hardly intemperate Elihu Root told a New York crowd that "there are men walking about the streets of this city tonight who ought to be taken out at sunrise tomorrow and shot for treason."[2] In such an atmosphere, the peace progressives had no chance of enacting their own program, yet the war years proved crucial to the formation of a consistent dissenting ideology. The perceived excesses of the Wilson administration sharpened the group's antiexecutive outlook, in particular causing senators such as Borah and Johnson to reexamine their Rooseveltian fascination with a powerful President. The other Western progressives were not as comfortable with this approach, and by 1919 both Cummins and Jones were well on their way to becoming conservative Republicans.

Wilson's endorsement of conscription, after toying with the idea of a volunteer army, shocked the Western progressives. Borah, who led the opposition, charged that the draft would "transform this republic into an autocracy"; he found it "perfectly repulsive . . . to conscript a man and drive him into the European trenches . . . for any grounds yet advanced or suggested" by the administration. In sharp contrast to the prewar period, when the senator had warned against overrating the dangers posed by militarism, Borah now termed conscription "the most dangerous virus against which republics have to guard." Thomas Hardwick, another prowar senator, joined Borah in opposing conscription. Bacon's successor, Hardwick had compiled a curious foreign policy record in the prewar era, siding with the peace progressives only occasionally; yet evidence exists that he participated in the armed ship bill filibuster, consuming time by delivering a long speech in favor of the resolution. Once the United States entered the conflict, Hardwick broke entirely with the President, agreeing with Borah that the draft represented the "beginning of a militarism from which we will not soon escape," leading to the establishment of an "autocracy in this country greater than that you have started out to demolish across the seas." Like Borah, Hardwick defined American war aims very narrowly, contending that the United States had entered the conflict only because of the German policy of injuring American commerce; he favored concluding peace with Germany the minute Berlin rescinded unrestricted submarine warfare. Given these limited aims, the senator opposed sending a large army to Europe, calling instead for American financial aid to the Allies, mobilization of the Navy, and perhaps the dispatch to France of one volunteer Army division for moral support. Both Hardwick and Borah viewed the declaration of war as only one of a number of American efforts to deal more firmly with Germany and not as a turning point in American foreign policy; therefore, no need to enact a radical new military policy existed.[3]

The war years erased the split on military policy that had existed among the peace progressives, as emerged in the remainder of the debate on conscription. La Follette contended that the draft reflected the thinking of "that coterie of military gentlemen" who wanted to install militarism in the American way of life. He agreed with Borah and Hardwick that the United States did not need to send a large army to fight in Europe, urging instead that it imitate Japan and not send troops overseas. Vardaman predicted that "there will be no freedom in America when the professional soldier shall be allowed to determine the military policy of this Republic," while Gronna harked back to earlier dissenters by calling conscription "involuntary servitude" and doubted, as had the Free Soil Whigs in an earlier time, that a democratic government could survive while some of its citizens existed in slavery.[4]

Although unity eluded the peace progressives on the final draft vote, they did not divide for ideological reasons. Norris surprised observers by voting for the draft even though he agreed with La Follette and Vardaman that conscription could prove "a step toward a permanent compulsory military service." But with the war raging, the Nebraska senator conceded that the government needed to raise an army, although he did support numerous amendments that would have weakened the bill. Kenyon and Jones gave even more lukewarm endorsements, announcing that passage of the bill was inevitable and urging their progressive colleagues to pick fights that they could win. Nonetheless, the peace progressives who voted for the draft did not challenge the majority's assumptions about the superiority of the volunteer system, the limited nature of America's war aims, or the potentially evil effects of militarism on American democracy. Given this ideological cohesion, unity became possible as the initial effects of the war evaporated. The peace progressives agitated throughout 1918 for increasing the minimum draft age, which had been lowered to eighteen. After the defeat of their amendments, Borah called for a World War I version of the GI bill, urging the government to pay the educational expenses of drafted men; but his proposal received little support.[5]

Wilson's successful efforts to increase government power over the press and public information drew an equally strong response from the peace progressives. The Espionage Act, introduced in the Senate by onetime Southern dissenter Charles Culberson, gave the executive the power to censor the press, to punish any activity that interfered with the conduct or recruitment of the armed services, and to prevent treasonable material from passing through the mails. Opposition to the bill marked the brief emergence of Hiram Johnson as a peace progressive leader. The former California governor, more representative of the dominant strain of California progressivism than his predecessor Works (who had opposed his nomination), viewed himself as presidential material. This ambition piqued his interest in domestic affairs that he thought could fulfill his political as well as ideological goals. He took a moral ground in opposing censorship, claiming to speak for "the man and the woman who see their boy conscripted . . . to do a man's work." He damned the bill as making "a crime of the truth," charging that Wilson chiefly desired to prevent legitimate criticism of his administration as part of an "excursion into autocracy." Johnson worried that the bill represented part of a trend in which Congress "has forgotten much of its initiative and has abdicated much and many of its functions"; when pressed on this claim, he contended that it would be "infinitely better" to have falsehoods or sensitive information about the war published "than that the citizens of the United States be gagged or the press be muzzled." The California senator concluded by rejoicing that the recent Russian revolution had proved once again that the United States was the "beacon light" for democracies around the world, but feared that this law would show that the leaders of the world's greatest democracy believed that "democracy cannot be trusted." Privately, he admitted that "the convictions of a lifetime were involved in this censorship fight." Lewis Seibold of the New York *World* described Johnson's main speech in opposition to the bill as one of the most impressive delivered in the Senate during his coverage of the institution.[6]

Other peace progressives shared Johnson's concern. Borah contended that the bill violated the Bill of Rights and would function as "a certain shield or cover" for administration mistakes, since the censorship board "would be composed undoubtedly of those whose acts ought to be criticized."[7] Cummins added that the bill would sacrifice "the well-established advantages of publicity" by failing to distinguish between legitimate military secrets, which deserved protection, and political national security issues, which were subjects of legitimate public debate. Although Borah felt the measure "so bad that the modifications will not help it much," the peace progressives attempted to water down the bill once it became clear that administration forces had the votes necessary to pass. After the amendments narrowly failed, the more politically conscious of the group—Cummins, Gore, Johnson, Jones, and Kenyon—voted for the bill. Borah sided with five radicals in voting against it. On the testing amendments the peace progressives voted unanimously for weakening the act. Although they failed to prevent its passage, the peace progressive fight against the Espionage Act marked a significant point in the emergence of a consistent anti–executive power element in their ideology. The Espionage Act debate also showed how, in the war era, the previous distinction between domestic and foreign policy became blurred. As a result the peace progressives were far more united and aggressive in opposing administration policies than they had been in reacting to Wilson's foreign policies before 1917.[8]

The wartime hysteria that produced this unity, however, proved costly. On September 20, 1917, La Follette traveled to St. Paul to speak before a conference called by the Nonpartisan League to discuss the high cost of living. The senator's speech consisted of nothing new; he again denied that the United States should have entered the war, repeated his argument that Americans should have sacrificed their "technical" rights under international law in the name of peace, and alleged that Congress had turned over too many of its powers to the executive. According (incorrectly) to the Associated Press dispatch from St. Paul, La Follette also said that the United States "had no grievance against Germany." Traditional La Follette enemies seized upon the reports to discredit him. Theodore Roosevelt called the senator "the Grand American neo-copperhead" and, charging that La Follette was "at the moment loyally serving one country—Germany," advocated exiling the senator and "shadow huns" like Gronna to Germany. Frank Kellogg, Clapp's Senate successor, introduced the resolution for expulsion shortly thereafter, on September 29.[9] Though eventually exonerated, the charges temporarily removed La Follette from any position of influence within the Senate, and he delivered only one major speech, on freedom of speech in time of war, for the remainder of the conflict.[10]

Peace progressives' policy toward civil liberties, censorship, and the Espionage Act revealed a great deal concerning their feelings on the Wilsonian way of war. Borah called for prosecuting the war "according to American methods," which translated into doing as little as possible to disrupt normal peacetime existence and maintaining the power of the Senate against the natural wartime tendency toward increased executive influence. This stand matched the group's very limited war aims and general lack of enthusiasm about the conflict. Perhaps more importantly, as Thomas Knock observes, Wilson's policies on these issues had shattered the progressive internationalist coalition that had sustained the President's foreign policy vision in the prewar era. These disenchanted liberals and radicals began to look elsewhere in the political spectrum for allies, and began to turn to the peace progressives. In a sense, the losing battles over civil liberties and military issues represented the initial stages of what would become a powerful 1920s coalition between the peace movement and the peace progressives.[11]

War finance became another issue in which domestic and international affairs intersected. Liberals were drawn to the peace progressives because of their support for radical taxation to finance the war, in opposition to Wilson's more moderate program of mild tax increases and bonds to pay the government's new expenses. The peace progressives contended that the administration had reneged on its earlier promises to finance half the cost of the war through direct taxation at the behest of the same business interests that had carried the country into the war. Unlike on military-related issues, both Borah and Johnson eschewed caution during war finance debates, and although the peace progressives failed to alter Wilson's policies, they delivered a blistering critique that proved to Wilson that ignoring his left flank had domestic political costs.[12]

Radicals such as La Follette, Vardaman, and Gronna urged a war profits tax of 80 percent combined with a 50 percent tax on corporate profits and a graduated income tax starting at 1 percent for annual incomes of $5,000 up to 35 percent for incomes of $47,500 or more. Dismissing administration arguments that the amendments represented proof of his disloyalty to the war cause, La Follette argued that "loyalty to this government is not devotion to the owners of big incomes and the producers of immense war profits." The senator feared that World War I, like the Civil War, could lead to the creation of a new generation of millionaires, and that this new aristocracy could retard American reform efforts as had the Goulds, the Morgans, the Vanderbilts, and the Rockefellers during the Gilded Age. Vardaman used a similar appeal to oppose financing any of the war through bonds, since "if war taxes could be fixed upon the generations that bring about war it would be a strong incentive for world peace." Finally, this group of peace progressives wanted to use war finance as a way to strike back at the interests that they believed had caused American intervention. The more moderate peace progressives had few disputes with either the ideology or the tactics of their more radical brethren. Johnson's biographer contends that La Follette's arguments about the influence of big business on the war declaration (Johnson later wrote that during the declaration debate "the one argument that stood faith was that of La Follette") swayed the California senator to crusade for a war profits tax. Apart from a minor difference in rates (Johnson proposed 73 percent, La Follette 80 percent), little separated the finance positions of the two senators. Johnson urged the Senate to "have the same enthusiasm for conscripting the wealth of the Nation" as it did for the draft and, in remarkable rhetoric for a senator who had voted for the war, demanded an immediate war tax to prevent "those who coined our blood in this war" from reaping wartime profits. During Senate debate, Borah also defended La Follette's loyalty from the "bitterly personal" attacks leveled against the Wisconsin senator by several Democratic senators. The peace progressives had raised many of these themes in the years before 1917, but debate over war finance revealed the greater appeal—both within the group and for liberals as a whole—of the economic-based arguments associated with La Follette.[13]

As occurred with military policy and civil liberties, the peace progressives had little success after the initial finance votes placed the Senate on record behind Wilson's program, although unlike their experience with other two issues, on war finance their cause became noticeably more popular as the war progressed. Even Wilson warned of a "most unsound policy to raise too large a proportion" of government finances through bonds and conceded the need for "equitably distributed taxation." La Follette praised the President's "trenchant address" and gloated that all "profiteering 'patriots' " who in the past had urged loyalty to Wilson would have to support a peace progressive–oriented bill. La Follette introduced such a measure, but it failed to come to a vote before the armistice and received tepid support when it came before the Senate in December 1918. This response flowed in part from the weakness of La Follette's political position. Even Johnson worried about the political implications of appearing too close to the Wisconsin senator, writing that "La Follette is simply impossible . . . His attitude upon the war and every question in connection with it has tainted him so that his leadership even in a just cause, or even his advocacy, will militate against that cause." Even though they lost on war finance, however, the group again showed surprising unity, accepting (apart from Cummins) the argument that economic factors explained the American intervention in the war and that future peace could occur only if the government checked the power of large business interests. When combined with the antimilitarism evident in draft bill debates and the antiexecutive opinions dating from the attempts to restrict wartime civil liberties, a powerful, radical, and fairly unified ideology, largely on the prewar lines of the Middle Border progressives, was emerging. The peace progressives continued to attack Wilson where they perceived the President to be the most vulnerable, looking to accelerate the estrangement between Wilson and his prewar liberal supporters.[14]

Cummins and Jones departed from this pattern, although both men remained loosely affiliated with the movement until the League of Nations fight. Norris recalled Cummins as a man with "an analytical mind not surpassed by any man with whom I have ever come into contact in my public life," but also as a senator unusually susceptible to flattery from conservative forces, who gradually "enveloped him in the meshes of their stand pat tendencies." Sadly the Nebraska senator watched his colleague "gradually go over to the other side." Cummins' call for the registration of every man under sixty to prevent slackers reflected his growing conservative tendencies, as did his acceptance of the basics of the war effort, which as early as September 1917 he called "righteous and just"; he added in 1918 that it was "vitally important" that the United States win the war "completely, overwhelmingly" to disarm Germany. Jones, terrified by labor violence associated with the Industrial Workers of the World (IWW), moved to the right even more rapidly, and he seemed to endorse a Yakima mob's tarring and feathering of an IWW organizer with the comment that the people could "take the law into their own hands to suppress traitorous conduct." One of the few Republicans to praise the administration's 1918 "slacker raids," joint actions by soldiers, sailors, and private agencies against those suspected of resisting the draft, Jones argued that "we should commend these actions as patriotic American citizens." The Washington senator tended to join with his old colleagues regularly only on votes relating to war finance.[15]

The remaining peace progressives—Borah, Gore, Gronna, Hardwick, Johnson, Kenyon, La Follette, Norris, and Vardaman— joined forces as well in trying to forge an alternative to Wilson's war aims, illustrating both the continuing limits of the peace progressive agenda and the strength of the idealistic element of the President's appeal. The peace progressives exhibited considerably less unity in this arena than they had on other wartime issues; apparently they had not yet resolved the conflicts over American sovereign rights and prospective membership in an international organization that had plagued them before 1917. While the peace progressives squabbled, Wilson appeared before Congress in early 1918 to spell out his vision for a postwar world, outlining the fourteen points that he felt necessary to ensure permanent peace. Calling for open diplomacy, freedom of navigation, equality of nations, self-determination, and a League of Nations, Wilson's program did not differ all that markedly from that of the left-wing peace progressives, but he delivered his speech with a greater degree of cohesion than was ever achieved by the La Follette group. The President promised an end to conquest and secret covenants and requested a postwar peace that made the world "safe for every peace-loving nation which, like our own, wishes to live its own life, determine its own institutions, be assured of justice and fair dealing by the other peoples of the world as against force and selfish aggression." Wilson viewed the United States as "partners of all the governments and peoples associated together against the Imperialists," and he confirmed his support for "the principle of justice to all peoples and nationalities, and their right to live on equal terms of liberty and safety with one another, whether they be strong or weak." The appeal of such rhetoric made it highly unlikely that the peace progressives could win support for their plan (if they could agree on one) outside their faction.[16]

La Follette made the first wartime attempt to define the group's war aims.[17] Stimulated by leftist European rhetoric, the Wisconsin senator resolved to have the Senate affirm its commitment to democratic peace terms. (He had begun to drift away from the President after learning of Wilson's refusal to call for an abrogation of all secret treaties.) To force Wilson to act, La Follette introduced an August 1917 resolution calling for the Senate "to determine and to declare definitely" American war aims by disavowing American willingness to continue the war for territorial annexations or indemnities, establishing a common fund by all belligerents for the restoration of areas devastated by the war, and demanding a public statement of Allied peace terms. Vardaman called the resolution's terms "just right," although other peace progressives did not comment upon it, and the resolution really had no chance of serious consideration because of continuing public hostility toward the dissenters who had voted against the war. The *New York Times* called La Follette the "leader of the pacifists in Congress" and hinted that his resolution would give aid and comfort to the enemy. La Follette's position was called "queer as well as very personal," while the *Times* quoted a G.O.P. senator as saying that since "Gronna doesn't know what any of these national and international questions mean," the North Dakota senator blindly followed La Follette on everything. The "provincial" Hardwick and Vardaman, meanwhile, opposed the war only because they liked being different so that they would be noticed. The peace progressives had little hope of successfully defining the aims of a war that most of them had opposed.[18]

The combination of disloyalty charges against La Follette and the success of the Fourteen Points in galvanizing the same national and international liberal opinion to which La Follette hoped to appeal placed the peace progressives on the defensive in their 1918 attempts to define war aims. With La Follette on the sidelines, Borah increasingly took the initiative on this issue, introducing a January 1918 resolution calling for the Senate to affirm American war aims along the lines of the Fourteen Points. Borah, however, defining the points differently from Wilson, wanted to prevent the postwar peace conference from "recognizing the advantages of the stronger powers regardless of the rights of other peoples" by bartering "away the interests of weaker nations." Therefore, the Allies needed to pledge both the right of each nationality to separate representation at the peace conference and international respect for civil liberties and freedom of religion (none of which Wilson had promised). On the self-determination points, Borah, like Wilson, termed Poland the critical test of whether the postwar system would honor people's rights "to associate themselves together according to their lives and languages." Open diplomacy formed the other central plank of Borah's plan. Fearful that Wilson and mainstream Republicans would collaborate to consider an imperialistic postwar treaty in executive session, Borah introduced a resolution to have all treaties conducted in open session unless two-thirds of the senators present voted to the contrary. Borah's transformation of the administration's points did not escape Wilson, who prodded his Secretary of State, Robert Lansing, to construct a "careful and conclusive" rebuttal to Borah's plan for open consideration of treaties. The President said that by open diplomacy he had not meant to imply that there would be "no private discussion of delicate matters."[19]

Borah's resolution and remarks indicated the increasing antiimperialism in the European outlook of the dissenting senators, a sharp change from the years before 1917. Nonetheless, forging a liberal alternative to Wilson's peace proposals represented a daunting task for the peace progressives, and by the end of the war they clearly had not solved their problems on this issue. Both La Follette and Borah attempted to outmaneuver Wilson, but the President's adroitness at preempting his critics, combined with popular suspicions of their loyalty, made their task difficult.[20] For the most part, in any case, by mid-1918 the peace progressives seemed content to hope that in this instance Wilson would live up to his rhetoric and not disappoint them at the peace conference.[21] In the process, they altered their definition of the aims of the war from the exceedingly narrow scope offered in mid-1917 to the broader, anti-imperial visions associated with the La Follette and Borah resolutions. Wilson's decision to send troops into Russia changed the situation drastically, eroding peace progressive confidence in the President's ability to create a permanent, liberal peace.

As was the case with most American liberals, the first Russian revolution had excited Wilson, and he had done his best to prop up the moderate governments first of Prince Lvov and then of Alexander Kerensky against their foes on both the left and the right. Kerensky's overthrow by the Bolsheviks posed a series of dilemmas for the President. The Bolsheviks represented a serious leftist challenge to Wilson's liberal internationalist world order, and their military weakness both endangered the Allied war effort and seemed to encourage Japanese expansionism in Northeast Asia. Under pressure from the Allies and most of his key foreign policy advisers, Wilson reluctantly agreed to minor military interventions in both Siberia and northern Russia, totaling around 15,000 American soldiers.[22]

The peace progressives did not differ from other American liberals in their enthusiasm for the Kerensky regime. La Follette justified his war aims resolution in the name of aiding Kerensky in his fight against anti-imperialist propaganda within Russia, and after Kerensky's fall Borah excoriated the administration for not doing enough to aid the democratic Russians, asking whether the Americans could "content ourselves with anesthetizing the Bolsheviki and shut our ears to the wail of the masses." He concluded that what Russia "needs now is leadership . . . advice and counsel such as will help to bring about order," and proposed sending a commission of Americans sympathetic with the aims of the revolution to aid in carrying it out successfully. Privately, the Idaho senator believed that the United States could not "stand idle while one of the great peoples of the earth is struggling to establish a sound and stable democracy." Agreeing with La Follette that German propagandists had made good use of Wilson's failure to liberalize Allied war aims during 1917, Borah equated the German success with the belief that the Bolsheviks, who advanced similar arguments, had to be German agents. He even hinted at a limited military intervention to protect Allied war materiel.[23]

Borah's miscalculation about the true origins of the Bolsheviks reflected a general lack of information about the exact situation in Russia, and throughout 1918 obtaining accurate Russian political intelligence became an obsession of the group. Raymond Robins, who returned from Russia in mid-1918 after serving as head of the American Red

Cross in the war-torn country, in part satisfied their curiosity about Soviet conditions; he met with La Follette on August 18, and the senator left the conversation with forty-seven cards of scribbled notes reflecting Robins' belief that the Bolsheviks "were seeking to attain industrial democracy." La Follette spent the rest of the year trying to think of a way to force the Foreign Relations Committee to summon Robins as a witness, but Robins consistently demurred, partly because he did not want to offend Hiram Johnson, to whom he also was passing information, and partly because of administration pressure. At some risk to himself, Robins forwarded the California senator large caches of confidential documents pertaining to the Russian situation, including a copy of a pre-Brest memorandum in which Trotsky had spelled out rather conciliatory conditions for remaining in the war. By the end of 1918 the administration still had more access to detailed information about Russia than did the peace progressives, but the Robins connection gave them firsthand material from Russia and dispelled any beliefs they may have entertained earlier that the Bolsheviks were political opportunists doing the work of the Kaiser.[24]

Armed with this knowledge and brilliantly led by Johnson, the peace progressives went on the attack in an attempt to cut off funds for the stationing of American troops in Russia. Johnson began the process with a mid-1918 speech accompanying a resolution to compel the Secretaries of State and War to furnish the Senate with the relevant documents on the intervention. He decried the "anomalous situation for the great democracy of the world demanding open diplomacy and justice for all peoples" but having no open discussion of vital foreign policy issues at home; critical unanswered questions (clearly flowing from information supplied by Robins) included whether the Soviets sought American aid to avoid Brest-Litovsk, whether they offered the United States most-favored-nation status, and whether American Red Cross representatives were safe in Russia before the intervention. Although the senator dismissed the Bolsheviks as "worse than ridiculous," he argued that the United States needed to deal with the conditions that spawned Bolshevism—"oppression, and poverty, and hunger"—rather than wildly intervening with no clear idea about a replacement regime. He detected a "concealed" policy of a "war against revolution in all countries, whether enemy or ally, to prevent the agitation of revolution from spreading," and wondered how this differed from the German policy of imposing governments on alien peoples by military force.

Johnson concluded that he wanted "no American militarism to impose by force our will upon weaker nations."[25]

Johnson's speech set the stage for a number of anti-Wilson addresses by other peace progressives that employed similar though occasionally more radical tones.[26] La Follette emerged from his self-imposed silence to join Johnson in opposition, charging that international wealth "at this time fears above all things . . . the principles attempted to be established by the soviet government of Russia." Kenyon and Norris agreed, while Vardaman described the policy as American troops fighting the lower class of Russia in violation of both international law and the Constitution so that international corporations could collect some of the $10 billion in claims owed them by the imperial Russian government. Privately, La Follette reasoned that the policy made a "mockery" of Wilson's Fourteen Points, and scoffed at the hypocrisy of using an army drafted to make the world safe for democracy "to crush the Soviet Government that is struggling to establish an industrial democracy"; the intervention represented "the crime of all crimes against democracy, 'self-determination,' and the 'consent of the governed.' " Borah fell somewhere between Johnson's skepticism for the Bolsheviks and La Follette's sympathy for them, although like both of his colleagues the Idaho senator bitterly opposed the intervention. In response to critics who contended that Wilson needed to intervene as part of a forceful stance against domestic radicalism, Borah charged that Wilson's "lawlessness" was itself responsible for the rise of the extreme left in the United States, since the President had engaged in a "plain usurpation of power to maintain troops in Russia." The senator doubted that the American people could respect the authority of the government if the government did not follow constitutional procedures. He lamented that "we are as brutal as the Bolshevists and call it Christianity." This comment triggered a strong response from William King (D–Utah), the most persistent senatorial opponent of the Soviet regime, who dismissed Borah's arguments and held that Bolshevism was condemned "even by hell itself." Borah retorted that "the Senator from Idaho is not familiar with that region. He has no communication with it."[27]

Johnson summed up the case while pleading for his second resolution, which would have cut off funds for the intervention. The California senator dismissed Wilson's promise in the Fourteen Points not to intervene in Russia as "given not only to lull the Russian people into a false sense of security, but to lull the American people as well"; fearing that "self-determination has fallen by the wayside," he warned his colleagues against perpetuating the "psychology of war" by conceding to the President the right to wage an undeclared conflict. He ridiculed the "fantastic doctrine" of those who argued against the Johnson Resolutions on the grounds that the Russians were making war against American men (which technically was true), asking what else the Russian soldiers could have done after the American troops landed. He also denied that Wilson's policy could ever succeed given the ideological nature of the Bolsheviks' appeal, since "you cannot shoot or hang a state of mind." Both of Johnson's resolutions failed, but in defeat the peace progressives achieved perhaps their most important victory to that point. The Senate tabled the first Johnson resolution by a vote of thirty-seven to thirty-two; the far more important resolution, to cut off funding for the intervention, failed on a thirty-three-to-thirty-three tie vote. In both cases Wilson enjoyed but a Pyrrhic victory. In January 1919, Acting Secretary of State Frank Polk, recognizing the "critical spirit in Congress" regarding Russia, predicted that regardless of the fate of the Johnson Resolution, the Senate would never appropriate additional funds for the occupation. Wilson's policy had eroded domestically the very anti-Bolshevik coalition that the President had hoped to construct.[28]

Wilson's Russian policy also injured the President at home by tainting his liberal appeal at a time when he needed it most. The Russian intervention stood as the most recent example of collective security when Wilson presented the League of Nations proposal to the Senate, and the fear of sanctioning another Russia by supporting the League weighed heavily on the minds of the peace progressives. Although the Russian intervention alone did not cause any of the peace progressives to oppose the League outright, it played the crucial role in conditioning them to oppose a League unless Wilson could convince them otherwise. Johnson stated that a "Paris informant" had told him that "the first thing contemplated by the League of Nations was to have an American army of half million or thereabouts sent into Russia," and he agreed that "in this Russian situation we have exactly the League of Nations. This League has decreed the Russian expedition against our vote." Borah inferred from Winston Churchill's assertion that the success of the League depended on what happened in Russia that "the first task of the league of nations will be to take part in the internal affairs of a great nation for the sole and exclusive reason" of preventing the spread of Bolshevism. Peace progressives previously more open to an international organization expressed similar reservations. La Follette termed Russian policy an example of "secret covenants secretly arrived at" and feared that arrangements at Versailles would have similar consequences; Norris and Gronna also linked Russian policy to the League. The intervention put the peace progressives in an anti-imperialist frame of mind to respond to a treaty unusually vulnerable to an anti-imperialist critique.[29]

Although the Russian intervention represented the senators' primary international policy concern apart from World War I before the consideration of the League of Nations, they occasionally commented on other issues. Using an anti-imperialist outlook, they provided the only sustained opposition to the 1917 Webb-Pomerene Act, which exempted businesses engaged in the foreign export trade from antitrust laws. La Follette charged that the "real author" of the legislation, George Rublee, the first graduate of Groton School and a man of an infinitely different world outlook from the Wisconsin senator, "proposes to give *our exploiters* the right to combine in order the better to compete with other foreign exploiters (in combinations) to extend foreign trade." The senator predicted that passage of the act would lead to "a bigger navy to 'protect foreign trade'—and thence it is but a short step to absolute imperialism." The peace progressives united around a Cummins amendment to weaken the act; when that failed they voted en masse against the bill, with only Jones dissenting. Wilson succeeded in overcoming Democratic opposition by arguing for the bill as a war measure to permit American producers to compete financially and effectively for trade once held by Germany.[30]

Central American issues also attracted La Follette's attention. Alarmed at the increasingly belligerent policy toward Mexico pursued in 1918 and 1919 by Wilson and Lansing, he hoped that the administration would remember that throughout its history Mexico had been "exploited through contact with stronger, more advanced peoples," and that even diplomatic intervention to protect private interests was "never justified" unless the host country had denied justice to American economic concerns, which Mexico had not done. La Follette also questioned Wilsonian policy toward Costa Rica, subjected to a quiet blockade after General Federico Tinoco overthrew the elected government and established military rule in mid-1917. Reports of border clashes between the pro-American Nicaraguan regime and Tinoco's forces prompted La Follette to introduce a July 1919 resolution instructing the State Department to release all information on "why Nicaragua, a country over which the United States is maintaining a protectorate, has been and is now permitted, with armed forces, to invade and threaten with invasion the territory of Costa Rica." After excising the comment about the protectorate status of Nicaragua, the Senate passed the resolution by a voice vote.[31]

The Russian intervention (and Webb-Pomerene, to a far lesser degree) performed an important function in the formation of a coherent peace progressive ideology; as the comments of Borah and Johnson reveal, those Western peace progressives who remained with the group had embraced a considerably stronger anti-imperialist vision than they had entertained in the years before 1917. Even Johnson, the peace progressive furthest from La Follette politically, personally, and ideologically, agreed with the Wisconsin senator that "the real thing behind the scenes in this Russian situation is the international banker."[32] By causing Borah and Johnson to modify their views on anti-imperialism, the Russian intervention unified the group around an anti-imperialist ideology while for the first time showing the usefulness of applying that ideology to a critique of European events. As the spring of 1919 approached, then, the peace progressives had coalesced on issues relating to relations with weaker states, military policy, executive authority, and war powers under the Constitution. Only on American participation in an international organization did substantial disagreement persist. The debate over the League of Nations changed that.

The peace progressives entered the League of Nations debate in their weakest political position since coming to national prominence in the middle of the Taft administration. While Cummins and Jones had drifted away from the movement, other members of the group had experienced retribution for opposing Wilson's war policies. Surprisingly, Norris survived his 1918 reelection campaign, in large part because of the failure of his prowar Republican opponents to unite behind a single primary candidate, but other peace progressives did not fare as well. Vardaman, ill and already with a sizable Mississippi constituency opposing him from his days as governor, saw his opponents (including Wilson) unite around the primary candidacy of Representative Pat Harrison, who charged that "every disloyal man is for Vardaman."

Aided by a public letter from Wilson to Mississippi Democrats comparing a Vardaman victory to a "condemnation of my Administration," Harrison narrowly triumphed despite a desultory campaign by the incumbent. Hardwick also fell to the Wilson-sponsored primary challenge of William Harris. Although Vardaman and Hardwick remained in the Senate during the initial portion of the League of Nations discussion, by the time of the key debates during the summer and fall of 1919, only Borah, Gore, Gronna, Johnson, Kenyon, La Follette, and Norris remained to oppose the League.[33]

The peace progressives who joined the irreconcilables, those senators who opposed the League under any conditions, entertained varying opinions about the League until the summer of 1919.[34] While the peace progressives did have different opinions about the League throughout 1917 and 1918, by the summer of 1919 all those who opposed the League did so for the same reasons and with the same ends in mind. Thus the League of Nations debate served as the final, perhaps crucial element in the formation of a unified peace progressive ideology of anti-imperialism.

The peace progressive least likely to endorse the League of Nations was Hiram Johnson, a man endowed with a conspiratorial outlook of foreign affairs and a deep distrust of Wilson. Johnson doubted whether Wilson accurately reflected American ideals, summarizing the Fourteen Points as "a most excellent presentation of Great Britain's war aims," and he charged that Wilson's League offered nothing for the United States, while "pledging our country in various directions, which will require us to keep troops possibly in Togo Land, the Samerian [sic], and even in the Dardanelles."[35] Despite these sentiments, Johnson did not publicly commit himself against the administration until the spring of 1919 (and he briefly conceded that the idea of a league appealed to him), when he charged that since it was "imposed upon us by the superior cunning and diplomatic school of England," he had no choice but to oppose it. Johnson then outlined what he perceived as the multitude of problems with the League. He opposed the United States' guaranteeing the political independence of all nations, or putting "the world in a straight jacket irrespective of America's part in it"; the senator also feared that the League would "expressly or implicitly [commit the United States] to police the world with American boys." More nationalistically, he contended that the League would abrogate the Monroe Doctrine by submitting questions of importance to the United

States to the governments of England, France, Italy, or Japan, and that it would place American soldiers under foreign commanders. The senator speculated that the League fight had developed into a contest between nationalism and internationalism, with Wilson representing the un-American internationalist strain. Yet, like so many terms associated with the League debate, Johnson's definition of internationalism was less precise than the word suggested. For Johnson, Wilsonian internationalism represented a foreign policy controlled by businessmen and international bankers; he noted with interest in April 1919 that virtually every major figure who had taken him to task for opposing the Russian intervention now supported the League. Clearly, a narrow vision of nationalism accounted in part for Johnson's opposition to the League, but anti-imperialism played a key role as well; the senator firmly believed that Versailles represented "the most imperialistic document put forth since the world commenced."[36]

Anti-imperialism played a more important role in the path that Borah took to opposing the treaty, although, like Johnson, the Idaho senator never came close to winding up among backers of the League. Even so, until the spring of 1919, although he did criticize Wilson's League, Borah targeted his barbs at Taft's League to Enforce Peace, which he described as "Prussianism pure and simple" in a series of short Senate addresses. Starting from a politically maladroit comment by Taft that the proper response to the Bolsheviks might be to "kill them off," Borah did not find it surprising that someone like Taft would "advocate a league . . . which will go into Russia, which will go into this country and into that country, and adjust the internal affairs of that particular nation in accordance with the [antirevolutionary] program of the league." Borah hoped that the United States could recognize that revolutions represented the "legitimate outgrowth and offspring of the injustice and oppression, the hideous, prolonged, and insistent cruelty of the governments which preceded" and come up with a better solution than "killing them off." He noted with dismay how quickly many prowar people had abandoned their professed wartime idealism; their new program, which Borah contended bore a considerable resemblance to the Holy Alliance vision for South America, replaced disarmament with a large navy, dismissed open diplomacy, and assigned only "a most limited application" to self-determination. The Idaho senator also wondered what Taft would recommend if the American people rebelled against the militarism, large navy, and large taxes needed to support the LEP program. Perhaps Taft then would say to "kill them off" too.[37]

Borah doubted that the United States ever could lead through military force as the LEP proposed, and he recommended that instead the United States lead through "influence and counsel"; this policy, he claimed, amounted to a dose of "old-time Americanism" against the evils of internationalism. Like Johnson, however, Borah defined internationalism oddly, referring to it as similar to Prussianism, Bolshevism, and other evil Old World forces. (He wrote that the LEP represented a combination of the Lenin/Trotsky and Wilhelm/Ludendorff doctrines.) Given that Wilson conceived of his League as a liberal alternative to Bolshevism, he was thinking along lines not entirely dissimilar to Borah's;[38] in December 1918 Borah, though suspicious of Wilson's League, criticized it for its lack of enforcement power (comparing it to "an old ladies' quilting society"), not for having the ill effects he attributed to the LEP. As late as January 1919, Borah contended that two types of League advocates existed, those who would organize the moral forces of the world and those who would rely solely on military force. Taft clearly belonged to the latter category, but at this point Borah believed that Wilson (like the senator himself) apparently advocated achieving peace only through the exercise of moral force.[39]

Although Borah steadfastly denied that any of his criticisms of the LEP were also directed against the League of Nations, he transferred the arguments when its provisions became clear. Borah's letters from the first three months of 1919 reveal an increasing skepticism about the League, which he backed in principle but doubted "in practice" could reflect "American" doctrines; he cited an "illustration of the league of nations in the conglomerate army now in Russia." Also, like Johnson, Borah came to oppose the League for nationalistic reasons, fearing that European nations had hoodwinked Wilson from a desire to have the United States "both finance and police Europe for a number of years." Although this echoed his traditional fare of opposing an international organization out of fear of American entanglement in traditional power politics, Borah's other reasons for deciding against the League reflected newer concerns similar to the anti-imperialist rhetoric that he espoused in criticizing the Russian intervention. The Idaho senator found "not a word of the principle of self-determination" in the League charter, and he alleged that "no subject nationality could ever get its independence except by fighting through the League." Although the Irish were the nationality to which he referred most often in such statements, he increasingly spoke of the plight of Egypt as he received more information on the "monstrous" policy pursued by England toward its protectorate. In March 1919 the senator promised that he would oppose "any document which would place small nations and governments of peoples in a strait jacket and rivet them there by military power."[40]

The role played by anti-imperialism in reinforcing Borah's and Johnson's opposition to the League becomes apparent by contrast with the League positions of the two Western peace progressives who moved away from the ideology, Cummins and Jones. Cummins opposed the argument that "any form of internationalism is an unwise invasion of nationalism," since the world was now a much smaller place, and he saw some good in the League, particularly in its provisions for arbitration and disarmament; he even signed on to the idea of League sanctions against a power that refused a cooling-off period in a nonarbitrable dispute. Cummins' concern that the League could "gridiron the earth with an inflexible territorial pattern" flowed from a fear that the League could block expansions that the "decree of civilization demanded," like that of the United States into New Mexico. He took a somewhat indecisive position on Wilson's overall proposal, criticizing Articles X and XIX as unconstitutional and worrying that Japan could use the League to force changes in American immigration policy; but overall his sovereignty-based isolationism was shaken. As late as July 1919 Jones argued that the United States could not "refuse to join our power and wealth with the other peoples and Governments to preserve the world's peace." Although he eventually came to favor "strong, clear, and definite reservations," the senator hoped in December that Congress and the President would compromise "in such a way that we can safely go in" the League, which he felt "ought not to be difficult." In the interim, Jones urged a foreign policy based upon "unalloyed Americanism" directed toward driving the aliens "out of this country entirely." Without the anti-imperialist rationale supplied by Borah and Johnson, the traditional Western argument against an international organization proved considerably weaker in the postwar world.[41]

While Borah and Johnson had staked out firm positions against the League by early 1919, the route to irreconcilable status for other peace progressives proved considerably more difficult. In contrast to the Western progressives, these senators had favored American participation in a postwar international organization and had shown none of the concern with the loss of American sovereign rights that had characterized the opinions of Borah and Johnson. They thus were inclined to support the League initially, and only after convincing themselves that the League represented an imperialistic plot did most of them change their minds. In the process they abandoned their earlier position on an international organization and accepted the basics of the Borah argument that a league of nations contained more dangers than benefits both to American rights and to the developing peace progressive anti-imperialist vision.

Alone in Washington during late 1918 and early 1919, La Follette poured out his thoughts about the League to his family in long letters written daily at the end of Senate sessions. Unlike Borah and Johnson, La Follette worried much more about the peace terms themselves rather than the League of Nations alone; he wanted a lenient peace, including humanitarian aid to Germany. He doubted that the League could function if one of the great powers were "permitted to retain a *great navy*," since a British "monster navy" would produce only a destabilizing naval race between Britain and the United States. These two interests dovetailed with La Follette's other "big question"—the treatment of Russia by the peace conference. The senator worried that the provisional peace terms released from Versailles in January 1919 "make Wilson's 14 peace proposals look like an ancient ruin," and he feared that the President was content with "bowing and smiling and juggling with words" while Italy, France, and England set the peace terms. He also criticized the lack of news coverage coming from Paris, given the Russian precedent of "secret covenants secretly arrived at." Yet despite his criticism of the "bum peace," La Follette was still "reserving judgment" on the League until June 1919. An April 1919 British trade union proposal for a liberal peace combined with a British withdrawal from Russia encouraged him; he termed it the "only alternative" to a harsh peace that *"will certainly produce revolution."* He hoped that Wilson too was thinking along the same lines, conceding that perhaps the Wilson European speeches that he had criticized were "campaigning" to bring pressure on the reactionary European leaders. Although it would be "difficult to agree" with the man whom he viewed as a "bigoted boss," if Wilson returned from Europe with a tenable position, he had no choice but to support the President. By June, however, he had swung clearly into the opposition ranks, agreeing with Borah that the League represented an "autocracy" to "secure the spoils for the victors" by imposing a harsh peace upon Germany and preserving Western European colonial dominance over Africa and the Middle East. La Follette described the League as little more than "an alliance among the victorious governments, following a great war, by which their conquered enemies may be kept in subjugation and exploited to the utmost." A combination of bitter personal dislike for Wilson and a newfound conviction that the League would further imperialism caused La Follette to change his mind and come out against the League. Like Wilson, La Follette argued that only a liberal peace would foreclose the possibility of postwar revolution, but the senator showed no willingness to recognize the diplomatic difficulties under which Wilson labored in Paris, preferring to assign the most devious of motives to the President's compromises with the Allies.[42]

Other peace progressives from the Middle Border and the South arrived at conclusions similar to La Follette's. Only scattered comments survive of the thinking of Gronna during this period. In March 1919 the North Dakota senator promised that "I will die before I will vote for the League of Nations," but he did not elaborate why he had come to occupy such a bitterly anti-League position two months before other Middle Border progressives did. As he left the Senate, Hardwick announced that all those who favored "the sturdy principles of Americanism" would oppose the treaty, since it favored the European insistence that the United States "must take the major portion of these police duties" arising from the war. Vardaman offered more insights about his position, urging a liberal peace that would treat Germany as charitably as possible, abolish conscription, and institute a war referendum in all countries. He called on the President to bring American troops home and "give up this idea of trying to regulate the whole of Europe." Vardaman also denounced the League as both unconstitutional and an "unprecedented instrument" that would rob the United States "of its sovereign powers and subject it to the yoke of a foreign and novel dominion," depriving it of the opportunity to pursue a foreign policy based more on ideals and less on the force-oriented diplomacy that he argued characterized European international relations.[43]

The remaining left-wing peace progressives—Norris, Kenyon, and Gore—underwent a much more painful process before arriving at their opinions on the League. To a greater degree than La Follette, Norris retained his affinity for American participation in an international organization until well into 1919. Norris believed that the "peace of the world can be maintained if six or seven of the leading civilized powers of the world will enter into a League that will be effective in keeping the peace between themselves," and although he retreated from his prewar support of an international navy, the senator adopted the old John Works proposal that the leading nations of his organization agree "to an economic ostracism of any nation that goes to war contrary to the agreement." The Nebraska senator did have specific demands for his international organization, urging the abolition of secret diplomacy and opposing any agreement that would require standing armies in the "semi-civilized countries" of Eastern Europe or Western Asia, but he believed that "all nations must be willing to surrender to some extent, their freedom of action in international affairs." Given these attitudes, Norris was in "entire sympathy" with the League throughout the spring of 1919, and intended to resolve every doubt in its favor. Though recognizing that the League had its defects, he could not oppose it "simply because . . . the administration has been so objectionable and so subject to just criticism," and he accepted Wilson's claim that the alternative to the League was military preparation "at a rate that will stagger the imagination." In his only springtime comments about the treaty on the Senate floor, Norris defended the League, noting that the "history of the world has shown that we have gotten into a good deal of trouble by staying out" of international politics. He came out firmly against the treaty only when he saw the provisions relating to the transfer of German rights in China's Shantung province to the Japanese (the Japanese had occupied the province, granted to Germany under a treaty arrangement, since the onset of the war); in the end, as with La Follette, anti-imperialism overcame an initial tendency to support American membership in the League.[44]

Kenyon and Gore entertained perspectives similar to that of Norris, but upon reflection they arrived at considerably different conclusions and in so doing drifted away from the peace progressive movement. Always among the quietest of the peace progressives, Kenyon appeared the least likely member of the group to chart a radically independent course, but he began doing so after his politically inspired vote for the war in April 1917. The Iowa senator contended that the United States under Wilson's leadership could play a positive and active world role in aiding weaker peoples; he also believed that only through a generous policy toward its European allies could the United States accomplish this goal. Along these lines, Kenyon in May 1918 introduced a resolution to forgive all French indebtedness assumed during the war, which he hoped would increase the likelihood of a pro-American stance by French leaders at the postwar peace conference. His other significant wartime foreign policy initiative was an August 1917 resolution asking the Senate to affirm its commitment to postwar Bohemian independence; the senator also expressed his sympathy for the Czech troops trapped in Russia during preliminary debate over the Russian intervention in June of 1918. Kenyon differed from the other peace progressives in that he was prepared to trust both Wilson and the Allies to act in accordance with their stated principles, and he maintained this belief, with varying intensity, until Wilson's departure from the presidency. These feelings gave him a fairly moderate view of the League of Nations throughout 1919. The Iowa senator always desired reservations, particularly concerning the Monroe Doctrine and Article X (which he termed a "war breeder" that could lead to "the boys of the United States [being] sent into any part of the world to fight for some miserable monarchy that has no license to exist"); but he argued that the question centered not on whether the United States should enter the League, but on how to modify the entrance so as to protect American rights. (Unlike most Republicans, Kenyon praised aspects of Wilson's performance in Paris, singling out his opposition to the demands of Italy.) The Iowa senator criticized both Democrats and Republicans for overpoliticizing the issue; he believed that instead the "whole thing ought to be fought out before the American people," to be capped off with a referendum so that the people would "have a chance to express themselves on this matter." His opinions cost him a seat on the Foreign Relations Committee, whose chair, Henry Cabot Lodge (R–Massachusetts), considered Kenyon too lukewarm on the League to be trusted and obviously did not appreciate the Iowa senator's criticism of Republican partisanship.[45]

Gore occupied a position somewhere between those of Kenyon and the remaining peace progressives. In March 1919 the Oklahoma senator predicted that the League of Nations would involve the United States in forty wars over the next hundred years, although, like Kenyon, he preferred to modify the League through reservations rather than to discard it entirely. Gore specifically pushed a reservation to "democratize war" by establishing a war referendum in all League countries. Without a referendum reservation, he feared that the League could extend "the ancient European balance of power to Asia and to the Americas." He also criticized Article XVI (economic sanctions), arguing that "economic isolation punishes the innocent as well as the guilty." Nonetheless, he said that he would support American membership in both an international legislative council to meet annually to codify and clarify principles of international law and a permanent court of arbitration. In addition, the senator favored directing the "enlightened public opinion of mankind" against nations that refused to arbitrate and perhaps economic sanctions for those countries whose people voted affirmatively in a war referendum. Because of the closely divided nature of the Senate in 1919, Gore came to occupy an important position on many votes on reservations; Taft barked that the senator was "such a contemptible thing that it is irksome to have to deal with him," but that pro-League forces had no choice. The former President recommended putting the "fear of God" in Gore about his reelection, but the senator knew the political risks that he was taking, and such tactics had little effect.[46] The positions of Kenyon and Gore suggest how close some of the other peace progressives might have come to supporting the League, particularly if Wilson had done a better job at framing his document in an anti-imperialist fashion. Also, the desire for positive American action on behalf of weaker peoples under the League's aegis expressed by Kenyon and Gore bore some similarity to the peace progressive program of the 1920s. The Kenyon position also stood much closer to the peace progressive ideology than the other two peace progressive spinoffs, the conservatism of Cummins and Jones and the extreme nationalism adopted in the 1920s by Hiram Johnson. By the spring of 1919 the peace progressives other than Kenyon and Gore, having resolved to oppose the League, did so to their fullest, and for similar reasons—a desire to protect American sovereignty and fulfill their anti-imperialist ideals. This unanimity led them to concentrate their fire on what they considered the two most obnoxious articles of the League covenant, Articles X and XI.

Woodrow Wilson considered Article X, which committed League members "to respect and preserve as against external aggression the territorial integrity and existing political independence of all Members of the League," the "king pin" of the covenant. The article likewise attracted the concern of the League's conservative opponents. Lodge argued that it would require "compulsive force" to execute, and worried that it would supersede both the Monroe Doctrine and the congressional power to declare war. He considered as an alternative the idea of two Leagues, one for each hemisphere. Cummins agreed with his new conservative brethren, writing that Article X stood "in conflict with every precept of liberty and democracy and there are no circumstances under which I could be brought to defend it or support it."[47]

Like its other opponents, the peace progressives employed a battery of arguments against Article X, joining conservatives in questioning the constitutionality of Wilson's policies. (La Follette wondered who best knew the meaning of the Constitution, the great soldier and statesman Washington or the "school master" Wilson.) The dissenters had no trouble in acting alongside League opponents led by Lodge who sought to emasculate Article X with a protective resolution, and the faction (including Kenyon and Gore) voted unanimously in favor of the Lodge reservation to the article. They also (Kenyon here dissenting) enthusiastically endorsed a much stronger reservation by Borah stating that the United States would possess no "legal or moral" obligation under Article X. As has been suggested most prominently by John Chalmers Vinson, the opposition of the peace progressives to Article X reflected a broader anti-European sentiment, best exemplified by Hiram Johnson. The California senator maintained that the United States needed to make a choice between internationalism and "narrow Americanism" by ratifying a reservation he introduced protesting the voting inequality between the United States and the British Empire in the League assembly, although he never decided whether he wanted England trimmed down to one vote or the American contingent increased to six. Borah worried that the American representative to the League might not reflect American public opinion or might be tricked by the wiles of British-French diplomacy into sacrificing American interests. Gronna added that the United States should not become involved in European political affairs because of the danger of stirring up immigrant groups within the United States, while all peace progressives except for Norris also mentioned the need to maintain the Monroe Doctrine as a reason for opposing Article X. Borah summed up the occasionally virulent anti-European sentiments of the group when he remarked that if the Europeans wanted a harsh peace, "let Europe guarantee it."[48]

In addition to these more nationalistic reasons for opposing Article X, the peace progressives also feared that it would, in Hiram Johnson's words, "freeze the world into immutability and put it into a straightjacket," leaving "subject peoples . . . subject until the crack of doom." Borah addressed this issue in greatest detail, charging that the League architects had contemplated nothing less "than the maintenance of the territorial integrity of all these nations by force," which would make Article X a war-making provision dedicated to the "idea of maintaining the status quo by force." He again used the Russian example to illustrate what he felt the League framers had in mind with the workings of Article X. As Robert James Maddox has observed, Borah contended that in the postwar world nationalism would rise as a powerful force in international affairs, and he feared that Article X would place the American military on the side that was bound to lose in the long run. Despite this impressive array of rhetoric, though, the peace progressives would have opposed the League just as strongly had the covenant not contained Article X. The group just as fervently opposed Article XI, which escaped the mention of virtually every other Senate opponent of the League. Their opposition to Article XI distinguished their ideology from that held by the other irreconcilables, and best illustrated the role played by anti-imperialism in solidifying peace progressive opposition to the League.[49]

The peace progressives feared that Article XI would prove far more powerful than Article X, which in theory became operative only when an interstate war broke out. Article XI, which vaguely stated that "any war or threat of war, whether immediately affecting any of the Members of the League or not, is hereby declared a matter of concern to the whole League," also gave any League member the "friendly right" to bring to the League's attention "any circumstance whatever affecting international relations which threatens to disturb international peace or the good understanding between nations upon which peace depends." Wilson himself championed the article on his Western speaking tour, telling audiences to treat "Article XI in conjunction with Article X." The President made it clear that Article XI, his "favorite article in the treaty," stood as the chief protection in the Covenant for weaker nations, since it permitted the United States to "mind other peoples' business, and . . . force a nation on the other side of the globe to bring to that bar of mankind any wrong that is afoot in that part of the world." The peace progressives interpreted this as sanctioning League intervention in the domestic affairs of states not deemed peaceful by the great powers. La Follette and Borah both agreed that Article XI was the key to the Covenant; the Idaho senator said that he would oppose the League as long as the article, the "very acme of tyranny," remained in place. Gronna argued that the article "undertakes to dictate and regulate the affairs of every nation on the face on the globe," and that under its provisions, with "limitless autocracy and oligarchy complete, self-determination will forever be a thing of the past." La Follette added that the "cunningly conceived" wording would make the first act of revolution in Korea, Egypt, Ireland, or India a threat of war and compel the League to act. Borah cited an ill-timed July 1919 letter by French Premier Georges Clemenceau to embattled Polish President Josef Pilsudski seeming to offer a French guarantee about internal Polish stability to prove his point that under Article XI "the United States would be called upon to mix in the affairs of other countries in the League."[50]

This intense reaction to Article XI reflected a broader conviction of the peace progressives that the League Covenant had sacrificed the Wilsonian ideals that most of them had supported during the war. The peace progressives believed that the only way to judge the Executive Council, which would make the key decisions about enforcement of Article XI, was to examine the performance of the powerful nations at Paris. La Follette delved into this point in considerable detail during two of his principal speeches against the League, faulting the peace-makers for their "grotesque partition" of Austria-Hungary, under which the Czech state received Germans, Italy was granted Tyrol, Rumania won predominantly-Hungarian Transylvania, and the Polish state did not receive enough territory. A "secret conclave" at the peace conference had accomplished all this, and then created a "league of nations to stand guard over the swag." He reasoned that the United States had been "powerless to serve oppressed people at Paris" and doubted that American effectiveness would increase in the new League. The Wisconsin senator also feared the aggressiveness of minor victor states such as Italy and Rumania, and speculated that they would not accept American ideals easily.[51]

The record of the peace conference reinforced a peace progressive fear of how Article XI would affect the American place in the postwar world, best spelled out in a long speech by Gronna. The North Dakota senator contended that he would support the treaty if it had not added "to the power of the stronger nations as against the weaker nations," but that, as it existed, he would not sacrifice his "most cherished ideal," the "opportunity of independent and separate nationalities who love liberty and freedom to establish governments fit for free peoples to live in." He asked what had become of the Fourteen Points, particularly those dealing with self-determination, and he refused to become bound to a superstate "which establishes a principle of status quo in every kingdom and monarchy." Gronna recommended instead that the United States "should mind our own business and not interfere with the affairs of foreign nations *unless it is for the purpose of assisting the weak and the oppressed* [emphasis added]." The North Dakota senator had much more in mind with that clause than a purely negative policy, and he was not the only peace progressive to express sentiments along these lines. Borah confessed that he opposed the United States' maintaining the territorial integrity of any nation in Europe or Asia, but that somehow, even if the treaty did not so provide, nations such as Poland, Ireland, and Egypt should be able "to establish themselves as a people." La Follette introduced a reservation guaranteeing the right of revolution "to the people of Ireland, India, Egypt, Korea, or any other people living under a Government which, as to such people, does not derive its powers from the consent of the governed," despite the provisions of Article XI; the Wisconsin senator despaired that "patriots" of past times such as Kossuth and Kosciuszko who had sought American aid in the cause of human freedom would now be branded "international outlaws." He left little doubt that if asked again the United States should provide such aid. The peace progressives viewed the United States as the leader of an international bloc of weaker states and colonial peoples, perhaps including Scandinavia, Russia, and Germany, lined up against the victorious, "imperialist" Allies, celebrating the virtues of nationalism and democracy against the reactionary and monarchical states of Western Europe. The peace progressives ruled out military intervention virtually anywhere, but they never precluded the possibilities of either military or economic aid to rebelling subject nationalities, and they promised American moral and possibly diplomatic assistance for virtually every nationalistic colonial revolution. This proposed foreign policy of having the United States actively hostile to the Western European states obviously did not reflect American power or national interests as interpreted by most at the time, but to view peace progressive statements on issues like these as political demagoguery or poorly thought-out musings would be a mistake. Both the peace progressives and American supporters of Article XI agreed that the United States should have a right to interfere in the domestic conflicts of the world's weaker states; the two sides disagreed about which faction in the affected nations the United States should support.[52]

This almost revolutionary ideology also helps explain the considerable importance attached by the peace progressives to the sections of the treaty making concessions to the great powers. The provision granting previous German concessions in Shantung to Japan serves as the best example of this point; both Norris and Gronna said that Shantung represented the most important reason for their opposing the treaty. In a wild three-day address, arguably the most intemperate speech delivered in his Senate career, Norris termed the provision "one of the most dishonorable things that has ever occurred in history." The Nebraska senator noted that the Japanese (to whom he referred as "Japs" throughout the speech) had directed their fire "against the Christian religion and the Christian church," quoting a letter from an American missionary in Korea charging that "the Japs hate American missionaries in China with a special virulence." Condemning the "devious ways and dark alleys of Japanese diplomacy," Norris looked to Korea, where "Japan, by her militaristic course which would have made the Kaiser blush," had crushed a local independence movement just as Christianity was on the verge of triumphing, for a preview of Japanese policy toward Shantung. He made broader arguments, contending that the Shantung provision betrayed China and sowed the seeds for future conflict as the German annexation of Alsace-Lorraine had before World War I, and he termed the provision a violation of the key principle for which the United States had fought the war, "to equalize the weak and the strong."[53] For the most part, though, he concentrated his fire on the "so many elements of sin and wrong" of the treaty against "higher law" and the anti-Christian policy of the Japanese. Gronna agreed that the Japanese wanted the destruction of Christianity in East Asia, while Borah concurred in Norris' description of Japanese diplomacy, terming it "Machiavellianism in its utmost refinement."[54]

Other anti-League senators, including most conservatives, attacked the Shantung provision. Less common was the peace progressive strategy of criticizing the concessions granted by the treaty to the British Empire. La Follette, noting the irony that a war "waged to protect the rights of the weak against the strong" had ended by satisfying "the most ambitious plans of British imperialists . . . in Africa," criticized the way in which British policy had affected the more "venerable" cultures of Asia and Africa, and doubted that the native populations would consent to bondage for much longer. This explained Britain's desire for the League as a vehicle to protect the empire from its inevitable revolutions. Of particular concern to the peace progressives were the British colonies in Ireland and Egypt. Borah, overlooking the wartime attitudes of neutrality held by most Irish, asked why the peace conference had denied a seat to a people who had struggled for independence for the previous 700 years. The Idaho senator reasoned that since the League would uphold the British position, the Irish could receive their freedom only through the aid of an outside power (the United States?), which Article XI prohibited. Norris speculated that World War I, by making "men and nations more inhuman than they were before," explained the "almost barbarous policy" practiced in Ireland by the British. Quite unlike other anti-British senators, the peace progressives devoted as much or perhaps more time to protesting the situation in Egypt. Norris contended that the British had violated wartime promises to grant Egypt its independence, and questioned why Egypt, consisting of a clearly defined nationality, did not receive its freedom whereas a nation with many races like Czechoslovakia did. The Nebraska senator compared British policy in Egypt with Japanese policy in Korea, and blasted Wilson for betraying the Egyptian people at the peace conference after the Egyptians had believed what the President said about the postwar rights of smaller states. These sentiments represented a considerable refinement of their earlier ideas about anti-imperialism, and showed that the peace progressives had devoted considerably more time to the issue than they had in the years before the war.[55]

Administration supporters attempted to neutralize the peace progressives' anti-imperialism by pointing out that their opposition to the League would lead to the United States' declining its League mandate over Armenia, a Christian enclave threatened by the Islamic Turks. The peace progressives disagreed with the premise of the critique on Armenia,[56] and behind this opposition lay skepticism about Wilson's mandate program, which La Follette equated with annexation under another name. Gronna proposed as an alternative to mandates having the League oversee the granting of independence to all Asian and African states; he worried that under the mandate system, Africans and Asians "shall be denied the right of self-determination and must submit to the mandates of this [League] council, regardless of how brutally they may be oppressed and how just their causes for freedom and liberty may be." (Vardaman had made a similar proposal in 1916, during debate over policy toward the Philippines.) La Follette tried to amend the mandate article through a reservation to prohibit any mandate from granting a concession on natural resources to its mother country, reflecting a broader peace progressive concern with the role played by large economic interests in shaping the League. Johnson had "no doubt at all that the international bankers are behind the League of Nations," citing Dwight Morrow and Elihu Root as examples; he described the League itself as a "huge war trust, backed by international capitalists who prefer to have an international clearing house." Borah charged that greed had caused the League backers—"miserable traitors who would sell their country for thirty pieces of silver"—to abandon American interests in favor of their own. The peace progressives theorized that the capitalists wanted the League as a superstate to protect their exploitative concessions in underdeveloped countries, an expansion on arguments advanced by La Follette since 1915.[57]

The new degree of unity also manifested itself in the actions of former peace progressives now out of the Senate. Joseph Bristow toured Kansas and Nebraska denouncing the League as "infected with European autocracy," and he accurately predicted that support for the League had undermined Democratic senator Gilbert Hitchcock's political base in Nebraska. Thomas Hardwick served as one of the few Democrats on the board of directors of the anti-Wilsonian League for the Preservation of American Independence. John Works, who during the war years had championed independence for Ireland, described the League as a "far-reaching alliance and entanglement with European nations," but like the peace progressives he chose to go beyond what he described as narrow issues such as constitutionalism and nationalism in his anti-League position. Works worried that under Articles X and XI the United States would become the "defender of the *politics* as well as the territory of every monarchy of Europe, however despotic it may be," and he chastised Wilson for saying that entering the League would confirm the American great power status earned after the annexation of the Philippines. Works nonetheless contended that since the European war had destroyed isolationism once and for all, the United States had a duty to make a better postwar world, but "to render this worldwide humanitarian service we must of necessity preserve our ... freedom to act according to our understanding of conditions as they may arrive." Though not as explicit as Gronna or Borah, Works too seemed to recommend that the United States take an active anti-imperialist role against the leading League powers. Vardaman opposed the League even more passionately than Works, listing the need for the United States to help Ireland effect an "internal revolution" as one of his key reasons for opposing the League, and rebuking Wilson for not pushing harder at Versailles for application of his self-determination principles to Egypt, India, Russia, Shantung, Korea, Burma, Ceylon, Madagascar, Vietnam, Persia, Syria, Iraq, and Macedonia.[58]

The role played by the peace progressives in defeating the approval of the Versailles Treaty has been told in great detail elsewhere.[59] Teaming with several conservatives to form the irreconcilables, the peace progressives then formed a fragile alliance with Lodge, who in turn held the mild reservationists[60] within the anti-League coalition while satisfying the demands of the irreconcilables. The irreconcilables supported the Lodge reservations, modifying the League so as to make it unacceptable to Wilson, and then turned around and voted against the League both with and without reservations. When Wilson launched his nationwide speaking tour to drum up popular support for the League, Borah and Johnson followed, delivering speeches to enthusiastic and quite large audiences—in Chicago they drew 10,000 people. When Wilson and Lodge refused to compromise, the irreconcilables retained their position in the Senate balance of power and helped prevent approval of the Versailles Treaty on three separate occasions in 1919 and 1920.[61]

Potential oblivion stood as the principal problem of the peace progressives in the wake of their League success. Both Gronna and Gore lost in 1920 primaries, and although Gronna's eventual successor, Edwin Ladd, proved sympathetic to the peace progressive cause, the Oklahoma seat went to a conservative Republican, John Harreld.[62] Despite their small numbers, however, the peace progressives managed to form an ideology more global and much more detailed than that of any previous group of congressional dissenters, uniting behind a program that applied fairly well to all areas of the world. Many of the ideas offered by the peace progressives from 1917 through 1919 reflected themes common to American thought about international affairs since the Revolutionary era, but the way in which the peace progressives structured their dissent was quite original. They also established a left-wing alternative to Wilsonianism and enjoyed substantial success in exposing the contradictions within the President's liberal world vision, as occurred with issues like the debate over Article XI. (At the same time, though, the often rigid stance of the senators blinded them both to the positive aspects of the League of Nations and the common points between their ideals and those of Wilson.) Unlike the period from 1913 through 1917, the dissenters also began proposing more positive alternatives of their own, in the process bringing anti-imperialism to a prominent place in the liberal mindset of the era, triggering its increasingly widespread acceptance as the dominant ideology of the American peace movement during the 1920s. The story of left-wing foreign policy activism during the decade in large part centers on the dual themes of the peace progressive ideological challenge to Wilsonianism and the American peace movement's increasing acceptance of anti-imperialism as the precursor to solving the international problems of the postwar era.

4

Alternative to Imperialism

Although farmers had held their own economically during the war, by 1921 American overproduction combined with a resurgence in international competition had created a worldwide agricultural depression. The price of wheat declined from $2.83 per bushel in July 1920 to $1.26 per bushel in December 1921; during a similar period, the per bushel price of corn fell from $1.55 to .48 while rye tumbled from $2.23 to .86.[1] The peace progressives took advantage of the opening caused by the economic distress, and by 1927 they again occupied a prominent place in the Senate. Once in place, the movement looked to expand upon the anti-imperialist critique developed in the League of Nations fight, and the dissenters found in the inter-American and East Asian policies pursued by the decade's Republican administrations a wide array of policies to which they could apply their new ideology fruitfully.

In the process, the peace progressives began to eclipse the Wilsonians as the most important spokesmen of the American left on foreign policy issues. In contrast to divided responses coming from followers of the former President, the dissenting senators articulated consistent and, to the decade's peace activists, appealing responses to the policies of the decade's Republican administrations toward the USSR, Mexico, Nicaragua, and China. At the same time the dissenters continued, as in the League of Nations battle, to affect policy through the tenacity of their opposition. Their fierce dissent helped force the administration of Calvin Coolidge to back down in early 1927 from an aggressive policy toward Mexico, and, using their parliamentary skills, they launched an ultimately successful crusade to cut off Senate funding for the occupation of Nicaragua. Though less successful in influencing the administration's position on Soviet and Chinese affairs, the peace progressives established themselves by 1929 as most important congressional players on issues relating to the underdeveloped world, a bloc that policymakers could afford to ignore only at their own peril.

The first new radical to win election during the decade, Edwin Ladd, proved to be the least reliable peace progressive. After arriving in North Dakota in 1890 as a professor in the Chemistry Department of the North Dakota Agricultural College, Ladd led a campaign against the adulteration of food that led to his appointment as North Dakota's first pure food administrator. The fight against business interests on this issue made him sympathetic to the political appeal of the Non-Partisan League, and in 1920 he received crucial tactical support from the NPL in his campaign against Gronna. Once in Washington, Ladd compiled a curious record; Peter Norbeck (R–South Dakota), hardly a radical himself, remarked in late 1922 that Ladd was "becoming conservative as fast as any progressive who ever came here." At the same time, however, the North Dakota senator delivered several strong attacks on Harding administration foreign policy that placed him in line with peace progressive thinking, and he did risk his committee seats by endorsing the La Follette presidential candidacy in 1924. When Ladd died suddenly in June 1925, few could speak with any certainty about his personal ideology.[2]

The 1922 elections saw six new senators join Ladd as members of this second generation of peace progressives.[3] Minnesota elected Farmer/Labor candidate Henrik Shipstead, a second-generation Norwegian who was a dentist before entering politics as the NPL-endorsed candidate in a 1918 House contest and the 1920 G.O.P. gubernatorial race. In 1922 the radicals gave up their attempt to conquer the G.O.P. from within and formed the Farmer/Labor Party. The party fielded Shipstead against the prime target of the peace progressives in 1922, Frank Kellogg, who began the campaign with a comfortable advantage and strong backing from the national administration. The FLP received crucial help from La Follette, who attracted crowds in excess of 10,000 on a state speaking tour denouncing Kellogg. Shipstead broadened the attack to call for new leadership in Washington to avoid involvement in another European war, charging that Kellogg's policies had left the United States "economically and politically entangled in foreign alliances and intrigues of foreign nations." Because of Kellogg's ties with the Harding administration and the senator's decision to make an attack on La Follette's war record as one of the centerpieces of his campaign, the election attracted national attention, and commentators viewed it a significant win for La Follette when Shipstead scored a comfortable victory of 47 to 35 percent.[4]

Meanwhile, North Dakota elected the NPL-endorsed Lynn Frazier, who had served just over a term as a reform-minded governor before losing a 1921 recall election in a conservative counterattack. Frazier edged out four-term conservative Senator Porter McCumber in the G.O.P. primary, arguing that the senator had sold out the interests of the farmer first through his support for the League of Nations and then by his authorship of the 1922 Fordney-McCumber Tariff. In the general election Frazier faced an articulate conservative-endorsed Democrat, John O'Connor, in what the *New York Times* called the most bitter senatorial contest of 1922. Frazier called for an active foreign policy, dismissing "talk of America's 'detached and distant situation' " as "nonsense." He believed that the United States had been drawn into World War I and would be drawn into future wars unless the great powers worked out an agreement for universal disarmament. In a very close election that many observers had predicted would go to O'Connor, Frazier triumphed by just under 9,000 votes; the Democratic state chairman fumed that La Follette's campaign tour had made the difference.[5]

North Dakota's western neighbor also witnessed a political comeback in 1922. The decision by conservative Democrat Henry Myers to retire paved the way for an old Myers foe, Burton Wheeler, to win election to the Senate. A Massachusetts-born lawyer, Wheeler tangled with the Anaconda Mining Company forces in the Montana state legislature; he was rewarded when progressive Thomas Walsh won the 1912 senatorial contest with an appointment as a U.S. Attorney. Although Wheeler supported American entry into World War I, he declined to use his position to prosecute antiwar activists under the Sedition and Espionage Acts, and in so doing became a political liability to Walsh, who persuaded him to resign before the 1918 campaign. Wheeler proceeded to capture the 1920 Democratic gubernatorial nomination with the support of the Montana NPL, but in a bitter fall campaign he garnered barely 40 percent of the vote. Two years later he was back, calling himself a "Wilson Democrat" and denouncing G.O.P. foreign policy; he narrowly defeated a weak Republican nominee, in large part because of a ten-to-one margin in labor areas. As would become clear, Wheeler's definition of a "Wilson Democrat" differed from that of Walsh, who had campaigned actively for him; shortly after the election the new senator said that American membership in the League of Nations would sanction the "status quo of a divided central Europe and a wholly unsound economic system," and proposed in its place the creation of a European federation.[6]

Washington sent another radical Democrat to the Senate in 1922. Clarence Cleveland (C. C.) Dill had represented the Spokane district in the House of Representatives from 1915 through 1919; his House downfall came after he fulfilled his 1916 campaign pledge to vote against American participation in a European war. The Washington congressman argued that the Allies had gone to war for "trade and territory," and he described American entrance into the war as the "greatest crime ever perpetrated upon a free people." After the war declaration, he assailed the draft and expressed skepticism about the League of Nations, becoming the first member of either branch of Congress to raise the idea of a war referendum reservation, later picked up by Thomas Gore. The congressman proposed a "world league of peoples and peace" to improve upon and ultimately replace Wilson's "league of governments," unworkable since it depended "entirely upon force." Back in private life, Dill briefly published a magazine called *Let the People Vote on War*, which spoke of the need to "crystallize the peace sentiment" behind the adoption of a war referendum amendment. Running for the Senate in 1922 in a state in which the FLP had outpolled the Democrats in several 1920 contests and which had never before elected a Democratic senator, he seemed unlikely to win. Like Wheeler, however, he faced a weak opponent in incumbent Senator Miles Poindexter, who, like Dill, had been an irreconcilable opponent of the League. The Democrat reaffirmed his opposition to all wars, given that "statesmen" started wars but innocent boys did the fighting, and he used his opposition to World War I as the central tenet of his platform. Unsurprisingly, given the radical foreign policy record of his opponent, international affairs played a prominent role in the Poindexter strategy. The Spokane *Spokesman-Review* reflected the Poindexter approach when it asserted that Dill's support came from "Kaiser-worshippers" and "ultra-radical elements." Like the North Dakota and Montana contests, this race was tight, with Dill prevailing by just under 4,000 votes.[7]

In addition to Wisconsin, which overwhelmingly reelected La Follette despite his wartime record, two other states sent peace progressives to the Senate in 1922. The Iowa seat held by William Kenyon opened when the senator surprisingly accepted a federal judgeship, and agrarian leader Smith Wildman Brookhart jumped into the race. Brookhart had served in both the Spanish-American War and the 1916 anti-Villa expedition, and spent World War I as a rifle instructor in the Army. Calling himself a "cowhide radical," he almost beat Albert Cummins in the 1920 Senate primary and became the logical progressive candidate to succeed Kenyon; La Follette, Norris, Ladd, Borah, and Kenyon himself all endorsed him in a six-way primary. Brookhart made agricultural subsidies the cornerstone of his campaign, charging that the federal government "owes it to agriculture to go into the Treasury . . . to make right the wrong it has done." Although his style would eventually wear on observers (H. L. Mencken called him a witless "mouthpiece"), at the time he enjoyed enormous popularity in Iowa, and won the primary with 41 percent of the vote, 25 percent ahead of his nearest challenger. Brookhart too attacked administration foreign policy in his campaign, although it did not receive the central place that it did in Dill's.[8]

As predicted three years earlier by Joseph Bristow, support for the League had eroded Gilbert Hitchcock's political base in Nebraska, benefiting the final peace progressive elected in 1922, Robert Beecher Howell. A crusader for municipally owned public utilities, Howell billed himself as an "advanced progressive." Though an active supporter of Roosevelt in the 1912 primary season, he stayed with Taft in the general election and earned spots on both the state and national Republican party committees. By 1922 his increasingly successful program for municipal ownership made him much less acceptable to conservatives (Howell served as the spokesman for the Nebraska NPL in 1921), but having assisted Norris in taking over the state G.O.P., Howell no longer needed the regulars' support. Howell made taxation policy, foreign affairs, and public ownership the centerpieces of his campaign; his domestic agenda called for public ownership of selected railroads as a way to force rates down, while in international affairs he blasted Hitchcock's support for the League and criticized postwar French foreign policy. He won easily.[9]

The peace progressive political upswing abated over the next few years. The death of longtime senator Knute Nelson in 1923 opened up his Minnesota seat for a special election, and the FLP nominated Magnus Johnson, a Swedish immigrant who worked as a glass blower and dirt farmer before coming to prominence within the party. In an appeal mailed to 400,000 Minnesotans, La Follette contended that the peace progressives needed Johnson in the Senate to help "curb militarism and imperialism—the twin inequities which overwhelm the people with taxation, beget foreign complications, and inevitably breed foreign wars." Johnson proved a quite ineffective senator, however, and failed to win a full term in 1924. Brookhart also ran into trouble in his bid for a full term. The senator faced an articulate conservative Democrat, Daniel Steck, who attacked him for his stance on Russian recognition and for the senator's belated decision to endorse the La Follette presidential candidacy. Brookhart narrowly won the election and was certified by the Iowa Secretary of State, but Democrats challenged the result in the Senate, and after an eighteen-month delay a coalition of partisan Democrats and conservative Republicans unseated Brookhart and awarded the election to Steck. Retaliating by declaring a primary challenge to Cummins for his seat the next day, Brookhart comfortably bested the former peace progressive en route to a new six-year term in 1926.[10]

The only peace progressive victor in 1924 was William McMaster (R–South Dakota), a banker who had won election as governor in 1920 on a platform pledged to reorganizing state government to aid agricultural interests. Once in office, he created controversy when he ordered the state to sell gasoline to the public in order to force down gas prices charged by the large oil companies, which he denounced as guilty of "highway robbery." McMaster ousted former Progressive Thomas Sterling in the 1924 G.O.P. primary and by the fall was "openly flirting" with La Follette adherents; conservative Republicans backed his Democratic opponent, U. S. G. Cherry. In a three-way contest, Cherry proved unable to overcome South Dakota's traditional G.O.P. leanings, and McMaster drew enough liberal votes to compensate for his loss of conservatives.[11]

Ladd's death opened his seat in North Dakota, and Governor A. J. Sorlie appointed a young NPL newspaper editor, Gerald Nye, to the seat. Nye had backed American entry into World War I and, despite reservations, endorsed both the League and the peace treaty. He returned to national issues in 1924, when he ran on La Follette's ticket as a candidate for Congress, drawing 47 percent of the vote. Upon arriving in the Senate, he quickly moved into the mainstream of the peace progressive camp. Up for election in 1926, Nye reversed himself on membership in an international organization, opposing American participation in the World Court, and won a narrow victory in the primary followed by a solid win in the general election. Despite Nye's prominence in foreign policy battles of the 1930s, though, the North Dakotan did not take an active role in most foreign policy debates during the 1920s; only McMaster was less visible among the peace progressives.[12]

Wisconsin also had an open seat in 1925 after the death of Robert La Follette. When his widow, Belle Case La Follette, rejected overtures to succeed her husband, La Follette's son, "Young Bob" La Follette, announced his candidacy. La Follette made Congress and foreign policy one of his key issues. He asserted that Congress should exercise its constitutional right to the "authoritative voice in foreign affairs" to achieve friendly relations with all countries, especially those in Latin America; promote treaty agreements to outlaw war; defeat all forms of imperialism, especially those that involved the use of American armed forces "to aid in the exploitation of weaker nations"; abolish conscription; and provide for a war referendum. Despite active conservative primary opposition, La Follette easily captured the G.O.P. nomination, although he proved a rather cautious senator, going out of his way to get along with conservatives in the Senate G.O.P.[13]

The vacuum created by the death of the elder La Follette, however, did not remain unfilled for long. Of all the decade's contests won by a peace progressive, the 1926 Wisconsin G.O.P. primary focused the most on foreign policy issues and played the most important role in sustaining the movement. Irvine Lenroot, who had once associated with the La Follettes but by the start of the war had broken with his onetime political mentor, won election to the Senate in 1918 and reelection in 1920 over the intense opposition of the La Follette machine. Lenroot attracted the state's three-term Republican governor, John Blaine, as his opponent. The son of a former abolitionist, Blaine as governor supported a host of progressive reforms; he also was the only governor to refuse to allow his National Guard to participate in Defense Day exercises in 1924, calling instead for a "demonstration that would lead the way for foreign nations to universal peace," since no reason existed for the American government to promote armaments through "prop-

aganda and demonstration" at a time when the world needed disarmament. Blaine exhibited extraordinary activity on foreign policy issues
for a state governor. A bitter opponent of World War I, he aroused
hostility in 1922 when he pardoned every veteran whose imprisonment
(according to the governor's judgment) resulted from conditions caused
by his service in the military. In 1925, when Congress was debating
settlement of the French debt, the governor fired off a telegram to
Calvin Coolidge urging the President to withdraw the measure from
the Senate until the French had stopped their military offensive against
Riff rebels in Morocco and had agreed to American disarmament principles. Blaine outlined a radical foreign policy plan as the centerpiece
to his challenge to Lenroot, opposing the League and the World Court,
listing a war referendum as the first step to outlawing war, condemning
excessive defense expenditures as "encouraging imperialism and pro-
vocative of war," and urging the reduction of the Army and Navy to a
size needed only to prevent an invasion of the United States. Blaine
also pledged his "unalterable opposition" to universal military training
or "any other militaristic system" and criticized the G.O.P. policy of
offering protection to Americans who invested their money overseas.
After a whirlwind campaign in which Lenroot vigorously counterattacked, Blaine prevailed by 18,000 votes, attributing his victory to
public opposition to the World Court. The election sent an effective
and aggressive radical to the Senate who would rival Norris and Borah
as the most important peace progressive over the next few years.[14]

Despite their small numbers, the newly elected peace progressives
had high expectations; as Howell noted, although their contest with
conservatives would be one-sided "were it not for the rules of the
Senate," those rules "highly protect the minority and thus augment our
strength far beyond that due to our numbers."[15] Conservatives such as
William Howard Taft feared that Republican ineptitude had allowed
"these yahoos of the West" to take control of the Senate, but Taft's
nightmare never materialized. In a series of events that have been analyzed in considerable detail elsewhere, the peace progressives failed
either to forge a coalition with the Democrats to achieve ideological
control of the Senate or even to articulate a consistent domestic agenda
of their own.[16] Nonetheless, certain elements of their domestic agenda
had an impact on their foreign policy positions. Blaine, for example,
was the Senate's leading opponent of capital punishment, long an issue

associated with peace activism.[17] Wheeler, McMaster, and especially Frazier also applied their international concerns for the rights of weaker peoples to the domestic scene by supporting a generous federal policy toward Indians. Domestic policy proposals also piqued peace progressive interest in foreign nations that had already enacted systems similar to those desired by the senators, causing them to champion cross-national cultural and ideological exchange. Brookhart, who touted farm cooperatives as a way to address the nation's agricultural problems, proposed an international cooperative exchange agency with cooperative associations from all countries doing business with the United States; the Iowa senator also believed that Americans could learn from the agricultural policies of the Soviet Union and Denmark and the tactics of English cooperatives. Both Norris and Howell pointed to Ontario's experience with public power to justify their positions on turning the Muscle Shoals facility in Alabama into a public power plant. The peace progressives also viewed foreign and domestic developments as inseparable. Blaine saw the four key issues of the 1928 campaign (in which he endorsed Democratic nominee Al Smith) as hydroelectric energy and water power, "reestablishing the great law of morality in our international relations," preventing the nation from being "corrupted and debauched," and taxation, all of which "dovetail together, as we find upon analysis and consideration of the ramifications of selfish interests that have brought these problems to us."[18]

This second generation of peace progressives also shared several characteristics relating solely to international affairs. Although foreign policy had played a prominent role only in the Dill-Poindexter contest in Washington (where it worked to the disadvantage of the peace progressive candidate) and the Blaine-Lenroot primary battle in Wisconsin, international affairs, in sharp contrast to the 1910s, had appeared in all of their platforms and campaigns, and all indicated an acceptance of the basics of the peace progressive ideology that had emerged from the battles associated with the war and the League of Nations. All, therefore, came to the Senate fairly well versed in foreign affairs, decreasing the likelihood of a rerun of the prewar period, when unity had eluded the bloc. In addition, all except Howell had some kind of association with the elder La Follette, reinforcing the foreign policy consensus.[19] These twin characteristics—unity on foreign policy and an affiliation with La Follette—gave the peace progressivism of the

1920s a more radical and aggressive quality than its 1910s counterpart, as became clear in the group's critique of inter-American policy during the decade.

The military occupations of Haiti and the Dominican Republic began as two of the least noticed military maneuvers in American history. Haiti had long interested American expansionists, who had coveted the harbor at Môle St. Nicholas. The Môle declined in importance for the United States after the acquisition of Guantanamo Bay, but Washington still kept a watchful eye out for possible foreign schemes to lease the harbor. Meanwhile, Haitian politics, stable if repressive during most of the nineteenth century, suddenly imploded; from 1911 through 1915 Haiti had seven different presidents, producing disastrous consequences during the Wilson administration. As David Healy has argued, Wilson desired stability in the Caribbean Basin above all else, and after a particularly gruesome revolution in July 1915, Wilson ordered Admiral William Caperton ashore. Caperton soon proceeded to go far beyond a mandate of securing law and order, and by 1916 had established a puppet government under Sudre Dartiguenave. Events followed a slightly different course in the neighboring Dominican Republic, where Wilson worried that Germany could use political turbulence to maneuver into a position to control the harbor at Samaná Bay. Using the treaty of 1906, Wilson intervened personally and staked American prestige behind the weak government of Juan Jiménez. When Jiménez appeared on the verge of being overthrown in 1916, the Marines landed, but there the parallels with Haiti ended. The Dominican Congress refused to elect a puppet, and so Caperton abolished it and instituted a formal military dictatorship under Captain Harry Knapp.[20]

The occupations suddenly became front-page news in 1920, when the Democratic nominee for Vice President, Assistant Secretary of the Navy Franklin Roosevelt, boasted that he had written Haiti's constitution himself. Warren Harding seized upon the impolitic remark, declaring that if President he would not "empower an Assistant Secretary of the Navy to draft a constitution for helpless neighbors in the West Indies and jam it down their throats at the points of bayonets borne by U.S. Marines." Although a combination of factors led Harding's Secretary of State, Charles Evans Hughes, to begin negotiations with Dominican nationalists, the new administration exhibited little tendency to pull out of Haiti. The political storm raised by the campaign remarks, however, required some alteration in Haitian policy. Accordingly, a special Senate committee to investigate the two occupations was formed under administration ally Medill McCormick (R–Illinois). The committee took over one thousand pages of testimony, much of it quite critical of the occupations, but its recommendations never were much in doubt. When it released its 1922 report calling for the occupation to continue with cosmetic changes—Washington appointed a new high commissioner while another client, Louis Borno, an admirer of Mussolini, replaced Dartiguenave—the public furor over Haiti temporarily died down.[21]

This satisfied most in the Senate but not the peace progressives, who, though late coming to the issue, led a furious if futile battle to end the occupation. Johnson began by introducing a February 1921 resolution calling for the investigation of American civilian and military authorities in both halves of Hispaniola. Technically satisfied by the McCormick Committee report, the resolution progressed no further, and the peace progressives went on to unite behind an amendment sponsored by William King (D–Utah) that would have cut off all funds for the occupation, with Borah emerging as the key peace progressive figure in the fight. Detecting "powerful influences" behind the McCormick Committee decision to maintain a military government, Borah termed the imposed constitution the first step toward permanent occupation, desired by these interests, he wildly charged, since Haiti had the most fertile soil in the world. On a more sustainable note, the senator fretted that the current American policy of granting sizable loans to the client government would perpetuate the occupation, predicting that "the influence which took us there will not be nearly so strong as the influence will be which will hold us there." Borah detected an international trend of financial interests urging their governments to assume control of resource-rich but weak peoples, citing Siberia, Syria, and Iraq as other examples, part of a pattern in which "we have some two or three [foreign] policies . . and those policies are adjusted to the size and strength of the people." A strong antimilitarist line of thinking also pervaded the Borah critique. He characterized American rule as "sheer brutal despotism," a "shameless tyranny" that possessed "exactly the authority which any military despot has over a helpless people." Finally, from an antiexpansionist angle, Borah contended that administration policy logically would conclude with the United States' taking control of every island between Florida and the Panama Canal, "wrecking" the local governments and furnishing them with "no government instead" as the Japanese had done in Korea. For immediate remedies for Haiti, Borah urged a change to civilian government coupled with free elections and a re-abolition of foreign ownership of land. Few other senators were persuaded; the King Amendment failed on a vote of forty-three to nine,[22] with the five peace progressives then in the Senate unanimously in favor.[23]

Despite the overwhelming defeat, the peace progressives claimed a moral victory. Borah said that he did not expect to receive many votes, but he expressed confidence that the people would oppose the policy "when they are thoroughly informed." He attempted to hasten this process with a May Day 1922 speech in Carnegie Hall, broadcast nationwide by radio, which attracted a crowd of 3,500 people to hear him charge the Marines with atrocities—to be expected when following a policy of imperialism. When he termed the activities of the Marines "a disgrace to the American people," he received a minute's worth of applause. Borah predicted that the occupation would continue "unless American opinion brings us out," although he feared that European concerns had distracted too many people from more important events in the Western Hemisphere.[24]

This anti-imperialism occasionally led the peace progressives to take unusual positions; the year before their protest of the Haitian occupation, they had opposed a treaty that most Latin Americans considered necessary to rectify a past act of American imperialism. The United States since 1906 had been attempting to resolve its long-standing dispute with Colombia over the actions of the Roosevelt administration during the Panamanian revolt of 1903. Wilson had overseen the negotiation of the Thomson-Urritia Treaty of 1914, which called for a onetime American payment to Colombia of $25 million, but the treaty ran into trouble in the Senate when friends of Roosevelt, led by Henry Cabot Lodge, contended that it besmirched the former President's name. The issue revived late in the Wilson administration, and impetus for ratification continued into the early stages of the Harding presidency, with conservatives who once had opposed the treaty seeing merit in the argument that the United States needed to make concessions to avoid a nationalistic Colombian oil policy. Only the peace progressives, a few die-hard Republicans, and some renegade Democrats opposed, and although this bloc put up a vigorous fight, the treaty passed by a margin of sixty-nine to nineteen.[25]

The peace progressives denied that their opposition implied an endorsement of imperialism, while the split between the La Follette/Norris faction and Roosevelt weakens the traditional argument that these senators acted on Roosevelt's behalf. Rather, the anti-imperialism that caused the group to oppose most Caribbean Basin policies later in the decade led them to oppose this treaty. Norris charged that Hughes needed the treaty to ensure greater American access to Colombian oil, and he also worried that the precedent could be used if the much larger oil deposits of the Middle East went up for bidding. He also dismissed any argument that Colombia deserved American sympathy. Borah defended Roosevelt's intervention in the 1903 revolt, describing Panama as one of Colombia's "dissatisfied colonies" that the dictatorial regime of General Rafael Nuñez had forcibly incorporated under Colombia's control in 1880. Since then Panama had been ruled by "ruthless despots" who spared "no kind of punishment or persecution" in an effort to keep the Panamanians in line; Panama was therefore "entitled to her independence by every rule of international morality, justice, and every maxim of liberty and independence." The peace progressives were the only Senate opponents of the treaty to raise this point. Privately, Borah speculated that the treaty had come into being because "more oil concessions in Colombia are now held by citizens of this country than ever before." He did not deny that the United States should give fair encouragement to its citizens seeking oil concessions, but he rebuked the oil companies for wanting ratification of the treaty only in order "to make their oil concessions more available and valuable."[26]

The peace progressives did not confine their activity on issues of expansion to the Caribbean Basin, and they enjoyed better luck when they led the fight against the Harding administration's proposal to set up a financial receivership over Liberia through a $5 million loan. In a sparsely attended debate that required frequent quorum calls to sustain, Borah predicted that the money would go to J. P. Morgan, to whom the Liberian government already owed a sizable sum, and he worried that "this imperial scheme of finance" could lead to a prolonged American military occupation of a country three thousand miles away. The Idaho senator preferred to see the money invested in the United States to remedy agricultural distress "unless it can be demonstrated beyond peradventure that it is to be directly beneficial to the people who are to receive it abroad." To further ensure that the bill would not pass, Borah and Norris joined forces with Democrats to tack on a series of farm relief measures to the bill; in the end the bill was recommitted to the Finance Committee.[27]

The opposition to the Liberian loan reflected a broader peace progressive concern, expressed in the 1910s, about the excessive influence that the group felt powerful business interests employed over the making of foreign policy. In 1921 La Follette introduced an amendment calling for increased taxes on capital invested overseas (in contrast to a Finance Committee recommendation that corporations that did 80 percent or more of their business abroad should pay no taxes at all). Like Borah, La Follette believed that the domestic market offered more than enough investment opportunities for the "captains of industry," though not the "fabulous profits" available only in "underdeveloped or war-stricken countries." He conceded that the Senate legally could do nothing to restrain the "exploiters," but he also hoped that the government would do nothing to encourage them either. Conservatives bitterly attacked the amendment. Porter McCumber reasoned that since "we are seeking to expand our commerce," commercial interests needed some tax breaks; the powerful Reed Smoot (R–Utah) described the amendment as "virtually an embargo against any American citizen doing business in a foreign country." On the vote, however, the Democrat–peace progressive alliance that would defeat the Liberian loan held, and the La Follette Amendment prevailed by a tally of thirty-five to thirty.[28]

The peace progressives made more assertive suggestions concerning Harding administration policy toward Ireland, where the group closely watched the British-Irish negotiations in the early 1920s over home rule. Norris' service on the American Commission on Conditions in Ireland (along with other notable progressives such as Jane Addams and Norman Thomas) acquainted him with the "brute" British policy; he compared the "crime of permanently holding in subjection against their will a people of a nation" to slavery. (Norris was not the first nor would he be the last peace progressive to make the comparison between imperialism and slavery.) He did not specify, however, what positive action the United States should take, although La Follette, who worked closely with Norris on this issue, spelled out in much greater detail what the duo had in mind about American policy, introducing a resolution in early 1921 calling for the Senate to compel Harding to recognize Irish independence. The Wisconsin senator asked senators to recognize their moral obligation to aid Ireland given that the United

States entered World War I to aid the Allies "in the fight for small nationalities." Citing the long tradition by which the United States, using its recognition policy, "has lighted the way for the struggling democracies of the world," he contended that his resolution would fulfill the traditional American policy of promoting "the establishment of new nations throughout the world founded upon the consent of the governed." When the negotiations became deadlocked in the summer of 1921, La Follette prepared a much stronger speech to accompany the reintroduction of his resolution, calling for a settlement to be imposed "by events beyond the control" of England and Ireland. Although he hoped that the "great force" of world public opinion would suffice to compel the British to back down, he implied that he would back a more assertive American role if necessary, since the United States had a right to express its views when negotiations occurred between any two parties that "directly or indirectly affected its interests." This definition of United States power, which emphasized the force of American ideas, reflected themes long present in American foreign policy reform movements and illustrates one of the ways in which the anti-imperialism of the peace progressives had moved beyond the economics-dominated perspective of the years before 1917. The negotiations shortly went back on track, and in 1922 the Irish Free State became independent. Although La Follette continued to agitate for inclusion of the six Ulster provinces in the new Free State, the issue by and large receded from the peace progressive agenda for the remainder of the decade.[29]

Most of the themes raised by the peace progressives during the Harding administration resurfaced in the closing weeks of the La Follette 1924 presidential campaign. Although he started his campaign focusing on domestic issues, he began to shift to foreign affairs in Cincinnati on October 10, pledging to "bring all diplomacy out into the open, . . . [ensure] the democratic control of foreign policy . . . [and] at all times keep Congress fully advised and concede to it its constitutional share in the conduct of foreign relations."[30] This line of thinking reached its climax in an October 30 appearance before an enthusiastic crowd of 10,000 in Boston, where La Follette recounted the various victims of American "imperialism" during the preceding thirty years—the Philippines, Haiti, Nicaragua, the Dominican Republic—and predicted that other Central and South American nations soon would follow as long as the "traitors to American ideals" remained in control of the executive branch. The senator said that he would not oppose American overseas investment, but cautioned that "if it has to be defended, they [the financiers] have to go over there and defend it themselves." However, La Follette was a bit vague about how to replace the current policy, merely promising to "offer help and encouragement to those peoples to establish self-government" and stating his hope to "end the causes of war." A week later he had finished a disappointing third in the presidential race, and within a year he was dead.[31]

La Follette's passing marked a turning point in the peace progressive movement. The Wisconsin senator had played a critical role in the origination of the movement during the 1910s and had likewise assumed a prominent place in the dissenters' embracing of anti-imperialism during the Russian and League of Nations contests. Nonetheless, he was never able to shed the tendency shown by the peace progressives during the 1910s to interpret foreign policy matters solely through the lens of their domestic ideology. This tendency led him to adopt several foreign policy positions in the early 1920s that bordered on the bizarre. For example, he termed the proposal for a bankers' consortium to make loans to China in the early 1920s a "wicked agreement" negotiated by international capital to keep China in bondage after the ratification of the Versailles Treaty. This plan for the "joint exploitation" of China by American, Japanese, British, and French financiers only proved his long-standing theory that American foreign policy had become "a plaything of the international bankers," with the Army and Navy holding down the "harsh duty of the debt collector."[32] Though ideologically consistent, this criticism offered little insight into the nature of Chinese-American relations during the early 1920s, nor did it suggest any positive policy alternatives for the United States when dealing with China. In addition, the Wisconsin senator's political courage and willingness to experiment with new ideas had been an asset to the movement in the 1910s, but by the 1920s his controversial politics and personality impeded coalitions with other liberal forces. When coupled with the early 1920s departure from the movement of the increasingly nationalistic and isolationist Hiram Johnson, La Follette's death enabled the peace progressives to begin articulating responses more suited to the individual foreign policy crises at hand, while also allowing for the rise of new and innovative thinkers among the dissenters, such as Blaine, Dill, and Shipstead. This crystallization of peace progressive thought helped complete the evolution of the dissenters' anti-imperialist ideology from the populist, domestic-centered alternative that they forwarded in the mid-1910s to the broad critique of the structure of American foreign relations and the place of the United States in the world that they came to offer by the late 1920s. In the five years after La Follette's defeat, the peace progressives turned their attention to Latin American and East Asian affairs with increasing frequency, launching a virtual anti-imperialist crusade by the middle of the Coolidge administration.

During the early 1920s the peace progressives had exhibited a sporadic interest in Mexico, where the government of Álvaro Obregón, which had taken power in a 1920 military coup, still had not received the diplomatic recognition of the United States. In July 1921 La Follette again introduced a resolution protesting possible use of the American military to back up oil companies in their never-ending dispute with the Mexican government, winning the senator the public thanks of a number of Mexican senators. Just over a year later, Edwin Ladd laid out the case for recognition in a tightly reasoned address that recalled "when Americans were mindful of their own revolutionary origin and as a matter of right and principle were the first to extend the fraternal hand of welcome to republics which deposed tyrants, no matter in what quarter of the globe." The senator denounced the shortsightedness of a policy that aided a small number of American firms while damaging long-term commercial prospects; he felt that recognition "undoubtedly would swell our already important commerce with Mexico," a boon to "our languishing foreign commerce . . . [and] our idle factories." He called for a congressional recognition of Mexico if necessary, since the executive "has no right to withhold arbitrarily recognition from a friendly Republic." Although Ladd's speech did not bring about the public outcry for recognition that he hoped it would, administration supporter Tasker Oddie (R–Nevada) reported that the North Dakotan's position was gaining strength in Congress, prompting the State Department to leak information implying that Obregón and not the United States was holding up recognition. Mexico received recognition in 1923 only after Obregón ratified an agreement between Thomas Lamont and Mexican Foreign Minister Adolfo de la Huerta that worked out a plan for dealing with the Mexican foreign debt.[33]

These activities only served as a precursor for the tangle that developed between the peace progressives and the administration when

Plutarco Elías Calles succeeded Obregón as President and received James Sheffield as the American ambassador in Mexico City. Calles' most ambitious program centered on a positive attempt to implement Article 27 and replace perpetual Porfirian oil concessions with either fifty-year leases or outright annulments, depending on conditions. This matter deeply concerned Sheffield, who characterized the Mexicans as "Latin-Indians who . . . in the final analysis recognize no argument but force," and promised to support a policy of firmness that would not "have the United States make all the advances and do all the overlooking and all the forgiving." This attitude, when combined with Sheffield's belief that "the carrying on of foreign affairs is distinctly the province of the Executive branch of the Government," was bound to produce tensions, which the stiff and legalistic style of Frank Kellogg, now Secretary of State, only compounded. Kellogg termed the Calles policies "lacking in the essential elements of justice usual in the law and procedure of nations," striking "at the very root of the system of property rights which lies at the basis of all civilized society." Although he claimed that his protests arose "from a genuine wish for friendliness and cooperation" and consistently denied that he was cooperating with the oil companies in their attempts to get around the oil licensing laws, Kellogg's policies did little to reduce tensions between the two nations.[34]

As the cries for intervention increased and the State Department seemed unwilling or unable to quiet them, the peace progressives attempted to alter the administration's policy. They explained the State Department's apparent tendency to back up the oil companies by contending that, in Frazier's words, "behind the scenes certain selfish interests are pulling hidden strings." Borah began pushing Kellogg for a more complete publication of the American-Mexican diplomatic correspondence early in 1926, while Norris tried to embarrass the administration by authoring (and securing passage of) a resolution requesting Kellogg to furnish the Senate with the names of all American companies that had abided by the new Mexican laws, those that had not, and those that had written to the State Department requesting assistance. Complaining that the Senate seemed to be "constantly passing resolutions asking me for information" and conceding that with "both Borah and the Mexican Ambassador . . . insisting on publication" he had little flexibility, the Secretary complied with the first two requests but refused the third, privately worrying that publication could prejudice the case of the corporations in their legal battle with the Mexican government. (This is probably what Norris had in mind.)[35]

Faced with this congressional flurry, Kellogg tried to regain the initiative. He first denounced the American-Mexican antismuggling treaty in a move that Norris interpreted as "nothing more than an invitation to all those who desire to ferment a revolution" in Mexico. The Secretary more spectacularly gambled that he could swing American public opinion against both the Calles regime and the peace progressives by proving that the Mexican government had Communist leanings. On January 12, before an executive session of the Senate Foreign Relations Committee, Kellogg argued that anti-interventionist rhetoric both in the United States and in Latin America formed part of a Moscow-directed plot orchestrated by the Third International, which desired "the destruction of what they term American imperialism." Wheeler, who sat in on the hearing though not a member of the committee, scoffed that "ever since the Swedes up in Minnesota threw him out of the Senate, Kellogg has been seeing a red behind every bush"; the anti-interventionist *St. Louis Post-Dispatch* agreed, blasting the testimony as a "smoke screen" designed to allow Kellogg an "easy escape from the incompetence of his own acts." Even administration supporters had little good to say about Kellogg's performance. The *New York Times*, accusing Kellogg of "a singular lack of perspective," termed it "humiliating" that the American government had to justify its foreign policy "by admitting that it stands in dread of the hand of Soviet Russia"; while Walter Edge (R–New Jersey), one of the Senate's strongest supporters of administration inter-American policy, privately remarked that "to suggest without proving the existence of this bogey was futile and did more harm" than good.[36]

The peace progressives now realized that to succeed in their Mexican policy they would have to bring Kellogg down. Wheeler led the charge, denouncing the "faulty logic" and "fevered imagination" of the Secretary of State, who seemed most interested in making "a mouth-filling slogan in case of actual hostilities"; he lamented that "realities . . . crushingly refute Mr. Kellogg's diplomatic romances." The Montana senator contended that the Secretary had made a bad situation much worse and should resign. The most vitriolic attack came from Lynn Frazier, who argued that Kellogg had abused his official position by making the unsubstantiated charges. Frazier went on to comment on Kellogg's "singularly nervous disposition," a key reason for the people of Minnesota to have replaced him with Shipstead; anyway, "those of us who know Mr. Kellogg best also know that it is not impossible to dupe him on false evidence." While these remarks brought testy rejoinders, particularly from Walter Edge, they did help keep the administration on the defensive.[37]

The peace progressives also led a congressional effort to usurp control of Mexican policy from the executive, which Wheeler justified on the grounds that the framers "intended for the legislature to be the dominant branch of the government" in foreign affairs. The first step in implementing this plan was a Frazier resolution to express the sense of the Senate that the President should not employ the armed forces in resolving the Mexican dispute during the congressional recess. In a Foreign Relations subcommittee hearing on the resolution technically overseen by Shipstead, Frazier guided friendly witnesses who portrayed a just and kind Mexican regime persecuted by an overly legalistic American executive branch that wished to deny that "Congress is a coordinate branch of government." The resolution drew harsh attacks from conservatives, led on the committee by Frank Willis (R–Ohio), who believed that its passage would constitute "the grossest possible insult to the President." Enough Democrats agreed that the resolution stood no chance of passage, and the peace progressives were forced to settle down for a watered-down version of a resolution authored by Senate Minority Leader Joe Robinson (D–Arkansas), until a few days earlier a supporter of the Kellogg policy, which expressed the sense of the Senate that the United States and Mexico should arbitrate their differences. Robinson worded his resolution so vaguely that it passed the Senate without a dissenting vote, but nonetheless its passage did represent a type of victory for the peace progressives; Chandler Anderson, a Sheffield confidant then in Washington lobbying for United States intervention, fumed that the resolution "changed the entire situation and no doubt gave considerable comfort and encouragement to Calles."[38]

Rebuffed on the Frazier Resolution, the peace progressives returned to the principle of open diplomacy as a way to ensure that the administration would have no choice but to fulfill Frazier's provisions. A Norris resolution forced the State Department to release some of its information on the oil controversy; two days later the Mexican Foreign Ministry released an amended list of companies that had abided by the new Mexican law. Norris also urged Kellogg to release all relevant documents on current American-Mexican negotiations over the oil laws, worrying that secrecy allowed millionaires to "steal oil lands in Mexico without anybody knowing it." Borah agreed, holding that publication of all notes would reduce tension; this argument was somewhat paradoxical given the stern nature of some of Kellogg's proposals, and more likely the peace progressives hoped to embarrass the administration by forcing it to reveal publicly the tenuous nature of many of its arguments. Wheeler clearly hoped for this, urging the "moral force of an aroused public opinion," similar to that which had destroyed slavery, to overwhelm Coolidge's power and force the revision of Dollar Diplomacy.[39]

The peace progressives also united behind a Borah proposal to have the Foreign Relations Committee tour both Mexico and Central America during the congressional recess to assemble an unbiased opinion about the crisis. The senator could not control his own committee, however, and two Democrats sided with eight Republicans to vote the plan down by ten to eight. Although a "dreadfully disappointed" La Follette confided that he felt "helpless and apprehensive" about what Coolidge might do, Borah had an alternative, writing Calles directly to request the information on the oil companies that he wanted to assemble on his trip; Calles gladly furnished him with the data. Borah's action prompted a conservative outcry accusing him of "traitorous and treasonable" activity by violating the Logan Act, which prohibited American citizens from negotiating with a foreign government; but the Idaho senator maintained that as Foreign Relations Chair he had the right to obtain information from any sources that he deemed appropriate. Even the anti–peace progressive London *Times* conceded that the dissenters' constant pressure had challenged the "rigidly conservative" position of the Kellogg State Department and had helped block a more aggressive American response.[40]

The peace progressives never contended that Mexico lay beyond the American sphere of influence; they only reasoned that Washington was exerting its influence incorrectly. Borah agreed that "we are responsible for order in Central America" and that the United States possessed a "peculiar interest" in Mexico, but argued that the United States should foster these goals through friendship and not through the "suicidal . . . old doctrine of force." Dill likewise termed the Coolidge policy "indefensible" and urged the President to trade the "big bully" for the "big brother." From a "purely selfish commercial point of view," La

Follette saw the policy costing the United States exports to South America, which had totaled $450 million in 1926. Wheeler appealed to "legitimate" American business to recognize that the United States, as the greatest creditor nation in the world, needed a broader policy that looked after the totality of its new economic interests, not just those of the more politically entrenched groups. These themes of security and economics would resurface in the peace progressive critique of Nicaraguan policy.[41]

By late 1927 the administration too had tired of the Mexican controversy; in mid-1927 the embattled Sheffield finally was replaced by New Jersey corporate lawyer Dwight Morrow. La Follette termed the Morrow appointment "the most flagrant avowal of domination by the international bankers which any President has ever dared to make," while Frazier agreed that Morrow "would not harmonize our relations" with Mexico. Morrow had some progressive support, however; activist Alexander Gumberg wrote La Follette urging him to reconsider, while Borah broke ranks and issued a public endorsement. In the end, Borah was right and La Follette wrong; Morrow proved well suited to handling the task. Morrow's tact, combined with a conservative shift within the Calles government, eased tensions so much that by 1928 the ambassador remarked that "Calles is the best President the country has had since Díaz." The final controversy over American holdings in Mexico was delayed until 1938 and the administrations of Franklin Roosevelt and Lázaro Cárdenas, sparing the peace progressives the dilemma of attempting to reconcile their ideology with a program considerably more nationalistic than any put forth by Latin American nationalists during the 1920s.[42]

By mid-1927, in any case, the State Department had a much more serious inter-American crisis on its hands. Political instability following the death of Nicaraguan President Diego Chamorro in 1923 led to the creation of a fusionist ticket of Conservative Carlos Solórzano for President and Liberal Juan Sacasa for Vice President that easily captured the 1924 presidential election over Emilio Chamorro, who headed a rump group of Conservatives. The State Department, though not pleased with the election result, did not intervene to overturn it, and by August 1925 the American Marine Legation Guard, which had stood in Managua since 1912 as a symbol of the American presence in the country, returned to the United States. Chamorro never accepted defeat, and in January 1926, after Sacasa had fled for Guatemala and the intimidated Solórzano had resigned, Chamorro was awaiting U.S. recognition of his new regime, although Kellogg had maintained that the United States would not recognize a government that came to power via unconstitutional means. Chamorro had not counted on Kellogg's legalistic stubbornness, and in October Chamorro finally resigned. Kellogg wrote his chargé in Managua, Lawrence Dennis, that he would consider recognition if Adolfo Díaz replaced Chamorro, and within a week Díaz was the new Nicaraguan President and Washington had extended recognition. The recognition infuriated Sacasa, who had established an alternative regime; when Sacasa's representatives wrote Kellogg requesting recognition, the Secretary coldly informed them that the United States supported Díaz and that if Sacasa threatened the government the United States "could not consider him other than a revolutionist." Mexico did not agree, however, and extended recognition to Sacasa, adding another and more serious angle to the problem. As the situation deteriorated in late December 1926 and early January 1927, Kellogg and Coolidge considerably expanded the American presence, confident that Díaz would "offer no objection." A bloody five-year occupation had begun.[43]

The peace progressives initially believed that Kellogg, in the words of Norris, was "anxious to make what they call a 'firm stand' in Nicaragua in order to impress Mexico." La Follette cautioned that with the action Mexico had stepped forward as the champion of Latin American states and that the American policy would thus inevitably lead to conflict with its southern neighbor unless reversed. Because of this belief, the peace progressives refrained from strongly criticizing Nicaraguan policy in December 1926 and concentrated their fire on Mexican affairs.[44] As it became clearer that the occupation could last for some time, Wheeler introduced two resolutions, one demanding withdrawal and terming Solórzano and Sacasa Nicaragua's legal rulers, the other calling for a Senate investigation of the "often unjustifiable" concessions granted American firms in the Caribbean Basin. The final important peace progressive resolution, introduced by Henrik Shipstead in April 1926, called for an investigation of all U.S. loans to underdeveloped countries and demanded that the executive desist from directly or indirectly aiding any "financial arrangement" by U.S. citizens. The Minnesota senator urged its consideration promptly given that American armed forces seemed on the verge of backing up one of these loans with force.[45]

Wheeler began for the peace progressives in a brief address for his resolution in early January, agreeing with Coolidge that the United States had a duty to protect its citizens, but denying that Sacasa's forces threatened any Americans. Having dismissed the Coolidge argument, Wheeler then posited that the United States was "simply bullying the Nicaraguan people because Nicaragua is a small nation" and because the State Department wanted to protect American concessions granted by Díaz. He argued that the State Department would have to tell business interests with foreign investments either that "you have to take the chances with the kind of government that you find there" in the host country or the United States would wind up regularly sending troops to protect the property of the companies that had made overseas investments. Meanwhile, on January 13 Borah publicly broke with Kellogg in a Senate speech that attracted national attention. The Idaho senator had given signs of his unhappiness as early as January 7, when he met with Coolidge and told the President that the United States should withdraw from Nicaragua and recognize Sacasa. (Kellogg dismissed the arguments of the Foreign Relations Committee Chair as "absolutely wrong.") Borah did not deny that Central America constituted a "peculiar concern to us," nor that the United States had a right to protect the property of its citizens under international law, but he reasoned that the present policy went "far beyond" that. Also, if the United States had to intervene, "we ought to make an effort to prop up and sustain the expressed will and purposes of the people of Nicaragua," although he did not spell out the extent to which he wanted the United States to aid Sacasa. Like Wheeler, he called for consistency from the State Department, and felt that the United States should try to apply the same principles toward "powerless and helpless countries" that it used toward the powerful. An overoptimistic William Howard Taft commented that the Borah speech "fell dead" and predicted that the Senate would devote little more attention to Nicaraguan affairs. The former President found it "really humorous" to listen to peace progressive comments that good government would result from a Sacasa presidency, contending that "the only time when any of those countries seems to thrive is when the United States is lending a hand to guide it." Although Taft dismissed the impact of the peace progressive criticism, reports persisted into early 1927 that a "deeply concerned" Coolidge was contemplating a change in policy partly in response to suggestions by dissenting senators that the Senate should conduct an investigation of Nicaraguan affairs. Occupation supporter

Simeon Fess (R–Ohio) admitted that "if it had not been for Borah, the country would never have known about the landing of marines in Nicaragua."[46]

While the debate raged in the Senate, Shipstead oversaw a series of congressional hearings that further embarrassed the administration. The senator's star witnesses were Toribio Tijerino, a prominent financial official in the Martínez and Solórzano governments, and Thomas Moffat, who had served as the American consul at Bluefields during the Nicaraguan revolt of 1909 and 1910. Tijerino claimed to have proof of U.S. monetary and military involvement in the revolt that toppled Zelaya, and he described a sordid tale of embezzlement, betrayal, and deceit that came back to the thesis that the investment firm of Brown Brothers, in conjunction with Díaz and Chamorro, had assumed a virtual protectorate over Nicaragua. Shipstead concluded that he had "never heard a better financial statement made." (Kellogg responded that his 1922 opponent spent all his time condemning the administration "about many matters of which he has little if any knowledge.") Moffat charged that "Nicaragua has been sadly hampered through dictation, intrigue, and greed, ever the adjuncts of a diplomacy founded on and dominated almost entirely by financial considerations"; he explained that the influence of financial interests associated with Philander Knox had caused both American interventions. Unlike Tijerino, who passed through his testimony largely unscathed, Moffat was subjected to a demanding cross-examination by Frank Willis (R–Ohio), who scored points by forcing Moffat to concede that indeed the 1909 revolt had threatened some foreign, but non-American, property. Nonetheless, the hearings cast considerable doubt upon the origins of American involvement in Nicaragua at the very time when the administration needed all its resources to convince the Senate of the justness of the present intervention. The hearings also formed a critical part of the peace progressive strategy. Realistically recognizing that they lacked the votes in the Senate to force an end to the occupation, the peace progressives used the hearings to present enough controversial information to arouse public opinion, which they hoped would in turn pressure Democratic and moderate Republican senators to come out against the administration's policy.[47]

Despite peace progressive claims to the contrary, Kellogg did not wish to see U.S. Marines stationed in Nicaragua indefinitely, and, unhappy with the competence of his advice from the scene, he and

Coolidge sent Henry Stimson to Nicaragua in April 1927 with an extraordinary grant of power to negotiate a lasting solution to the Nicaraguan problem. (The only restriction Kellogg placed upon Stimson was a demand that the emissary not return to the United States with anything that the administration would have to submit to the Senate for approval.) Upon his arrival in Nicaragua, Stimson discovered the Conservatives near collapse and pressed Kellogg for the authority to commit the United States to overseeing the 1928 presidential election coupled with a "firm military attitude" against the Liberals in the short term and in the long term an American organization of an independent Nicaraguan constabulary. He persuaded the leading Liberal general, José Moncada, to commit his forces to lay down their arms and live under a Díaz government in exchange for American supervision of the 1928 election, and confidently predicted that only scattered opposition of bandits to the accord would exist. The peace progressives had a mixed reaction to the Tipitapa accords. Shipstead noted that the "executive agent of the President has long been a convenient tool" to do things legally forbidden to diplomats; he doubted that the United States could supervise a fair election given its policy of selling arms to Díaz. Norris denied that anything that Stimson had negotiated bound Congress in any way, while La Follette correctly noted that Stimson's actions represented a desperate gamble to save a policy that was about to collapse. Borah, however, departed from the consensus, terming Tipitapa "the best plan possible" given that Kellogg had made it clear that he would not recognize Sacasa. The Idaho senator conceded that generally an American overseeing of an election "would only be another and a more sly and subtle form of imperialism," but he denied that this would occur in 1928, since if the United States kept at a distance the Díaz forces would "have every advantage."[48]

Stimson failed to predict that one of Moncada's generals, Augusto Sandino, would refuse to abide by the accords and instead launch a guerrilla campaign against the American forces, leading to an increasingly bloody military campaign. As press reports about the severity of the fighting began trickling into the United States, the peace progressives began to question the implications of Tipitapa. La Follette accused Kellogg of trying "to explain in a very light and casual manner a very serious matter"; despite Kellogg's denials, La Follette believed that the State Department had ordered the Marines to pursue Sandino, although "we have no more legal right to bomb rebels in Nicaragua than

Nicaragua would have to bomb rebels in the United States." The campaign only increased in severity when Coolidge appointed General Frank McCoy as head of the American mission to supervise the election. McCoy, in the words of the *New York Times* "as much at home in an embassy room as on the parade ground," hoped that a free election would stifle Latin American critics and undermine domestic opposition while paving the way for a graceful withdrawal from Nicaragua with American hegemony still intact, although he also pushed his military colleagues for more aggressive action against Sandino. Designed as a face-saving tactic, the electoral mission under McCoy substantially increased the American presence in Nicaragua, and throughout 1928 the general served as a virtual proconsul.[49]

While McCoy was establishing himself in Managua, two peace progressives spent mid-1927 exploring alternatives to the traditional framework of inter-American relations, revealing the increasing range of the anti-imperialist position put forth by the dissenters. Shipstead toured the Caribbean Basin in the early summer of 1927, making stops in Haiti, Costa Rica, and Nicaragua, and upon his return touted the idea of American sponsorship of a federation as a way to solve the region's instability. The Minnesota senator contended that a Central American federation would remove most of the causes of political rivalry that had plagued the region over the preceding century. He believed that the United States could serve as a catalyst for the federation's creation by acquiring Belize from England in exchange for part of its wartime debt to the United States and then presenting the former British colony to the federation; once established, Shipstead urged the conclusion of a reciprocity treaty with Central America since free trade would benefit both sides. The federation formed one element of Shipstead's broader program for the Western Hemisphere, which involved the creation of what he called a republican-oriented alliance dedicated "to the cause of representative government." Accordingly, Washington should "seek to maintain representative government throughout the Western Hemisphere" by every means at its disposal short of internal intervention, although he conceded that the United States ought not to intervene "even in order to improve the type of representative government." Shipstead saw it as being in the American economic and strategic interest to maintain close relations with the other republics of the world. The senator warned that "good-will alone" would not improve trade—only a friendly spirit and "an intimacy of political relationship" could accomplish that—and so the United States would have much to lose "from a policy of isolation as regards the other American countries."[50] At the same time, he urged a "policy of non-support for Americans who engage in foreign business" as a way to end the exploitation of foreign governments by overseas capital and improve the region's stability. Shipstead's pan-American vision as outlined in 1927 rivaled anything put forward in the preceding decade, including that of Woodrow Wilson.[51]

Borah did not share Shipstead's creativity, but he too thought more broadly about inter-American issues during the spring and summer of 1927, striving to place the issue in more of a global framework. The Idaho senator, who spent the year learning Spanish so he could correspond with Latin Americans more freely, called for the same policies toward large and small nations based on the principles of open diplomacy and diplomatic relations with all countries. Borah recognized it as "inevitable" and mutually beneficial that Americans would secure investments in Latin American countries, but he also noted that "material interests do not override" the traditional American policy of friendship. Given this, the senator recommended a policy by which Americans who acquired property in foreign lands would have to submit to local laws "or at most to arbitration," and forfeit any claim to military intervention to back up their claims. Borah also denied that the "narrow, sordid theory that we must have dollar for dollar" should form the basis of an acceptable settlement for claims; "substantial justice" would do. He hoped that with such a pacific policy, the United States "would in the long run gather respect and confidence and reap both the moral and material wealth far beyond that which can ever be gathered under a policy of exploitation and force." The Shipstead and Borah programs, by indicating a far more sophisticated approach to foreign economic policy than evident in the populistic anti-imperialism offered by La Follette in the 1910s, illustrates the how the anti-imperialism of the peace progressives evolved during the 1920s into a far more potent ideology than that espoused by the group in much of the preceding decade.[52]

The enlargement of the occupation (1,148 more Marines arrived in Nicaragua in January 1928, raising the total number of U.S. troops to more than 2,500) led the peace progressives to introduce several other pieces of legislation designed to bring the intervention to a speedy close.[53] John Blaine authored the two most significant of these, and the debate surrounding Latin American policy in 1928 marked his brief emergence as the most innovative thinker of the radical wing of the movement. The Blaine Resolution outlined the peace progressive principles for inter-American policy, maintaining that U.S. citizens engaged in trade or commerce with foreign countries had to obey the laws of those countries and that investments made by U.S. citizens in foreign countries would be subject to native laws. It also stated that the U.S. government would not assume responsibility for seeing that contractual obligations between American citizens and foreign governments were fulfilled, and that U.S. citizens could not appeal to their own government until they had exhausted legal remedies in the host country. Even then arbitration would represent the most extreme American response, since "in no event" would the United States "have recourse to arms or resort to force in any manner." Having faced the legalistic arguments of Kellogg for the past year, the peace progressives resolved to move beyond international law in a way that they had begun to do in the days before American entry into European war, calling for a revision of international law along lines long demanded by nationalist Latin Americans. On a more specific level, the Wisconsin senator proposed an amendment to the 1928 naval appropriations bill, modeled on the various King Amendments toward Haiti, cutting off funding for the occupation as of Christmas 1928.[54] The dissenters indicated a consistent desire for the United States to play an active role in hemispheric affairs as the champion of the smaller states, as shown by their support for Sacasa and their constant fear of the diminution of American moral power in the world. To these principles the peace progressives added a less altruistic concern with the deleterious effects of imperialism on American foreign trade. The combination, which addressed elements of strategic, economic, and moral power, proved quite complete, although debate over Nicaraguan policy would test it severely. Proposals such as Shipstead's Western Hemisphere alliance, Borah's desire for diplomatic assistance for Sacasa, and Blaine's call for a revision of international law also revealed the internationalist side of the anti-imperialist ideology of the peace progressives, as did their strong interest in Latin America, something not shared by most members of the Senate in the 1920s.

The first manifestation of these ideas in 1928 came in what the *Baltimore Sun* called an "extraordinarily spirited" exchange between Dill and

William Cabell Bruce (D–Maryland), the strongest Democratic supporter of the Nicaraguan occupation. Citing the pro-Sandino articles
by Carleton Beals as the source for much of his information, Dill began
by defending the Sandinists, noting that "they are called bandits because they would not sell their ammunition and their right to fight for
what they believed to be self-government in their own country." He
added that he would sanction the use of force only to get Americans
"out" of a revolutionary country. This brought in Bruce, who charged
that "the Senator would have our nationals scurry out of the country
like so many frightened rats"; Dill disputed the wording but not the
premise, and shot back that the Bruce policy would wind up having
American Marines appearing in every country in the world that had a
revolution. The Maryland senator stated that the only opponents of
present Nicaraguan policy "are the extreme pacifists and the radicals,"
and he defended previous American occupations of Caribbean Basin
nations as carrying "a blessing" (which Dill retorted amounted to "the
blessing of bullets"). Pressed by Dill, Bruce became more extreme, recalling the suppression of the Boxer Rebellion as "one of the most
glorious episodes in the history of the people of the United States" and
describing Coolidge's Mexican and Nicaraguan policy as "nothing less
than a new era in the history of mankind." Dill dismissed Bruce's remark as glorifying "the dying of American boys in the name of American investors," and concluded by terming the intervention as "in violation of the precedents and historic policy of this Government."
Besides its spectacular nature, the debate also marked the decline of an
issue that had weakened the anti-imperialism of the peace progressives
during the 1910s: how to protect foreign nationals overseas. At various
points earlier, Borah, Jones, and even Works had advanced Bruce-like
arguments to justify American intervention in Mexico; Dill indicated
that the peace progressives instead now wished to alter international
law as a way of showing respect for the rights of small nations.[55]

The Senate delayed debate on Nicaragua during the Sixth Pan-
American Conference, held in Havana from January 16 through February 20, 1928. Kellogg appointed a distinguished delegation headed
by Charles Evans Hughes to represent the United States, and he and
Borah persuaded Coolidge to travel to Havana to address the conference in person. Coolidge cited Cuba as the best example of progress in
the Western Hemisphere, since it had advanced from a colony to an
"independent, free, prosperous, peaceful," and self-governing nation in

the span of thirty years. The President committed himself to working toward the "establishment and expansion of the spirit of democracy" in which the weak and small would share power. Kellogg's hand appeared in the closing portions of the address, which called for bringing inter-American relations under the rule of law, "the surest refuge of the weak and the oppressed." Any mention of Nicaraguan or Mexican policy stood conspicuously absent from the speech. In a significant diplomatic victory for the United States, the conference adjourned without a condemnation of the American action in Nicaragua.[56]

Blaine gave the peace progressive response in a two-day address, on February 2 and 3, 1928. He charged that the President had warped the Monroe Doctrine, a "doctrine of inherent fairness and justice that the strong must not ride down the weak," into a dictum that "exalted greed," which in turn weakened American moral power. Americans, as the "monsters of imperialism," could no longer denounce French atrocities in North Africa, British policies in India and other colonies, or even Japanese excesses in East Asia (because of "our indefensible extraterritorial policy" in China). Blaine ridiculed the technical distinctions made between formal imperialism and what he called "imperialism of the dollar," the informal financial power rapidly being assumed by American firms, in many cases under the aegis of the State Department, in virtually every country of the Western Hemisphere. He cautioned that only a small group would receive the financial advantages from this policy, which discriminated against both the "vast majority" of American business and American labor by allowing industrial development in countries with "cheap labor." Blaine then retraced the history of U.S. policy in the region, implying that Washington, Monroe, and Millard Fillmore all had anticipated the dangers that foreign concessions in Latin America would pose, employing long quotations from Fillmore to justify his claim.[57] The only imperialist Presidents before McKinley had been Andrew Johnson, who had exhibited "either fits of madness or even less honorable characteristics," and U. S. Grant, before Sumner had checked his plans; Blaine used several quotations from Sumner's "dance of blood" speech in his address. He reserved particular praise for Grover Cleveland, who came from "the ranks of those who believed . . . in America's traditions" and could have intervened on behalf of foreign concessionaires but did not; Blaine hailed Cleveland for referring to great nations when he spoke of international wrongdoing (as in the Venezuela crisis), unlike

Roosevelt, who equated chronic wrongdoing only with the weak. Cleveland evidently was the last President to conduct a moral foreign policy. McKinley lacked the political courage to resist imperialism, while Roosevelt, despite the positive attributes of supporting arbitration and opposing the use of force to collect debts, contradicted his own logic by refusing to deny the use of force; out of the "womb" of this contradiction "the imperialistic policy of America was born." Blaine concluded by ripping apart the Latin American policies of Taft, Wilson, and Harding. In addition to revealing the peace progressive mindset at the dawn of the Nicaraguan debate, the Blaine interpretation of Cleveland further illustrates the peace progressives' goal of an activist foreign policy in the region on behalf of weaker states.[58]

This speech set the stage for the fight over the Blaine Amendment, described by the pro-occupation *Christian Science Monitor* as "good theater . . . a rare ingredient of the unusual, the perplexing, and the intriguing." In a weeklong series of debates, which prompted a worried Kellogg to rush off a cable to McCoy demanding information to combat a "great deal of criticism in this country," the peace progressives made their strongest critique yet of the Nicaraguan affair. Norris opened by cautioning that allowing the intervention to stand would set a dangerous precedent: the congressional right to declare war would be "entirely taken away by the executive department." The Nebraska senator vigorously disputed the doctrine that "we must not criticize the President, particularly in matters relating to foreign relations"; quite to the contrary, he believed that "criticism is a healthy thing" tending to strengthen the basics of the governmental system. Blaine spelled out the most restrictive view of executive power, prompting Thaddeus Caraway (D–Arkansas) to joke that perhaps his Wisconsin colleague would prefer an executive commission rather than a unitary executive. Blaine defined the Commander-in-Chief's role as a purely military one of personally leading the Army or Navy into battle. He theorized that Congress maintained the ultimate power over the military, since if it denied appropriations, the President would lead "painted ships upon a painted ocean." The Wisconsin senator conceded that usually the President possessed more power during war, but he maintained that these powers came from congressional authorization, since "the Commander-in-Chief is only the agent of Congress under the Constitution." The increased peace progressive emphasis on the limits of presidential power flowed in large part from their controversial tactics of trying to end the occupation through a cutoff of appropriations; as Dill said, the "suggestion that the Senate is without authority to do these things is the suggestion of those who do not want to meet the issue."[59]

The peace progressives then proceeded to denounce the tactics employed by the American military, whose role Wheeler compared to that of the Hessians in the Revolutionary War. Lynn Frazier scoffed at those who spoke as if the Marines "were welfare workers, engaged in philanthropic missions here and there about the world." He conceded that although the situation probably would destabilize further if American forces withdrew, thus increasing the threat to American property, he maintained that Nicaragua and the United States would benefit in the long term from placing their relationship upon a more equal basis. A strong defense of Sandino that approximated overt sympathy for the Nicaraguan's cause accompanied this rhetoric. Wheeler doubted the success of squelching a rebellion based upon "exactly the same principles of liberty and free government" that had motivated the founding fathers. Norris, comparing Sandino to George Washington and his army to Washington's at Valley Forge, chastised Coolidge for using American armed forces "to destroy human life, to burn villages, to bomb innocent women and children from the air." He suggested that the military was distorting reports coming back from Nicaragua in an attempt to influence the Senate vote. The sentiments represented an important evolution in the thinking of the peace progressives on Nicaraguan politics. Through 1927 they had sympathized with the Liberals, but by early 1928 all save Borah sided with Sandino and hinted that the mainstream Liberals had betrayed their country and thus forfeited the right to govern. In addition, Sandino, as a leftist but non-Communist nationalist whose sympathies lay against big business and with the agrarian sector of his country, represented the type of figure that most appealed to them. Confidence that Sandino would prevail if the United States withdrew from Nicaragua led the peace progressives to call for unequivocal withdrawal, and not a beneficial intervention (diplomatic or otherwise) of the type that they had had in mind to aid Sacasa in early 1927.[60]

The peace progressives suffered a critical defection, however, when Borah came out against the Blaine Amendment, denying the group the use of the Foreign Relations Committee as a sounding board against administration policy. Borah affirmed that despite his opposition to the amendment he still believed that Congress had "a war-making power and is necessary in all matters which relate to the use of the Army and the Navy," but he focused on the need to deal with the present and not to base judgment on the wisdom of the initial occupation. The senator contended that he was "occupying the same position" he had always occupied, and that he disagreed with the other peace progressives only with regard to "the best manner of accomplishing" their common goals; unlike his dissenting colleagues, he maintained an overt sympathy for the Liberals. A steady stream of correspondence and visits with leading Nicaraguan Liberals dating from 1925 convinced him that the Liberals represented the best interests of the people of Nicaragua. Moncada himself, exiled in Costa Rica at the time, informed Borah that the Chamorro regime was "protected by American interests" while the Liberals would "fight for liberty and social welfare and are in duty bound with American democracy." During the debate Borah defended the Liberals more strongly than any other member of the Senate. (In fact he was virtually the only senator to have anything positive to say about them; pro-occupation senators regarded them with suspicion because of the Sacasa connection, while the other peace progressives believed that the Liberals had betrayed their country at Tipitapa.) The Idaho senator contended that for fifteen years American marines "had kept in power those who represented not the people . . . so much as foreign capitalists who were investing in Nicaragua." Given the Conservative control of the government, the Idaho senator saw American supervision as the only way to ensure a free election, and thus a Liberal victory; otherwise "we would leave the Liberals in Nicaragua absolutely subject to the dictation and the power of those who had driven them out prior to the time that Díaz became President." Though still lacking enthusiasm for the occupation, Borah believed that without American troops "the people who *ought* to rule Nicaragua would be practically destroyed"; therefore, the United States could not withdraw "without doing an almost incalculable injustice to those who have trusted us." He also doubted that the Nicaraguan people would oppose this final round of interventionism, again citing his correspondence with the Liberals. As early as January 1926, one former Liberal senator had urged Borah to back the "friendly assistance" of the United States in returning Sacasa to power.[61]

Alongside this Liberal partisanship rested Borah's conviction that a Liberal victory represented the best hope for a permanent U.S. withdrawal from Nicaragua; therefore, a fair election, "the great object in my mind," was the key to ending the occupation, his "ultimate and dominant idea." The senator conceded that he did not know what would happen if, after the election, Chamorro and Díaz revolted again, but he hoped that the Liberals, "supported by [Nicaraguan] public opinion and . . . [by] our moral support by recognizing the government," would have the strength to hold power. A sense of desperation pervaded Borah's thinking. After receiving a stinging letter from Oswald Garrison Villard denouncing his position, he admitted that "what we can do effectively with reference to Nicaragua is not by any means clear to me"; he asked Villard what the editor suggested as an alternative. Though uncomfortable in his position as the defender of an undeclared war, Borah hoped that his gamble would terminate the occupation and leave Nicaragua dominated by a nationalist government with domestic policies he desired. He constantly promised that he would not support an occupation that continued for very long after the election. His opposition was enough to doom the Blaine Amendment, which nonetheless drew twenty-two votes, the best to date of any amendment designed to cut off funds from an existing overseas military operation. The United States supervised the 1928 election, which Liberal José Moncada won quite easily.[62]

Borah had not taken his position without one final attempt to avoid compromising his principles and voting to sustain the occupation. Unlike the administration, the senator did not equate support of an American-supervised election with a continuation of the military campaign against Sandino; he instead sought to swing peace progressive support behind his idea through a successful venture in private diplomacy, much as he believed he had helped cool U.S.-Mexican tensions a year earlier through his public correspondence with Calles. His vessel for the effort was the Christian pacifist Nevin Sayre, in Nicaragua during January 1928 with several other members of the Fellowship of Reconciliation in an attempt to mediate an end to the war. Sayre, who opposed Sandino because of the guerrilla's reliance on force, and thus sympathized with Sacasa, mirrored Borah's beliefs perfectly; a January 5 telegram from Sayre (overoptimistically) predicting the possibility of success in his "adventure of peace" drew an excited response from Borah, who "desperately" wanted to find some way "to stop the fight with Sandino." Although Sayre's mission collapsed shortly thereafter when American authorities in Managua refused him permission to travel into the military zone, the incident did reveal the lengths to which Borah was

willing to go to achieve his twin goals of a Liberal government in Nicaragua and a quick end to the war.[63]

Events thereafter did not follow Borah's predicted course. Both the
Sandinist revolt and the Marine occupation continued. Although
throughout 1929 and 1930 the anti-Sandino forces appeared to be getting the upper hand, Moncada showed no inclination either to call for
the withdrawal of the Marines or to enact the kind of sweeping reform
program that he had promised Borah in 1926. The peace progressives
thus united around Dill's amendment to the 1929 Navy bill to cut off
funds for the occupation, which initially passed but was reversed as a
result of administration pressure. Its passage nonetheless signaled the
beginning of the end of the occupation, with Borah, as promised, voting
with the majority against the administration.[64]

Peace progressive policy toward Cuba late in the decade shows that
Borah was not the only dissenter who considered backing American
intervention on behalf of Latin American democracy. In April 1928
Shipstead, despite his own earlier warnings that the United States
should not intervene to promote anti-imperialism, introduced a resolution requesting the Senate to use American power under the Platt
Amendment to investigate whether the Cuban regime of Gerardo
Machado had protected American lives and property sufficiently. Shipstead aimed chiefly, however, at employing American pressure to oust
Machado; the Minnesota senator cited "specific charges" from "reliable
sources" that the Machado government had suppressed all freedom of
speech and the press, denied essential rights, closed the national university, and engaged in "numerous assassinations," imprisonments, and
exiles. The resolution aroused a furor in both Washington and Havana.
In the Senate Borah, recently the target of Shipstead's barbs for promoting Caribbean Basin democracy through affirmative means, now
returned the favor, questioning whether the United States could conduct an investigation and still "act with respect for the integrity and
sovereignty of a friendly nation." The Idaho senator noted that between
those who wanted increased American involvement in the Caribbean
Basin and those who wanted the United States out of the region altogether it was difficult for the Foreign Relations Committee to establish
a permanent policy, especially given that the same people had urged
both options on differing occasions. Machado's representatives, recognizing Shipstead's motive, reacted with greater consternation. The
Cuban ambassador in Washington, Orestes Ferrara, dismissed Ship-

stead's sources as "radical malcontents"; he further argued, with some justification, that one could "regard the words of the proposition of Senator Shipstead as an aggression." The combination of Borah's hesitance, the Cuban reaction, and State Department opposition doomed the resolution, although Shipstead continued to press the matter for a couple of years through his position as chair of the Cuban Relations Subcommittee.[65]

The decade ended much as it had begun, with the peace progressives criticizing the occupation of Haiti. After his 1927 visit, Shipstead questioned the wisdom of attempting to "civilize" the Haitians, contending that "a simple economic and political existence is probably best suited to them." Administration sources criticized the senator for attempting "to bring all political and social phenomena into line with philosophical theories which he possesses." Frustrated by the continuance of the occupation without congressional authorization and fearful of "a great wrong being consummated" under American authority, Borah wrote in April 1928 that he could not see "what we can do in the way of effectuating any change in the situation. We can make inquiry and investigate, but this is a situation which seems to require something more than that." (This came at a time when his "something more" for Nicaragua was his gamble on the supervised election.) Conditions changed when riots broke out in Port-au-Prince in December 1929; after temporizing, Hoover appointed a commission headed by W. Cameron Forbes to investigate affairs. Borah pressed for immediate changes of the same type that he had desired in 1922—appointment of a civilian high commissioner and a free election. Frazier supported the commission idea in the abstract but, pointing to the lessons of the McCormick Committee, hoped that "it will be one interested in the welfare of the people rather than in the financial and military interests of the United States." Blaine was more skeptical, noting that it did not take "very much intelligence to determine [that] . . . the trouble in Haiti is the United States itself." All three senators demanded withdrawal after a free election, which squared with the tenor if not the specifics of the Forbes Commission report. Much had changed since Medill McCormick had traveled to Haiti in the early 1920s.[66]

Throughout the 1920s the peace progressives made their appeal more acceptable to the mainstream by not denying that the United States possessed a "peculiar" strategic and economic interest in the Caribbean Basin. As early as 1923, Shipstead said that he would support "anything that will bring the potent large markets of those countries closer to our producers"; by 1927 this line of reasoning had become regular fare for most peace progressives. At the same time, of course, they supplemented their argument that anti-imperialism represented the best policy economically with constant references to its increasing American moral power. In addition, perhaps because it had occurred to them so often on the domestic scene, they proved quite capable of distinguishing between Latin American nationalism and Bolshevism. Finally, the peace progressives succeeded in removing some of the flaws from their 1910s program. Their increasingly well-developed anti-imperialism allowed them to propose positive policy alternatives— Shipstead's Central American federation and republican alliance, Wheeler's use of moral power through recognition, Dill's hands-off approach in Nicaragua to allow a Sandino victory, general support for free Haitian elections before withdrawal—that had eluded their critique of Wilsonian policy in the region, although their major failure did come from Borah's attempt to construct a positive alternative. Also, they resolved their earlier conflict between nationalism and anti-imperialism by modifying their views on sovereign rights under international law, arguing that the United States should evacuate its citizens from revolutionary areas and that American nationals overseas should accept the laws of the country in which they did business. (In 1931 Borah, the champion of sovereign rights during the 1910s, informed a press conference that when American citizens went into underdeveloped countries "they thereby consent to accept the laws and the kind of government that the people have.") All told, the program was quite complete.[67]

The peace progressives attempted to apply their foreign policy principles to all nations, not just those in Latin America; two of the more straightforward applications involved the USSR and China. The senators advocated diplomatic recognition of the Soviet state more strongly than any other group in the Senate at the time, and they also emerged as the most prominent Senate supporters of the nationalist Kuomintang (KMT) party in China. In the process they articulated the final component of their anti-imperialist ideology—a desire to offer the United States as the alternative to Bolshevism in the underdeveloped world.

Warren Harding had campaigned against Wilsonianism in foreign affairs, but his administration willingly continued its predecessor's Soviet policies. Charles Evans Hughes, Harding's Secretary of State, made no secret that he despised the Communist regime and would do nothing "to place the seal of approval on the tyrannical measures" it had adopted. Although Hughes claimed that he did not want to interfere in the domestic politics of the USSR, he noted that Soviet respect for the liberties of foreigners, which he termed a precondition to recognition, "will most likely be accompanied by appropriate respect for the essential rights and liberties of the Russian people themselves." The peace progressives considered this policy dangerously shortsighted, but they faced a difficult task in building enough popular support for their cause. They began with an attempt to show that the Soviet government enjoyed wide popular support and had virtues not generally communicated to the American public. Borah originated the tactic, at various times contending that the government enjoyed the support of 85 percent and 90 percent of the peasantry. Describing the Soviet government as the most stable in Europe, Borah also asked antirecognition forces to consider the alternative to the Communists—civil war and "another five or ten years of indescribable misery." In any case, the Idaho senator believed that the principle of Communism "obtains now only in a limited degree" in Russia, since "the farmer in Russia . . . has destroyed or modified communism." Although "we would all like to see revolutions take place in an orderly [and] bloodless way," Borah felt that conditions in Russia were improving. Finally, as part of what he called "spiritual disarmament," he cited recognition as one way to put the intolerance of the Great War behind; the alternative "is to foment and keep alive the spirit of distrust and war and to justify the piling up of armament."[68]

Activity increased during the congressional recess of 1923, when La Follette, Ladd, Brookhart, and Wheeler all visited Russia and came back supporting recognition.[69] Brookhart went so far as to assert that "the Soviet government has abandoned the communistic plan for that of the cooperative," and when he returned home he hailed Leon Trotsky as "a greater financial genius" than any found on Wall Street. He added that the Bolshevik financial program had produced "excellent crops" and increased "comfort and attractiveness" for the average villager. When pressed by conservatives in the United States about his statements possibly condoning revolution, Brookhart retorted that he liked "their government better for that reason." Although he conceded that the Soviet government needed improvement, he noted that the

Americans had done similar work on their political structure through constitutional amendments. Wheeler agreed with his Iowa colleague that the USSR represented "the most stable government in Europe today," and he painted a picture of a country not all that dissimilar to the United States. The "naked facts" were that, contrary to antirecognition propaganda, no reign of terror or religious persecution existed in Russia; on the contrary, entrepreneurs in Petrograd and Moscow were copying American methods and desired American capital. Wheeler also defended the continuing Soviet restrictions on freedom of speech and the press "until outside pressure is released, until outside nations cease assisting the enemies of the Government." Like Borah, the Montana senator alleged that the Soviet government "has practically abandoned the communistic theory as unworkable," as shown by the adoption of Lenin's New Economic Plan. Borah also dismissed the administration argument about Soviet propaganda, contending that it was no worse than the propaganda put out by the British or the French. Brookhart went much further to advance the fantastic argument that the Soviets had the legal right under international law "to meddle in our Government, and even to destroy it if they wish to," triggering a stinging rebuke from Henry Cabot Lodge. Although the peace progressives abandoned this naive vision of Soviet society later in the decade, their decision to portray the USSR in a favorable light rather than to concentrate on a purely technical case for recognition that did not seem to involve praise of the USSR did nothing to aid the cause of recognition throughout the early 1920s.[70]

Borah rejoined the fray as chair of a Foreign Relations subcommittee considering a Borah-sponsored resolution to recognize Russia, sparring with Robert Kelley, head of the State Department's East European desk, in an attempt to disprove some of the State Department's statements about the USSR. Borah denied that the Communist party controlled the Soviet government, noting that the Soviet constitution did not "recognize the power of the Communist party to interpose in the affairs of the Government"; the unprepared Kelley could not cite an instance in which the Communist party had interfered with a decision of a Soviet court. The two also disagreed over whether the Third International constituted an arm of the Soviet government, an important point since the Third International and not the government was issuing most of the anti-American propaganda; Kelley stated that he did not believe Soviet denials about the connection, prompting Borah to remark that the Assistant Secretary believed only what he wanted to. Borah repeatedly tried to compare Soviet governmental and party institutions to similar ones in the United States. In addition to showing the senator's appalling lack of knowledge about actual conditions in Russia, the hearings demonstrated how far the peace progressives were prepared to go to make the public case that the Soviet Union was a fairly responsible government, although they hastened to add that diplomatic recognition did not imply political support of the government recognized. In part this strategy came from the weak position of the peace progressives on this issue in both Congress and the executive branch. As the American correspondent for the London *Times* perceptively noted, the dissenters delivered the constant string of speeches on Russia because on matters of diplomatic recognition, given the structure of the American government, they "must look to the President for action and to the force of an educated public opinion to persuade the President."[71]

Although a rather naive outlook characterized most of the public statements by the peace progressives, alongside the rhetoric lay a rather strong anti-Bolshevist ideology; they disagreed with all the means of the Hughes policy, but with few of its ends. Virtually every peace progressive (except Brookhart) believed that the United States had the power, through recognition, to use its moral influence to undermine Bolshevik rule. As early as 1922 Borah wrote that "the best way to get rid of the Bolshevik rulers is for the great governments to get in touch with the Russian people" as a way of helping them "to get away from both communism and the old regime." Throughout the 1920s the Idaho senator maintained the belief that recognition would "do more to undermine it [Bolshevism] and destroy it than any other possible thing we could do." Wheeler added that withholding recognition "also encourages and strengthens the elements of communism which derive their power, at the expense of the more moderate elements, from the fact that the United States and other powers seem to be opposing the present regime." Recognition thus formed a central component of the peace progressive arsenal of moral power, and they desired to use it as a tool to moderate extremist regimes of the left in the same way that they did not oppose the use of nonrecognition (as in the Chamorro case) to dispose of extremist regimes of the right.[72]

As the decade progressed, the peace progressives (except Brookhart) placed greater emphasis on anti-Bolshevism. In 1927 Borah publicized his point that "the best friends Lenin and Trotsky ever had were the foreign nations which have stood in the way of trade recognition or relation with Russia"; he termed U.S.-Soviet trade the "most distinctive force which you could possibly bring against the Bolshevistic movement." At the same time, he continued to defend the revolution as a necessary transition period from tsarism to "a sane democracy." Despite the rhetoric, the Soviet government began to view Borah as its best American friend, and for a time the senator functioned as a de facto Secretary of State in dealing with the Soviet Union. By 1928 Borah was helping to obtain the release of American citizens imprisoned there; in 1929 he asked the Kremlin to cease its campaign of persecution against top Catholic officials, and for a time the Soviets complied. The *New York Times* reported that a letter from Borah gained American travelers to Russia access to areas denied even to nationals of countries with which the USSR had diplomatic relations. Borah gradually ceased these contacts in the early 1930s, fearing that by providing an informal diplomatic channel between the United States and Russia he was delaying formal recognition.[73]

Although the peace progressives failed to secure recognition for Russia, their agitation for recognition illuminates both their conceptions of moral power and their desire to position the United States somewhere between Bolshevism and traditional American foreign policy, including Wilsonianism, as a way of counteracting the Bolshevist appeal both in its home base and in the underdeveloped world. In addition, the arguments used to justify the call for recognition show, as in the Latin American cases, the extent to which the peace progressives believed that anti-imperialism served American economic as well as strategic and moral interests; economics was crucial to both their public and private critiques of administration Soviet policy. Although economics did not play as central a role in their dissent from Frank Kellogg's China policy, the anti-Communist element reappeared.

Instability in China climaxed in early 1927, when tensions between the KMT and the Chinese Communists forced the powers to decide how best to protect their nationals operating in China, particularly in Shanghai. The State Department rejected the emerging peace progressive position on such matters—the brief landing of American forces to help evacuate American nationals out of the danger zone—arguing that such an action "would, of course, paralyze American business interests there and would be most disastrous." Nor did Kellogg exhibit any enthusiasm for resolving Chinese domestic instability by positioning the United States behind the KMT, describing the party as little more than the rulers of "individual provinces or groups of provinces." Since the Secretary believed that "Bolshevik agitators and propagandists are back of this anti-foreign demonstration in China," he felt little need to alter his passive diplomacy, resolved to preserve American freedom of action by committing the United States to neither side in China. (To those who complained, Kellogg blandly responded that the only Americans more interested than himself in restoring full sovereignty to China were "pro-Chinese cranks.") After the debate over the Washington Treaties in 1922, the China issue had dropped out of the peace progressive repertoire until 1925, when Borah unexpectedly called for the cession of American extraterritorial rights "as speedily as possible" to show respect to Chinese nationalism and integrity. The United States maintained its extraterritorial privileges (in large part, the senator believed, because of the "thoroughly organized propaganda" of the American Chamber of Commerce), but Borah still believed it "contrary to the spirit of the times and the modern conception of national integrity"; the senator warned that the foreign powers needed to adjust their policies to the fact that Chinese nationalism was powerful and would not go away. The position drew public criticism from, of all people, Kaiser Wilhelm, who predicted that "Senator Borah will be hailed as a champion of colored nations and will be acclaimed by the Moscow Third International, for his statement asserts the principle that the Bolsheviki are at pains to spread over the whole world, namely, the equality of the colored races with the white race"; Wilhelm asserted that Borah's proposal was part of an Asian/Bolshevist plot to take over Europe through a devastated Germany. Borah retorted that the ex-Kaiser's views would lead to a worldwide race war.[74]

As the political situation in China crystallized, the peace progressives urged the administration to recognize the Nationalist government; the KMT slogan "China for the Chinese," which in Norris' view expressed the same concepts that the founding fathers had, particularly appealed to them. Borah said that the KMT deserved recognition promptly even though it did not control all of the country. Shipstead described the Nationalists as "the forces of democracy in China," while Howell reported that "early pacification of China [by the KMT] . . . is the hope of all Americans." Only Wheeler, who also urged prompt recognition of the Canton government, expressed some skepticism about the quality of the KMT leadership, writing that Chiang Kai-shek "did not seem big enough for the stupendous task he had before him." Still, the Montana senator, who toured East Asia in 1927, found KMT Foreign Minister C. C. Wu "one of the most sensible and conscientious Chinamen" he encountered. The peace progressives had nothing good to say about Chiang's rivals in China. Borah argued that Chang Tso-lin, "the military dictator of Manchuria," wanted to "strengthen the hold of the militarists and weaken the hold of the liberal forces in China." Wheeler said that Chang resembled "the one-time Western frontier gambler— slick, suave, cunning, insincere," and speculated that the Japanese were financing the northern armies opposed to the KMT. This rhetoric resonated in Nationalist-held areas. Walter Lippmann, who visited China in mid-1926, reported back to Borah that the extraterritoriality remarks had been widely circulated in China, in both the foreign- and Chinese-language press, and that the Borah speech, by showing the Chinese that they had some international friends, had increased American prestige in East Asia. Meanwhile, one American traveler to China, who received an open letter of introduction from Borah, recalled that the senator's "reputation for liberalism and anti-imperialism was nowhere greater than in China," and that the letter constituted the "best introduction to the leaders of the national revolution."[75]

The administration's decision in 1927 to send the Marines to Shanghai to protect American nationals triggered a sharp peace progressive protest, although Kellogg had no desire to intervene in China's domestic politics. Borah feared that sending troops might antagonize nationalist forces and make the situation more difficult; he contended that the United States could protect its nationals best "by bringing them out of danger until the danger is passed." Norris agreed that the United States should limit its military involvement to evacuating U.S. citizens from the war zone, and he urged Kellogg to announce that "we sympathize with those who believe that foreigners should not make laws for an unwilling people, simply because they are too weak to defend themselves." The peace progressives particularly worried that the Marines would wind up fighting the Nationalists. Wheeler saw the KMT as the only group in China besides the Communists who could hold out some hope to the Chinese people that conditions would improve. Given that improving the living conditions of the Chinese people formed the only way to stamp out the seeds of Bolshevism, he said that the United States must help "in every way possible" to promote a "sane and liberal" China, although he declined to specify how that was to be done; Howell, too, saw the KMT as the logical alternative to the "twin evils" of imperialism and communism. McMaster advocated authorizing the Federal Farm Board to purchase $25 million of wheat and flour to donate to China for famine relief, arguing that such a policy "would create a friendly feeling toward this nation in every section of the globe" while also having a "tremendous economic effect" at home. The peace progressives dismissed conservative allegations that Chiang's forces also were Communist; Borah said that, as in Mexico and Nicaragua, it was not communism "but the spirit of nationalism which is aflame." Distinguishing between genuine nationalists and Communists so as to determine which side deserved American aid formed a critical tenet of the peace progressive critique of China policy.[76]

By the end of the decade, then, the peace progressives had constructed an ideology that combined a blistering critique of American military interventionism with an active worldwide program of American moral and economic intervention to aid nationalist, democratic forces. The senators argued that their policy served the moral interests of the United States by allowing it to preserve the ideals that had made the country the model for progressive forces around the world during the first 150 years of its existence. During the 1920s the senators added two other components to this line of thought. They argued that antiimperialism served the economic interests of their constituents, contending that a policy of forceful interventionism aided a few large business interests that desired government help with risky endeavors, but hurt most of American business by causing anti-American boycotts of varying intensity. These in turn denied American farmers and small manufacturers the foreign markets they seemed to need so desperately. Finally, the peace progressives reasoned that American strategic interests justified a policy of anti-imperialism. The senators believed that a world of independent, nationalist-minded nations would create a peaceful, economically open world order, and that the imperialism of the Western European states and Japan, which retarded the creation of such a world, thus threatened long-term American security. By the same token, Bolshevism, at least in its purest form, threatened the United States in the same way. Therefore, they argued that the United States needed a policy that would diminish the threats of both of these "twin evils"; the anti-imperialism that they espoused did so. Though vague when discussing how far the United States should go to implement this ideology, they did believe that an active program of moral, diplomatic, and, if absolutely necessary, economic power would work. This radical anti-imperialism, unique in its consistency and forcefulness in the annals of the congressional dissent, established the peace progressives as important thinkers on issues of peace. This ideology also explicitly challenged the perspective of Woodrow Wilson in the underdeveloped world. The former President too had looked to position the United States somewhere between communism and imperialism in international affairs while using American moral power to achieve strategic and economic goals.[77] The peace progressives, however, expressed a far greater willingness to oppose conservative foreign governments than Wilson ever thought feasible; the outlines of this dispute had appeared in the contrasting interpretations of Article XI during the League of Nations debate. While the ideological divisions on liberal policy toward East Asia and Latin America generally featured only the peace progressives and Wilsonians, in matters relating to Europe a third bloc offered a foreign policy agenda. The search for a peace progressive alternative to the business-oriented European policy pursued by the decade's Republican administrations completed the foreign policy agenda of the senators during the 1920s.

George Norris. The Nebraska senator's passionate speeches against the Armed Ship Bill and U.S. entrance into World War I aroused the hostility of nationalist Democrats, who accused him of treason.

Asle Gronna. The most radical of the peace progressives during the 1910s, the North Dakota senator offered the most forthright anti-imperialist critique of the League of Nations during debate in 1919.

William Kenyon. The Iowa senator drifted away from the peace progressives during the League of Nations fight, contending that the group's anti-imperialist principles dictated a more favorable interpretation of Wilsonian diplomacy.

Robert La Follette and John Blaine with Wisconsin progressive leader Herman Ekern. The elder La Follette spent the 1910s expanding his domestic antibusiness ideology into an anti-imperialist foreign policy perspective. After his death in 1925, Blaine took his place as the leader of the radical wing of the peace progressives.

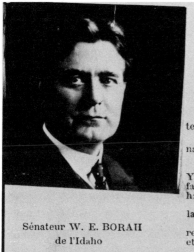

Voici la photographie de l'éminent Sénateur BORAH de l'Idaho.

C'est notre Nouveau Charles Sumner au Sé-
nat Américain.

Il a pris en main la cause d'Haïti.

Après un récent meeting qu'il a tenu à New-
York à Carnegie Hall, le 1er Mai 1922, il a
fait faire un pas gigantesque à la question
haïtienne. Sa devise est: «Il faut sortir d'Haïti».

C'est l'éminent candidat du parti libéral à
la présidence des Etats Unis pour 1924.

Peuple haïtien, le Sénateur Borah inspire confiance, car c'est un champion ardent
et convaincu du Droit et de la Justice.

Sénateur W. E. BORAH
de l'Idaho

William Borah. A 1923 publication of the Union Patriotique called Borah the
Charles Sumner of his generation and proposed the Idaho senator for president of
the United States in 1924.

Burton Wheeler with the exiled vice president of Nicaragua, Juan Sacasa, in 1926.
The peace progressives defended Sacasa's claim to the Nicaraguan presidency in
1926, arguing that the United States should intervene diplomatically on the Liberal
leader's behalf. By mid-1927, however, all except Borah soured on him and turned
to Augusto Sandino as their preferred choice in Nicaragua.

Smith Brookhart with a group of Russians during his 1923 visit to the Soviet Union. The peace progressives emerged as the foremost congressional champions of diplomatic recognition of the USSR; several of them traveled there with Brookhart at various times during the 1920s.

Henrik Shipstead. The Minnesota senator emerged as the group's leading expert on economic diplomacy during the 1920s, structuring the peace progressive position on how the United States could aid Germany in its economic recovery.

John Blaine. The impatient Wisconsin senator articulated the strongest anti-imperialist alternative to Coolidge administration policies in both Europe and Latin America.

Gerald Nye, William Borah, and Lynn Frazier were well known for their positions on decreasing the role of force in international affairs. Borah preferred an international treaty to outlaw war, Frazier called for an amendment to strip the war power from the Constitution, while Nye in the 1930s came to favor restrictions on American munitions makers.

5

Alternative to Corporatism

The anti-imperialism of the peace progressives provided a stark alternative to the G.O.P.'s often heavy-handed Latin American and East Asian policies. As writers of the corporatist school have observed, however, the European policy of the Republicans operated quite differently, with the Harding and Coolidge administrations attempting to use economic diplomacy to achieve peace without American political or military commitments to the continent.[1] Unsurprisingly, the peace progressives placed a sinister spin on this link between business and foreign policy, and spent the decade attempting to prevent the mainstream Republicans, led by Secretary of Commerce Herbert Hoover, from achieving their foreign policy goals. Although they divided more often on European questions than on those dealing with the underdeveloped world, the peace progressives assembled an alternative to business-oriented internationalism that combined anti-imperialism, anti-militarism, and a different kind of economic diplomacy with initiatives to align the United States more closely with neutrals and political opponents of the Allies, particularly Germany. In the process the dissenters articulated a third way, apart from both business internationalism and Wilsonianism, for the United States to deal with European issues, and the senators also enjoyed a good deal of success at frustrating the initiatives of both groups of their ideological opponents.

In their European program, however, the dissenters experienced difficulties that they had avoided in their Latin American and East Asian agendas. Although the senators came up with their share of creative proposals for the proper U.S. policy toward Europe, they overestimated the ability of American nonmilitary initiatives to influence events in France, England, and Italy; and the peace progressive program, if adopted, would in all likelihood have increased tension with both the British and the French without necessarily producing any tangible benefits for the United States. In addition, the dissenters supplemented their European program with disarmament proposals that grew progressively more extreme through the decade and that offered no guarantee of having the transforming effect on international affairs that the senators predicted. Finally, the suspicion of involvement in a European-dominated political organization, carried over from the League of Nations fight, led them to divide on all five of the major treaty votes of the decade and led some of them to oppose treaties that seemed to satisfy their overall foreign policy goals. For these reasons the peace progressives generally failed to increase the level of support for their European agenda—either in Congress or among the peace movement—as the decade progressed; these drawbacks also help explain why no later group of dissenters resurrected their European policy proposals, unlike the case with their Latin American and East Asian frameworks. The peace progressives managed through their European policy suggestions to structure a truly global ideology, but in terms of policy toward Europe their legacy was far more contradictory.

The early 1920s witnessed a culmination of the historical revisionism on the nature of American war aims begun by the peace progressives during the League debates. Ladd said that the United States could fulfill its wartime promises by aiding the weaker states on whose behalf the United States had fought the war; Borah went further, with the incredible (for him) comment that Wilson had gone to Europe with "an American program announcing American principles" on behalf of small nations only to be rejected at Versailles. Their anti-imperialist principles led the peace progressives to attack the political leaders they believed were obstructing fulfillment of their vision. Borah charged that former French Prime Minister Clemenceau, who toured the United States in 1922, really wanted the United States to return to the European scene so that Paris could use American troops to dismember Germany; this scheme fitted into Clemenceau's general theory that "there

is no means in this world by which to govern men except that of force."
Borah urged the French to concentrate on reforming their policy,
"which is bringing Europe to utter ruin." At the same time, as in the
League debate, anti-imperialism led to an interest in European affairs.
In a speech in Chicago Borah urged Harding to tell England and France
that their policies of imperialism "shall find no sympathy or succor in
this corner of the globe." The senator charged the Allies with reneging
on wartime promises to grant independence to former Ottoman vassal
states such as Syria; instead, Syria had been made a French mandate,
an action that could "only be justified upon principles of imperialism,
and the most obnoxious and indefensible imperialism." He reminded
his listeners that "these are the policies which we are invited to go to
Europe and enforce."[2]

French policy in Europe did not escape the senators' criticism. All
the peace progressives condemned the French occupation of the Ruhr.
Describing the action as "a crime against peace, against humanity, and
against international decency," Borah argued that since Germany had
accepted an armistice on American principles articulated by Wilson,
the United States had an obligation to prevent a clear violation of armistice terms by "the most destructive and ruthless method of militarism." He called for "bold and determined action" from the State Department, which would involve at the very minimum the United States'
marshaling "the moral forces of the world" to oppose the French action. The American correspondent for the London *Times* remarked that
on the Ruhr issue, Borah, "this shrewdest of judges of the public mind,"
had seemed to capture American sentiment exactly. La Follette, who
toured the area during his European visit in 1923, contended that the
French wanted permanent possession of the Ruhr, which could create
a dangerous situation by turning the traditionally democratic socialist
population of the region into revolutionaries. The Wisconsin senator
also charged the French forces with a variety of atrocities.[3]

The French actions did not surprise the peace progressives, who by
the mid-1920s had come to view France as the consummate imperialist
power. Borah contended that French Prime Minister Raymond Poincaré represented as "great a menace to the peace of the world" as had
the Kaiser; he described the "vicious" French leaders as "enemies of
humanity, enemies of peace and good order throughout Europe." La
Follette elaborated, contending that Poincaré wanted to dismember
Germany while permanently occupying the left bank of the Rhine,

which he would exploit jointly with German capitalists; to enforce this obviously unjust solution, Poincaré planned the creation of a "huge army" supplemented by African troops and military forces from the anti-German states of Eastern and Central Europe. The senator urged a strong condemnation of Paris to foil Poincaré's attempt to create the impression that the United States approved of the present French "imperialistic enterprises." Most of the peace progressives believed that the French people were being kept in the dark by what Wheeler described as a public press that spouted "a systematic propaganda of hate." All the peace progressives also viewed the French political system as dangerously flawed. Shipstead believed that French industrialists held total control of the government, where "they can use . . . their power" to provoke a war in the name of the "white man's civilization" for access to raw materials in Europe or in the underdeveloped world; his only solace was that Paris "stands revealed to the world clothed in the armor of imperialism and conquest."[4]

These anti-French opinions did not translate into a general anti-European viewpoint, as is shown by peace progressive opinions about England. On the one hand, the Wisconsin progressives in particular attacked British foreign policy. La Follette noted the "startling difference" between the aggressive Middle Eastern policies of the British and pacific Soviet initiatives in the same region. Blaine argued that the British invented "the policy that a strong nation has a right to ride down a weaker nation, the stronger nation being the judge of every question," and he cautioned against a close identification with the "arrogant imperial policy" of the British Empire. Whereas the peace progressives feared France beyond redemption, however, they did not have as pessimistic a view of England. Although Borah publicly feuded with Winston Churchill, who ranked just behind Clemenceau and Poincaré on the peace progressive list of undesirables, all the dissenters hoped that England could reform under the leadership of the Labour party and particularly Ramsay MacDonald. When MacDonald criticized the Ruhr occupation, Borah announced that he was "greatly pleased" with the Labour leader's recognition of the value of moral leadership. MacDonald's elevation to Prime Minister in January 1924 led La Follette to hope that he would inaugurate a foreign policy devoted to peace, while Borah urged the Coolidge administration to learn from Labour's precepts. Norris interpreted MacDonald's return to leadership in 1929 as a repudiation of the Versailles Treaty and the "unjust and indefensible treatment of Russia" by the Western powers. Dill, arguing that MacDonald represented the hopes of the "masses of people in this country," looked to the Labourite to join with the peace progressives in providing leadership for the cause of peace internationally.[5]

The peace progressives had little hope that a MacDonald would emerge to lead Fascist Italy out the ranks of imperialist powers; unlike most Americans of their day, they had nothing but contempt for the government of Benito Mussolini. La Follette went to Rome during his European tour and questioned Mussolini about Fascist restrictions on freedom of the press. He commented later on the similarity between Fascist political repressiveness and that which he had witnessed in the USSR, although he did not see in Italy any of the benefits to society that he had seen in Russia. His son continued the anti-Italian crusade after his father's death, although he feared that the dictator had entrenched himself in power and threatened world peace. Borah seconded this conclusion, blasting the Italians for the size of their army and criticizing Mussolini personally during a July 1927 speech in Denver; this brought a reply from the Italian ambassador that Borah was meddling in Italian domestic affairs.[6]

This negative view of the principal European powers dating from the League of Nations battle (combined with an equally unflattering, though rarely articulated, opinion of Japan) gave the peace progressives a poor opinion of organizations and policies that they perceived as dominated by these countries. Borah lamented that the conflicting imperialist desires of England, France, and Italy ruined any chance of peace; Shipstead added that Lloyd George, Poincaré, Mussolini, Lenin, and Ludendorff, the "quacks who have charge of the world," were not helping matters. La Follette described the League of Nations as nothing more than a "tool of French imperialism" manipulated by the same "forces of hate" that had wrecked any chance of peace in the wake of the Great War. Brookhart agreed, and added that the powers needed to remove the World Court from the control of League "reactionaries" to further the cause of peace. Still, the peace progressives believed that the people of Europe, "like the people of America," wanted peace, although most election results did not reflect this because "the channels of publicity, the public press, are damed [sic] up and only those things which the ruling class in each country desires to publish is allowed to get out."[7]

The peace progressives also had dim opinions of countries they viewed as vassals of France, in the process revealing an overestimation of French power in the decade's European affairs. Borah feared that the large loans made by the French to Poland and the Little Entente nations throughout the decade proved that France desired to make "Poland a powerful militaristic state." La Follette in 1921 filed a memorandum with the Foreign Relations Committee on Polish "atrocities and persecutions in East Galicia," and he later dismissed Poland as "one of the favored countries under the Versailles Treaty" that had received Silesian coal as its "share of the spoils of war." The Wisconsin senator also reported that Rumania "has a regulation white terror [as a result of a] combination of big banks and big land owners" that dominated the political system. Wheeler, describing the Balkan countries as "virtually armed camps," accused the French and Italians of manipulating the region for power-political aims, but he hoped that popular movements for a Balkan union signaled that the people of the region "are more farseeing and peacefully inclined than their governments." On the other hand, the peace progressives sympathized with the East European countries they felt had been victimized by the postwar treaties. La Follette hailed the struggle of the Austrian Socialists to preserve democracy against the combined forces of monarchists and "Allied money lenders," while in the later part of the decade Borah campaigned for a revision of the Treaty of Trianon, which he argued was "made in violation of the most fundamental principles upon which America entered and fought the war." A Prague paper quoted the senator as favoring a revision of Trianon to allow each East European country to annex the territories of its nationals.[8]

The peace progressives believed that the postwar treaties treated Germany the most unfairly. Borah argued that the "real problem" in Europe after the war "is the destruction of a great nation" and the punishment of a people "who were not responsible for the war"; he called for restoring the property of German nationals confiscated during the war and by the late 1920s urged a revision of Versailles on the basis of new evidence that he claimed exonerated the Germans from sole responsibility for starting the war. La Follette wanted the United States to employ the "traditional" American foreign policy and "express our sympathy and lend our moral influence" to encourage German democracy. He sought to achieve this through a $10 million relief package for Germany, which he argued would serve both the strategic interests of the United States and humanitarian concerns. The Wisconsin senator reasoned that since "hunger is the firebrand of revolution," a severe famine could weaken the "enlightened" Weimar state and strengthen the alternatives, "communism or monarchy." Howell sponsored a similar plan, calling for a $25 million government-sponsored loan to Germany for the purchase of American grain and other food products to help prevent German famine. At the same time the peace progressives defended the election of former Field Marshal Hindenberg as Weimar President in 1925, which Shipstead speculated resulted from nationalist reactions to the "shameful invasion of the Ruhr and the indefensible Treaty of Versailles." The Minnesota senator argued that the real "menace to world peace" was the fact that "Germany is disarmed, but is surrounded both on the east and west by large standing armies whose Governments still resort to enforced military service."[9]

In other parts of the world, most peace progressives welcomed the reconciliation with Turkey offered by the 1926 Lausanne Treaty, with Borah favoring "establishing friendly relations with all nations and all peoples" as a way of bringing non-Christian nations into contact with Christian principles. In addition to the strong peace progressive sympathy for Syria and North Africa, Borah favored establishing a Jewish homeland in Palestine and chastised the British for a shortsighted policy, which he argued had played into the hands of fanatical Arab nationalists. Blaine emerged as the most prominent Senate backer of Indian independence, describing British colonial policy as the "most atrocious conduct known to history." The Wisconsin senator introduced several resolutions urging the Senate to express its sympathy for independence for India, "mindful of the struggle for independence that gave birth to our Republic," although none progressed very far.[10]

The peace progressives reserved their most positive appraisal for the Scandinavian nations. Shipstead and Brookhart praised the Scandinavian cooperative movement, with the Iowa senator terming cooperatives the "only constructive movement that has survived the war," since they highlighted the "spirit of service and democracy." He hoped that the international cooperative exchange in Scandinavia could be extended to include the United States, Germany, Russia, Mexico, and Turkey as part of a new alignment that could stand as an alternative to the League of Nations system of "statesmanship guided by economic power and greed." Norway was the only country whose foreign policy received consistent praise from the peace progressives. Blaine, describing the Norwegians as "lovers of freedom and independence," compared the Norwegian revolution of the 1810s to the American Revolution, although the outcome differed when Norway fell victim to the "intrigues against the smaller nations" practiced by the great powers, much like Shantung after the Great War. Nonetheless, the Norwegians managed to live in harmony with Sweden and Denmark, which proved that onetime enemy nations "might yet join in an agreement . . . for peace and world brotherhood, laying that agreement . . . on the foundation of a progressive an ultimate disarmament." Blaine hoped that the tenacity of the Norwegians, who had struggled several hundred years before achieving full independence in 1905, would "inspire the struggling peoples of other countries and sustain them in their struggles for a national existence." He declared that a celebration of Norwegian independence would keep alive the "spirit of liberty and independence" in a Europe in which the "right of self-determination is denied to peoples who have an organic unity of mankind and who thus constitute a state entitled to its freedom and its independence." La Follette cited Norway as an example of a democracy that did not need a strong military establishment because it had "no schemes for the exploitation of weaker peoples which would tempt her to seek entrance into any entangling alliance."[11]

When the peace progressives spoke of Norway, they seemed to describe an ideal foreign policy. The senators did not, however, envision the United States as another Norway. As their German, Indian, and Soviet policies indicated, they did not wish the United States to withdraw politically from international affairs, nor even to take a purely economic and cultural approach as they saw Norway doing. On the contrary, they wanted the United States to employ its leverage gained from the war to foster changes in the international climate that would promote a more peaceful world. To achieve this, the dissenters proposed a quite interventionist policy directed primarily against the powers they viewed as most threatening to the world peace, particularly France. Like their opponents, they hoped to use American economic might for diplomatic purposes, but their overall goals differed markedly from those of the decade's Republican administrations.

Wartime credits had left the major European powers owing the U.S. government between $10 billion and $11 billion, which European leaders pressured the United States to scale downward or cancel alto-

gether. The Harding administration and Senate Republican leaders settled upon the creation of a Foreign Debt Commission, which allowed
the administration to negotiate with European nations for debt adjustment so long as the final settlements contained interest rates at a minimum of 4.25 percent and the debtor nations repaid all principal and
interest within twenty-five years.[12] The peace progressives assailed this
policy, charging that the administration had created a debt bill "pe-
culiarly in the interest of the international bankers," since with the
European economic distress the "specter of REPUDIATION of allied debts
spread terror through the Wall Street banking groups." The dissenters
also registered less programmed complaints, fearing that through the
commission the United States would sacrifice its chief leverage for influencing European policies.[13] Howell argued that policymakers incorrectly considered the debt "a commercial, rather than a political, debt."
The peace progressives made no such distinction; believing in the in-
tertwined nature of the strategic, economic, and moral elements of foreign policy, they argued that the administration had made a false and
potentially dangerous distinction. Borah lamented the "misfortune" of
settling "these debts divorced from other problems"; with the debt
question out of the way, "we are at their mercy." The Idaho senator
wanted to consider the debts as part of a larger package to include a
European program of disarmament and recognition of the USSR,
hoping that a "definite, determined policy" by the United States would
lead the major European powers "to reflect, and ultimately to modify
and revise their programs." As things existed, he denied that conditions
entitled the European states to any favorable treatment, since the constant insistence on alliances and the "brutal and insane . . . militaristic
and imperialistic policies" rendered the Europeans unprepared to help
themselves. Cancellation could "aggravate the present conditions" by
freeing up debt money for other purposes; the Europeans "would be
much better off in using the money to pay their debts than they would
in using it in the manner in which they are now using it."[14]

The peace progressives failed to prevent passage of the bill creating
the debt commission, and the newly created commission first renego-
tiated the British debt, which policymakers on both sides of the Atlantic
viewed as essential to restoring economic prosperity and stability. Led
by La Follette, the peace progressives attacked the arrangement. In a
four-page editorial in *La Follette's Magazine* the Wisconsin senator predicted that eventually the deal could commit the United States to pre-

serving the "vastly over-extended and shaky structure of the British Empire" and would "foster and stimulate imperialism" by allowing the British to "extend their monstrous schemes of conquest." He reasoned that as a creditor Washington should "inquire into the CHARACTER OF EXPENDITURES which the British Government is making" while pleading its inability to pay. Ladd, seizing upon an impolitic remark by British Prime Minister Stanley Baldwin, who had suggested that difficulties in debt negotiations had arisen primarily because of rural American politicians, sarcastically commented that "the ruralite may even be intelligent enough to recognize points of difference in his treatment as compared with the generous concessions made to Great Britain." He speculated that the British attacked Congress because they viewed executive officials "as being disposed to be reasonable (easy marks?)."[15]

The senators also rebuked leading British politicians who questioned the generosity of the settlement. Borah charged Winston Churchill with conducting a "Gallipoli campaign for cancellation" by adopting wartime propaganda efforts to persuade the American public to change its mind on the issue; the senator noted that England had received 3.805 million square miles as a result of the Versailles Treaty and for Churchill to turn around to complain about the conduct of a country that had received no spoils of war only proved that at Versailles both the United States and England "were true to their ideals." Borah came up with a number of schemes for preventing further debt revision. In March 1926 he urged Kellogg to initiate a counterclaim against the British and French for violations of American neutral rights before 1917, and in August he argued that Europeans should cancel all reparations payments before the United States even considered cancellation. Howell, who increasingly emerged as a leading player on this issue, denied that England had any right to complain given that London had regularly met (the much smaller) payments to J. P. Morgan at over twice the rate of interest paid to the U.S. government. He also accused the British of waging economic warfare against the United States through manipulation of the world rubber market. This alone offered a reason why the United States should not forgive any more of the British debt.[16]

If the British debt debate featured the peace progressives at their least creative, their response to the broader foreign economic policy offered by the G.O.P. administrations showed the dissenters at their most penetrating. They showed particular astuteness with regard to the Dawes

Plan, which recommended reducing German reparation payments by using a scientific formula to calculate German capacity to pay. Shipstead emerged as the leading Senate critic of what he called a "gold brick loaded with dynamite"; dismissing the arguments of plan supporters that it would promote peace in Europe, he wondered if that were so "why is it not stipulated in the contract that Europe disarm before she gets the money." Shipstead searched in vain for any evidence in their recent conduct that indicated the major European countries would use additional American loans for peaceful purposes; he charged that "France is spending money . . . as quickly as we send it to her," noting with particular interest a recent loan of 4.5 billion francs to her "small allies." La Follette agreed, charging that international bankers had constructed the plan for their own exclusive financial benefit; he termed it "extraordinary" that Coolidge would create a commission "entirely controlled by Morgan influences" without any vestige of congressional sanction. Shipstead asserted that the peace progressives preferred "a real American policy in our foreign relations that will have for its purposes the establishment of world peace and safety of humanity." (To this, the *Wall Street Journal* replied that Shipstead "obviously never read" the text of the Dawes Plan, "and, if he did read it, [he] could never understand it," although he did not care about the truthfulness of his statements "so long as it went down with an audience as ignorant as himself.")[17]

The peace progressives did not propose cutting off American capital from Europe. Rather, they expressed enthusiasm for a 1925 Shipstead proposal for government control of all overseas U.S. financial transactions as a way to promote world peace. The Minnesota senator argued that the war, by giving the United States control over the credit of the world, made the question of whether Washington would employ its financial power for good or evil purposes the only pertinent one. Given this viewpoint, Shipstead wanted "unlimited" American loans to finance European productive industries, food, and construction, provided the Europeans would disarm, disband their "large standing armies, quit building battleships and get down to a peace basis." Under such a system, financial power could become "the genuine power for world peace," greater than any conceivable military might, since "we are in a position to dictate that policy of peace. If the governments want our money, let them pay for it by guaranteeing world peace." This too attracted scorn from business interests; the New York *Journal of Com-*

merce noted with derision that the plan would have "the United States play the role of nursemaid or even preceptor to incorrigibly belligerent European nations." The reversal of positions was doubly ironic given that in the case of Latin American policy the peace progressives had criticized the State Department for seeming to give approval to loans and for attaching political conditions to the receipt of American credit.[18]

Given this attitude, the peace progressives not surprisingly opposed the other debt settlements of the 1920s, attracting the most Democratic support in their battle against the refinancing of the Italian debt. Dill criticized the proposal for offering Italy the same interest rate on loans as that given Germany under the Dawes Plan, even though Germany deserved a better deal because the Weimar regime did not spend nearly as much on its military. After surveying the European scene, Shipstead could not understand why Italy needed to spend over $100 million per year on armaments, while Borah predicted that every dollar conceded by the United States would "go to build up great military establishments and push us on the way to the . . . day when those military establishments will be called into action." He reiterated that the United States had every right to comment on Rome's "international policies"; La Follette agreed, and also went one step further, saying that Washington also should do nothing to aid Mussolini's "despotic rule." The peace progressives reiterated their earlier position that the United States needed to use the debts to force European powers to change their policies. Hoping to give the United States a veto power over the Italian defense budget, Howell proposed an amendment to give the Secretary of the Treasury the power to compel the Italian government to float bonds at American demand to repay the debt more quickly. The Nebraska senator also wrote that the Senate needed to consider "what Italy spent on her African Empire, and what is her income therefrom," and deduct both totals from the amount of debt forgiven. La Follette suggested government requirements for approval of foreign loans as a way to block loans to Italy for rearmament and still permit American credit for "productive purposes." Shipstead fretted that the United States was overtaxing its own people to help maintain "the same old game of intrigue and militaristic imperialism." No excuse for such a policy existed while the United States possessed "control of the greatest power in the world" through its position as the world's leading creditor.[19]

The peace progressives reserved their greatest fury, however, for the French debt, which the Senate did not vote upon until 1929. The arrangement ultimately worked out in 1926 gave Paris lucrative concessions on interest rates (the sixty-two-year average totaled only 1.64 percent) and short-term repayments, but the French government balked at the deal, desiring greater overall reductions. Thus a further settlement was delayed by three more years. In addition to spelling out their case most completely for the kind of European role they envisioned for the United States, the senators also demonstrated their influence by helping to decrease the flexibility of American negotiators, making a final agreement much more difficult to achieve. The peace progressives began by reviving their critique of French foreign policy, particularly in the Middle East and North Africa. Borah noted that since the war the French had built more airplanes than the United States, England, and Japan combined, while having 200,000 men fighting the Riff rebels in Morocco and subjecting their Syrian mandate to "the terrific weight of [French] military forces." Norris called the French African policy "stupendous and altogether unnecessary." Support for the Riffs accompanied a strong displeasure with French diplomacy and society in general. Shipstead wondered how French loans to the Little Entente nations could serve "the interest of peace," while Howell repeatedly badgered administration sources for information on French loans to Eastern European nations and also on the French policy of war debt settlement with states to which it was a creditor, like Rumania. Given these attitudes, the peace progressives took a much more aggressive stance in calling for French repayment than they did for England or Italy. Howell detected "a conspiracy" between French imperialists, international bankers, and the Commerce Department behind the settlement; he reasoned that the silence of most major newspapers on the issue only "outlines in bold relief the biased foundation upon which public opinion largely rests at the present time." A desire to treat what the administration viewed as a commercial debt as a political debt remained the chief peace progressive objection to the French settlement. For the elder La Follette, economic leverage formed the perfect alternative to the use of force to achieve the anti-imperialist aims of the peace progressives when, as in the French case, moral and diplomatic power had failed; he exclaimed that "we have in our hands effective means for compelling compliance without recourse to arms." Although La Follette contended that such a policy would not constitute a political entanglement, opponents of the peace progressives had little trouble refuting the claim, and the peace progressives themselves never conceded the fundamental inconsistency between their specific economic policy proposals for Western Europe and for the rest of the world.[20]

Anti-imperialism provided the crucial point of distinction between the peace progressives and the administration position, the most hard-line articulation of which came in a Toledo speech by Herbert Hoover in 1922. Hoover dismissed cancellation as a possibility since the European governments owed their debts to the American taxpayers, and he hinted that the United States would consider relief in interest payments only with a European guarantee to "bring about an atmosphere of peace in replacement of an atmosphere of war," including general disarmament. The Commerce Secretary also stressed that most European nations possessed a capacity to pay as a result of the significant American trade relations with the continent. Hoover did not, however, tie debt forgiveness in any way to specific European foreign policy initiatives, nor did he mention European military activities in the underdeveloped world. This, and not a gulf between "isolationism" and internationalism, separated the Secretary from his Senate critics.[21]

The peace progressives also united behind a set of initiatives to redefine U.S. policy toward Germany. In late 1922, hoping to avert a French invasion of the Ruhr, Borah proposed an international economic conference to deal with war debts, reparations, the restoration of international trade, and disarmament, a program clearly unacceptable to the French. The idea nonetheless excited several peace progressives; Brookhart, Ladd, and Norris were reported strongly in favor, and the newly elected Shipstead and Frazier also had positive comments on the proposal. Both Borah and Frazier denied that the idea signaled a departure from traditional American foreign policy—Frazier argued that it represented a manifestation of the ideas in the Farewell Address—and all the peace progressives contended that the Borah conference represented a way for the United States to exert its influence on behalf of Germany and European peace without committing itself to an imperialistic program. The White House received the idea frostily, as did the French, and when administration diplomacy failed to prevent invasion of the Ruhr, the peace progressives pounded away at Harding and Hughes for not having accepted the Borah plan.[22]

The next peace progressive initiative on behalf of the Weimar government came in 1924 with a La Follette amendment to allow the government to grant money directly to Germany for famine relief. The Wisconsin senator viewed aid to Germany as vital to what Borah called spiritual disarmament—the purging "of the passions and hate engendered by war"—without which the world would remain in turbulence. Although La Follette sympathized with the German people, he did not act from purely or even primarily humanitarian motives. He asserted that German impoverishment "has reached the point where it seriously affects the grain exports from the United States," since the German government could not import food because of difficulty in getting overseas credit. La Follette also characterized his resolution as vital "to those who are bravely struggling against great odds to maintain a democratic form of government in Germany," people who had lost ground to both the monarchists and the Communists as a result of Versailles and the Ruhr occupation. Although the proposal received bitter attacks from both Democrats and mainstream Republicans—Thomas Heflin (D–Alabama) was particularly stinging in his opposition to aiding a country whose soldiers had killed American men—it attracted unanimous peace progressive support and, along with the Shipstead and Howell proposals on American economic aid to the continent, completed the group's alternative to the Dawes Plan.[23]

La Follette argued that his resolution could help make up for the United States' having failed the German people at Versailles; later in the decade the peace progressives returned to this theme with a Shipstead resolution ridiculed by the *New York Times* as a "somewhat comic illustration of the Senate's self-complacency." First introduced in 1928, the resolution called for a Foreign Relations Committee inquiry into war guilt or, if that was not possible, for the United States to urge the submission of the question of war guilt to a commission of neutrals. The resolution alleged that recently opened archival material had proved that Article 231 of the Versailles Treaty, which condemned Germany as guilty for starting the war, was based upon "hysteria, hypocrisy, and falsifications." Shipstead argued that the U.S. government had a right to seek to overturn the clause since it was a party to the treaty; he termed the establishment of the true facts "vital to a reconciliation" in Europe and to the continent's "moral disarmament." Although the Shipstead resolution, like La Follette's, enjoyed broad support from the peace progressives, it never progressed out of committee.[24]

Given their historical reputation as bitter opponents of American involvement in Europe, the peace progressive program of the 1920s stands as something of an irony. Their anti-imperialism led them to unite behind a series of proposals—stringent debt readjustment, aid to Germany—that would have involved the United States in the domestic politics of Europe more deeply than the policy proposals of their mainstream opposition. At the same time, conditions in Europe made it extremely unlikely that the peace progressives would have been able to achieve their goals even if their program had been adopted. Certainly their hope that a stringent debt policy would tip the balance in France and England in favor of anti-imperialist forces bore little resemblance to the political reality in the two countries given that nothing close to a majority in either the British Labour party or the French Socialist party favored immediate decolonization. The peace progressives also failed to explain in sufficient detail why antagonizing the two closest allies of the United States on behalf of groups like the Riffs or the Syrians would serve U.S. national interests. However, they did explore in far greater detail than any other mainstream political group in the 1920s an issue that would plague American policymakers after World War II—whether to antagonize traditional allies when the actions of those allies, particularly with regard to colonial matters, conflicted with U.S. ideals. Finally, their agenda overestimated America's power to influence events on the continent, perhaps because it was better suited to a critique of U.S. policy in Latin America, where the United States was the unquestioned dominant power. Nonetheless, the ideology also gave them a united view of Europe, one considerably more nuanced than many of their critics either at the time or since suggested. Oddly, in light of their stances in the 1930s, they disagreed over whether the economically and morally based program would suffice, or whether the United States should also form political links with the Western European governments. Their desire for international peace suggested supporting any vehicle that would work toward that goal, but their anti-imperialism cautioned them against entering into international arrangements with disagreeable states such as England and particularly France. They never resolved this dilemma fully, and on all major treaties and protocols of the 1920s that involved political cooperation with England and France—the Berlin Treaty, the Four Power Treaty, the World Court, the Kellogg-Briand Pact, the London Naval Treaty—the peace progressives offered a divided response.

Occasionally anti-imperialism did point the peace progressives solidly in one direction concerning treaty relationships. Borah and Shipstead expressed skepticism about the 1926 treaty on international arms traffic, even though the group had criticized the Coolidge administration in vitriolic terms for supplying arms to the Obregón government in 1924. Shipstead wondered if under the treaty the Riffs, the Moroccan rebels than fighting the French, could purchase arms in the United States, while Borah worried that the treaty would "make it practically impossible for any revolutionary movement to get arms," citing India as a possible example. Although the peace progressives backed the idea of international disarmament and recognized the need for the United States to preserve a position of moral leadership on the traffic-in-arms issue, they did not wish to commit the United States to anything that could restrict American freedom of action in dealing with revolutionary movements. On the other hand, both senators were "very much in favor" of the 1928 treaty to forbid the production of poison gas, which failed to win ratification because of combined pressure from the Army, Navy, American Legion, and chemical industry.[25]

Beyond these two relatively minor treaties, the peace progressives split. Debates over treaties revealed both the drawbacks of the dissenters' extreme ideological posture and the continuing strength of the perennial fear of American foreign policy reformers concerning the dangers of excessive involvement in traditional power politics. During the initial years of the Harding administration, haunted by the specter of entering the League of Nations through the "back door," the senators questioned the wisdom of the 1921 Treaty of Berlin, which ended the technical state of war still existing between the United States and Germany. The major peace progressives argued that the treaty committed the United States to "every conceivable question which can arise in Europe." Generally, however, the senators were left to making unsubstantiated charges about the allegedly devious motives of the Hughes State Department and to rehashing some of their old arguments about Versailles. Borah also argued that approving the Berlin Treaty without insisting on a repudiation of Versailles would result in Washington's giving "its moral sanction" to a treaty that "comes as near creating a complete autocracy based upon military force" as possible. He did not spell out, however, how American refusal to end its state of war with Germany would force the European nations to revise Versailles beyond a cryptic comment that ratification would weaken the long-term American appeal to Europe because the European people had become accustomed to looking to the United States to oppose the "harsh and reactionary" policies of Versailles. La Follette refused even to concede this much, and articulated one of the few bald isolationist pronouncements to come from the group at any point during the 1920s. The Wisconsin senator called for a return to domestic affairs and charged that the government had paid too much attention to "foreign policy, in which the international bankers and imperialists of Wall Street have billions at stake." In the end, Ladd (without explanation) defected and voted to approve; the peace progressives united only behind an unsuccessful amendment sponsored by James Reed (D–Missouri) stating that under the treaty the United States would assume no obligation for the final amount of reparations demanded from Germany. Without the non-European issues provided in the 1919 fight, the peace progressive appeal was limited; as of 1921, they had not come up with any firm ideas about the proper role of the United States in Europe.[26]

This pattern continued during the ratification debates over the treaties associated with the Washington Conference of 1921 and 1922. Ironically, the conference was launched with a resolution introduced by Borah himself, urging the State Department to call a conference of the United States, England, and Japan to address the question of naval disarmament. The senator stated that because of executive unwillingness, the Senate needed to act, not "loiter around like satellites of royalty until we are bid to act and to profess and to pretend to think." Seeing that it had no chance to defeat the resolution, the incoming Harding administration adopted it as its own, although Hughes broadened it considerably to include France and Italy in naval disarmament talks and a host of other countries in discussions of the general East Asian situation. The conference ultimately produced a naval ratio of 5:5:3; other Washington treaties included the Four Power Treaty, a vaguely worded document designed to supersede the Anglo-Japanese Alliance; and the Nine Power Treaty, which committed the signatories to a unified front when dealing with Chinese nationalism.[27]

Although the peace progressives initially had shown a good deal of enthusiasm for the work of the conference, they became increasingly skeptical about the Four Power Treaty, which committed the United States to consultation on Pacific issues with England, France, and Japan. Borah, La Follette, and Johnson were convinced that the treaty represented an alliance; Johnson fumed that George Washington knew the difference between foreign relations and a political alliance even if Charles Evans Hughes did not. (A deep distrust of Hughes, whom Johnson characterized as a man of "diabolical cunning," compounded the peace progressives' fear that the Secretary of State desired something more than a pact of consultation.) The California senator denied that political relations should be a goal of American foreign policy (citing equal opportunity with all nations for trade and commerce as the proper goal). Borah termed the treaty "nothing but a naked combination of military powers to dominate the Orient" with the aim of "underwriting . . . imperialism in the Pacific," and when pressed on the issue by Irvine Lenroot, he compared Article II (which provided for consultation among the signatories to deal with any threats to their Pacific possessions) to Article XI of the Versailles Treaty. Given the similarity of the provisions, it stood to reason that the same forces that had proposed the Versailles Treaty were behind this arrangement as well. La Follette contended that the genesis for the treaty lay with the international bankers, since many of the treaty's chief negotiators, such as Hughes, Elihu Root, Henry Cabot Lodge, and Oscar Underwood, were "representatives of the imperialistic policies of the big banking interests." As in the Versailles fight, La Follette reasoned that the "lustful eyes of these new partners of ours," seeing the natural resources in underdeveloped areas, had needed to devise a scheme under which they could secure American military backing for their imperialistic ventures. The senators finally charged that despite the public claims of Hughes, the disarmament provisions of the treaty had accomplished little. La Follette described the results as a "naval holiday—neither more nor less," while Borah insisted upon "real disarmament" to include the weapons "of war with which the next war will be fought": submarines, poison gas, and "airbombs." Borah argued that great powers always denounced political pacts when it served their interests to do so, and that therefore anyone who relied solely upon such treaties for American security logically would have to support a large Army and Navy as well. These comments built on an argument offered by John Works in the 1910s to the effect that reforming the conduct of international relations, both by nation-states and individuals within those nations, far outweighed any document in the likelihood of achieving international peace. The peace progressives had no doubt that the conference would have made more substantial progress toward disarmament had its progress not been clouded by what Hiram Johnson called "the vexatious Far Eastern question."[28]

One of these "vexatious" issues was the Yap Treaty, which formally gave Japan mandatory rights over the former German island colonies of the Carolines, Marshalls, and Ladrones. Johnson contended that the treaty represented part of a tradeoff for Pacific islands orchestrated by England and Japan, and asked his colleagues to look at Japan's treatment of the people of China and Korea who lived under its colonial rule. Borah alleged that the United States entertained the treaty only because of fear that if it did not pacify the Japanese they would attack the Philippines, proving his long-standing thesis that the annexation the Philippines compelled the adoption of "all the methods and customs and practices of imperialists" in later policies. The Yap Treaty, however, revealed the fragile nature of the anti-imperialist critique of the whole Washington System. Both Norris and Ladd, one-third of the peace contingent in the Senate at the time, backed the treaty. Norris praised the document, arguing that he would prefer to see the Japanese as a mandatory power rather than outright owners of the islands, since this would place some obligations on Tokyo, such as allowing missionaries on the islands. Since he did not see the United States in a position to alter the situation in any more positive fashion without the use of military force, Norris recommended that "we ought to be practical and take things as we find them" and agree to the best deal possible. Norris and Ladd used the same spirit to back the Four Power Treaty itself, arguing that the Senate should consider it as part of a package that in total did more good than harm.[29]

Debate over the Washington Treaties revealed that while the peace progressives shared an anti-imperialist conception of the world order, the question of political cooperation with European nations was not one answered easily. This issue resurfaced in 1925 when the Senate considered American membership in the World Court. In a major address, Hughes proposed "universal law" as the way to achieve peace; he conceded that international law probably could not prevent conflict between the larger powers, but maintained that under international law "small powers, if their cases present minor or isolated interests, may be disciplined." Kellogg, in his first public speech after taking over as Secretary of State, agreed, remarking that "civilized nations are now beginning to recognize the real principles of international law." Both men opposed the peace progressive argument that the United States should put off World Court membership until a codification of international law had been completed, arguing that such a program "puts hurdles in the way of progress."[30]

The peace progressives obviously had little interest in a framework of international law that would punish weaker states but not affect the major powers. In a 1923 editorial La Follette expressed doubt that the United States could do anything internationally to further the cause of peace until Versailles was "obliterated" and the reactionary governments of Europe replaced; the United States should curb its own imperialism and return to a "living example of the happiness and prosperity that is possible under genuine democracy." Norris admitted that he had approached the idea of a World Court with a "friendly heart" but by early 1924 did not "feel as though an agreement with such peoples [the Western Europeans] and such Governments would be carried out in good faith." Like La Follette, the Nebraska senator believed that "we ourselves have not shown the right kind of spirit that a civilized country ought to show to those who are weak and those who cannot defend themselves." These sentiments, from dissenters once associated with a pro-Court position, mirrored the positions taken by other peace progressives during the Harding and early Coolidge administrations. The remarks also reflected the continuing stress placed by the peace progressives on not compromising American ideals so that these ideals would remain useful in resolving foreign policy crises in the future to the advantage of the United States.[31]

Borah took the most active role among the peace progressives in opposing Court membership once the issue came before the Senate. He repeated the by now consistent refrain that membership in the Court would presage membership in the League, although he maintained that he would support a Court "divorced" from the League entirely. This, he claimed, could be accomplished by eliminating the Court's ability to deliver advisory opinions to the League Council upon the latter's request, which would remove the danger of the Court's functioning as "the judicial arm of the league." Having established (to himself, at least) that the Court formed the equivalent of the League, Borah proceeded, with much greater force than in the Four Power Treaty fight, to raise the anti-imperialist banner that the peace progressives had used so effectively against the League itself. In 1919 the Europeans had faced the alternatives of Wilson "at his most idealistic," advancing principles that "might have been of great help to Europe,"

and Clemenceau; by 1925 the League and its "lackey" clearly represented the "true culmination" of the Clemenceau policy. Therefore,
"autocratic power seems to have reached its zenith," with the Court
functioning as the judicial guarantor of the arbitrary acquisitions of
territories made through the "unrighteous fruit of the vicious secret
treaties." Borah further blasted the Court for its ultimate reliance upon
force to back up its decisions, citing the preferable alternative of the
U.S. Supreme Court, which enforced its decisions through public
opinion. The idea of peace through force stood as a legacy to "the days
when governments were founded upon force and the people had no
voice"; the failure of European governments and some Americans to
move beyond traditional power politics meant that no difference cur-
rently existed between advocates of peace and advocates of war. The
senator also explicitly denied that the Court could ever aid smaller
nations, since it lacked the compulsory jurisdiction clauses that weaker
states needed to check the might of the great powers.[32]

Several other peace progressives also employed the anti-imperialist
theme. Shipstead feared that the business of the Court was "to decide
that loot acquired as a result of the last war has been legally acquired,"
reasoning that the major powers needed a Court monopoly of international law to preserve a situation "with half of Europe reduced to the
status of Shantung or Haiti." (The Minnesota senator most often associated the idea with Elihu Root, whom he charged with seeking a
"judicial tyranny" that would permit the "new autocracy of financial
power that now sits on the throne" to solidify its power through international law.) Given that the great powers dominated both the League
and the Court, the newly elected Young Bob La Follette doubted its
effectiveness in the cause of peace, particularly since the "fundamental
cause of modern war is imperialism." Since all the major powers were
"guilty of the same offenses under the Versailles Treaty," none could
permit the creation of a precedent, such as one in favor of Syria against
France, that a mandate state could later use against them. Therefore,
the Court could never help to establish lasting peace. This line of argument fitted in with the general peace progressive tendency, which
had begun as early as 1916, to question the traditional progressive reliance solely on international law as a way to further the cause of
peace.[33]

It was only a short step from sentiments such as these to isolationist
pronouncements, and a few of the peace progressives did voice these.

If membership were approved, Borah called for equality of representation, given that the Europeans and Japan would vote together; equal representation would allow the United States to preserve what it had "in view of the great competition of economic affairs in the coming years." Nye spoke of the European ability to win over America's "keenest minds" through the wiles of secret diplomacy, and he called for the United States to "continue to stand as it is today, a free and independent nation." He speculated that the framers would have opposed the World Court, since it did not give the United States sufficient voting strength. Despite these sentiments, isolationism formed an important part only of Nye's critique, and for every statement like Nye's there existed a counterpart like the call by his colleague Lynn Frazier for an "international police of the seas." Frazier felt that international disarmament with the exception of this force would serve peace much more effectively than the World Court.[34]

Frazier's plan indicated one of a number of alternatives to the World Court considered by the peace progressives. Brookhart called for the United States to take the lead in changing the international economic system to one grounded on cooperative principles, which would ensure democracy, limit the earnings of capital, and evenly distribute the net profits from sales back to consumers and producers. Shipstead proposed a treaty to outlaw militarism, which would bind all nations to abolish conscription for thirty years, confirming the American position as "the beacon light giving hope to oppressed people all over the world" by striking at the "foundation of militarism." Others forwarded the idea of war outlawry. Shipstead remarked that it was "plain that the World Court does not outlaw war," and that instead it formed a "very carefully planned program for making war" by protecting the spoils of war. Nye, Frazier, and Borah raised similar points.[35]

Four peace progressives, however, rejected these arguments. The most important of these was Norris, who reversed his earlier position and came out in favor of the Court in late December 1925. (The New York Times noted that his decision caused "greater demoralization to the World Court opposition" than anything else that yet had occurred.) Norris reminded people that "fundamentally" he had favored the League of Nations because of his opposition to war, but that he could not support the plan because of the postwar imperialistic activities of the leading powers. He said that its opponents "wonderfully overestimated" the danger posed by the World Court, although he also doubted that the membership would make much of a difference one way or the other beyond giving American moral support to the institution. McMaster spoke for "proper reservations" but otherwise supported the Court, as did Howell and Wheeler. Perhaps out of respect to their colleagues, none actively participated in the debate, although all seemed to agree that infusing a slightly disagreeable institution with American ideals could improve the Court.[36]

After the vote, the World Court issue remained alive through the primary contest between Blaine and Lenroot, which attracted national attention as a referendum on Lenroot's vote in favor of American membership. Blaine made the issue the centerpiece of his campaign, charging that it only had validated the "harsh and unconscionable terms" of Versailles, leaving "weaker peoples . . . subjugated and made vassals." Blaine also expanded upon the peace progressive challenge to international law as a panacea for peace. Pointing to what he considered unconstitutional decisions made by the Supreme Court in the Dred Scott case and various World War I rulings, he denied that the World Court could render unbiased decisions in the name of peace when a case seriously threatened the national interests of any leading European power. Blaine lamented that the Court "offers no hope for peace," describing it as a "phantom" and a "fraud." The Blaine victory all but ended any chance for a revival of the World Court issue during the decade.[37]

More so than on any other European-related issue, the peace progressives became best known during the 1920s for their ardent support for outlawing war, a concept championed most persistently by Chicago attorney Salmon Levinson. On the broadest of scales, outlawry fitted in with their general 1920s pattern of trying to modify international law to standards more to their liking; on a specific level outlawry provided another alternative to unacceptable ideas like the League and the World Court. As Robert James Maddox has observed, a considerable degree of the peace progressive enthusiasm for outlawry came for their desire to present a positive program to stave off other disagreeable ideas (although the peace progressives were not alone in this: Levinson himself conceived the plan during the war years as an alternative to the League of Nations). Shipstead spelled out this theme shortly after his election, confessing that he knew nothing about the "so-called Borah court . . . except that . . . it was to be constructed on the idea that war was a crime"; from this limited information, he was "inclined to think it is all right." More important, he needed some type of plan to answer Wilsonian critics who "are saying that I am against Peace because . . . I am opposed to international cooperation." Yet the idea also genuinely appealed to the peace progressives; as Borah later said, outlawry represented "the only kind of treaty the United States could sign." The senator doubted that the world could stop or check war until international law allowed the world community to hold those who started wars responsible as international criminals. Borah felt that outlawry succeeded where all other peace plans had failed—since it called for the "substitution of law and judicial tribunals for politics and force in international affairs," it would not "speedily become nothing more than a military alliance." He compared the outlawry movement to the earlier crusade against slavery, and reasoned that to end war, as with slavery, the world needed to look beyond governments to "that educated, aroused, and well-directed public opinion."[38]

Three other peace progressives, however, had quite different conceptions of outlawry. In 1926, disgusted by the ratification of the Italian debt bill, Frazier, working closely with the Women's Peace Union, proposed a constitutional amendment stripping all war powers from the federal government. This represented the most extreme manifestation of the peace progressive contention that in international relations ideas and ideals, if properly handled, could serve American aims as well as traditional tools of foreign policy such as the military and diplomatic conventions. Frazier feared that outlawry as constructed by Borah would not suffice, since the "interests which profit by wars might still continue to finance them"; he reasoned that as long as the United States was prepared to use its military force, wars could not "be codified into common sense or disciplined into decency." When pressed on why his amendment would not subject the United States to instant attack, the senator responded that once the United States adopted the amendment, it would "be immediately followed by many other nations." Even if a nation such as Japan refused to follow, he could not imagine "an attack on us if we disarmed in good faith," although he had no doubt that if such an attack occurred "the rest of the family of nations would sit upon [the attacker] at once." Frazier did not specify exactly what to "sit upon" would imply.[39]

The North Dakota senator fleshed out his ideas during 1928 debate. He defended his decision not to modify the amendment so as to allow for war to counter invasion, noting that such a move would justify increased armament spending in the name of self-defense. This would mean that American boys would still "protect business interests and alleged property rights away from home." Whereas Borah had criticized earlier peace plans for relying too much upon force, Frazier contended that the Borah proposal did not go far enough since it left the United States with the constitutional power to wage war and thus "attempt[ed] to reconcile war and peace." The senator reasoned that the airplane, by making victory in warfare not worth the price of fighting, had ended the right of self-defense; he hoped that the world would recognize that all sides could profit if instead of killing one's neighbors, nations increased commercial contact with them, as the United States and Canada had done. He added that the United States needed to set an example to overcome the "tremendous stupidity" known as modern warfare. The senator predicted that only those who believed "in the divine right of a government to plunge its people into war" or those who valued property over life would oppose his amendment.[40]

Frazier's ideas represented the extreme of the decade's Senate spectrum. But the opinions of John Blaine were closer to the peace progressive mainstream, and he too questioned whether the Borah outlawry proposal went far enough. The Wisconsin senator argued that the world would outlaw war only when it outlawed imperialism, since "the main causes of war arise out of international exploitation." Blaine also doubted that war could occur if every country in the world instituted a war referendum, abolished conscription, and ceased all forms of military training. He reasoned that a general international policy of "letting the adventurers of exploitation submit to the jurisdiction to which they choose to go in their journeys of exploitation" would do considerably more to end war than would the Borah plan adopted in its entirety. Dill, who championed what he called a "patriotism of peace," concurred. The Washington senator argued that modern international society "is so bound together" that the United States needed a citizenship "that will be tolerant of the ideals and purposes of other parts of the world." This perspective translated into a foreign policy whereby the United States would set an example to the rest of the world and disarm while also being ready, as Asle Gronna had recommended nine years before, "to lend a helping hand when necessity requires to those who struggle against tyranny anywhere on the face of the earth." Dill also asserted that preventing financial interests from dragging nations into war constituted the best way of ending international conflict. The ideas of Blaine and Dill foreshadowed the next serious peace progressive breach on issues associated with 1920s "internationalism."[41]

In 1927 French Foreign Minister Aristide Briand, building upon the ideas of Levinson and Borah, proposed a bilateral treaty with the United States renouncing war. Borah had no interest in Briand's initiative, terming a two-power treaty "at war with the whole theory of outlawry," but the plan appealed to Kellogg as a way to mollify his increasingly vocal domestic critics and at the same time improve prospects for European disarmament and security arrangements. After Kellogg broadened the pact to include all nations willing to ratify, Borah agreed to serve as the point man during Senate debate over the treaty. He hoped that worldwide adoption of outlawry would nullify Article X of the League of Nations and permit the League to resurrect its "dominant principle" of peace. At the same time, though, he stressed that the treaty permitted wars waged for purposes of self-defense, and he denied conservative charges that the treaty would supersede the Monroe Doctrine. (Borah did concede, under questioning from Hiram Johnson and several Democrats, that quite often in the recent past several Presidents had "misconstrued" the Doctrine and applied it in a way that did not exemplify American self-defense.) Beyond this, the senator clearly believed that Kellogg-Briand accommodated the major peace progressive foreign policy principles. He also affirmed that the treaty fundamentally altered existing international law, since it condemned "war as an institution," opening up the way for "a different psychology in international affairs," which would facilitate later moves toward disarmament and open diplomacy.[42]

Robert James Maddox has suggested that Borah forwarded the outlawry plan at this time to guard against a resurgence of support for American membership in the World Court; a more likely scenario is that he and other peace progressives favored adoption of Kellogg-Briand as a way to pry away votes from the 1929 cruisers bill. Norris, "exceedingly anxious" to have the treaty considered before the cruisers bill (as ultimately occurred, in exchange for a peace progressive promise not to filibuster), asked why the United States should continue naval expansion "if we are sincere in the treaty." Borah thought that only outlawry could tame public sentiment for war, "an institution which has come to dominate international affairs and to a marked degree domestic affairs." The pact thus could help to reduce the defense budget and free money for other priorities. Blaine (who opposed Kellogg-Briand) agreed, noting that "it would be ironical if America were to become the first nation to prepare for war" after adopting the treaty. The Wisconsin senator went further, arguing for increasing the effectiveness of the treaty by decreasing arms production so as to "suspend" the right of wars for self-defense, which he viewed as one of the treaty's principal flaws.[43]

Most important, the peace progressives who favored Kellogg-Briand argued that the treaty embraced anti-imperialism. Borah contended that the treaty would solve the problem of strong versus weak that had plagued the world since the end of the war, since a "just and humane policy towards small nations" and outlawry complemented each other. On a more specific level, both Borah and Brookhart made the case that ratification of the treaty constituted a de facto recognition of the Soviet Union, since Moscow too had indicated its support for Kellogg-Briand. The Iowa senator delivered his usual address about the wonders of cooperative economics, and rebuked those who continued to oppose recognition on the grounds of Soviet revolutionary propaganda, arguing that "propaganda as to overthrowing the world . . . has an American sound to me" given the traditional American sympathy toward revolutions. When the United States and the USSR became the first two countries to ratify the pact, Brookhart expressed a hope that "these two great revolutionary countries will now proceed to outlaw war throughout the world."[44]

Although they all ultimately supported it, Kellogg-Briand attracted considerable skepticism from the traditional peace progressive foes during Senate debate.[45] The strongest critique, however, and the only vote against the treaty's passage, came from the extreme anti-imperialist Blaine, who concentrated his attack upon Paragraph 10 of the British interpretive note to the treaty, which reserved the British right to send troops to "certain regions of the world the welfare and integrity of which constitute a special and vital interest of our peace and safety." The Wisconsin senator introduced a reservation to the treaty stating that since Paragraph 10, which legalized British rule "over 400 million people without their consent and against their protest," did not prejudice British freedom of action in their colonies, American adherence to the treaty did not compromise American freedom of action in dealing with future disputes between England and its colonies. Blaine tangled with Borah over the issue, particularly with reference to Indian affairs;

Borah admitted that England should not have written the reservation and that as stated only "the public opinion of the world" and not the treaty could censor a British military action in India. The Idaho senator nonetheless reminded his colleague that the treaty would not prevent the United States in such a circumstance from recognizing Indian independence.[46]

Blaine vigorously disputed Borah's contention in an address that the London *Times* remarked would "make Cassandra seem positively cheerful by comparison." Attacking the heart of the Borah argument, the Wisconsin senator dismissed the treaty as "a mere skeleton, inert and impotent," too weighed down by reservations to have any effectiveness. He predicted that since "we cannot promote peace by mere words," the world could outlaw war only when the causes of war—protectorates, mandates, spheres of influence, foreign concessions, exploitation of natural resources, monopoly of trade routes, and an increase in tariff barriers—were outlawed. Blaine contended that Paragraph 10 went well beyond Article X, which only guaranteed against external aggression, to the most dangerous of realms, internal stability, attacked by the peace progressives earlier in the form of Article XI. Blaine commended the Senate for rejecting American membership in the League because it did not want to deny "other nations—smaller and weaker nations—the right of self-determination"; by doing so, the United States remained as the beacon for national revolutions. Blaine proceeded to quote letters received from Indians and Egyptians backing his policy, and he charged that American acceptance of the note would unite the two largest English-speaking nations in the world behind a policy of imperialism.[47]

After the ratification of Kellogg-Briand, Blaine, who continued to entertain "grave apprehensions of the ultimate consequences of the Treaty," decided to accept it in "good faith" and thus oppose all military appropriations bills, since "if nations are sincere and not all liars, under the Treaty there should be no wars." Frazier was less content and, if anything, pushed his version of outlawry more strongly after the treaty's adoption. He argued that adoption of his amendment would mean "simply the carrying out of the honest intention of the Peace Pact," since the treaty, while a "gesture in the right direction," contained its share of "high sounding platitudes and ever present glittering generalities." The North Dakota senator orchestrated a second Judiciary Committee hearing upon the amendment in 1930, personally appearing and consulting with his WPU colleagues in excruciating detail over the order and number of witnesses to testify for the plan. Frazier believed that a hearing "would be the very best kind of publicity that could be had," and he refused to rule out the possibility of a favorable committee report, since "conditions have changed to a wonderful extent" since 1927. One convert to the cause was Dill, who had been cool toward the amendment in 1929 but the next year agreed to begin inserting WPU petitions into the *Congressional Record.* He told WPU leaders that the time had come to start "taking such extreme steps" as adoption of the Frazier Amendment, since the "future of the white race depends upon preventing another great war," because technological advances would cause whites to be wiped out if another war occurred, leaving the planet to the control of the "yellow, black, and brown peoples who have not learned how to murder their fellow-men so rapidly."[48]

The mainstream effort for peace culminated in the London Naval Treaty of 1930, which altered the naval ratio among the United States, Britain, and Japan to 10:10:6.975. Unlike the Washington Conference, the London Conference did not broaden its scope to deal with non-disarmament issues, and so the peace progressives generally had a more favorable (and in a few cases very favorable) outlook on the proceedings. Borah most actively supported the Hoover administration. Asking "what is national security when the world is armed to the teeth," the senator contended that by increasing suspicion huge armaments stood counter to the spirit of the Kellogg-Briand pact. He implied that the conference represented the final hope for the appearance of the peaceful world public opinion that he hoped would sustain Kellogg-Briand; accordingly, Borah urged patience and told his constituents to have confidence in the London negotiations. Other senators also raised this point, most ironically Blaine, who reasoned that the United States needed to interpret Kellogg-Briand "in the spirit of peace" and oppose a further naval buildup. Borah and the other peace progressives also contended that the United States needed to sacrifice the concept of parity, based on "national pride more than national security," in order to ensure real progress toward disarmament. During the Foreign Relations Committee hearings on the treaty, Borah and La Follette (a recent committee appointment) hammered away at this theme, leading to sharp peace progressive questioning of whether the treaty would wind up increasing the naval budget. Blaine explored this issue in the greatest detail, and only after satisfying himself that the treaty did not compel the United States to increase the size of its Navy did the Wisconsin senator endorse it.[49]

Peace progressive support for the treaty faltered almost entirely when Henry Stimson, now Secretary of State, declined a request from Norris to release to the Senate all documents relating to the negotiations. The Nebraska senator worried that the conferees had concluded secret deals, and balked when Joe Robinson introduced a compromise resolution requesting Stimson to release all documents if not incompatible with the public interest. Norris responded that the Constitution required the President to furnish the Senate with all relevant information on treaties. Shipstead then chimed in with a long speech attacking the administration for not having consulted the Senate all along, since, unlike in monarchical systems, the "sole and exclusive" power of treaty negotiation did not rest with the President. He termed the documents the joint property of the Senate and the executive, and he saw Senate support for the Robinson Resolution as part of a pattern in which Congress delegated more and more power to the executive, thus "drifting away from the ancient landmarks"; Haiti and Nicaragua also served as examples. The senator called for a return to the "democratic mode of treaty-making" present in the Articles of Confederation government. Despite the peace progressive protests, the Robinson Amendment passed by a vote of thirty-eight to seventeen, and Norris then settled for a reservation conditioning Senate approval of the treaty upon its containing no secret arrangements. Norris' reservation did not satisfy Shipstead, however, who wrote a blistering dissenting report when the Foreign Relations Committee recommended approval, and voted against the treaty on the floor.[50]

The peace progressives did not achieve the degree of unity that characterized their war debt positions on the votes relating to political cooperation with Europe. How to deal with treaties with allegedly imperialist powers represented the most difficult foreign policy dilemma for senators devoted to an anti-imperialist ideology, and the peace progressives never succeeded in resolving the issue completely. These divisions did not, however, substantially weaken the peace progressive case on American-European relations. Throughout the decade they viewed their economic and diplomatic initiatives (such as their positions on debt renegotiation and aid to Germany) as more important than purely political issues. Also, they looked to move beyond the mainstream position by achieving international peace through a radical program of disarmament, which they hoped would achieve the goals of the Washington and London negotiators through the arousal of public opinion around the world. This represented the final element of their alternative program to the decade's business-oriented internationalism.

The peace progressives' case for disarmament early in the decade relied upon traditional antimilitarist themes.[51] Given that framework, the peace progressives found no use for a large army, and so Borah sponsored a series of resolutions calling for reducing the 175,000-man force first to 150,000 and eventually to 100,000. La Follette guessed that the Army would be "sent out to Haiti and Mexico and Nicaragua to make good the shaky investments of the great bankers and oil magnates," while Borah feared that the "sheer waste" of military spending motivated by a "very pronounced propaganda in this country in favor of an increased or enlarged" military delayed needed funds for agricultural relief. The peace progressive distrust of the Army remained constant throughout the decade. On the tenth anniversary of American entry into the Great War, Norris, the only senator who had voted against Wilson's declaration still in the Senate, remarked that the "brave army" sent to France "has been superseded by another army, fighting a weak nation in the jungles of Nicaragua and parading our power and military greatness through the streets of ancient Chinese cities." The senator believed that one of the "great lessons of the war is the evil of huge military preparations." Brookhart, in an extreme manifestation of the peace progressive faith in the ability of the United States to use nonmilitary means to defend its interests, went so far as to argue that Americans would be "better defended" than European states with large armies "if we did not have any army."[52]

Yet the peace progressives did not oppose funding for all branches of the military. Norris favored transferring more funds to the National Guard, since "if we get into war, it is the citizen soldiery of the country upon which we must depend"; Brookhart insisted on including Guard figures in military calculations of the "first line of defense." Blaine praised the Guard for "sustaining the proud achievements of the past" by remaining "free from every semblance of a militaristic policy." A remarkable transformation came from Borah, who reversed his position of the 1910s and called for the Guard to "take a more prominent place in the national defense . . . at the expense of some of the unessential things which are being maintained." The dissenters held an even more favorable opinion of the Army Air Corps. Borah contended that only those "interested in armament contracts . . . and the bureaus and bureaucracy" opposed air power; after backing Billy Mitchell's 1921 air power demonstration plan, the senator expressed a suspicion that the "steel lobby is back of battleship advocates." Norris blasted both the Army and the Coolidge administration after the Mitchell court-martial, saying that the aviator "has done a great good for our country" by bringing attention to "appalling conditions," while the elder La Follette described Mitchell's program as "preparation for defense rather than aggression." The peace progressives expressed more ambivalence toward the other new weapon of the age, the submarine, generally arguing that its negative features outweighed its positive ones.[53]

The attitude of leading naval figures, who opposed the Mitchell ideas, only reinforced what by the 1920s had become a near state of paranoia felt by the peace progressives toward the service. In his critique of the 1921 Navy bill, Borah argued that the Navy absorbed too high a percentage of government expenditures, ballooning the defense budget to a such a level that 93 percent (he used this figure loosely— at other points in the decade it was 80 or 85 percent) of the federal budget, counting expenditures for wartime debt and war pensions, went to war-related measures. The Idaho senator wondered how long "a republican form of government can exist under that state of affairs." He offered a resolution to suspend naval construction for six months while leading military minds studied what a modern navy needed, terming it useless to build massive numbers of battleships that planes could destroy in thirty minutes. All peace progressives denied that the United States faced any conceivable international threat. The elder La Follette, in an address that spanned portions of four days, contended that "by building a reasonable number of submarines and airplanes at small cost to supplement coast defenses, this country will remain absolutely secure from enemy attack"; in the modern era, with "surface craft almost useless," nothing contained in the bill besides the "trifling amount" for submarines and airplanes "will be effective." He also called for the creation of a Chief of the Bureaucratic of Aeronautics appointed from the ranks of the military (clearly intended to be Mitchell) and sponsored a series of unsuccessful amendments to increase the power of "flying officers." Having established to his satisfaction that the Navy was both needless and obsolete, La Follette was left to ponder why so many of his colleagues desired to increase its appropriations. The senator speculated that "powerful influences" wanted a large Navy to protect private loans to foreign governments and foreign investments such as railroads, land, and oil. Since air theory had proved that the Navy could not fight against any country with a strong air force, La Follette reasoned that the Navy was designed "for intimidating small and weak nations." Along these lines, he proposed two more amendments to the 1921 bill, one stating that the President could use no battleship to "coerce or compel the modification of the constitution or the laws of any foreign government," the second that no battleship could be used to collect "any pecuniary claim of any kind" of private American interests. This rhetoric resembled that of the 1910s, but added both an anti-imperialist element and the trendy air argument to broaden its appeal, and drew support from a much wider range of the movement.[54]

The contests over defense policy in the early 1920s set the stage for the most important domestic disarmament battle of the decade, the tangle over Coolidge's 1929 naval bill, which authorized the construction of fifteen light cruisers and one aircraft carrier. The President had spelled out the details of his naval policy in a 1928 Armistice Day address, calling for more cruisers to adhere to "world standards of defense and eliminating all competition." He doubted that preparedness led to war, and contended that in any case "peace is of little value if it is constantly accompanied by the threatened or actual violation of national rights." Coolidge also denied that a Navy for defense implied a Navy for aggression, and concluded that Americans possessed a "duty to ourselves and to the cause of civilization . . . to maintain an adequate army and navy." A Navy Department report issued the next day spelled out the details, calling for a Navy second to none "maintained in sufficient strength" to support American policies and overseas commerce, and urging "ocean-wide control of the sea." Initially proposing a $1 billion program spread over five years, the administration compromised and reduced its appropriations request to $750 million to pacify congressional opposition.[55]

Blaine set the tone of the peace progressive response in a March 1928 address charging that the Coolidge administration "has gone war mad" as a result of the combined influence of militarists and big business. Blaine predicted that the new Navy "will be used as the international sheriff to collect the money due private investors in foreign countries," which meant that the "naval program is a threat against the independence and the liberty of weaker and smaller peoples." At about the same time Norris, Borah, Howell, and Nye challenged the statement of Admiral Charles Plunkett that "war is inevitable so long as we travel along the lines we are traveling today" by keeping too small a Navy. Borah described the Plunkett sentiment as "mischievous to the last degree" and warned that such bombastic rhetoric, when combined with enlarged navies, went a long way toward bringing on war. Norris predicted that if the United States increased the size of its Navy, the British would "immediately start" enlarging theirs, leading to a financial crisis on both sides of the Atlantic. Despite their distrust of the British, the peace progressives emerged as the voices of moderation in this debate; they consistently maintained that whatever their differences the two sides needed to settle all disputes by peaceful means.[56]

Given such sentiments, the peace progressives had no intention of supporting any increase in the Navy, much less a bill for fifteen cruisers that the President regarded as a compromise, and they eagerly took up Coolidge's challenge. In the process they most comprehensively articulated their vision of a proper military strategy, and though ridiculed by James Reed as the "pacifist military experts of the Senate," they succeeded in spelling out an alternative to the Coolidge doctrine on military policy.[57]

They began with traditional antimilitarist sentiments. Nye addressed this issue in the greatest detail, denying the chief argument of the bill backers, best articulated by Simeon Fess, that construction of the cruisers would promote peace. The North Dakota senator contended that no instrument could serve both the cause of war and the cause of peace. He also ridiculed the notion that the Senate should listen to the "naval heads" on proper naval policy, reasoning that they could not "present an unprejudiced analysis" and would demand only what they wanted, not what the United States needed. (Nye did not specify to whom the Senate should listen in the place of naval experts, although the implication was dissenters within the Navy such as Admiral William Sims, who argued that airplanes and submarines constituted the weapons of the future.) He attributed the success of the Washington Conference to the ability of Charles Evans Hughes to retain control of the Navy representatives, and he dismissed the Senate Naval Affairs Committee "love feast" hearings on the bill as a new low in congressional fact-finding. As usual, the peace progressives saw the industrialists working in tandem with the militarists to impose their plan upon the American taxpayer. They then went after the majority's rationale for supporting the bill, dissenting from the notion that the United States needed to have as large a navy as the British. Borah denied that any possibility for war with the British existed unless "these enlarged naval programs in connection with declarations from the navies of the respective countries that war is inevitable" continued. In searching for an answer for the puzzling escalation in rhetoric, Frazier detected a plot orchestrated by naval officers in both England and the United States "who want some nice cruiser to sail on." For Nye, two choices existed: postpone construction and "put to shame the militarists of Great Britain," in the process leading to an understanding between the two governments; or trigger a naval race, for surely other nations "will not ignore our program of naval armaments." The peace progressives also dismissed the argument of naval bill supporters that the United States needed more cruisers to enforce its neutral rights regarding commerce during wartime. Finally, the dissenters feared that the bill would stall what most of them viewed as an important trend toward international goodwill in the wake of the passage of the Kellogg-Briand Treaty. Brookhart termed it a mockery to ratify the peace pact and then "adopt a system which would nullify that treaty"; Shipstead wondered under what article of the peace treaty the United States would use the cruisers. Blaine repeated his argument about the need to accept the pact in good faith, and he rebuked peace organizations for not expending the same amount of energy fighting this bill as they had to gain support for Kellogg-Briand. Frazier considered it "nothing short of hypocrisy" even to consider the cruisers bill in light of the peace pact's ratification.[58]

The specific peace progressive responses to the bill occasionally bordered on the bizarre. McMaster proposed an amendment to draft, upon the declaration of war, every member of Congress under fifty-five, every American male between thirty and fifty-five with property holdings of $5 million or more, the chief executive of every American corporation valued at $5 million or more, and the next ten male highest stock owners in all such corporations. The South Dakota senator reasoned that his amendment would end what he called the exercise of despotic power by old men, and would bring home to the wealthy the meaning of modern warfare. McMaster worried that the consistent policy of nations' sending their young off to die had created widespread disillusionment and had made the generally older leaders too likely to resort to war as a recourse to settling international disputes. In an unusual twist on the group's anti-imperialism, he urged passage of his amendment on the grounds that it would increase the power of youth over foreign policy. The senator believed that American youth, unlike the older generation, recognized that as long as force dominated international relations the "small nations of the earth have no voice in the determination of their own affairs." McMaster's rationale reappeared in a constitutional amendment introduced by Dill to "equalize the burden and to minimize the profits of war" through the drafting of capital during wartime, which the Washington senator argued would respond to the "universal demand in this country that property shall be treated the same as men."[59]

A more serious attempt to derail the bill came through a Norris amendment to call for a British-American naval conference to discuss the cruisers issue, with an understanding that the Navy would build no cruisers until diplomacy had received a chance to slow down the arms race. Norris hoped that the U.S. declaration of its intention to hold such a conference "would stop the building of naval vessels everywhere in the civilized world" by removing any excuse for other nations to build ships. He sarcastically noted that the alternative to his proposal would be to send Naval Committee Chair Frederick Hale (R–Maine) around to other countries to offer his Senate rationale that the cruisers bill served the interests of peace. Hale did not appreciate the ridicule; neither did Claude Swanson (D–Virginia), who equated the Norris Amendment with the United States' begging the British for disarmament. When the amendment attracted a scant nine votes, Norris unsuccessfully proposed a substitute to reduce the number of cruisers built. The group's final fallback position came in an amendment introduced by Pat Harrison (D–Mississippi) to delete the "time limit" provision of the bill, which compelled the construction of some of the cruisers immediately. This too failed, though on a closer vote of fifty-four to twenty-eight; Borah reasoned that under the amendment the President could have negotiated with the "paper authority" to build the ships without ever actually constructing them.[60]

The peace progressives' intense opposition to the proposal flowed in part from their defensive military strategy. Nye noted that "the next war will make a cruiser or a battleship worth just as much as a decoy duck"; Brookhart and Frazier drew the same conclusions. The peace progressives argued that the government should move most of the money intended for cruiser construction out of the defense budget and spend the rest on the Air Corps; when challenged by Navy supporter Millard Tydings (D–Maryland) on the life expectancy of a fighting plane, Wheeler retorted that it "would last long enough to sink these 15 cruisers." The most extreme manifestation of this rationale came from Nye, who argued that since the "leaders in aviation" wanted the air service to "contribute to world amity," appropriations for the Air Corps should go to the Department of Commerce rather than to any of the war bureaus, given the similarity of the goals of Commerce and the airmen. The peace progressives also wondered how, in Brookhart's words, the cruisers could serve a strategy of "merely maintaining a defensive attitude and an armament that would defend us against aggression." The Iowa senator, "not ashamed to stand up in the Senate and say I am a pacifist," wanted an "efficient defense," not an "aggressive army and navy." A profound antimilitarism reinforced these ideas. Shipstead cautioned that, as for individuals, "too much power in the hands of any nation is a dangerous thing"; Norris feared the "national arrogance that always follows the ownership of large navies and the existence of large standing armies."[61]

An alternative conception of preparedness, which focused more on economic and moral elements, complemented this defensive military strategy. The two most conservative peace progressives, Borah and Howell, backed what Howell called "financial preparedness." The Nebraska senator said that "the only real preparedness we may look forward to is an abundant credit and a full treasury," while Borah posited that "armaments are but an incident now in real preparedness," which also included the physical, mental, and moral well-being of the people. He predicted that the strongest economic and financial power would win the next war, and worried about the United States' "depleting our economic power" through excessive spending on needless cruisers. Brookhart took a variant on this approach, stressing American economic might and reasoning that the United States did not need a large Navy since "we have an economic power [presumably through debt and trade leverage] to disband all the armies and to sink all the navies."[62]

Borah and Shipstead also resurrected the proposal for a codification of international law that they had made during the World Court fight; the issue became a near-obsession for Borah as a necessary appendage to the Kellogg-Briand Treaty. The Idaho senator reasoned that an agreement on the wartime rights of neutrals based on "a minimum of belligerent rights [and] a maximum of neutral rights" would provide a way to protect American commerce by peaceful means and thus neutralize one of the central arguments of the backers of the cruisers bill. Borah worried that the "lawless" condition of the sea adversely affected relations between the "English-speaking races," and to avoid what he termed an inevitable naval race, he proposed an amendment to the cruisers bill (which passed by eighty-one to one, with only William Cabell Bruce dissenting) calling for the convening of a conference to discuss disarmament and the codification of international law. Shipstead disagreed slightly with Borah's rationale, doubting that any agreement could be structured that would guarantee the protection of neutral commerce during wartime; the cruisers thus formed "symptoms of a deep-seated disease." Even so, he favored Borah's codification as a way to protect the weak, reasoning that during a future war belligerent nations were more likely to trample on the rights of smaller states than on those of the United States. (This had long been the Latin American position on codification of international law.) Shipstead also hoped that codification would protect the rights of the weak by defusing the "same old battle . . . to control the raw materials and the trade routes of the universe," which often concluded with the exploitation of smaller states.[63]

Finally, and most fervently, the peace progressives called for using American moral power in preparedness calculations. Nye termed a need to promote "a better spirit of good will" the leading argument against the bill; he saw the United States presented with a great opportunity to seize the initiative by abandoning an economically and morally unsound cruisers program and setting an example that would help public opinion in other countries "shame their war lords." Frazier agreed that the United States should "take the lead for world peace" and expressed doubt that such a program would affect American security adversely, pointing to the lessons of 1914 to prove the inability of navies to prevent war. Norris worried that under the current policy "small nations which do not have the financial ability to build big navies can well question our good faith." The argument on the moral nature of the bill featured both positive and negative aspects; the senators feared the bill's effects on American ideals, but they also wanted the government first to try to use those ideals to achieve international peace. This was a terribly important point to the peace progressives, since they had united around the position that the United States should begin disarming unilaterally and hoped that the moral force created by this move would weaken the positions of big-navy forces in other countries. Once this occurred, these countries too would begin disarming, accomplishing the goals of the disarmament and peace pacts without tarnishing the American moral image. Although they obviously overemphasized the impact of unilateral American disarmament, their disarmament package stood as something broader than a traditional antimilitarist desire to scale back the military budget. Rather, it complemented their anti-imperialist and economic diplomacy proposals for the proper policy for the United States to pursue toward Europe.[64]

Democratic diplomacy formed the other element of the peace progressive plan to achieve international peace through unilateral American action. The senators agitated throughout the decade for a literal fulfillment of Wilson's open diplomacy principle, to which they added a renewed call for a war referendum. Apart from Frazier, who spent a good deal of time on these and related issues, the other dissenters devoted only a cursory amount of attention to the problem. Nevertheless, all but Howell, who did not comment on the matter, issued a statement at some point during the 1920s in support of a war referendum. Unsurprisingly, given his previous interest, shortly after arriving in the Senate Dill introduced a constitutional amendment for national referenda both on war and on any issue that could lead to war. He also pushed the idea of an international treaty under which all the signatories would pledge not to go to war until their people had ratified the decision through a vote. Either he or Frazier introduced a similar amendment during every congressional session for the remainder of the decade. Reversing his earlier position, Borah endorsed the idea as early as 1924; in 1927 he commented that "no war should begin, except in absolute defense, until the question has been submitted to those who are to do the fighting." Like La Follette, Borah reasoned that referring "the business of declaring war to the judgment and control of the people" would make peace more certain.[65]

The peace progressives proposed a number of other ideas along similar lines. Shipstead spent 1924 calling for an abolition of secret diplomacy and a return to "popular control of Foreign Affairs," which he said would fulfill the more widely accepted goal of "popular control of Government." The Minnesota senator denounced the "very laborious procedure" under which the Senate could obtain foreign policy information from the Secretary of State, and he called for the Secretary to sit in the Senate at least once a week, prepared to answer foreign policy questions along the lines of the British model. Such a system would provide a free and easy exchange between the Senate and the Secretary of State, replacing the current system of "secret diplomacy," in which only the representatives of privilege received information from the State Department. Borah seconded the call for "as much open diplomacy as is practically possible," arguing that "a continued and sustained interest upon the part of the people in our foreign affairs" would guarantee peace, since it would minimize the chances that the public would be swayed during tense times by "passion" or "manipulators of our foreign affairs." In the belief that opening the United States to foreigners with radical views would help achieve this proposal, Borah called for repeal of the war-era law that gave the Secretary of State the right to exclude visitors on grounds of national security.[66]

The peace progressives thus expanded considerably on traditional antimilitarist themes in two ways. First (most clearly through the dissent of Blaine), they made an anti-imperialist case for disarmament. Second, they contended that unilateral disarmament could serve the interests of world peace, and not just peace in the United States, as earlier dissenters such as the Free Soil Whigs had maintained. This argument formed the final aspect of their alternative plan to the 1920s G.O.P. foreign policy. The dissenters reasoned that the United States, by carefully calibrating all elements of its European policy along anti-militarist and anti-imperialist lines, could achieve peace without any of the sacrifices that they viewed as being associated with the programs of the business internationalists and the Wilsonians. They thus managed to integrate most aspects of their foreign policy into a cohesive whole. This achievement did not, however, come without a price. In their attempt to outperform the decade's Republican administrations on disarmament questions, the dissenters became increasingly extreme on the issue. While the European element of their program had little chance of fruition because of political conditions in Europe, their disarmament agenda had no chance of winning adoption in the United States because of political conditions at home. One peace activist commented that the peace progressive disarmament proposals actually hurt the cause, since "most Americans will be antagonized and frightened off by such an extreme measure."[67] Since they felt that disarmament treaties did not go far enough, the peace progressives had little choice but to forward the agenda that they did. Although they achieved ideological consistency, they enjoyed fewer successes in their European and disarmament policies than they managed in Latin American affairs.

The ideological cohesion associated with military policy did not apply to the peace progressive approach to tariff and immigration questions, which did not fit in with the group's general anti-imperialism. Rather, the tariff and immigration existed as foreign policy issues at all only in the vaguest of terms; the peace progressives instead preferred to view them as domestic issues and applied to them the same (unsuccessful and internally divisive) remedies that they used for internal American affairs. Despite their desire to view these issues solely in the domestic framework, this oversight revealed a fundamental inconsistency in the peace progressives' 1920s ideology that foreshadowed their movement away from anti-imperialism in the 1930s.

Opposition to high industrial tariffs had formed a defining element of the dissenters' ideology since their emergence during the Taft administration,[68] although the peace progressives always believed in the essentials of the tariff system, as they demonstrated in the 1910s. Norris conceded that tariff protection was a "selfish policy," but he cautioned that its alternative, free trade, "equalizes living conditions of the countries between which it operates"; since the United States had a higher standard of living than most other countries, "we are justified in levying a tariff upon the products of other countries where the standard of living and the cost of production are lower than ours." Meanwhile, he hoped to inject the spirit of domestic progressive reforms into tariff policy, as can be seen in his attacks on the São Paulo coffee valorization scheme. Rather early on, then, a pattern of parochialism appeared in peace progressive policy toward foreign economic issues that did not exist when the group dealt with other affairs. Since these issues directly affected the dissenters' constituents, either as producers or as consumers, the peace progressives were inclined to look after the interests of their constituents first, even at the risk of alienating a foreign government.[69]

This rather narrow, domestically based vision of the tariff also appeared when the peace progressives attacked the 1922 Fordney-McCumber Tariff. Borah articulated a strong case for the opposition. He conceded that "the protection system . . . as announced by Hamilton and magnificently expounded by Clay [odd heroes for the group] is sound," but charged that this bill provided protection only to big business interests. The senator also vigorously opposed the "flexible" tariff idea (designed to give the President the power to raise and lower rates unilaterally within fixed guidelines), which he insisted stood "clearly and directly in contravention of the constitutional principles of our Government." La Follette made an even more passionate plea against the bill in a three-hour address in which he argued that Fordney-McCumber would harm consumers by establishing "robber rates of tariff." Ladd and Johnson disagreed. The North Dakota senator called for "real protection" for the North Dakota–based flax industry, which he contended had floundered without it. In the process he articulated a vision that justified his votes for high tariffs on all goods. Ladd reasoned that "we cannot have industrial prosperity by forcing the wage earners . . . into competition with the low-waged foreigner and low conditions of living." Johnson also regularly backed increased levies for industrial products, something all other peace progressives except Ladd refused to do, prompting the *New York Times* to thank the California senator, the "great progressive," for the fact that "every American who buys will have to pay" for California's prosperity. This kind of economic nationalism also became associated with Brookhart, who shortly after his election called for "a high tariff wall erected to keep out food products from abroad. The miller and the middlemen would have to purchase to farm products then either from the farmers or from the Government." Somewhat inconsistently, he touted this idea as the first step in his international cooperative scheme.[70]

With the growing antibusiness rhetoric coming from the group, the Johnson/Ladd position on industrial rates quickly became untenable, and by the mid-1920s the majority of peace progressives had united around the position assumed by Borah in 1922. Besides Brookhart and Borah, Shipstead and McMaster became the most active on this issue. As early as 1926, the South Dakota senator stated that farmers had not received enough from the 1922 tariff, which he alleged increased the price of all needed purchases without increasing the prices of the goods the farmers sold. In 1928 he introduced a resolution calling for instant tariff revision on behalf of agriculture, since under the present system the farmer had been "gouged by the machine trust." (Reed Smoot characterized the amendment as "an attack in the dark without a redeeming feature.") Meanwhile, Borah argued that "one of the most effective means [of] helping the agricultural and livestock interests in this country is to revise the tariff on such things upward." In addition to the McMaster Resolution, this group liked the export debenture plan, which provided for an export bounty to guarantee the price of all agricultural products at the tariff level (with the difference between the actual price and the tariff rate coming out of the Treasury).[71]

At the same time, however, a smaller bloc of peace progressives was beginning to revise its thinking on tariff, and, as often occurred on issues in the late 1920s, Blaine played an active role. The Wisconsin senator argued in 1926 that "tariffs, so far as they apply to dairy products or any other produce which comes from the farm, are a deception," since only controlling the surplus, not high tariff rates, would guarantee agricultural prosperity. Therefore, a "drastic reduction of the exorbitant duties" on both manufacturing and agricultural items was needed. Norris had long before reached the same conclusion about the importance of the surplus, although he never went as far as Blaine in backing an across-the-board lowering of rates, holding that the farmer needed to benefit from the tariff as long as the industrialists did. He preferred a government corporation to purchase the farmers' surplus and keep it off the market, thus stabilizing prices (an idea not that dissimilar to the São Paulo valorization scheme, which he had earlier criticized). In any case, he, like Blaine, had grown increasingly skeptical that high agricultural tariffs served the farmers' interests. The peace progressives thus entered debate over the Hawley-Smoot tariff divided on the issue of agricultural tariffs. Blaine, La Follette, and Norris voted against the higher rates more than 80 percent of the time (the figure for Blaine approached 90 percent); among the other peace progressives, only Wheeler did better than 40 percent, while Brookhart, Frazier, Nye, and Howell favored the higher rates in nearly 80 percent of the votes.[72] The majority of the group began their battle with a June 1929 resolution by Borah (which fell short by only one vote) calling for limiting tariff revision to farm products so as to frame to tariff bill "to give the home market to the American producer whatever the products may be." Since agricultural duties had "manifestly been too low," increasing them afforded "the most immediate and definitive relief we can give to the American farmer." Howell, "favorable to raising of the tariff on cattle, all kinds of meat products, and hides," called for an "equitable adjustment of rates that will prove a benefit to agriculture generally." Other peace progressives confined themselves to more parochial issues. Frazier backed an increase in the tariff on bread and also on mustard seed, "an infant industry" that needed protection; Brookhart called for hikes in the rates for oleomargarine and lard, since the "farmers ought to receive twice as much for their labor as they are now receiving." This rhetoric took the place of a position based on sensitivity to the American consumer, which David Thelen has argued had characterized earlier progressivism. Borah remarked that he would support an increase in the duties on hides, although he had opposed one in 1922, since it would "scarcely be felt" by consumers. Brookhart engaged in a heated debate with David Walsh (D–Massachusetts) concerning the effect upon the laboring class of an increase in the lard duty, maintaining that consumers "are with me in all these farm rates," since labor recognized that farmers had suffered from underemployment throughout the 1920s and thus was willing to pay higher prices.[73]

The one peace progressive with different parochial interests was Dill, who wanted high agricultural rates for eastern Washington but concentrated upon securing what he described as a "competitive tariff" for lumber. In the process he and other lumber-state senators allied with sugar-state and oil-state senators to trade their votes and ensure higher rates for all three commodities. Although Norris had warned at the start of the debate that "some of these insurgents will necessarily have to go along the selfish route, in order to maintain themselves in Congress," Dill was subjected to withering public and private criticism from the group. The Washington senator shot back, dismissing his sugar tariff vote as "nothing to get excited about" and quoting Alexander Hamilton to prove that the "tariff that leaves out any industry that needs protection is unjustifiable and indefensible." He blasted *The Nation* for singling him out as among the "betrayers of the public trust" while saying "nothing about such progressives as Blaine and La Follette and Brookhart who switched their votes on hard wood flooring." He conceded that everyone ate sugar, but "so does everybody eat wheat and such Progressives as Norris, Borah, Frazier, Nye . . . McMaster, and Wheeler all voted for a tariff on wheat." He contended that these senators had acted as they did out of fear of political retaliation in their home states; perhaps they would be more attuned to the wishes of the common people if they "were to run for election of the Democratic ticket . . . as I do in my state." Dill also took his case to the Senate floor, ripping Norris as a hypocrite for the Nebraskan's public criticism of the Dill lumber tariff vote; he scoffed that "these 'progressive' senators, who are so loud in protecting the farmer against a tariff on the timber he must buy, are very anxious to protect him against competitors in the milk and butter and the eggs . . . which millions of people living in the great centers of this country must buy." This was sharp criticism of a fellow dissenter, and it showed the power that economic issues could have in altering the perspectives held by the peace progressives.[74]

Although Dill targeted all the other peace progressives for criticism, three of them—Blaine, La Follette, and Norris—came as close to forming a free trade bloc as any in the group ever did, with Blaine coming the closest to advocating free trade.[75] The Wisconsin senator contended that the manufacturer received all the rewards from the tariff, but that the "presumptions and assumptions that conceal the actual facts" had fooled many farmers into believing that they too benefited. Blaine feared that the tariff bill, a "prohibitive" rather than a "protective" measure, had "goldbricked" the farmer. La Follette agreed that agricultural tariffs were "in many cases ineffective" and "carry with it the obligation to pay higher prices upon almost every article that is used upon the farm"; he charged that "the farmer has been made the excuse by which industrial lobbyists have secured new and higher tariff rates to the benefit of the special interests which they represent." Ideally, however, La Follette wanted to "block further un-justifiable increases in the industrial rates, and grant to agriculture rates which could be presumed to be effective." Norris confronted a similar gap between ideal and reality; he still believed in "the right kind of a protective tariff" but doubted that he ever would see one enacted. All three opposed most agricultural hikes and vigorously opposed the final bill.[76]

Both the Blaine and Borah blocs tried to make the case that the tariff did not concern foreign policy at all, although occasionally they admitted even to themselves that it did, and when they did so they did not sound much like the committed anti-imperialists of the Nicaraguan debate. Borah advocated increasing the tariff on bananas to protect American growers, although he realized that "in all probability" Latin Americans "won't like the bill." Nonetheless, "we cannot ask our farmers to forgo their right to a reasonable protection against the cheaper products" from the south, given that "there are a tremendous amount of agricultural products which come into competition with the cheapest labor in the world." Borah conceded that foreigners had the right to complain about the tariff, but stated that he would pay much more attention to domestic criticism than "to objections from abroad." Other peace progressives took a far softer line. La Follette remarked that the tariff bill was "driving the nations of Europe into a movement to create a customs union whose barriers will be built primarily to exclude our products." Wheeler noted that Americans needed "the finding of world markets [a central tenet of Wheeler's anti-imperialism], rather than the building of a tariff wall around the United States" for prosperity, while Norris worried that the tariff bill had "increased the enmity of all the nations of the world in the unreasonable and discriminatory rates which it contains." Comments such as these might have represented the beginning of a peace progressive attempt to apply anti-imperialist principles to the tariff through the lowering of the (primarily agricultural) rates that directly affected the weaker states, which the peace progressives spent much of the decade championing in other ways. Anti-imperialism never became central, however, to the low-tariff group, and the economic nationalism of Borah and Howell appealed in hard times. This blind spot in the peace progressive world outlook would assume more importance as the 1930s progressed.[77]

The peace progressives devoted even less attention to immigration reform, on which they rarely spoke during the 1920s. In the abstract, the dissenters vehemently opposed unlimited immigration, and most supported the 1924 Immigration Act. Borah professed himself "very much opposed" to any liberalization of immigration laws, while Norris said that he had always favored restriction with an eye toward bringing "in the lowest number of immigrants from Southern European countries." The peace progressives also showed no hostility toward restricting nonwhite immigrants. Dill, reflecting the opinions of his Washington constituents, called for complete exclusion of Japanese, since the Pacific coast felt the sting of the "Japanese menace" more acutely than the rest of the country. Shipstead blasted the 1907 Gentlemen's Agreement for giving Japan "the right to control the immigration policy of the United States," and all peace progressives supported an amendment abrogating it in 1924. Later in the decade, Wheeler emerged as a leading backer of Mexican restriction, lamenting that Mexicans entered the United States under the pretense of being farmhands and then migrated north to take the jobs of "white miners, American citizens." Yet the peace progressives, with the possible exception of Dill, were never entirely comfortable in this position. Only Dill and Wheeler endorsed a narrowly defeated 1930 amendment introduced by Hugo Black (D–Alabama) calling for the elimination of all immigration to the United States except that from Canada. Borah led the opposition to a 1930 Bingham amendment to allow unrestricted immigration from all Western Hemisphere nations except Mexico; the Idaho senator opposed "singling out one nation" and worried that the "indefensible" discrimination of the amendment would hurt the image of the United States throughout Latin America. Early in the decade, Hiram Johnson spoke for all peace progressives in sponsoring an amendment to override any quota restrictions for aliens who could prove they were the objects of religious or political persecution in their homelands. For the most part, however, the peace progressives tried to avoid this issue, perhaps sensing their contradictory stance. As in the case of the tariff, the considerable peace progressive opposition to large-scale immigration from the weaker states revealed that the dissenters, like other senators, seemed to apply a different standard to foreign policy issues that directly affected their constituents. Oddly, few of their opponents took them to task over the issue.[78]

Unlike some of their harshest critics among conservatives, the peace progressives attempted to construct a foreign policy ideology that applied similar principles to all areas of the world. They argued that the European war had shattered the old world order, and that the United States needed to adjust to the new nationalism of the underdeveloped world; this belief formed the basis of much of their critique of 1920s Latin American and East Asian policy. Yet they did not abandon old dissenting arguments, borrowing liberally from traditional antimilitarism, adding to it their preoccupation with moral power, and combining the result with fairly interventionist ideas based upon anti-imperialism to form their European agenda. The resulting, rather peculiar, policy stood as the peace progressive contribution to the traditional American search for alternative conceptions of power in international relations. The dissenters' inter-American, European, Asian, and disarmament policies existed as part of a well-calibrated anti-imperialist program, not as an awkward mixture of nationalism, isolationism, and anti-imperialism. With its emphasis on moral and economic power, disarmament, the rights of weaker peoples, and the dismissal of any strategic threat to the United States, the program also fitted very smoothly with the spirit of the 1920s. Yet the peace progressive European agenda also suffered from three flaws. First of all (in addition to adhering to a quite peculiar view of the American national interest), it overestimated the ability of the United States to dictate the foreign policies of the European countries and underestimated the political strengths of sympathizers with the peace progressive programs in those countries. Second, the domestic element of the program (radical disarmament) proved politically untenable, even in the environment of the 1920s. Finally, the agrarian domestic agenda of the dissenters, which led them to adopt positions on the tariff and immigration inconsistent with their anti-imperialism in its most advanced form, weakened their overall approach. The increasing importance of domestic concerns in the early 1930s tested the level of commitment to their 1920s ideology; when combined with changes to a more unfavorable international political environment, this set the stage for the peace progressive turn away from anti-imperialism.

6

Anti-Imperialism and the Peace Movement

P eace progressive political skill and the unusual split of the Senate in the 1920s obviously increased the senators' strength on foreign policy issues, but the peace progressives also benefited from events largely beyond their control. The 1920s witnessed the transformation of the American peace movement into a bloc more radical, unified, antimilitarist, and anti-imperialist than during the years before American entry into the European war. The peace movement both helped spread the peace progressive ideology and supplied the senators with new ideas and relevant foreign policy information. The increasingly parallel world outlooks of the peace progressives and a substantial section of the peace movement confirmed the importance of ideology—as opposed to regionalism or ethnicity—in shaping the dissenters' foreign policy beliefs, and it also illustrated the importance of the role played by the peace progressives in shaping the decade's peace agenda in the United States.

The twentieth-century American interest in peace originated in large part with the progressive movement. The initial indications of the formation of a progressive plan for world peace came in the Lake Mohonk Conferences on arbitration, which began in 1895, and then, most important, in the 1907 founding of the American Society for International Law. The dominant figures in this movement became Roosevelt's Secretary of State, Elihu Root, and Columbia University president Nicholas Murray Butler. The agenda they articulated expressed a fundamentally conservative view of the world, cherishing stability over change. These international legalists, who united under the banner of the Carnegie Endowment, all but ignored the outbreak of the European war, and by 1916 they had resolved to prepare for international peace in the postwar world rather than try to stop the war at hand. The directors of the Endowment urged American intervention on the British side, although both Root and Butler clung to the idea that a world court, backed up by a new and strengthened code of international law imposed by the victorious Allies, could ensure a postwar peace. Others of a similar ideological bent doubted that the legalist program would suffice, and in 1915 they founded the League to Enforce Peace (LEP), which differed from Root and Butler in its belief that policy questions, not legal issues, caused serious international conflicts between nations. The LEP hoped for a league in which the United States and England would play the key roles, branding nations that refused to arbitrate their differences as aggressors and then dealing with the threat to the peace in a united way.[1]

As the progressive movement began to splinter and radicalize, domestic opponents of these legalists began to question their international program. The radicals never came up with a coherent alternative, however, and did not really begin to address the questions of war and peace until 1914. Women activists took the first step in this direction. Jane Addams, a progressive reformer who had made a name for herself as head of Chicago's Hull House, emerged as the leader of one group, which organized itself into the Women's Peace Party (WPP) in 1915. The Women's Peace Party called for neutral mediation of the war through a continuing conference of neutrals staffed by experts; it also advocated democratic control of foreign policy, a postwar policy of self-determination, and an international organization backed by an international police force. In late 1915 the WPP was joined by the American Union against Militarism (AUAM), later called by Borah the "brains" of the war-era peace movement. The AUAM focused on opposing preparedness campaigns and urged popular control over foreign affairs; it held its own in the preparedness debates until early 1917 when Germany resumed unrestricted submarine warfare. Much like the peace progressives during the period 1914–1917, the radical peace activists might have succeeded in an era of peace, but the changing course of international relations during this period made their task impossible.[2]

The early twentieth-century American peace movement also tended to focus on European issues and events. Virtually all the international legalists supported an assertive U.S. policy in Latin America and East Asia, while their more radical colleagues generally paid little attention to such issues. Those who searched for alternatives to the Latin American and East Asian policies of the McKinley, Roosevelt, and Taft administrations tended to be quite conservative themselves. Such a description fitted most of the members of the Anti-Imperialist League; it also applied to Hiram Bingham, one of the more innovative thinkers in the United States on inter-American affairs in the years before World War I and a figure who obviously played a role in 1920s inter-American policy as well. Bingham in 1913 was a professor of Latin American history at Yale when he published *The Monroe Doctrine: An Obsolete Shibboleth*. He argued that the Doctrine insulted the stronger nations of Latin America, particularly the Southern Cone states, and he doubted that a European threat to the continent continued to exist; if the United States needed to intervene to ensure Central American stability, it should do so in concert with the ABC states (Argentina, Brazil, and Chile). Although in 1914 Bingham advocated uniting "with the leading American republics" to deal with all hemispheric questions, he soon thereafter began to retreat. Later in 1914 he criticized revolutionary Mexicans for lacking "the stuff . . . to establish a satisfactory republic," and in 1916 he urged an active U.S. presence in the Caribbean to combat alleged German schemes. Bingham's reversals indicated a more general shift by international legalists away from any tampering with the traditional American role in the Caribbean Basin.[3]

While elements of this peace movement survived in the postwar era, those affiliated with international legalism before the war now seemed unsure about what program to offer. In particular, they split over the wisdom of cooperation with the 1920s Republican administrations. Hamilton Holt, formerly of the LEP, led a group that sold the League of Nations as an alternative to Bolshevism and celebrated Wilson's covenant as "unquestionably the greatest document since the Declaration of American Independence." After failing to pressure the Democrats to make the 1922 elections a referendum on the League, Holt joined with retiring Supreme Court Justice John Clarke and Raymond Fosdick, who had served in Newton Baker's War Department, to form the League of Nations Non-Partisan Association (LNNPA), with Clarke at its head. By avoiding a concrete position on Article X, the new organization proved flexible enough to attract pro-League Republicans such as Taft's Attorney General, George Wickersham; and by the fall of 1923 the group was publishing a biweekly newsletter, the *League of Nations Herald*, which at its peak attained a circulation of 35,000. Attempting to refute the arguments of the League's anti-imperialist opponents, Holt suggested that the League had done a great deal for persecuted minorities and smaller states, such as Austria, while the "most efficacious" mandate system had allowed developing peoples to be "held as a 'sacred trust' of humanity." Despite Holt's success in defusing some of the anti-imperialist concerns with the League, and although the LNNPA maintained a strong following throughout the decade, the organization struggled to achieve its goals. Frustrated, in 1925 Holt accepted the presidency of Rollins College, and in 1927 Clarke too retired, leaving Wickersham with the unenviable task of trying to explain to a public enthused by the Kellogg-Briand Treaty why the League could do more for American peace than outlawry.[4] In retrospect the most significant achievement of the LNNPA was to keep alive Wilson's ideas on political internationalism in their purest form. During the 1920s, if anything, it became less powerful. The LNNPA gambled that the question of political cooperation with Europe would dominate the American international agenda for the decade; with the exception of the World Court fight, this did not happen. It struggled to deal with issues like disarmament, anti-imperialism, or economic cooperation with Europe apart from the framework of the League, and so wound up influencing only those likely to be swayed by the pro-League agenda in the first place.

The legalists formed a more important element of the decade's peace movement; Nicholas Murray Butler maintained public influence through his position as head of the Carnegie Endowment, and he capped off his career by sharing the 1931 Nobel Peace Prize with Jane Addams. Butler's attitude toward the League fluctuated; in early 1919 he seemed to endorse the idea but thereafter backtracked, calling instead for a return to the "constructive international policies" of the McKinley, Roosevelt, and Taft administrations. As an alternative to the League, he proposed dividing the world into three spheres of influence (the Western Hemisphere, Europe, and Asia), with the leading power in each sphere policing it. As before the war, he showed much more interest in a World Court, and his arguments on this issue persisted almost unchanged from the prewar era. Unlike the peace progressives, the connection between the Court and the leading European powers did not trouble Butler, who had warm things to say about all the former American allies. Throughout the 1920s he urged U.S. economic aid to France, contending that no two modern nations shared such a "community of ideas and ideals." Butler also hailed Mussolini as a latter-day Oliver Cromwell, a "great personal force, violative of constitutional procedure and rising above the laws which are only imperfectly law . . . working to save the nation in spite of itself"; given Butler's normal reverence for the law, this was strong praise.[5]

Butler also possessed an optimism that only increased after Briand's proposal in the summer of 1927 for a French-American outlawry pact. Over a seven-month period in 1927 and 1928 he delivered thirteen major speeches endorsing the idea, urging complete acceptance of the Briand plan, accompanied by the Locarno definition of an aggressor so as to not "pretend to outlaw war in a merely rhetorical way." (Borah's plan, on the other hand, was dismissed: "we might as well pass a resolution to outlaw hypocrisy.") The ratification of the Pact of Paris, however, moved Butler a bit to the left, and he broke with Hoover and endorsed Al Smith in the 1928 presidential contest in large part because of Hoover's support of the cruisers bill. Butler also called for curbing the power of the "so-called naval experts" as part of a broader antimilitarist program to abolish compulsory military service and decrease the size of armies to that needed for policing purposes. Butler's move toward antimilitarism did not imply an acceptance of anti-imperialist principles. He admitted in 1925 that he possessed "absolutely no knowledge of the conditions" in Mexico, but instinctively trusted the James Sheffield vision of Mexican politics. He also denied that all peoples were equally suited for "orderly self-government," identifying the key dilemma facing the advanced nations as maintaining relations with "less advanced" peoples without appearing patronizing or controlling.[6]

Another general framework associated with the prewar conservative peace ideology continued in the form of the National Conference for the Cause and Cure of War and its head, Carrie Chapman Catt, who turned her attention to peace full-time after the passage of the suffrage amendment.[7] Catt strongly supported the traditional progressive paths to peace, urging American participation in both the League and the World Court. As with her previous suffrage tactics, Catt tried to bring as many differing viewpoints as possible under the umbrella of peace, an effort that restricted her to only very general pronouncements about possible policy options. Her chief innovation, the various National

Conferences on the Cause and Cure of War held throughout the decade, fitted this pattern. Catt likewise offered a mixed view on the question of anti-imperialism, espousing at times some rather radical rhetoric, as when she described the Monroe Doctrine as "false in theory and pernicious in application." At the same time, however, she defended specific American policymakers, praising the "clear analytical mind" of Hughes for his "modifications" of the Doctrine, excusing Coolidge's intervention in Nicaragua on grounds of precedent, and in general reasoning that "when and if the United States is imperialistic, it is because all other nations are imperialistic." When pressed, Catt merely called for all nations to find a way to protect life and property without resorting to imperialism, without suggesting specifics on how to accomplish this beyond the adoption of "decent international manners." She also occupied a middle position on questions of disarmament. Although she criticized both compulsory ROTC training and the equation of patriotism with "a constant preparation for war," she also denied that she or her organization advocated American disarmament in advance of an international agreement, and she harped on the fact that the disunity in the 1920s peace movement had allowed "radical and hysterical" elements to come to the fore. Catt's chief proposal on this issue was to call for a one-week conference to include the leading peace activists and the upper levels of the Army and Navy. After a few days of haggling, she predicted that the military men would learn that "very few [pacifists] want to interfere with legitimate preparedness for honest defense," while the pacifists would "discover that militarists are honest advocates of peace and high-minded, noble Americanism." Catt never seemed to recognize that the critical points of difference between the "pacifists" and the "militarists" came over terms like "legitimate preparedness for honest defense."[8]

Along with the LNNPA and Butler, Catt formed a part of the peace movement that operated under premises quite similar to those of the 1910s, attempting to employ progressive solutions such as public information and reverence for the law to achieve peace. Unlike in the 1910s, however, the traditionalists found themselves under heavy attack. Although they may have begun the decade as the most prominent members of the peace movement, they ended the 1920s challenged both ideologically and tactically, and in the distinct minority of a movement that they once had controlled.

In contrast to the traditional peace activists who attempted to adapt their ideology to the postwar setting, a substantial number of former progressives rejected the solutions that they had found appealing during the 1910s. Although this group varied considerably in terms of both personality and proposals, all found the peace progressives to be their most reliable political allies on foreign affairs during the 1920s. The convergence of ideas between this group of ex-progressives—who almost uniformly did not share either the domestic political outlook, the Upper Midwest regional background, or pressures from German or Scandinavian constituents—offers further proof of the danger of taking too narrow an approach in analyzing the peace progressive ideology of the 1920s.

For most of the decade, the figure from this group closest to the dissenters in the Senate was Chicago attorney Salmon Levinson, the "captain" of the war outlawry movement. His idea for outlawry came from his reading of Charles Sumner, but it expanded under the pressure of what Levinson called the "necessity for a counter constructive program" to the League of Nations. Although outlawry became a favorite program of the peace progressives, Levinson did not hold a particularly radical conception of outlawry initially, as is shown by his selection of Philander Knox, then a Pennsylvania senator, as its Senate champion. The proposal, which Levinson described as a "real American foreign policy," included the codification of international law to include a provision making aggressive war punishable as a crime, the establishment of an international tribunal, general disarmament, and the abolition of secret treaties. (He wanted to exclude issues such as the Monroe Doctrine, the tariff, and immigration from the jurisdiction of the international court so as "not to surrender our basic principles and traditions nor to sell out our nationality for a mess of pottage with poison in it.") Levinson also initially allowed for a citizen-soldier force allegedly along the Swiss model, which he argued would "destroy militarism, not . . . promote it"; only after vociferous opposition from Borah did he drop the idea. His conception of outlawry even bore some resemblance to Wilson's Article X. When pressed by Borah on how outlawry would function if Japan were to invade Siberia, Levinson speculated that the international court could hear the case, and if it decided for Siberia, then "all the other nations signatory to the code would have the right (not the duty) to join in the defense of Siberia." He also did not view outlawry as part of a global anti-imperialist crusade. Responding to a critique from Oswald Garrison Villard that only a policy of anti-imperialism could bring lasting peace, Levinson contended that "the question of subject peoples is purely a domestic one and has no more to do with the theory of the outlawry of war than the question of immigration of the tariff"; he had not set out "to cure all the ills of the world."[9]

Disappointed by Harding's failure to name Knox Secretary of State, Levinson emerged as a strong critic of the President's diplomacy. He also began working much more closely with Borah after Knox's death. Levinson termed Borah's disarmament conference resolution "the biggest single crystallized effort for peace" since 1914, but he quickly soured on the work of the resulting Washington Conference. He contended that the ambitions of Charles Evans Hughes, whom he detested, "cripple him for service to the world"; since Hughes needed a successful disarmament conference for his reputation, he had not stood up to the militarist nations, particularly France. Although he failed to have an impact on the Senate debate against the treaty, Levinson did forge closer ties to Borah, initiating a sometimes frustrating ten-year relationship. Out of a need to win Borah's backing for his plan, he began to alter it enough to reconcile it to peace progressive thought. Levinson also began to cooperate with Raymond Robins, soon the chief public spokesperson for the cause. A self-described "social economist," Robins, a prominent figure in Chicago reform politics, had initially come into contact with the peace progressives in 1919, when he supplied them with information on conditions in revolutionary Russia. Robins first joined Levinson in the fight for Borah's disarmament plan and converted to outlawry because "it is nonrevolutionary in character" yet still could be applied immediately. With Levinson's funding, Robins delivered hundreds of speeches on behalf of outlawry from 1922 through 1928, reasoning that the world could solve the problem of war only through "an international code based on equality and justice for . . . peaceful settlement by law," just as outlawing "the slave institution" had eliminated "the fundamental trouble with our domestic social order in 1850." (He did not mention that a war had produced this outlawing.) He called on the Republican party, which had "won the historic ascendancy fighting for the abolition of the domestic slave system," to expand that fight to the international arena and join the crusade for outlawry.[10]

At the same time, both Levinson and Robins distinguished their plan from the League and especially from what they called the League

Court. Robins ridiculed the "fake character of this League of Nations Court, back door into the League of Nations, proposal of the crafty and crooked Hughes"; he said that outlawry constituted "the only alternative to the League of Nations or absolute isolation." The conviction that the League "must be destroyed or future wars are inevitable" naturally led to a suspicion of the major European powers not dissimilar to that held by the peace progressives. In 1923 Robins wrote of France that he had "not met anywhere except in Germany ten years ago such a spirit of brutal and ruthless militarism," while Levinson likewise committed himself to a "patriotic crusade to keep this country out of European entanglements so long as the war game is legal." Their experience with the League and with their alternative to it led them closer to the peace progressive world conception than they were prepared to admit.[11]

The preoccupation of Levinson and Robins, however, remained outlawry. Levinson called the Coolidge policy toward Nicaragua "absolutely disgusting," but he argued that all questions involving it "will be automatically taken care of when the Treaty is signed by the Latin-American countries." Robins devoted slightly more attention to the issue, calling in 1928 for a platform plank urging an end to the application of force to Latin American and East Asian problems. He further recommended a concerted effort, similar to that attempted by Burton Wheeler, to show American businessmen who wanted new foreign markets that the use of force created anti-American sentiment overseas. Both Levinson and Robins opposed the 1929 cruisers bill but did so in halfhearted terms. Levinson noted that he had never opposed the building of cruisers, but failed to see why Coolidge desired so many; he wanted an adequate defense "with a minimum of friction and jingoism." Since he had always emphasized that "outlawry is in no sense a non-resistant movement," he could not justify having the United States "in a burst of ultra-pacific spirit reduce her armaments by example." He told Villard as early as 1924 that despite the importance of disarmament, it could only "work out as a corollary to a reordered world in which war is eliminated." Levinson eventually split with the peace progressives over both foreign policy and domestic issues, revealing that he never had abandoned a legalist conception of world affairs; but throughout the 1920s their cooperation remained solid.[12]

While Levinson and Robins focused on outlawry, no one worked harder for Russian recognition than Alexander Gumberg, whose connection to the political scene came through Robins, whom he met in Russia in 1917. Gumberg maintained that the United States could not compete economically in Russia if it did not grant recognition; he especially targeted this argument to conservative groups such as the Chamber of Commerce and export businesses. Like Levinson and Robins, he too bombarded the peace progressives with information on his cause. Gumberg aided Borah, particularly in the early 1920s, in obtaining assistance for Americans detained by the Soviets, and he also worked closely with Brookhart and Wheeler throughout the decade in helping them build their public cases for recognition. Gumberg's focused strategy enabled him to increase his power, and by the end of the decade he had emerged as one of the more influential national figures on the issue.[13]

Another former progressive who sided with the peace progressives was Lynn Haines, who held even more impeccable progressive credentials than did Levinson, Robins, and Gumberg. Executive secretary of the National Voters' League, Haines served as editor of the Voters' League monthly publication, *Searchlight on Congress*. Although his magazine concentrated primarily on domestic affairs, Haines dabbled in foreign policy, beginning the decade by opposing both the Four Power Treaty and the World Court. About the only good thing Haines could uncover about either battle was the "illuminating" speeches by Borah in opposition. He noted the Court's "most intimate" association with the League and predicted that the Court's "surface popularity" would vanish once Borah and other peace progressives intensified their opposition. He agreed with Borah that the Court lacked the "authority to hale the more powerful nations into Court," and reasoned that only the "international bankers and their clients" would really benefit from American participation.[14]

Like Levinson and Robins, Haines grew increasingly suspicious of the major European powers in the years following the war. He criticized the French invasion of the Ruhr as the culmination of French "decadence," which only "verified what Borah forcefully foresaw," and he agreed with the Idaho senator that the United States should have "exercised far-reaching moral leadership" in an attempt to solve the crisis. Haines unsurprisingly blasted the British debt deal as "an entanglement [too] portentous to contemplate," which had rewarded London for "vastly" strengthening its position through the spoils of Versailles, and he recommended that the United States call in all its debts at once so that the "war-breeding countries would be compelled to divert their available funds from militarism to this better purpose of paying us." Haines also criticized the Italian debt plan, which he scoffed Coolidge desired so much because he shared with Mussolini a sense of "undisputed executive domination of everything pertaining to public affairs."[15]

Haines held a more deeply rooted antimilitarism than either Levinson or Robins. He questioned the idea of compulsory military training and endorsed Borah's "deeply significant" proposals for reduction of the Army as a strike against "rampant militarism." (The magazine's sections on the 1921 Navy bill amounted to little more than a reprint of Borah's speeches.) Haines also opposed increased expenditures for poison gas, another favorite Borah position. The editor proved more active on Caribbean Basin issues than did the outlawrists. Criticizing the McCormick Committee recommendations on Haiti for making John Russell "virtually a dictator," he supported the 1922 King Resolution. Later in the decade Haines praised the Shipstead Hearings for proving that the State Department "exercises an unrighteous, unwarranted interference, through the power of money" in many Latin American states. An opponent of the Nicaraguan occupation, he published several articles by Amy Woods critical of it.[16]

Other progressives of the pre-1917 period also began to question the course of American foreign policy during the 1920s. One such figure was Walter Lippmann, the consummate Eastern progressive crusader during the 1910s. Swept up by Wilsonian idealism, Lippmann felt betrayed by the peace that Wilson brokered at Paris; he chastised the President for violating promises of self-determination and criticized Article X for committing the United States to guaranteeing the status quo. As things stood, he predicted that the League would function as "a bureau of the French foreign office, acting as a somewhat vague alliance of the Great Powers against the influence and the liberty of the people who live between the Rhine and the Pacific Ocean." Despite the similarity of the rhetoric, Lippmann was no peace progressive (although he did supply Hiram Johnson with copious amounts of material during the League debate), and he later regretted siding with the dissenters during 1919. Rather, he abandoned his progressive idealism and tried to apply a *realpolitik* interpretation to the decade's foreign policy, which led him to articulate a middle-of-the-road European policy. Lippmann did not regard the World Court "as intrinsically of world-standing importance," but he nonetheless backed membership on the grounds that the United States needed to demonstrate a willingness to participate in world political affairs. He took a more mixed line on the debt question, pronouncing himself "morally certain" that peace progressive attempts to couple the debt with disarmament proposals would fail, but also endorsing large segments of the dissenters' debt positions, including their calls for decreased German reparations payments. He also shared with the peace progressives a view of Mussolini's Italy as "the supreme menace to the peace of Europe . . . a dictatorship which has had to become more dictatorial the longer it has held power" (although his friendship with Thomas Lamont tempered his opinion on Italy late in the decade). Finally, Lippmann, like Borah, raved about disarmament in general and the London Naval Conference in particular; the editor praised Ramsay MacDonald for achieving a "stupendous vindication . . . of the idealism of 1919" and bitterly condemned the American admirals who opposed the pact for overstepping their military authority.[17]

Lippmann parted company from the peace progressives on outlawry of war, ridiculing the Borah position as "so illogical [it] must be a political accident"; he could not understand how anyone who had attacked the League as a superstate could author a plan that, if carried to its logical conclusion, would establish a world court with broad and undefined powers. He noted that Borah's exceptions to outlawry—the tariff, immigration, the Monroe Doctrine, and, most important, wars of liberation—were so broad as to all but guarantee that the program could at best represent "a moral crusade in favor of complete moral disarmament." He would concede only that outlawry possessed "intangible possibilities" and that Kellogg-Briand perhaps could compel the United States to consult with the other signatories should a breach of the treaty occur. Rather than attempting to achieve the impossible, Lippmann advocated a more limited approach to peace, structuring an international system with pacific methods for altering the status quo, as had occurred in French-German relations in the aftermath of Locarno. A stable world environment with some kind of international government would help in achieving this end; in any case, outlawry did not even begin to address the issue.[18]

Lippmann's analysis of American foreign policy led him into much closer cooperation with the peace progressives in inter-American relations, where he sharply attacked the "new and radically different principle" on Latin American affairs offered by Kellogg. This principle concerned Lippmann enough that he spent much of early 1927 (working with George Rublee, the elder La Follette's nemesis from the Webb-Pomerene fight) taking apart Kellogg's policy and, more importantly from his perspective, coming up with an alternative that would safeguard American interests sufficiently to force Coolidge to overrule a Secretary who both Lippmann and Rublee believed "represents American oil companies" and not the public interest. Lippmann argued that Kellogg's position, in essence, amounted to saying that the right of property stood "superior under international law to the right of sovereignty." He feared that this policy would mean that "a nation's social developments would be frozen in status quo," guaranteeing the permanent enmity of Latin American nationalists. (Ambassador Sheffield termed this argument "unwarranted, unpatriotic, and dangerous" and urged a prompt administration response.) Lippmann looked to turn Kellogg's reliance on international law against him by proving that the Secretary's case had no merit. Privately, he teamed with Rublee, Lamont, and Dwight Morrow to defuse the crisis without U.S. military intervention. The easing of tensions with Mexico did not alter Lippmann's perspective on Kellogg's diplomacy. He questioned how the imposition of free elections upon supposedly sovereign and independent peoples could bring about long-term peace and stability, although from there Lippmann departed from the peace progressive consensus. He believed that the United States was essentially a disinterested observer that truly desired inter-American cooperation along the Roosevelt/Root lines but had become sidetracked by bungling diplomacy. Therefore, he recommended joint pan-American action when intervention became necessary, and called for the appointment of qualified diplomats to Central American posts. Nonetheless, the decade's anti-imperialist sentiment touched even Lippmann, who spent much of the 1920s attempting to determine an American foreign policy devoid of sentimentality. Throughout 1928 he pressed Borah for investigations of Honduran and Haitian affairs, arguing that a congressional initiative could succeed, since in the aftermath of the Mexican and Nicaraguan debates "public opinion is much more sensitive about Latin American affairs now than it was a year ago." In the summer of 1928 he confessed to Rublee that he found himself "curiously fascinated by Mexico," remaining "vitally interested" in Mexican affairs despite the easing of tensions. Because of opinions like these, Hiram Bingham described

Lippmann, "the near socialist" who regularly associated with "individuals belonging to what Roosevelt used to call the 'lunatic fringe of reform'," as "one of our most dangerous editorial writers."[19]

The magazine that best represented the thought of the Eastern progressives, the *New Republic*, reflected a point of view rather similar to Lippmann's throughout the decade. Although the *New Republic* did not make the Haitian issue a crusade, it did comment that the American intervention there bore "a remarkable likeness to that of the Japanese conquest of Korea." The editors found "no excuse and no defence" for the McCormick Committee report, which they explained by ridiculing the intellectual abilities of the committee members.[20] Later in the decade, noting that the American-imposed constitution actually represented "a long step away from democratic government and toward dictatorship," they praised the various King amendments for helping to keep Haiti in the public eye. The critique of Haitian policy fitted into an overall condemnation of the "sordid and nationalistic" Hughes policy in the region. The editors dismissed the Hughes interpretation of the Monroe Doctrine as "unillumined and disappointing" for failing to recognize that the United States, and not Europe, posed the greatest current threat to Latin American independence. Like the peace progressives, the *New Republic* also chastised the 1924 decision to send arms to the Obregón government. The diplomacy of Frank Kellogg, which the *New Republic* found almost indescribably ineffective, only confirmed the editors' worst fears. The magazine noted that the United States had a fairly good case against Mexico on the retroactive laws, but charged that Kellogg's blundering had created the impression that the United States was interfering in Mexican domestic politics. The editors stepped up their criticism of Kellogg's "arrogant and unyielding attitude" by the end of 1926; obviously a policy of encouraging American citizens to disobey Mexican law did not hold out long-term prospects for success. The editors very much liked the 1927 Frazier resolution calling on Coolidge not to wage war against Mexico while Congress was out of session, passage of which they hoped would demonstrate to Coolidge the extent of his policy's unpopularity. Kellogg's Nicaraguan policy likewise earned the magazine's calculated disapproval. In a long critique of Kellogg's diplomacy published in 1927, two-thirds of which was devoted to Latin American affairs, the *New Republic* rebuked the Secretary for placing American prestige in the region at a "disastrously low level" by practicing a policy of "ruthless imperialism," the reasons for which were often "mutually contradictory and . . . in no case convincing or even plausible." The editors noted that in Nicaragua Kellogg had taken a "reasonably simple legal question and . . . puffed it up into an international crisis" on morally indefensible terms.[21]

The *New Republic* also sided with prevailing anti-imperialist sentiments on Russian recognition and German policy. In the "protracted battle" between the cooperatives and the Soviet bureaucracy, the magazine saw the cooperatives winning out, from which "it follows that peasant communism must finally prevail over urban communism in the actual organization of economic life." Criticizing the Hughes rebuff to the 1923 Soviet initiative for recognition as "unworthy of the Secretary of State" in both tone and content, the editors urged, as did the peace progressives, recognition on the grounds that it would undermine communism by encouraging foreign economic and cultural penetration. Like the peace progressives, the *New Republic* also tilted toward post-Versailles Germany, openly sympathizing with the Germans during the Ruhr occupation, calling for the United States to remain entirely aloof from European affairs until the Allies revised the Versailles Treaty in Germany's favor. By the end of the decade the editors were endorsing virtually all German territorial claims, advocating the nullification of the "indefensible" Saar and Rhineland settlements, the return of Danzig to Germany, and the permission of a German-Austrian union. The magazine's attitude toward the French thus was predictable; the critique began early in the decade and continued unabated throughout the 1920s. Dismissing Clemenceau as a man of "narrow outlook . . . inaccurate mind . . . [and] obviously failing intellectual powers," the *New Republic* reasoned that the French should stop whining and attribute the anti-French attitude in the United States "to the indefensibility of their own cause." The editors understood the French desire for security, but since Paris apparently would not consent to give security to anyone else, the peace of Europe was threatened by a France "armed to the teeth." The magazine, however, declined to equate French policy with the conduct of the League. Throughout the 1920s it called for a realistic and flexible response to the American role in Europe, including American World Court membership, although the editors also bitterly criticized Versailles and called for England and the United States to remain aloof from European affairs and use isolationism "as an instrument of coercion" against the makers of an unjust European peace, forcing the French to alter Versailles and thus permit an American entrance into a new European system.[22]

The European perspectives of the *New Republic* and of individuals such as Robins, Gumberg, Levinson, and even (to a degree) Lippmann overlapped with those of the peace progressives, indicating that the dissenters' proposals (as odd as some of them may seem in retrospect) did accord with the spirit of the times. This similarity in outlook toward Europe (and particularly Latin America) also calls into question any argument that contends that the peace progressives adopted the foreign policy positions they did because of regional or ethnic factors; obviously neither of these issues affected the 1910s progressives who had moved to the left in the 1920s and had begun to affiliate on many matters with the Senate dissenters. The search of these 1910s progressives for foreign policy allies in the 1920s also illustrates the political power of the peace progressives during the decade. Although Robins, Levinson, Lippmann, and the *New Republic* all occupied positions on most foreign policy issues to the right of the Senate dissenters and could in no sense be classified as anti-imperialists, they found no other political bloc particularly appealing, and so gradually, if fitfully, drifted into the peace progressive orbit. This development played a vital role in creating an intellectual and political alliance between the peace progressives and the peace movement during the 1920s.

During the 1920s at least, the decline of the traditional progressives worked most to the advantage of their emerging radical foes from the 1910s, who grew both more aggressive and more powerful as the decade progressed. The 1920s featured the rise of a number of extreme peace groups ranging from the War Resisters League (WRL), whose members took a pledge "never to take part in war" in any form, to the Women's Peace Society (WPS), which condemned all war with the dual platform of absolute American disarmament and worldwide free trade. The most important of these radical pacifist organizations was the Women's Peace Union (WPU), whose influence came through its alliance with Lynn Frazier, with whom it worked on behalf of a constitutional amendment stripping the war power from the federal government. The group believed that there "can be no compromise with war" and that "to be civilized we must abandon the ways of savagery"; like Frazier, its members argued that if the United States took the lead on the issue, other nations would follow.[23]

The National Council for Prevention of War, with an annual budget as high as $100,000 and at its peak twenty-one member organizations, occupied the other extreme of the peace movement during the 1920s.

Headed by the extremely active Frederick Libby, the NCPW functioned as a clearinghouse for diverse elements within the peace movement. It therefore looked for compromise and shied away from extreme
views; as its legislative secretary remarked concerning disarmament issues, NCPW member "organizations have been agreed on these objects
only as general principles, and in the days when we tried to make them
definite, we found it impossible to do so." The NCPW reached the
height of its influence in the 1920s when it helped mobilize public
opinion against the Coolidge Mexican policy. It sent out over 450,000
pieces of literature on the issue during the spring of 1927, threatened
a nationwide protest if Coolidge lifted the arms embargo; promoted
arbitration at the grassroots level through mass meetings, forums, discussions, and addresses by foreign policy experts; and worked inten-
sively with lawyers to get major legal organizations to apply pressure
on the White House for arbitration. Even here, though, Libby was said
to have "felt his hands so tied because the Council as such could not
have a clear cut, definite program," and he declined at any point in the
decade to sever his ties with his "high-class acquaintances" in more
conservative organizations such as the Foreign Policy Association. Finally, the effort required to sustain the fairly large bureaucracy associated with the NCPW—Libby estimated that the Peace with Mexico
campaign alone cost over $9,000—required the already harried director
to devote large amounts of time to fundraising; he quipped that "it
would be amusing if we were so busy with our routine that we had no
time to stop a war."[24]

Nonetheless, the NCPW obviously played an important role in sustaining the decade's peace movement. In addition to its activities on
behalf of Mexican arbitration and its consistent agitation for American
membership in both the League of Nations and the World Court, the
group played a prominent role in the cruisers bill fight, working to
augment the strength of what Libby called the "serious opposition" in
the Senate. In addition to the lobbying effort, Libby took his case to
the public, debating future Secretary of State Christian Herter on the
wisdom of abandoning the "crudely nationalistic" doctrine of naval
parity with England and scrapping the bill. (Herter countered that the
United States had fought two of its five wars with England and needed
to be prepared.) For his effort, Libby was denounced as "unpatriotic"
by the Daughters of the American Revolution and termed the "arch
slacker" by the American Legion. The NCPW also experimented as a

more modern-style special interest group by providing direct support to peace-oriented congressional candidates. But because the NCPW existed as a coalition of individual peace groups, it could not set policy for the peace movement, leaving other organizations to set the ideological tone. The first such organization was the American branch of the Women's International League for Peace and Freedom (WILPF), which throughout the 1920s remained under the leadership of Jane Addams. More flexible than many left-wing peace activists in her attitude toward the League of Nations, Addams urged the peace movement to work with the League in an attempt to reform it, and supported American participation in League-sponsored disarmament conferences and American cooperation with other League organizations. To left-wing critics who worried that the League could lead the United States into unwanted wars, she responded that the League would use military sanctions "only under such very remote and exceptional circumstances that it may never be worked, as it never has been."[25]

Beyond that, Addams kept to the very general, but she did offer an indication that she was thinking along fairly radical lines. She sympathized with international anti-imperialism, citing Gandhi as an example that a "national movement of self-determination may be successfully conducted by moral energy ignoring brute force." Addams also hoped that the protection of foreign nationals through civil procedure "will deal a body blow at imperialism all over the world." This also would aid the cause of disarmament, since imperialism "is the mother of modern militarism"; she feared that otherwise the decade's disarmament conferences would fail because of the excessive influence of naval men over the delegations. Addams also explored a range of issues that the peace advocates in Congress attempted to avoid, notably the tariff and immigration. She contended that unrestricted economic intercourse between nations would promote goodwill (although she was not as passionate on this issue as the WPS), and she called on Coolidge to lift most immigration restrictions. In general, Addams hoped for a world patriotism "founded on internationalism" that would usher in an era of cooperation between all nations and all races.[26]

Addams decreased her involvement in the day-to-day operations of the organization as the 1920s progressed, and as her subordinates, particularly Dorothy Detzer and Emily Balch, assumed larger roles, the WILPF moved toward a more explicit anti-imperialist stance.[27] Oswald Garrison Villard credited Detzer, an intensive propagandist and effective lobbyist, with doing more to end the Nicaraguan occupation than any other single person. Along with Balch, she also turned the attention of the WILPF to Haiti at a time (the mid-1920s) when public interest in Haiti had waned and even the peace progressives despaired about ending the occupation. The WILPF had always shown interest in inter-American policy; Detzer's predecessor, Amy Woods, had worked with both Ladd and Shipstead trying to fortify their opposition to Hughes and Kellogg policies toward Central America. Detzer picked up where Woods left off, describing the Kellogg Nicaraguan policy as "a stupid and obsolete method for settling a difficult problem." She denied that the United States could produce Nicaraguan democracy by applying force, and urged a joint campaign by peace organizations to compel Kellogg's resignation. Detzer also unsuccessfully urged a "free and open discussion" of all U.S. policies toward the Caribbean Basin at the Havana Conference, which she termed an "extraordinary opportunity to help adjust a bitter and tragic situation." She concluded the decade by touting an unarmed border between the United States and Mexico and organizing a campaign for WILPF members to live in Mexico for a time in the hopes of easing tensions by creating a greater American understanding of Mexican culture. In general, Detzer believed that the Monroe Doctrine, "originally a healthy document," had become "misused and distorted" and was no longer relevant.[28]

In 1926 the WILPF also undertook a mission to Haiti to investigate the progress of the McCormick Committee's suggested reforms. The committee, headed by Balch and including future Illinois Senator Paul Douglas, then a confidant of William King, unsurprisingly recommended the termination of the occupation and the restoration of Haitian self-government. Balch lamented that despite American claims, the occupation had done nothing to aid Haitian society materially while instituting an educational policy "making it impossible for Haitians to continue to have an educated class." (In 1927 the committee published a book, *Occupied Haiti*, in which the State Department found both a "considerable number of errors" and "little evidence of a real appreciation of the difficulties which have been faced" by the occupiers.) The WILPF kept up the campaign, redoubling its efforts when the 1929 Port-au-Prince riots broke out. Balch personally lobbied all liberal senators, urging them to speak on the Haitian issue; she had some influence at least with Hugo Black (D–Alabama). The effort did not cease until the Roosevelt administration withdrew the Marines in 1934.[29]

Detzer and Balch also succeeded in moving the American WILPF to the left on disarmament issues. The WILPF had questioned the Frazier Amendment when the North Dakota senator had first secured hearings for it in 1926, but in 1930 the organization reversed its position and sent Detzer to testify before the Judiciary Committee on the amendment's behalf. Detzer argued that "war now is morally obsolete" and therefore should be discarded; she compared it to slavery, an institution once perceived as beneficial to some but clearly recognized as no longer effective. She recommended that "our best method of defense is to prove our faith in the Kellogg Treaty" by eliminating the war power, thus abolishing the means with which to violate the treaty. Detzer earlier had cooperated with the peace progressives in a massive public relations campaign against the cruisers bill, when she privately argued that the peace movement would be better off sacrificing Kellogg-Briand rather than have it passed alongside a naval increase.[30]

The Fellowship of Reconciliation (FOR) rivaled the WILPF in importance for the 1920s peace movement, and it too embraced a much more pronounced anti-imperialist position as the decade progressed. Patterned on a British group founded in 1914 to aid conscientious objectors, by the end of the war the Fellowship espoused a radical program for both domestic and foreign policy. It assumed a more national role when John Nevin Sayre, an Episcopal minister active in aiding conscientious objectors during the war, took over as executive secretary in 1924. The FOR spent much of the early 1920s opposing Republican military policy, championing cross-cultural intellectual and religious understanding combined with a respect for human rights as the way to bring peace. Sayre argued that the United States should work for an international disarmament agreement, but, failing that, Washington "should disarm anyhow and set the example," allowing "the magnetism of friendship to have full play." Like the peace progressives, he compared his crusade to the earlier one to abolish slavery, and he joined the dissenters in the belief that disarmament formed "itself a potent cause for peace, for the psychological effect of the abolishing of a professional military class . . . would have a powerful effect for the depopularity of war." (He continued his efforts along these lines throughout the 1920s, ending the decade as an enthusiastic supporter of the Frazier Amendment.) In European affairs, like the peace progressives, the FOR adopted an anti-French position. The entire European agenda of the organization mirrored that of the peace progressives.[31]

In 1924 the FOR turned its attention to a "new subject," "the question of imperialism in relation to the development of world brotherhood." Over the next eight years, prodded by Sayre, the organization undertook two major initiatives in inter-American affairs. The first was Sayre's "adventure of peace" in late 1927, an attempt to meet with Sandino and negotiate a peaceful end to the Nicaraguan conflict. Sayre told Nicaraguans that since "the resemblances between peoples are more important and more fundamental than their differences," the stronger powers needed to cease "using that power to crush weaker fellows." On the basis of what he had witnessed, the FOR head believed that Nicaragua had a bright future provided that the American military could be curbed, although he warned that "as long as we follow a course of economic imperialism, the welfare, political integrity, and economic independence of weaker nations is constantly in danger." In addition to immediate withdrawal of the Marines and a "thorough" Senate investigation of the whole affair, Sayre urged a program of immediate American financial assistance to Nicaragua for nonmilitary concerns such as education, railroads, roadbuilding, and agriculture, singling out the work to improve Nicaragua's health care system undertaken by the Rockefeller Foundation as the type of initiative that he desired. Like the peace progressives, Sayre challenged the administration's international law justification, contending that with so many deaths caused by the conflict "something more than technical justification is needed" for the United States to continue the occupation.[32]

Sayre felt so strongly about ending the occupation that he feared that peace movement activism in the Kellogg-Briand and cruisers bill fights would "swamp the Nicaraguan situation." To avoid this he established a Latin American division of the FOR headed by Charles Thomson, making the FOR the first American peace organization to establish a branch in Latin America. Instructing Thomson to "be careful not to identify . . . the Fellowship with Sandino's use of violence," Sayre called on the Latin American branch to concentrate on reinforcing strong local personalities, assisting in peaceful educational programs, and "showing up" militarism and imperialism by using the "weapon of truth." The Latin American Fellowship struggled to overcome cultural and religious gulfs separating its generally Anglo-Saxon Protestant leadership and the Spanish Catholics it attempted to recruit, but it expanded its membership in each of its three years. Thomson also proved particularly adept at attracting attention to his cause, as occurred when he got himself arrested by U.S. Marines in Nicaragua in 1931 for protesting the occupation or when he visited Haiti in 1930 to protest against the "arbitrary" and "awkward" imperialism that had failed to take into account that "no people like to be reformed by the military forces of a foreign power." Beyond protesting the American occupation of Haiti and Nicaragua upon the scene, he attempted to establish American cultural centers in Central American capitals to give Central Americans a "more realistic and less stereotyped picture of the United States." Thomson recognized that his "venture represents a relatively new approach to the promotion of international cooperation and understanding," but he hoped that the emphasis on the cultural and nonviolent aspects of international relations would bring dividends.[33]

As the FOR turned toward inter-American issues, its work on disarmament was increasingly taken over by the Committee on Militarism in Education (CME). The organization, founded to combat obligatory ROTC participation at land grant colleges, was launched in 1925 with a pamphlet by Winthrop Lane sponsored by Borah, La Follette, Norris, and Shipstead. Lane contended that the ROTC program, by leading impressionable young men into "an alignment with the world's forces of militarism," was making the United States a militarist society without the public's knowledge. Lane also worried that War Department grants of money would give the military too much power over the kinds of courses taught at universities: "to let the camel of militarism thus get his nose under the tent of academic independence seems a dangerous experiment." Another CME official, Professor Carlton J. H. Hayes of Columbia, charged that ROTC fed off nationalism, "a religion with a special brand of worship" organized around the "cult" of the flag; he stressed the importance of proper education for peace, since "the preservation of the nationalistic faith [required that] the common people should be kept in ignorance." To replace ROTC, the CME urged colleges to "promote a dynamic education for peace" by offering "popular orientation courses in the problems of building a peaceful world community," to include "practical field work" for the student, perhaps "participating in some local peace education campaign." The CME never advocated that its program be compulsory, but it did see the battle for the college mind as important given that the "decisions as to whether America in the future shall be a *peace-thinking* or a *war-thinking* nation" were occurring at the college level. This antimilitarism appeared in other CME causes as well. The CME opposed the idea of a national Defense Day (against which Blaine had fought), arguing that it "greatly favors militarism" by leading to the interpretation of "patriotism in terms of war service"; the organization also opposed the cruisers bill. As had the peace progressives, the CME turned toward earlier moral crusades for guidance, arguing that military propaganda could be "perhaps best understood as a close parallel to the pro-slavery agitation which was carried on by advocates of slavery in this country." Like the FOR and the WILPF, the CME assumed positions on most foreign policy issues subscribed to in the Senate only by the peace progressives in the 1920s.[34]

A small but quite powerful group of historians who sought throughout the 1920s to alter the American perception of both the causes of the European war and the reasons for the American intervention in it allied themselves with these peace activists. The revisionists, partly serious historians, partly peace propagandists, essentially advanced the theory that the peace progressives who voted against the war had analyzed the conflict correctly, and that therefore by implication the 1920s European policy of the Senate dissenters also had some technical merit. The revisionists, whether of the moderate or hard-line variety, all agreed that Article 231 of the Versailles Treaty, which held Germany guilty for the outbreak of the war, did not stand up under historical analysis. The less scholarly efforts tended to claim that the fault for the origination of the war lay with the Allies, and that therefore the United States had possessed no reason to enter the conflict. The most important of these early revisionists, Harry Elmer Barnes, a professor of historical sociology at Smith College, made the case that the United States had gone to war to protect Allied bonds, and that the Allies were primarily responsible for the outbreak of the war. Much more so than any of the other revisionists, Barnes attracted an enthusiastic following in American liberal circles. By the end of the decade his branch of the revisionists became as interested in avoiding a future conflict as in writing serious history. Frederick Bausman, another revisionist and a contemporary of Dill as a power in the Washington Democratic party, spent the 1920s trying to root out the influence of alleged British propaganda in the U.S. system, while Barnes attacked the power of militarism in American society and celebrated the war outlawry movement. Also, the war debt controversies, particularly with France, strengthened the case of a group that argued that countries like France bore responsibility for the war. The revisionists at least implicitly contributed to the anti-French feeling fed upon by the peace progressives.[35]

The radical peace activists and the revisionists combined to create an intellectual atmosphere quite similar to that experienced by Woodrow Wilson during the preceding decade. They and the dissenters enjoyed close relationships, regularly exchanging ideas and assisting one another whenever possible. By giving the ideas of the Senate dissenters a wider audience, these groups increased the level of public support for the peace progressives; by addressing issues that the peace progressives had not considered, they gave the senators new fodder for use in debate. They also presented a radical and thorough critique of American foreign relations that fitted well with the general peace progressive mindset, particularly in the increasing attention given to anti-imperialism and relations with Latin America.

Though clearly stronger and more focused in the 1920s, factions with proposals similar to those of some of the radical groups had existed during the late 1910s. Another element of the 1920s radical coalition was peculiar to the decade. Called by one of their number the "muckrakers of imperialism,"[36] these figures, alternatively historians, publicists, journalists, and lobbyists for their causes, helped give the anti-imperialist ideas of the peace progressives a wider public forum. In a different and technically more objective way from the peace activists and the dissenting senators, these men and women introduced the American public to Latin America.

Oswald Garrison Villard, the pacifist editor of *The Nation* who reached the height of his influence during the 1920s, gave the anti-imperialists constant editorial support and employed several of them—either as editors or as freelance writers—during the decade. Unsurprisingly, given his interests, Villard commented on a wide variety of issues, regularly touching upon European and military developments as well as Latin American matters. The editor consulted with all the leading peace progressives on his frequent visits from New York to Washington, and although he did not agree with the dissenters on all issues, he generally supported their foreign policy positions in the pages of his journal, which enjoyed something of a circulation boom during the 1920s.[37]

The Nation became the magazine most identified with the campaign to end the Haitian occupation. Villard justified his activism on the basis of his doubts that anyone "could get the truth out of a Marine officer in Haiti." After the "whitewash" of the McCormick Committee and the failure of the King Amendment, when most others lost interest in Haiti, Villard did not, blasting Louis Borno in 1926 for overseeing a government that made Haiti "safe for almost everybody except the Haitians." When the issue revived after the Port-au-Prince riots in 1929, Villard personally and through Gruening lobbied two members of the Forbes Commission (James Kerney and William Allen White), worrying that a commission led by a man "extremely tarred with the Leonard Wood point of view" again could produce a whitewash. (Kerney supplied him with confidential information from the commission for the duration of its existence and, telling Freda Kirchwey that he viewed it as his "job to kick the Marines in the rump," said that he would "put the Marines out of Haiti for [Villard] or bust a gut.") Villard's opposition to the Haitian occupation formed a small part of his larger disgust with administration Caribbean Basin policy. He lamented that Hughes, "ruined by office and ambition," had made a "rapid descent" from this days as a progressive-oriented governor and had based his Mexican policy upon an "antiquated conception" of private property, while Obregón stood for a "generous conception of human rights." *The Nation* sympathized "unreservedly with the Mexican government"; Villard could not remember the United States' ever acting "so openly and unblushingly at the behest of the a portion of Big Business" as in its attempt to force Obregón to overturn Article 27.[38]

These attitudes naturally led to a strong opposition to the Kellogg Nicaraguan policy, which Villard compared to the French efforts to remove the Syrian "bandits." He called for Congress to assert its constitutional rights in the way that Dill had done when he "had much the best" of his debate with Bruce; *The Nation* also wanted the government to begin negotiations with Sandino, a man "of the breed of George Washington and the other great rebels of the past." Villard chastised the "shameless hypocrisy" of Coolidge's Havana address, wondering if the President thought that he was speaking to the American Legion. He also stung Borah for changing his mind, reminding the senator that the "first duty we owe" was to stop Kellogg's "private war." When Borah was not persuaded, Villard criticized him publicly, writing that Coolidge probably guffawed when he heard senators like Borah "stand up and with straight faces announce that the Marines must stay in Nicaragua to teach the benighted Latins all about voting"; from Villard's point of view, the Marines were killing people, not teaching democracy.[39]

Villard shared the peace progressive perspective on many other foreign policy issues as well. The distrust of the military shown in his critique of Nicaraguan affairs spilled over into Villard's disarmament positions; he wanted to "strip war both of its glory and its appeal to the ideal." Calling for vigilance in light of the fact that "military and naval propaganda is unceasingly at work," Villard urged the creation of a Department of Peace, which he hoped would balance the propaganda put out by the War Department; the department could establish an International Peace University to offset West Point, sponsor world friendship cruises to counter stops by the Navy, and authorize the building of peace monuments to compete with war memorials.[40] Villard also shared the negative view of the French and Italians held by the peace progressives, rebuking the "cowardly and stupid militarism" of France's "cynical, cold-blooded . . . plan to . . . enslave millions" of Ruhr Germans and condemning the French for practicing a Syrian policy that amounted to "raining death from the air upon defenseless villages." On the reverse side, he praised the Germany as the brightest spot of Europe and commended the Germans for their complete repudiation of militarism. Villard did not, however, support keeping the United States from all European political commitments, and he rather consistently supported American membership in the World Court.[41]

Anti-imperialism remained at the core of Villard's foreign policy ideology. In a critique of outlawry in 1922, Villard called for a "thorough-going campaign against imperialism" that would "require the advocate of peace to get to the root of imperialism." Peace among the great powers could not occur until imperialism ceased, since "no nation can bully the weak in the economic or political field, and then expect to be able to lay the economic or spiritual basis for world peace among the strong." Villard openly sympathized with revolutionary movements in the underdeveloped world, terming the rise of Gandhi of "unique significance," since the Indian sought not just political freedom but economic and cultural independence as well. Early in the decade Villard called revolts of weaker peoples against unjust settlements the most encouraging trend since the war, and he hoped that the "newly awakening race consciousness" would end colonialism soon.[42]

One of Villard's closest confidantes was Ernest Gruening, who became extremely active on behalf of Haitian independence after Villard named him managing editor of *The Nation* in 1921. To investigate matters firsthand, Gruening visited Haiti in late 1921, admitting that he desired to screen witnesses who would testify before the McCormick Committee (hoping to "eliminate" shaky material) while performing what he called a "diplomatic function," mediating between Haitian opposition groups with differing ideas on how to end the occupation. Gruening questioned the morality and practicality of a policy that amounted to making an American military man "supreme legislator, supreme judge, supreme executor" in both Haiti and the neighboring Dominican Republic; he wondered how the Haitians could learn democracy given that the military authorities defined an agitator as "anyone opposed to the presence of an alien military, to martial law, to the overthrow of Haitian sovereignty." Proof that "the United States clearly tried to gain control of these republics" for economic reasons lay in the American-sponsored changes in the Haitian land law that had dispossessed Haitian peasants of their lands in favor of American-owned corporations. Gruening went well beyond merely telling the story, serving as a prominent opposition witness during the McCormick Committee hearings; fluent in French and well traveled in Haiti, he told the committee that all Haitians except a few collaborators opposed the occupation, wanted an abrogation of the 1915 Haitian-American treaty and 1917 American-imposed constitution, and did not desire further American loans or customs collection lest such measures perpetuate the occupation. After the committee failed to recommend withdrawal, Gruening, through his position on the Advisory Council to the Haiti–Santo Domingo Independence Society, "played a leading role in the formation of a Haitian resistance movement," coordinating antioccupation activities in the United States, helping to raise money for the Union Patriotique, and suggesting many of the English-language slogans used by Haitian protesters when the McCormick Committee members visited Port-au-Prince. Gruening spent several months in Washington lobbying on behalf of the King Amendment. He also organized Borah's antioccupation speech in Carnegie Hall, in the process meeting most of the leading peace progressives.[43]

Although Gruening was unsuccessful in his efforts concerning Haiti, his contacts served him well; after Villard had to lay him off because of financial difficulties at *The Nation*, Gruening signed on as national publicity director for the 1924 La Follette presidential campaign. The editor had begun the year working with Villard to reestablish the moribund Anti-Imperialist League along significantly more radical lines, aiming at the "restoration of full liberty to all countries within the sphere of our economic influence and the exposure of the mechanics of the United States imperialism under which the machinery of the Government is used to further purely private interests." During the presidential campaign Gruening regularly produced press releases assuring that a La Follette presidency would stand "against the imperialism that leads to oppression and war" while solving the "discontent with the efforts to destroy our democracy, to override the Constitution." Gruening also promised that a La Follette State Department would favor "arbitration and conciliation" while helping in "turning out old-time diplomacy and creating new and liberal governments."[44]

Election day found Gruening off to Mexico City, where he observed the inauguration of Plutarco Calles as the President's personal guest. The editor described the Calles administration as "the most important four-year period in Mexican history" and dismissed those who raised the charge of Bolshevism, a "convenient term to qualify any method (other than ours) to try to bring archaic governmental and social forms up to date." Although he conceded that a difference existed between the Mexican and American "races," Gruening denied that the Mexicans were inferior, and as the 1920s progressed he seemed to begin believing the opposite. Calles earned even greater praise than Obregón for his "epoch-making" decision to decrease the power of the Army, proving that a fairly large nation could conduct an antimilitarist policy. Gruening sharply criticized the Kellogg-Sheffield Mexican diplomacy. He worked for an alternative policy by inviting prominent Mexicans, such as Secretary of Industry Luis Morones, widely perceived as the most radical figure in the Mexican cabinet, to the United States for small meetings (often held at the New York City Harvard Club) with friendly American journalists. This activity earned him the ire of the administration. The State Department file on Gruening listed him as a "radical and professional propagandist" and issued instructions that he was to be "watched carefully" by the embassy in Mexico City to obtain some "definite proof" that this "chief of Calles' press agents in the United States" was in the pay of the Mexican government. Sheffield, who believed it a "moral certainty" that Gruening was a key figure in a multimillion-dollar Mexican propaganda program designed to sway public opinion in the United States, needed no further encouragement, and the ambassador had his consuls throughout the country looking for damaging information on one-third of "a Jewish radical trinity which has been active in Mexico in recent years." Kellogg confined himself to the more substantive charge that a member of the Foreign Relations Committee (probably Shipstead) was using Gruening as a conduit to funnel confidential information to Calles that, despite administration rhetoric, the United States would not break diplomatic relations. Even Sheffield, though, conceded that "we are governed in America by public opinion" and that Gruening and his allies had persuaded the American public to such an extent that the public "would not support a movement for armed intervention in Mexico."[45]

Although he concentrated on Haiti and Mexico, Gruening fell within the mainstream of the peace progressive movement on other issues as well. He rebuked Borah for reversing his long-standing opposition to the Nicaraguan occupation "over a technicality," noting that it was "always possible for those who perform an illegal act to allege a commitment." By 1929, though, he praised the Idaho senator's work on behalf of Kellogg-Briand and blasted the cruisers bill, teaming with Frederick Libby in the national campaign against the naval increase. Gruening argued that "we must have faith in diplomacy and in suasion to keep others from building too recklessly," and contended that the United States, with no conceivable foreign threats, should make a four-year commitment to pressuring other nations to disarm before adding any more ships to the Navy. Gruening also expressed disappointment with the London Naval Conference, where he felt that "our delegation talked the archaic language of diplomacy" at a time when bold action was needed; he termed the American refusal to scrap more battleships "grotesque."[46]

Sheffield also kept a watchful eye on Carleton Beals ("an alleged radical socialist"), who within two years would emerge as the most prominent of the muckrakers of imperialism. Like Gruening, Beals sympathized with the Mexican revolutionary leaders, and he had particular praise for the Calles foreign policy. Although he denied that Mexico had ever interfered in the internal affairs of another Latin American country, he conceded that Mexico City had "assisted" in the installations of both the Solórzano and Sacasa Puerto Cabazas regimes. Nonetheless, Beals found it "difficult to think" of Mexico playing an imperialist role in the region, and he argued that Mexican expansion differed from its American counterpart in that the Mexicans stressed cultural expansion with a heavy dose of pan-Americanism. Since Mexico relied on cultural power and Washington on military force, Beals saw the United States outmaneuvered "diplomatically and morally" in Central America, a situation he felt would continue until the State Department initiated a consistent, culturally based policy toward Latin America. Beals portrayed Mexico as a peaceful and evolving nation engaging in a long-needed social revolution that presented no threat to the United States and actually in some ways could serve as a model for American policy.[47]

Beals attracted the most public attention, however, for his multiple-part series in *The Nation* on Sandino, which appeared just when U.S. Marines were combing the American countryside in search of the guerrilla leader and the Senate was considering the Blaine Amendment. Beals found Sandino "utterly without vices" and possessed of an "unequivocal sense of personal justice," a brilliant general whose abilities, luck, and excellent intelligence would allow him to remain in the field indefinitely. Beals then quoted Sandino at length, giving the guerrilla an unparalleled opportunity to speak directly to the American public. Sandino charged that Coolidge's claim of protecting American life and property merely constituted a "pretext" for intervention. The guerrilla leader claimed that "we are no more bandits than was Washington," and if the American public could not recognize this, it had "become calloused [*sic*] to justice"; he denied that Nicaragua could ever have a free election under Marine supervision and with a "constitution Made-in-America." Sandino reserved his most bitter criticism for the American military, which he charged considered "every civilian a combatant and treat[ed] him accordingly"; Beals backed him up (on this as well as virtually every other point), describing in detailed (unproved) Sandinist stories of Marine atrocities. The articles had considerable effect. Almost immediately after their publication C. C. Dill cited them for his description of Nicaraguan politics in his Senate debate with Bruce; later Norris borrowed Sandino's characterization of himself as the George Washington of Nicaragua. Sandino obviously did not win universal praise in the United States—Kellogg spoke for many conservatives when he remarked that the rebels represented "in effect nothing more than common outlaws," while Henry Stimson bitterly complained that the "comparative superiority of facility enjoyed by revolutionist propaganda in reaching America had quite seriously warped the accuracy of American news." But by giving the American public a view of Sandino that squared with the one presented by the peace progressives in Senate debate and strongly differed from the one offered by Kellogg and Coolidge, Beals strengthened the peace progressives' political position in the Senate.[48]

Anti-imperialism was also an element in the efforts of the NAACP and its executive secretary, James Weldon Johnson, to end the occupation of Haiti. Johnson included a racial element in his critique, doubting that Washington ever "will win absolute confidence and goodwill of the Latin American people so long as there is in this country a Negro problem." He toured Haiti during the spring of 1920 and returned to publish a series of articles in *The Nation* that denounced the harshness of American military tactics, charged the National City Bank with initiating the occupation, and posited that the occupation stood counter to traditional American ideals. The articles also helped to inject the Haitian issue into the 1920 presidential campaign and may have contributed to vice-presidential candidate Roosevelt's faux pas of claiming to have authored the Haitian constitution. Johnson and the NAACP strongly pushed a congressional investigation of the occupation following Harding's inauguration, which the President, since he had raised the issue so prominently during the campaign, had little choice but to endorse. (At the same time, though, Johnson refused a request by Gruening to have the NAACP organize a letter-writing campaign on behalf of the King Amendment, saying that the anti-lynching bill stood as his highest priority and he did not want to spread his organization too thin.) After the committee's failure to recommend an end to the occupation and the defeat of the King Amendment, Johnson charged that the Senate had refused to address the question of "the international and moral right of the United States to usurp, substitute, or control the government of any country against the will of the people," and he continued to work closely with Union Patriotique forces in both Washington and Port-au-Prince, arousing the ire of John Russell, who charged in a report to Hughes that Johnson, Gruening, and Villard bore some of the responsibility for continued Haitian unrest.[49]

In addition to books and articles by Gruening, Beals, and Johnson, a host of other works critical of American policy in Latin America appeared during the 1920s. The radical line of thought, which included works by former Senator Pettigrew and, more important, Scott Nearing, culminated in Parker Moon's massive 1926 study, *Imperialism in World Politics*, which placed U.S. policy toward the Caribbean Basin in the context of a worldwide imperialist trend that had begun in the nineteenth century; Moon's central argument was that "imperialism seeks to relieve the pressure of surplus goods and surplus capital on a temporarily saturated market." After the book's publication, Moon turned to chairing the Research Committee on Latin America, a theoretically nonpartisan organization sponsored by Columbia University designed to fund original research in Latin American affairs. (Moon, ironically, had remained sympathetic to Wilsonianism through the League of Nations fight but, like many Wilsonians, was attracted by the vibrancy of the 1920s anti-imperialist movement.) A number of more specialized studies also appeared during the 1920s. The American Fund for Public Service sponsored a series of books edited by Harry Elmer Barnes that examined the effects of American foreign investments on "the civilization, culture, and political institutions of the countries involved," with particular attention devoted to the relationship between American investors and State Department policy; as Barnes observed, "it was natural that [the series] should first turn to Latin America." Margaret Marsh's *The Bankers in Bolivia* traced Bolivian relations with the American banking community during the 1920s, sympathetically describing the plight faced by the various weak La Paz regimes that desperately needed foreign capital for economic development and political survival. La Follette cited her book in 1928 in his critical survey of U.S.–Latin American relations. Studies of Cuba and the Dominican Republic offered a similarly sympathetic perspective.[50]

All of these works, and the articles and newspaper editorials that accompanied them, aided the peace progressives by keeping the Latin American interventions before the public eye, in sharp contrast to the 1910s, when comparatively little was published in the United States on Latin American policy.[51] The anti-imperialists served a broader role, however; in the days before large congressional staffs, they, along with elements of the peace movement, helped provide the peace progressives with the details needed to sustain the dissenting case in Senate debate. Perhaps the best example of this was Burton Wheeler's habit of holding conferences of peace activists in his Senate office to discuss the future of inter-American affairs,[52] but Levinson, Gumberg, Gruening, Detzer, and officers of the FOR, WILPF, and NCPW all regularly supplied the peace progressives with statistical and factual information on foreign policy matters that they felt would be helpful to the senators in

Senate debates on international relations. They also acted as de facto public relations operatives for the peace progressive position, much as the better-known muckrakers had done for the domestic positions of the progressives in the 1900s and early 1910s. The senators and the anti-imperialists had a mutually beneficial relationship, with each strengthening the other's position;[53] both sought to make Latin America an important issue for the American public.

Finally, the decade featured the rise of individual or group activists who aimed solely at improving American relations with Latin America. Samuel Guy Inman, a Protestant missionary and instructor in the Columbia University Extension School who served as Director of the Committee on Cooperation in Latin America (CCLA), developed a broad critique of Latin American policy. Inman prodded the CCLA, which up until the early 1920s had been concerned solely with Protestant missionary work in Latin America, to become "active with a larger version of its task than ever before" and to work to move inter-American relations "away from political complications and . . . commercial dominance" and toward social and cultural issues with a long-term goal of creating "a collective conscience" in the Western Hemisphere. He went public with these sentiments in a controversial but widely discussed *Atlantic Monthly* article in 1924, singling out for exploration countries over which the United States exercised financial control but "not yet" military dominance. He also criticized (and correctly analyzed) the Hughes-Kellogg policy of attempting to incorporate Latin America completely into the American sphere by using "refunding" loans that lessened the influence of European capital in the region, and by increasingly supplying the Latin American states with U.S. arms, of which the American naval mission to Brazil served as the most recent example. Inman hypothesized that such a policy weakened the standing of the United States in the world and encouraged the Latin American states to move away from it and try to increase their political ties with Europe. Blaine used these theories in 1928 Senate debates. Like Gruening, Inman also invited prominent Mexicans (in his case mostly professors and literary figures) to New York for small lunches with sympathetic Americans. From Mexico City, James Sheffield called on the State Department to do something to combat such "professorial propaganda," while the Hughes State Department prepared both a public and private response to the "glaring untruths" and "irresponsible criticism" contained in the Inman arguments.[54]

Inman's organization worked to inform the American public better about conditions in Latin America. A similar group with an even more pro–Latin American viewpoint was the Committee on Cultural Relations with Latin America (CCRLA), described by Gruening as the decade's "most useful and vital project in promoting international relations, especially inter-American relations." Founded by Hubert Herring, executive secretary of the Social Relations Department of the Congregational Church, the CCRLA promoted "the furthering of mutual understanding and appreciation between the peoples of the United States and of the Latin American republics" by increasing American knowledge "of the life and culture of the Latin American peoples." It made a mark in late 1926 when it sent a thirty-member mission (selected by Herring to include members who "will be able to exert wide influence on American public opinion") to Mexico at the height of the tensions over Calles' oil and land laws, believing that "each country has much to offer the other through the interchange of cultures and ideas." Herring rebuked the "arrogance" of Kellogg's "reiterated insistence on legal rights," which he contended had poisoned what should have been a "free and open attitude of friendly cooperation." The mission drew front-page headlines in the United States when Calles met with it in early January 1927 and stated his willingness to arbitrate U.S.-Mexican differences, increasing public pressure on Coolidge and helping to smooth the way for passage of the Robinson Resolution. After the success of the initial conference, Herring, who believed that it was "idle to talk of peace" when U.S.-Mexican relations remained tense, made the event an annual one, guiding over 200 (generally prominent) Americans through a series of lectures and field trips on Mexican culture and the role that a celebration of culture could play in international relations. He also expanded the program to include a Seminar on the Caribbean, designed as a "cooperative study of the chief Caribbean peoples with special reference to their relations with the United States." Gruening and Beals were regular lecturers at the seminars (which took place in the host country), as was Moises Sáenz, Mexico's Minister of Agriculture and brother of Kellogg's nemesis in the Mexican Foreign Ministry. Even at the decade's end, when inter-American tensions had eased somewhat, the CCRLA maintained that "there is no more important aspect of our international relations than in the Latin American field." The effectiveness of the CCRLA was shown in part by the fury that it aroused. Kellogg complained that the "cranks" who belonged to the group "are *never* in favor of their own country," while Sheffield likewise fumed that CCRLA members "seem to care more for the interests of other countries and other peoples than their own."[55]

The emergence of the anti-imperialists cemented the intellectual bond that had developed between the organized peace movement and the peace progressives. The anti-imperialists, like the dissenting senators, sought in the end to decrease the importance of traditional power politics and to increase the role played by cultural and ideological exchange in international relations. Although the CCRLA addressed the issue the most squarely, all the anti-imperialists sought to improve the image of Latin Americans in the United States with a hope that if Americans thought of their southern neighbors as human beings with common ideals and shared characteristics they would be less likely to support military interventions in Latin America. This vision obviously separated the peace activists from their conservative opponents, who consistently depreciated Latin American culture. (Sheffield characterized Mexico as "four hundred years behind the times," while William Howard Taft worried that the Stimson Tipitapa mission might fail because Stimson lacked sufficient experience "with Spanish-descended mongrels.") The cultural perspective also provided the key distinction between the anti-imperialists and the peace activists who retained the 1910s perspective, for whom Carrie Chapman Catt spoke when she remarked (upon hearing of plans to endow a series of university chairs in Spanish-American literature as a way to foster closer inter-American relations) that "it is not that I do not appreciate the value of culture, but that is not my line."[56] Meanwhile, virtually all peace activists believed that solving Latin American issues peacefully formed a critical step in achieving their overall program for the reform of U.S. foreign policy. In this sense the anti-imperialists and the peace activists worked toward the same end throughout the decade.

A series of developments within the peace movement during the 1920s worked to the advantage of the peace progressives. First of all, the fracturing of the prewar conservative progressive peace ideology, which was hostile to the peace progressive perspective during the 1910s and remained so (to a lesser degree) during the 1920s, opened up the way for more radical groups to become key players within the peace movement. Second, the increasing attention that the activists of these groups gave to anti-imperialism and antimilitarism, the two key peace progressive issues during the decade, substantially strengthened the foreign policy public attuned to peace progressive ideals. Third, the Senate dissenters benefited from the willingness of members of many of these organizations to function as de facto foreign policy staffs for the dissenting senators. This intellectual alliance thus aided the peace progressives during the 1920s in the same way that it had bolstered Woodrow Wilson during the 1910s. Finally, the convergence of ideas between the peace progressives and diverse elements of the peace movement (even on European affairs, clearly the weakest spot of the dissenters) casts serious doubt on any theory that the dissenting senators adopted the foreign policy positions that they did because of regional or ethnic biases.

7

The Collapse of Wilsonianism

Logic would have dictated that the peace movement turn for political support to the opposition party in the Senate, the Democrats, whose national party platforms in both 1924 and 1928 bitterly condemned Republican foreign policy. The 1924 platform supported a national war referendum, the drafting of capital during wartime, and a "strict and sweeping reduction of armaments by land and sea"; in 1928 the platform took issue with Coolidge for using the marines to enforce "unratified" arrangements with foreign governments.[1] Yet this rhetoric papered over substantial Democratic divisions so deep that in the course of the 1920s at least six separate Democratic foreign policy ideologies emerged, revealing the almost complete collapse of Wilsonianism in the party in which the ideology was founded. The Democratic performance during the decade thus calls into question any assumption that the Wilsonianism of the 1910s was linked with its counterpart in the 1930s.[2] What Young Bob La Follette termed the "patent collapse of the Democratic Party in Congress" reinforced the peace progressive position as the alternative to G.O.P. foreign policy.[3] As Akira Iriye[4] has established, Wilsonianism maintained broad appeal during the 1920s, but, in sharp contrast to the 1910s, at least within the Congress, Wilsonianism did not possess a partisan political vehicle.

A Democratic core did exist, coalescing around a centrist bloc that contained some of the biggest names in the decade's Senate. Headed

236

by Claude Swanson (Virginia), dubbed by the *New York Times* "the party's chief spokesman in the Senate on international affairs," and Minority Leader Joe Robinson (Arkansas), this bloc also featured Key Pittman (Nevada), chair of the Foreign Relations Committee during the 1930s, and Wilson's Secretary of the Treasury, Carter Glass (Virginia). Although they called themselves Wilsonians, the centrists reduced the Wilsonian agenda to support for the League and particularly the World Court. Swanson was the most important Senate backer of Court membership even though the Coolidge administration formally sponsored it. The Virginia senator addressed several of Borah's criticisms, specifically denying that any more linkage existed between the Court and the League than between the Congress and the Supreme Court, describing the League as "simply . . . an agent" used by the Court to facilitate the selection of judges. Swanson also persuaded more skeptical Democrats to accept the compromise fifth reservation (which allowed the United States to prevent the Court from entertaining requests for advisory opinions on matters in which the United States claimed an interest) while strongly opposing what he called the dilatory reservations put up by the peace progressives. He aimed in the long term for a Court with broad powers to assist in collective security, since "the right and wrong of war is largely gauged by the way the nation involved has violated or followed international law." Backing up his colleague, Robinson structured a deal with G.O.P. leaders to enact cloture, cutting off the peace progressive–led filibuster. After the refusal of League powers to accept American membership with the submitted reservations, other members of the center group, Carter Glass and Park Trammell (Florida), led the Senate fight to remove the fifth reservation and allow the United States to enter the Court.[5]

The centrists' view of Wilsonianism went little beyond this point, however; they supported League entry much more weakly. Pittman, through his position on the platform committee, helped frustrate attempts to get an unequivocal pro-League plank inserted into the 1924 Democratic platform, telling the convention that all genuine supporters of the League should seek to make the issue a nonpartisan one. This left the centrists to rhetoric such as Carter Glass's comment that he favored the League "body and soul" or to acting on their own to increase public support for the League, as when Morris Sheppard (Texas) gave a five-hour address in 1921 describing in the most minute detail all the League's accomplishments since its founding. In general, though, the centrists had no trouble with letting the League issue wane, and instead concentrated on increasing American cooperation with existing League agencies. Swanson urged American participation in League disarmament conferences as the only possible route to effective disarmament, while Robinson pushed American membership in the League-backed Reparations Committee, which he viewed as a positive step in aiding American commerce and stopping the spread of "continued revolution" in Europe. While proposals like these made the centrists considerably more pro-League than either their Republican or peace progressive colleagues, they did not mirror the LNNPA platform either.[6]

Although the positions of the centrists on League-related issues may have pleased most elements in the peace movement, few of the group's other positions reflected the idealistic strains of Wilsonianism, in large part because of Swanson's influence. Although the Virginian served as ranking senator on both the Foreign Relations and Naval Affairs Committees, the Navy was his passion. Swanson, denouncing the "folly" of leaving "our national safety and our vital interests only to peace preachments," believed that American naval parity with other leading powers formed the "best guarantee . . . of a continuation of peace." In general, he felt that "there has been too much unjust criticism of naval people and naval activities." He looked to rectify this in his defense of the Navy leadership for its handling of the Mitchell case, blocking a congressional investigation on Mitchell's behalf on the grounds that the Navy always conducted its inquiries "fairly and completely." During the cruisers bill debate, he served as a virtual cosponsor of the bill with Frederick Hale, proving considerably more effective than the Maine senator in spelling out a case for a larger Navy. Swanson contended that the United States, as the world's strongest power, needed a larger Navy than in the past, particularly in order to guarantee the overseas trade routes vital to the American economy. Given these needs, he ridiculed those, such as the peace progressives, who advocated more money for air defenses and submarines and less for battleships, since the "object of the Navy is to control the surface of the sea," the key to keeping trade routes open. Without the powerful Navy, "our diplomacy must be vacillating and humiliating," particularly if the British formed a naval pact with either the Japanese or the French. Swanson's influence within his party carried a number of wavering votes with him; despite the fury surrounding the cruisers bill, only five Democrats opposed the administration. In general, the centrists proved consistently hostile to decreasing military spending, regularly siding with the administration on defense votes, and occasionally advocating more funding than the Republicans requested.[7]

On two other issues, the center vigorously fought the peace progressive position. Swanson blasted the dissenters' pro-German leanings and targeted the La Follette 1924 German aid bill for defeat. The Virginia senator saw no evidence of German starvation; on the contrary, Germany stood in a better position than the nations that it had overrun during the war. Swanson wondered why La Follette had not proposed aid for Serbia or Rumania; perhaps "the sympathy is all where the vote is." Although he harbored no "ill will" toward the Germans, he contended that the United States should aid its friends first, and in any case the United States had already exhibited more than enough generosity toward Weimar by not demanding reparations for "Germany's outrages." Later in the decade Swanson, joined by F. M. Simmons (North Carolina), led the opposition to Borah's proposal to return property confiscated from German nationals during the war, contending that Germany had violated international law from 1914 through 1918 and thus had no right to expect any concessions from the United States. The Virginia senator also hinted that Hindenberg's triumph in the 1925 German presidential election "puts Germany under suspicion" and made European affairs "uncertain and possibly threatening." Despite Swanson's pronounced anti-British leanings, then, neither he nor any other member of the center bloc entertained the prospect of an understanding with the Germans.[8]

Nor did the faction favor recognition of the USSR. Key Pittman, praised by the London *Times* as "a singularly able Democrat," conceded the "enticing" nature of Russian resources but argued that "the great question involved is one not of expediency but of principle," namely, the need to combat the Communist party, the "antithesis of our government." Pittman noted that the party, "in its fanaticism, has made slaves of its people, brought on famine, deluged their great country with atheism, blood, and death" to consolidate control. Despite these horrors, though, he said that he would support recognition were it not for the Soviet confiscation of American-owned property, which had "ridiculed the moral principle of international law." The senator added that the United States should recognize only after the Soviet government committed itself to noninterference and abolished the Third International; Duncan Fletcher (Florida) carried Pittman's critique one step further and posited that the State Department should delay recognition until the Soviet government accepted the "sound economic principles" offered it by Herbert Hoover. This proposal went beyond that demanded by Hughes, and obviously it stood a long way from the peace progressive perspective.[9]

The centrists could have made things difficult for the Republican administrations on the debt renegotiations, but they rarely used their power, in large part because Carter Glass provided critical support on both the Italian and French debt votes. The Democrats began the decade by fiercely criticizing the Debt Commission, with thirty-three of thirty-four Democrats agreeing with F. M. Simmons' concern that the bill gave "sweeping, unlimited powers" to the Secretary of the Treasury. After that, however, Glass, described by one commentator as a "sound Democrat" who shared "all of [Grover] Cleveland's fundamental economic soundness," took over, outlining the basics of debt policy to which he would return later in the decade in what the *New York Times* described as an "impassioned plea" for the British debt bill. The Virginia senator supported passage on the admittedly "sentimental" grounds that the United States owed England a moral debt and with the more calculating argument that refinancing would serve the best economic interests of the United States. Glass also doubted the wisdom of criticizing the British for their alleged imperialist activities in the Middle East, hoping instead that London would do "a service to civilization by driving every one of these savage creatures [the Turks] into the unmeasured depths of the Mediterranean Sea." The backing of the prestigious Glass, the acknowledged Democratic leader on foreign economic questions, frustrated Robinson's efforts in 1926 to make the Italian debt vote a referendum on the "sordid, selfish, partisan, and unpatriotic" G.O.P. foreign policy. Beyond that, the centrists often deferred to the peace progressives during debt bill debates, with their only original argument, raised by Swanson and Andrieus Jones (New Mexico), linking solution of the debt problem to opening up the American market by lowering the tariff. In any case the group tended to support the British settlement, oppose the more controversial Italian deal, and divide on the French vote, although on all of these occasions only Glass and Robinson, on opposite sides of the issue, played prominent roles in the Senate debate.[10]

The power political viewpoint associated with the beliefs of Swanson and Glass reappeared in the centrist appraisals of both the Kellogg-Briand Pact and the London Naval Treaty, about which they showed little enthusiasm. Glass characterized Levinson's plan, which he described as a "wan gesture in the direction of peace," as "one of the numerous subterfuges to prevent this nation from joining the League of Nations or the World Court." When the treaty reached the Senate floor, the Virginia senator dismissed it as a "worthless, but perfectly harmless thing." He expressed "no confidence whatsoever in the accomplishment of any good by this alleged pact," since no peace pact "that has not behind it the potential use of the military powers of those nations combined" could ever work. Alben Barkley (Kentucky) delivered only a slightly more positive appraisal of the treaty, offering a very narrow interpretation of the pact under which any aggressive act by any foreign country interpreted by the United States as contrary to its interests would make the treaty null and void; the senator certainly could not sanction the United States' renouncing war if that meant "permitting an infringement of its rights." Barkley further minimized the treaty's impact by claiming that it did not supersede "any obligation that is carried under the League of Nations or the treaty of Locarno," but he favored approval on the grounds that it might contribute in a vague way to the spirit of peace. Both Swanson and Robinson stood closer to Borah during Senate debate on the treaty, although they too expressed skepticism about outlawry at various other times.[11]

While the centrists offended the outlawrists with their position on the Kellogg-Briand Pact, they did little to win anti-imperialist support with their stances on inter-American issues. As on the debt question, this bloc potentially possessed a tremendous amount of power to influence policy, as was shown in 1927 by its unified action on behalf of the Robinson Resolution for arbitration with Mexico. The centrists' coalescing behind the Robinson position came as something of a surprise given their positions on inter-American policy before 1927. All centrists except Lee Overman (North Carolina) voting on the 1922 King Amendment had opposed it, although no bloc member participated in the Haitian debate of that year; as late as 1926, Fletcher continued to defend the occupation as necessary to maintain order. The Florida senator exhibited similar sentiments toward revolutionary Mexico, urging nonrecognition on the grounds that Obregón had "manifested no disposition to get away from [Article 27,] that harsh and absurd provision of the Mexican Constitution." As U.S.-Mexican relations began to worsen in 1926, the centrists sent conflicting signals. Swanson opposed intervention in mid-1926 but backtracked later in the year with the cryptic comment that if Mexico did not "carry out her understandings and keep faith with the conditions under which recognition was accrued," the United States could then consider "what action would be necessary to give proper protection to property and citizens." Robinson, always less keen on intervention than Swanson, played the key role in uniting the bloc around arbitration, saying that his resolution would allow the Senate to prove to the world that the United States did not bully its neighbors and immediately use force for resolving disputes; the Arkansas senator asked his colleagues to keep in mind the fact that "for some reason, just or unjust, the United States has grown unpopular" in Latin America.[12]

Robinson's comment revealed an ambivalence about the American position in Latin America that also appeared during debate on Nicaraguan policy. Quite unlike the peace progressives, the centrists recognized the political weakness of the United States in the region, but never could understand why Latin Americans did not like the United States. Although the Nicaraguan occupation troubled the centrists, most sided with the administration on the Blaine Amendment vote. Glass termed it a "very grave mistake" to repudiate the moral obligation of the United States, while Fletcher worried that the amendment's vague wording could deny funding for a "perfectly friendly intervention" in a country like Haiti, China, or Panama. Swanson agreed with Borah (to whom he deferred consistently during the debate) that the United States needed to carry out Tipitapa to "keep national faith," and he also dismissed Blaine's constitutional arguments. Less important centrists, however, disagreed with their leaders. Pittman supported the Blaine Amendment out of fear that its defeat would prove foreign charges of American imperialism, although he obtained from Blaine for the price of his support a rider amendment stating that the President maintained the right to act without congressional assent "in case of actual physical attacks upon American citizens or their property." Other centrists were more aggressive; both Walter George (Georgia) and Thaddeus Caraway (Arkansas) persistently and effectively questioned Swanson and Borah during the latters' attempts to justify their support for Kellogg. Only in the early 1930s did the centrists become aggressive opponents of G.O.P. Nicaraguan policy; as with Mexican arbitration, Robinson's decision in 1931 to sponsor a Blaine-like amendment for Nicaragua indicated a shifting of political forces within the Senate and spelled the end of congressional authorization for the occupation.[13]

Alongside these centrist beliefs existed a sometimes sharp nationalism that did not fit particularly well with the group's claim as the Senate bloc most "adhering to the principles of Woodrow Wilson." Nearly all favored stringent immigration restriction. W. J. Harris (Georgia), probably the strongest Senate supporter of the cause, protested against "unrestricted immigration" when "there are millions of Americans seeking a chance to work," while Sheppard opposed any further immigration "from the overcrowded and pauperized sections of the globe," since the "old pre–Civil War American stock is diminishing." (Sheppard's comment foreshadowed a broader centrist critique of the Four Power Treaty on the grounds that its consultative clauses could force the United States to give up immigration restriction.) Occasionally, bald anti-European rhetoric also crept into centrist comments. Early in the decade Harris, Simmons, and Trammell all called for rigorous collection of the wartime debts; Simmons feared that the Europeans would use "all the power and all the ingenuity so characteristic of European diplomats and financiers" to force cancellation. As with Latin America, the centrists seemed unable to understand the anti-American feeling in Europe, and so began attributing it to anti-American propaganda orchestrated by European politicians to distract attention from domestic problems. The sometimes intemperate Caraway leveled this charge in 1922, but the far more moderate Swanson concurred in 1926. The peace progressives occasionally issued similar statements, but generally they tied them to their more global policy rather than simply leveling them alone, and in any case the peace progressives did not claim to stand as the heirs of Wilsonian internationalism.[14]

Even the centrist performance on the issue that most interested many of the senators—the tariff—indicated a trend away from a Wilsonian position. Swanson and Glass compiled the two most extreme low-tariff records of any senator during votes on Hawley-Smoot amendments, and several other centrists also provided articulate defenses of the party's traditional low-tariff position. As early as 1922, however, Pittman argued that there were "very few, if any, absolute free traders in the Democratic party in the Senate"; six years later, as the party's national campaign spokesman on the issue, he revealed that as of 1928, since the "theory of the low tariff has ceased to exist," both parties "are in favor of a tariff and both are opposed to free trade or an unreasonably high tariff." The Nevada senator stated that the Congress had a "duty to allow all of our industries to prosper without fear of destruction from foreign goods manufactured by cheap labor," and he called for a tariff policy that "goes further" than merely equalizing the cost of production between the United States and foreign nations. Pittman's position flowed from his overall view that economic competition formed the central tenet of American foreign policy. Not all Democratic senators agreed with Pittman's analysis, but enough did so that by 1930 and Hawley-Smoot a substantial faction of Democrats favored higher tariffs, more than making up for the slight peace progressive trend in favor of freer trade.[15]

A small group of Democrats aligned with the centrists took the group's nationalist and partisan tendencies far more seriously and spent much of the decade trying to use foreign policy to embarrass the Republicans. Chief among the demagogues was "Cotton Tom" Heflin (Alabama), who believed that the Jesuits were plotting to poison him to quiet his exposé of attempts by the Catholic Church, through the Knights of Columbus, to foment a war between the United States and Mexico. Later in the decade he investigated an alleged attempt by Mussolini to extend "Fascist terrorization tactics" and other "intrigues" to the United States. Heflin loudly opposed the Kellogg policy in Mexico and later appeared as one of the strongest Senate supporters of the peace progressives during the Nicaraguan debate; both policies he attributed to a mixture of two "devilish interests," the "money power" of Wall Street and the hierarchy of the Roman Catholic Church. In European matters, Heflin supported World Court membership and detected a plot behind the expressions of Senate opposition, although he also criticized all the debt refinancing schemes, the work of "certain innocent, raw, and inexperienced Republican diplomats" trying to sell the country out to the Europeans. Unlike the peace progressives, however, Heflin was not merely anti-France; the Alabama senator attempted to revive wartime fervor in a long speech against the La Follette plan for economic assistance to Germany. The sincerity of most of Heflin's foreign policy positions was open to question. While blasting Coolidge over Nicaragua, for example, he maintained that he nonetheless wanted the President "to be foot-loose and free" in the protection of the rights of American nationals overseas. Also, Heflin supported the Nicaraguan canal idea just as strongly as he had opposed the occupation one year earlier, congratulating Walter Edge on his good work. While toying with the antimilitarist feelings in vogue during the decade, Heflin also called for a Navy sufficient to carry American cargoes all over the world. No other centrist held the demagogic or nationalist sentiments of Heflin, but he did reflect feelings present to a degree in the larger group.[16]

The Democratic center offered an example of both the power and the weakness of Woodrow Wilson. During his presidency Wilson commanded a remarkable degree of unity from Senate Democrats, approaching 90 percent on most second-term foreign policy issues. By 1921, his eight years in the White House had shattered the previously existing Democratic orthodoxy—the ideology of the Bacon/Rayner era—while also instilling in the party a deep and genuine commitment to internationalism through the World Court. Wilson failed, however, to reshape the party completely; the center had few core beliefs on questions not relating to political cooperation with Europe. In addition, the senators often either shied away from international affairs altogether—only Swanson, Glass, and Robinson played important foreign policy roles, and quite often they supported the administration—or made their foreign policy decisions in the context of local political needs. Perhaps the most crass example of this came in "Cotton Ed" Smith's 1929 votes on naval and Nicaraguan matters; when chastised by Burton Wheeler for supporting the administration to ensure a steady supply of work for the Charleston Naval Shipyard even though he disagreed with its policy, the South Carolina senator freely admitted that he had engaged in pork-barrel politics, though adding that he had only copied this kind of strategy from the Republicans.[17] Smith's case was extreme but by no means unique. The center's lack of interest in foreign policy contributed to the de facto Democratic decision to forfeit its opposition role on foreign policy matters, creating a vacuum eventually filled by the peace progressives. The senators also attempted to modify the teachings of Wilson along what they viewed as more conservative and realistic lines. They certainly did not carry the Wilsonian banner against an anti-Wilsonian series of Republican administrations.

While the center did not present a unified ideological alternative to the Republicans, another Democratic faction did. The decade featured the rise of a small group of Wilsonian idealists headed by Thomas Walsh (Montana), Pat Harrison (Mississippi), and, after 1927, Hugo Black (Alabama), who accepted Wilson's statements at face value and applied them to the foreign policy questions of the day. In Walsh and Harrison, the idealists had two of the more prominent national Democrats of the decade. Walsh first gained national attention as a spokesman for Western progressivism with his election to the Senate in 1912; during the war he stayed faithful to the President, and during the League of Nations fight he emerged as one of Wilson's most trusted lieutenants. When faced with peace progressive attacks about his support for Articles X and XI, Walsh responded that the articles could hasten the independence of colonial states, including Ireland, by removing the fears held by the colonizers that independence would open the former colonies to attack from a hostile power. This highly unusual attempt to integrate anti-imperialism with the League marked Walsh as one of the debate's more creative thinkers on foreign policy issues. Though not sharing Walsh's foreign policy expertise, Harrison throughout the 1920s fought hard to move the Democratic caucus to the left on international issues. Beyond Walsh and Harrison, however, the group's political strength weakened. Robert Owen (Oklahoma), the most liberal member of the 1910s Senate not to affiliate with the peace progressives, retired from the Senate in 1924. Earle Mayfield (Texas), after winning a narrow election in 1922, spent his first three years in the Senate fighting off an investigation that alleged he owed his victory to massive vote fraud organized by the KKK and his last three years campaigning for reelection.[18] Neither he nor his West Virginia colleague, M. M. Neely, elected in the same year, played an important role in any 1920s foreign policy debate. Elmer Thomas (Oklahoma), elected in 1926, also generally refrained from participating in Senate debate. Only Black, who replaced conservative leader Oscar Underwood in the 1926 elections, developed a strong interest in foreign policy, especially on issues relating to the Navy and Haiti. Taken as a whole, however, the idealists exhibited far less interest in international affairs than did the peace progressives; they tended to follow the peace progressive lead (except on the World Court) rather than the reverse.[19]

Like the centrists, the idealists paid tribute to Wilson through their support of the League and its Court. In tones considerably more enthusiastic than those of the centrists, Walsh described the League as a "powerful agency for peace," a "harbinger" of things to come, when war would no longer exist. Along these lines, he began the decade by unsuccessfully proposing the linking of Borah's disarmament conference with the League, although when his amendment was rejected

Walsh supported most of the work of the Washington Conference, except for the Four Power Treaty. Both Neely and Harrison spoke on the Senate floor in favor of World Court membership, but here again Walsh played the most prominent role of the group, challenging anti-Court arguments that the Court would decide on all great international political controversies and that its decisions would inevitably lead to the use of force. Walsh also directly addressed the anti-imperialist argument, denying that the Court acted as a tool of the great powers. Here he built upon an earlier case made by Robert Owen, who, citing Irish independence, Egyptian autonomy, and the return of Shantung to China, contended that the League had satisfied the objections made in 1919 by its anti-imperialist critics; by institutionalizing the principles of Wilson's Fourteen Points, "the doctrine of the right to rule without the consent of the governed has been almost completely abandoned throughout the world," replaced by the doctrines of democracy and liberty in international relations. At the same time, however, the idealists were flexible enough to back non-Wilsonian peace initiatives such as Kellogg-Briand. After an initial coolness toward the idea, Walsh grew closer to Levinson and emerged as one of the plan's most enthusiastic backers by 1929. Dismissing those senators who viewed the treaty "as something in the nature of a pious wish," Walsh confessed that he saw it in "quite a different light" as a "revolution in international law" that would help change the attitude of average people toward war, increase the importance of world public opinion, and foster closer international cooperation. The idealists also called for applying Wilson's open diplomacy principles; Owen contended that the worldwide adoption of Wilsonian ideals would lead to a disarmed, stable, and prosperous Europe.[20]

Walsh's structuring of favorable arguments for the League from an anti-imperialist standpoint, virtually unique in the Senate of the 1920s, indicated a general idealist sympathy with anti-imperialism. Teaming with the peace progressives to champion Irish independence in the early 1920s, he cautioned that groups like the English-Speaking Union and awards such as the Rhodes Scholarship formed parts of a massive "propaganda organization" designed to blind the United States to British excesses; he hoped that the British would remember that historically the United States befriended those "endeavoring to free themselves of a hated dominion and set up a government of their own." Comparing the Irish to United States and South American revolutionaries, Walsh, like La Follette and Norris, urged American aid for their cause. Owen, meanwhile, launched a public campaign against the Haitian occupation, arguing that it had transformed the Monroe Doctrine so that "we become not protectors but oppressors." The Oklahoma senator reasoned that it violated the Constitution and "closes our mouths when we condemn imperialism"; he added that "they are negroes and have valuable property but still 'noblesse oblige.' "[21]

Walsh allowed his newfound anti-imperialism to revise his earlier view of Mexico, and by 1926 he called for a settling of "deplorable" conditions by arbitration, not by American intervention on behalf of "adventurers with a predatory disposition."[22] He took a much more moderate stance on Nicaragua, doubting in 1927 the likelihood of war between Washington and Managua (as Marines were on the ground) and conceding that no proof existed that Conservative forces had driven Sacasa from the country; two years later he chastised Dill and Blaine for overstating the likelihood of Nicaraguans' attacking canal surveyors, given that both the Liberals and the Conservatives wanted a Nicaraguan canal. By this time, though, other idealists had staked out their anti-imperialist credentials. In 1930 Black attacked the Haitian occupation with the charge that Americans had forced the Haitians to change their constitution "not by a bona fide vote of the people but at the point of a bayonet." He also called for Filipino independence from an idealistic perspective, reminding his colleagues that the American colonists had revolted in 1776 in part because they lived under a commercial monopoly by the mother country. The group also sported a strongly anti-imperialist voting record. Despite this, the idealists never gained recognition as the Senate's leading anti-imperialists, in large part because they almost never took part in Senate debate on any of these questions. Nonetheless, on inter-American issues they provided far more reliable votes for the peace progressives than for the Democratic center.[23]

The idealists also shared the peace progressive perspective on naval policy, where they showed slightly more activity, although their anti-militarism did not flower until relatively late in the decade. In 1928 Walsh denounced the Army for sending soldiers bulletins containing not only military matters but "a whole lot of matters entirely foreign thereto and generally combatting the efforts of what are called 'pacifists.' " He amplified on these thoughts a year later when he opposed the cruisers bill as unnecessary because of the new spirit of Kellogg-

Briand, denouncing the "strange vanity" held in some circles that the United States would live up to the treaty while other nations would not. Walsh called for obtaining naval parity by scaling down, not building up, and, in a major concession to the peace progressives, admitted under fierce questioning from William Bruce that effective disarmament could occur through a non-League conference, particularly since the United States could count on the support of lesser powers there. This anti-Navy perspective carried over to the London Naval Treaty, which the four idealists remaining (Neely and Mayfield failed to win reelection in 1928) endorsed from a perspective not dissimilar to that of the peace progressives. Black joined Shipstead and Norris in opposing the Robinson Amendment, which he said would make the Secretary of State more powerful than the Senate and thus further advance the government "along the Hamiltonian pathway of concentration." According to Black, the framers wanted the Senate as the dominant branch in treaty making, and he added that only an increase in the Senate's role in foreign affairs would satisfy the people's desire for "escape from . . . the thralldom of secret diplomacy." Walsh entertained similar reservations, noting that a program of naval expansion made no economic sense and could "conceivably give rise to international suspicions and ill-will."[24]

Like the peace progressives, the idealists elected not to apply their principles fully to foreign economic and social policy. In large part because of his ties to Montana labor, Walsh consistently called for restrictions on Mexican immigration (as did his colleague Burton Wheeler); Black carried the nativist sentiments several steps further in 1930 by proposing an amendment to suspend all immigration for five years on economic grounds. The idealists sported mixed records on the tariff. Both Walsh and Harrison, strong free traders in 1922, retreated from their positions on agricultural issues by 1930. Walsh publicly defended increases in the mustard seed tariff, terming it an "opportunity to do the farmer some good" and a chance to have "a little bit of reciprocity" with European industries already protected. Harrison called for decreases in the sugar tariff in a rather bitter debate with the Louisiana senators, but then turned around and supported higher rates for long-staple cotton. Black also backed the higher cotton rates, and Elmer Thomas, part of the high-tariff bloc of sugar, lumber, and oil-state senators to which Dill also belonged, backed higher tariffs on all of those products in addition to glass, cotton, and agricultural oils. The group's interpretation of Wilsonianism, then, stopped short of accepting the President's teachings on foreign economic policy.[25]

The idealists tried to provide a liberal alternative to peace progressivism, but their sporadic interest in international affairs made their attempt a quite halfhearted one. The senators represented an ideological bridge between the Wilsonians of the 1910s and those of the 1930s, but their major impact for the 1920s came through generally increasing the voting strength of the peace progressive position, not through existing as independent actors in the foreign policy debates of the era.

The idealists also failed to emerge as the principal Democratic alternative to the vague positions offered by the center. That honor fell instead to a group of conservatives who possessed sufficient voting strength to eliminate any chance of a Democrat/peace progressive foreign policy coalition. A loose alliance of conservative Southern Democrats, traditional "Bourbon" Democrats, and a few onetime domestic liberals disillusioned with the foreign policy solutions offered by their ideological comrades, the conservatives did not form as tight a bloc as the idealists, but they presented a far more consistent and unified foreign policy program than did the center until their sudden political collapse in the last few years of the 1920s.

The most prominent figure of the Democratic right, Oscar Underwood (Alabama), first made his name as a tariff reformer during the Wilson administration. Underwood grew increasingly skeptical of both the President's domestic and foreign policies; by the early 1920s, one Democratic activist saw "no difference (outside the party label) between Senator Underwood and Senator Edge." After Underwood's retirement in 1926, William Cabell Bruce, who ran in 1922 as an "Underwood Democrat," became the leader of the faction, joined later in the decade by his Maryland colleague Millard Tydings; New Jersey Democrat Edward Edwards, a leading New Jersey banker and Prohibition opponent; and Thomas Bayard, winner on a platform committed to the preservation of states' rights and descendant of a host of other Bayards elected to the Senate from Delaware.[26] (Hiram Bingham described Bayard as "an old Yale man and a delightful person" and found few issues on which he disagreed with his Delaware colleague.) These Bourbon Democrats held deeply conservative positions on both foreign and domestic issues, and compiled voting records virtually indistinguishable from those of rightist Republicans, except on Prohibition.

Southerners who joined Underwood in this faction included Lawrence Tyson (Tennessee), a brigade commander during the war with close ties to the chemical industry; Joseph Ransdell (Louisiana), a man with strongly conservative foreign policy leanings who, like Tyson, had links to the chemical industry; and Edwin Broussard (Louisiana), whose chief interest in foreign policy lay in forming strong enough links with the Republicans to ensure a higher sugar tariff. Scattered foreign policy conservatives, such as Dan Steck (Iowa), who had defeated Brookhart in the disputed 1924 Iowa Senate election and was seated in the Senate through the votes of conservative Republicans, and Royal Copeland (New York), who entered the Senate with strong liberal support but quickly drew severe criticism from *The Nation* and its left-wing followers, rounded out the group. The conservatives showed considerably more interest in foreign policy issues than did the idealists, and assumed positions that indicated very little displeasure with the course chosen by the Republican administrations.[27]

The gap between the conservatives and the other Democratic factions revealed itself when the conservatives discussed political cooperation with Europe. Underwood, then Senate Minority Leader, served as the Democratic delegate to the Washington Conference and, comparing the Four Power Treaty to Versailles, led a unanimous conservative bloc in favor of the treaty. Ransdell agreed, praising the performance of Hughes in the negotiations and predicting peace upon the ratification of the treaty; the onetime "strong advocate" of the League of Nations argued that the League "is a matter of past history, however, and we must deal now with the living present." He said that he would agree "gladly" to a Twelve Power Treaty containing the world's twelve leading powers backed by force and "applying to all questions of international controversy." The conservatives also sought to move beyond Wilson's shadow on the World Court. In 1923 Underwood called for a "wise and progressive policy . . . not the laggard notion of a court of law" to relieve European financial distress, while Bruce favored entering the Court "under proper reservations" but deemed it a "matter of secondary importance." During Senate debate over membership, Bruce articulated a more spirited defense, ridiculing Borah's assertion that the great powers dominated the Court; he alleged that Borah had "really favored the World Court until he found out that 46 or so of the most highly civilized powers of the world agreed with him, and then he went off on his present target." (Bruce for one had tired of the peace

progressives' making "one idle, empty gesture of peace after another.")
The Maryland senator said that he had "no faith in this vain cry of
'Peace, peace, peace' not backed up by some real, essential military
agency adequate for the task of preserving international peace," although he confessed that he cared little about Court membership except as an "antechamber to the League of Nations." As it turned out,
however, Bruce's ideal of the League differed considerably from that
of Wilson or his 1920s followers. In an Armistice Day 1923 address,
the newly elected senator argued that perpetual peace would exist if
civilization consisted only of English-speaking lands and "highly enlightened states" such as Norway, Sweden, Denmark, Holland, and
Switzerland. Since it did not, the world needed a League of Nations
"clothed, in every respect, with the full measure of police authority
necessary to qualify it for the task of executing its mandates": "if the
world is to enjoy peace, it must be commanded." This power-domi-
nated conception of international affairs formed one of the central
tenets of the conservative foreign policy ideology.[28]

Given this line of reasoning, the conservatives had little good to say
about the decade's ultimate expression of moral power, the Kellogg-
Briand Pact. Again Bruce spoke for the group, laying out a compelling
case against the pact in a long colloquy with Borah. Noting that he had
seen no "indication that these moral forces upon which [Borah] is so
strongly disposed are as powerful as he seems to think they are," he
challenged the outlawrists to produce one historical example of a peace
pact that had functioned without the backing of force. The Maryland
senator believed that the world, just like cities, needed to be policed,
citing the policy of nineteenth-century England as his model; London
had "the prudence to keep its powder dry," maintaining a large military
for the protection of British liberties and also "for the progress of
human civilization itself throughout the world." He then attacked the
pact bit by bit, tearing apart Article I, which renounced war formally,
as "the last stage of nervous and degenerate effeminacy in the history
of the pacifist movement in this country." Article II he accused of
lacking explicitness in outlining what constituted the right of self-defense, a right that he "would as soon thrust my head into an incandes-
cent furnace" as give up; given this omission, he concluded that the
pact outlawed defensive warfare altogether, sneering that Borah evidently had "worked himself up to still a higher degree of pacifism."
Bruce not only saw the pact as "parchment futility" that had been

stripped of any value it might have had by the interpretive notes, but quite possibly harmful. The senator predicted that it could lull the American people into a false sense of security, strengthening the "lunatic fringe" of "imbecile pacifism" that hoped for peace through "sermons, Sunday school lectures, and parlor or pink-tea addresses." Nonetheless, just before the vote, Bruce, remarkably, announced that he would vote for the pact on the grounds that it might pave the way for American entrance into the League, an organization that he conceived of as based on the explicit idea of force renounced by Kellogg-Briand.[29]

The conservatives not surprisingly had a radically different conception of European affairs from that of the peace progressives. Underwood ridiculed the idea of recognition of a Russian "despotism" constructed in the name of communistic policies that had "plunged the people of Russia into poverty, hunger, and distress." The Alabama senator also called for the disposal of the property of German nationals seized during the war, rather than its return to Germany as recommended by Borah. All strongly opposed the La Follette and Howell plans for American aid to Germany; Nathan Dial said that if the United States were going to embark upon a foreign aid program, Germany should rank as the last country deserving of such assistance. Overall, the conservatives believed that cooperation with Europe amounted to "the question of opportunity for business development of our own people" and that the chief motive for American policymakers "is first the stability of [European] government and then the stability of finance." These tenets, remarkably similar to those held on foreign economic policy by the G.O.P. administrations of the 1920s, were reflected in the positions taken by the conservatives on the debt bills. The conservatives advanced a rather consistent nationalistic reason for favoring renegotiation—in the blunt rhetoric of Ransdell, passage of the bills would mean "that within 48 hours . . . the price of cotton will go up materially." Underwood added that he believed international financial stability represented the "most important question that is confronting the civilized world today," since only stabilized finance could ensure markets for American crops. Later in the decade, Royal Copeland emerged as one of the stronger backers of refinancing Italy's debt, remarking that the Senate should not consider Mussolini's style of rule in its vote; Copeland's further comment that the bill's opponents needed to address the human aspect of the problem brought an explosion from Dill.[30]

Power remained the central conservatives' concern, and they did all that they could during the decade to see the American share of it increase. Although all conservatives initially backed the Washington Treaties, by the end of the decade they had repudiated their earlier stance. (Bruce noted that in addition the conference had rendered the "truly unfortunate" result of decreasing the strength of the British fleet, "the most powerful arm that the liberty and civilization of mankind had.") Meanwhile, Tyson and Ransdell tenaciously fought the 1926 Geneva Convention to outlaw poison gas in warfare, playing (according to Borah) the pivotal roles in blocking ratification of the arrangement. Tyson noted that the protocol, undoubtedly "put forward by people who do not understand the inhumanity or the humanity of gas warfare," was backed by the administration only to "pacify the pacifists." He also disputed the convention's premises, describing gas "the most humane of all weapons," since it ensured a shorter end to all wars. As an alternative to the Convention, Ransdell recommended a massive expansion of American expenditures on poison gas, looking toward the development of a gas that airplanes could use to reach the civilian population as the "surest means of preventing war." All of this served as a warmup for the cruisers bill, which attracted the unanimous and enthusiastic support of the conservatives. Tyson belittled peace progressive arguments that the bill would provoke an arms race, and called for the immediate building of all the cruisers on the grounds that recent events had shown that disarmament conferences could not work as long as the United States did not possess the world's strongest navy. Dan Steck, meanwhile, joined Hiram Bingham in a pre–cruisers bill rally, delivering a slashing attack on "pacifist propaganda against national defense."[31]

Bruce's debate with Dill in early 1928 illustrated the main tenets of the group's feelings on issues relating to East Asia and Latin America. Ransdell upheld administration policy in Central America as early as 1926, when he commended the disarming of the Liberals and predicted Democratic support for the Díaz regime to oppose the "Communists of Mexico [who] are trying to implant their vagaries to Nicaragua, hoping that they may spread throughout Central America and result in a communistic union of Mexico with the other Central American states." Beginning in 1925 with Mexican policy, the Louisiana senator feared only that the administration had not implemented a forceful enough policy. In 1928 Copeland pronounced himself "very much concerned" about the deaths of U.S. citizens in Nicaragua and denounced the "mawkish sentimentality" of those who wanted to withdraw the Marines. The scattered conservative comments dealing with other areas of the world revealed a similar perspective. Bruce peppered William King with hostile questions during debate about withdrawal from Haiti, characterizing the Utah senator's position as a preference for Haitian freedom over Haitian civilization. The Maryland senator also challenged King on Filipino independence, describing American possession of the Philippines as "the best title that one country ever did have to the soil of another one."[32]

Finally, the conservatives (with the exception of Underwood, who remained true to his low-tariff principles) took a position on the tariff deviant from most other Democratic senators. Broussard, John Kendrick (Wyoming), and Ransdell, linked by their common desire for higher sugar rates, provided the only three Democratic votes or pairs in favor of the Fordney-McCumber tariff. In 1930 they continued their support for high tariffs, with Ransdell arguing that Thomas Jefferson and James Madison had first articulated protectionism; both men knew that the industries of the South could not survive without a high tariff because of the vulnerability of the Southern states to international competition. The Louisiana senator contended that world conditions made protection for all branches of agriculture mandatory. With the 1930 Democrats as a party slightly more favorable to protectionism than in 1922, the affirmative votes of four of the five conservatives then remaining in the Senate (Copeland voted for the tariff, Tydings opposed it) stood out less, but nonetheless only eight Democrats supported Hawley-Smoot in the final tally.[33]

Although Democratic conservatism continued long after the 1920s, a combination of retirements and narrow electoral defeats decimated this particular bloc by 1932. During the 1920s, however, they were a political force, at their height controlling around 30 percent of the votes in the Democratic caucus. Like the other Democratic factions, the conservatives had their share of members who paid little attention to foreign affairs, but as a whole they were far more active than the idealists and also provided three of the more articulate defenders (Underwood, Bruce, and Ransdell) of an assertive foreign policy. This vision, when compared with that offered by the peace progressives, illustrated the range of opinions on foreign affairs offered in the Senate during the 1920s. Based on the importance of force, the conservative world vision, along with the promilitary inclinations of the center, eliminated any chance of cooperation between the peace movement and the Democrats. The gap between the idealists and the conservatives also demonstrated the near impossibility of the Democrats' functioning effectively as a unified minority party on foreign policy matters.

The Democratic blocs, despite their rather loose nature, did not include three of the party's wild cards, all of whom exhibited a considerable interest in foreign policy throughout the decade and all of whom charted a course entirely independent of the Democratic party leadership, further weakening the party's ability to act as a cohesive and independent force on international affairs.

James Reed (Missouri), the most vitriolic of these senators, subscribed to a highly xenophobic and nationalistic ideology that set him apart from virtually all the major political figures of his day. Noting that Reed had come to the Senate after a phenomenally successful career as a Kansas City prosecuting attorney, Mark Sullivan hypothesized that for the senator, "there is always a criminal, a wholly evil devil," to which Reed could play the prosecutor. He opposed his first significant devil, the League of Nations, from a racist and nationalistic perspective as an organization that would transfer American sovereignty to a group of foreigners. The senator asked one correspondent to think of the United States' submitting vital questions "to a tribunal on which a nigger from Liberia, a nigger from Honduras, a nigger from India, or an unlettered gentleman from Siam, each have votes equal to that of the great United States of America." Reed expanded on this line of reasoning during debate over the Berlin Treaty, which he improbably contended would either bring the United States into the League of Nations, compel Washington to offer a territorial guarantee to France, or permit the three League powers to use the League to rearm Germany and then form a superalliance directed against the United States. To avoid these prospects, he called for the United States to "be prepared to defend itself against all comers" regardless of expense; in particular, it needed a large Navy to fend off England, a country that had violated American rights habitually over the preceding sixty years. The Missouri senator attacked the Washington Conference from the same pro-Navy, anti-British standpoint, adding that Hughes's handiwork "takes from us . . . the right to make ourselves the [naval] equal of the British Empire" while keeping America vulnerable to a possible British attack. He then analyzed the considerable advantages he saw gained by the Japanese, who had proved in their negotiations with Hughes that "the occidental mind is no match for oriental skill in diplomatic proceedings." In several other wild conspiracy theories, Reed hypothesized that the results of the conference would force the British to side with the Japanese in an American-Japanese war over immigration while the consultative organization set up by the Four Power Treaty would vote three to one to strip the United States of the Philippines and award them to either the British or the Japanese. The senator did not indicate how he had arrived at such conclusions.[34]

Reed also rejected the model for international peace offered by the decade's Republican administrations when he opposed all debt refinancing deals on the grounds that the United States was not a "country of inexhaustible wealth . . . [or] nurse for the remainder of the world." He termed the British deal a "practical cancellation" of the debt, orchestrated by international bankers to "deliver the United States bound hand and foot to the British government" while making dangerous concessions to a potential enemy. The Missouri senator likewise had little good to say about France, a "solvent but dishonest creditor" hoping to force a complete cancellation of the debt by a policy of "qualified" nonpayment. Reed also rejected the legalist peace plan, the World Court, as "a complete reversal of the ancient policies of this Government" that would hand over vital policy questions to foreigners. Although he agreed with the outlawrists about the World Court, he had no sympathy with their proposed solution to problems of war and peace either. In 1922 Reed attacked outlawry as an "International Plan," which, like all other such programs, "at first glance appears to be absolutely perfect, [but] when applied to concrete solutions [is] frequently found to be unworkable." He instead recommended dividing up the world into three spheres, with the United States maintaining its "most benevolent" protectorate over the Western Hemisphere; any other plan would collapse as a result of the "diversity of interest, racial instinct, and cultural and ethical standards" among the United States, South America, Europe, and Japan. Having rejected all peace programs put forth during the 1920s, Reed fell back on arming the United States to a degree sufficient that "no other nation can successfully attack our shores." During his brief 1928 presidential campaign, he called for a policy of staunch national defense and preparedness based upon an "adequate" Navy, since "experience of the ages demonstrated that paper treaties are no adequate defense against artillery of an enemy." He emerged the next year as an enthusiastic champion of the cruisers bill; when Brookhart protested that the United States should do nothing to hamper the desire of the world for peace, Reed shot back that it was "refreshing to find one or two gentlemen who can speak for the entire world."[35]

Reed's inter-American policy also employed a highly nationalistic framework. He condemned the 1921 treaty with Colombia for having taken Roosevelt's "white shroud and run it up as a white flag of surrender." Later in the decade he called for the United States to expand its presence in the Caribbean by demanding that England and France cede their Caribbean possessions; since Jamaica and Martinique "are not vital to their welfare," they could prove a testing ground for British and French professions of friendship. In 1927 Reed joined Republican stalwarts Walter Edge and George McLean (R–Connecticut) as the only three members of the Foreign Relations Committee to oppose the Robinson Resolution calling for arbitration with Mexico in the committee vote. He contended that since Coolidge had taken a correct stance in his Mexican policy by negotiating in "good faith," the Senate should not take any actions that the Mexicans could interpret as a congressional rebuke to the President. The Missouri senator also supported the Nicaraguan occupation.[36]

Reed's nationalist Democratic colleague Cole Blease articulated an even more xenophobic world vision than the Missouri senator. The then–South Carolina governor had questioned American entry into the European war in 1917, a position that probably lost him the 1918 Senate nomination to Nathan Dial. He gained his revenge six years later, easily besting the incumbent in the primary and then edging future governor, senator, Secretary of State, and Supreme Court Justice James Byrnes by just over 2,000 votes in the runoff. Described as the "type of demagogue which sometimes has humiliated the South in the Senate," Blease revealed his international perspective in his first major foreign policy speech, which opposed membership in the World Court. He observed that the Court contained judges who "do not speak our language, and so we could not tell what they were talking about"; they even could "cuss" at the American judge without the American knowing what the foreigners were saying. The South Carolina senator imagined a Court that could let foreigners "say whether Japs shall come over into Central America or not," while forcing a white American "to sit side-by-side with a full-blooded 'nigger' " and throwing "the destinies of Southern women and Southern men into the lap of a black man." If the United States were to join, it needed to have more power to name Court judges than representatives of a "nigger republic" like Haiti or Liberia, although the senator preferred to support the higher taxes needed for a larger Army rather "than be carried into a court with a nigger judge." Having rejected internationalism, Blease too turned to "a proper and adequate defense," including a "strong, well-equipped Army and Navy," as his solution to international tensions. The senator denounced "what are called these disarmament conferences" as "folly" that would cause the U.S. military to "disintegrate"; he recommended instead a strong Navy to respond to foreign insults, operating under a policy of "Americans standing for America, and standing prepared to take care of themselves." On a less flourishing note, Blease constantly harassed Naval Committee Chair Hale to increase the number of cruisers built at the Charleston Navy Yard.[37]

The nationalism and racism of Reed and Blease in no way represented the opinions of the majority of the Democratic caucus, although at the same time Reed enjoyed a national reputation as one of the party's leading foreign policy spokesmen. Reed and Blease most resembled the demagogues associated with the Democratic center, but unlike Heflin and Thomas McKellar they subscribed to a much more pronounced and much more consistent nationalism. Though difficult to fit on the foreign policy spectrum of the time, Reed and Blease did their best to pull the party away from any kind of cooperation with the peace movement or, except on the debt issues and the World Court, with the peace progressives.

Unlike Reed and Blease, David Walsh (Massachusetts) did not espouse ideas otherwise absent from the Democratic ranks, although he did articulate a combination of proposals that set him apart from his Democratic colleagues. In general, Walsh wanted to attune the party's foreign policy more closely to the interests of its small but growing urban, Northeastern constituency. The first Irish-American ever popularly elected to the Senate, Walsh, a Boston lawyer and one-term former governor, narrowly triumphed in the 1918 Massachusetts contest by combining a progressive, prolabor domestic policy with pro-Irish foreign sympathies, positions that led him to take one of the more unusual approaches to the League of Nations. Never formally an irreconcilable, Walsh maintained his support for the "principle" of a league and said that he would favor a compromise settlement between the Senate and the President. Still, he feared that the Paris Conference had represented only the "old order, with its evil diplomacy, its accursed materialism, and its cynical disregard of human rights." Most of Walsh's objections to the covenant fitted into the anti-imperialist category. He denounced the Shantung provision as "indefensible" and lamented that he found nothing in the covenant "which gives the slightest hope of the league of nations ever amicably adjusting the problems of subjugated peoples," particularly the Irish. The Massachusetts senator worried that Article X would "do violence to our own history and . . . give the lie to our traditional policy of helpfulness to the downtrodden and the oppressed"; he also joined the peace progressives in their critique of Article XI and proposed a reservation to limit the article's scope. Walsh did not support all the peace progressive anti-imperialist reservations, but he did back most of them, and his critique of the treaty came as close to the peace progressive position as that put forth by any other senator during the League debate.[38]

Walsh also became the most passionate Democratic proponent of low agricultural tariffs almost immediately after his arrival in the Senate, winning a reputation as the strongest congressional critic of the Fordney-McCumber tariff. He believed that a high tariff would impose "tremendous burdens" on consumers and allow larger, more centrally organized manufacturers to "exploit, crush, and destroy numerous small and independent industries." Walsh's 1922 voting record of opposing virtually all the committee amendments did not set him apart from most other Democrats, but unlike the rest of his party, he continued to agitate the issue long after Fordney-McCumber became law. He made his tariff position the central theme of his narrowly unsuccessful reelection campaign in 1924, a defeat he avenged two years later in a special election in which his tariff position again became the key issue of the contest. He thus had returned to the Senate to fight against Hawley-Smoot in 1930, which he charged ignored "the viewpoint of the average man and women, the consumers of this country." Attempts by rural senators to increase the agricultural rates particularly enraged Walsh, who reminded the farm bloc that "there is a serious difference between indefensible excessive protection and a defensible moderate protection." (He did praise Blaine and the other peace progressive free-traders, noting that the Wisconsin senator had taken into account the "capacity of the poorer classes and the middle classes to pay exorbitant prices for the necessities of life.") By 1930, however, Walsh conceded that he would vote for some higher industrial rates for Depression-ravaged industries where evidence existed of "increasing imports destroying the American market"; his vote for higher rates for shoes, an important manufacturing product of Massachusetts, enraged rural senators used to Walsh's barbs for supporting high rates for products of their constituents.[39]

As with the tariff, Walsh exhibited a regionally based concern with immigration, opposing all attempts to restrict European immigration (although he supported curtailing the number of immigrants from Japan and Mexico) from a belief that such measures discriminated against the poor "in the spirit of intolerance, largely racial and in part religious." As with the tariff, Walsh gained the cooperation of the other Northeastern Democrats on this issue. Rhode Island's Peter Gerry teamed with his Massachusetts colleague to oppose both the 1924 Immigration Act and the equally important Harrison Amendment, which called for allotting immigration quotas on the basis of the 1890 rather than the 1910 census. Royal Copeland, pushing for an increased quota for Jewish immigrants, proposed an unsuccessful 1924 amendment to raise the number of Central and Eastern European immigrants by 100,000 annually (on the assumption that most of those emigrating would be Jewish). Under hostile questioning from W. J. Harris, Copeland said that as much as possible the Senate should "let America be an asylum and a home" for Jewish refugees. When debate concluded, he remarked that "it is eminently proper that a Senator from New York should be the one to speak for the Jews."[40]

Quite apart from these regional perspectives, Walsh, unlike his Northeastern colleagues, articulated a different foreign policy agenda on broader issues as well. In the 1920s the senator amassed an anti-imperialist voting record blemished only by his opposition to the Blaine and Heflin Amendments in 1928. Walsh began the decade by opposing the Liberian loan and breaking with his party by supporting the King Amendment; two years later he earned an endorsement from La Follette because of his anti-imperialist credentials. Walsh opposed intervention in Mexico despite the anti-Catholic policies of the Calles government, and in 1927 he questioned the basis of Kellogg's Nicaraguan policy. Although he voted against the Blaine Amendment because of its overly "strict limitation" upon the President, he professed himself "in very hearty accord with the general principle" of the Wisconsin senator; the next year he supported both Dill Amendments and opposed the Nicaraguan canal appropriation. In 1930 he turned his attention to Cuba, which he termed "the most important [question] before the American government" for the year. Admitting that he wanted to overturn the Machado regime, Walsh called for the United States to use its power under the Platt Amendment to compel free elections and assure "the Cuban people the right to exercise their basic privilege to declare who shall govern them," since "all liberty commences at the ballot box."[41]

Although Walsh endorsed the general anti-imperialist principles of the peace progressives, he never made them the central tenets of his foreign policy ideology, and his position on military issues diverged from that of the dissenting senators. The senator sided with the peace progressives on the need to increase funding for the air corps, but he did not want to slash funds for the Navy overall. He agreed with conservative Arthur Robinson (R–Indiana) about the "inadequacy of our naval defenses," which he blamed on the economy program pursued by the Republican administrations. He urged Hale to have a roll call vote on building up to Washington Treaty limits to allow the people to "see who is voting to keep down the Naval Establishment of the country below the line of safety." Walsh revealed a bit more about the reconciliation of his propeace and pro-Navy views during debate over the Kellogg-Briand Treaty. He became the only senator to contend that the treaty and the cruisers bill would serve the same purpose—the promotion of peace through freedom of the seas, important since its "vast shipping interests" mandated that the United States not leave "its commerce in jeopardy." The Massachusetts senator reasoned that in the meantime the United States needed the world's largest military to compel the peace, noting that "aside from the militaristic group" all senators believed "that the passage of the bill would do more than anything else to bring about naval disarmament in the near future." He nonetheless confessed that he was "not enthusiastic" about the bill while finding himself "more and more enthusiastic" about increasing public sentiment for peace. A year later, though, Walsh cast one of the four Democratic votes against the London Naval Treaty, worrying that "we are growing indifferent to our national security because of the propaganda of pacifists"; he called for a middle ground between the "extreme militarists" and the "well-meaning pacifists" by attaching to the treaty a rider reservation stating that the Senate would build up to treaty limits by 1936. He conceded that world peace and military reduction complemented each other, but still explicitly targeted those such as the peace progressives "who really believe that the less strength our Navy has the more likely we are to promote world peace by our example of disarming." Walsh thus became the only Senate anti-imperialist of the decade to support naval increases regularly. He eventually found these two positions irreconcilable and in early 1931 began distancing himself from the peace progressives, charging that their "suicidal" overreliance on outlawry had "hoodwinked" Americans into believing that London had not left the country with an almost "insignificant" navy of "markedly inferior strength" to those of the other great powers.[42]

Unlike the centrists, the idealists, and the conservatives, neither Walsh, Reed, nor Blease was considered a Wilsonian during the 1910s, and so none of their viewpoints in the 1920s can be viewed in the context of a fracturing of the Wilsonian ideology. But their increased political power—as seen in Reed's presidential campaign or Walsh's position in the Democratic caucus—indicated that even mainstream Democrats had conceded the influence of these admitted anti-Wilsonians in a way that would have been anathema to the party in the 1910s. In addition, all articulated foreign policy visions at variance with those of the major Democratic factions, adding to the cacophony of voices coming from the Democratic side of the aisle. They obviously did not possess the voting strength of any of the Democratic blocs, but Reed, Blease, and Walsh were willing to fight for the causes in which they believed, and so, not unlike the peace progressives, they enjoyed considerably more influence than their numbers would have suggested.

The Democratic senator who spoke the most on foreign policy issues during the 1920s declined association with any bloc. The author of a variety of anti-Haitian occupation amendments and the implacable foe of high naval spending, William King, a conservative (by national standards) Mormon who had practiced corporate law in Salt Lake City before entering Congress, did not fit the profile of a classic Senate dissenter. Since he closely followed Woodrow Wilson during the war years while making a name for himself as an intense Red-baiter and a fairly consistent if nondescript defender of the League of Nations, little in his career before 1921 would have suggested his articulation of a series of foreign policy views that set him apart entirely from all other senators of the 1920s.[43]

On naval, Nicaraguan, Haitian, and East Asian issues King cooperated wholeheartedly with the peace progressives. He spoke more against a large Navy and the Haitian occupation than did any other dissenter. The Utah senator spelled out his feelings on the Navy in 1921, calling for an international policy "of peace and amity with all nations" with the United States as the moral leader of the world, and he shared the dissenters' fears that the new Navy would be used for "imperialistic policies" in disregard of the rights of smaller states. In 1924 he criticized the Washington Conference on the grounds that it had produced too high a naval budget (making him the only non–peace progressive to raise this point) given that the treaty had eliminated Japan completely as a potential enemy. The next year he demanded a full-scale congressional investigation of the Navy Department over its handling of the Mitchell affair and reintroduced his annual resolution for the United States to take part in a League of Nations disarmament conference. King strongly attacked the cruisers bill, cautioning against the rise of an international militaristic spirit while chastising Coolidge for practicing a policy of "militarism which finds expression in larger appropriations for the navy and army than any country in the world" at a time when the government was making "professions for world peace" and there existed "no menace to our security." King concluded the decade by expressing disappointment with the American delegation to the London Naval Conference for placing too much emphasis on parity and taking an inflexible bargaining position that failed to take into account the views of other nations.[44]

King felt passionately about ending the Haitian occupation and devoted far more time to the cause than any other member of the Senate in the 1920s. He said that the United States "must pursue a course so generous, so unselfish, indeed, so noble, as to command, not only the esteem, but the confidence and the affection of the peoples of all lands," since "we can afford to deal with small states and with backward peoples in a most generous and helpful manner." Unlike the peace progressives, who generally moved away from the issue after 1922, King kept up the fight, bringing a rejoinder from Tasker Oddie, who hoped that the antioccupation senators "will further study the subject and get their information from the real and legitimate sources" instead of from people like Ernest Gruening, whose articles King had inserted into the *Congressional Record* as a "calm, judicial presentation of the salient facts of the case." In 1923 the Utah senator urged peace activists and other "public spirited persons" to raise the needed money to send a "competent investigator" (clearly Gruening) to Haiti to "get the facts" or else bring Union Patriotique leaders to the United States so that they could lobby Congress directly. Unsuccessful in all of his attempts to end the occupation, King turned to a different approach in late 1925, hoping to tap into antimilitarist sentiment through a resolution demanding an investigation of the powers held by John Russell. Russell retaliated two years later, when King announced that he planned to visit Haiti during the 1927 congressional recess; the occupation head prevailed upon Louis Borno to deny the Utah senator access to the country as an "undesirable." From the Supreme Court, William Howard Taft, who described King as having "no real conception of statesmanlike policy, and only the gift of unlimited gab," chortled that the whole United States "will break into a guffaw if [King] attempts to go into Haiti and is prevented." Contrary to Taft's hopes, however, the move fooled no one, and backfired by drawing the Haiti issue back to the front pages of newspapers when King accused the State Department of orchestrating the entire charade "to keep alive the fiction of Haitian independence." King also emerged as a consistent critic of G.O.P. policies in Nicaragua, East Asia, and the Middle East, although Haiti always remained his chief example of the dangers of imperialism.[45]

Beyond this, however, King departed from the peace progressive consensus. Unlike the peace progressives, who tried to view the world as a whole and to construct a policy applicable to its entirety, the Utah senator (beyond his antimilitarism) saw the world in layers. With regard to the weaker states, he preferred the anti-imperialist solution of the peace progressives. His ardor for Wilsonianism had not cooled, however, and he followed Wilson's teachings when analyzing Republican foreign policy toward Western Europe. He began the decade with a blistering attack on the Four Power Treaty, which he viewed as one of the "pitiful efforts" of the G.O.P. to turn public attention away from the League; the senator stated his preference instead for a "world alliance, an alliance which involves force." King also championed American participation in the World Court, defending England from charges made by Court opponents that London had manipulated the Court to its advantage in Middle Eastern decisions. Although King also favored the Kellogg-Briand Treaty, he did not comment on it publicly beyond a vague reference praising Briand's initial proposal for a bilateral American-French pact outlawing war. The Utah senator also entertained a positive view of the major European powers, particularly the French.

He rationalized French foreign policy as a logical reaction to the American rejection of Versailles, and reminded Paris' critics of the need to understand French fears of "the danger of invasion from a regenerated Germany." This friendly attitude toward Europeans carried over to the foreign debt question. He sharply challenged Howell's attempts to link debt policy with the conduct of Mussolini's government in Italy, worrying that it "does not make for good will and fellowship to denounce other peoples and other rulers and other forms of government"; in any case, he saw Mussolini as "an extraordinary character and a powerful figure" who had fended off the forces of Italian Bolshevism.[46]

King's combination of Wilsonianism, antimilitarism, and anti-imperialism was rather similar to the ideology of the Democratic idealists, with whom he cooperated frequently in foreign policy debates, although the Utah senator's positions had an intensity and a consistency unmatched by the idealists'. In addition, further differentiating him from the idealists, the senator's division of the world did not stop with a separation of the weak from the strong. He added a third grouping—international outlaw states, nations powerful enough to be held accountable for their own actions (unlike the weaker states) but which refused to abide by the accepted principles of international law (unlike the great powers). For these countries he had no mercy, and recommended a policy of forceful action, unilateral if necessary.

King began the decade with a vision of Soviet Russia as the chief international outlaw. After the Soviet consolidation of power, King continued to support a policy of nonrecognition, since history did "not furnish a parallel to the Soviet debacle," a government of "moral and material degeneracy." A tour of the USSR in 1923 (accompanied by Edwin Ladd) softened his attitude somewhat. He continued to oppose recognition, but the harsh anti-Soviet rhetoric moderated, and he reversed himself to favor the formal establishment of Soviet-American trade relations, although he doubted that they would amount to much. By this time Turkey had replaced Russia as King's candidate for the world's most reckless nation. King called the Senate's attention to Turkish atrocities against Greeks and Armenians "which should excite the interest of all Christian peoples," urging unilateral American action of an unspecified nature on behalf of the "strong, vigorous, intellectual, and progressive" Armenians. He charged that the "insolent . . . cruel . . . cunning Turk" had played upon the imperialistic sympathies of the Europeans; by not protesting more forcefully, Harding too had apparently "taken refuge behind the ramparts of materialism and alleged self-interest." King wrote the text in the 1924 Democratic national platform that opposed the Lausanne Treaty on the grounds that the Turkish rulers stood "totally unable to orient themselves" to the West. After his success in helping to block Lausanne, King's tirades about the "cunning Turk" tapered off, although he did place a number of anti-Turkish articles into the *Congressional Record*.[47]

The third country that drew this line of criticism from King was Mexico, and the Utah senator continued his criticism of the Mexicans for violations of the rights of Americans long after he had earned his anti-imperialist reputation for his Haitian policy. Early in the decade he praised Hughes's "wise and statesmanlike course," arguing that any government that could not protect the rights of foreigners did not deserve recognition. The Utah senator dismissed the Obregón regime as little more than a combination of "military chieftains and corrupt politicians." He urged a more assertive response from Hughes, perhaps seizing "one or more ports and collect[ing] import duties" until Mexico was "brought to her senses." King believed that the high point of Mexican history had come during the Díaz presidency; Díaz's successors seemed motivated by communistic theories as espoused in the 1917 Constitution, and spent most of their time "constantly seizing" private property. The Utah senator charged that Calles had "deliberately entered upon an official policy of confiscation of American property" as part of the "purely" communistic agrarian reform program. Denying that he desired intervention in Mexican domestic affairs (similar denials had come during his Russian and Turkish critiques), he stated that he only wanted Mexico to "do her duty to her people and to other nations" and uphold international law. King's peculiar, three-tiered ideology generally led him to keep his own counsel throughout the decade, but his keen interest in almost all foreign policy questions gave him some influence among the Democrats.[48]

In his study of 1920s Democrats and domestic policy, David Burner has argued that the Democrats of the era articulated provincial solutions while making the transition from the traditional conservatism of the prewar years to the liberalism associated with the New Deal.[49] Burner's thesis does not apply as well to foreign policy issues. Although the Democrats often did come up with provincial solutions to the problems of international affairs, they did not appear to be making any sort of foreign policy transition in the years from 1921 through 1930. The

Democrats during the 1920s never resolved the issue of how closely they should adhere to Wilson's teachings, and through this failure they forfeited the opportunity to appeal to foreign policy liberals as Wilson had succeeded in doing during the decade before.[50] Although elements of Wilsonianism existed in some of the Democratic positions of the 1920s, the Senate Democrats in no way carried the Wilsonian banner during the years between Wilson and Roosevelt. Their combined division and lack of interest led to an extraordinary situation in which the peace progressives functioned as the opposition party on all major foreign policy questions except that of the World Court, setting the agenda for the opposition and leading the debate; the various Democratic factions then chose to adhere to either the peace progressive or (more often) the administration position. Because of their aggressiveness and unity on foreign policy, the peace progressives had the ability to influence 1920s diplomacy one way or the other, but had they not filled a foreign policy vacuum created by the Democrats, they would have had a less substantial impact.

8

The Decline of Anti-Imperialism

The stock market crash of 1929 and the ensuing Great Depression shattered the international environment of the 1920s. For the peace progressives, on its most immediate level, the Depression worsened the already severe hardships for their rural constituents, polarizing the politics of most of the Middle Border states and sending several dissenters to defeat in either primary or general elections.[1] This combination of economic hardship and political insecurity led the peace progressives to search harder for ways in which foreign policy could serve the interests of their constituents. At the same time, international events made anti-imperialism a much more difficult ideology to sustain. Much like the mainstream Republican ideology of the 1920s, the anti-imperialism of the peace progressives assumed an active American presence in a relatively peaceful and stable world order. With the rise of aggressive regimes in Germany and Japan, the requisite international conditions no longer existed. The peace progressives could have expanded their anti-imperialism by reorienting their world views, classifying Japan and Germany as imperialist powers, and advocating a strong American presence to counter their expansionism. Instead, however, somewhat fitfully, they moved away from anti-imperialism and in the process embraced a more nationalistic vision of world affairs. This choice had the added benefit of seeming to meet many of the economic needs of their constituents. By 1935 the anti-imperialism associated with the peace progressive critique of the 1920s had waned, leaving the senators with a considerably different framework through which to interpret the international events leading up to World War II.

Arguably the most important change for the peace progressives ushered in by the Great Depression had nothing to do with foreign policy. The dissenters, all but invulnerable politically during the 1920s, had enjoyed a balance of power position in the Senate from 1923 through 1929. Their political influence peaked after the 1926 elections, when the votes of Henrik Shipstead and Lynn Frazier decided which party would organize the Senate. Both of these conditions vanished during the early 1930s. The national Democratic upswing gave the Democrats a comfortable Senate majority after the 1932 elections, while a combination of voter discontent and conservative counterattacks in battles for control of state Republican organizations made the peace progressives suddenly vulnerable at home.

What the *New York Times* described as the "first definite referendum on insurgency" since the stock market crash came in South Dakota. After requesting a "vote of confidence in Northwestern Progressive Republicans who voted with Democrats against administration policies," McMaster barely survived a primary battle against a self-described "Hoover Republican." He nonetheless continued the theme during his fall campaign, hoping as well to benefit from the public support of La Follette and Blaine. The senator's opponent, two-term Democratic Governor W. J. Bulow, shot back that peace progressive political tactics had failed, challenging McMaster to name "one single thing that he has obtained for the people of this state" while in Washington; Bulow promised to "support the President, be he a Republican or a Democrat, in any reasonable policy." In the closing days of the campaign, Bulow began attacking McMaster for devoting too much attention to foreign policy, saying that the senator had wasted his time attempting to send wheat to China when the state needed his influence on domestic issues. McMaster refused to back down, touting his support for the London Naval Treaty and his opposition to the cruisers bill, and he chastised Bulow for "pussyfooting and straddling" on all major foreign policy questions. Bulow responded that he did not have to state specific positions on international issues, since they were not important to the campaign. Though expected to prevail, McMaster lost by almost 7,000 votes, running well behind the rest of the state Republican ticket.[2]

McMaster's defeat energized Midwestern conservatives, who then targeted two of the three peace progressives up for reelection in 1932, Brookhart and Blaine. Brookhart presented the more inviting prey. The Iowa senator lacked any constructive legislative accomplishments during his eight years in Washington, and he opened himself up to charges of nepotism when he placed five of his family members on the Senate payroll. In an attempt to revive his previous reform constituency, Brookhart campaigned on a radical platform, calling for paper-money inflation, redistribution of wealth through taxation, limitation of all private annual salaries to $10,000, and federal price fixing for agriculture. Conservatives worked hard to attract a challenger capable of appealing to Brookhart's traditional rural base; they settled upon Henry Field, host of a statewide radio farm program. Norris wrote two letters to Field—one six pages long—urging him not to make the race, but Field demurred, and despite strong peace progressive support for the incumbent, Field trounced Brookhart in the primary 45 percent to 33 percent.[3]

Blaine's loss came as more of a surprise. The senator campaigned on a platform that combined a radical domestic critique with boasts of his opposition to Kellogg-Briand, the World Court, and the occupation of Nicaragua; rather than retreating from his support of Al Smith, he issued a late July statement that as a "Lincoln Republican" he would endorse Franklin Roosevelt in 1932. To compensate for the anticipated loss of conservatives, the senator brought in Wheeler and Shipstead to urge Democratic and independent voters to vote in the G.O.P. primary; Wheeler asked "progressive voters to forget all about party affiliations." The senator faced a weak opponent in State Representative John Chapple, an extreme conservative who pointed to Blaine's stance in favor of Soviet recognition as proof that the primary represented a choice between whether "we are going to keep on the American road or take the communistic road." Chapple also claimed that Blaine, "a man without a party," had betrayed the farmer with his votes against high agricultural tariffs. The race attracted virtually no national attention, with even Wisconsin conservatives conceding that Chapple had little chance of winning; Blaine spent as much time campaigning for progressive gubernatorial candidate Phil La Follette as he did for his own seat. When La Follette lost the primary by more than 100,000 votes to Walter Kohler, however, Blaine could not overcome the associative effect, losing in a stunning upset by 10,000 votes.[4]

Two years later Dill declined to stand for a third term despite having assumed the chairmanship of the Interstate Commerce Committee in 1933. Considered a shoo-in for reelection, he said that the "Senate has lost its thrill," adding that he wanted to get out while he still had a chance at a second career. The congressional correspondent for the *Washington Post* disagreed, contending that Dill was retiring because he had been "outprogressived" in the New Deal Senate, where no place existed for a "timid progressive" like Dill. The senator denied the charge, claiming that he was "just as progressive as . . . ever," but he did admit that "the political issues that divide us have changed" since he had entered the Senate in 1923. In addition to the retirement and defeats, the peace progressives lost a fifth member of their 1920s contingent when Howell died of pneumonia in early 1933.[5]

The departures of Blaine, Brookhart, Dill, and McMaster reflected peace progressive political weaknesses new to the 1930s. Conservative forces scored well with the charge that the peace progressives paid too much attention to foreign affairs. Meanwhile, as was shown particularly in the Field campaign, standpatters began attacking the peace progressives as not crusaders for the public good but as congressional obstructors making it more difficult for the government to function in hard times. This critique struck at the heart of peace progressivism; as Wheeler observed, the ideological and educational accomplishments of the peace progressives accumulated over time and could not be measured by immediate achievements. Finally, the Dill retirement reflected the increasing discomfort felt by many traditional progressives with New Deal liberalism, which became more clear later in the 1930s when several peace progressives drifted into the conservative camp. The South Dakota, Wisconsin, Iowa, and Washington contests indicated that with the onset of the Great Depression the political environment that had sustained 1920s peace progressivism had withered away.[6]

Only one new peace progressive won election: Homer Bone (D–Washington) crushed (60 percent to 32 percent) the onetime dissenter Wesley Jones in 1932. A well-known public power activist, Bone served briefly as a state representative under the Farmer-Labor Party banner, ran for the House in 1928 in a Republican primary, and backed Dill in both 1922 and 1928 although he did not belong to the Democratic party in either year. Dill returned the favor by arranging to have the Democratic National Committee funnel support to the cash-starved Bone during his primary battle against a conservative

Democrat. In 1932 Bone cast himself as the "bitter protester" campaigning against the "ruthless exploitation of the whole nation by the coterie of business crooks who run national affairs." The Democrat also accepted the peace progressive teachings on foreign policy, urging a massive cut in military expenditures, attacking the French for loaning money to their East European allies for military spending, and criticizing the World Court as "an engine of war." Since it was "too much to expect that a court, consisting in the *main* of judges appointed by foreign dictators, would from the start be unbiased," Bone believed that "for the United States to take part in deciding questions of conflicting European interests is definitely dangerous." Bone did not view foreign policy as particularly important, although he urged pro–World Court voters to support him because of his positions on the more "compelling domestic issues." With his prolabor, proconsumer rhetoric, Bone joined Norris and La Follette as the only peace progressives able to bridge the gap between the group's 1920s domestic ideology and 1930s liberalism.[7]

Finally, the political arithmetic confronting the peace progressives in 1933 differed markedly from that of the 1920s. After the 1932 elections the Senate balance stood at fifty-nine Democrats, thirty-six Republicans, and one Farmer-Laborite; the 1934 elections only increased the Democratic majority. Although by voting as a bloc the peace progressives still had some influence, their greatest potential came through an alliance with the conservative minority, a prospect that interested them only rarely before 1937. The newly elected Franklin Roosevelt wooed them during his first term in large part because their agenda stood much closer to his than did the ideologies of conservative Senate Democrats. This power, however, did not equal that enjoyed by the group in the Senate of the 1920s. Political insecurity did not cause the peace progressives to turn away from anti-imperialism, but when combined with other international and national events it made the shift considerably more likely.

The peace progressives had always assumed that a policy of anti-imperialism would serve the economic as well as the moral and strategic interests of the United States, but the 1930s shattered this belief. The first sign that economic nationalism was tempering their anti-imperialism came in their opinions regarding the Philippines; the peace progressives divided over the applicability of the tariff to the islands while still an American colony and later split on the reasons for granting the Filipinos their independence.

Several peace progressives viewed the Philippines as a threat to the economic well-being of the American farmer and called for the application of the Hawley-Smoot tariff to the islands. Borah, scoffing that "these Eastern industrialists not only want their high protection, but they want free raw material and cheap food stuffs," favored granting domestic producers a bounty while denying one to growers from Hawaii or the Philippines, whereas Nye wanted a tariff on Filipino agricultural oils as a way to protect continental farmers. This view of the Philippines as a threat to U.S. agriculture peaked in 1932 with a Shipstead amendment to levy an emergency tariff on most Filipino agricultural products, which the Minnesota senator said would rectify a situation in which "the farmers of the United States are compelled to pay indirectly the cost of maintaining the Philippines under the American flag." The Shipstead group consistently denied that its policy would injure the average Filipino. Howell contended that affluent companies would bear the brunt of the burden under the amendment, while Shipstead maintained that the cost would fall to the "Oil Trust." Dill denounced the hypocrisy of trying to exclude Filipino goods when the islands were still under the American flag, but he supported restricting the rights of Filipinos in another way, by barring Filipino immigration to the United States. The Washington senator termed the matter a "most serious question" for Pacific Northwest labor, since Filipino immigrants went into lumber camps to "work for wages upon which a white man cannot live." Simply because those "interested in exploiting the Philippines" had succeeded in unjustly delaying independence for the islands, he saw "no reason why in the meantime this kind of oriental labor should be permitted through our gates." Dill went on to charge wildly that the immigrants had brought spinal meningitis into the United States and therefore represented a health risk; he concluded that the Senate needed to "protect our own people and our own country."[8]

A relatively small group of peace progressives, led by Norris and Blaine, expressed horror at the abandonment of the group's traditional perspective on the Philippines. Blaine termed the idea of a tariff on Filipino goods a "betrayal" of American principles; "since America dominates the political and economic life of the Philippine Islands, we have no right to tax them without their consent, any more than the British had a right to tax our colonies without our consent." Norris, dismissing the Shipstead Amendment as an "absolutely indefensible" contravention of the "fundamental principle of our existence," pleaded that "we ought to be fair enough to a weak people whom we are holding without their consent." He also criticized the Dill Amendment, contending that the United States could not "on the one hand . . . hold them in subjection" and on the other deny Filipinos the freedom to travel. Norris and Blaine, however, did not oppose the rationale motivating the other peace progressives. Norris said that he sympathized with the principle of the Dill Amendment, while he joined Wheeler and Blaine in implying support for a tariff on Filipino sugar. They maintained, however, that the Senate could not consider such proposals until after it had granted the Filipinos their independence.[9]

These fissures also appeared when the Senate considered independence apart from the tariff bill, as occurred sporadically from 1929 through 1932. All the peace progressives except Howell, who wavered, supported independence, but they did so for differing reasons, signaling the first major anti-imperialist issue since the war on which the peace progressives differed substantially among themselves. A case for independence based upon anti-imperialist principles, most thoroughly espoused by Wheeler, La Follette, and Norris, continued to come from the dissenters. The other peace progressives did not disagree with these sentiments, but, unlike in 1916, they no longer found them the single most compelling reason for granting independence.[10] Terming it a "burning question on the Pacific coast," Dill wanted independence "at the earliest possible date that will not be seriously destructive of American interests." Borah called independence a matter of "supreme importance" to American agriculture and thus favored independence by the mid-1930s so that the United States could tax Filipino exports; Howell agreed that Filipino products "depress certain agricultural products of this country." A degree of isolationism also crept into the rhetoric of this group. Shipstead termed the Philippines "the weakest link in our position of self-defense," while Borah opposed a Dill/Wheeler scheme to neutralize the islands following independence on the grounds that it would not serve American interests to "have an island of western culture in the midst of an oriental ocean" unless the United States was willing to fight to protect its outpost. Howell made the strongest statement, saying that he was "inclined to say 'amen' if we can wash our hands of the islands completely and be freed of all obligations as to their future."[11]

In 1934 all the peace progressives united around the nationalist position, supporting a Shipstead amendment to place a three-cent-per-pound "processing tax" on Filipino coconut oil, which the Minnesota senator contended would rectify the unfair "advantage over foreign countries" held by the Philippines. Despite a charge from Millard Tydings that the "purpose of this tax is to destroy the Philippines," even Norris endorsed the Shipstead proposal with a perfecting amendment that turned over all revenues from the tax to the Philippine treasury. The Nebraska senator conceded that "it is very difficult to do justice both to our wards, the Filipinos, and to the American farmer," but if an injustice had to be done, it "would be better to do that injustice to the Filipinos rather than to the American farmer." Denying that his proposal constituted a morally unacceptable tariff, the Nebraska senator reasoned that it only asked of the Filipino people a sacrifice like that given by farmers who had curtailed crop production under the Agricultural Adjustment Administration.[12]

Peace progressive comments on the Soviet Union likewise revealed a gradual movement away from anti-imperialism and toward a foreign policy based more upon economic necessities. Wheeler, who toured the USSR for the second time in 1930, returned with a much bleaker view than he had held in 1923, although he retained his fundamentally optimistic view of the future of the Soviet Union. Wheeler praised Soviet efforts in education and agriculture and predicted that "eventually there will emerge from it all a democratic form of government patterned after our own." Despite all its faults, Borah believed that the Soviet government was looking out for the "welfare of the Russian people," and he too guessed that the Soviet regime "will continue to modify its views until there will be established in Russia a democracy, not such a democracy as we believe in, but such a democracy as will best fit the lives of the Russian people." Some peace progressives had few objections to the Soviet Union as it existed. Norris maintained in early 1934 that on peace and disarmament "Russia is more in accord with the United States . . . than most any other foreign nation," while Brookhart contended that the Soviets had only inherited their Communist ideology from the early Christians. This rhetoric represented a slight modification of the traditional peace progressive viewpoint on Soviet affairs. By the early 1930s the senators seemed to believe that the Soviet Union had moved toward a democratic government on its own, and that U.S. diplomatic recognition was not required to undermine communism. Earlier they had predicted Soviet progress toward democracy but had consistently maintained that only through recognition could the United States ensure the undermining of the hard-line Bolshevik factions in Moscow. The rhetoric also indicated a continued overoptimistic view of developments inside the USSR.[13]

This left economic grounds as the prime peace progressive rationale for recognition. Wheeler believed that Americans were "suckers" for not realizing that "Russia is the greatest potential market for American goods in the world"; he worried that nonrecognition only denied the Soviet market to small businesses, since large and influential American firms could deal with the Soviets in any event. Borah saw a great potential market in the USSR as a result of the expected success of the Five-Year Plan, and argued that the Depression mandated a policy "to cultivate friendly relations and develop trade with every nation under the sun." Even Norris conceded that although "there is a higher reason for recognizing Russia than the trade advantages[,] . . . in this day of terrible stress" the United States could not overlook the potential economic gain from the policy. He predicted that the United States could do an "immense amount of business" in Russia.[14]

While the newly prominent economic nationalism did not alter the ultimate policies that the peace progressives had recommended for the Philippines and the USSR, the same did not hold true for China. Wheeler led a bloc of Western senators that agitated for the remonetization of silver as a way to combat the "Oriental countries" that had captured "our foreign textile markets and invade[d] our home market, because their lower production costs, due to their depreciated currencies and low-priced silver, enable[d] them to offer their goods at a price far below our cost of production." The senator also hoped that remonetization would increase the purchasing power of people in East Asia and stifle the trend toward industrialization in both China and Japan. He further argued that the United States should remonetize "independently and alone" to derive the maximum advantage in preventing "the Orient from dumping their products upon us."[15] Wheeler's silver policy, deliberately designed to injure the Chinese economy, best illustrated how the new economic nationalism of the dissenters could alter their anti-imperialist perspective.

The shift from anti-imperialism to economic nationalism revealed itself also in early 1930s peace progressive comments about debt refinancing. The major debt-related initiative of the Hoover administration came in 1931, when the President announced a one-year moratorium on debt repayments during the congressional recess. Although most peace progressives unenthusiastically supported the moratorium as a necessary gamble to alleviate worldwide economic distress, they sharply criticized Hoover for legislating through "private conferences" with congressional leaders; Blaine reminded the President that, in contrast to his days running a coal mine in China, the American government ran "by law and not by the edict of a dictator." Shipstead and Norris agreed that Hoover had committed a serious constitutional offense and had overstepped his "authority and power." The dissenters further wondered why Hoover had granted the moratorium unilaterally. Shipstead contended that the European nations could repay their debts if they cut their defense budgets by 10 percent rather than having American taxpayers pay "for the armies and navies of Europe"; the Minnesota senator singled out France, with "heaps of gold, sitting on top of which she dictates her policy to the world," for utilizing its "financial power" for nonpeaceful purposes. Borah and Blaine agreed that the moratorium would serve little purpose if not accompanied by "drastic disarmament." Norris devoted the most attention to this issue, urging Hoover to use the debts to bring about a spirit of peace, which neither international law nor arms could create. The Nebraska senator added that the only practical way the United States could prove its desire for peace "is to stop building warships and equipping large standing armies."[16]

The peace progressives also used the moratorium issue to make their final plea for a pro-German turn in American foreign policy. Borah wired Hoover that he would oppose the moratorium if, as some had rumored, the French tied it to some sort of American commitment to "follow France in her continued demand for security." He reasoned that France really desired "nothing less than the destruction of Germany, Austria, and Hungary." Blaine charged that France "has sucked almost all of the lifeblood out of Germany," in effect taking a mortgage on the German economy (not unlike the bankers in Nicaragua) and obtaining access to territory and resources "under the harsh and unconscionable terms of the Versailles Treaty." The Wisconsin senator argued that Germany "presents a somewhat different picture" for American policy in Europe, because the Germans had spent far less on their military than on their international debts. The peace progressives united around a Howell amendment refusing a renewal of the moratorium without an affirmation from the European nations for "reformation of the Versailles Treaty." The amendment failed miserably, as did a Shipstead sense of the Senate resolution declaring Article 231 historically inaccurate. The senators fell back on a dramatic if not entirely new proposal by Borah to link the debt payments with reparations. In a reversal of his 1920s positions, the Idaho senator said that he would not insist on French disarmament as a precondition for cancellation, but he did imply that he expected a revision of Versailles to form part of the overall package. Wheeler and Shipstead instantly endorsed the proposal, with the Minnesota senator sharply castigating Hoover for not attending more closely to German reparations payments.[17]

A degree of nationalism had always existed in the peace progressive critique of debt refinancing, but it became a bit sharper in 1931. It focused on Gerald Nye, among the least prominent of the group during the 1920s, who introduced an amendment to couple the debt moratorium with a moratorium on farmers' private debts. Charging that the United States had drifted away from a policy of supporting American interests, Nye maintained that Hoover had to look out for Americans (especially farmers) first. Although he was the only peace progressive to express solely nationalistic sentiments, Nye's arguments resonated throughout the movement. Shipstead held that "economic salvation—like charity—should begin at home," while Blaine contended that public officials were "no less than traitorous . . . in their failure to bend *every* effort toward the rehabilitation of our own people." Norris charged that the Hoover administration "seems to be more interested in saving Europe than it is in saving America." It did not take too much to travel from this rhetoric to more hard-line policy of withdrawal from all European affairs, as revealed in Borah's comment in late 1931 that if the Europeans did not reduce armament spending and reparations quickly, then the United States "had better come out of Europe and stay out."[18]

The debt moratorium battle marked one of the final times when the peace progressives relied primarily upon 1920s-type arguments in criticizing debt policy. Perhaps the last such occasion came in 1932, in a series of initiatives by Borah, who chastised Hoover for not making more of an effort to scale back reparations payments. The Idaho senator worried about the economic effect of the payments upon the German economy, but he expressed the most concern about their political effect, contending that reparations constituted a form of "intellectual, emotional, and spiritual" warfare against Germany. Borah recognized that the United States could not put off a final resolution of the debt question much longer; he asked only that before cancellation became a reality, "some program ... be presented which deals with the real problem involved in world recovery," the link between the scaling back of reparations and disarmament. Shipstead followed up Borah's speech with a July 1932 resolution to offer debt cancellation conditioned upon a 5 percent annual cutback for ten years in the defense budgets of the forgiven nations, the abolition of all military conscription for thirty years (an idea that he had first proposed in 1925), and the cancellation of reparations. In the fall of 1932 Borah met with high-level officials from the Hoover administration and informed them that he would campaign actively for the G.O.P. ticket if and only if the President said that in his second term he would revise his position on debt renegotiation to support 50 percent world disarmament, a reduction in German reparations, and the stabilization of all currencies by international action. After some thought, the administration rejected the offer.[19]

Borah's rhetoric differed quite substantially when he next returned to the subject, in early January 1933. He still criticized the French for spending too much money on armaments, and still charged that the division of territory at Versailles "will torment the world for decades," but he concentrated on how the United States could use the debts to its own national advantage. He denied that a spirit of compassion compelled cancellation, contending that the European nations, with their comparatively small budget deficits and unemployment rates, enjoyed greater prosperity than the United States. Despite these concerns, Borah said that he would favor cancellation if in exchange the Europeans opened their markets to American farmers. Other desirable points included a more general revival of trade, the reestablishment of sound monetary systems, and a decrease in armaments, but the senator stressed that the Senate needed to begin discussion of the issue from the viewpoint of the farmer. He knew that it would take "gigantic efforts" to end the Depression, but he thought that his package might work.[20]

Borah's plan to use the debts to pry open markets for the farmers represented a feature entirely absent from the debt policy that the peace progressives offered in the 1920s. In late 1932 Borah wrote that the United States needed to do something with the debts to help the farmers, since "without a prosperous, independent, successful class of farmers, Republican institutions will be imperiled." He wanted to "trade these debts for real prosperity," favoring complete cancellation and possible American tariff revision "if a program could be worked out which would reopen the markets of the world and reestablish commodity prices." On the other end of the peace progressive ideological spectrum, Blaine advanced similar ideas, arguing that the United States should entertain suggestions for debt revision only when "our debtor countries cease building their armies and navies," stop conscription, revise Versailles, scale down reparations, and "remove the unfair discrimination against American products." The first four points in Blaine's list were familiar, but his fifth demand first appeared only in 1932. Like Borah, Blaine began retreating from the idea of using the debts to reshape the world in an anti-imperialist image toward a more narrow vision of employing the leverage gained by promising refinancing to extract economic concessions from the Europeans. This rhetoric increasingly gave way to an even more nationalistic view on debt renegotiation, symbolized by a Howell comment in April 1932 that Hoover needed to reiterate to the Europeans that every dollar not paid by Europe would have to be paid by American taxpayers, who were "not in as good a position to pay those dollars as are the well-fed and well-clothed Europeans." Frazier agreed that the peace progressives should do all that they could to get members of Congress more interested in making their debt adjustments in the United States and not abroad.[21]

By 1934 all the peace progressives remaining in the Senate shared this pervasive sense of frustration, and the group finally abandoned its long-articulated position that the United States should use the debts for some positive international purpose. Borah reasoned that the European governments had made up their minds not to pay, with encouragement from the United States, who had not forced the issue. The peace progressives decided that the so-called Johnson Act represented the best avenue for forcing the issue. Introduced by the former peace progressive Hiram Johnson, the act, aimed at "those European welchers," prohibited private American loans to European nations that defaulted on debts owed to either the U.S. government or American private interests.[22] The bill passed the Senate on a voice vote and effectively ended the debt controversy; by denying all loans to European governments that were in a state of partial as well as full default, the

Johnson Act took away any incentive for the Europeans to continue funding the debt. The peace progressives did not play a prominent role in the passage of the Johnson Act, but it did illustrate one way in which their newly empowered nationalism tempered their previously held anti-imperialism.

The decline of anti-imperialism in the peace progressive ideology might not have occurred so quickly if Herbert Hoover had won the 1932 presidential election. Hoover's defeat opened the way for the institution of Franklin Roosevelt's Good Neighbor Policy in Latin America, which, although it got off to a shaky start, quickly fulfilled the major wishes of the peace progressives. Their desire to end American military intervention in the Caribbean Basin satisfied, the peace progressives gradually lost interest in the region that more than any other had defined their stances in the 1920s.

Hoover had offered some rhetorical concessions to Latin American nationalism. In 1929 he remarked that "it ought not to be the policy of the United States to intervene by force to secure or maintain contracts between our citizens and foreign states or their citizens," and he also authorized the publication of the Clark Memorandum, which renounced the Roosevelt Corollary. Nonetheless, he continued the policy of nonrecognition toward unelected regimes until 1932, and although Henry Stimson conceded that the Marines could no longer protect all American property in Latin America, he also blasted the peace progressives and promised that what remained of the policy would "not be poisoned and rendered of no effect by ignorant or partisan attacks in the United States." Although Hoover reduced the number of troops stationed in Nicaragua, the Marines did not come out until Congress made them withdraw in 1932.[23]

While praising Hoover for the steps that he did take, the peace progressives chastised the President for not going far enough. Borah publicly commended Stimson's repudiation of the Wilson nonrecognition policy, but the next year the peace progressives bitingly criticized a Frederick Hale amendment (backed by the administration) to increase expenditures for the Marine force occupying Nicaragua in time to supervise the 1932 Nicaraguan election. Nye and Wheeler wondered how long the United States would continue a policy motivated solely by the desire to protect "American dollars." La Follette, meanwhile, provided the only public opposition to a Hoover reservation (supported and defended by Borah) that exempted all previous treaties between the United States and Latin American countries from the scope of the 1932 Pan-American Arbitration Treaty. The Wisconsin senator charged that the reservation would "make the treaty a hollow shell," since it would exclude virtually any attempt by Haiti, Cuba, Nicaragua, and Panama to arbitrate anything with the United States; he wanted Washington to prove that its oft-stated sentiments favoring the judicial settlement of international controversies actually meant something. La Follette failed in his attempt to have the Senate overturn the reservation.[24]

The peace progressives showed more patience with Roosevelt, who in 1932 had enjoyed the support or the benevolent neutrality of all in the group except Howell. Because of his role in the Haitian occupation and his ill-timed remark in the 1920 campaign, Roosevelt did not enjoy a reputation as a sympathizer with anti-imperialism. He had, however, somewhat modified his views in a celebrated 1928 article in *Foreign Affairs*, admitting that the occupation did not constitute "another forward step" in inter-American relations. In place of the old ideas, Roosevelt recommended a policy of mutual security, agreeing that "it is not the right or duty of the United States to intervene alone," since the United States "must accept . . . a newer and better standard in international relations." He nonetheless continued to justify the initial decision to occupy Haiti out of the need to prevent revolutionary disturbances from spreading to Cuba, and he expressed surprise that instead of thanking the United States, most Latin American governments "disapprove of our intervention almost unanimously." Although Roosevelt in his 1932 inaugural address promised a new Latin American policy based upon the principle of the "good neighbor," the policy remained remarkably vague throughout 1933. The administration's first Latin American policy test, in Cuba, did little to clarify matters. Sumner Welles, the President's top adviser on Latin American affairs and his first ambassador to Cuba, quickly orchestrated Machado's ouster, but when the successor regime was overthrown, Welles persuaded the administration not to extend diplomatic recognition to the new revolutionary government, headed by Ramón Grau San Martín. The general pattern of Cuban policy repeated itself in early Roosevelt policy toward Haiti, with the President taking little interest in the matter other than to support the efforts of Assistant Secretary of State William Phillips to wind down the occupation on terms negotiated by the Hoover State Department.[25]

These policies began to arouse opposition from a peace progressive contingent initially inclined to offer the administration the benefit of the doubt. Borah specifically chastised Welles's handling of the Grau recognition issue. Contact between the Idaho senator and Cuban opposition politicians had existed since 1931, when he reversed his opposition to the Shipstead position and called for American action against Machado, whom he accused of reviving "the old practices of five centuries ago" by denying "the simplest rights" to most Cubans. In September 1933 Borah denounced Roosevelt's "disappointing and disastrous" Cuban policy as a "departure from the principles of the Constitution" and called for the United States to abrogate the Platt Amendment at once. He then authored a public letter to Grau, telling the Cuban president that "Cuba can best solve her own problems and is entitled to live her own life in her own way . . . The policy of exploitation upon the part of certain private interests and the period of interference with your governmental affairs ought to have an end." Borah also worked closely with Ernest Gruening, then busily arranging an opposition bloc to the proposed Haitian arrangement, agreeing with the publicist on the need for a "new deal" for Latin America and pronouncing himself "very much in sympathy . . . [with] the termination of our financial occupancy of Haiti."[26]

This revival of peace progressive interest in Latin America coincided with the seventh annual Inter-American Conference, scheduled for Montevideo in December 1933. The administration initially did not plan a major revision of policy for the conference; State Department instructions were similar to those given the delegates to the 1923 and 1928 conferences. Hull led the American delegation; Gruening served as his adviser on Latin American affairs. Given that Gruening several months earlier had denounced the proposed Haitian treaty for leaving the United States "in complete control of the economic and fiscal life of the country" and permitting the use of American military and diplomatic power "for the collection of a debt for private bondholders," the appointment represented a considerable concession to the peace progressives. (Dorothy Detzer observed that Gruening's appointment represented "convincing evidence of a new deal in United States policy toward Latin America.") Gruening and Hull traveled together to Uruguay, and Gruening urged the Secretary to make a definitive statement against intervention. Hull disagreed, asking what he would do when "chaos breaks out in one of these countries and armed bands go roaming around, pillaging and murdering Americans." When

Gruening pressed, Hull confided that he had his own weaker proposal, and added that he had worked out a private deal with Argentina's foreign minister, Carlos Saavedra Lamas, to have Saavedra act as a shield against anti-American resolutions in exchange for the United States' signing an antiwar pact authored by the ambitious Argentine. Saavedra did not live up to his end of the bargain; instead he issued a ringing condemnation of intervention and supported the report of the Committee on Rights and Duties of States, which forbade intervention in the internal or external affairs of another state and affirmed that foreigners had to abide by local law. This move left Hull in the awkward position of having to accede to a report far more radical than he preferred or admitting that the Good Neighbor Policy constituted no real change; he chose the former option. Gruening's role in this decision remains unclear, but it was no coincidence that Hull adopted in his speech many of the proposals promoted earlier by Gruening. Roosevelt reinforced the Secretary's remarks over the next month. In a December 28 speech the President asserted that "the definite policy of the United States from now on is one opposed to armed intervention," and he admitted that he could understand why Latin American nationalists criticized the United States, an important concession given the type of rhetoric that came from centrist Democrats during the 1920s.[27]

A case can certainly be made that domestic politics, and not international relations, provided the key motivation for Roosevelt's change in direction. By late 1933 Roosevelt needed the peace progressives on domestic votes, and he had already made it clear that, in contrast to the dissenters, Latin American policy did not stand high on his list of priorities. The President also feared that "Progressive Republicans like La Follette . . . Nye, etc. . . . are flirting with the idea of a third ticket . . . with the knowledge that such a third ticket would be beaten but that it would defeat us, elect a conservative Republican, and cause a complete swing far to the left before 1940." When combined with the fact that the December rhetorical shifts had received a positive response in Latin America, the politics of the move also must have appealed to Roosevelt. Regardless of whether or not Roosevelt acceded to the change in his Latin American policy for domestic political reasons, by early 1934 the Good Neighbor bore some similarity to the 1920s positions of the peace progressives; the administration implicitly conceded the right of expropriation and explicitly forfeited the treaty rights with Nicaragua, Haiti, and Cuba.[28]

This program proved more than powerful enough to win over most of the anti-imperialist wing of the peace movement, which had so plagued Kellogg and Coolidge and had questioned Roosevelt's course in Cuba. *The Nation*, now under the stewardship of Freda Kirchwey with Villard as only a contributing editor, termed the role played by Welles in the overthrow of Machado an "auspicious beginning" for a new policy; Hubert Herring agreed to the need for a "continuation of the mediation so intelligently launched by Mr. Welles." The nonrecognition doctrine, however, did not please the group. Both Samuel Guy Inman and *The Nation* praised Grau's government, and Gruening agreed that "our policy should be to recognize any regime which the Cubans set up, try to work with it, and help it succeed." Nor did the anti-imperialists like what they saw elsewhere in the Caribbean. Herring blasted James Farley for playing patronage politics with Puerto Rican appointments, and contended that American treatment of Puerto Rico constituted a key test of the alleged good intentions of the Good Neighbor Policy. He also criticized the proposed executive agreement with Haiti as a "betrayal of Haiti's hopes and legitimate aspirations," noting that apparently a New Deal for Haiti meant that "the chicanery of the past is solemnly reenacted."[29]

Even at this early stage, however, the anti-imperialist movement began to fracture. The *New Republic* praised Roosevelt for not sending the Marines into Cuba, largely out of fear that it would weaken the American moral position in Manchuria vis-à-vis Japan. The radical rhetoric of the Grau regime perturbed the editors, and they expressed some sympathy for Roosevelt's handling of the situation. Meanwhile, a bitter critique of the policy came from Carleton Beals, who accused Welles of setting "up an illegal government which looked legal," symbolic of an "interventionist attitude not one whit different" from the G.O.P. of the 1920s. Beals also ridiculed Welles's rhetoric about seeking a regime that represented the wishes of the Cuban people, claiming that Welles really wanted a "government subservient to Washington." This foreshadowed what became a penetrating critique of the Good Neighbor Policy which argued that the tariff reciprocity championed by Hull demanded of the Latin Americans "that for the sake of American merchants they ... remain dutiful little colonies under Uncle Sam's tutelage." By mid-1934, then, one element of the anti-imperialist coalition had abandoned the movement, while Beals had staked out a position far more radical than that of any of his counterparts. Gruening wondered if his onetime colleague had not "succumbed to the conspiracy complex."[30]

The Montevideo Conference and subsequent policy moves, particularly Gruening's appointment as Director of the Division of Territories and Island Possessions in 1934, transformed all the anti-imperialists except Beals into enthusiastic champions of the Good Neighbor Policy. Inman praised Hull's "astounding" success at Montevideo for creating a "greater degree of amity between our country and [Latin America] than at any other period in our history"; *The Nation* championed Roosevelt's Wilson Foundation address as an "unprecedented and tremendously significant step forward in American foreign policy." With the renunciation of intervention, the anti-imperialists attempted to come up with positive steps to advance inter-American relations, and in doing so they revealed a sharply different perspective from the 1920s. Both Gruening and *The Nation* wanted a more active American presence combatting dictatorial regimes in the Caribbean, pointing in 1935 to the continuance of obnoxious governments in Cuba, the Dominican Republic, and Haiti as the chief failures of the Good Neighbor Policy. Meanwhile, Villard praised Hull's "tremendously important" reciprocal tariff idea in phrases that sounded like those of an economic imperialist. He called for incorporating the Caribbean into an American free trade zone as the first step toward a Western Hemisphere economic bloc, since "if the United States has a manifest destiny it is that it should find its best markets in Central and South America." Inman began attempting to settle German intellectual refugees in Latin America, while Gruening decided to reform the system from within and accepted Roosevelt's job offer, which made him the top American official in Puerto Rico and the Virgin Islands. Ironically, his attempt at widespread economic and social reforms drew accusations of imperialism from his political enemies in Puerto Rico, who criticized him for employing too many Americans in Puerto Rican relief efforts and pushing "wildly radical, impractical, and visionary schemes for which the people [of Puerto Rico] are not yet ready." By 1935, anti-imperialism as a movement in the 1920s sense had ceased to exist.[31]

Although some elements of the anti-imperialist movement, notably the new editors at *The Nation*, disagreed with the Villard perspective on Hull's reciprocal tariff agreements, none of the anti-imperialist rhetoric resembled the rather sharp opposition the plan received from most peace progressives. Borah favored building up foreign trade, but "with due regard to domestic interests," and he refused to sanction anything that would take from the Senate its taxing power and leave him "powerless to serve my constituents." The Idaho senator predicted disastrous consequences for treaties with nations that had "very little to send into this country except that of which our people produce a surplus." Dill and Hiram Johnson united on an amendment to subject all reciprocity agreements to congressional ratification, since neither wanted to grant the President sole power to control the tariffs on goods "competing with the products of the people of the United States." The only free-trade voice in the group came from Homer Bone, who asked his colleagues to remember the fact that although South American agriculture had an advantage over its American counterpart, American manufactured goods enjoyed a similar advantage in South American markets. (Norris stayed with the administration on all key votes but admitted that he would not support the bill "if we were not in the midst of a depression.") After the vote Borah predicted that reciprocity "would open up the markets of this country to the agricultural and livestock production of other countries to the utter destruction of our own," but it did not have the effect that Hull had hoped or that Borah had feared.[32]

The reciprocity debate did not provide the only evidence that the peace progressives had moved away from the anti-imperialism of Borah's early critique of the Good Neighbor Policy toward a more nationalist stance. By the mid-1930s Wheeler and Nye became active on behalf of bondholder committees fighting for repayment of Latin American securities in default. They denied that their attacks on Cuba, Mexico, and Brazil constituted imperialism, maintaining that they wanted to protect the smaller investor who lacked the influence of the international bankers. Meanwhile, perhaps as a result of obligations assumed to American Catholic leaders in their joint fight against U.S. membership in the World Court, Borah in 1935 introduced a resolution calling for an investigation of antireligious activities by the government of Lázaro Cárdenas in Mexico. Claiming that his resolution was entirely consistent with his Mexican policies of the preceding two decades, he maintained that he only wished to protect American citizens affected by "this brutal and barbarous fight on religion in Mexico"; the senator could not "understand why we should be indifferent to a situation which involved life, property, and religious freedom for our own people as well as for the people of Mexico." The Borah resolution led to editorial outcry in the United States and a stinging response from the Mexican government. Mexico's Foreign Minister Emilio Portes Gil charged that it "was tantamount to abolishing the wise policy of the 'good neighbor.'" Although he quickly lost interest in the matter (in part because of the strong reaction it produced), Borah's resolution indicated how far and how quickly the group had moved away from its 1920s anti-imperialism.[33]

Virtually the only remnant of anti-imperialism in peace progressive statements came in connection with an issue that represented the past and not the future. In 1935 the Senate voted on the promotion of John Russell, former commander of the American occupying forces in Haiti. Shipstead called for denying promotion because of Russell's responsibility for the 1927 incident in which Borno had prevented William King from entering Haiti, and he denounced the arrogance of Russell to ask for a promotion given his conduct during the occupation. Despite Shipstead's rhetoric, an idealist Democrat, Hugo Black, fought the hardest to block the promotion, threatening a filibuster and offering a long and bitter speech questioning Russell's qualifications and conduct. A Black motion to recommit the promotion failed, and in any case opposition to the Haitian occupation represented a fight over a dead issue given Roosevelt's commitment to withdraw.[34]

The vote on the reciprocal tariff bill revealed an evolving pattern in peace progressive policy toward Latin America. Satisfied that they had won a major victory with the adoption of the Good Neighbor Policy, the majority of peace progressives simply turned their attention away from the region to focus on domestic or European affairs. This occurred largely as a result of another broad theme raised by the reciprocity issue: the shift in inter-American relations away from political, military, and (to a lesser extent) cultural relations and toward economic ones. In this new environment, the 1920s anti-imperialism of the peace progressives offered little guidance, allowing the economic nationalism that the senators had exhibited in earlier tariff debates to come to prominence. For those who continued to pay attention to the region, Latin America became another avenue for the group's growing nationalism, as shown by their conduct in the bondholders issue. In a rather ironic twist, the success of the senators in moving the United States away from an interventionist policy contributed to their drift away from the ideology that had originally motivated their opposition.

On the surface, the element of the peace progressive ideology least affected by the group's increasing nationalism was its antimilitarism, but even on this issue the senators' beliefs gradually underwent transformation. Though defeated badly on the cruiser bill votes, the peace progressives maintained the offensive throughout the Hoover administration. In close cooperation with the peace movement, Frazier continued his work to have antimilitarism adopted as official government policy. In 1931 he proposed an amendment to the War Department appropriations bill to forbid compulsory military training at all non-military colleges, contending that ROTC perverted the meaning of education, since colleges could not provide both learning and military training. This issue also worried Nye, who charged that ROTC programs forced college men to "listen to a lot of doctrine that I think is unpatriotic." Though unsuccessful, the amendment attracted the support of all peace progressives except McMaster, who argued that the Senate should leave the decision to the states.[35]

The peace progressives also continued to put forth as an alternative to arms increases solutions that they had offered in the 1920s. In 1932 Frazier introduced an amendment to place the United States on record as favoring a one-year moratorium on naval building (similar to the debt moratorium) as an inducement for other nations to do the same. At the same time, all peace progressives except Borah expressed enthusiasm about the disarmament talks that took place in Geneva late in the Hoover administration. Frazier insisted that if the passive American delegation took the lead "several other nations would gladly join them" in obtaining a "world-wide treaty providing for an immediate drastic cut in arms and steadily progressing disarmament, looking toward total disarmament." Norris agreed that the American delegation should "take the initiative," and he called for a shuffling of the negotiators to include delegates less linked to military interests. The Nebraska senator also wondered against whom the military would direct its new weapons, as did Nye, who in 1932 reasoned that the government had "no right to go" beyond the level of armaments needed to protect the country against invasion. He cited China (a rather odd choice) as an example of a country that could survive without a large military.[36]

Meanwhile, the effects of the Depression appeared in Blaine's contention that "permanent restoration and stability of economic life and public welfare" demanded an "immediate and drastic reduction in arms." Such a perspective had formed a relatively minor element of the 1920s peace progressive critique. Shipstead quizzed Frederick Hale on the government's ability to afford the 1932 naval bill in light of the economic downturn and the smaller-than-expected debt payments by European countries, while La Follette denounced the hypocrisy of the "economy bloc" senators who called for decreased social spending but believed that "every dollar wasted" in the domestic side of the budget should go to the Navy. Concern about the cost of the naval budgets had always formed a part of the peace progressive critique of the military, but never before had it enjoyed the role that it did during the 1932 debates. As Borah explained, disarmament remained a moral issue but by 1932 stood "in a higher sense" as an economic problem.[37]

The peace progressives had one of their first substantive breaks with the Roosevelt administration over the 1934 Vinson bill to increase funding for the Navy, which all of them except the retiring Dill vehemently opposed.[38] Frazier believed that the vessels the Vinson bill authorized amounted to "floating palaces for the officers who have charge of those new ships," which "one well-directed bomb" would sink, since recent "sham battles" had proved that airplanes not only were superior to the battleships but also were invulnerable. The chief objection to the bill, however, of all peace progressives except Frazier lay in the alleged evil ties between the government and munitions manufacturers. This represented a theme that several peace progressives had raised during the 1910s but one almost entirely absent from their critiques of Republican military policy during the 1920s. Borah based his entire public opposition to the bill on this issue, denouncing the "power, and influence, and activities of munition manufacturers in the building up of armaments, and in questions affecting peace." The Idaho senator blamed the tensions between England and Germany before 1914 on the "sordid" propaganda from arms makers "seeking a market for their instruments of murder," and committed himself to foiling similar plans to provoke a conflict between the United States and Japan. Bone followed up with an even wilder speech charging that munitions makers, their patriotism "plastered all over with dollar signs," regarded the government as "an agency that exists merely for the purpose of enriching them at public expense." The senator who would become most associated with this cause, Gerald Nye, dismissed the Vinson bill as "a bill for the relief of the munitions makers of the United States." In response to pro-Navy forces who argued that the United States needed the bill because of the repeated failures of earlier disarmament conferences, Nye shot back that the conferences had failed only because of manipulation "by lobbyists for the munition makers who do not want, above all things else, anything resembling disarmament." All three senators implied that the world could achieve peace only when it checked the power of the munitions makers.[39]

This rhetoric coincided neatly with that of the Nye Committee, then just beginning its hearings. Although the idea of a Senate investigation of the munitions industry enjoyed fairly broad support, Dorothy Detzer played the most important role in persuading Nye of the plan's merits. A resolution authorizing an investigation of the issue set up a special committee that elected Nye as its chair although it contained a nominal Democratic majority. The committee undertook a wide-ranging investigation of the connection between the munitions industry, the government, and international peace. It spent $130,000 and questioned almost two hundred witnesses, including J. P. Morgan, whose appearance Nye said proved that "bankers were in the heart and center of a system that made our going to war inevitable." The Munitions Committee gradually transformed its mission from looking into arms manufacturers into a probe of the reasons for the American entry into World War I. This eventually brought the investigation to a close, since Nye's charge that Wilson and Lansing had "falsified" their knowledge of the secret treaties undermined the committee's claim of impartiality on general foreign policy matters. Although the committee generally failed to prove its central charges, its ability to produce a few spectacular instances of bribery by munitions makers or immoral arms lobbying led to a public notion that the committee had reached the truth. Cordell Hull later wrote that the hearings had the "disastrous effects" of arousing "an isolationist sentiment that was to tie the hands of the Administration just at the very time when our hands should have been free to place the weight of our influence in the scales where it would count."[40]

Whatever else their impact, the hearings furthered the peace progressive movement away from anti-imperialism: their tenor and outcome would have been very different had they occurred in the 1920s (the Shipstead hearings on foreign loans provide a basis for comparison). Beyond the obvious point that Nye, as one of the two or three least prominent peace progressives, would not have played a leading role in 1920s hearings, the basic premise of the committee's investigation differed markedly from the peace progressive mindset of the anti-imperialist era. In the fall of 1934 Nye stated that "there may be doubt as to the degree but there is certainty that the profits of war itself constitute the *most serious challenge* to the peace of the world." This remark differed sharply from the 1920s peace progressive belief that a more complex combination of commercial expansionism, militarism, great-power dominance of international relations, and imperialism threatened peace. Although many of the villains remained the same, the Nye hearings boiled down the 1920s beliefs and singled out arms manufacturers (eventually, Nye decided, in partnership with elements within the government) as the sole problem. Implicitly, this critique of the international environment also solved the problems of how to achieve peace without cooperating with the Western European powers and running the risk of involvement in traditional power politics. The peace progressives of the earlier decade had settled upon anti-imperialism as the most fruitful vehicle to achieve this goal; by the mid-1930s they had rejected their earlier internationalism and turned to a purely domestic solution—curbing the powers of American manufacturers of arms—as a way to bring about peace. This reinforced the inward-looking nature of the peace progressive position also evidenced in the group's increasing economic nationalism.[41]

Nye justified his committee's work in a long speech blaming the repeated failures of postwar disarmament conferences as well as the inability of the 1920s peace progressives to block any of the decade's naval bills on the influence of the munitions industries (Shipstead concurred here), and he predicted that the country could eliminate the danger of war "if we can find the way somehow to make for less dollar prosperity in time of war." The North Dakota senator contended that the United States should take advantage of its geographic position and spend less money on national defense. He called for the nationalization of the munitions industry, noting that the United States could do a great deal to achieve peace irrespective of an international agreement. Bone, meanwhile, doubted that "moral suasion," a key element of the 1920s program of the peace progressives, could provide international peace, since "the private profit motive is overwhelming and seems to have submerged practically all other considerations"; therefore, the "only practical answer . . . is to take the profit out of war and preparation for war."[42]

The Nye Committee also did not worry about antagonizing foreign governments in its zeal for exposing the truth; the amoral connection between munitions makers (regardless of nationality) and foreign armed forces formed one of the committee's chief areas of interest. The hearings focused particularly in this respect on Latin American governments, and implicated a wide range of Central and South American public officials in international arms trafficking, often on flimsy evidence. The actions drew protests from Argentina, Peru, China, and

Mexico, prompting the Associated Press to remark that "whatever else it may have done, the . . . Senate inquiry into munitions deals has struck a good many sore spots in South and Central America." An Argentine admiral said that the committee "respects others' reputations so little" that obviously it did not care about its own; the Kuomintang minister in the United States, Alfred Sze, formally protested to Hull about a Nye charge that China had used funds derived from American wheat and cotton loans to purchase ammunition. The committee thus helped sweep away the remnants of the 1920s peace progressive vision of a global anti-imperialist front with the United States at its head.[43]

The committee also marked the growing importance of Nye in the peace progressive movement. The senator became something of a national celebrity, regularly appearing on the national lecture circuit. This too had important consequences, as the less nationalistic members of the movement—Norris, Dill, Wheeler, Blaine, La Follette—began either to pay less attention to foreign policy or to embrace nationalism along with Nye.[44] The North Dakota senator, the chief peace progressive spokesperson against the 1935 military appropriations bill, urged the President and Congress to work together and take from the military the power "to define an adequate defensive Navy." He repeated his call for curbs on the power of munitions makers, buttressing his point with the charge that "no one man was more responsible" for the world war than the notorious arms dealer Sir Basil Zaharoff. If Americans "could divorce ourselves from our American militarists," Nye predicted peace, even with Japan, where he also detected the influence of arms manufacturers in fomenting discord.[45]

As in 1915 and 1925, the peace progressives in 1935 represented the congressional bloc most hostile to increases in the military budget, and their antimilitarism remained even when their anti-imperialism faded. Yet their increasingly inward-oriented approach also had an impact on their opinions on defense issues, as shown in the Nye Committee's handling of foreign governments and in the beliefs of Nye, Borah, and many other peace progressives that the United States could achieve peace by limiting the powers of the munitions makers. Although the peace progressives succeeded in reconciling antimilitarism with a more nationalistic handling of foreign policy matters, they had to alter their arguments about military matters to do so.

The increasingly rigid nationalistic stance of the group explains the rapprochement between the peace progressives and their most prominent former member, Hiram Johnson. The California senator, acidly referred to by the London *Times* as the "most irreconcilable of irreconcilables," had drifted away from the movement in the early 1920s. He reversed his position on anti-imperialism (correctly viewing it as another form of internationalism) and criticized the peace progressives for taking too soft a stance concerning the Navy. The relationship between Johnson and the peace progressives, though never completely antagonistic because of their common dislike for mainstream Republicanism, cooled substantially after 1923. Norris pronounced himself "very much disappointed" with Johnson's post-1920 work, which "did not measure up to what his prior record indicated he ought to be." Raymond Robins, abandoning their earlier friendship, classified the California senator with James Reed as part of a breed of "narrow nationalists who are in fact American militarists," while Oswald Garrison Villard remarked that Johnson "seems bound to throw away what remains of his reputation" with his decision to abandon anti-imperialism for isolationism. For his part, Johnson consistently expressed disappointment in the "pacifists, who constitute the Insurgent group and who hate the Navy." The California senator reserved some of his bitterest criticism for Borah, complaining that the Idaho senator was acclaimed as "a great statesman . . . while I am still a nasty little demagogue." Undoubtedly an element of personal antipathy intensified the split between Johnson and the peace progressives, but sharp ideological differences played the most important role in driving the onetime allies apart.[46]

Although Johnson had participated in the anti-imperialist critique of Wilson's Russian and Haitian policies, by the mid-1920s he decided that isolationism and anti-imperialism could not mix. Critical in this transformation was his strongly negative view of revolutionary Mexico. The senator denounced the 1924 arms sale to Obregón as immoral and unconstitutional, and, unlike the peace progressives, he also expressed sympathy for Obregón's political foes. In 1926 he returned to the issue, requesting a Senate inquiry to look into rumors of a Mexican land grant to the Japanese in lower California. Anti-Mexico sentiment led him to support the Nicaraguan occupation, on which he sided with the administration in both the 1928 and 1929 votes. The senator, who made virtually no public statements on Nicaragua, privately argued in 1927 that "having undertaken to maintain ourselves . . . in that nasty little place, if we withdraw, what prestige we have in Latin-America is gone, and unless some scheme is agreed upon, to be ultimately upheld by our

Marines, Mexico will assume the paramount position in the land adjacent to the Panama Canal." He repeated this point a year later, denying that the fight against Sandino represented anything new in the history of U.S.-Nicaraguan relations and worrying that if the Marines pulled out they would leave "Mexican influences predominating." Beyond this, Johnson simply ceased commenting (either publicly or privately) on the countries where he had led anti-imperialist crusades early in his career, the Soviet Union and Haiti.[47]

Having abandoned anti-imperialism, Johnson turned to a form of nationalism that on most European questions resulted in an isolationist position. The senator ridiculed Borah's 1923 proposal for an international economic conference as a Wilsonian scheme to "make our country part of Europe" by dumping "into America's lap the economic ills of Europe and the reparations muddle." He reasoned that any movement by the United States toward involvement in European matters logically had to lead to League membership. He denounced internationalists (a term that he generally used to refer to anyone who opposed him) as people either "unconsciously distorted by cunning intrigue, and pervasive, iniquitous propaganda" or intellectuals who "contemptuously scorn all petty virtues and who scoff at patriotism," and dedicated himself to "maintaining America just as America has ever been." The senator foresaw "another bloody war" in Europe caused by a "clash of selfish ambitions and the yet existing racial feuds," and he warned Americans to stay out of "the turmoil, the strife, and the controversies." Unlike the peace progressives, who had hoped to use American power to reform Europe in the 1920s, Johnson had written the continent off as beyond hope shortly after the League fight. He thus framed the choices for the United States as adopting an isolationist position or participating in European power politics in their most unseemly form. Such an attitude naturally led this "most intractable of all the isolationists" to oppose American membership in the World Court, agitation for which he attributed to the influences of foreign propaganda. Johnson also feared taking "this hated creditor nation into a World Court dominated by its hating debtors." His recommended debt policy did little to appease the hated debtors; he blasted the "cynicism of Paris and London" for assuming that ordinary citizens of the American West and Midwest would shoulder increased tax burdens on their behalf. He therefore urged both Harding and Coolidge to keep the country away "from Europe's politics, from Europe's wars, from Europe's agreements." On both Latin American and European issues, Johnson exhibited a markedly different perspective from the peace progressives during the 1920s. He also tended to show considerably less interest in foreign affairs than did the dissenters.[48]

The senator also wished to shut the United States off from the world through its tariff and immigration policies. Johnson always emphasized the need to cultivate foreign markets, arguing that "we must of necessity market much of this surplus abroad, if our general prosperity and our standards of living are to be maintained." On the other hand, he took a more rigidly protectionist position than any peace progressive in 1922, and he turned in a similar performance in 1930 while fighting especially hard for the protection of California agricultural products (such as cherries). Like many other Western senators, he also stridently urged the elimination of Japanese immigration, celebrating the 1924 Immigration Act as a triumph for California "in the long struggle for the protection and preservation of its own." Johnson also called for avoiding future racial conflicts by limiting the number of Filipinos eligible to enter the United States. He worried about Filipinos "with their peculiar habits and their singular mode of living, different from ours, [trying] to supplant those who are part of the community, and who have made the community what it is." He also wanted to figure in the number of Mexicans who entered the country illegally when calculating the Mexican immigration quota.[49]

Johnson, then, held a highly nationalist and conspiratorial view of the world, convinced that foreign powers were out to manipulate American public opinion and through it the country's foreign policy out of a "hatred of the United States." Like James Reed, who shared similar beliefs, Johnson saw a powerful American Navy as his answer to the country's problems. The California senator blasted the "neglect and deterioration of our Navy" dating from the Washington Conference, which, by forcing the scrapping of "beautiful, completed battleships," had left the American Navy "so far inferior [to England and Japan] as to humiliate the national pride and imperil the national safety." Since the United States, as the world's leading creditor nation, had earned the enmity of most other countries, it needed a "maximum of naval strength" to maintain peace. Johnson concluded by denouncing the "experiment" of the United States' leading by example and called for the "international pacifists" to stop worrying that the United States might precipitate an international arms race and instead to begin considering the very real possibility of a joint European-Japanese alliance against the United States. In the end, "our foreign policy rests for its foundation not upon our will but upon our ability to defend that will."[50]

Johnson amplified on these themes when he twice parted company from the peace progressives in early 1929, to dismiss Kellogg-Briand and to support the cruisers bill. He voted for the treaty only after publicly ridiculing those who stand "agog . . . with the idea that . . . ratification . . . is going to bring in a new era" and privately dismissing the pact as "just a piece of bunk utilized by so-called statesmen the world over to fool their people." Meanwhile, he enthusiastically championed the cruisers bill, which he termed essential for the protection of U.S. "trade supremacy . . . in the good old American way," since "the spirit of commerce, after all, is the spirit of conquest." "Sick and tired of gestures made in this body, gestures without substance in them," such as the Borah/Blaine argument that the cruisers bill ran contrary to the Kellogg Pact or the general peace progressive belief that the bill would trigger an arms race, Johnson contended that the bill would further the cause of disarmament by putting the American Navy on a par with its competitors. Most important, the senator preferred a strong Navy to diplomatic methods in dealing "with very delicate questions in which our defense may be involved with foreign nations."[51]

Johnson's final attack against the disarmament sentiment of the 1920s came with his spirited opposition to the London Naval Treaty, or "another piece of international bunk." Fearing that "everybody is singing paeans of praise to peace, and without the slightest knowledge of the details of the treaty," he orchestrated testimony against the treaty by a parade of active and retired admirals during the Foreign Relations Committee hearings on ratification. In contrast to the peace progressives, who criticized the treaty (if at all) for constitutional reasons, Johnson squarely took on the idea of disarmament conferences. In a stinging Minority Report (with conservatives George Moses and Arthur Robinson concurring), Johnson contended that the treaty reinforced a pattern first begun at the Washington Conference, where "our sacrifices were infinitely greater than those of any other nation"; "hysterical internationalists" Stimson and Hoover had "scrapped the American policy at London" and permitted the United States to remain in an inferior position. Though particularly agitated about the "unjustified and unfair" ratio given to Japan, the senator believed that the treaty as a whole "imperils our sea-borne commerce and endangers our national defense." As previously, he offered no alternative other than to recommend increasing the strength of the American Navy. Johnson showed more activity in opposing the treaty than he had in any foreign policy fight since 1922, boasting to his son of the "impregnable" case that he made against the arrangement, the "wickedest thing" since the League. He particularly reveled in his position in the minority; as he had earlier admitted privately, "perhaps the Lord made me a normal rebel, perhaps just I'm an obstinate ass, but I just have to go my own way."[52]

Although Johnson did not hide his scorn for the 1920s peace progressive alternative to Republican foreign policy, by 1935 the California senator had renewed his alliance with the dissenters. This did not come about as a result of a change in his personal beliefs. Apart from toning down his pro-Navy rhetoric slightly, the Johnson of the 1930s did not differ from the Johnson of the 1920s. As late as 1931 he pointedly declined, despite prodding from William King, to urge the withdrawal of the Marines from Nicaragua; four years later he enthusiastically supported John Russell during the promotion debate. With anti-imperialism and disarmament less important issues, however, the peace progressives found the nationalistic elements of the rest of Johnson's program attractive. Johnson retained his economic nationalism, and he also joined the anti-free-trade peace progressives in their opposition to the 1934 reciprocity bill. He repeated the constitutional objections against the bill but conceded that he had more "selfish and provincial" reasons for his position. The senator recalled that he had fought throughout his career for high tariffs so that California "might be prosperous and in order that it might meet competition from abroad," and he had no intention of denying Californians the tariffs "which we require for our very life."[53]

His investigation of foreign loans, which operated under the premise that "our people have been soaked unmercifully for the profit of these international bankers," also brought him closer to the peace progressives. The investigation, which occurred under the auspices of the Finance Committee, uncovered links between the State Department and Colombian oil concessions as well as irregularities in the marketing of European and Latin American securities in the United States. The California senator had continued his fight against debt readjustment during the Hoover and Roosevelt administrations, criticizing the debt moratorium as the "first step that these international bankers wish us to take

... the step towards dictatorship" and urging the Senate not to "be Europe minded when distress stalks in our land." The remarks drew praise from Dill, Nye, and Wheeler, and the sentiments that he expressed reflected the increasingly nationalist position taken on the issue by the peace progressives.[54]

This reconciliation with the Johnson framework figured most prominently in the peace progressive responses to the international crises of the early 1930s. The dissenters no longer believed that the United States had the ability to influence world developments on the scale necessary to bring peace; therefore, they recommended doing everything possible to make sure that the country would not become involved in what they viewed as an increasingly inevitable great power conflict. In one way, this represented a return to the positions held by the peace progressives during World War I, when the entire group had feared U.S. involvement in traditional power politics and had sought to structure various alternatives to such a prospect. But important differences existed by the early 1930s. In particular, the group had far less confidence in some of the bolder solutions that they had forwarded during the 1910s, such as economic embargoes against aggressive states, U.S. participation in an international navy, or even an anti-imperialist alliance with like-minded nations. This distrust of the international scene left the dissenters increasingly inclined to attempt to seal the United States off from Europe as the best way to avoid American participation in any forthcoming conflict. A few peace progressives had toyed with such ideas during the 1910s, but never with the intensity of the group of the 1930s. In addition, those who had considered such an option during the World War I era, notably Borah, had formed a distinct minority of the group. By the 1930s the dissenters were all but unanimous on the wisdom of this position. With the decline of the anti-imperialist perspective, they felt as if no other policy choice existed that could fulfill their foreign policy goals.

The peace progressive response to events in Asia served as the first indication that the solutions of the 1920s had fallen out of favor. On September 18, 1931, the Japanese Kwantung Army, violating both the Kellogg-Briand Pact and the Nine Power Treaty, invaded Manchuria and eventually set up the puppet state of Manchukuo. Only on October 14 did the League (along with the United States) criticize the Japanese and call for a return to the pre-September status quo; it also authorized a commission headed by England's Lord Lytton to investigate the affair. Stimson had desired stronger action, including economic sanctions against the Japanese, but Hoover feared that the policies could lead to an American-Japanese war. The Secretary thus settled for a statement affirming that the United States would not recognize any territory gained by Japan through conquest.[55]

The peace progressives divided in their initial response to the Manchurian Incident. The majority sided with Borah, who condemned the Japanese for having "violated every international law" but confidently if vaguely predicted that the Kellogg Pact and the Nine Power Treaty would solve the situation. The Idaho senator opposed strong American action against the Japanese, particularly if it meant changing the "peace pact into a military pact" and putting it into operation "whenever the fertile mind of some ambitious schemer can find an aggressor." Borah also questioned the wisdom of economic sanctions, contending that a boycott would turn "the face of the American people towards another war," taking the United States "in the realm where the 'force' people are anxious apparently to find us." The senator admitted that Americans had "gone as far as we can go" under Kellogg-Briand and would have to rely on "time and public opinion" ultimately to settle the crisis. Shipstead, even more critical of the course pursued by the administration, charged that Stimson had violated the Nine Power Treaty by consulting with the League rather than with the treaty signatories; as things stood in December 1931, in a bizarre rationale, Japanese good faith in the pact "has been proved to be as good as that of any other nations . . . in fact . . . better than most." (The Minnesota senator also denied that the Japanese had violated Kellogg-Briand, positing that both Japan and China had claimed self-defense, which was all that the pact required.) Shipstead had no solutions, however, expressing a deep pessimism about the possibility of long-term peace given that "under the guise of self-defense, wars of conquest can still be carried on." Borah added that recognition of the USSR, which he predicted would lead to the "friendly cooperation of Russia . . . in the Orient," constituted the "limited field within which we can properly move."[56]

Other peace progressives wanted a more active American stance. Norris praised Stimson for "making protest and taking peaceful action against Japan," and only wished that the League powers had cooperated more with the United States. Brookhart took an even more internationalist standpoint, urging a "strong protest" to Japan and a joint effort between the United States and the League of Nations to demand that the Japanese cease all hostilities. In February 1932 the Iowa senator gave his conditional approval for a breaking of diplomatic relations with Japan and repeated his plea for a united front, to include the League powers and the Soviet Union, to stop Japanese aggression. Dill attempted to weave together these disparate positions by introducing a resolution to place an embargo on all American arms shipments to East Asia, an idea that he had first floated in 1929. The Washington senator won the support of the Borah group by not tying the United States to the League, but he defended his resolution as anti-Japanese (on the grounds that Japan could afford to purchase considerably more American arms than could China) and so earned the backing of Brookhart and Norris. To appeal to a wider Senate audience, Dill also agreed to modify his resolution to make the embargo subject to presidential discretion. Along with Soviet recognition, the arms embargo, blocked in early 1933 by the tenacious opposition of Hiram Bingham, represented the peace progressive response to the Manchurian Incident.[57]

The peace progressives' indecision reflected a broader sense of unease within the peace movement, which struggled to come up with a coherent response to the Japanese invasion. Both Dorothy Detzer and the pacifist *The World Tomorrow* urged the United States and the League to threaten a break in diplomatic relations with Tokyo if Japanese forces did not withdraw, while Tucker Smith of the Committee on Militarism in Education supported an American boycott of Japanese goods to promote antimilitarist feeling in Japan. After asking "of what earthly concern of ours is the Sino-Japanese squabble" and endorsing "the deliberate refusal of all sane Americans to engage" in a war against Japan as the only way to prevent American military involvement in the crisis, Ernest Gruening one month later said that economic sanctions represented the only proper American response against a Japan "arrogantly sure of its own righteousness." Villard disagreed, believing that the United States only needed to "exercise tremendous moral pressure and Japan will collapse economically, perhaps inside of ninety days." Increasingly others in the peace movement sided with him; both Frederick Libby and Nevin Sayre worried that an aggressive policy could play into the hands of their domestic enemies. Walter Lippmann preferred to see collective security invoked but doubted the willingness of the European powers to take a stand, and so championed nonrecognition as a way of allowing the United States to "sit and wait, leaving

Japan indicted and on the defensive." He soon retreated, however, contending that the United States could not stop the Japanese short of going to war, which would be "sheer folly." Levinson, meanwhile, pronounced himself "totally" opposed to an anti-Japanese boycott, and by the spring of 1932 convinced himself that the crisis had proved "a great demonstration of the peace treaty," since an aroused world public opinion had "frightened" the Japanese into not extending their conquests beyond Manchuria.[58]

In contrast to this disunity in the peace movement, the peace progressives clung to the arms embargo as a way to solve the crisis, although increasingly they viewed it less as Dill's anti-Japanese vehicle and more simply as a way for the United States to steer clear of an East Asian war.[59] Borah criticized the Japanese denunciation of the Washington Treaties as "sheer madness," but he added that Americans "ought not to make the mistake of interpreting Japan's act as indicating a warlike attitude toward the United States"; the Idaho senator still believed that munitions makers had caused most of the American-Japanese tensions, as he alleged had occurred during the 1910s. Nye took a much more pro-Japanese stance, endorsing Japanese demands for naval equality in late 1934; in early 1935 a Tokyo newspaper quoted the North Dakota senator as saying that "Japan has a right to feel secure, with a free hand in the Far East and the same degree of freedom from intervention from without that America enjoys in the western hemisphere." Nye also predicted that the "only lasting solution to the naval problem" lay in permitting "both America and Japan to float a navy big enough for defense but not big enough for offense." By early 1935 most peace progressives advocated appeasing the Japanese and keeping the United States as far away from the conflict as possible, agreeing with Hiram Johnson that the lesson of Manchuria was that Americans needed "to put our trust in ourselves, and be prepared for any eventuality."[60]

The peace progressives also adopted a deeply pessimistic view of European matters, reversing a basically optimistic outlook on world affairs that for some had persisted through the early 1930s. For example, in a February 1931 address Brookhart praised the efforts of Woodrow Wilson to make the world safe for democracy and noted that many good things had come out of the war: German democracy, led by Hindenberg, "the George Washington of Germany," had replaced German autocracy; a "dictatorship of the people . . . declared for economic equality as well as political equality" had eclipsed the "autocratic tyranny" of the tsars; and Kellogg-Briand had ensured that perhaps the Great War had ended all wars. Another significant expression of these ideas came during Borah's August 1932 Minneapolis address, when he outlined his plans for dealing with reparations and debts as part of one broad package and squarely rejected the option of withdrawing from European affairs, arguing that this solution would create economic problems.[61]

Most peace progressives, however, began expressing frustration with international conditions by the end of the Hoover administration, and they reacted by calling for a withdrawal of the United States from the world. Borah lashed out at European intransigence on reparations and disarmament, confessing that he was "through with all the temporizing on these questions"; he promised no compromise with "the short-sighted, intolerant, revengeful policies of Europe." Shipstead, in a long interview after Roosevelt's election, shared his colleague's pessimism, noting that since in the aftermath of Manchuria "the law of conquest is international law . . . isolation is not without merit in such a situa-tion." He could foresee international cooperation playing a prominent role only through cooperation among the central banks of the world to restore the integrity of currency. More radical peace progressives har-bored similar doubts about the world situation. Dill hoped that Roosevelt would preside over an "administration with the interests of America first," while Blaine lamented that Manchuria had proved (as he had predicted) that Kellogg-Briand represented no more than "a pious gesture without any potency for world peace," its ineffectiveness illustrated by the suggestions of many of its original backers "that ma-chinery should be set up that would make it an instrument of force to enforce peace and thus make it an instrument of war instead of peace."[62]

These sentiments hardened during the early years of the Roosevelt administration, while the coming to power of Hitler in Germany only intensified the revulsion felt by the peace progressives toward Europe. Borah organized a quiet campaign to help German Jews by doing any-thing possible "in ameliorating this awful situation." He called for the United States to express its moral outrage with Nazi policy by dealing "mercilessly" with anti-Jewish propaganda in the United States, since "the venomous snake of racial intolerance should not be permitted to coil itself into American life." This hostility toward Germany stood in sharp contrast to the 1920s, when the peace progressives had viewed

Germany as one of the most important potential allies in an anti-imperialist front; with Germany passed over to the other side and the increasingly unfavorable peace progressive view of Stalinist Russia, the senators had relatively few European regimes with which to sympathize. Borah kept up his campaign for a revision of the "injustice" associated with the "cursed" Treaty of Trianon, but centering American policy toward Europe around Hungary hardly seemed like a promising prospect. Instead, the dissenters began viewing all European powers as evil in one way or another, and so could see no other alternative for the United States but to disassociate itself from them. In part, this policy shift resulted from changes in the international scene, where the cultural and economic diplomacy associated with the 1920s had declined, replaced by a world in which military might played a far more prominent role in international affairs. Nonetheless, this strand of thought, reflecting the peace progressive hostility to what they perceived as an immoral European balance of power system, had always existed in the ideology of the dissenters. With the Great Depression and subsequent changes to the international system, it became far more pronounced.[63]

Accordingly, the peace progressives gave up on their attempt to reform Europe and began trying to distance the United States from the continent. The formerly low-tariff Wheeler termed it "absolutely impossible" for the United States to agree on tariff reduction until the New Deal had received a chance to increase commodity prices. Borah expanded on this theme during a January 1934 speech before the Council on Foreign Relations which advanced the dual thesis that nationalism had triumphed over internationalism and that most world problems centered on Europe, where "the outside world cannot reach them." The Idaho senator argued that initially two breeds of internationalists existed—people like Woodrow Wilson, "those who sincerely believed that the new course was the high and honorable and most beneficial course to pursue," and that "strange figure known as the 'unofficial observer,'" who represented the interests of international finance. During the 1920s the second type of internationalist had gradually prevailed over the first, leading to an "un-American and humiliating" policy; the fact that world conditions had not changed at all since 1915 proved that internationalism, "another revolution" in foreign affairs, had not succeeded. Borah believed that the fight against nationalism "had to fail," because the Europeans differed from Americans "in everything which makes for the community spirit, for social understanding, for political accord." The Idaho senator therefore called for a return to nationalism in American policy, with the country turning its attention to domestic affairs. Norris, who inserted the speech into the *Congressional Record*, termed it a "rather remarkable" address.[64]

Only Dill continued to search for solutions in line with the spirit of the 1920s. Despite his strong and continuing hostility to both the League of Nations and the World Court, the Washington Democrat returned in his final year of service to the war referendum, the issue with which he was most identified during his House career. Dill still believed that outlawry, not curbing munitions makers, represented the only way to make war impossible, and he argued that Kellogg-Briand had failed only because it did not provide a mechanism for allowing "the people of the country whose rulers want war . . . to vote on it." He urged Roosevelt to take the lead on negotiating a treaty to ensure a war referendum in all countries as a way of combatting the "same forces of industrial and commercial rivalry which brought on" the world war. Dill did not underestimate the task ahead, but he continued to believe that a strong American effort would accomplish the desired result. With Dill's retirement from the Senate, the final peace progressive adherent to this aspect of the beliefs of the 1920s departed.[65]

The two major foreign policy initiatives of 1935, the World Court and the Neutrality Act, revealed the depth of the group's fear that the United States might become involved in European concerns. For the most part, the debate over the World Court repeated arguments made by the peace progressives in the 1926 fight against the Court, although the stress that they laid on differing aspects of their position differed. For example, Borah noted that the World Court dealt mostly with questions "purely European in character" that did not "concern us in the slightest." Shipstead picked up on this theme, warning that the world had entered a time "when history is about to repeat itself," when "war makers make war in the name of peace . . . [and] ammunition makers control disarmament conferences and peace conferences." He urged his colleagues to keep the United States as far away from that world as possible. Johnson, who spoke "not as a citizen of the world" but "as a citizen of the United States" endeavoring "to preserve the traditional policy of the American Republic and to keep this country free and independent in its very action," equated World Court membership with a propensity "to meddle and muddle, under an hysterical internationalism, in those controversies that Europe has and Europe will never be rid of." Describing the turmoil in Germany, Italy, and the Soviet Union, coupled with the weakness of Britain and France, Johnson noted that "we are different over here. Why go abroad?"[66]

Norris provided the most spectacular change from 1926; Frederick Libby termed the Nebraska senator's actions "largely responsible for the defeat of the Court." Norris began by introducing an amendment to compel the President to receive a two-thirds majority from the Senate before submitting any matter to the Court, which he argued would leave "our country free from any danger of European entanglements" and ensure against the United States' being "plunged into war, perhaps, on account of hasty action taken by the President when the Senate was not in session." When the amendment failed by a close vote (forty-seven to thirty-seven), Norris announced his opposition to membership. He said that he could not countenance submitting unknown future controversies to a Court "composed mostly of men not familiar with American questions . . . but constituted of men who have grown up under a different civilization." He expanded this point to include all European matters, opposing entangling the United States in European questions, since Europeans "are living in a different world and are part of a different civilization." For Norris, "one of the saddest things in the world now is that two of the so-called leading nations seem to be bent on the destruction of . . . civilization," although even more distressing was that "the people of these countries are behind their governments in their irresponsible and illogical attempts to destroy the freedom, even the existence, of other nations." Before 1929 the peace progressives had not issued blanket condemnations of all European governments, much less the entire European populace; the remarks of Norris, in many ways the most tolerant of the group, indicated how deeply the European events of the 1930s had affected the dissenters.[67]

This desire to quarantine the country from Europe manifested itself again in the strong peace progressive support for neutrality legislation designed to restrict American neutral rights during wartime. The administration succeeded in sidetracking the peace progressive proposals, replacing them with a bill authored by Key Pittman that included a mandatory arms embargo, but the peace progressives still urged support for the watered-down measure. Bone, fearing that Europe, still filled with "doddering old men over there in positions of power, along with a sorry lot of confirmed megalomaniacs," seemed about to explode again, announced that he would prefer to "temporarily abandon all world commerce" rather than enter another war. Norris seconded Bone's call for entertaining the embargo idea, and hailed effective neutrality legislation as "the only way in which we can prevent the slaughter of our own people on the battle fields of Europe." Nye wondered why since 1917 "we have not as a Government, or as a legislative body, taken a single step to remedy the evil which existed then and which permitted our being drawn into that conflict." He did not say why the group that logically should have structured such an alternative, the peace progressives, had not done so to his satisfaction during the 1920s. Borah, who later in the decade questioned the neutrality program, in 1935 condemned the Foreign Relations Committee for not prohibiting all American citizens from traveling on belligerent ships during wartime, worrying that an incident involving an American citizen could contribute "to a feeling of war psychology" that could bring the United States into conflict. Only Johnson did not think a legislated neutrality program could keep the United States out of war, but he rejoiced that the law served an important purpose by marking the "triumph of the so-called 'isolationists,' and . . . the downfall . . . of the internationalist who has been devoting his gigantic energy in the last 17 years to involving us in machinations abroad." Strengthened by public opinion energized by the Nye hearings, the act passed by a vote of seventy-nine to two. When searching for historical examples to explain their support for neutrality legislation, the peace progressives bypassed the 1920s and looked back to the 1910s. Norris argued that opponents of neutrality legislation, like those who had supported American entrance into World War I, were "those who are interested in carrying on trade for profit." In 1910s-like language, he characterized the dispute as one over the old "question of money against lives."[68] The vote thus marked the final demise of their 1920s perspective, since by seeking to cut the country off from Europe, the peace progressives gave up once and for all on their earlier attempts to reform the world along anti-imperialist lines.

The anti-imperialism articulated in the 1920s by the peace progressives embraced strategic, economic, and moral elements, and their movement away from that ideology involved a rejection of all three facets of their earlier anti-imperialism. Strategically, they viewed it as too dangerous for the United States to continue playing an active world role given that another European (and probably Asian) conflict appeared likely. They hoped to learn from the lessons of the Great War and to keep the United States out of trouble by steering clear of all possible controversies. Economically, they no longer believed that anti-imperialism served American interests, particularly those of its rural citizens; a policy of friendship with weaker but predominantly agricultural nations could have disastrous consequences in hard times. Rather, the dissenters adopted a much narrower vision than they had in the 1920s and tried to use foreign policy as a means of improving the economic conditions of their constituents, at the expense, if necessary, of broader international goals. Finally, as was most clearly shown in the Norris speech on the World Court, they moved away from their belief that most people sought freedom and thus deserved American assistance; they also abandoned their once strongly held conviction that most countries in the world (apart from Japan, England, France, Italy, their allies, and Latin American states ruled by banker-controlled dictators) shared common values with the United States and had the potential to join in a (very) loosely organized worldwide bloc of peaceful, economically prosperous, and nationalist-democratic regimes. By 1935 little evidence remained to sustain that vision, with both the international and domestic environments radically different from the 1920s. With the underpinnings of the peace progressive anti-imperialist ideology no longer in place, a more isolationist perspective came to predominate.

Epilogue

On July 24, 1945, Burton Wheeler, criticizing the United Nations Charter as a "mechanism to legalize and perpetuate the brutal realities which now afflict friend and foe alike," warned that "the present trend in power politics" would produce a major war. Dismissing the "hypocrisy" of "pious intentions," the Montana senator cautioned that unless the Truman administration altered its policies, the "tragic mistakes of Versailles [would] merely be aggravated and earlier set in motion." Wheeler charged that the Charter both enslaved the German people and permitted "the subjugation of Latvia, Lithuania, Estonia, Poland, and Bulgaria." The senator detected a parallel between the abandonment of the Fourteen Points after World War I and the ignoring of the principles of the Atlantic Charter by the Soviet Union in Eastern Europe and by Britain in Africa and India after World War II. He feared that "we shall sign our own death warrant" with an endorsement of such an unstable arrangement, since ratification would also rob Congress of its power to declare war and "take away from the people of America the right to be heard on the crucial issues of war and peace." The biting anti-imperialism of the critique rivaled the rhetoric of the peace progressives in the 1920s, but in contrast to his actions in that decade, Wheeler concluded his address by announcing that he would support U.S. membership in an international organization dominated by the major powers. Also in contrast to the earlier period, the dissenters received minuscule popular support and had virtually no influence on the Senate debate.[1]

Wheeler's speech illustrates the cruel fate that befell the peace progressives after the mid-1930s. After the battle over the World Court, the peace progressives continued their opposition to the Roosevelt foreign policy, and they increasingly criticized the President's domestic agenda as well; Wheeler himself led the fight against Roosevelt's scheme in 1937 to pack the Supreme Court. This domestic and international agenda led the senators to form alliances with conservatives whom they had considered anathema in the 1910s and 1920s. A similar shift occurred in the politics of many of the states represented by the peace progressives, which moved sharply to the right in the 1940s. By 1945 the domestic climate in which peace progressivism had flourished no longer existed, and the senators became politically vulnerable to conservative opponents. William Langer ousted Lynn Frazier in a 1940 primary contest in North Dakota in which Langer attacked the incumbent from the left and Frazier accepted assistance from the same conservative forces that had opposed him in 1922, 1928, and 1934. Norris failed to win reelection in 1942; Bone, sensing his vulnerability, accepted Roosevelt's offer of a federal judgeship in 1944, the same year in which Nye lost in a three-way contest in North Dakota. In 1946 the three remaining peace progressives in the Senate, Wheeler, La Follette, and Shipstead, all failed to survive their party primaries. Meanwhile the peace progressives themselves seemed unable to reconcile their arguments with the world as it existed; perhaps sensing that they were lost, they attempted to return to the kind of moralistic and anti-imperialist arguments that had characterized their 1920s dissent. Their activities over the previous ten years, however, had robbed them of their credibility, both as foreign policy thinkers and as politicians.

Anti-imperialism did not vanish from the dissenters' arsenal in the years following 1935, although the senators all but ceased to comment on inter-American affairs. Under Nye's leadership several peace progressives opposed the Roosevelt administration's course toward the Spanish Civil War, calling for the United States to structure a policy using an international arms embargo that would aid the Spanish Republican government but not involve Americans directly in the conflict. Several years later many of these same senators expressed sympathy for the Finns in their Winter War against the USSR. For the most part, however, the Nye/Wheeler bloc articulated what Manfred Jonas refers to as a "timid" isolationist position, calling for the United States to withdraw itself entirely from European affairs and to sacrifice American neutrality rights if necessary to keep out of the impending conflict. The rhetoric associated with this position, however, represented a much harder-line perspective than that of the World War I critique, and Borah, as he had during the earlier era, broke away from the dissenters in the years before his death and called for a vigorous enforcement of

American neutrality rights. A third branch of the movement followed Norris, who had become increasingly dependent on the Roosevelt administration for his political survival, and inched toward support of the President's foreign policy. All of these perspectives built upon sentiments prevalent in the 1910s and 1920s, but the specific policies recommended by the dissenters did not bear any particular resemblance to the 1920s peace progressive dissent.[2]

The almost pathetic nature of Wheeler's United Nations address should not cause historians to dismiss the peace progressives as intellectual relics, out of place in post-1898 America. The economic, political, and international tensions associated with the Great Depression exposed weaknesses within the ideology of the senators that ultimately contributed to their political downfalls. Before 1935, however, the senators articulated a creative foreign policy that built upon themes prevalent among foreign policy reformers since the eighteenth century. Along with many of their ideological opponents, the peace progressives recognized the fundamental way in which World War I had affected the role of the United States in the world. In particular, the dissenters, along with figures such as Herbert Hoover, Thomas Lamont, and Charles Dawes, agreed that the United States should involve itself in European affairs while refraining from political ties with the continent. Although the European program put forth by the dissenters was in many ways an unrealistic one, with little chance of success and no relevance for future liberal activists, the program did enjoy some support throughout the 1920s, even from figures such as Salmon Levinson and Walter Lippmann, who clearly stood to the right of the peace progressives on most international questions. When combined with the fracturing of the Democratic party on foreign affairs and the emergence of the peace progressives as the principal alternative faction to the decade's Republican administrations, the peace progressive European record suggests that a slight revision of much of the corporatist historiography is in order. An underlying assumption of much of the corporatist writing has been that the central foreign policy debate in the 1920s United States centered upon the question of whether political or economic links should govern American relations with Europe. The preceding chapters have suggested that the real window of debate was far narrower, with all the important players in the foreign policy arena accepting the contention that diplomatic, economic, and cultural factors should predominate. (The peace progressives also added moral concerns to this list.) Thus the corporatist European program was hardly original; it merely represented the consensus of its time.

Second, the intellectual communion between the peace progressives and the quite active 1920s peace movement deserves mention, particularly by historians of peace studies. The fifteen years preceding the Civil War and perhaps, as Thomas Knock contends, the few years of Wilson's greatest power in the mid-1910s represented earlier periods of cooperation between peace activists and powerful political forces;[3] but the degree of convergence between the peace progressives and the 1920s peace movement stood out even against these two earlier examples. With the sole exception of World Court membership, the agendas of the dissenting senators and the foreign policy left were virtually identical; equally important, the two sides shared ideas and engaged in mutually beneficial political strategies. In addition, the peace progressives made an important contribution to the ideology of the American quest for peace by linking anti-imperialism with other strands of thought prevalent in American dissent, specifically the hostility to traditional power politics. Other groups earlier, such as the Garrisonians, the Free Soil Whigs, and (to a lesser extent) both the Anti-Imperialist League of the 1890s and the Wilsonians of the 1910s, had made such a connection, but with none of the force and consistency managed by the peace progressives. The peace progressives—at least for a few years in the late 1920s—also became the first bloc of congressional dissenters to articulate a truly global foreign policy ideology. That they did so by resorting to unworkable disarmament proposals and a European program that did not stand the test of time obviously weakens the impressiveness of this achievement, but, nonetheless, they did succeed where most earlier dissenting groups had failed.

Finally, the peace progressives joined the Wilsonians as the liberal American pioneers in exploring the relationship between the stronger and weaker powers, and it is here that their dissent retained relevance long after they had passed from the scene. Wilson's Fourteen Points address outlined in its most idealistic form the President's solution for dealing with these problems, but the President's mandates program, his willingness to intervene in the Caribbean Basin, and his Eurocentric interpretation of Articles X and XI of the Covenant indicated that Wilson's liberal vision of the world did not envision many of the weaker states as full partners in the international order. The peace progressives responded with a policy that they felt would reconcile legitimate American moral, economic, and strategic interests with the rise of Latin American and East Asian nationalism. They contended that all these interests justified a more favorable U.S. attitude toward nationalism in the less developed world, even if this meant offending traditional European allies. The peace progressives, then, were not just an additional mutation of Wilsonianism. Peace progressivism came into existence as a self-conscious left-wing alternative to Wilson's foreign policy agenda, and despite the similarity between the rhetoric of Wilson and the dissenting senators on issues such as disarmament, anti-imperialism, and open diplomacy, a deep gap (initially illustrated by their conflicting interpretations of Article XI of the Covenant) divided the two forces from 1919 onward. Peace progressivism remained throughout the 1920s as an *alternative* to Wilsonianism, not an evolution of it, and the battle between Wilson and the peace progressives illuminated the two principal approaches of the twentieth-century American left to international affairs. This debate continued throughout the century and is unlikely to be resolved any time soon. Both Wilson and the peace progressives attempted to structure a foreign policy that served the country's security interests without compromising its ideals, but the interpretations that they offered on how to deal with weaker states differed radically. Although the peace progressive position has rarely enjoyed anything majority support in the United States since 1933, it has lingered—most notably among Senate dissenters in the 1960s and early 1970s, and to a certain extent in Jimmy Carter's early-term experiments in human rights diplomacy.

This vision of international relations deserves its proper place in the historiography of 1920s U.S. foreign affairs. The peace progressives proposed a stark alternative to the inter-American policies pursued particularly by the Coolidge administration, and their attempts to reconcile the protection of American national rights with the demands of Latin American nationalism look impressive even seven decades later. Their suggestions for 1920s European policy, considerably less impressive in retrospect, still did not represent a knee-jerk isolationism. Their alternative to corporatism, combining disarmament and anti-imperialism with elements of American moral, diplomatic, and economic power deserves recognition at least for its originality, if not for its realism.

In one of his less caustic moods, Hiram Johnson once encouraged George Norris to "dream on."[4] Like most congressional dissenters, the peace progressives were idealists, but unlike many of their predecessors in dissent, they went out of their way to propose an alternative overall framework to the policies that they criticized. By declining simply to oppose, they forced themselves to think deeply about international affairs. In the process, they articulated a powerful and sustained left-wing dissenting vision that held its own in ideological and political battles with two of the more innovative foreign policy programs ever offered by the executive branch, Wilsonianism and 1920s business internationalism. Historians have recognized the role played by these two ideologies in shaping the postwar American perspective on international affairs. The addition of peace progressivism to this picture would make the story complete.

APPENDIX

NOTES

SELECT BIBLIOGRAPHY

INDEX

Appendix:
Congressional Votes on Foreign Relations, 1914–1932

Keys to the columns precede each table.

Throughout, D = Democrats, PP = peace progressives, y = voted for (yea), n = voted against (nay), + = paired for, − = paired against, ay = announced for, an = announced against, ? = did not vote or otherwise make position known, xx = insufficient votes to compile, *CR* = *Congressional Record.*

Senators are recorded as paired for or against when they arranged a pair, under which two senators on opposite sides of a given vote refrained from voting. Generally, one (and sometimes both) of these senators was absent for the vote. Senators are recorded announced for or against when their position on a vote was announced by a colleague immediately before the roll-call vote, but they were unable to arrange a pair. In the following tables, the final vote is given, but when tabulating peace progressive and Democratic totals, pairs and announced positions as well as the actual votes are recorded.

Finally, in Tables A.6 and A.7 the votes of Democrats from the 72d Congress (1931–1932) are not included, since the large number of Democratic senators elected in 1930 had no connection to the discussion of the Democratic perspective on 1920s foreign relations in Chapter 7.

Table A.1   Votes on anti-imperialist issues, 1914–1919

A. *Affairs in Mexico. H.J. Res. 251.* Amendment by La Follette, R–Wis., to disclaim any U.S. intention to exercise sovereignty, jurisdiction, or control over any portion of Mexico, and to assert a determination to withdraw after the completion of "pacification." Rejected 39–44 (including pairs, PP 11–3; D 2–42). April 21, 1914. 51 *CR*, 63d Cong., 2d sess., p. 7008.

B. *Affairs in Mexico. H.J. Res. 251.* Stone, D–Mo., motion to pass the joint resolution. Accepted 72–13 (PP 10–4; D 44–0). April 21, 1914. 51 *CR*, 63d Cong., 2d sess., p. 7014.

C. *The Government of the Philippines. S. 381.* Norris, R–Neb., amendment to disclaim U.S. possession of coaling stations or naval bases in an independent Philippines. Rejected 14–58 (PP 8–6; D 7–36). February 1, 1916. 53 *CR*, 64th Cong., 1st sess., p. 1945.

D. *The Government of the Philippines. S. 381.* Stone, D–Mo., motion to pass the bill, committing the United States to granting independence to the Philippines within five years. Accepted 52–24 (PP 10–3; D 45–0). February 4, 1916. 53 *CR*, 64th Cong., 1st sess., p. 2121.

E. *Naval Appropriations. H.R. 15947.* La Follette, R–Wis., amendment to prohibit any naval vessels appropriated from acting to "coerce or compel the collection of any pecuniary claim" or to enforce any such claim. Rejected 8–44 (PP 7–0; D 2–35). February 18, 1916. 53 *CR*, 64th Cong., 1st sess., p. 11350.

F. *Nicaraguan Canal Route.* Motion in executive session to approve the Bryan-Chamorro Treaty between the United States and Nicaragua, granting the United States access to a canal route across Nicaragua in exchange for a refunding loan to the Nicaraguan government. Accepted 55–19 (PP 0–12; D 43–3). February 18, 1916. 53 *CR*, 64th Cong., 1st sess., p. 2770.

G. *Government of Porto Rico. S. 8148.* Clapp, R–Minn., amendment to strike out the clause prohibiting Puerto Ricans who failed the required literacy test and who did not pay more than $3 per year in taxes from voting. Accepted 31–16 (PP 10–3; D 17–11). February 17, 1917. 54 *CR*, 64th Cong., 2d sess., p. 3476.

H. *Promotion of Foreign Trade. H. 2136.* Cummins, R–Iowa, amendment to permit the establishment in foreign countries of commercial selling agencies consisting of U.S. firms, but to disallow an exemption from the Sherman Antitrust act from any selling agency that has exported goods from the United States. Rejected 18–43 (PP 9–1; D 6–24). December 12, 1917. 56 *CR*, 65th Cong., 2d sess., p. 180.

I. *Promotion of Foreign Trade. H. 2136.* Pomerene, D–Ohio, motion to pass the bill, the so-called Webb-Pomerene Act. Accepted 51–11 (PP 0–7; D 29–4). December 12, 1917. 56 *CR*, 65th Cong., 2d sess., p. 186.

J. *American Troops in Russia. S. Res. 411.* Fletcher, D–Fla., motion to table (kill) Johnson, R–Calif., resolution stating that the Senate feels that American troops should be withdrawn from Russia "as soon as practicable." Accepted 33–33 (PP 0–11; D 35–1). February 14, 1919. 57 *CR*, 65th Cong., 3d sess., p. 3342.

K. Percentage of votes for the anti-imperialist position.

	A	B	C	D	E	F	G	H	I	J	K
Peace progressives											
Borah	y	y	y	y	n	?	y	y	n	n	89
Bristow	y	n									100
Clapp	y	y	y	y	n	+	y				86

	A	B	C	D	E	F	G	H	I	J	K
Peace progressives (cont.)											
Clarke	n	y	n	y	n	?					40
Cummins	y	y	n	n	n	?	y	y	n	n	67
Gore	n	y	n	?	?	?	–	y	?	n	33
Gronna	+	–	y	n	n	y	y	y	n	n	90
Johnson (Calif.)								y	?	n	100
Jones (Wash.)	y	y	n	n	n	?	y	n	y	n	44
Kenyon	y	y	y	y	n	y	y	y	n	n	90
Kirby							n	?	?	y	0
La Follette	y	n	y	y	n	y	y	y	n	n	100
Lane	y	y	y	+	an	y	y				86
Norris	y	n	y	y	n	y	y	y	n	n	100
Vardaman	n	y	y	y	n	y	n	+	n	n	70
Works	y	n	n	y	an	?	y				83
Democrats											
Ashurst	n	y	n	y	y	n	?	?	y	y	13
Bankhead	n	y	n	y	y	n	–	n	y	y	10
Beckham			n	y	y	–	?	n	y	y	14
Broussard			–	y	y	n	n	–	+		14
Bryan	n	y	n	y	?	?	y				40
Chamberlain	–	+	?	?	n	y	y	n	y	n	50
Chilton	n	y	n	y	y	n	?				17
Culberson	–	+	–	+	?	–	n	?	?	?	17
Fletcher	n	y	n	y	y	n	?	n	y	y	11
Gay										y	0
Gerry								?	?	+	0
Hardwick			n	y	?	?	?	?	?	n	67
Henderson										+	0
Hitchcock	n	y	y	y	y	–	y	y	n	+	50

	A	B	C	D	E	F	G	H	I	J	K
Democrats (cont.)											
Hollis	n	y	n	y	y	n	?	?	y	?	14
Hughes	n	y	?	y	y	—	y	?	?		33
Husting			y	y	y	n	y				60
James	n	y	n	y	ay	n	n	n	y		11
Johnson (Maine)	n	y	n	y	ay	n	—				14
Johnson (S.D.)			y	y	y	?	n	n	?	y	33
Jones (N.M.)								n	y	y	0
Kendrick								?	?	y	0
Kern	n	y	n	y	y	n	y				29
King								y	n	y	67
Lea	n	y	+	y	ay	—	y				43
Lee	n	y	n	y	y	n	n				14
Martin	n	y	n	y	y	n	y	?	ay	+	22
Martine	n	y	n	+	n	y	y				57
McKellar								n	y	y	0
Myers	—	+	n	y	y	n	+	n	y	y	20
Newlands	n	y	—	y	y	?	?	n	y		14
Nugent										y	0
O'Gorman	n	y	+	y	y	?	?				20
Overman	n	y	n	y	y	n	n	?	y	y	11
Owen	n	y	?	?	y	?	?	?	?	?	0
Phelan			n	+	y	n	—	?	+	?	17
Pittman	n	y	n	y	y	?	y	?	?	y	29
Pomerene	n	y	n	y	y	n	y	n	y	y	20
Ransdell	n	y	n	y	y	n	?	n	y	y	11
Reed	n	y	n	y	y	n	y	y	n	?	44
Robinson	n	y	n	y	y	n	n	n	y	y	10
Saulsbury	n	y	?	y	y	?	?	n	y	y	14

	A	B	C	D	E	F	G	H	I	J	K
Democrats (cont.)											
Shafroth	n	y	n	y	y	n	y	y	y	y	30
Sheppard	n	y	n	y	y	n	y	n	y	y	20
Shields	n	y	n	y	y	n	?	n	y	+	11
Shively	n	y	?	?							0
Simmons	n	y	n	y	y	—	?	n	y	?	13
Smith (Ariz.)	—	+	y	y	y	n	?	n	y	?	25
Smith (Ga.)	n	y	n	y	y	n	?	y	y	y	22
Smith (Md.)	n	y	?	+	y	?	?	n	y	?	17
Smith (S.C.)	n	y	n	y	y	n	?	?	?	y	14
Stone	—	+	n	y	y	n	?	n	y		13
Swanson	n	y	n	y	y	n	?	n	y	y	11
Thomas	y	y	y	y	n	?		?	?	y	71
Thompson	n	y	n	y	y	?	n	n	y	y	11
Tillman	—	+	?	y	y	n	?	?	?		20
Trammell								y	n	y	67
Underwood			n	?	?	?	?	n	?	+	0
Walsh (Mont.)	n	y	n	y	y	n	n	?	?	?	14
Williams	y	y	n	y	y	?	y	?	?	y	43
Wolcott								?	?	y	0

Table A.2 Votes on preparedness issues, 1914–1917

A. *Naval Appropriations. H.R. 14034.* Vardaman, D–Miss., amendment to reduce the number of first-class battleships authorized by the bill from two to one. Rejected 16–42 (including pairs, PP 10–3; D 11–24). June 2, 1914. 51 *CR*, 63d Cong., 2d sess., p. 9641.

B. *National Defense. H.R. 12776.* Hitchcock, D–Neb., amendment to cap the number of enlisted men in the Army at 150,000, from the 200,000 suggested in the bill. Rejected 13–66 (PP 6–6; D 7–35). April 18, 1916. 53 *CR*, 64th Cong., 1st sess., p. 6349.

C. *National Defense. H.R. 12776.* Brandegee, R–Conn., amendment to increase the number of enlisted men allowed in the Army from 200,000 to 250,000. Accepted 43–37 (PP 0–12; D 21–23). April 18, 1916. 53 *CR*, 64th Cong., 1st sess., p. 6359.

D. *National Defense. H.R. 12776.* Lewis, D–Ill., amendment to strike out Section 56, calling for the establishment of military instruction camps for civilians. Rejected 37–40 (PP 11–1; D 23–20). April 18, 1916. 53 *CR*, 64th Cong., 1st sess., p. 6372.

E. *Naval Appropriations. H.R. 15947.* Cummins, R–Iowa, amendment to reduce the number of first-class battleships authorized from ten to two and to reduce the number of battle cruisers authorized from six to four. Rejected 14–60 (PP 12–1; D 2–43). July 21, 1916. 53 *CR*, 64th Cong., 1st sess., p. 11367.

F. *Naval Appropriations. H.R. 15947.* Shafroth, D–Colo., to extend the time allowed for the construction of the authorized vessels from three years to five years. Rejected 21–57 (PP 10–2; D 10–36). July 21, 1916. 53 *CR*, 64th Cong., 1st sess., p. 11378.

G. *Naval Appropriations. H.R. 15947.* Naval Affairs Committee amendments to construct ten battleships and six cruisers. Accepted 61–15 (PP 2–11; D 38–6). July 21, 1916. 53 *CR*, 64th Cong., 1st sess., p. 11379.

H. *Naval Appropriations. H.R. 15947.* Motion for passage of final 1916 naval bill. Accepted 71–8 (PP 5–8; D 46–1). July 21, 1916. 53 *CR*, 64th Cong., 1st sess., p. 11384.

I. *Naval Appropriations. H.R. 15947.* Swanson, D–Va., motion to table (kill) the Norris, R–Neb., amendment to hold that construction of the vessels authorized shall not commence until the President has made a sincere effort to secure agreement for a permanent international court of arbitration. The amendment also states that the U.S. government desires to participate in a postwar peace treaty to promote the arbitration court, a limitation of armament and the "establishment of an international navy to enforce the decrees of such court." The amendment also authorizes the President to turn over part of the U.S. Navy to the international navy. Accepted 35–11 (PP 2–8; D 24–4). July 17, 1916. 53 *CR*, 64th Cong., 1st sess., p. 11192.

J. *Army Appropriations. H.R. 16460.* Chamberlain, D–Ore., amendment to create a council of national defense to coordinate industries and resources for the national welfare. Accepted 39–13 (PP 1–10; D 29–2). July 25, 1916. 53 *CR*, 64th Cong., 1st sess., p. 11564.

K. *Naval Appropriations. H.R. 20632.* Swanson, D–Va., amendment to increase the amount of money permitted for the Navy to borrow for naval construction from $115 million to $150 million. Accepted 50–24 (PP 1–9; D 36–3). March 2, 1917. 54 *CR*, 64th Cong., 2d sess., p. 4737.

L. Percentage of votes against higher defense spending.

	A	B	C	D	E	F	G	H	I	J	K	L
Peace progressives												
Borah	n	n	n	n	n	n	y	y	?	?	n	22
Bristow	y											100
Clapp	+	n	n	y	y	y	n	n	–	n	n	91
Clarke	+	+	–	+	+	?	–	–	?	?		100
Cummins	y	n	n	y	y	y	n	y	n	n	?	80
Gore	?	?	?	?	+	+	–	–	+	+	?	67
Gronna	+	y	n	y	y	y	n	n	n	n	n	100
Jones (Wash.)	–	n	n	y	y	n	y	y	y	n	n	55
Kenyon	y	n	n	y	y	y	n	y	n	n	?	80
Kirby											y	0
La Follette	y	y	n	y	y	y	n	n	n	n	n	100
Lane	y	n	n	y	y	y	n	y	n	n	n	82
Norris	y	y	n	y	y	y	n	n	n	n	n	100
Vardaman	y	y	n	y	y	y	n	n	–	n	n	100
Works	n	y	n	y	y	y	n	n	?	–	n	90
Democrats												
Ashurst	y	n	y	y	n	n	y	y	?	?	y	22
Bankhead	?	n	n	y	n	y	n	y	?	?	y	50
Beckham		n	n	n	+	n	y	y	?	y	?	25
Broussard		n	y	n	n	n	y	y	n	?	y	11
Bryan	n	?	?	?	n	n	y	y	?	?	y	0
Chamberlain	n	n	y	n	n	n	y	y	n	y	n	22
Chilton	n	n	y	y	n	n	y	y	?	y	?	11
Culberson	?	n	n	y	n	n	?	y	?	?	y	29
Fletcher	?	?	?	?	n	n	y	y	y	y	y	0
Hardwick		n	y	y	–	y	y	y	+	?	y	30
Hitchcock	n	y	n	n	–	+	–	?	n	?	?	63
Hollis	?	n	n	n	n	n	y	y	y	+	y	10
Hughes	n	n	y	y	–	–	+	+	?	+	y	10

	A	B	C	D	E	F	G	H	I	J	K	L
Democrats (cont.)												
Husting		n	y	n	n	n	y	y	?	y	y	0
James	?	n	y	y	n	n	y	y	?	y	y	11
Johnson (Maine)	−	n	y	n	n	n	y	y	y	+	?	0
Johnson (S.D.)		n	y	n	n	y	y	y	y	?	y	11
Kern	?	n	n	n	n	y	y	y	y	n	?	33
Lea	n	−	?	?	−	−	+	+	+	+	y	0
Lee	n	n	y	y	n	n	y	y	y	n	y	18
Martin	n	?	?	?	n	n	y	y	y	y	y	0
Martine	n	n	y	y	n	y	y	y	y	y	n	27
Myers	y	y	n	y	n	y	n	y	?	y	y	60
Newlands	?	?	?	n	?	?	?	y	?	?	y	0
O'Gorman	n	n	y	n	an	?	?	?	?	y	?	0
Overman	n	y	n	y	?	n	?	y	y	y	?	37
Owen	?	?	n	y	n	n	y	y	−	?	y	37
Phelan		n	y	n	n	n	y	y	y	+	y	0
Pittman	+	n	y	n	n	n	y	y	y	?	y	10
Pomerene	n	n	n	n	n	n	y	y	y	?	y	10
Ransdell	+	n	n	y	n	n	y	y	y	?	?	33
Reed	n	y	n	y	n	n	y	y	?	y	y	30
Robinson	−	y	n	y	y	y	n	y	+	?	y	60
Saulsbury	n	an	+	+	−	−	+	+	?	y	y	10
Shafroth	y	n	n	y	n	y	y	y	?	y	y	40
Sheppard	y	n	y	n	n	n	y	y	y	y	y	9
Shields	−	?	−	−	n	?	?	y	?	?	y	18
Shively	n											0
Simmons	n	n	y	y	n	n	y	y	+	y	y	9
Smith (Ariz.)	n	n	y	y	n	n	y	y	y	?	?	11
Smith (Ga.)	n	n	y	y	?	n	y	y	y	y	y	10
Smith (Md.)	?	n	y	n	n	n	y	y	?	y	y	0

	A	B	C	D	E	F	G	H	I	J	K	L
Democrats (cont.)												
Smith (S.C.)	+	n	n	y	n	n	y	y	?	y	y	30
Stone	+	y	n	y	n	n	y	y	?	y	?	44
Swanson	n	y	n	y	n	n	y	y	y	y	y	27
Thomas	+	n	n	n	y	y	n	n	y	y	n	64
Thompson	y	n	n	?	n	n	y	y	?	?	y	25
Tillman	n	?	n	y	n	n	y	y	y	y	y	20
Underwood		n	n	?	n	y	n	y	?	?	?	50
Walsh	n	n	n	n	n	n	y	y	y	?	y	11
Williams	y	n	y	n	n	n	y	y	y	y	y	9

Table A.3   Votes related to World War I, 1917–1919

A. *War with Germany. S.J. Res. 1.* Hitchcock, D–Neb., motion to pass the joint resolution. Accepted 82–6 (including pairs, PP 7–5; D 47–1). April 4, 1917. 55 *CR*, 65th Cong., 1st sess., p. 261.

B. *Punishment of Espionage. S. 2.* Cummins, R–Iowa, amendment not to apply the terms of the act to members of Congress or debate therein. Rejected 34–40 (PP 11–0; D 4–34). April 20, 1917. 55 *CR*, 65th Cong., 1st sess., p. 886.

C. *Punishment of Espionage. S. 2.* Thomas, D–Colo., amendment to strike out the punishment clause from the act. Rejected 37–43 (PP 10–1; D 7–35). April 20, 1917. 55 *CR*, 65th Cong., 1st sess., p. 887.

D. *Increase of Military Establishment. S. 1871.* McKellar, D–Tenn., amendment authorizing the President to raise an army of 500,000 men by volunteers, and authorizing the use of conscription only if after ninety days that total has not been met. Rejected 18–69 (PP 9–2; D 4–52). April 28, 1917. 55 *CR*, 65th Cong., 1st sess., p. 1489.

E. *Increase of Military Establishment. S. 1871.* Chamberlain, D–Ore., motion to pass the bill and inaugurate conscription. Accepted 81–8 (PP 5–5; D 46–3). April 28, 1917. 55 *CR*, 65th Cong., 1st sess., p. 1500.

F. *Increase of Military Establishment. S. 1871.* La Follette, R–Wis., amendment in the form of a substitute for the bill, including a provision for a national referendum on whether conscripted men should be sent to the European front. Rejected 4–68 (PP 4–2; D 0–38). May 1, 1917. 55 *CR*, 65th Cong., 1st sess., p. 1624.

G. *Increase of Military Establishment. S. 1871.* McCumber, R–N.D., amendment striking from the bill the clause allowing conscientious objectors. Rejected 17–54 (PP 1–7; D 11–24). May 1, 1917. *55 CR*, 65th Cong., 1st sess., p. 1625.

H. *Punishment of Espionage. H.R. 291.* Hardwick, D–Ga., amendment to strike out Section 1, declaring seditious printed material "nonmailable matter." Rejected 28–39 (PP 10–1; D 3–38). May 10, 1917. *55 CR*, 65th Cong., 1st sess., p. 2072.

I. *Punishment of Espionage. H.R. 291.* Borah, R–Idaho, amendment to reconsider the vote on the Hardwick amendment. Rejected 29–52 (PP 11–0; D 3–42). May 14, 1917. *55 CR*, 65th Cong., 1st sess., p. 2270.

J. *Punishment of Espionage. H.R. 291.* Motion to pass the bill. Accepted 77–6 (PP 6–6; D 45–1). May 14, 1917. *55 CR*, 65th Cong., 1st sess., p. 2270.

K. *War Revenue. H.R. 4280.* Johnson, R–Calif., amendment to levy a tax of 73 percent on war profits. Rejected 17–62 (PP 10–0; D 6–34). September 10, 1917. *55 CR*, 65th Cong., 1st sess., p. 6857.

L. *War Revenue. H.R. 4280.* La Follette, R–Wis., amendment in the form of a substitute, to establish a graduated income tax, a war income tax, a 76 percent war profits tax, and a war tax on distilled beverages, cigars, and tobacco. Rejected 15–65 (PP 10–0; D 5–38). September 10, 1917. *55 CR*, 65th Cong., 1st sess., p. 6879.

M. *Punishment of Seditious Acts and Utterances. H.R. 8753.* France, R–Md., amendment stating that nothing in the act shall be construed "as impairing the right of any individual to publish or speak what is true, with good motives and for justifiable ends." Rejected 31–33 (PP 6–1; D 7–30). April 9, 1918. *56 CR*, 65th Cong., 2d sess., p. 4826.

N. *Punishment of Seditious Acts and Utterances. H.R. 8753.* Overman, D–N.C., motion to agree to the conference report. Accepted 48–26 (PP 1–8; D 41–1). May 4, 1918. *56 CR*, 65th Cong., 2d sess., p. 6057.

O. *Limitation of Debate—Amendment of the Rules. S. Res. 235.* Borah, R–Idaho, amendment to have treaties considered in open session. Rejected 23–50 (PP 10–0; D 3–37). June 12, 1918. *56 CR*, 65th Cong., 2d sess., p. 7657.

P. *Army Appropriations. H.R. 12281.* Hardwick, D–Ga., amendment to keep the minimum draft age at twenty-one instead of twenty. Rejected 33–41 (PP 7–3; D 27–13). June 28, 1918. *56 CR*, 65th Cong., 2d sess., p. 8411.

Q. *Changes in the Draft Age. H.R. 12731.* Kirby, D–Ark., amendment to keep minimum draft age at twenty instead of eighteen. Rejected 12–60 (PP 7–2; D 4–33). August 27, 1918. *56 CR*, 65th Cong., 2d sess., p. 9570.

R. *Post Office Appropriations. H.R. 13308.* Borah, R–Idaho, amendment to suspend the rules and repeal Section 1 of the 1917 Espionage Act and Section 4 of the 1918 Espionage Act, allowing the Postmaster General to exclude seditious materials from the mails. Rejected 25–33 (PP 8–1; D 0–32). February 8, 1919. *57 CR*, 65th Cong., 3d sess., p. 2969.

S. Percentage of votes for the administration position.

	A	B	C	D	E	F	G	H	I	J	K	L	M	N	O	P	Q	R	S
Peace progressives																			
Borah	y	y	y	y	y	n	?	?	y	n	y	y	y	n	y	y	y	y	94
Cummins	y	y	y	y	y	y	?	n	y	y	?	?	y	−	y	n	y	y	73
Gore	an	y	y	n	y	n	y	?	?	y	y	y	?	?	+	y	y	y	86
Gronna	n	y	y	y	y	n	y	n	y	n	y	y	?	n	y	y	ay	y	100
Hardwick	y	y	n	y	y	n	?	?	y	y	+	y	y	n	?	y	ay	y	80
Johnson (Calif.)	y	y	y	y	y	y	?	?	y	y	y	y	y	n	y	n	n	y	69
Jones (Wash.)	y	y	y	y	n	y	n	y	y	y	y	y	y	n	y	y	y	?	50
Kenyon	y	y	y	y	n	y	?	?	y	y	y	y	?	n	y	n	n	?	57
Kirby	y	n	n	n	y	n	?	n	n	y	y	n	y	y	n	y	y	n	41
La Follette	n	y	y	y	y	n	y	n	y	n	y	y	?	−	+	?	?	y	100
Lane	n	?	?	?	?	?	?	?	+	−									100
Norris	n	y	y	y	y	n	n	n	+	an	y	y	y	n	y	y	y	y	94
Vardaman	n	y	y	y	y	ex	y	n	y	n	y	y	y	?	y	y	y	?	100
Democrats																			
Ashurst	y	?	y	n	n	y	?	n	n	y	y	−	n	y	n	y	n	n	25
Bankhead	ay	?	?	n	n	y	?	y	n	y	n	n	?	y	n	y	n	n	7
Beckham	y	n	n	n	n	y	n	?	n	y	n	n	n	y	n	n	n	n	15
Broussard	y	n	n	n	n	y	n	?	n	y	n	?	−						0
Chamberlain	y	n	n	n	n	y	n	n	n	y	n	n	n	y	y	y	n	−	17
Culberson	y	?	?	?	n	y	n	n	n	y	n	−	?	y	n	y	y	?	23
Fletcher	y	n	n	n	n	y	n	n	n	y	n	n	n	n	y	?	n	n	6
Gay																		n	0
Gerry	y	n	n	n	n	y	n	y	n	y	n	n	n	y	?	?	n	?	0
Guion														y	n	n	n		0
Hitchcock	y	n	n	−	?	y	n	n	−	?	n	−	y	y	n	n	n	−	13
Hollis	ay	−	−	n	n	y	n	n	n	y	y	y	n	y	?	y	?	?	27
Hughes	y	n	n	−	an	ay	?	−	+	?	?	?							26
Husting	y	−	−	n	n	y	n	n	n	y	y	y							25

	A	B	C	D	E	F	G	H	I	J	K	L	M	N	O	P	Q	R	S
Democrats (cont.)																			
James	y	n	n	–	n	y	n	y	n	y	n	y	n	n	?	+	?	?	?	0
Johnson (S.D.)	y	n	n	?	n	y	n	n	–	ay	y	n	–	?	y	y	n	?	27
Jones (N.M.)	y	n	n	n	n	y	n	y	n	y	n	n	?	y	–	?	n	n	0
Kendrick	y	n	n	n	ay	ay	n	n	n	y	n	n	?	+	n	y	y	n	24
King	y	y	y	n	n	n	y	n	y	n	y	n	n	y	y	n	y	?	n	24
Martin	y	?	?	n	n	y	n	n	n	y	n	n	n	ay	n	y	?	n	13
McKellar	y	n	n	n	y	y	n	n	n	n	y	n	n	n	y	n	y	n	n	17
Myers	y	n	n	n	n	y	n	n	n	y	n	n	n	y	n	?	an	n	6
Newlands	ay	?	?	?	?	ay	–	?	n	y	n	n							0
Nugent													n	?	y	n	n	?	25
Overman	y	n	n	n	n	y	n	n	n	y	n	n	n	y	n	n	n	n	6
Owen	y	n	n	–	n	y	?	?	n	y	n	?	–	y	n	+	n	?	7
Phelan	y	n	n	y	n	y	?	?	n	y	n	?	?	y	n	n	n	–	7
Pittman	y	n	n	n	n	y	n	y	n	y	n	n	n	y	?	n	n	n	0
Pomerene	y	n	n	n	n	y	n	n	n	y	n	n	?	y	n	y	y	n	18
Ransdell	y	n	n	+	n	y	n	n	n	y	n	n	n	y	n	n	n	n	11
Reed	y	y	y	n	y	y	n	y	y	y	?	y	y	n	n	?	n	?	47
Robinson	y	n	n	n	n	y	n	n	n	y	n	n	n	+	n	y	n	?	12
Saulsbury	y	n	n	?	n	y	n	n	n	y	n	n	n	y	n	an	n	?	6
Shafroth	y	n	y	n	n	y	?	n	n	y	n	n	n	y	n	y	n	n	18
Sheppard	y	n	n	n	n	y	n	n	n	y	n	n	n	y	n	y	n	n	11
Shields	y	y	y	n	n	y	n	?	n	y	n	n	n	y	n	y	n	?	19
Simmons	y	n	n	–	n	y	n	n	n	y	n	n	n	y	n	y	n	n	11
Smith (Ariz.)	y	?	?	y	n	y	n	y	?	y	?	?	n	ay	n	y	n	n	15
Smith (Ga.)	y	n	n	–	n	y	n	y	n	y	n	n	y	y	n	?	n	n	6
Smith, (Md.)	ay	?	+	?	n	y	n	?	?	y	n	n	?	y	n	y	?	?	9
Smith (S.C.)	y	n	n	+	n	y	n	n	n	y	n	n	n	ay	n	y	?	n	18
Stone	n	?	?	n	n	y	?	n	n	y	n	n	+						30
Swanson	y	n	n	n	n	y	n	n	n	y	?	n	n	y	n	+	?	n	13

	A	B	C	D	E	F	G	H	I	J	K	L	M	N	O	P	Q	R	S
Democrats (cont.)																			
Thomas	y	y	y	y	y	n	n	y	y	–	?	+	n	?	n	y	n	n	56
Thompson	y	n	n	n	n	y	n	?	n	y	y	n	n	y	n	y	?	n	13
Tillman	ay	?	?	?	an	ay	?	?	?	?	?	?	?	n	y	n	?		0
Trammell	y	?	n	n	y	n	?	y	n	y	?	n	n	y	n	y	n	n	20
Underwood	y	–	–	n	n	y	n	?	n	y	n	n	n	y	n	y	n	n	6
Walsh (Mont.)	y	n	n	n	n	y	n	n	?	y	?	+	?	y	–	+	n	n	20
Williams	y	n	n	n	n	y	?	?	n	y	n	n	n	y	?	n	?	?	0
Wolcott	y	n	n	n	n	y	n	?	n	y	?	n	?	?	–	+	n	?	8

Table A.4 Votes on the League of Nations and related issues, 1919–1920

A. La Follette, R–Wis., amendment to delete the labor clauses from the treaty. Rejected 34–47 (PP, including Gore and Kenyon, 7–0; D 4–39). November 5, 1919. 58 *CR*, 66th Cong., 1st sess., p. 7969.

B. Gore, D–Okla., amendment to mandate the League members to agree to a three-month cooling-off period in all disputes, as well as to submit all war declarations to an "advisory vote of the people." Rejected 16–67 (PP 6–1; D 1–41). November 6, 1919. 58 *CR*, 66th Cong., 1st sess., p. 8013.

C. Borah, R–Idaho, amendment to require ratification of U.S. reservations by all four major powers (England, France, Italy, and Japan). Rejected 25–63 (PP 5–2; D 2–41). November 7, 1919. 58 *CR*, 66th Cong., 1st sess., p. 8069.

D. McCumber, R–N.D., amendment to strike out the requirement that U.S. reservations need to be ratified by any foreign power. Rejected 40–48 (PP 0–7; D 40–3). November 7, 1919. 58 *CR*, 66th Cong., 1st sess., p. 8068.

E. Borah, R–Idaho, amendment to state that the United States assumes no "legal or moral" responsibility for the workings of Article X. Rejected 18–68 (PP 6–1; D 2–42). November 10, 1919. 58 *CR*, 66th Cong., 1st sess., p. 8212.

F. Lodge, R–Mass., reservation to weaken Article X by stating that each nation is "free to accept or reject" advice given by the League council under Article X and that the United States could act under the article only through a declaration of war by Congress. Accepted 46–33 (PP 7–0; D 4–39). November 13, 1919. 58 *CR*, 66th Cong., 1st sess., p. 8437.

G. Lodge, R–Mass., reservation to disclaim any American responsibility for the disposition of the former German colonies. Rejected 29–64 (PP 4–3; D 3–41). November 17, 1919. 58 *CR*, 66th Cong., 1st sess., p. 8635.

H. Lodge, R–Mass., reservation to allow the United States freedom to decide which issues to submit to arbitration by the League of Nations court. Rejected 36–56 (PP 6–1; D 2–42). November 17, 1919. 58 *CR*, 66th Cong., 1st sess., p. 8641.

I. Owen, D–Okla., reservation to make U.S. participation in the League conditional on the granting of independence to Egypt. Rejected 37–45 (PP 7–0; D 5–33). November 17, 1919. 58 *CR*, 66th Cong., 1st sess., p. 8644.

J. Johnson, R–Calif., reservation to make U.S. participation in the League conditional on the United States' receiving equal voting strength to that of the British Empire. Accepted 43–36 (PP 7–0; D 4–39). November 18, 1919. 58 *CR*, 66th Cong., 1st sess., p. 8738.

K. Phelan, D–Calif., reservation to make the Fourteen Points the basis for the postwar peace. Rejected 12–79 (PP 5–2; D 2–40). November 18, 1919. 58 *CR*, 66th Cong., 1st sess., p. 8741.

L. Jones, R–Wash., reservation to prohibit the U.S. representative to the League from taking actions without the consent of the Congress. Rejected 34–50 (PP 7–0; D 3–38). November 18, 1919. 58 *CR*, 66th Cong., 1st sess., p. 8744.

M. Gore, D–Okla., reservation to hold that nothing in the ratification of the League would constitute U.S. entrance into an "entangling alliance." Rejected 28–50 (PP 7–0; D 3–35). November 18, 1919. 58 *CR*, 66th Cong., 1st sess., p. 8746.

N. La Follette, R–Wis., reservation stating that the United States would assume no responsibility for the enforcement of Article XI as it applies to Ireland, India, Egypt, and Korea. Rejected 24–49 (PP 6–1; D 3–34). November 18, 1919. 58 *CR*, 66th Cong., 1st sess., p. 8749.

O. La Follette, R–Wis., reservation stating that the United States would withdraw from the League within one year unless all member states abolish conscription. Rejected 21–54 (PP 7–0; D 3–35). November 18, 1919. 58 *CR*, 66th Cong., 1st sess., p. 8750.

P. La Follette, R–Wis., reservation stating that the United States would withdraw from the League within five years unless all member states spending more than $50 million annually on their 1919 military budgets have not reduced those budgets by at least 20 percent. Rejected 10–60 (PP 5–2; D 0–34). November 18, 1919. 58 *CR*, 66th Cong., 1st sess., p. 8751.

Q. La Follette, R–Wis., reservation stating that the United States would withdraw from the League if any League member forcibly acquires additional colonies. Rejected 19–51 (PP 7–0; D 2–32). November 18, 1919. 58 *CR*, 66th Cong., 1st sess., p. 8752.

R. La Follette, R–Wis., reservation stating that the United States would withdraw from the League if any mandatory power exploits the natural resources of its mandate. Rejected 23–51 (PP 7–0; D 2–36). November 18, 1919. 58 *CR*, 66th Cong., 1st sess., p. 8753.

S. Walsh, D–Mass., reservation stating that the provisions of Article XI "shall in no respect abridge the rights of" free speech, press, or religion. Rejected 36–42 (PP 7–0; D 5–34). November 18, 1919. 58 *CR*, 66th Cong., 1st sess., p. 8754.

T. Lodge, R–Mass., motion to approve the treaty with the Senate reservations. Approval rejected 49–35 (PP 2–5; D 22–21). March 19, 1920. 59 *CR*, 66th Cong., 2d sess., p. 4599.

U. *Armenian Mandatory. S. Con. Res. 27.* Hitchcock, D–Neb., motion to recommit the bill with instructions that the United States will accept a mandate over Armenia. Rejected 34–43 (PP 1–6; D 38–5). June 1, 1920. 59 *CR*, 66th Cong., 2d sess., p. 8070.

V. Percentage of votes for the Wilson administration position on League-related matters.

	A	B	C	D	E	F	G	H	I	J	K	L	M	N	O	P	Q	R	S	T	U	V	%
Peace progressives																							
Borah	y	y	y	n	y	y	y	y	y	y	y	y	y	y	y	y	y	y	y	y	n	n	0
Cummins	y	n	y	n	y	y	n	n	n	y	y	n	y	y	+	+	+	+	+	+	+	–	24
Gore	y	y	n	n	y	y	n	y	y	y	y	n	y	y	y	y	n	y	?	y	y	–	20
Gronna	y	y	y	n	y	y	y	y	y	y	y	y	y	y	y	y	y	y	y	y	n	–	0
Johnson (Calif.)	+	+	y	n	y	y	y	y	y	y	y	y	y	y	y	y	y	y	y	y	n	–	0
Jones (Wash.)	y	y	n	n	n	+	n	y	y	y	n	y	y	y	y	y	n	y	y	y	y	n	29
Kenyon	y	n	n	n	n	y	n	n	n	y	y	n	y	?	n	y	n	y	y	y	y	y	55
La Follette	y	y	y	n	y	y	y	y	y	y	y	y	y	y	y	y	y	y	y	y	n	–	0
Norris	y	y	y	n	y	y	y	y	y	y	y	y	y	y	y	y	y	y	y	y	n	n	5
Democrats																							
Ashurst	n	n	n	y	n	n	n	n	n	?	n	n	–	?	?	?	?	?	?	?	y	y	100
Bankhead	–	–	?	?	–	–	n	n	?	n	n	?	?	?	?	?	?	?	?				100
Beckham	–	?	–	+	n	n	n	n	n	n	n	n	n	n	n	n	n	n	n	n	y	y	100
Chamberlain	n	n	n	y	–	–	n	n	y	n	n	n	n	n	?	n	n	n	n	n	y	y	95
Culberson	n	n	n	y	–	–	n	–	–	–	–	?	?	?	?	?	?	?	?	?	n	–	100
Dial	n	n	n	y	n	n	n	n	n	n	n	n	n	n	n	n	n	n	n	n	n	y	100
Fletcher	n	n	n	y	n	n	n	n	n	n	n	n	n	n	n	n	n	n	n	n	y	+	100
Gay	n	n	n	y	n	n	n	n	n	n	n	n	n	n	n	n	n	n	n	n	n	y	100
Gerry	n	?	n	y	n	n	n	n	n	n	–	n	n	n	?	?	?	?	n	?	+	y	100

Democrats (cont.)

	A	B	C	D	E	F	G	H	I	J	K	L	M	N	O	P	Q	R	S	T	U	V
Harris	n	n	n	y	n	n	n	n	n	n	n	n	n	n	n	n	n	n	n	n	y	100
Harrison	n	n	n	y	n	n	n	n	n	n	n	n	n	n	n	n	n	n	n	n	y	100
Henderson	n	n	n	y	n	n	n	n	n	n	n	n	n	n	n	n	n	-	n	y	y	100
Hitchcock	n	n	n	y	n	n	n	n	n	n	n	n	n	n	n	n	n	n	n	n	y	100
Johnson (S.D.)	n	n	n	y	n	n	n	n	?	n	n	n	?	n	n	n	-	n	n	n	+	100
Jones (N.M.)	n	n	n	y	n	n	n	n	n	n	n	n	n	n	n	?	?	n	n	+	+	100
Kendrick	n	n	n	y	n	n	-	n	n	n	n	?	n	n	n	n	?	n	n	y	y	100
King	n	n	n	y	n	?	n	n	n	n	n	n	n	n	n	n	n	n	n	y	y	100
Kirby	n	n	n	y	n	n	n	n	n	y	n	-	-	n	n	n	n	n	n	n	+	91
McKellar	n	n	n	y	n	n	n	n	n	n	n	n	n	n	n	n	n	n	n	n	y	100
Martin	-	?	?	?	?																	100
Myers	y	n	n	y	n	n	n	n	-	?	?	n	n	n	n	?	n	n	n	y	y	94
Nugent	n	n	n	y	n	n	n	n	?	n	n	n	n	n	n	n	n	n	n	y	y	100
Overman	n	n	n	y	n	n	n	n	n	n	n	n	n	-	n	n	n	n	n	n	y	100
Owen	n	n	n	y	n	n	n	n	n	y	n	y	n	n	?	n	?	-	-	y	+	89
Phelan	n	-	n	y	n	n	n	n	y	y	y	n	n	?	n	-	n	n	y	y	y	79
Pittman	-	n	n	y	n	n	n	n	n	n	n	n	n	n	n	n	-	-	n	y	y	100
Pomerene	-	n	n	y	n	-	n	n	n	n	n	n	n	n	n	n	n	n	n	y	y	100
Ransdell	n	n	n	y	n	n	n	n	n	n	n	n	n	n	n	n	-	-	n	y	y	100
Reed	y	y	y	n	y	y	y	y	y	y	y	n	y	y	y	y	n	y	y	n	n	10
Robinson	n	n	n	y	n	n	n	n	n	n	n	n	n	n	-	n	n	n	n	n	y	100
Sheppard	n	n	n	y	n	n	n	n	n	n	n	n	n	n	n	n	n	n	n	n	y	100
Shields	?	an	+	-	+	+	y	y	y	y	n	y	y	y	n	?	?	?	y	n	n	18
Simmons	n	n	n	y	n	-	n	n	n	n	n	-	?	?	?	?	?	?	-	n	y	100
Smith (Ariz.)	n	n	n	y	n	-	n	n	n	n	n	n	n	n	n	n	n	n	n	-	y	100
Smith (Ga.)	n	n	n	y	n	y	n	n	n	n	n	n	n	-	-	-	n	n	y	y	y	91
Smith (Md.)	-	n	n	y	n	n	n	n	n	n	n	n	n	-	n	n	n	n	n	y	y	100

	A	B	C	D	E	F	G	H	I	J	K	L	M	N	O	P	Q	R	S	T	U	V	
Democrats (cont.)																							
Smith (S.C.)	n	n	n	y	n	n	n	n	n	n	n	n	n	n	n	n	n	n	n	n	n	y	100
Stanley	?	—	—	+	n	n	n	?	?	n	?	n	n	n	n	n	n	n	n	n	n	y	100
Swanson	n	n	n	y	n	—	n	n	n	n	n	n	n	n	n	n	n	n	n	n	n	+	100
Thomas	y	n	n	y	n	n	n	n	n	n	n	n	n	n	n	n	n	n	n	n	n	n	90
Trammell	n	n	n	y	n	n	n	n	n	n	n	n	n	n	n	n	n	n	n	n	y	y	100
Underwood	n	n	n	y	n	n	n	n	?	n	n	n	n	n	n	n	n	n	n	n	n	y	100
Walsh (Mass.)	y	n	n	n	n	y	y	y	n	y	y	y	n	y	y	y	y	n	y	y	y	y	38
Walsh (Mont.)	n	n	n	y	n	n	n	n	n	n	n	n	n	n	n	n	n	n	n	n	y	y	100
Williams	n	n	n	y	n	n	n	n	n	n	n	n	n	n	n	n	n	n	n	n	n	n	95
Wolcott	n	n	n	y	n	n	n	n	n	n	n	n	n	?	—	—	?	?	?	—	y	y	100

Table A.5   Votes on anti-imperialist issues, 1921–1929

A. *Treaty with Colombia.* Motion to approve. Accepted 69–19 (including pairs, PP 1–4; D 32–4). April 20, 1921. A "yea" vote is interpreted as the anti-imperialist position on this vote, although several peace progressives who opposed the treaty employed anti-imperialist arguments in doing so. 61 *CR*, 67th Cong., 1st sess., p. 487.

B. *Tax Revision. H.R. 8245.* La Follette, R–Wis., amendment to delete the Committee amendment granting tax breaks to "foreign traders" and "foreign corporations." Accepted 35–30 (PP 4–0; D 31–1). October 20, 1921. 61 *CR*, 67th Cong., 1st sess., p. 6548.

C. *Liberian Loan. H.J. Res. 270.* McNary, R–Ore., amendment to recommit the bill, excepting the Borah amendment to provide $20 million for reclamation purposes. Rejected 34–38 (PP 5–0; D 30–1). November 27, 1922. 63 *CR*, 67th Cong., 3d sess., p. 287.

D. *The Four Power Treaty.* La Follette, R–Wis., reservation to ratification, granting independence to the Philippines and requiring England and Japan to respect the sovereignty of the islands. Rejected 27–60 (PP 4–0; D 23–8). March 24, 1922. 62 *CR*, 67th Cong., 2d sess., p. 4493.

E. *The Four Power Treaty.* La Follette, R–Wis., reservation to ratification, stating that the United States would withdraw from the treaty if any signatory forcibly acquires any more Pacific colonies. Rejected 27–59 (PP 4–1; D 23–8). March 24, 1922. 62 *CR*, 67th Cong., 2d sess., p. 4492.

F. King, D–Utah, amendment cutting off funds for the Marines' occupations of Haiti, the Dominican Republic, and Nicaragua after December 31, 1922, unless the lives of U.S. citizens are threatened, and then only for the protection of those citizens. Rejected 9–43 (PP 5–0; D 2–15, 21 not voting). June 19, 1922. 62 *CR*, 67th Cong., 2d sess., p. 8974.

G. *Naval Appropriations. H.R. 12286.* Blaine, R–Wis., amendment cutting off funds for the Marines' occupation of Nicaragua after February 1, 1929, even if the Nicaraguan government invited the Marines to stay longer, unless the lives of U.S. citizens are threatened, and then only for "strictly protective purposes." Rejected 22–52 (PP 11–1; D 15–21). April 25, 1928. 69 *CR*, 70th Cong., 1st sess., p. 7192.

H. *Naval Appropriations. H.R. 12286.* Heflin, D–Ala., amendment cutting off funds for the Marines' occupation of Nicaragua immediately, until the submission of a declaration of war by the President to Congress. Rejected 15–60 (PP 10–2; D 9–28). April 25, 1928. 69 *CR*, 70th Cong., 1st sess., p. 7193.

I. *Naval Appropriations. H.R. 16714.* Dill, D–Wash., amendment stating that no part of the appropriations shall be used to maintain the Marines in Nicaragua except to transport them back to the United States. Accepted 38–30 (PP 11–0; D 28–6). February 22, 1929. 70 *CR*, 70th Cong., 2d sess., p. 4046.

J. *Naval Appropriations. H.R. 16714.* Dill, D–Wash., amendment stating that no part of the appropriations shall be used to maintain the Marines in Nicaragua except to transport them back to the United States; reconsideration of vote. Rejected 32–48 (PP 11–0; D 25–15). February 23, 1929. 70 *CR*, 70th Cong., 2d sess., p. 4119.

K. *Second Deficiency Appropriations. H.R. 17223.* Edge, R–N.J., amendment to appropriate $150,000 for a survey of a possible site for a Nicaraguan canal. Accepted 54–19 (PP 0–9; D 25–7). February 28, 1929. 70 *CR*, 70th Cong., 2d sess., p. 4669.

L. Percentage of votes for the anti-imperialist position.

	A	B	C	D	E	F	G	H	I	J	K	L
Peace progressives												
Blaine							y	y	y	y	n	100
Borah	n	y	y	?	y	y	n	n	y	y	n	70
Brookhart							+	+	y	y	n	100
Dill							y	y	y	y	n	100
Frazier							y	y	y	y	n	100
Howell							y	y	?	?	?	100
Ladd	y	?	y	y	n	y						80
La Follette, Sr.	n	y	y	y	y	y						83
La Follette, Jr.							y	y	ay	+	?	100

	A	B	C	D	E	F	G	H	I	J	K	L
Peace progressives (cont.)												
McMaster							y	n	y	y	n	80
Norris	n	ay	y	y	y	y	y	y	y	y	n	92
Nye							y	y	+	y	n	100
Shipstead							+	+	ay	+	?	100
Wheeler							y	y	y	y	n	100
Centrist Democrats												
Ashurst	y	y	y	y	y	n	n	n	y	n	y	58
Barkley							y	n	y	y	n	80
Caraway, T.	y	y	y	?	y	n	y	n	y	y	y	60
Culberson	y	+	y	?	y	?						100
Fletcher	y	+	y	y	y	?	n	n	?	+	y	67
George							+	?	+	+	y	75
Gerry	y	y	?	y	y	n	y	n	y	y	y	70
Glass	y	y	?	?	y	?	?	−	y	y	y	71
Harris	y	y	y	y	y	?	y	n	y	y	y	80
Heflin	y	y	y	?	?	n	y	y	y	y	y	78
Jones (N.M.)	y	y	y	−	−	?						60
McKellar	y	y	y	y	y	?	y	y	y	y	y	90
Overman	y	y	y	y	?	y	n	n	y	y	?	75
Pittman	y	+	y	y	y	?	y	n	?	y	?	88
Robinson (Ark.)	y	+	?	y	y	?	?	?	?	y	y	83
Sheppard	y	y	y	y	y	n	y	y	y	y	y	80
Simmons	n	y	y	y	y	n	?	?	?	y	?	71
Smith	y	?	y	y	y	n	?	?	y	n	−	75
Stanley	y	+	?	?	?	?						100
Stephens							+	+	y	+	?	100
Swanson	y	y	y	y	y	−	n	n	y	y	y	64
Trammell	−	?	?	y	y	n	?	?	y	y	y	57
Wagner							n	n	n	n	y	0

	A	B	C	D	E	F	G	H	I	J	K	L
Idealist Democrats												
Black							y	y	y	y	y	80
Harrison	y	?	y	y	y	?	?	?	?	y	?	100
Mayfield							y	y	y	y	y	80
Neely							+	+	y	y	n	100
Owen	+	+	y	y	?	?						100
Thomas (Okla.)							y	y	y	?	n	100
Walsh (Mont.)	+	?	y	y	y	y	n	n	y	y	y	70
Conservative Democrats												
Bayard						n	n	+	n	y		20
Bratton							n	n	y	y	y	40
Broussard	y	y	+	n	n	n	n	n	n	n	?	30
Bruce							n	n	n	n	?	0
Copeland							–	–	?	?	y	0
Dial	n	y	n	n	n	n						16
Edwards							n	n	?	–	?	0
Hawes							n	n	n	n	y	0
Kendrick	y	y	?	n	n	n	n	n	n	n	y	20
Hayden							n	n	y	?	?	33
Ransdell	y	y	y	y	n	–	n	n	n	n	y	36
Steck							n	n	y	n	?	40
Tydings							–	n	?	n	y	0
Tyson							n	n	y	n	y	20
Underwood	y	y	y	n	n	?						60
Wild-card Democrats												
Blease							n	n	y	n	n	40
Reed (Mo.)	n	+	y	y	y	–	?	?	?	n	?	57
Shields	+	y	+	y	y	?						100
Walsh (Mass.)	y	y	y	y	y	y	n	n	y	y	n	82
King	y	y	+	y	?	y	y	y	y	y	n	100

	A	B	C	D	E	F	G	H	I	J	K	L
Other Democrats												
Ferris							?	?	?	?	?	0
Hitchcock	y	y	y	y	y	?						100
Myers	y	n	y	n	n							40
Pomerene	y	y	y	n	?	n						60
Watson (Ga.)	n	y	?	y	y	?						75
Williams	y	y	+	n	n	?						60
Moderate Republicans												
Capper	n	y	n	n	n	n	n	n	y	y	y	29
Couzens							n	n	n	n	n	50
Cummins	–	y	n	n	n	?						20
Cutting							n	n				40
Johnson (Calif.)	n	?	?	y	y	y	n	n	n	n	?	46
Jones (Wash.)	n	–	n	n	n	+	n	n	y	n	y	23
Kenyon	n	y										50
Lenroot	n	y	?	n	n	n						20
McNary	n	n	y	n	n	n	n	n	n	n	y	29
Norbeck	n	?	?	n	n	n	n	n	n	n	n	25
Pine							?	?	y	?	n	100
Schall							n	n	n	n	y	0
Sterling	y	?	n	n	n	n						20
Thomas (Id.)									y	n	y	50

Table A.6   Votes on disarmament, 1921–1932

A. *Naval Appropriations. H.R. 4803.* King, D–Utah, motion to recommit the naval bill with instructions to reduce the appropriations by $100 million. Rejected 25–43 (including pairs, PP 4–0; D 20–14). June 1, 1921. 61 *CR*, 67th Cong., 1st sess., p. 1971.

B. *Army Appropriations. H.R. 5010.* Wadsworth, R–N.Y., amendment to increase the amount allotted for Army pay from $72 million to $83 million. Accepted 34–30 (PP 1–4; D 3–26). June 7, 1921. 61 *CR*, 67th Cong., 1st sess., p. 2193.

C. *Army Appropriations. H.R. 5010.* Wadsworth, R–N.Y., motion to agree to conference report on the bill. Accepted 58–13 (PP 0–4; D 20–9). June 22, 1921. 61 *CR*, 67th Cong., 1st sess., p. 2894.

D. *War Department Appropriations. H.R. 10871.* Wadsworth, R–N.Y., amendment to increase the appropriations for poison gas from $500,000 to $750,000. Accepted 46–22 (PP 1–3; D 6- 24). June 2, 1922. 62 *CR*, 67th Cong., 2d sess., p. 8019.

E. *War Department Appropriations. H.R. 10871.* Wadsworth, R–N.Y., amendment to increase the size of the Army from 115,000 to 133,000. Accepted 49–21 (PP 1–4; D 10–23). June 2, 1922. 62 *CR*, 67th Cong., 2d sess., p. 8032.

F. *Naval Appropriations. H.R. 15641.* Hale, R–Maine, amendment to increase appropriations from $13.75 million to $14.95 million, to allow for the construction of additional cruisers. Accepted 49–27 (PP 0–8; D 30–7). February 1, 1927. 68 *CR*, 69th Cong., 2d sess., p. 2676.

G. *Construction of Cruisers. H.R. 11526.* Harrison, D–Miss., amendment to strike the clause mandating completion of the construction program within five years. Rejected 28–54 (PP 12–0; D 11–30). February 4, 1929. 70 *CR*, 70th Cong., 2d sess., p. 2762.

H. *Construction of Cruisers. H.R. 11526.* Hale, R–Maine, motion to agree to the bill, providing for construction of fifteen cruisers by 1934. Accepted 68–12 (PP 0–11; D 37–5). February 5, 1929. 70 *CR*, 70th Cong., 2d sess., p. 2854.

I. *London Naval Treaty.* Motion to approve. Accepted 58–9 (PP 11–1; D 29–4). July 21, 1930. 73 *CR*, 71st Cong., special sess., p. 378.

J. *War Department Appropriations. H.R. 15593.* Frazier, R–N.D., amendment to prohibit use of funds from the act toward compulsory military courses or training at any civilian school of college. Rejected 7–62 (PP 7–1; D 1–25). January 29, 1931. 74 *CR*, 71st Cong., 3d sess., p. 3468.

K. *Navy Department Appropriations. H.R. 16969.* Hale, R–Maine, amendment to increase appropriations from $23.6 million to $31.1 million. Accepted 63–10 (PP 2–10; D 28–4). February 21, 1931. 74 *CR*, 71st Cong., 3d sess., p. 5615.

L. *Naval Building Program. S. 51.* Frazier, R–N.D., amendment to establish as U.S. policy a one-year naval moratorium rather than build up to Washington and London Treaty limits. Rejected 17–58 (PP 11–0; D 8–27). May 5, 1932. 75 *CR*, 72d Cong., 1st sess., p. 9369.

M. *Naval Building Program. S. 51.* Hale, R-Maine, motion to agree to bill for 1932 Navy. Accepted 44–21 (PP 0–10; D 19–18). May 6, 1932. 75 *CR*, 72d Cong., 1st sess., p. 9711.

N. *War Department Appropriations. H.R. 11897.* Frazier, R–N.D., amendment to decrease the number of Army officers by 2000. Rejected 16–51 (PP 10–0; D 7–23). June 9, 1932. 75 *CR*, 72d Cong., 1st sess., p. 12429.

O. *War Department Appropriations. H.R. 11897.* McKellar, D–Tenn., motion to recommit, with instructions to decrease to appropriation by 10 percent. Rejected 23–47 (PP 10–0; D 10–19). June 9, 1932. 75 *CR*, 72d Cong., 1st sess., p. 12448.

P. *Naval Appropriations. H.R. 11452.* King, D–Utah, motion to recommit, with instructions to decrease to appropriation by 10 percent. Rejected 22–27 (PP 10–0; D 11–12). June 16, 1932. 75 *CR*, 72d Cong., 1st sess., p. 13175.

Q. *Naval Appropriations. H.R. 11452.* Hale, R–Maine, amendment to increase appropriations for the naval reserve from $3.077 million to $3.727 million. Accepted 34–26 (PP 0–11; D 10–20). June 16, 1932. 75 *CR*, 72d Cong., 1st sess., p. 13171.

R. Percentage of votes in favor of disarmament.

	A	B	C	D	E	F	G	H	I	J	K	L	M	N	O	P	Q	R
Peace progressives																		
Blaine							y	−	+	y	n	y	n	y	y	y	n	100
Borah	y	n	n	n	n	n	y	n	y	?	n	y	?	y	y	+	−	100
Brookhart							y	n	y	y	n	+	−	y	?	y		n	100
Dill						n	y	n	+	?	−	y	n	y	y	?		n	100
Frazier						n	y	n	ay	y	n	y	n	y	y	y		n	100
Howell						?	ay	?	y	?	y	y	n	?	y	y		n	88
Ladd	y	n	?	y	n													75
La Follette, Sr.	y	n	n	n	n													100
La Follette, Jr.						n	+	an	y	y	n	y	n	y	y	y		n	100
McMaster						n	y	n	y	n	an							83
Norris	y	n	n	n	n	?	y	n	y	y	n	y	n	y	y	y		n	100
Nye						n	y	n	ay	y	n	y	n	y	y	+	−	100
Shipstead						n	y	n	−	?	y	y	−	+	y	y		n	82
Wheeler						n	y	−	+	+	n	+	−	y	y	y		n	100
Centrist Democrats																		
Ashurst	y	n	n	y	y	y	y	n	y	+	n	y						36
Barkley							n	+	ay	n	y							20
Caraway	+	−	y	n	n	n	y	y	y	n	?							70
Culberson	?	?	?	y	−													50
Fletcher	n	?	y	−	−	y	−	+	y	n	y							30
George							y	n	y	y	n	?						20
Gerry	n	n	n	−	y	y	n	y										25
Glass	y	−	y	n	?	y	+	−	y	n	ay							60

	A	B	C	D	E	F	G	H	I	J	K	L	M	N	O	P	Q	R
Centrist Democrats (cont.)																		
Harris	y	n	y	y	n	y	n	y	y	n	y							36
Heflin	y	–	y	n	y	n	n	y	?	y	y							50
Jones (N.M.)	+	n	?	n	n	n												100
McKellar	y	+	y	–	–	y	n	y	n	n	y							27
Overman	+	n	y	n	–	y	n	y	y									55
Pittman	n	–	–	–	+	ay	n	y	–	?	y							27
Robinson (Ark.)	?	–	?	n	n	?	n	y	y	n	y							44
Sheppard	y	n	y	y	y	n	y	y	y	n	y							45
Simmons	n	n	y	n	n	+	n	y	ay	n	y							45
Smith	n	–	y	n	y	y	y	y	ay	?	y							40
Stanley	y	–	y	?	n													75
Stephens						y	n	y	+	?	?							25
Swanson	n	n	y	?	n	+	n	y	y	n	y							30
Trammell	n	?	y	?	–	y	n	y	y	n	y							22
Wagner							n	y	y	?	y							25
Idealist Democrats																		
Harrison	y	–	n	n	n	y	y	–	y	?	ay							82
Black							y	n	y	n	?							75
Mayfield						–	y	y										67
Neely						?	y	y										50
Owen	+	?	?	?	–													100
Thomas (Okla.)							y	n	y	n	–							80
Walsh (Mont.)	n	n	?	–	n	y	+	n	y	n	–							70
Conservative Democrats																		
Bayard						y	n	y										0
Bratton						y	n	y	+	n	y							20
Broussard	n	n	y	?	n	y	?	ay	–	n	y							22

	A	B	C	D	E	F	G	H	I	J	K	L	M	N	O	P	Q	R
Conservative Democrats (cont.)																		
Bruce						y	n	y										0
Copeland						y	n	y	−	n	y							0
Dial	y	n	?	n	n													75
Edwards						y	an	y										0
Hawes						y	n	y	+	?	?							25
Hayden							n	y	?	n	y							0
Kendrick	y	−	n	n	y	y	n	y	y	n	y							45
Ransdell	+	+	y	y	−	+	n	y	ay	n	y							27
Steck						y	n	y	ay	?	?							25
Tydings							n	y	+	n	y							25
Tyson						y	n	y										0
Underwood	n	n	y	n	y	?												40
Wild-card Democrats																		
Blease						?	?	y	?	n	−							33
Reed (Mo.)	n	?	?	−	?	y	n	y										25
Shields	+	?	n	−	−													100
Walsh (Mass.)	n	n	n	n	n	y	n	y	n	?	y							40
King	y	n	y	n	n	n	y	−	y	?	n							90
Other Democrats																		
Brock									y	n	?							50
Bulkley											y							0
Connally									ay	n	y							33
Ferris						n												100
Hitchcock	y	n	+	n	n													80
McGill											y							0
Morrison											ay							0
Myers	?	y	y	y	y													0
Pomerene	y	n	n	n	?													100

	A	B	C	D	E	F	G	H	I	J	K	L	M	N	O	P	Q	R
Other Democrats (cont.)																		
Watson (Ga.)	y	n	n	n	n													100
Williams	n	?	y	?	?													0
Moderate Republicans																		
Capper	y		y		n	n	y	y	y	n	y	y	n	y	y	y	n	73
Couzens						y	n	y	y	n	y	n	y	n	y	+	y	25
Cummins	y		y															50
Cutting									ay	?	?	n	n	n	n	?	?	40
Johnson (Calif.)	?	+	n	?	y	y	n	y	n	n	y	n	y	n	n	−	?	7
Jones (Wash.)	n		n			n	y	y	y	n	y	n	y	n	n	n	+	28
Kenyon	y	n	?															100
Lenroot	y	y		n														67
McNary	?		y			y	y	y	y	n	y	n	?	n	?	n	y	18
Norbeck			?			−	y	y	?	n	n	?	?	?	?	y	n	71
Pine						n	?	y	n	?	+							25
Schall						y	n	y	y	n	y	n	y	−	n	n	y	8
Sterling	n																	
Thomas (Id.)						y	y	y	?	y	−	+	n	y	y	y		40

Table A.7   Votes on European issues, 1921–1931

A. *Treaty of Peace with Germany.* Reed, D–Mo., amendment to disclaim any American responsibility for all provisions of the Versailles Treaty. Rejected 7–71 (including pairs, PP 4–0; D 4–24). October 18, 1921. 61 *CR*, 67th Cong., 1st sess., p. 6418.

B. *Treaty of Peace with Germany.* Lodge, R–Mass., motion to table (kill) King, D–Utah, amendment to replace the Berlin Treaty with the Versailles Treaty, coupled with the Lodge Reservations. Accepted 59–25 (PP 3–0; D 5–28). October 18, 1921. 61 *CR*, 67th Cong., 1st sess., p. 6435.

C. *Treaty of Peace with Germany.* Lodge, R–Mass., motion to approve the treaty. Accepted 66–20 (PP 1–4; D 16–20). October 18, 1921. 61 *CR*, 67th Cong., 1st sess., p. 6438.

D. *Adjustment of Foreign Loans. H.R. 8762.* Smoot, R–Utah, motion to create a commission authorized under certain conditions to "refund or convert obligations" owed by foreign governments to the United States. Accepted 39–26 (PP 0–4; D 1–33). January 31, 1922. *62 CR*, 67th Cong., 2d sess., p. 1978.

E. *The Four Power Treaty.* Lodge, R–Mass., motion to approve. Accepted 67–27 (PP 2–3; D 13–23). March 24, 1922. *62 CR*, 67th Cong., 2d sess., p. 4497.

F. *World War Foreign Debt Settlement. H.R. 14254.* Smoot, R–Utah, motion to modify the Foreign Debt Act to permit the refunding of the British debt over sixty-two years at a rate from 3 percent to 3.5 percent. Accepted 70–13 (PP 1–4; D 26–9). February 16, 1923. *64 CR*, 67th Cong., 4th sess., p. 3787.

G. *Confirmation of Ambassador Kellogg.* Lodge, R–Mass., motion in executive session to confirm Frank Kellogg as U.S. ambassador to the United Kingdom. Confirmed 75–9 (PP 2–7; D 31–2). December 11, 1923. *65 CR*, 68th Cong., 1st sess., p. 235.

H. *Relief of Distress in Germany. H.J. Res. 180.* La Follette, R–Wis., motion to discharge the resolution, calling for a $10 million U.S. loan to Germany, from the Foreign Relations Committee. Rejected 23–53 (PP 10–0; D 7–30). June 6, 1924. *65 CR*, 68th Cong., 1st sess., p. 10994.

I. *The World Court.* Moses, R–N.H., reservation to disclaim any U.S. responsibility for the outcome of advisory opinions of the World Court and to support the disassociation of the Court from the League of Nations. Rejected 21–72 (PP 9–2; D 3–33). June 27, 1926. *67 CR*, 69th Cong., 1st sess., p. 2821.

J. *The World Court.* Motion to approve the protocol. Accepted 76–17 (PP 4–7; D 35–2). June 27, 1926. *67 CR*, 69th Cong., 1st sess., p. 2825.

K. *Indebtedness of Italy to the United States. H.R. 6773.* Howell, R–Neb., amendment to compel Italy to issue bonds upon U.S. demand not to exceed the amount due that year and unpaid previous balance. Rejected 24–55 (PP 9–0; D 15–13). April 21, 1926. *67 CR*, 69th Cong., 1st sess., p. 7902.

L. *Indebtedness of Italy to the United States. H.R. 6773.* Smoot, R–Utah, motion to agree to the bill. Accepted 54–33 (PP 0–10; D 14–23). April 21, 1926. *67 CR*, 69th Cong., 1st sess., p. 7902.

M. *French Debt Settlement. H.R. 6585.* Smoot, R–Utah, motion to agree to the bill. Accepted 53–21 (PP 1–11; D 16–11). December 16, 1929. *72 CR*, 71st Cong., 2d sess., p. 720.

N. *Foreign-Debt Moratorium. H.J. Res. 147.* Howell, R–Neb., amendment to allow no further postponement of the debt unless and until the European nations assented to a "reformation" of the Versailles Treaty. Rejected 16–63 (PP 10–1; D 4–33). December 22, 1931. *75 CR*, 72d Cong., 1st sess., p. 1120.

O. *Foreign-Debt Moratorium. H.J. Res. 147.* Shipstead, Farmer-Labor–Minn., amendment to state the sense of the Congress that "in light of the documentary evidence accumulating since 1919" the United States no longer acquiesces in the charge made by Article 231 of the Versailles Treaty "to the effect that Germany alone was responsible for the war." Rejected 10–64 (PP 9–2; D 2–34). December 22, 1931. 75 *CR*, 72d Cong., 1st sess., p. 1126.

P. Percentage of votes for the European positions assumed by the Harding, Coolidge, and Hoover administrations.

	A	B	C	D	E	F	G	H	I	J	K	L	M	N	O	P
Peace progressives																
Blaine													n	y	y	0
Borah	y	y	n	n	n	n	?	?	y	n	?	n	n	n	n	17
Brookhart						y	y	n	y	n			y	y	y	25
Dill						y	n	+	−	y	n	n	y	n		11
Frazier						n	y	n	y	n	y	n	n	y	y	0
Howell						?	y	y	n	y	y	n	n	ay	+	33
Johnson (Minn.)							y	n								0
Ladd	+	?	+	?	y	?	y	y								60
La Follette, Sr.	y	y	n	n	n	n	y	?								0
La Follette, Jr.									y	n	y	n	n	y	y	0
McMaster									n	y	y	n	n			40
Norris	?	?	−	n	y	n	y	n	y	y	ay	−	n	y	y	15
Nye									y	n	y	n	n	y	y	0
Shipstead						y	n	y	n	y	n	an	+	+		0
Wheeler						y	n	y	y	y	n	n	y	y		11
Centrist Democrats																
Ashurst	y	n	y	n	n	n	y	?	n	y	n	n	?	n		50
Barkley													y	n		100
Caraway	n	n	n	n	n	y	n	y	n	y	y	n	n			46
Culberson	n	n	n	−	n	ay										50
Fletcher	n	n	y	n	y	y	n	y	n	y	+	−	y	n		79
George						n	y	n	y	y	n	y	n			75
Gerry	n	n	y	−	n	n	n	y	n	y	n	y				75
Glass	n	n	n	n	n	y	n	y	n	y	n	y	y	n		79
Harris	n	n	n	n	n	−	n	?	n	y	y	n	n			46
Heflin	n	n	n	n	n	n	n	?	n	y	y	n	n			42

	A	B	C	D	E	F	G	H	I	J	K	L	M	N	O	P
Centrist Democrats (cont.)																
Jones (N.M.)	n	n	n	n	+	y	n	y	?	y	n	y				82
McKellar	n	n	n	n	y	n	n	y	n	y	y	n	n	n		57
Overman	n	n	n	n	n	y	n	y	n	y	?	n	?			64
Pittman	?	n	n	n	n	y	y	y	n	y	?	?	y	?		60
Robinson (Ark.)	?	?	−	−	n	y	n	?	n	y	?	−	?	?		50
Sheppard	n	n	n	n	n	y	n	y	n	y	y	n	n	n		57
Simmons	n	n	n	n	n	ay	n	?	n	y	?	n	y			64
Smith	?	?	+	?	n	y	n	?	n	y	?	n	n	n		67
Stanley	n	n	n	n	n	y	n	?								57
Stephens							n	y	n	y	y	n	n	?		57
Swanson	?	−	−	−	n	y	n	y	n	y	?	n	y	?		64
Trammell	n	n	y	−	y	n	n	y	n	y	y	n	n	n		64
Wagner													y	y		50
Idealist Democrats																
Black													n	n		50
Harrison	n	n	n	n	n	y	n	n	n	y	y	n	?	n		62
Mayfield							n	y	n	y	y	n				67
Neely							n	y	n	y	y	n			−	77
Owen	?	−	y	−	y	y	?	?								75
Thomas (Okla.)													?	n		100
Walsh (Mont.)	n	n	n	n	n	n	y	y	n	y	?	n	y	n		54
Conservative Democrats																
Bayard							n	y	n	y	n	y				100
Bratton							n	y	n	n	−	n				67
Broussard	n	y	y	n	y	y	n	y	n	y	n	y	?	n		85
Bruce							−	y	n	y	n	y				100
Copeland							y	n	y	y	n	y	y	y		50
Dial	?	?	y	−	y	y	−	y								83

	A	B	C	D	E	F	G	H	I	J	K	L	M	N	O	P
Conservative Democrats (cont.)																
Edwards							y	y	n	y	n	y				83
Hawes													y	n		100
Hayden													y	n		100
Kendrick	n	n	y	?	y	ay	y	y	n	y	n	y	y	n		92
Ransdell	?	n	y	n	y	y	—	y	n	y	n	y	y			92
Steck											?	ay	?			100
Tydings											?		?	n		100
Tyson									n	y	?	n				67
Underwood	n	n	y	—	y	y	—	y	n	y	?	+				91
Wild-card Democrats																
Blease									y	n	y	n	n			0
Reed (Mo.)	y	y	n	n	n	n	+	?	y	n	ay	an				0
Shields	?	y	y	—	n	y	n	—	n							57
Walsh (Mass.)	y	y	y	n	n	n	n	y					y	n		50
King	n	n	n	n	n	y	n	y	n	y	y	y		n		69
Other Democrats																
Ferris							?	n	n	y	n	y				80
Hitchcock	n	n	+	—	n	n										50
Myers	n	n	y	n	y	y										83
Pomerene	n	n	y	n	y	y										83
Watson (Ga.)	y	y	n	n	n											0
Williams	n	y	n	ay	y	y										67
Moderate Republicans																
Capper	n	y	y	y	y	y			n	y	n	y	y	n		92
Couzens						y			y	y	y	y	y			67
Cummins	n	y	y	+	y	?			n	y						88
Cutting													y	y		50
Johnson (Calif.)	y	y	n	—	n	y			y	n	y	n	?	y		9

	A	B	C	D	E	F	G	H	I	J	K	L	M	N	O	P
Moderate Republicans (cont.)																
Jones (Wash.)	+	?	+	y	y	y	y		n	y	n	y	y	n		91
Kenyon	?	y	y	?												50
Lenroot	n	y	y	ay	y	y			n	y	n	n				80
McNary	n	y	y	y	y	y			n	y	n	y	y	n		92
Norbeck	?	+	y	+	y	ay			n	y	n	y	?	y		80
Pine									y	n	n	y	?			50
Schall									y	n	an	ay	y	y		50
Sterling	n	y	y	y	y	y										83
Thomas (Id.)													y	n		100

Table A.8 Votes on the Hawley-Smoot tariff, 1930

A. Wheeler, D–Mont., amendment to decrease the ad valorem rate on rayon from 45 percent to 35 percent. Rejected 23–52 (including pairs, PP 11–1; D 14–19). January 27, 1930. 72 *CR*, 71st Cong., 2d sess., p. 2445.

B. Barkley, D–Ky., amendment to decrease the rate on straw hats valued at less than $8/dozen from $4 and 50 percent ad valorem to 60 percent ad valorem. Rejected 38–39 (PP 12–0; D 25–5). January 29, 1930. 72 *CR*, 71st Cong., 2d sess., p. 2623.

C. McMaster, R–S.D., amendment to place cement on the free list. Accepted 40–35 (PP 11–1; D 29–6). January 31, 1930. 72 *CR*, 71st Cong., 2d sess., p. 2773.

D. Barkley, D–Ky., amendment to decrease the rate on sheet glass from 1.875¢/lb. to 1.25¢/lb. Accepted 41–40 (PP 11–0; D 32–5). February 11, 1930. 72 *CR*, 71st Cong., 2d sess., p. 3428.

E. Walsh, D–Mass., amendment to decrease aluminum rates: on scrap and crude from 5¢/lb. to 2¢/lb; on coils plates, sheets, bars, rods, etc. from 9¢/lb. to 3.5¢/lb. Accepted 41–39 (PP 12–0; D 30–6). February 17, 1930. 72 *CR*, 71st Cong., 2d sess., p. 3774.

F. Grundy, R–Pa., amendment to increase the rate on pig iron from 75¢/ton to $1.40/ton. Rejected 31–42 (PP 0–11; D 3–29). March 12, 1930. 72 *CR*, 71st Cong., 2d sess., p. 5070.

G. Barkley, D–Ky., amendment to place hollow steel bars on the free list. Accepted 35–26 (PP 11–0; D 26–0). March 12, 1930. 72 *CR*, 71st Cong., 2d sess., p. 5074.

H. Thomas, D–Okla., amendment to take crude petroleum off the free list. Rejected 29–38 (PP 0–12; D 8–26). March 19, 1930. 72 *CR*, 71st Cong., 2d sess., p. 5604.

I. Copeland, D–N.Y., amendment to increase the rate on wire fencing from 50 percent ad valorem to 90 percent ad valorem. Rejected 28–38 (PP 0–10; D 2–25). March 21, 1930. 72 *CR*, 71st Cong., 2d sess., p. 5812.

J. Total percentage for lower industrial tariff rates on all 66 industrial rate votes (minimum 20 votes), including test votes and 71 *CR* 4778 (tannic acid), 4893 (cellulose sheets), 4931 (paints), 5194 (earthenware), 5222 (rolled glass), 5238 (pig iron), 5309 (beams and girders), 5345 (screws), 5509 (shingles), 5524 (watch movements), 5544 (spring clothespins); 72 *CR* 1121 (wool yarn), 1174 (silk woven fabrics), 1935 (plain basic paper) 2299 (leather gloves), 2446 and 2447 (rayon), 2622 and 2680 (straw hats), 3077 (acetic acid), 3230 (lead pigments), 3369 (brick), 3442 (plate glass), 3749 (wire rods), 3775 (aluminum ware), 4061 (manila cordage), 4142 (wool yarn), 4151 (woolen clothing), 4155 (wool fabrics), 4207 (silk clothing, silk manufactured goods) 4210 (silk pile fabrics), 4220 (pipe organs), 4290 (fur hats), 4916 (cement), 4945 and 4946 (earthenware), 5060 (sheet glass), 5063 (plate glass), 5155 (clothespins), 5190 (wool fabrics), 5204 (rayon), 5280 (cartridges), 5382 (boots and shoes), 5384 (leather), 5398 (umbrellas), 5577 (cement), 5622 (laces), 5714 (acetic acid), 5725 (tiles), 5790 (plate glass), 5795 (china ware), 5803 (brick), 5815 (pincers), 5813 (cotton blankets), 5898 (wool fabrics), 5910 (photographic paper), 5929 (matches).

K. Thomas, R–Idaho, amendment to increase the rate on various agricultural oils. Rejected 26–49 (PP 6–4; D 11–19). January 28, 1930. 72 *CR*, 71st Cong., 2d sess., p. 2548.

L. Connally, D–Tex., amendment to increase the rates on cattle: below 700 pounds from 2¢/lb. to 2.5¢/lb; above 700 pounds from 2.5¢/lb. to 3¢/lb. Accepted 71–4 (PP 12–0; D 24–4). February 18, 1930. 72 *CR*, 71st Cong., 2d sess., p. 3867.

M. Brookhart, R–Iowa, amendment to increase the rate on lard from 3¢/lb. to 4¢/lb. Rejected 23–53 (PP 6–5; D 4–23). February 20, 1930. 72 *CR*, 71st Cong., 2d sess., p. 3982.

N. Smoot, R–Utah, amendment to increase the rate on wool from 40 percent ad valorem to 45 percent ad valorem. Accepted 45–28 (PP 5–5; D 4–25). February 24, 1930. 72 *CR*, 71st Cong., 2d sess., p. 4142.

O. Jones, R–Wash., amendment to increase the rate on lumber by $2 per 1,000 feet. Rejected 34–39 (PP 1–11; D 9–24). February 27, 1930. 72 *CR*, 71st Cong., 2d sess., p. 4414.

P. Smoot, R–Utah, amendment to increase the rate on sugar from $1.24/lb. to $1.7125/lb. Accepted 47–39 (PP 4–8; D 9–27). March 5, 1930. 72 *CR*, 71st Cong., 2d sess., p. 4780.

Q. Goldsborough, R–Md., amendment to decrease the rate on mustard seed from 3¢/lb. to 1¢/lb. Rejected 28–39 (PP 3–6; D 9–16). March 13, 1930. 72 *CR*, 71st Cong., 2d sess., p. 5162.

R. Smoot, R–Utah, amendment to increase the rate on long-staple cotton by 10¢/lb. Accepted 44–32 (PP 6–4; D 21–12). March 13, 1930. 72 *CR*, 71st Cong., 2d sess., p. 5166.

S. Sheppard, D–Tex., amendment to take various agricultural oils used for mechanical or manufacturing purposes off the free list. Rejected 28–39 (PP 7–4; D 8–16). March 22, 1930. 72 *CR*, 71st Cong., 2d sess., p. 5943.

T. Total percentage for lower agricultural tariff rates on all 43 agricultural rate votes (minimum 20 votes), including test votes and 71 *CR* 3926 (wheat), 4517 (wheat flour), 4560 (avocados and mangoes), 4867 (casein), 4977 and 4978 (olive oil), 5509 (shingles), 5543 (maple, birch, and beech flooring), 5715 (tobacco), 5801 (cotton rags), 5904 (wools); 72 *CR* 376 (wool coils), 377 (wool thread), 378 (wool cord), 459 (wool rags), 461 (wool), 523 (wool hair), 1690 (sugar), 2278 and 2292 (hides), 3353 (starch), 3915 (dates), 4138 (wool), 4626 (cotton), 4636 (planed lumber), 4860 (casein), 5091 (maple, birch, and beech flooring), 5145 (sugar), 5274 (maple sugar), 5404 (beeswax), 5828 (broomcorn), 5832 (grapes), 5848 (flax, jemp, hute), 5951 (mangoes, avocados, pears free from Cuba).

U. *Revision of the Tariff.* H.R. 2667. Motion to agree to passage of final vote on tariff bill. Accepted 53–31 (PP 5–7; D 8–29). March 24, 1930. 72 *CR*, 71st Cong., 2d sess., p. 6015.

	A	B	C	D	E	F	G	H	I	J	K	L	M	N	O	P	Q	R	S	T	U
	Industrial Tariffs										*Agricultural and Lumber Tariffs*										
Peace progressives/moderate Republicans																					
Blaine	y	y	y	y	y	n	y	n	n	100	n	y	n	n	n	n	?	n	n	88	n
Borah	y	y	y	y	y	n	y	n	n	97	y	y	y	y	n	n	?	?	?	42	y
Brookhart	n	y	y	y	y	n	+	−	n	92	y	y	y	y	n	n	n	n	y	27	y
Capper	y	y	y	n	y	n	y	y	n	68	y	y	y	y	n	n	n	y	y	40	y
Couzens	n	n	y	y	n	y	?	n	n	53	n	y	n	y	n	y	y	n	?	63	y
Cutting	y	y	+	y	y	n	y	+	n	92	?	y	?	y	n	n	n	y	+	50	+
Dill	y	y	n	y	y	y	n	y	−	91	?	?	n	n	y	y	y	y	n	36	n
Frazier	y	y	y	y	y	n	y	n	n	92	y	y	y	y	n	y	n	y	y	26	y
Howell	y	y	y	+	y	n	y	n	n	95	?	y	y	y	−	y	n	y	y	21	y
Johnson	?	?	n	?	y	n	?	y	?	40	n	y	?	?	+	y	n	y	y	15	y
La Follette	y	y	y	y	y	n	y	n	n	100	n	y	n	n	n	n	y	n	n	84	n
McMaster	y	y	y	y	y	n	y	n	n	100	y	y	y	n	n	n	n	y	y	40	n

	A	B	C	D	E	F	G	H	I	J	K	L	M	N	O	P	Q	R	S	T	U
				Industrial Tariffs									*Agricultural and Lumber Tariffs*								

Peace progressives/moderate Republicans (cont.)

	A	B	C	D	E	F	G	H	I	J	K	L	M	N	O	P	Q	R	S	T	U
Norbeck	y	y	y	y	y	n	y	n	n	98	y	y	n	n	n	n	n	?	y	53	n
Norris	y	y	y	y	y	n	y	n	n	100	n	y	n	n	n	n	y	n	y	81	n
Nye	y	y	y	y	y	n	y	n	?	89	y	ay	y	y	y	n	y	n	y	23	y
Shipstead	y	y	y	?	+	?	?	—	—	97	y	ay	?	?	—	—	?	?	?	xx	—
Wheeler	y	y	y	y	+	n	y	n	?	98	n	y	n	?	—	n	n	n	n	67	n

Democrats

	A	B	C	D	E	F	G	H	I	J	K	L	M	N	O	P	Q	R	S	T	U
Ashurst	+	y	n	y	y	y	n	n	n	96	n	y	n	n	y	y	n	y	?	44	n
Barkley	y	y	y	y	y	y	n	n	n	100	n	y	?	n	n	n	n	n	n	88	n
Black	y	y	y	y	y	y	n	n	n	100	n	y	n	n	n	n	n	y	?	73	n
Blease	?	y	+	y	y	y	—	n	n	100	n	y	n	n	—	—	y	n	n	80	n
Brock	n	?	—	y	n	?	—	—	?	81	?	y	n	—	n	n	n	y	?	77	—
Broussard	n	?	n	n	n	?	y	y	y	5	?	y	?	y	y	y	?	y	?	13	y
Bratton	y	y	y	y	y	y	n	?	—	96	n	y	n	y	n	n	n	y	y	50	y
Caraway	?	y	y	y	y	?	n	+	n	100	y	y	n	n	n	n	?	?	y	72	n
Connally	n	y	y	y	y	y	n	y	n	97	y	y	?	n	n	—	n	y	y	44	n
Copeland	n	n	n	y	n	y	y	n	y	37	n	n	n	n	?	n	y	n	n	90	y
Fletcher	y	+	y	y	y	y	n	n	n	93	y	y	y	n	y	y	n	y	n	38	+
George	—	y	?	+	y	y	n	n	n	97	y	y	n	n	n	n	n	y	n	68	n
Glass	n	?	y	y	y	y	n	—	n	98	n	?	n	n	—	n	?	n	n	94	n
Harris	n	y	y	y	y	y	n	n	n	97	y	n	n	n	n	n	y	y	y	72	n
Harrison	n	y	+	y	y	y	n	?	n	98	n	y	n	n	n	n	n	y	n	79	n
Hawes	—	y	y	—	+	?	n	n	—	73	n	y	n	?	n	n	n	y	n	70	n
Hayden	+	?	+	y	y	?	n	n	n	96	+	y	?	?	n	y	n	y	n	53	n
Heflin	n	y	y	+	+	y	n	n	n	91	y	?	?	n	n	n	n	y	y	61	n
Kendrick	y	n	y	y	y	?	?	y	n	37	n	y	y	y	+	+	?	?	n	18	y
King	?	?	+	+	+	?	?	?	?	xx	?	?	?	?	—	y	?	?	?	xx	—
McKellar	n	y	n	y	y	y	n	—	—	92	y	y	n	?	n	n	n	y	?	65	n
Overman	n	y	y	y	?	?	?	n	n	100	n	?	n	n	—	n	?	n	?	86	—

	A	B	C	D	E	F	G	H	I	J	K	L	M	N	O	P	Q	R	S	T	U
				Industrial Tariffs										*Agricultural and Lumber Tariffs*							

Democrats (cont.)

	A	B	C	D	E	F	G	H	I	J	K	L	M	N	O	P	Q	R	S	T	U
Pittman	?	?	?	+	y	+	−	y	?	81	?	y	y	?	y	n	?	y	?	33	y
Ransdell	n	n	n	n	−	?	?	y	?	15	y	y	?	?	y	y	?	y	y	16	y
Robinson (Ark.)	?	?	+	+	+	?	?	?	?	xx	?	?	?	?	?	?	?	?	?	xx	−
Sheppard	y	y	y	y	y	y	n	y	n	97	y	y	y	n	n	n	n	y	y	34	n
Simmons	n	y	y	y	y	y	n	n	n	98	n	ay	n	−	?	n	?	n	?	87	n
Smith	y	y	y	y	+	+	−	−	−	98	n	ay	n	n	n	n	+	−	?	86	n
Steck	y	y	y	y	y	?	n	n	n	98	n	?	?	?	?	n	?	+	?	70	n
Stephens	+	+	+	y	y	y	−	−	?	100	?	?	n	n	y	n	n	y	?	74	−
Swanson	n	y	y	y	y	y	n	n	n	98	n	?	n	n	n	n	y	−	n	92	n
Thomas	y	y	y	n	y	+	−	y	?	86	?	?	n	n	y	y	y	y	y	58	n
Trammell	n	y	y	n	y	+	n	n	?	80	y	y	y	n	y	y	?	y	n	44	y
Tydings	n	y	y	y	n	y	n	−	n	92	n	y	n	n	n	n	y	n	n	94	n
Wagner	n	n	y	y	n	+	y	n	?	60	n	n	n	−	n	n	y	n	n	92	n
Walsh (Mass.)	n	n	y	y	y	y	n	n	?	80	−	n	n	y	n	n	y	n	n	89	n
Walsh (Mont.)	y	y	y	y	y	y	n	n	n	98	n	y	n	n	n	n	n	n	n	72	n

Notes

Introduction

1. 47 *Congressional Record* (hereafter *CR*) 1911, 62d Cong., 1st sess., pp. 2676–2710. For more on Gronna, see William Phillips, "Asle J. Gronna: Self-Made Man of the Prairies" (Ph.D. diss., University of Missouri, 1958), p. 339.
2. 70 *CR* 1929, 70th Cong., 2d sess., pp. 4043–46, 4119; *New York Times*, Feb. 23 and 24, 1929; New York *World*, Feb. 24, 1929.
3. This interpretation was first made by Robert Seager, "The Progressives and American Foreign Policy" (Ph.D. diss., Ohio State University, 1957). Ralph Stone similarly used the term in *The Irreconcilables: The Fight against the League of Nations* (Lexington: University Press of Kentucky, 1970).
4. Wayne Cole, *Roosevelt and the Isolationists, 1932–1941* (Lincoln: University of Nebraska Press, 1983); idem, *America First: The Battle against Intervention, 1940–1941* (Madison: University of Wisconsin Press, 1953). See also Manfred Jonas, *Isolationism in America, 1935–1941* (Ithaca: Cornell University Press, 1966); and Justus Doenecke, "American Isolationism, 1939–1941," *Journal of Libertarian Studies: An Interdisciplinary Review* 6 (1982):207–215.
5. On this point I disagree with Cole, who contends that the group reached its high point during the 1930s. See Wayne Cole, "Isolationism," in idem, *Franklin D. Roosevelt: His Life and Times; An Encyclopedic View* (Boston: G. K. Hall, 1985), pp. 211–213.
6. For this argument see William Appleman Williams, *The Tragedy of American Diplomacy* (Cleveland: World, 1959); idem, "The Legend of Isolationism in the 1920s," *Science and Society* 18 (1954):1–20; Barton Bernstein and Franklin Leib, "Progressive Republican Senators and American Imperialism, 1898–1916: A Reappraisal," *Mid-America* 50 (1968):163–205.
7. Daniel Patrick Moynihan, *On the Law of Nations* (Cambridge, Mass.: Harvard University Press, 1990), p. 50.
   A number of studies give some attention to William Borah but do not communicate the sense that he was part of a larger congressional bloc articulating an alternative foreign policy vision. For a particularly good mainstream discussion of Borah's role in the decade's foreign policy de-

bates, see Frank Costigliola, *Awkward Dominion: American Political, Economic, and Cultural Relations with Europe, 1919–1933* (Ithaca: Cornell University Press, 1984).

8. This study focuses on the Senate because the key foreign policy battles of the decade were fought there. As peace progressive Robert La Follette, Jr., remarked in 1926, the House "has become merely a registrative body pliant to the will of the executive" because of its large membership and increasing adoption of gag rules, making the Senate the only "forum where the minority could be heard"; *La Follette's Magazine*, April 1926. La Follette obviously is not an objective source here, but the point is incontrovertible.

9. David Pletcher, "Caribbean 'Empire,' Planned and Improvised," *Diplomatic History* 14 (1990):458.

10. Michael Hogan, *Informal Entente: The Private Structure of Cooperation in Anglo-American Economic Diplomacy, 1918–1929* (Columbia: University of Missouri Press, 1977); Melvyn Leffler, *The Elusive Quest: America's Pursuit of European Stability and French Security, 1919–1933* (Chapel Hill: University of North Carolina Press, 1979).

11. See especially Lloyd Gardner, *Safe for Democracy: The Anglo-American Response to Revolution, 1913–1923* (New York: Oxford University Press, 1984); and Thomas Knock, *To End All Wars: Woodrow Wilson and the Quest for a New World Order* (New York: Oxford University Press, 1992). A negative appraisal of Wilson's policies that nonetheless sees the President as a central figure in fashioning the U.S. response to nationalism in the non-European world is Robert Freeman Smith, *The United States and Revolutionary Nationalism in Mexico, 1916–1932* (Chicago: University of Chicago Press, 1972).

12. Robert David Johnson, "Ernest Gruening and the Tonkin Gulf Resolution: Continuities in Dissent," *Journal of American–East Asian Relations* 2 (1993):111–135.

13. Lawrence Wittner, "Peace Historians and Foreign Policy: The Challenge to Diplomatic Historians," *Diplomatic History* 11 (1987):355–370; Robert Beisner, *Twelve against Empire: The Anti-Imperialists, 1898–1900* (New York: McGraw-Hill, 1968); Peter Brock, *Pacifism in the United States from the Colonial Era to the First World War* (Princeton: Princeton University Press, 1968); Charles Chatfield, *For Peace and Justice: Pacifism in America, 1914–1941* (Knoxville: University of Tennessee Press, 1971); Charles DeBenedetti, *Origins of the Modern American Peace Movement, 1915–1929* (Millwood, N.Y.: KTO Press, 1978); Sondra Herman, *Eleven against War: American Internationalist Thought, 1898–1921* (Stanford: Hoover Institution Press, 1969); C. Roland Marchand, *The American Peace Movement and Social Reform, 1898–1918* (Princeton: Princeton University Press, 1972).

14. An exception to this pattern is John Schroeder, *Mr. Polk's War: American Opposition and Dissent, 1846–1848* (Madison: University of Wisconsin Press, 1973).

15. Charles DeBenedetti with Charles Chatfield, *An American Ordeal: The Antiwar Movement of the Vietnam Era* (Syracuse: Syracuse University Press, 1990).

16. Ray A. Billington, "The Origins of Middle Western Isolationism," *Political Science Quarterly* 60 (1945):44–64; William Carleton, "Isolationism and the Middle West," *Mississippi Valley Historical Review* 33 (1946):377–390; George Wilbur Garvid, "Politics in Minnesota and American Foreign Relations, 1921–1941" (Ph.D. diss., University of Minnesota, 1967); Paul Holbo, "They Voted against War: A Study in Motivations" (Ph.D. diss., University of Chicago, 1961); George Grassmuck, "Sectional Biases in Foreign Policy" (Ph.D. diss., Johns Hopkins University, 1951).

17. Carleton, "Isolationism and the Middle West"; Robert Wilkins, "The Non-Ethnic Roots of North Dakota Isolationism," *Nebraska History* 44 (1963):205–211.

18. Selig Adler, *The Isolationist Impulse: Its Twentieth Century Reaction* (New York: Abelard-Schuman, 1957); Wayne Cole, *Senator Gerald P. Nye and American Foreign Relations* (Minneapolis: University of Minnesota Press, 1962).

19. LeRoy Ashby, *The Spearless Leader: Senator Borah and the Progressive Movement in the 1920s* (Urbana: University of Illinois Press, 1972).

20. Williams, *The Tragedy of American Diplomacy*; idem, "Legend of Isolationism in the 1920s"; Bernstein and Leib, "Progressive Republican Senators"; Laurence Hauptman, "To the Good Neighbor: A Study of the Senate's Role in American Foreign Policy" (Ph.D. diss., New York University, 1972). While Williams and others of this school, such as Orde Pinckney, occasionally do mention the European positions of the dissenters, their portrayal of those positions is so present-minded as to be of little value. See Williams, *The Tragedy of American Diplomacy*; and Orde Pinckney, "William E. Borah: Critic of American Foreign Policy," *Studies on the Left* 1 (1960):48–61.

21. Robert James Maddox, *William E. Borah and American Foreign Policy* (Baton Rouge: Louisiana State University Press, 1969); idem, "Another Look at the Legend of Isolationism in the 1920s," *Mid-America* 53 (1971):35–43; Thomas Guinsburg, *The Pursuit of Isolationism in the United States Senate from Versailles to Pearl Harbor* (New York: Garland, 1982); John Chalmers Vinson, *The Parchment Peace: The United States Senate and the Washington Conference, 1921–1922* (Athens: University of Georgia Press, 1955); idem, *Referendum for Isolation: The Defeat of Article Ten of the League of Nations Covenant* (Athens: University of Georgia Press, 1961).

22. A more sophisticated though narrower approach comes from historians such as Ralph Stone, Richard Lowitt, and LeRoy Ashby. All three have contended that peace progressive foreign policy exhibited some combination of anti-imperialism and nationalism that often existed in conflict with each other. Of this group, however, only Stone examines the group

as a bloc (doing so at its weakest point numerically, 1919), and he contends that the senators described in this study as peace progressives failed to present internally consistent ideological reasons for opposing the League. Ashby and Lowitt, by focusing on individual senators in biographies that concentrate primarily on domestic affairs, do not communicate a sense of an organized congressional bloc opposing mainstream foreign policy; because of their approaches, they also cannot examine the intensity of the peace progressive opinions. Ashby, *The Spearless Leader;* Stone, *The Irreconcilables;* Richard Lowitt, *George W. Norris: The Persistence of a Progressive, 1913–1933* (Urbana: University of Illinois Press, 1971).

23. 70 *CR* 1929, 70th Cong., 2d sess., pp. 2411–23.

1. Patterns of Dissent

1. Felix Gilbert, *To the Farewell Address: Ideas of Early American Foreign Policy* (Princeton: Princeton University Press, 1961), pp. 44–56; James Hutson, "Intellectual Foundations of Early American Diplomacy," *Diplomatic History* 1 (1977):1–19; Reginald Stuart, *War and American Thought from the Revolution to the Monroe Doctrine* (Kent: Kent State University Press, 1982).

2. Drew McCoy, *The Elusive Republic: Political Economy in Jeffersonian America* (Chapel Hill: University of North Carolina Press, 1980), pp. 210–218.

3. Ibid., pp. 185–208.

4. Merrill Peterson, *The Jeffersonian Image in the American Mind* (New York: Oxford University Press, 1960); Thomas Hietala, *Manifest Design: Anxious Aggrandizement in Jacksonian America* (Ithaca: Cornell University Press, 1985).

5. "Brutus," in *New York Gazette*, Oct. 18, 1787, in Herbert Storing, ed., *The Anti-Federalist: Writings by the Opponents of the Constitution* (Chicago: University of Chicago Press, 1981), p. 115; "Brutus," in *New York Gazette*, Jan. 3, 1788, ibid., pp. 146, 148; "Agrippa," in *Massachusetts Gazette*, Dec. 25, 1787, ibid., pp. 243–245; "Impartial Examiner," in *Virginia Independent Gazette*, Feb. 27, 1788, ibid., p. 284; Mason speech, June 14, 1788, in Robert Rutland, ed., *The Papers of George Mason, 1725–1792* (Chapel Hill: University of North Carolina Press, 1970), vol. 3, p. 1073; Norman Graebner, "Isolationism and Antifederalism: The Ratification Debates," *Diplomatic History* 11 (1987):337–353. For more on the antimilitarism of the Revolutionary era, see Charles Royster, *A Revolutionary People at War: The Continental Army and American Character, 1775–1783* (Chapel Hill: University of North Carolina Press, 1979).

6. Henry Adams, *Life of Gallatin* (Philadelphia, 1879), p. 197.

7. 7 *Annals of Congress* 1798, 5th Cong., pp. 1119–32; Gerry quoted in Hutson, "Intellectual Foundations of Early American Diplomacy," p. 8.

8. 23 *Annals of Congress* 1812, 12th Cong., 1st sess., pp. 441–454, 511–515, 668–675; Roger Brown, *The Republic in Peril: 1812* (New York: W. W.

Norton, 1971), pp. 150–154, 229. For more on the Old Republicans, see Norman Risjord, *The Old Republicans: Southern Conservatism in the Age of Jefferson* (New York: Columbia University Press, 1965); Robert Dawidoff, *The Education of John Randolph* (New York: W. W. Norton, 1979); and David Carson, "That Ground Called Quiddism: John Randolph's War with the Jefferson Administration," *Journal of American Studies* 20 (1986):71–92.

9. 17 *Congressional Globe* (hereafter *CG*) 1848, 30th Cong., 1st sess., pp. 122–126; 17 *CG, Appendix* 1848, 30th Cong., 1st sess., pp. 81, 122–124, 341–342, 364; Richard H. Sewell, *John P. Hale and the Politics of Abolition* (Cambridge, Mass.: Harvard University Press, 1965), pp. 52–85, 112; David Herbert Donald, *Charles Sumner and the Coming of the Civil War* (New York: Alfred A. Knopf, 1960), pp. 108–110. On the Navy, see 26 *CG* 1853, 32d Cong., 2d sess., pp. 485–486; 29 *CG* 1856, 34th Cong., 1st sess., pp. 1697, 1739, 2057–58.

10. Timothy Matthewson, "George Washington's Policy toward the Haitian Revolution," *Diplomatic History* 3 (1979):321–336.

11. Peggy Liss, *Atlantic Empires: The Network of Trade and Revolution, 1713–1826* (Baltimore: Johns Hopkins University Press, 1983), pp. 105–111; Arthur Whitaker, *The United States and the Independence of Latin America, 1800–1830* (Baltimore: Johns Hopkins University Press, 1941), pp. 189–247; Wolfgang Mommsen, *Theories of Imperialism* (Chicago: University of Chicago Press, 1980), p. 5.

12. 29 *Annals of Congress* 1816, 14th Cong., 1st sess., p. 790; 31 *Annals of Congress* 1818, 15th Cong., 1st sess., pp. 1474–99.

13. 41 *Annals of Congress* 1824, 18th Cong., 1st sess., pp. 1085–97; E. M. Earle, "American Interest in the Greek Cause, 1821–1827," *American Historical Review* 33 (1927):46–48.

14. 7 *Annals of Congress* 1798, 5th Cong., p. 1129; 41 *Annals of Congress* 1824, 18th Cong., 1st sess., pp. 1104–12, 1131–34; Adams quoted in John Milton Cooper, Jr., *The Vanity of Power: Isolationism in America, 1914–1917* (Westport, Conn.: Greenwood Press, 1969), p. 13.

15. 44 *Register of Debates* 1826, 19th Cong., 1st sess., pp. 236–253, 277–291, 1237–40, 2084. The most complete coverage of the public response to the Panama Congress is Piero Gleijeses, "The Limits of Sympathy: The United States and the Independence of Spanish America," *Journal of Latin American Studies* 24 (1992):481–505.

16. Garrison to Charles Whipple, July 19, 1946, in Walter Merrill, ed., *The Letters of William Lloyd Garrison* (Cambridge, Mass.: The Belknap Press of Harvard University Press, 1973), vol. 3, p. 353; 15 *CG, Appendix* 1846, 29th Cong., 1st sess., pp. 826–827; 16 *CG* 1846, 29th Cong., 2d sess., pp. 643, 683, 812, 916; 17 *CG* 1847, 30th Cong., 1st sess., pp. 122–124. For House debate over the pro-Haitian petitions, see *CG*, 25th Cong., 3d sess., pp. 41, 47, 56, 62, 137. The most complete coverage of the Whig

dissent from the Mexican War is John Schroeder, *Mr. Polk's War: American Opposition and Dissent, 1846–1848* (Madison: University of Wisconsin Press, 1973).

17. *Speeches, etc., of John P. Hale, 1846–1865* (Washington, D.C., 1848–1865), Feb. 15, 1853; *CG* 1858, 35th Cong., 1st sess., pp. 1705, 1727–29; *CG* 1859, 35th Cong., 2d sess., pp. 1179–87; Preston to Lewis Cass, April 4, 1859, in William Ray Manning, ed., *Diplomatic Correspondence of the United States: Inter-American Affairs, 1831–1860* (Washington, D.C.: Carnegie Endowment for International Peace, 1932–1939), vol. 9, pp. 968–969. The antiexpansionist consensus broke down, however, when slavery played no part in the Democrats' Caribbean policy, as in a mid-1850s dispute with Great Britain over the applicability of the Clayton-Bulwer Treaty to British protectorates over the Miskito coast in Nicaragua and the Bay Islands in Honduras, revealing that the group's anti-imperialism activated only when they perceived that American expansion would serve the interests of slavery. For Free Soil Whig comments on 1850s disputes between the United States and England over Central America, see *CG, Appendix* 1855, 34th Cong., 1st sess., pp. 73–74 (Collamer), 81–84 (Foot), 84–87 (Wilson), 301–306 (Fessenden).

18. Sewell, *John P. Hale*, pp. 199–200.

19. *CG* 1870, 41st Cong., 3d sess., pp. 226–231; *CG* 1871, 42d Cong., 1st sess., pp. 294–305.

20. *CG* 1859, 35th Cong., 2d sess., p. 1354; *CG* 1870, 41st Cong., 3d sess., pp. 193–196, 225–226, 257–270; *CG, Appendix* 1870, 41st Cong., 3d sess., pp. 25–34; *CG* 1871, 42d Cong., 1st sess., pp. 524–534; Robert Beisner, "Thirty Years before Manila: E. L. Godkin, Carl Schurz, and Anti-Imperialism in the Gilded Age," *Historian* 30 (1968):561–577. Domestic concerns beyond racism also played a key role in shaping the Democratic opposition. Thurman called the resolution "another one of the mighty strides that have been taken toward centralizing all power in the General Government," putting the United States on a road "toward a consolidated despotism in this land"; Bayard added that given both the domestic and foreign policies of the Republicans, "perhaps a reference to the Constitution may be considered ... not particularly important or of much weight," but announced that he would make such an appeal anyway; *CG* 1870, 41st Cong., 3d sess., pp. 249, 256.

21. Donald Marquard Dozer, "Anti-Imperialism in the United States, 1865–1895: Opposition to Annexation of Overseas Territories" (Ph.D. diss., Harvard University, 1936), pp. 76, 141, 153–155. One Cleveland biographer has observed that "the celerity with which Cleveland set about to reverse the trend toward participation in power politics indicated beyond question of reasonable doubt that he had a clear understanding of the policy he meant to enforce in this respect"; George Roscoe Dulebohn,

Principles of Foreign Policy under the Cleveland Administrations (Philadelphia: University of Pennsylvania Press, 1941), p. 91.

22. 32 *CR* 1899, 55th Cong., 3d sess., pp. 733–740.

23. 32 *CR* 1899, 55th Cong., 3d sess., pp. 1530–32, 1738; 34 *CR* 1901, 56th Cong., 2d sess., pp. 3116–18.

24. Robert Beisner, *Twelve against Empire: The Anti-Imperialists, 1898–1900* (New York: McGraw-Hill, 1968), pp. 25–31, 76–80; E. Berkeley Tompkins, *Anti-Imperialism in the United States: The Great Debate, 1898–1920* (Philadelphia: University of Pennsylvania Press, 1970).

25. 32 *CR* 1899, 55th Cong., 3d sess., pp. 494–501, 1840–46; 33 *CR* 1900, 56th Cong., 1st sess., pp. 4278–5206. Theodore Roosevelt spoke of "such men as Hoar [as] little better than traitors . . . He can be pardoned only on the ground that he is senile"; Roosevelt to Henry Cabot Lodge, Jan. 26, 1899, in Elting Morrison, ed., *The Letters of Theodore Roosevelt*, 8 vols. (Cambridge, Mass.: Harvard University Press, 1951), vol. 2, pp. 923, 925. The most complete coverage of Hoar's career is Richard Welch, *George Frisbie Hoar and the Half-Breed Republicans* (Cambridge, Mass.: Harvard University Press, 1971).

26. 40 *CR* 1906, 59th Cong., 1st sess., pp. 2125–37 (Bacon). Roosevelt to John Hay, March 30, 1905, in Morrison, *Letters of Theodore Roosevelt*, vol. 4, pp. 1150–51. Roosevelt still worried that Bacon, "backed by the average yahoo among the Democratic senators . . . wholly indifferent to national honor or national welfare . . . [and] primarily concerned in getting a little cheap reputation among ignorant people," could block his treaty out of spite using demagogic arguments designed to undermine his popular consensus. He waited until he was sure he had the votes to introduce the treaty in 1906, although a more spirited Democratic opposition might have defeated it anyway. Roosevelt to Joseph Bucklin Bishop, March 23, 1905, ibid., pp. 1144–45.

27. 40 *CR* 1906, 59th Cong., 1st sess., pp. 793–800.

28. The Democrats were not helped here by their constant contention that they (and not the Republicans) were the true followers of Roosevelt domestically. See John Wiseman, *Dilemmas of a Party out of Power: The Democrats, 1904–1912* (New York: Garland, 1988).

29. 33 *CR* 1900, 56th Cong., 1st sess., pp. 767–770, 805–810; 34 *CR* 1901, 56th Cong., 2d sess., pp. 2951, 3109–15; C. Vann Woodward, *Tom Watson: Agrarian Rebel* (Savannah: Beehive Press, 1973), pp. 289–290.

30. Bryan address, Lincoln, Neb., Dec. 31, 1898, in *Bryan on Imperialism* (Chicago: Bentley, 1900), p. 8; *New York Journal*, Dec. 25, 1898, ibid., pp. 25–30; *New York Journal*, Jan. 15, 1899, ibid., pp. 39–43; *New York Journal*, Feb. 12, 1899, ibid., pp. 55–58; Bryan speech, Indianapolis, Aug. 8, 1900, ibid., pp. 85–90; Kendrick Clements, *William Jennings Bryan: Missionary Isolationist* (Knoxville: University of Tennessee Press, 1982), pp. 23–39; LeRoy Ashby, *William Jennings Bryan: Champion of Democracy*

(Boston: Twayne, 1987), p. 82; Paolo Coletta, *William Jennings Bryan: Political Evangelist, 1860–1908* (Lincoln: University of Nebraska Press, 1964), pp. 213–237.

31. Clements, *William Jennings Bryan*, pp. 41–53; Ashby, *William Jennings Bryan*, p. 85.

32. Peterson, *The Jeffersonian Image*, pp. 259–260; Clements, *William Jennings Bryan*, pp. 40–58; Ashby, *William Jennings Bryan*, p. 164.

33. 47 *CR* 1911, 62d Cong., 1st sess., pp. 196–200 (Rayner), 448, 1132–34 (Bacon), 448–449 (Stone), 5662, 5665 (Bacon). Rayner responded by charging that the Bacon course would produce a war between the United States and Mexico.

34. For the Southern Democrats and Taft's European policies, see 48 *CR* 1911–12, 62d Cong., 2d sess., pp. 370 (Culberson), 370, 2865–75 (Bacon), 474–477, 963–966 (Rayner). For the Senate Democrats and Taft's military policies, see ibid., p. 4686.

2. The Emergence of the Peace Progressives

1. 42 *CR* 1908, 60th Cong., 1st sess., p. 5224. On Clapp's personality, see James Holt, *Congressional Insurgents and the Party System, 1909–1916* (Cambridge, Mass.: Harvard University Press, 1967). Clapp also had an unusual interest in civil rights for a Minnesota senator; through this cause he met Oswald Garrison Villard, publisher of *The Nation. Washington Post*, May 3, 1913; *St. Paul* (Minn.) *Pioneer*, Jan. 13, 1914, Reel 1, Moses Clapp Papers, Minnesota State Historical Society, St. Paul.

2. Padraic Colum Kennedy, "La Follette's Imperialist Flirtation," *Pacific Historical Review* 29 (1960):131–140; John Milton Cooper, Jr., "Progressivism and American Foreign Policy: A Reconsideration," *Mid-America* 51 (1969):268–270; William Phillips, "Asle J. Gronna: Self-Made Man of the Prairies" (Ph.D. diss., University of Missouri, 1958), p. 220; A. Bower Sageser, *Joseph L. Bristow: Kansas Progressive* (Lawrence: University Press of Kansas, 1968), pp. 53–64; Robert Seager, "The Progressives and American Foreign Policy," 2 vols. (Ph.D. diss., Ohio State University, 1956), vol. 2, pp. 107, 133. On the pre-1908 progressives and foreign policy, see William Leuchtenberg, "Progressivism and Imperialism: The Progressive Movement and American Foreign Policy," *Mississippi Valley Historical Review* 39 (1952):483–504. Leuchtenberg's thesis does not apply particularly well to the years following 1908.

3. Holt, *Congressional Insurgents*, pp. 29–43; David Sarasohn, *The Party of Reform: Democrats in the Progressive Era* (Jackson: University Press of Mississippi, 1989), pp. 59–86.

4. La Follette, draft speech, 1911, Box B-215, La Follette Family Papers, Library of Congress, Washington, D.C.; *New York Times*, May 18, 1911; Seager, "The Progressives and American Foreign Policy," vol. 2,

pp. 173–176; Barton Bernstein and Franklin Leib, "Progressive Republican Senators and American Imperialism, 1898–1916: A Reappraisal," *Mid-America* 50 (1968):163–205; Holt, *Congressional Insurgents*, p. 39; Padraic Colum Kennedy, "La Follette's Foreign Policy: From Imperialism to Anti-Imperialism," *Wisconsin Magazine of History* 66 (1963):287–293. For more on Borah's early career, see Marian McKenna, *Borah* (Ann Arbor: University of Michigan Press, 1961), chaps. 1–5. For La Follette's early career, see David Thelen, *Robert La Follette and the Insurgent Spirit* (Boston: Little, Brown, 1976); and Belle La Follette and Fola La Follette, *Robert M. La Follette*, 2 vols. (New York: Macmillan, 1953), vol. 1. For the insurgents and the Honduran treaty, see David Healy, *Drive to Hegemony: The United States in the Caribbean, 1898–1917* (Madison: University of Wisconsin Press, 1988), p. 150.

5. Works to L. A. Seward, April 17, 1911; Works to Taft, May 6, 1911; Works to N. R. Martin, March 21, 1912; Works to Knox, May 22, 1912; Works to M. M. Gleason, June 5, 1912; all in Box 1, John Downey Works Papers, Bancroft Library, University of California, Berkeley. For California Progressivism, see Richard Coke Lower, *A Bloc of One: The Political Career of Hiram W. Johnson* (Stanford: Stanford University Press, 1993), pp. 1–91; George Mowry, *The California Progressives* (Berkeley: University of California Press, 1951); Spencer Olin, *California's Prodigal Sons: Hiram Johnson and the Progressives* (Berkeley: University of California Press, 1968).

6. Cummins in *Des Moines Register*, March 25, 1911, Scrapbook 5, Albert Cummins Papers, Iowa State Historical Society, Des Moines; 47 *CR* 1911, 62d Cong., 1st sess., pp. 2574 (Borah), 2677, 2689, 2708 (Gronna), 2767 (Clapp), 3145 (La Follette); Phillips, "Asle J. Gronna," p. 339.

7. Joseph Smith, *Unequal Giants: Diplomatic Relations between the United States and Brazil, 1889–1930* (Pittsburgh: University of Pittsburgh Press, 1991), pp. 88–93.

8. 51 *CR* 1914, 63d Cong., 2d sess., pp. 7532–7538 (Norris), 9724, 9726 (Vardaman), 9728, 9730 (Borah) 10229 (Bristow), 10052 (Clapp).

9. Kendrick Clements, *William Jennings Bryan: Missionary Isolationist* (Knoxville: University of Tennessee Press, 1982), pp. 77–112; Cooper, "Progressivism and American Foreign Policy," p. 267.

10. Clements, *William Jennings Bryan*, pp. 113–126; Sarasohn, *The Party of Reform*, p. 60; Cooper, "Progressivism and American Foreign Policy," pp. 266–267; John Milton Cooper, Jr., *The Vanity of Power: American Isolationism and the First World War, 1914–1917* (Westport, Conn.: Greenwood Press, 1967), pp. 86–98.

11. Jerome Clubb and Howard Allen, "Party Loyalty in the Progressive Years: The Senate, 1909–1915," *Journal of Politics* 29 (1967):575; Timothy McDonald, "The Gore-McLemore Resolutions: Democratic Revolt against Wilson's Submarine Policy," *Historian* 26 (1963):50–74; Monroe

Lee Billington, "The Gore Resolution of 1916," *Mid-America* 47 (1965):89–98.

12. Taft to Gus Karger, July 20, 1919, Reel 211, William Howard Taft Papers, Library of Congress. For Vardaman's early career, see William Holmes, *The White Chief: James Kimble Vardaman* (Baton Rouge: Louisiana State University Press, 1970). For Gore's early career, see Monroe Lee Billington, *Thomas P. Gore: The Blind Senator from Oklahoma* (Lawrence: University Press of Kansas, 1967). For Clarke and Kirby, see Richard Niswonger, *Arkansas Democratic Politics, 1896–1920* (Fayetteville: University of Arkansas Press, 1990). On the limits of the Southern appeal, see Ruth Warner Towne, *William J. Stone and the Politics of Compromise* (Port Washington, N.Y.: National University Publications, 1979), pp. 208–209; Cooper, *The Vanity of Power*, p. 112.

13. Holt, *Congressional Insurgents*, p. 124; Cooper, *The Vanity of Power*, pp. 27, 110; David Kennedy, *Over Here: The First World War and American Society* (New York: Oxford University Press, 1980), p. 22; 52 *CR* 1915, 63d Cong., 3d sess., pp. 3631–33; 53 *CR* 1916, 64th Cong., 1st sess., pp. 10931–33.

14. Robert James Maddox, *William E. Borah and American Foreign Policy* (Baton Rouge: Louisiana State University Press, 1969), p. 16; William Forth, "Wesley L. Jones: A Political Biography" (Ph.D. diss., University of Washington, 1962), pp. 253, 328, 332; Howard Arthur DeWitt, "Hiram W. Johnson and American Foreign Policy, 1917–1941" (Ph.D. diss., University of Arizona, 1972), p. 15. For more on the link between progressivism and nationalism, see Cooper, "Progressivism and American Foreign Policy," pp. 261–264.

15. For American policy during the latter stages of the Taft administration, see Friedrich Katz, *The Secret War in Mexico: Europe, the United States, and the Mexican Revolution* (Chicago: University of Chicago Press, 1981), pp. 92–118. On Wilson's attitudes, see Wilson address, Latin American Policy, Mobile, Oct. 27, 1913, in Arthur Link, ed., *Papers of Woodrow Wilson* (hereafter *PWW*), 68 vols. (Princeton: Princeton University Press, 1966–1993), vol. 28, pp. 448–452; Sir Cecil Arthur Spring Rice to Sir Edward Grey, *PWW*, vol. 29, pp. 229–231. For a sympathetic portrayal, see Kendrick Clements, "Woodrow Wilson's Mexican Policy," *Diplomatic History* 4 (1982):113–136.

16. Works to William Jennings Bryan, Dec. 27, 1913, Box 1, Works Papers; Works speech, March 6, 1914, Box 9, ibid.; 50 *CR*, 63d Cong., 1st sess., pp. 2592–93 (Jones), 4228, 5847 (Bristow); *New York Times*, Aug. 9, Sept. 5, Sept. 16, and Oct. 30, 1913. For Bristow's early career, see Sageser, *Joseph L. Bristow*. Works also fretted about the "apparently friendly relations" between Mexico and Japan, although again he urged no action. See Works to Bryan, Dec. 27, 1913, Box 1, Works Papers.

17. For Wilson's motives, see Clements, "Wilson's Mexican Policy," pp. 122–136; Katz, *Secret War in Mexico*, pp. 156–203; and Frederick

Calhoun, *Power and Principle: Armed Intervention in Wilsonian Foreign Policy* (Kent: Kent State University Press, 1986), pp. 34–68.

18. 51 *CR* 1914, 63d Cong., 2d sess., pp. 6973–75 (Works), 6999–7000 (Norris), 6996–98 (Bristow). For Norris' early career, see Richard Lowitt, *George W. Norris: The Making of a Progressive* (Syracuse: Syracuse University Press, 1963). Works's public statement contradicted several private comments that he had made in the weeks before Veracruz contemplating the possibility of American intervention.

19. Borah to James Clark, April 27, 1914; Borah to F. J. Hagenbarth, April 29, 1914; both in Box 11, William Borah Papers, Library of Congress; 51 *CR* 1914, 63d Cong., 2d sess., pp. 6996–7002 (Clapp), 7121–23 (Borah); *New York Times*, April 26, 1914; Forth, "Wesley L. Jones," p. 314; Billington, *Thomas P. Gore*, p. 67. Ironically, Bristow, perhaps the most vehement opponent of the resolution, also opposed the way in which Wilson got out of the crisis, through the ABC powers. He asked how the United States could "arbitrate with a bandit whom we do not recognize to be anything more or less than a murderer"; *New York Times*, April 26, 1914.

20. *La Follette's Magazine*, Jan. 1916, Aug. 1916; 53 *CR* 1916, 64th Cong., 1st sess., pp. 3887, 11343–46; Kennedy, "La Follette's Foreign Policy."

21. Works to D. M. Utter, March 12, 1915; Works to Manuel Calero, Jan. 25, 1916; both in Box 1, Works Papers; Cummins speech, March 8, 1915, Scrapbook 6, Cummins Papers; Cummins quoted in *Portland* (Iowa) *Journal*, n.d.; Cummins campaign speech, early 1916; both in Box 17, ibid.; Borah to Dr. Mason, Nov. 3, 1915, Box 21, Borah Papers; Jones to M. N. Knuppenberg, May 25, 1916, Box 7, Wesley Jones Papers, Allen Library, University of Washington; Jones to Thomas Sammons, Jan. 29, 1917, Box 34, ibid.; 52 *CR* 1915, 63d Cong., 3d sess., pp. 1500–02; *New York Times*, Jan. 16 and 21, 1916. For Cummins' early career, see Ralph Sayre, "Albert Baird Cummins and the Progressive Movement in Iowa" (Ph.D. diss., Columbia University, 1958).

22. Norris to C. E. Carhart, Feb. 24, 1916, Box 1, George Norris Papers, Nebraska State Historical Society, Lincoln (hereafter Norris Papers [Nebraska]); Borah to John Hofflinger, Jan. 9, 1914; Borah to James Clark, April 27, 1914; both in Box 11, Borah Papers; 51 *CR* 1914, 63d Cong., 2d sess., pp. 7123–30, 11614; *New York Times*, July 22, 1913, July 7, 1914. For Wilson's Nicaraguan policy, see Healy, *Drive to Hegemony*, pp. 183–187.

23. Norris to Carhart, Feb. 24, 1916, Box 1, Norris Papers (Nebraska); *La Follette's Magazine*, June 1915. For differing interpretations of the pan-American nature of Wilson's policies, see Thomas Knock, *To End All Wars: Woodrow Wilson and the Quest for a New World Order* (New York: Oxford University Press, 1992); Mark Gilderhus, *Pan American Visions: Woodrow Wilson in the Western Hemisphere, 1913–1921* (Tucson: University of Arizona Press, 1986).

24. 53 *CR* 1916, 64th Cong., 1st sess., pp. 768–771, 773, 1075, 1443,

1497–1501 (Vardaman), 781, 1253, 1507, 1796–99, 1942 (Clapp). For policy toward the Philippines during Wilson's first term, see Peter Stanley, *A Nation in the Making: The Philippines and the United States, 1899–1921* (Cambridge, Mass.: Harvard University Press, 1974), pp. 202–225.

25. Borah to Aulbach, Feb. 22, 1916, Box 31, Borah Papers; Borah to Gipson, Feb. 24, 1916, Box 32, ibid.; 53 *CR* 1916, 64th Cong., 1st sess., pp. 607, 771, 1438–45 (Borah), 766–768, 772–778 (Kenyon), 1624–26 (Clarke); Stanley, *A Nation in the Making*, pp. 221–225. Clarke's amendment passed the Senate but failed in conference.

26. Jones to J. Frank Ross, Aug. 20, 1914; Jones to James Hoge, March 4, 1916; both in Box 153, Jones Papers; 53 *CR* 1916, 64th Cong., 1st sess., pp. 780, 1933–39 (Cummins), 1942–44 (Gronna).

27. See John Blassingame, "The Press and American Intervention in Haiti and the Dominican Republic, 1904–1920," *Caribbean Studies* 9 (1969):27–43.

28. Norris to William Daily, Jan. 25, 1916, Box 1, Norris Papers (Nebraska); Works to Robert Lynch, Aug. 28, 1915; Works to Dwight Loughborough, Dec. 23, 1915; both in Box 1, Works Papers; *New York Times*, Nov. 27, Dec. 12, and Dec. 14, 1915. For La Follette on this issue, see *La Follette's Magazine*, Feb. 1915, Sept. 1915, Nov. 1915. The fullest coverage of this issue in the secondary literature is Walter Sutton, "Republican Progressive Senators and Preparedness, 1915–1916," *Mid-America* 52 (1970):155–176.

29. 53 *CR* 1916, 64th Cong., 1st sess., pp. 1497, 4017, 10950, 11167–70 (Vardaman), 4671 (Works), 6214, 11352 (Gronna), 11204–05 (Clapp), 11319–21 (Lane), 11330–42 (La Follette); *La Follette's Magazine*, Sept. 1916, Oct. 1916; Phillips, "Asle J. Gronna," p. 439; Holmes, *The White Chief*, pp. 305–309. The final senator in this group was Thomas Gore; for his views on preparedness, see Gore, "The True Basis for America's World Influence," *Annals of the American Academy of Political and Social Science* 66 (1916): 133–135. The peace progressives undoubtedly formed the stoutest defenders of Japan in Congress at this time; all mentioned that the threat of war with Japan was ridiculous and was only manufactured by prop-preparedness forces as a means to push their program through with the aid of public hysteria. Clapp went so far as to term the United States the "natural ally" of Japan; 53 *CR* 1916, 64th Cong., 1st sess., p. 11205.

30. Borah to Dr. Mason, Nov. 3, 1915; Borah to W. H. Cowles, Nov. 24, 1915; both in Box 21, Borah Papers; Cummins quoted in *Clinton* (Iowa) *Herald*, 19 Sept. 1915, Scrapbook 7, Cummins Papers; Cummins quoted in unidentified articles on Oct. 15 and Nov. 4, 1915, ibid.; Kenyon quoted in Seager, "The Progressives and American Foreign Policy," p. 302; *New York Times*, July 25, 1915 (Jones); Cummins, "Defense and Revenue in the Next Congress," *Review of Reviews*, Nov. 1915, pp. 554–558. The *New York Times* contended that the pro-Navy, anti-Army arguments of this group "cannot be taken seriously at this hour," and scoffed at the fear of the

"bogey of militarism" held by such "small politicians"; *New York Times*, April 17, 1916.

31. *Douglas* (Ariz.) *International*, Dec. 18, 1915; *Des Moines Register*, Jan. 15, 1916; *Minneapolis Journal*, Feb. 15, 1916; *Des Moines Register*, April 3, 1916; all in Scrapbook 7, Cummins Papers; Kenyon quoted in *Clinton* (Iowa) *Herald*, early 1916, copy in ibid.; 53 *CR* 1916, 64th Cong., 1st sess., pp. 5514, 5706, 11179 (Kenyon), 11311–13 (Cummins).

32. Borah to W. S. Tukey, Jan. 28, 1916; Borah to F. R. Fouch, March 18, 1916; both in Box 31, Borah Papers; Borah to Colonel Asa Gardiner, Dec. 6, 1916; Borah to Mrs. Victor Johnson, May 26, 1917; both in Box 42, ibid.; Jones to C. B. Blethen, Jan. 12, 1916, Box 1, Jones Papers; Jones to E. F. Blaine, June 12, 1916, Box 144, ibid.; Jones to Thomas Sammons, Sept. 18, 1916, Box 34, ibid.; 53 *CR* 1916, 64th Cong., 1st sess., pp. 11198, 11209 (Jones). Robert James Maddox makes the argument that Borah too desired intervention in Mexico to distract attention from Europe, although he offers no evidence to sustain his conclusion; Maddox, *William E. Borah*, chap. 1.

33. Norris to Charles Scranton, May 13, 1915, Box 1, Norris Papers (Nebraska); Works to A. H. Koebig, May 18, 1915, Box 1, Works Papers; *New York Times*, May 9, 1915 (Borah), May 10 and July 26, 1915 (Vardaman), May 12, 1915 (La Follette); Phillips, "Asle J. Gronna," pp. 430–431; Maddox, *William E. Borah*, p. 16; Warren Sutton, "Progressive Republican Senators and the Submarine Crisis, 1915–1916," *Mid-America* 67 (1965):75–88. Jones seemed to agree with the Works interpretation, noting that Germany could not repudiate the acts of her submarine officers, "and our policy from the beginning should have been determined on that basis"; Jones to W. W. Seymour, July 22, 1915; Jones to John Schloss, April 14, 1916; both in Box 126, Jones Papers.

34. Even before the war a few peace progressives had contemplated the prospect of an active American stance against traditional power politics. In 1911 Works praised the spirit of Taft's proposed treaties of arbitration with England and France, but criticized the administration's wording for excluding "almost every . . . matter of dispute of any consequence . . . by definition of justiciable questions." He proposed an alternative, recommending "an alliance between the great and powerful civilized nations . . . to ostracize any nation that goes to war" through economic and diplomatic sanctions, with the allied nations also committed "to tender their services to settle the dispute between the conflicting nations fairly and justly by peaceful means." Works's statement represented one of the first Senate calls for American participation in some kind of collective security organization; 48 *CR* 1912, 62d Cong., 2d sess., pp. 1834–37. Meanwhile, in 1913 Clapp participated in a conference denouncing the Rumanian government for its mistreatment of Rumanian Jews. The Minnesota senator argued that the United States should consider severing diplomatic relations with Bu-

charest, since policymakers needed to "recognize the principle of the brotherhood of man and the brotherhood of nations" and not sit idly by while another government persecuted its citizens; *New York Times,* Oct. 1, 1913.

35. Works to M. L. Field, March 9, 1916, Box 1, Works Papers; *La Follette's Magazine,* Sept. 1915; *New York Times,* Feb. 13, 1915, Jan. 28, 1916; Forth, "Wesley L. Jones," pp. 319–321; Cooper, *The Vanity of Power,* p. 110. James Clarke also backed an arms embargo, contending that the United States should set an example by "refusing to be a party, directly or indirectly, for commercial or other reasons, to the slaughter of human beings that is going on in the Old World"; 54 *CR* 1917, 64th Cong., 2d sess., p. 1615.

36. For more on this theme, see Sondra Herman, *Eleven against War: American Internationalist Thought, 1898–1921* (Stanford: Hoover Institution Press, 1969).

37. Works to Frederick Dixon, Sept. 27, 1915, Box 1, Works Papers; La Follette speech, Mt. Vernon, Wis., Arbor Day, 1916, Box B-218, La Follette Family Papers; 53 *CR* 1916, 64th Cong., 1st sess., pp. 3468–69 (Clarke).

38. Borah to H. Luther, Jan. 12, 1915, Box 24, Borah Papers; Jones to American Truth Society, Aug. 4, 1915, Box 126, Jones Papers; 53 *CR* 1916, 64th Cong., 1st sess., pp. 495–505, 3408 (Gore), 505–506 (Jones), 506–507, 3470–71, 4284 (Borah), 3408 (Clapp); Billington, *Thomas P. Gore,* pp. 70–72.

39. Borah to B. M. Hamlin, March 9, 1916, Box 36, Borah Papers; 53 *CR* 1916, 64th Cong., 1st sess., pp. 3468–69 (Clarke), 3886–90 (La Follette); *La Follette's Magazine,* March 1916. The *New York Times* called Clarke the ringleader of the anti-Wilson support of Gore-McLemore, as he had been the "leader of nearly every serious move" against Wilson's foreign policy in the past year. Though something of an overstatement, this does indicate that Clarke deserves more historical attention than he has generally received. *New York Times,* March 4, 1916.

40. Norris to A. F. Buechler, May 1, 1916, Box 1, Norris Papers (Nebraska); Norris to William Bayard Hale, May 1, 1916, Box 266, George Norris Papers, Library of Congress; 53 *CR* 1916, 64th Cong., 1st sess., pp. 7452–54 (Clapp), 11338 (La Follette); *La Follette's Magazine,* March 1916, May 1916. For more on the war referendum idea, see Ernest Bolt, *Ballots before Bullets: The War Referendum Approach to Peace in America, 1914–1941* (Charlottesville: University Press of Virginia, 1977).

41. Borah to William Bayard Hale, April 25, 1916, Box 36, Borah Papers; Norris to John Leyda, April 27, 1916, Box 46, Norris Papers; Kenyon quoted in *Clinton* (Iowa) *Herald,* early 1916, Scrapbook 7, Cummins Papers; 53 *CR* 1916, 64th Cong., 1st sess., pp. 7453–54 (Borah).

42. 52 *CR* 1915, 63d Cong., 3d sess., pp. 3631–33 (La Follette); *New York*

Times, Dec. 11, 1914 (Kenyon proposal), Feb. 10 and 13, 1915 (La Follette).

43. La Follette speech, Mt. Vernon, Wis., May 6, 1916, Box B-218, La Follette Family Papers; Works to Benjamin Wheeler, March 22, 1916, Box 1, Works Papers; 53 *CR* 1916, 64th Cong., 1st sess., pp. 10931–33 (Norris), 11187–92 (Norris Amendment); *La Follette's Magazine,* June 1916; Richard Lowitt, *George W. Norris: The Persistence of a Progressive, 1913–1933* (Urbana: University of Illinois Press, 1971), p. 48.

44. Works to Benjamin Wheeler, March 22, 1916, Box 1, Works Papers; Borah to William Jennings Bryan, Dec. 28, 1916; Borah to W. C. Bidwell, Jan. 31, 1917; Borah to J. C. Speight, Jan. 31, 1917; Borah to P. H. Newman, Feb. 6, 1917; all in Box 43, Borah Papers; Cummins speech, Iowa Wesleyan University, Oct. 28, 1915, Scrapbook 7, Cummins Papers; Cummins speech, Pittsburgh, Kan., July 4, 1916, Box 16, ibid.

45. *New York Times,* Jan. 26 and 27, 1917 (Clapp, Borah); DeWitt, "Hiram W. Johnson," pp. 13–15; Sayre, "Albert Baird Cummins," p. 459; Holmes, *The White Chief,* p. 313.

46. The first war-related peace progressive division came when Germany declined Wilson's peace overtures and resumed unrestricted submarine warfare on February 1, 1917, the President severed diplomatic relations with Berlin, and William Stone introduced a resolution sanctioning the move. The peace progressives split down the middle on the vote. La Follette, who joined William Jennings Bryan in a furious last-minute campaign designed to keep the United States out of the war, failed to see the logic behind the proposal, since "Germany is not interfering with our commercial rights as neutrals more than England." While the newly elected Arkansas radical William Kirby equated the resolution with a preliminary declaration of war, Clapp and Norris occupied a middle position, warning that if the President possessed the power to break relations unilaterally, "then in the President lies the real power to declare war"; but they decided that Wilson and his expressions for peace still deserved the benefit of the doubt and voted for the resolution. Borah, Cummins, Jones, and Kenyon harbored no such doubts—La Follette privately blasted "Borah's line of talk" in backing the resolution as a means of expressing support for American neutral rights—and confidently endorsed the resolution. La Follette to "Ones All," Feb. 2, 1917; La Follette to "Beloved Ones" Feb. 3, 1917; La Follette to "Hearts," Feb. 6, 1917; La Follette to "Family," Feb. 7, 1917; all in Box A-29, La Follette Family Papers; *New York Times*, Feb. 4, 1917 (Cummins, Kenyon), Feb. 8, 1917 (Kirby, Works); Lowitt, *George W. Norris: Persistence,* p. 58.

47. 54 *CR* 1917, 64th Cong., 2d sess., pp. 4777–78 (Vardaman), 4995–96 (Works), 4999–5002 (Clapp), 5002–03 (Lane), 5004–09 (Norris); *New York Times,* April 2, 1917. For the armed ship bill filibuster, see Thomas Ryley,

A Little Group of Willful Men: A Study of Congressional-President Authority (Port Washington, N.Y.: Kennikat Press, 1981).

48. Cummins press release, March 6, 1917; Cummins speech, March 17, 1917; Kenyon press release, March 6, 1917; all in Scrapbook 7, Cummins Papers; *Atlanta Journal*, March 6, 1917; 54 *CR* 1917, 64th Cong., 2d sess., pp. 4898–4905 (Jones), 4907–12 (Cummins). The strength of the filibustering coalition was fragile. La Follette predicted that passage of a Stone amendment to prohibit the arming of ships carrying munitions while leaving the rest of the bill intact probably would have won Kenyon, Cummins, Norris, Clapp, and "possibly" Works to support the bill, although the senator himself and Gronna "never" would have pursued such a course; La Follette to "Hearts," Feb. 6, 1917, Box A-29, La Follette Family Papers.

49. 55 *CR* 1917, 65th Cong., 1st sess., pp. 208–210 (Vardaman), 213–215 (Norris), 220–221 (Gronna), 223–224 (La Follette). Harry Lane also opposed the declaration but was fatally ill and did not participate in the debate. John Works, in an article published in July 1917, called American entry into the war "the most colossal mistake the Government has ever made . . . a disgrace to civilization and a crime against humanity." 55 *CR* 1917, 65th Cong., 1st sess., p. 5387.

50. 55 *CR* 1917, 65th Cong., 1st sess., pp. 219 (Kenyon), 220–221 (Kirby), 250 (Cummins), 252–253 (Borah); *New York Times*, April 1, 1917; DeWitt, "Hiram W. Johnson," pp. 25–26. On Kenyon, see Lowitt, *George W. Norris: Persistence*, p. 73.

3. Alternative to Wilsonianism

1. Borah to Frank Disney, April 7, 1917; Borah to W. A. Bower, April 9, 1917; Borah to T. A. Davis, April 14, 1917; all in Box 46, Borah Papers; Gore to Alger Melton, Aug. 23, 1917, *PWW*, vol. 43, p. 216; Kenyon quoted in diary of Josephus Daniels, Aug. 24, 1917, *PWW*, vol. 44, p. 49; Johnson quoted in Howard Arthur DeWitt, "Hiram W. Johnson and American Foreign Policy" (Ph.D. diss., University of Arizona, 1972), p. 27; Richard Coke Lower, *A Bloc of One: The Political Career of Hiram W. Johnson* (Stanford: Stanford University Press, 1993), pp. 100–109.

2. H. C. Peterson and Gilbert Fite, *Opponents of War, 1917–1918* (Madison: University of Wisconsin Press, 1957), pp. 10–20. The best coverage of these developments comes in David Kennedy, *Over Here: The First World War and American Society* (New York: Oxford University Press, 1980).

3. 55 *CR* 1917, 65th Cong., 1st sess., pp. 1319–29 (Hardwick), 1442–44 (Borah); *New York Times*, Sept. 1 and 8, 1917; Borah to J. W. Perry, April 9, 1917, Box 46, Borah Papers; Thomas Ryley, *A Little Group of Willful Men: A Study of Congressional-President Authority* (Port Washington, N.Y.: Kennikat Press, 1975), p. 126. Gore agreed with Borah and Hardwick that the United States should define its war aims narrowly and therefore did

not need a draft. The Oklahoma senator called for the United States to issue acceptable terms of peace and stop toying with "all this cloth-of-gold, peacock-feather, rainbow rhetoric about carrying democracy to people who would rather be dead than democrats"; Gore to Alger Melton, Aug. 23, 1917, *PWW*, vol. 44, p. 122.

4. 55 *CR* 1917, 65th Cong., 1st sess., pp. 1320–22 (Vardaman), 1355–63 (La Follette), 1490–91 (Gronna). Having voted against the war proved a serious liability to both La Follette and Gronna in their attempts to influence wartime military policy, as La Follette conceded; La Follette to "Beloved Ones," July 27, 1917, Box A-29, La Follette Family Papers.

5. 55 *CR* 1917, 65th Cong., 1st sess., pp. 1355 (Kenyon and Jones), 1496 (Norris); 56 *CR* 1918, 65th Cong., 2d sess., p. 4265 (Borah). On Hiram Johnson's political concerns, see DeWitt, "Hiram W. Johnson," p. 33. On peace progressive efforts to raise the minimum draft age, see 56 *CR* 1918, 65th Cong., 2d sess., pp. 8238 (Vardaman), 9463–65 (Borah). Only Jones evaded the issue of antimilitarism, saying that he wanted to vote for everything that would "prosecute this war as vigorously as possible to bring it to an early and successful conclusion," and that therefore, since he no longer had the "time to go into military matters much," he would "follow the recommendations of the Military Affairs Committee very largely"; Jones to Samuel Lemmon, May 1, 1917, Box 28, Jones Papers; Jones to Henry Suzzallo, April 16, 1917, Box 4, Henry Suzzallo Papers, Allen Library, University of Washington.

6. 55 *CR* 1917, 65th Cong., 1st sess., pp. 2097–99, 2112; *New York Times*, May 12, 1917; Lower, *A Bloc of One*, pp. 104–105.

7. Wilson's press secretary, Joseph Tumulty, wrote the President that Borah's argument was having some effect both in Congress and among the public at large; Tumulty to Wilson, April 20, 1917, *PWW*, vol. 42, pp. 106–107.

8. 55 *CR* 1917, 65th Cong., 1st sess., pp. 779–782, 2118–20 (Borah), 877 (Cummins); *New York Times*, April 29, 1917.

9. Wilson expressed "warm appreciation of the patriotic feeling and purposes embodied" in the movement for La Follette's expulsion, although he declined to issue a public statement on the matter; Wilson to Joseph Tumulty, Oct. 12, 1917, *PWW*, vol. 44, p. 365.

10. The most detailed coverage of this incident comes in Belle La Follette and Fola La Follette, *Robert M. La Follette*, 2 vols. (New York: Macmillan, 1953), vol. 2, pp. 761–853; a slightly more balanced account is in Peterson and Fite, *Opponents of War*, pp. 64–72. The rest of the peace progressives fought on to oppose the even more draconian censorship act of 1918, the Sedition Act, which David Kennedy has described as a "landmark of repression in American history." Hardwick summed up the peace progressive case, warning that the bill's "power is so broad and so arbitrary" that it granted Wilson "autocratic and despotic power." In one of the most bitter lines of the debate, the Georgia senator cautioned that under the Sedition

Act "free speech in a free country will simply mean that one man is perfectly free to advocate war to the end of eternity and another man cannot advocate peace without putting himself in a dungeon." Only Cummins appeared to backpedal, urging Iowa sheriffs to be tough on "treasonable utterances" and calling for complete loyalty, since "from now on the war is the chief business of the United States." 56 *CR* 1918, 65th Cong., 2d sess., pp. 5938–41 (Hardwick); *Des Moines Register*, Sept. 5 and 10, 1917; Kennedy, *Over Here*, pp. 85–87.

11. Borah to Charles Crane, April 19, 1918, Box 53, Borah Papers; Thomas Knock, *To End All Wars: Woodrow Wilson and the Quest for a New World Order* (New York: Oxford University Press, 1992), pp. 148–160.

12. La Follette to "Ones," Aug. 23, 1917, Box A-29, La Follette Family Papers; Kennedy, *Over Here*, pp. 108–111.

13. Borah speech, St. Paul, Sept. 19, 1917, Box 779, Borah Papers; La Follette to "Ones," Aug. 23, 1917, Box A-29, La Follette Family Papers; 55 *CR* 1917, 65th Cong., 1st sess., pp. 6184–85, 6497 (Johnson), 6201–11, 6273 (La Follette), 6209–10, 6269–6270 (Vardaman), 6473–76 (Gronna); *New York Times*, Sept. 20, 1917 (Gronna); *The Independent*, Sept. 8, 1917 (Johnson); DeWitt, "Hiram W. Johnson", pp. 32–33. Another point of unity between the radical and moderate peace progressives came in their opposition to Wilsonian plans to sell Allied war bonds to Americans. Both Gronna and Borah opposed the plan, arguing that an exchange of credits would perpetuate American involvement in Europe after the war; *New York Times*, April 18, 1917.

14. La Follette to "Loved Ones," Dec. 24, 1918, Box A-24, La Follette Family Papers; Johnson to C. K. McClatchy, Sept. 17, 1917, Box C-1, Hiram Johnson Papers, Bancroft Library, University of California, Berkeley; *La Follette's Magazine*, June 1918; Kennedy, *Over Here*, pp. 110–112.

15. Norris to David Locke, June 12, 1926, Box 143, Norris Papers; Cummins quoted in *Des Moines Register*, Sept. 5, 1917; Cummins in unidentified newspaper article, May 23, 1918; both in Scrapbook 8, Cummins Papers; Cummins 1918 speech, Box 16, ibid.; *New York Times*, March 22, 1918 (Jones); 56 *CR* 1918, p. 10063 (Jones).

16. *PWW*, vol. 45, pp. 534–539.

17. Borah was active on the issue at about the same time in a different way, committing himself to speaking tour in the West on behalf of the war if Wilson made a definite statement on idealistic war aims to include liberal peace terms; William Kent to Wilson, Aug. 11, 1917, *PWW*, vol. 43, pp. 432–433.

18. 55 *CR* 1917, 65th Cong., 1st sess., p. 5956; La Follette and La Follette, *Robert M. La Follette*, vol. 2, pp. 748–760; *New York Times*, Aug. 12 and 19, 1917. For the moment, however, the Wisconsin senator seemed satisfied with the Fourteen Points, praising Wilson for "a belated acknowledgement that war aims should have from the outset been clearly and frankly stated."

La Follette did not actively participate in the war aims debate again until much later in 1918. La Follette draft speech, Dec. (?) 1917, Box B-219, La Follette Family Papers; *La Follette's Magazine*, Jan. 1918.

19. Wilson to Lansing, March 12, 1918, *PWW*, vol. 46, p. 606; 56 *CR* 1918, pp. 7424, 7576; *New York Times*, Feb. 1, 1918; Borah address, Traffic Club (N.Y.), as quoted in *New York Times*, March 3, 1918. The Traffic Club address included extensive praise of George Washington, although at the same time Borah urged the United States to address the European masses and lead the way toward a "new Europe" that would be freer, more democratic, and conducive to a greater voice for the people on all issues, including foreign policy. How the United States would accomplish this and still adhere to the teachings of the Farewell Address Borah did not say, but the speech did suggest that the senator held a more flexible interpretation of Washington's foreign policy than is commonly intimated. Borah was less sure of himself on how to treat a defeated Germany. In March 1918 the senator praised Wilson for reiterating that the United States was at war with the "armed system" of the Kaiser's government, not with the German people. By May 1918, however, Borah had backed off slightly from this position, although he still hoped for a lenient peace or, better yet, a war ended not by triumph of arms but by the overthrow of militaristic governments by the people living under them. The gap between Borah and Cummins on this issue was a particularly wide one. The former peace progressive urged huge German reparations and a complete disarmament of Germany; he conceded that innocent Germans could suffer under such an arrangement, but otherwise "the millions who have died on the battlefields shall have died in vain." Unlike the peace progressives, who praised the Fourteen Points, Cummins argued that they were exactly what Germany wanted, and he urged instead the election of a G.O.P. Congress in 1918 to ensure a harsher peace. Cummins quoted in *Clinton* (Iowa) *Herald*, Oct. 14, 1918; Cummins quoted in *Iowa Times-Republican*, Oct. 31, 1918; both in Scrapbook 8, Cummins Papers; *New York Times*, March 3, 1918; Borah, "American Liberty's Crucial Hour," *Current History*, May 1918, pp. 278–281.

20. On this point I agree with Thomas Knock, who argues that Wilson was able to sustain his progressive internationalist vision on the foreign scene long after it had been eclipsed domestically; Knock, *To End All Wars*, pp. 179–181.

21. The exception was Vardaman, who praised the Fourteen Points but doubted that they could work, given Wilson's war program, since "the world will not take his big ideas by force of arms ... Moral reform must come by virtue of inherent merit and not by force of standing armies"; Vardaman quoted in John Milton Cooper, Jr., *The Vanity of Power: American Isolationism and the First World War, 1914–1917* (Westport, Conn.: Greenwood Press, 1969), p. 196.

22. For Wilson's policies toward the Russian Revolution, see Lloyd Gardner, *Safe for Democracy: The Anglo-American Response to Revolution* (New York: Oxford University Press, 1987); N. Gordon Levin, Jr., *Woodrow Wilson and World Politics: America's Response to War and Revolution* (New York: Oxford University Press, 1968), chaps. 1–3; and Betty Unterberger, *The United States, Revolutionary Russia, and the Rise of Czechoslovakia* (Chapel Hill: University of North Carolina Press, 1989).

23. Borah to John Cahill, Dec. 5, 1917; Borah to Helen Smith, Dec. 6, 1917; Borah to George Kebabian, Dec. 11, 1917; Borah to William Hunt, Jan. 10, 1918; all in Box 62, Borah Papers; Borah in *New York Times,* Dec. 2, 1917; Robert James Maddox, *William E. Borah and American Foreign Policy* (Baton Rouge: Louisiana State University Press, 1969), pp. 28–38.

24. Robins to Wilson, July 7, 1918, Reel 4, Raymond Robins Papers (microfilm), Wisconsin State Historical Society, Madison; La Follette notes on conversation with Robins, Box B-221, La Follette Family Papers. On La Follette's attempts to get Robins before the Foreign Relations Committee, see La Follette to "Loved Ones," Jan. 15, 1919, Box A-26, ibid.; Robins material to Johnson in Carton 12, Johnson Papers. For more on Robins' mission to Russia, see Neil Salzman, *Reform and Revolution: The Life and Times of Raymond Robins* (Kent: Kent State University Press, 1991), pp. 173–300.

25. *57 CR* 1918, 65th Cong., 3d sess., pp. 342–346.

26. La Follette welcomed the Johnson speech for making it easier for others to attack administration policy. La Follette to "Loved Ones," Dec. 12, 1918, Box A-24, La Follette Family Papers; La Follette to "Ones," 29 Jan. 1919, Box A-26, ibid. Johnson privately admitted that he was in a "quandary in reopening the subject" of the intervention, since he detested Lenin and Trotsky and did not want to defend Bolshevism in any way. Nonetheless, he felt compelled to act as he had because he did "not want an American army policing the world and quelling riots in all peoples' backyards"; Johnson to Roosevelt, Dec. 27, 1918, Part III, Box 2, Johnson Papers.

27. La Follette to "Loved Ones," Dec. 27, 1918, Box A-24, La Follette Family Papers; La Follette to "Beloved Ones," Feb. 1, 1919, Box A-26, ibid.; *57 CR* 1919, 65th Cong., 3d sess., pp. 1101–03 (La Follette), 1164–68, 3337–38, 4896–4902 (Borah), 3263 (Vardaman).

28. *57 CR* 1919, 65th Cong., 3d sess., pp. 2261–70, 3258–62; *Foreign Relations of the United States* (hereafter *FRUS*), 1919, Russia (Washington, D.C.: Government Printing Office, 1937), pp. 245–248. Wilson and Lansing sent back to Polk several arguments to use in lobbying, including maintaining economic predominance in Siberia, aiding the Czech troops, developing American commerce and preserving the open door, and watching the conduct of German prisoners of war, all of which represented a sig-

nificant retreat from the idealistic tones of Wilson's wartime pronouncements.

29. Johnson to Meyer Lissner, March 14, 1919; Johnson to Charles McClatchy, April 12, 1919; both in Part III, Box 2, Johnson Papers; La Follette to "Ones," Jan. 3, 1919, Box A-26, La Follette Family Papers; 58 *CR* 1919, 66th Cong., 1st sess., p. 4898 (Borah). Maddox also makes the point about the connection between the League and the Russian intervention, but he tends to understate its importance in altering the group's perception of the League; Maddox, *William E. Borah*, pp. 44–45.

30. La Follette to "Beloved Ones," Jan. 21, 1917, Box A-21, La Follette Family Papers; *Duluth News Tribune*, Dec. 14, 1917.

31. La Follette draft speech, Box B-223, La Follette Family Papers; 58 *CR* 1919, 66th Cong., 1st sess., p. 2145. For more on Wilson's Costa Rican policy, see George Baker, Jr., "Woodrow Wilson's Use of the Non-Recognition Policy in Costa Rica," *Americas* 22 (1965):1–19.

32. DeWitt, "Hiram W. Johnson," pp. 74–76.

33. On Norris' 1918 campaign in far greater detail, see Richard Lowitt, *George W. Norris: The Persistence of a Progressive, 1913–1933* (Urbana: University of Illinois Press, 1971), pp. 94–106. On Vardaman's 1918 campaign, see William Holmes, *The White Chief: James Kimble Vardaman* (Baton Rouge: Louisiana State University Press, 1970), pp. 350–355. See *New York Times*, Aug. 12, 1918, for Wilson's letter opposing Vardaman. The President asked Georgia Democratic leaders to tell their friends that he was "warmly in favor of electing Harris to the Senate"; Seward Livermore, *Woodrow Wilson and the War Congress, 1916–18* (Seattle: University of Washington Press, 1968), p. 139. For more on Wilson's plotting against Hardwick, see *PWW*, vol. 49, pp. 81–83, 114, 137, 143, 205–207; *New York Times*, Sept. 12, 1918.

34. Their paths differed so much that Ralph Stone, who has covered the group's opposition to the League in greater depth than any other historian, has classified the initial peace progressive opponents of the League—Borah and Johnson—in one bloc (the nationalists) while characterizing the rest as idealists; Ralph Stone, *The Irreconcilables: The Fight against the League of Nations* (Lexington: University Press of Kentucky, 1970).

35. Johnson to Hiram Johnson, Jr., Feb. 16, 1919, Part III, Box 2, Johnson Papers. Johnson was the only peace progressive openly and consistently critical of the points. He called for the United States to limit its war aims as much as possible in order to avoid prolonging the war. Johnson's criticisms troubled administration officials, particularly Colonel House, who for a time considered Johnson as a possible Republican representative on the peace commission. House conferred with Johnson in February 1918 and found the senator concerned that Wilson's Fourteen Points address had "committed us to helping European countries to territorial acquisition." House assured a "gratified" Johnson that this was not the case, and

the senator responded that he would consider backing the Wilsonian peace program. House diary, Feb. 10, 1918, *PWW*, vol. 46, p. 316.

36. Johnson to Charles McClatchy, Feb. 24, 1919; Johnson to Meyer Lissner, March 14 and April 11, 1919; Johnson to Hiram Johnson, Jr., April 20, 1919; all in Part III, Box 2, Johnson Papers; DeWitt, "Hiram W. Johnson," pp. 84–101; Lower, *A Bloc of One*, pp. 127–134.

37. Borah to Charles Gilkey, Dec. 30, 1918, Box 76, Borah Papers; 57 *CR* 1919, 65th Cong., 3d sess., pp. 1384–87, 1583, 2655–56.

38. At least one Wilson supporter recognized this. Key Pittman (D–Nevada) urged the President to appoint Borah as a delegate to the peace conference, remarking that Borah was "independent, fearless, and able," and "in complete accord with the principles espoused" by Wilson; Pittman to Wilson, Nov. 27, 1918, Box 68, Key Pittman Papers, Library of Congress. Even after the two had split, one Wilsonian told Borah "how much some of the President's personal friends appreciate the impersonal character of your opposition." This was one of the first signs of an odd rapprochement between Borah and the legacy of Wilson during the 1920s. Stone, *The Irreconcilables*, p. 32.

39. Borah to Charles Gilkey, Dec. 30, 1918, Box 76, Borah Papers; *New York Times*, Dec. 7, 1918; the distinction between Wilson and Taft is at 57 *CR* 1919, 65th Cong., 3d sess., pp. 1383–84. See also Borah, "Militarism in the League of Nations?" *Forum*, March 1919, pp. 297–306.

40. Borah to W. H. Cowles, Jan. 9 and 13, 1919, Box 76, Borah Papers; Borah to George Roberts, April 16, 1919; Borah to H. T. Kluck, Feb. 28, 1919; Borah to Patrick Walsh, July 17, 1919; all in Box 767, ibid.; *Des Moines Register*, March 17, 1919. On Borah and information from Egyptian sources, see Mahmoud Pasha to Borah, Nov. 3, 1919, Box 767, Borah Papers.

41. Jones to D. T. Ham, March 5, 1919, Box 25, Jones Papers; Jones to Thomas Sammons, March 29, 1919, Box 34, ibid.; Jones to W. H. Carruthers, March 31, 1919, Box 2, ibid.; Jones to Sol Smith, May 2, 1919, Box 12, ibid.; Jones to *West Side News*, July 18, 1919, Box 16A, ibid.; Jones to H. E. Gilman, Oct. 18, 1919, Box 4, ibid.; Jones to J. G. Lawrence, Dec. 15, 1919, Box 7, ibid.; 57 *CR* 1919, 65th Cong., 3d sess., pp. 4310–12; *New York Times*, July 5, 1919 (Jones); *Des Moines Register*, April 14, 15, and 23, 1919 (Cummins). For an alternative view on Cummins and nationalism, see *Dubuque Times-Herald*, May 6, 1919. Cummins stated that he would prefer an open alliance with France, viewed by the peace progressives as the most imperialist power in Europe, to the League of Nations; *New York Times*, May 11, 1919. On Cummins' indecisiveness, see La Follette to "Beloved Ones," Feb. 24, 1919, Box A-26, La Follette Family Papers.

42. La Follette to "Loved Ones," Dec. 4, 1918; La Follette to "Beloved Ones," Dec. 28, 1918; both in Box A-24, La Follette Family Papers; La Follette to "Ones," Jan. 3, 1919; La Follette to "Beloved Ones," Jan. 9, 1919; both

in Box A-26, ibid.; La Follette to "Ones," April 4, 1919; La Follette to "Beloved Ones," April 13, 1919; La Follette to "Mamma and Bobbie," April 18 and 19, 1919; La Follette to "Boys," June 10 and 21, 1919; all in Box A-27, ibid.; 57 *CR* 1919, 65th Cong., 3d sess., pp. 4981–83; *La Follette's Magazine*, Sept. 1919. The Wisconsin senator chose not to revive his prewar ideas about an international organization with armed force, and clearly opposed Taft's league as dangerous and reactionary. Using the Russian example, La Follette cautioned that the LEP would require a "big army to suppress every movement of the masses *any* where *abroad* and at *home* as well" because the "big interests . . . dread an uprising of the people for industrial democracy." Yet the senator did not at this time equate the LEP with the League of Nations. La Follette to "Loved Ones," Dec. 11, 1918, Box A-24, La Follette Family Papers.

43. 57 *CR* 1919, 65th Cong., 3d sess., pp. 3656–57; *New York Times*, March 4 and 6, 1919 (Gronna); *New York Times*, March 2, 1919 (Hardwick); *New York Times*, Feb. 19 and 26, 1919 (Vardaman); Holmes, *The White Chief*, pp. 361–365.

44. Norris to Walter Locke, March 18, 1919; Norris to "Dear Sir," March 25, 1919; Norris to "Dear Friend," March 27, 1919; *Nebraska State Journal*, March 30, 1919; all in Box 266, Norris Papers; *New York Times*, May 9, 1919; 57 *CR* 1919, 65th Cong., 3d sess., pp. 3749–50. Before July 1919, few seemed to have any idea exactly where Norris stood on the League. In a May 10 letter, Taft listed Norris as a League opponent; three weeks later he wrote another correspondent that Norris was "for the League as it was"; Taft quoted in Lowitt, *George W. Norris: Persistence*, p. 111.

45. Kenyon to William Logan, May 8, 1918, Folder 51, William Logan Papers, University of Iowa; draft of Kenyon League of Nations speech, Sept. 10, 1919, University of Iowa; Kenyon to Alson Secor, June 30, 1919, copy on Reel 210, Taft Papers; 58 *CR* 1919, 66th Cong., 1st sess., pp. 5150–55; *New York Times*, May 8 and June 20, 1918; *Des Moines Register*, March 18 and April 25, 1919. For Kenyon and the Foreign Relations Committee, see Stone, *The Irreconcilables*, pp. 96–98. For the evolution of Kenyon's thought during mid-1919, see *Des Moines Register*, May 8, 1919; *Dubuque Times-Herald*, July 18, 1919. The similarity between the ideological positions of Kenyon and Wilson did not escape some Democratic observers; see John Watson to J. W. Hill, Feb. 3, 1922, copy in Box 35, Folder 126, E. T. Meredith Papers, University of Iowa.

46. Taft to Gus Karger, July 21, 1919, Reel 211, Taft Papers; *New York Times*, March 6, 1919; *Dubuque Times-Herald*, March 31, 1919.

47. Cummins to D. W. Norris, Nov. 7, 1919, Box 14, Cummins Papers; *PWW*, vol. 59, p. 470; William Widenor, *Henry Cabot Lodge and the Search for an American Foreign Policy* (Berkeley: University of California Press, 1980), p. 316. On the Republicans and Article X, see *PWW*, vol. 56, pp. 157–159.

48. Johnson to Charles McClatchy, March 22, 1919; Johnson to Chester Rowell, July 21, 1919; both in Part III, Box 2, Johnson Papers; 58 *CR* 1919, 66th Cong., 1st sess., pp. 1729 (Borah), 7428 (Gronna), 8001–10, 8431 (La Follette); *Chicago Tribune*, Sept. 11, 1919. The isolationist angle is summarized in John Chalmers Vinson, *Referendum for Isolation: The Defeat of Article Ten of the League of Nations Covenant* (Athens: University of Georgia Press, 1961). Also, like the criticism of the six votes for the British Empire, peace progressive harping on the retention of the Monroe Doctrine combined an easy issue to demagogue, a genuine concern with protecting national sovereign rights, and a plank for their anti-imperialist ideology. The best example of the latter element came from James Vardaman, who worried that in sacrificing the Monroe Doctrine the United States could be leaving Latin America to the ambitions of the imperialistic European powers. Holmes, *The White Chief,* p. 365.

49. Johnson quote from address in Portland, Ore., *New York Times*, Oct. 8, 1919; 58 *CR* 1919, 66th Cong., 1st sess., pp. 1741–43, 7942–48 (Borah); Maddox, *William E. Borah,* p. 61.

50. 58 *CR* 1919, 66th Cong., 1st sess., pp. 7424 (Gronna), 8204–05 (Borah), 8727–28 (La Follette); Borah on Clemenceau in *New York Times,* July 3, 1919; *PWW,* vol. 58, pp. 189–199; Wilson addresses: Indianapolis, Sept. 4, 1919; San Francisco Civic Auditorium, Sept. 17, 1919; San Diego Stadium, Sept. 19, 1919; all in *PWW,* vol. 63, pp. 24–27, 331, 379. For more on Article XI, see Robert David Johnson, "Article XI in the Debate on the United States' Rejection of the League of Nations," *International History Review* 15 (1993):502–524. La Follette also commented that it involved "substantially the same obligation [as Article X] where the status quo is threatened by revolution," and he feared that even a reservation would not be sufficient to remove American liability from enforcement. Borah charged that Article XI involved stronger terms than the Holy Alliance and would make all revolutionary wars a concern of the League; 58 *CR* 1919, 66th Cong., 1st sess., pp. 2075–79. All used the Russian intervention as the kind of action they feared the most under Article XI. This distrust of Article XI was widespread throughout the movement. In one of his final Senate speeches, Hardwick claimed that the article "pledges the United States . . . to any action that the league may deem wise and effective whenever war occurs anywhere or is threatened anywhere"; 57 *CR* 1919, 65th Cong., 3d sess., p. 4700.

51. 58 *CR* 1919, 66th Cong., 1st sess., pp. 8428–33, 8719–28 (La Follette). Borah contended that the "acid test" of Versailles centered on "what rights would be granted to the subject nationalities of the victor nations"; 58 *CR* 1919, 66th Cong., 1st sess., p. 1729.

52. 58 *CR* 1919, 66th Cong., 1st sess., pp. 1742 (Borah), 7418–30 (Gronna), 8727 (La Follette on Kossuth), 8749 (La Follette Reservation).

53. Norris' comment and similar ones by Borah and Gronna illustrate the

historical revisionism practiced by the peace progressives during the Senate debate over the League. Wilson of course had made no such promise upon entering the war, and Borah, in his rather tepid speech endorsing the war resolution, explicitly denied that the United States was entering the war for any ideological reasons at all. Nowhere in the war resolution dissents of Norris and Gronna did they claim that to "equalize the weak and the strong" constituted the key reason for Wilson's entering the war; rather, the peace progressives had used limited war aims to justify much of their opposition to Wilson's wartime policies.

54. Norris to Gregg Sinclair, Sept. 16, 1919, File 752, Collective Documents Group A, Swarthmore College Peace Collection; 58 *CR* 1919, 66th Cong., 1st sess., pp. 4349–55 (Borah), 6788–6826 (Norris), 7002–04 (Johnson). On the influence of Protestant missionaries on Norris' opinion of the Japanese, see Norris to Rev. W. E. Gratz, Dec. 11, 1919, Box 1, Norris Papers (Nebraska).

55. Norris to B. F. Eberhart, Dec. 18, 1919; Norris to "Boys," Dec. 30, 1920; both in Box 1, Norris Papers (Nebraska); 58 *CR* 1919, 66th Cong., 1st sess., pp. 2077 (Borah), 8643 (Norris), 8719–28 (La Follette); 59 *CR*, 66th Cong., 2d sess., pp. 3565–76. Norris' letter to Eberhart consisted of a six-page justification of his opposition to the treaty, which touched solely on issues related to the underdeveloped world. The Irish nationalist group Sinn Fein rejoiced that both Borah and Johnson "are known to be outspokenly in favor of the Irish cause"; *New York Times*, Sept. 1, 1919. Borah conceded that "of course, there is politics" in his handling of the Irish issue, but this obviously did not apply for Egypt. Stone, *The Irreconcilables*, p. 106.

56. Norris expressed his sympathy for the "suffering people" of Armenia but blamed their difficulties upon the architects of the peace treaty, who had left the Armenian mandate with nothing more than barren desert while placing the nation's mineral-rich areas under French or British mandates in Syria or Iraq. La Follette was even colder, urging a congressional statement of sympathy for Armenia "as a restraining influence upon the Turks" but opposing any American military action to involve the United States "in the turmoil of intrigue and imperialism which exists in the Near east and the Old World generally." Norris to B. F. Eberhart, Dec. 18, 1919, Box 1, Norris Papers (Nebraska); La Follette to "Dear Sir," Nov. 20, 1919; La Follette form letter, Armenian affairs, Nov. 20, 1919; La Follette to George Montgomery, July 26, 1921; all in Box B-112, La Follette Family Papers

57. Johnson to Charles McClatchy, July 16, 1919; Johnson to Albert Beveridge, July 21, 1919; both in Part III, Box 2, Johnson Papers; Borah to Oswald Garrison Villard, Nov. 28, 1919, File 304, Oswald Garrison Villard Papers, Houghton Library, Harvard University; 58 *CR* 1919, 66th Cong., 1st sess., pp. 7418 (Gronna), 8722 (La Follette); DeWitt, "Hiram W.

Johnson," pp. 118–127. For Senate debate over mandates, see Rayford Logan, *The Senate and the Versailles Mandate System* (Washington, D.C.: Minorities Publishers, 1945).

58. Bristow to La Follette, Aug. 16, 1919, Box B-84, La Follette Family Papers; Works to Borah (articles enclosed), June 24, 1919, Box 767, Borah Papers; for Works and Ireland, see Thomas Watt Gregory to Wilson, July 19, 1917, *PWW*, vol. 43, p. 216; for Hardwick, see Stone, *The Irreconcilables*, p. 79; for more on Vardaman and the League, see *Vardaman's Weekly*, June 19, July 3, July 10, July 17, July 24, Aug. 21, Aug. 28, Sept. 11, Sept. 25, Oct. 2, Oct. 23, Nov. 20, Nov. 27, and Dec. 18, 1919; Jan. 15 and 20, 1920. Works too cited the Russian intervention as an example of the kind of action that he feared under the League. He opposed the League with or without reservations; Works to Borah, July 3, 1919, Box 767, Borah Papers. After opposing the war declaration, Works had spent the war years as an active member of the People's Council of America for Democracy and Peace, an organization founded in May 1917 by a coalition of antiwar Socialists and radical peace activists dedicated to committing American workers to the peace proposals put forth by the Bolsheviks: an immediate end to the war without indemnities or annexations. Louis Paul Lochner to Wilson, Aug. 28, 1917, *PWW*, vol. 44, p. 29.

59. See Stone, *The Irreconcilables*; Widenor, *Henry Cabot Lodge*, pp. 323–339; Lloyd Ambrosius, *Woodrow Wilson and the American Diplomatic Tradition: The Treaty Fight in Perspective* (New York: Cambridge University Press, 1987); Denna Fleming, *The Treaty Veto of the American Senate* (New York: Putnam's, 1930); idem, *The United States and the League of Nations, 1918–1920* (New York: Putnam's, 1930). As Ambrosius has observed, the combined stubbornness of Wilson and Lodge, not peace progressive political strength, defeated the League. Still, pro-League forces respected the potency of the dissenters; as early as May 1919, Taft expressed concern about the power over the treaty that Johnson, Borah, Norris, La Follette, Gronna, and Cummins [*sic*] would possess. This is an interesting comment given that the La Follette and Norris at least had not yet committed against the League. Taft to Horace Taft, May 10, 1919, Reel 209, Taft Papers.

60. For more on this bloc, see Herbert Magulies, *The Mild Reservationists and the League of Nations Controversy in the Senate* (Columbia: University of Missouri Press, 1989).

61. On the Chicago speech, see *Chicago Tribune*, Sept. 11, 1919.

62. Ladd, like Gronna, had opposed American entry into World War I, and Gronna lost mainly because he had failed to come to terms with the newly powerful North Dakota Non-Partisan League. On Gronna's defeat, see *New York Times*, July 9, 1920.

The *New York Times* noted the "elation of friends of President Wilson" at the defeat of the "Republican Democrat" Gore. During the campaign, Gore predicted that under the League "our boys will be drafted . . . our boys in khaki will be sent across the sea to die upon the burning deserts of Arabia and to die upon the frozen tundras of Northern Siberia, in wars which do no concern either our rights, our interests, or our honor"; *New York Times*, Aug. 5 and 7, 1920.

4. Alternative to Imperialism

1. *Statistical Abstract of the United States, 1921* (Washington, D.C.: Government Printing Office, 1922), p. 626. For a differing view on the peace progressive resurgence, see Erik Olssen, "Dissent from Normalcy: Progressives in Congress, 1918–1925" (Ph.D. diss., Duke University, 1970).
2. R. L. Morlan, *Political Prairie Fire: The Nonpartisan League, 1915–1922* (Minneapolis: University of Minnesota Press, 1955), p. 300; Dumas Malone, ed., *Dictionary of American Biography*, vol. 5, pp. 524–525; Olssen, "Dissent from Normalcy," pp. 152–154.
3. The *New York Times* rather dourly reported that as a result of the election the "austere" group that "had been thinned out until near extinction" would return to prominence, with La Follette "just now at the top of his career"; *New York Times*, Nov. 26, 1922.
4. Shipstead 1922 campaign pamphlet, Box 1, Henrik Shipstead Papers, Minnesota State Historical Society, St. Paul; *La Follette's Magazine*, Oct. 1922; *New York Times*, Nov. 5, 1922; *World's Work*, Aug. 1923; Barbara Stuhler, *Ten Men of Minnesota and American Foreign Policy* (St. Paul: Minnesota State Historical Society, 1973), pp. 76–79. The *New Republic* commented that although Shipstead said plain things, because of his "distinct and engaging Norwegian accent ... from him they come as revolutionary things, wrapped in philosophy and imaged deep from an ancient soil"; *New Republic*, Jan. 3, 1923. By the end of the decade, commentators would conclude that the philosophy was empty. In a searing 1929 critique, an anonymous correspondent in *American Mercury* classified Shipstead, "one of the worst bores in the Senate," by himself "for ponderous bombast," and remarked that he had done nothing in his first term except introduce "meaningless resolutions"; "The Progressives and the Senate," *American Mercury*, April 1929. Unless otherwise cited, all primary election results come from relevant issues of the *New York Times;* all general election results come from *Guide to U.S. Elections* (Washington, D.C.: Congressional Quarterly Publications, 1976).
5. *New York Times*, July 1, July 3, and Nov. 3, 1922; *Collier's*, March 10, 1923; Olssen, "Dissent from Normalcy," pp. 177–189.
6. *New York Times*, Nov. 3 and 11, 1922; *Helena Independent*, Oct. 20 and Nov. 3, 1922; John Anderson, "Burton K. Wheeler and United States Foreign Relations" (Ph.D. diss., University of Virginia, 1972), pp. 14–38; Olssen, "Dissent from Normalcy," pp. 179–182.
7. 55 *CR* 1917, 65th Cong., 1st sess., pp. 304–305 (war vote), 1408–11 (draft

bill); 57 *CR* 1919, 65th Cong., 3d sess., pp. 1824–25 (league of peoples and peace); Spokane *Spokesman-Review*, Oct. 26, Oct. 28, Oct. 29, Nov. 1, Nov. 5, Nov. 6, Nov. 7, 1922; *Seattle Post-Intelligencer*, Oct. 26, Oct. 28, Oct. 31, Nov. 1, Nov. 2, Nov. 5, 1922; *Let the People Vote on War*, March 15, 1919, Box 4, C. C. Dill Papers, Eastern Washington Historical Society, Spokane; Ernest Bolt, Jr., *Ballots before Bullets: The War Referendum Approach to Peace in America, 1914–1941* (Charlottesville: University Press of Virginia, 1977), pp. 86–89; Olssen, "Dissent from Normalcy," pp. 184–186; C. C. Dill, *Where Water Falls* (Spokane: C. C. Dill, 1970), pp. 56–92; Howard Allen, *Poindexter of Washington* (Carbondale: Southern Illinois University Press, 1981), p. 252; Robert Leslie Cole, "The Democratic Party in Washington State: Barometer of Social Change" (Ph.D. diss., University of Washington, 1972), pp. 58–74. For more on the role that the war vote played in Dill's 1918 defeat, see Robert Donald Saltvig, "The Progressive Movement in Washington" (Ph.D. diss., University of Washington, 1966), pp. 445–464. Although Dill criticized most of the Harding foreign policies, he did praise the Washington Conference disarmament provisions. He nonetheless worried about the secrecy associated with the Four Power Treaty, dangerous because "words do not mean the same when used by diplomats as when used by ordinary people"; Dill speech, "The Opportunity of the Democratic Party in 1922," Colfax, Wash., n.d., Box 3, Dill Papers.

8. *New York Times*, June 4 and 7, 1922; *World's Work*, Sept. 1923; *La Follette's Magazine*, April 1922; Reinhard Luthin, "Smith Wildman Brookhart of Iowa: Insurgent Agrarian Politician," *Agricultural History* 25 (1951):187–192; George McDaniel, "Smith Wildman Brookhart: Agrarian Radical in New Era America" (Ph.D. diss., University of Iowa, 1985). On La Follette's ties to the 1922 Brookhart campaign, see La Follette to Brookhart, June 12, 1922, Box B-118, La Follette Family Papers; *New York Times*, June 7, 1922.

9. Patrick G. O'Brien, "Senator Robert B. Howell: A Midwestern Progressive and Insurgent during 'Normalcy,'" *Emporia State Research Studies* 19 (1970):5–7; Olssen, "Dissent from Normalcy," p. 182; *World's Work*, Sept. 1923; *New York Times*, March 26, Oct. 28, Nov. 11, 1922.

10. *New York Times*, June 30, July 2, and July 15, 1923; June 4, June 5, and Oct. 28, 1924. The London *Times* ridiculed Johnson for merely "complaining loudly, instead of thinking, or trying to think, clearly"; *The Times*, Nov. 19, 1923.

11. *Review of Reviews*, March 1923, pp. 277–279; Patrick O'Brien, "William H. McMaster: Agrarian Dissenter during 'Normalcy,'" *Emporia State Research Studies* 20 (1972):24–39.

12. Wayne Cole, *Senator Gerald P. Nye and American Foreign Policy* (Minneapolis: University of Minnesota Press, 1962), pp. 13–49. Nye reported that the World Court and foreign debt settlements were the major issues in his

primary; Nye to Robert La Follette, Jr., June 4, 1926, Box C-5, La Follette Family Papers.

13. Patrick Maney, *"Young Bob" La Follette* (Columbia: University of Missouri Press, 1978), pp. 1–40; *La Follette's Magazine*, Aug. 1925; *New York Times*, Sept. 16 and 17, 1925. *American Mercury* assailed La Follette bitterly, noting that Senate reactionaries "didn't applaud and pat his father on the back" and charging that La Follette's "whole attitude is that of one who is playing safe," expressing radicalism on the pages of the magazine but not on the Senate floor; "The Progressives and the Senate," *American Mercury*, April 1929.

14. Blaine press release, Aug. 1927, Box 60, John Blaine Papers, Wisconsin State Historical Society, Madison; Blaine to La Follette, Jr., April 28, 1926, Box C-3, La Follette Family Papers; Blaine quoted in *St. Louis Post-Dispatch*, July 30, 1922, Box 68, Blaine Papers; *New York Times*, Aug. 3, 1924; Sept. 3, 9, 10, and 19, 1926; *Review of Reviews*, March 1923, pp. 277–279. The best summary of Blaine's career is Patrick O'Brien, "Senator John J. Blaine: An Independent Progressive during 'Normalcy,' " *Wisconsin Magazine of History* 60 (1976):25–41.

15. Howell to Andrew English, March 8, 1927, Box 30, Robert Beecher Howell Papers, Nebraska State Historical Society, Lincoln. McMaster agreed with his argument, fighting against excessive executive power since it was only in the Senate where a "vote of a senator from South Dakota is equal to the vote of a senator from New York"; O'Brien, "William H. McMaster," p. 33.

16. See especially LeRoy Ashby, *The Spearless Leader: Senator Borah and the Progressive Movement in the 1920s* (Urbana: University of Illinois Press, 1972); and Richard Lowitt, *George W. Norris: The Persistence of a Progressive, 1913–1933* (Urbana: University of Illinois Press, 1971).

17. For more on this theme, see Peter Brock, *Pacifism in the United States from the Colonial Era to the First World War* (Princeton: Princeton University Press, 1968).

18. Blaine press release (capital punishment), Aug. 1927, Box 60, Blaine Papers; Blaine speech, Waukesha, Wis., March 14, 1928, Box 61, ibid.; Brookhart speech, Jan. 26, 1923, Council on Foreign Relations, Box 1, Smith Brookhart Papers, Iowa State Historical Society, Des Moines; Howell, "Notes on Ontario's Electric System," Box 96, Howell Papers; Lowitt, *George W. Norris: Persistence*, pp. 260–264. On the interconnected nature of domestic and foreign policy issues, see also C. C. Dill to Edmond Meany, April 10, 1928, Box 43, Edmond Meany Papers, Allen Library, University of Washington. Blaine's initial thinking against Herbert Hoover centered on the nominee's foreign policy positions; he feared that Hoover's election could "bind America to the imperialism of the British Empire." He wrote that all other issues "pale in the shadow of the im-

pending menace"; Blaine to Gustav Haas, Sept. 19, 1928, Box 61, Blaine Papers.

19. La Follette spoke for the group's foreign policy three weeks after the election when he promised a program of "amity and good will with all nations" while attending to domestic business, and expressed a wish to carry American "democracy to the rest of the world, not upon the point of a bayonet, but by furnishing the most perfect example" of democratic government ever known. To achieve this, La Follette said that the group "must thwart the imperialistic schemes of our masters of finance" who had accumulated vast surpluses of capital by exploiting the natural resources of weaker peoples; *New York Times*, Nov. 26, 1922.

20. For Haitian policy, see David Healy, *Drive to Hegemony: The United States in the Caribbean, 1898–1917* (Madison: University of Wisconsin Press, 1989), pp. 164–202; idem, *Gunboat Diplomacy in the Wilson Era: The U.S. Navy in Haiti* (Madison: University of Wisconsin Press, 1976); Brenda Gayle Plummer, *Haiti and the Great Powers, 1902–1915* (Baton Rouge: Louisiana State University Press, 1988); and Hans Schmidt, *The United States Occupation of Haiti, 1915–1934* (New Brunswick, N.J.: Rutgers University Press, 1971), pp. 42–107. For Dominican policy, see Bruce Calder, *Impact of Intervention: The Dominican Republic during the U.S. Occupation, 1916–1924* (Austin: University of Texas Press, 1984), pp. 1–31.

21. Schmidt, *United States Occupation*, pp. 118–122. For an overview of the inter-American policy of Hughes, see Joseph Tulchin, *The Aftermath of War: World War I and U.S. Policy toward Latin America* (New York: New York University Press, 1971).

22. King believed that the vote did not reflect the accurate sentiment of the Senate, since many senators who he knew "bitterly opposed" the occupation stayed on the sidelines. Editor and activist Ernest Gruening speculated that at least ten other senators wanted to vote for the amendment but felt uncomfortable doing so before the McCormick Committee issued its report. King to Ernest Gruening, July 22, 1922; Gruening to Borah, June 26, 1922; both in "Imperialism, 1919–1941" box, Ernest Gruening Papers, Rasmuson Library, University of Alaska, Fairbanks.

23. Borah to Willis Sovett, Jan. 13, 1921; Borah to Oswald Garrison Villard, June 29, 1921; both in Box 90, Borah Papers; 62 *CR* 1922, 67th Cong., 2d sess., pp. 8941–44; *New York Times*, Feb. 8, 1921. The bulk of Borah's material came from Haitian opposition forces who had formed the organization Union Patriotique, especially Georges Sylvain, its director, and from Ernest Gruening, who also forwarded Borah large batches of letters from his informants in Haiti. See Gruening to Borah, July 1, 1922; Borah to Georges Sylvain, Oct. 20, 1923; both in Box 114, Borah Papers.

24. Borah to Ernest Gruening, June 20, 1922, Box 90, Borah Papers; Borah press release, Dec. 14, 1922, Box 779, ibid.; *New York Times*, May 2, 1922. Borah also hoped to revive the congressional hearing process, confessing

that he would not "regret at all having some incident arise which would justify a thorough investigation of this matter by a Senate Committee"; Borah to B. W. Huebsch, June 14, 1924, Box 24, ibid.

25. The best coverage of this is Richard Lael, *Arrogant Diplomacy: U.S. Policy toward Colombia, 1903–1922* (Wilmington, Del.: Scholarly Resources, 1987).

26. Borah to Thomas Latta, March 4, 1921; Borah to L. C. Caldwell, March 23, 1921; both in Box 90, Borah Papers; 61 *CR* 1921, 67th Cong., 1st sess., pp. 241–248 (Borah), 465-468 (Norris). Unlike Norris, Borah also felt deeply that the treaty would "dishonor the name of Colonel Roosevelt"; Borah to J. E. Ingham, March 15, 1921, Box 90, Borah Papers. Despite their historical reputation as nationalists, the peace progressives recommended a nationalist solution to only one Latin American issue during the 1920s, the 1925 treaty to return the Isle of Pines to Cuba. Borah and Shipstead led a majority of peace progressives in opposing the treaty. The Idaho senator said that ratification would amount to a confiscation of the property of the Americans, many "of limited means," who had settled there "in good faith," while Shipstead challenged the "eminent authorities on international law" who claimed that the Isle formed a part of Cuba. Norris, dissenting from this position, admitted that he had started out "prejudiced perhaps against the treaty," but worried that if the island really belonged to Cuba, "then it would not be honorable for our Government to take it away simply because Cuba is weak and we are strong." The Nebraska senator feared that any American action "unfair or dishonorable to a weak nation" would place the United States in an unfavorable light before the world. Borah to Lewis Gannett, Dec. 30, 1924, Box 252, Borah Papers; Norris to J. A. Austerman, Feb. 11, 1925; both in Box 42, Norris Papers; 67 *CR* 1925, 69th Cong., special sess., pp. 179–184 (Shipstead), 185 (Borah).

27. 62 *CR* 1922, 67th Cong., 2d sess., pp. 12338–43, 12383–84. For La Follette on Liberia, see draft speech, Box B-226, La Follette Family Papers. William Appleman Williams has contended that the the the rhetoric concerning the Liberian loan shows that Borah and other peace progressives preferred direct governmental grants to governmental loans and credits. While they did so prefer, they really wanted no action at all. William Appleman Williams, *The Tragedy of American Diplomacy* (Cleveland: World, 1959), pp. 89–90. For more on U.S.-Liberian relations at this time, see Emily Rosenberg, "The Invisible Protectorate: The United States, Liberia, and the Evolution of Neocolonialism, 1909–1940," *Diplomatic History* 9 (1985):191–214.

28. 61 *CR* 1921, 67th Cong., 1st sess., pp. 5868–78.

29. La Follette to Henry Cabot Lodge, July 13, 1921, Box B-114, La Follette Family Papers; La Follette draft speech, [July ?] 1921, Box B-223, ibid.; 61 *CR* 1921, 67th Cong., 1st sess., pp. 637–651 (La Follette), 2803–20

(Norris). La Follette alternatively described the battle in Ireland as "between imperialism and nationalism" and between imperialism and democracy, showing the danger of attributing an isolationist sentiment to the use of the word "nationalism" by the peace progressives. La Follette speech, Ancient Order of Hibernians, Milwaukee, March 20, 1921, Box B-224, La Follette Family Papers.

30. Copy of speech in Box B-228, La Follette Family Papers; *New York Times*, Oct. 11, 1924. La Follette acted in part as a result of prompting from Wheeler and campaign adviser Oswald Garrison Villard, who contended that his foreign policy message was his most popular appeal; Villard to La Follette, Sept. 13, 1924, file 2158, Villard Papers.

31. *New York Times*, Oct. 31, 1924 (Boston speech); *The Nation*, Oct. 29, 1924 (St. Louis speech). For the campaign's official foreign policy positions, see "The Facts," Box 7, Burton Wheeler Papers, Montana State Historical Society, Helena. The campaign drew extensive coverage in the British press, which generally portrayed La Follette as a demagogue guilty of "tempestuous intransigence" and openly rooted for a Coolidge victory. Quote from *The Times* (London), Oct. 13, 1924.

32. La Follette draft speech, n.d. [1922?], Box B-225, La Follette Family Papers.

33. 62 *CR* 1922, 67th Cong., 2d sess., pp. 10417–26 (Ladd); *New York Times*, July 7, 1921 (La Follette), July 26 and 27, 1922 (Ladd speech); for Oddie, see George Bealen, "The Harding Administration and Mexico: Diplomacy by Economic Persuasion," *The Americas* 41 (1984):188. Hughes told Harding that for the most part he had been silent on the issue to avoid provoking Mexico, but "there is a limit to the extent to which misrepresentation can go uncorrected particularly when voiced in the Senate" in the form of an "unfair attack"; Hughes to Harding, July 24, 1922, State Department Archives (hereafter SDA) 812.51/812. Events thereafter moved at a quick pace for the remainder of Hughes's tenure. Several months after recognition, de la Huerta led a revolt in an attempt to topple his onetime chief. Hughes, hoping to promote an antirevolutionary policy of inter-American stability, authorized the sale of American arms to uphold the regime, and shortly thereafter Obregón's forces squelched the rebellion. Despite their sympathy for Obregón, this policy met with harsh criticism from the peace progressives. La Follette hoped that "true friends of Mexico" would support Obregón in his effort to crush the reactionaries, but he termed the decision to sell arms a "wholly wicked" practice that the State Department could later use as a precedent to funnel arms to a group backed by American oil companies. Norris expressed concern that the action violated international law, while Shipstead worried that the United States had lost moral leadership on the traffic-in-arms issue by the "unprecedented and immoral act" of supplying weapons to Mexico. Shipstead speech, "Christianity in Politics," n.d., Box 22, Shipstead Papers; *La*

Follette's Magazine, Jan. 1924; *New York Times*, Jan. 1, 1924 (Norris); Robert Freeman Smith, *The United States and Revolutionary Nationalism in Mexico, 1916–1932* (Chicago: University of Chicago Press, 1972), pp. 210–227.

34. *FRUS*, 1926, vol. 2, pp. 613–622, 631–638, 643–650, 692–693; Sheffield to Nicholas Murray Butler, Nov. 5, 1925; Sheffield to Kellogg, July 1, 1926; both in Series 1, Box 5, James Sheffield Papers, Sterling Library, Yale University; Sheffield to Robert Olds, Dec. 22, 1927, Series 1, Box 6, ibid.; Smith, *United States and Revolutionary Nationalism in Mexico*, pp. 229–235; James John Horn, "Diplomacy by Ultimatum: Ambassador Sheffield and Mexican-American Relations, 1924–1927" (Ph.D. diss., State University of New York, Buffalo, 1969).

35. Frazier interview, *Nonpartisan* (North Dakota), May 18, 1927, copy in Gerald Nye Papers, Herbert Hoover Presidential Library, West Branch, Iowa; Norris to Joseph Pestal, Jan. 25, 1927, Box 34, Norris Papers; Association of Producers of Petroleum in Mexico to Norris, Feb. 17, 1927, Box 35, ibid.; Kellogg to Charles Warren, March 5, 1926, Reel 19, Frank Kellogg Papers, Minnesota State Historical Society, St. Paul; Kellogg to Clara Kellogg, June 17, 1926, Reel 20, ibid.; Kellogg to Borah, March 18, 1927, SDA 812.6363/1839; Kellogg to Coolidge, 1927, SDA 812.6363/2152. Norris (and others) tried to get around the State Department's tendency to withhold information considered "not compatible with the public interest" by making their demands for information to the Commerce Department or the Federal Reserve Board; Felix Frankfurter had written Norris recommending this in early 1927; Frankfurter to Norris, Feb. 14, 1927, Box 34, Norris Papers.

36. *New York Times*, Jan. 13, 1927; *St. Louis Post-Dispatch*, Jan. 13, 1927; Edge quoted in Arthur Schoenfeld to James Sheffield, Feb. 28, 1927, Series 1, Box 5, Sheffield Papers. For the complete transcript of Kellogg's testimony, see Reel 24, Kellogg Papers. The *Los Angeles Times*, perhaps the strongest newspaper supporter of an aggressive Latin American policy, did not run an editorial on the Secretary's testimony.

37. 68 *CR* 1927, 69th Cong., 2d sess., pp. 5523–25 (Frazier), 5575–80 (Wheeler); *New York Times*, Jan. 31, 1927 (Wheeler). Only Borah, who by this point had developed a close friendship with Kellogg despite policy differences, refused to join the anti-Kellogg bandwagon, informing Moorfield Storey that Kellogg's Mexican policy had not been colored by his ties with oil companies and that the Secretary was basically a decent man; Borah to Storey, Feb. 4, 1927, Box 232, Borah Papers.

38. Wheeler speech, Baltimore, Jan. 17, 1926, Box 15, Wheeler Papers; Chandler Anderson to James Sheffield, Feb. 5, 1927, Series 1, Box 5, Sheffield Papers; 68 *CR* 1927, 69th Cong., 2d sess., pp. 5526–27; U.S. Senate, Committee on Foreign Relations, 69th Cong., 2d sess., *Relations with Mexico*, pp. 1–32. On Robinson's supposed support for Kellogg on Mexico, see

William Howard Taft to James Sheffield, Jan. 14, 1927, Series 1, Box 5, Sheffield Papers. Borah played up the Robinson Resolution as much as possible, writing to William Allen White that the resolution expressed a desire to arbitrate "in as impressive a way as it was possible to do." Borah to William Allen White, Jan. 27, 1927, Box 232, Borah Papers.

39. 68 *CR* 1926, 69th Cong., 2d sess., pp. 2058 (Norris Resolutions), 5580, 5796–97 (Wheeler); *New York Times*, March 2 and 7, 1926.

40. La Follette to Villard, March 9, 1927, File 2159, Villard Papers; *New York Times*, Feb. 24 and 25, 1927; *The Times* (London), Jan. 25, 1927; Marian McKenna, *Borah* (Ann Arbor: University of Michigan Press, 1961), pp. 230–231. For the conservative counterreaction, see James Sheffield to Arthur Schoenfeld, March 1 and 7, 1927; William Howard Taft to Sheffield, March 16, 1927; all in Series 1, Box 5, Sheffield Papers.

41. Borah to George Herbert Mead, Feb. 4, 1927, Box 232, Borah Papers; Borah in Kellogg testimony, Foreign Relations Committee executive sess., Jan. 12, 1927, copy on Reel 24, Kellogg Papers; 68 *CR* 1927, 69th Cong., 2d sess., p. 5796 (Wheeler); *La Follette's Magazine*, Jan. 1927; *New York Times*, Jan. 15, 1927 (Dill), Jan. 31, 1927 (Wheeler).

42. *La Follette's Magazine*, Oct. 1927; *New York Times*, Sept. 21, 1927; *Journal of the Executive Proceedings of the Senate*, 70th Cong., 1st sess., vol. 2, p. 204; *FRUS*, 1927, vol. 2, pp. 187–193; Smith, *United States and Revolutionary Nationalism in Mexico*, pp. 250–258.

43. Kellogg telegram, Aug. 27, 1926, SDA 817.00/3738a; Kellogg statement, Nov. 17, 1926, SDA 817.00/4259; Kellogg telegram, Dec. 18, 1926, SDA 817.00/4267; *FRUS*, 1926, vol. 2, pp. 803–804, 804, 807, 809–810, 810–811, 812, 813. *FRUS*, 1927, vol. 3, p. 287. On Mexican policy, see Richard Salisbury, *Anti-Imperialism and International Competition in Central America, 1920–1929* (Wilmington, Del.: Scholarly Resources, 1989), pp. 67–98. For U.S.-Nicaraguan relations, see William Kamman, *Search for Stability: United States Diplomacy toward Nicaragua, 1925–1933* (South Bend: Notre Dame Press, 1968), pp. 1–86. The most concise summary of administration intentions can be found in a Robert Olds memo, Jan. 1927, SDA 817.00/5854.

44. Norris to John Leyda, Jan. 15, 1927, Box 34, Norris Papers; *La Follette's Magazine*, Jan. 1927. For other early peace progressive reaction to the intervention, see Borah press releases Dec. 24 and 29, 1926, Box 780, Borah Papers.

45. 68 *CR* 1926, 69th Cong., 2d sess., pp. 969–976, 1167 (Wheeler Resolutions); 67 *CR* 1926, 69th Cong., 1st sess., p. 7716 (Shipstead Resolution).

46. 68 *CR* 1927, 69th Cong., 2d sess., pp. 1272–75 (Wheeler), 1331, 1555–61 (Borah); "Bad Acting Is Bad Business," Box 15, Wheeler Papers; Taft to James Sheffield, March 16, 1927, Series 1, Box 5, Sheffield Papers; *New York Times*, Dec. 29, 1926, Jan. 6 and 8, 1927; New York *World*, April 5, 1927. For Coolidge's justification of the occupation, see *FRUS*, 1927, vol.

3, pp. 288–298. The *Chicago Tribune* scoffed that Borah's admiration of the weak meant that the senator "must have a very poor opinion of all events on this continent since 1492"; *Chicago Tribune*, Feb. 22, 1927. Meanwhile, Norris denounced the policy as hypocritical since the Marines were disarming Liberals and not Conservatives. When Hiram Bingham responded that the Marines had no choice, because of the dangerous levels of violence, the Nebraska senator asked Bingham if he thought that in Nicaragua "there is a revolution or it is a pleasure resort"; 68 *CR* 1927, 69th Cong., 2d sess., pp. 1565–70, 1641–45.

47. U.S. Senate, Committee on Foreign Relations, 69th Cong., 2d sess., *Foreign Loans*, pp. 1–93; Kellogg to Arthur Nelson, Aug. 17, 1927, Reel 27, Kellogg Papers. Senate G.O.P. leaders permitted Shipstead to hold the hearings as part of a deal struck by which Shipstead and Frazier, who held the balance in a Senate divided forty-nine to forty-seven, would vote with the Republicans in organizing the Senate. Tijerino's testimony did attract private State Department criticism from Robert Olds, who accused the Nicaraguan of being "incorrect in various particulars" of his testimony while engaging in outright falsehoods at other times; Olds memo, April 30, 1927, SDA 817.00/4746.

48. Shipstead speech, Aug. (?) 1927, Box 22, Shipstead Papers; Borah press releases, May 7 and June 7, 1927, Box 780, Borah Papers; *La Follette's Magazine*, Aug. 1927; Kellogg telegram, 27 July 1927, SDA 817.00/4953b; *FRUS*, 1927, vol. 3, 325, 328–329; Kamman, *Search for Stability*, pp. 97–118. For more on Stimson, see Alan Brinkley, "The Good Old Days," in Paul Boeker, ed., *Henry L. Stimson's American Policy in Nicaragua* (New York: Markus Weiner, 1991). The *New York Herald-Tribune* indicated the importance of Borah's position for the administration, noting that "if Borah can praise the Stimson pacification, few will be left to condemn it"; Laurence Hauptman, "To the Good Neighbor Policy: A Study of the Senate's Role in American Foreign Policy, 1972" (Ph.D. diss., New York University, 1972), p. 173. Borah still never retreated from his earlier position that "if we were going to take part in Nicaragua, we ought to have recognized and sustained those who were duly elected in 1924," although an honest election "may be able to compensate the Nicaraguans for the injustice which I feel we have done them." Borah to Maurice Heck, Aug. 6, 1927; Borah to John Marchand, Oct. 25, 1927; both in Box 234, Borah Papers. The Idaho senator took an active interest in preparations for the election, at one point urging Kellogg to do all that he could to ensure full voter registration. *New York Times*, Oct. 6, 1927.

49. *La Follette's Magazine*, Aug. 1927, Jan. 1928; Neill Macaulay, *The Sandino Affair* (Durham: Duke University Press, 1967), pp. 48–133; A. J. Bacevich, "The American Electoral Mission in Nicaragua," *Diplomatic History* 4 (1980):241–261; idem, *Diplomat in Khaki: Major General Frank Ross McCoy*

& *American Foreign Policy, 1898–1949* (Lawrence: University Press of Kansas, 1989), pp. 114–137.

50. Shipstead had raised this theme as early as 1924, when he called for more "agrarian diplomacy," which he defined as "diplomacy aimed not at making states, but at developing peace and commerce between states." Such a policy would benefit rural areas economically since farmers "have an active and definite interest" in a "sympathetic" policy towards Central and South America; Shipstead speech, n.d. [1923?], Box 23, Shipstead Papers.

51. Shipstead addresses, n.d.[1927], Boxes 21 and 23, Shipstead Papers; memo by W. W. Cumberland on conversation with Shipstead, March 29, 1927, SDA 838.00/2309. For the West Indies specifically, Shipstead recommended an end to all military occupations, the "closest possible trade and financial relations" provided these could be structured for the good of both sides, and a policy loyal to the Constitution and to the "ideals of representative government of the Western Hemisphere." Central American nationalists, particularly in Costa Rica, were advancing the federation idea at the same time for reasons not dissimilar to those of Shipstead; although there is no evidence that the senator met with any of these people during his tour, it seems quite probable that he did. For more on the Central American side of the movement, see Salisbury, *Anti-Imperialism*, pp. 99–130.

52. Borah press release, Feb. 20, 1927; Borah speech, Cleveland, May 9, 1927; both in Box 780, Borah Papers; *Washington Daily News*, March 22, 1927, Reel 5, Borah Scrapbooks (microfilm), Library of Congress. In the Cleveland speech, Borah went on to defend the right of Mexicans to expropriate agricultural lands, noting that the United States previously had confiscated foreign property through Prohibition and the World War I Alien Land Law. Borah's position on expropriation was remarkable given that as late as 1925 he was reported not satisfied with the protection of American property rights in Mexico and approved of a warning on the matter issued by Kellogg to the Mexican government, although Lewis Gannett said that Borah privately felt that Kellogg had mishandled the situation. Gannett to Ernest Gruening, June 15, 1925, "Imperialism, 1919–1941" box, Gruening Papers; *New York Times*, June 13, 1925.

53. For post-January increases in the number of U.S. military personnel in Nicaragua, see Navy Department memo, Feb. 15, 1929, SDA 817.00/6211.

54. 69 *CR* 1928, 70th Cong., 1st sess., p. 1223 (Blaine Resolution); Macaulay, *The Sandino Affair*, pp. 100–104. In late 1927 Nye also introduced a resolution that recycled the 1926 Shipstead Resolution. It demanded that the government never "guarantee nor protect by force the investments and properties of its citizens in foreign countries" and called on Coolidge to proclaim "this doctrine of self-determination as being an integral part of the policy of the United States from now on" in the hope that other nations

would follow; 69 *CR* 1927, 70th Cong., 1st sess., pp. 933–934. The *Fargo Forum* conceded that the Nye Resolution "so thoroughly encompasses the theories of a minority group of radical thinkers that it will secure somewhat more serious consideration" than earlier peace progressive motions, although it remained "wrong in theory"; *Fargo Forum*, Jan. 6, 1928, Box 80, Nye Papers. Although he supported Tipitapa, Borah did not indicate any disagreement with the Blaine-Nye principles, saying that a readjustment of relations with Mexico and Nicaragua into a "friendly, respectful, neighborly relationship" formed the most important foreign affairs question of 1928, since the "great powers" needed to learn that "public opinion will insist upon a paper respect for the independence and the rights of small nations"; Borah press release, Dec. 28, 1927, Box 781, Borah Papers.

55. 69 *CR* 1928, 70th Cong., 1st sess., pp. 1785–90; *Baltimore Sun*, Jan. 21, 1928. Meanwhile, Samuel Shortridge (R–California) blasted Dill for sanctioning a policy that would leave American citizens at the mercy of bandits; he dismissed Dill as "a type of American with which I am not in sympathy." Dill retorted that he did not care. 69 *CR* 1928, 70th Cong., 1st sess., p. 3917.

56. *New York Times*, Jan. 17, 1928 (full text of Coolidge speech); *FRUS*, 1928, vol. 1, pp. 534–584 (instructions to delegates); on Borah and Coolidge's decision to go to Havana, see *New York Times*, Jan. 10, 1928.

57. Although Fillmore had been to the right of the Free Soil Whigs, his foreign policy bore some similarity to their proposals, and the remark again shows the degree to which Free Soil Whig thinking influenced the peace progressives. For the most recent interpretation of Fillmore's foreign policy, see Adam David Chassin, "Expansion and the National Interest: American Attitudes toward Cuba, 1845–1860" (honors thesis, Harvard University, 1993).

58. 69 *CR* 1928, 70th Cong., 1st sess., pp. 2411–23.

59. 69 *CR* 1928, 70th Cong., 1st sess., pp. 3916, 6988–91 (Dill), 6451, 6524, 6686–90 (Blaine), 6848, 6966–75 (Norris); Kellogg to McCoy, March 3, 1928, SDA 817.00/5444a; *Christian Science Monitor*, April 20, 1928, Reel 5, Borah Scrapbooks. Conservatives strongly counterattacked on the constitutional issue. Walter Edge contended that the Blaine Amendment, and not Coolidge's policy, would amend the Constitution by delegating to some authority other than the President the power to interpret the Monroe Doctrine and international law; 69 *CR* 1928, 70th Cong., 1st sess., pp. 7155–58.

60. 69 *CR* 1928, 70th Cong., 1st sess., pp. 6523 (Wheeler), 6921, 6971 (Frazier), 6968–73 (Norris); Wheeler draft speech, n.d.[late 1927?], Box 15, Wheeler Papers. The peace progressives also repeated their concerns about the economic effects of the policy. Wheeler noted that American trade with the Western Hemisphere would increase only if "foreign nations feel that we are a fair and just nation," and he cautioned that "we cannot make

them trade at the point of a bayonet." Wheeler draft speech, ibid.; *New York Times*, Jan. 15, 1928 (Wheeler).

61. Borah to Ernest Gruening, March 12, 1928, Series 36, Box 3, Gruening Papers; Borah press release, Jan. 22, 1928, Box 781, Borah Papers; Borah report on Heflin Amendment, Box 257, ibid.; T. Seydel Vaca to Borah, Nov. 7, 1925, Box 188, ibid.; Senator Francisco Pariagua Prados to Borah, Jan. 18, 1926; Senator J. L. Salazar to Borah, March 23, 1926; José Moncada to Borah, May 30, 1926; all in Box 212, ibid.; C. Urcuyo (confidential agent of Sacasa in Costa Rica) to Borah, Dec. 31, 1926, Feb. 27, 1927, Box 234, ibid.; Borah to J. W. Bissell, March 16, 1928, Box 257, ibid.; Borah press release, March 7, 1928, Box 781, ibid. (emphasis added); 69 *CR* 1928, 70th Cong., 1st sess., pp. 6746–50; U.S. Senate, Committee on Foreign Relations, 70th Cong., 1st sess., *Use of the United States Navy in Nicaragua*, pp. 1–64. For messages of thanks to Borah from Central American Liberals, see Nicaraguan Liberals to Borah, Jan. 12, 1927; Costa Rican Congress telegram to Borah, March 24, 1927; both in Box 234, Borah Papers. For Borah's ambivalence about whether to support the Liberals or Sandino, see Borah interview in *St. Louis Post-Dispatch*, July 29, 1927, Reel 5, Borah Scrapbooks. Given the positive vision of the Liberals, Borah naturally held a negative view of Sandino, contending that Chamorro and Díaz were financing Sandino as a way to prevent the election; Borah to Villard, Jan. 17, 1928, File 304, Villard Papers. At the same time, Borah was pressing the State Department to apply diplomatic pressure against the Conservative regime in Honduras to prevent it from obstructing free elections, which the senator believed the Honduran Liberals would win; Borah to Frank Kellogg, June 2, 1928, copy in Box 4, Walter Lippmann Papers, Sterling Library, Yale University.

62. Borah to Villard, Jan. 17, 1928, File 304, Villard Papers; 69 *CR* 1928, 70th Cong., 1st sess., pp. 6747–49; *New York Times*, Feb. 12 and March 8, 1928. Borah was nonetheless placed in the awkward position of having to defend the administration, and the other peace progressives attempted as best they could to make him look foolish in the debate. Shipstead asked Borah whether he believed that the administration really wanted to leave; when Borah answered that top officials were more anxious to get out than to get in, the Minnesota senator sarcastically retorted that "then they must be very anxious to get out." Norris and Blaine also challenged Borah's contention that the Liberals represented the overwhelming majority of the Nicaraguan people; Blaine wondered, if that was so, "why is there not a veritable uprising of the people . . . to beat back" Sandino. Borah weakly responded that Sandino operated in such inaccessible terrain that neither the Marines nor a possible anti-Sandino popular movement could reach him. Dill asked why a negative vote on the Blaine Amendment would not "encourage Presidents in the future to disregard the law and to make other agreements which may involve us in international troubles," while Norris

lamented that "it almost seems as though we are at sea" when a senator as talented as Borah advanced arguments along the lines he now adopted. 69 *CR* 1928, 70th Cong., 1st sess., pp. 6745–61; *Christian Science Monitor,* April 20, 1928, Reel 5, Borah Scrapbooks. For favorable editorial opinion from the *St. Louis Post-Dispatch, Washington Star, Kansas City Times,* and *Providence Journal* on the 1928 Borah position, see ibid.

63. Borah's reactions to the Sayre message recorded in Paul Jones to Sayre, Jan. 6 and 10, 1928, Series E, Box 3, John Nevin Sayre Papers, Swarthmore College Peace Collection. For Sayre's dislike of Sandino and his backing of Sacasa, see Sayre press release, Jan. 7, 1928; Sayre to Charles Thomson, July 8, 1930; both in ibid. After Sayre released his peace terms (which centered on the U.S.-supervised election) to the press, Sandino publicly rejected them.

64. One more Nicaraguan fight occurred when Walter Edge, about to leave the Senate to become Hoover's ambassador to France, pushed for consideration of a $3 million appropriation for a commission to survey sites for a possible Nicaraguan canal. Edge attempted to ram the measure through at 8 P.M. on one of his final nights in the Senate, but Dill caught him and engaged in a six-hour filibuster. The Washington senator's chief worry was that the "real purpose" of the resolution was "to give an excuse for keeping the marines in Nicaragua," which would serve as an example to other Latin American countries that might be entertaining thoughts of a nationalist foreign policy. The filibuster failed to stop a fifty-four-to-nineteen vote authorizing the appropriation, although the onset of the Depression prevented the commision from being sent. 70 *CR* 1929, 70th Cong., 2d sess., pp. 4146–49, 4227–29, 4562–80.

65. 69 *CR* 1928, 70th Cong., 1st sess., pp. 7194–95; *New York Times,* April 18, 19, and 20, 1928. Shipstead actually was prescient in his analysis of the basis of U.S. policy toward Cuba; as Hoover's ambassador in Havana, Harry Guggenheim, noted, "a policy of non-intervention is interpreted as definite support of Machado." Historian Louis Pérez, Jr., has described the U.S. policy as "intervention by non-intervention"; Pérez, *Cuba under the Platt Amendment, 1902–1934* (Pittsburgh: University of Pittsburgh Press, 1986), pp. 275, 287.

66. W. W. Cumberland memo of conversation with Shipstead, March 29, 1927, SDA, 838.00/2309; Shipstead to Kellogg, April 27, 1927; Kellogg to Shipstead, Aug. 24, 1927; both in SDA 838.00/2313; Borah to James Weldon Johnson, April 11, 1928; Borah to Walter Lippmann, April 12, 1928; both in Box 247, Borah Papers; Borah press release, Jan. 8, 1930, Box 782, ibid.; Frazier to Emily Balch, Jan. 29, 1930, Series C, Box 15, File 35, Women's International League for Peace and Freedom Papers, Swarthmore Peace Collection (henceforth WILPF Papers); 72 *CR* 1930, 71st Cong., 2d sess., pp. 286, 938, 1114–15, 2138, 2851–52; *New York Times,* Dec. 8 and 24, 1929; Jan. 9 and 23, 1930.

67. Shipstead speech, n.d.[1923?], Box 23, Shipstead Papers; *New York Times,* April 18, 1931 (Borah).

68. Borah speech, Boston, Dec. 2, 1922, Box 179, Borah Papers; Borah to Samuel Gompers, Jan. 31, 1924, Box 167, ibid.; 62 *CR* 1922, 67th Cong., 2d sess., pp. 6298–6303, 6945–49; 64 *CR* 1923, 67th Cong., 4th sess., pp. 4154–61; 65 *CR* 1924, 68th Cong., 1st sess., pp. 445–449; *New York Times,* July 23, 1923.

69. La Follette did not share his colleagues' enthusiasm for the Soviet state, which he charged "had sacrificed the cardinal principles of democracy." The Wisconsin senator nonetheless favored recognition, if for no other reason than that he believed Russia "destined to play a large, if not a dominant, part in the international development of the next ten years." La Follette also wondered why Hughes seemed not to worry similarly about dictatorships of the right in Hungary, Spain, or Italy. La Follette diary, Sept. 4, 1923, Box B-1, La Follette Family Papers; *New York Times,* Aug. 21, 1923; *Washington Herald,* Dec. 16, 1923; *La Follette's Magazine,* Jan. 1924.

70. Brookhart interview, *Spotlight,* Aug. 1923; 65 *CR* 1924, 68th Cong., 1st sess., pp. 142–144, 615–620; *Washington Post,* June 7, 1923 (Wheeler); *Des Moines Register,* July 2, 6, and 18, 1923; Alfred Pearce Dennis, "The European Education of Senator Brookhart," *Saturday Evening Post,* Dec. 14, 1929; Ronald Briley, "Smith W. Brookhart and Russia," *Annals of Iowa* 42 (1974):541–556. Like Brookhart, Wheeler returned to his home state in the summer of 1923 and delivered speeches urging recognition; Wheeler to Alexander Gumberg, June 23 and Aug. 13, 1923, Box 3, Alexander Gumberg Papers, Wisconsin State Historical Society, Madison. Ladd also returned from Russia with good things to say about the state of Russian agriculture, prompting the *Chicago Tribune* to charge that the Soviets had placed 15,000 agents along his route to trick the North Dakota senator into believing that Russian prosperity existed so that he would help the Soviets get credits when he returned home; *Chicago Tribune,* Aug. 27, 1923.

71. U.S. Senate, Committee on Foreign Relations, 68th Cong., 1st sess., *Recognition of Russia,* pp. 1–158; *The Times* (London), Nov. 13, 1924. Borah and Kelley also had their share of ridiculous exchanges. They spent a few minutes disputing whether they should call the USSR the "Union" of Soviet Socialist Republics or the "Federation" of Soviet Socialist Republics; at another point Borah asked Kelley why he kept referring to the October Revolution if the revolution had occurred in November.

72. Borah to Samuel Dale, Dec. 7, 1922; Borah to W. W. Trumbull, April 14, 1923; both in Box 144, Borah Papers; Borah to Fred Badley, Nov. 19, 1924, Box 167, ibid.; *Washington Post,* June 7, 1923. Although the dissenters generally made the anti-Bolshevik argument only privately, they more publicly advanced another less than altruistic reason for recognition—the attractiveness of the Soviet market for American agricultural goods. Wheeler

contended that Russian trade would benefit Montana wheat farmers, while Borah hoped to introduce his 1924 resolution urging recognition as part of a package of agricultural relief legislation to increase congressional support. Meanwhile, Brookhart recognized the need of cooperation to prevent the USSR from flooding the world grain market and driving down prices for Americans. Borah to Alexander Gumberg, June 10, 1924; Gumberg to Borah (on Brookhart), June 18, 1923; Gumberg to Wheeler, June 18, 1923; all in Box 3, Gumberg Papers; *New York Times*, Dec. 30, 1923; Anderson, "Burton K. Wheeler," p. 12.

73. Borah speech, Cleveland, May 9, 1927, Box 780, Borah Papers; Borah press release, Nov. 7, 1927, Box 781, ibid.; Borah to Peter Bagnadoff, Jan. 29, 1930, Box 304, ibid.; Gumberg to Raymond Robins, March 16, 1928, Box 6A, Gumberg Papers; *New York Times*, June 29, 1929, Feb. 23, 1930. Borah correspondence with Boris Skvirsky, head of the Russian Information Agency in Washington, is in Boxes 326 and 349 of the Borah Papers. For more on Gumberg, Amtorg, and Borah, see Peter Filene, *Americans and the Soviet Experiment, 1917–1933* (Cambridge, Mass.: Harvard University Press, 1967), pp. 114–115.

74. Kellogg to Calvin Coolidge, June 26, 1925, Reel 16, Kellogg Papers; Kellogg to Silas Strawn, Nov. 2, 1926, Reel 22, ibid.; Borah quoted in (Boise) *Evening Capitol News*, June 29, 1925; Borah to C. E. Dant, July 10, 1925; Borah to Thomas Millard, July 20, 1925; Borah to Louise Harrison, Oct. 3, 1925; all in Box 175, Borah Papers; Borah to Walter Lippmann, June 29, 1925, Box 4, Lippmann Papers; Dorothy Borg, *American Policy and the Chinese Revolution, 1925–1928* (New York: Octagon Books, 1968), pp. 27–29. For fuller coverage of this period, see Akira Iriye, *After Imperialism: The Search for a New Order in the Far East, 1921–1931* (Cambridge, Mass.: Harvard University Press, 1965), pp. 1–253; *New York Times*, Oct. 18 and 20, 1925.

75. Borah to Arthur White, Dec. 8, 1926; Borah to James Yard, Dec. 24, 1926; both in Box 224, Borah Papers; Borah press releases, Dec. 31, 1926, Jan. 27, 1927, Box 780, ibid.; Walter Lippmann to Borah, June 23, 1926, Box 4, Lippmann Papers; Norris to John Maher, April 12, 1927, Box 46, Norris Papers; Wheeler article, *La Follette's Magazine*, Dec. 1927; *Butte Miner*, Aug. 20, 1927; Vincent Sheean, *Personal History* (New York: Literary Guild, 1935), p. 189; Howell to Paul Linebarger, June 27, 1930, Box 59, Howell Papers. Linebarger, a KMT confidant and biographer of Sun Yatsen, had looked for an American diplomatic position in China during the early part of the decade, but Kellogg had blocked the appointment, saying that he refused "to pick a man who had been writing the biography of a Chinese radical." Linebarger then began corresponding with the peace progressives, particularly Howell, on Chinese affairs. Kellogg to Milton Purdy, Oct. 6, 1926, Reel 22, Kellogg Papers.

76. Borah press release, Dec. 31, 1926; Borah speech, Brooklyn, April 25, 1927;

Borah speech, Cleveland, May 9, 1927; all in Box 780, Borah Papers; Wheeler article, *La Follette's Magazine*, Dec. 1927; Paul Linebarger, "Our Common Cause with China against Imperialism and Communism," copy in Box 19, Howell Papers; O'Brien, "William H. McMaster," p. 33. In other East Asian affairs, only the elder La Follette devoted any amount of time to the Philippines during the 1920s, bitterly criticizing Leonard Wood and his "cabinet of generals" and calling for independence based on the same moral grounds that he had raised during the preceding decade. Wheeler agreed that the American people should devote more attention to the issue, but he hesitated to call for immediate independence given the danger of a political "unrest that might be as disastrous as that in Russia." Nonetheless, the Montana senator conceded that given a choice between retention and freedom, he would favor freedom. Other peace progressives felt the same way. *La Follette's Magazine*, April 1924; *New York Times*, May 26, 1927 (Wheeler).

77. For more on Wilson and this theme, see N. Gordon Levin, Jr., *Woodrow Wilson and World Politics: America's Response to War and Revolution* (New York: Oxford University Press, 1968).

5. Alternative to Corporatism

1. For more on the corporatist school, see William Appleman Williams, "The Legend of Isolationism in the 1920s," *Science and Society* 18 (1954):1–20; also Frank Costigliola, *Awkward Dominion: American Political, Economic, and Cultural Relations with Europe, 1919–1933* (Ithaca: Cornell University Press, 1984); Michael Hogan, *Informal Entente: The Private Structure of Cooperation in Anglo-American Economic Diplomacy, 1918–1928* (Columbia: University of Missouri Press, 1977); Joan Hoff Wilson, *American Business and Foreign Policy, 1920–1933* (Lexington: University Press of Kentucky, 1971); Melvyn Leffler, *The Elusive Quest: America's Pursuit of European Stability and French Security, 1919–1933* (Chapel Hill: University of North Carolina Press, 1979); Emily Rosenberg, *Spreading the American Dream: American Economic and Cultural Expansion, 1890–1945* (New York: Hill and Wang, 1982); also John Lewis Gaddis, "The Corporatist Synthesis: A Skeptical View," and Michael Hogan, "Corporatism: A Positive Appraisal," in *Diplomatic History* 10 (1986):357–372; Michael Hogan, "Corporatism," in Michael Hogan and Thomas Paterson, eds., *Explaining the History of American Foreign Relations* (New York: Cambridge University Press, 1991), pp. 226–236; Michael Hunt, "The Long Crisis in United States Diplomatic History," *Diplomatic History* 16 (1992):115–140; Charles Maier, "The Two Postwar Eras and the Conditions for Stability in Twentieth-Century Western Europe," *American Historical Review* 86 (1981):327–367; Thomas McCormick, "Drift or Mastery? A Corporatist Synthesis for

American Diplomatic History," *Reviews in American History* 10 (1982):318–330.

2. Borah article, *Sunset* magazine, 1921; Borah press release, Nov. 22, 1922; both in Box 779, Borah Papers; Borah to S. H. Clark, May 31, 1921, copy in Box 3, Salmon Levinson Papers, Regenstein Library, University of Chicago; Borah to H. Kamphausen, Sept. 21, 1922, Box 112, Borah Papers; 63 *CR* 1922, 67th Cong., 3d sess., pp. 50–56; *New York Times*, Oct. 1, 1922 (Borah), Nov. 23, 1922 (Ladd).

3. Borah press releases, Jan. 22, Jan. 24, Feb. 22, 1923, Box 780, Borah Papers; Borah to Robert Thompson, Feb. 6, 1923, Box 132, ibid.; Borah to Villard, Feb. 9, 1923, File 304, Villard Papers; *La Follette's Magazine*, Jan. 1924; *The Times* (London), Jan. 24, 1923.

4. Borah to George Mallon, Jan. 19, 1923; Borah to Charles Smith, Feb. 2, 1923; Borah to C. B. Updegraff, Nov. 17, 1923; all in Box 132, Borah Papers; Borah press release, April 25, 1925, Box 780, ibid.; *La Follette's Magazine*, Feb. 1924; 65 *CR* 1924, 68th Cong., 1st sess., pp. 4707–08 (Shipstead).

5. La Follette press release, 1921, Box B-222, La Follette Family Papers; Blaine speech, German Club, Chicago, Oct. 20, 1923, Box 71, Blaine Papers; Borah to E. D. Morel, March 7, 1923, Box 132, Borah Papers; Borah press release, May 13, 1924, Box 780, ibid.; *La Follette's Magazine*, Feb. 1924; *New York Times*, June 1 and Oct. 5, 1929. Borah hailed MacDonald's return as the most important event since the end of the Great War, "indicative of the new era" in which war would not be used to resolve international disputes; *New York Times*, June 1, 1929. MacDonald reciprocated the compliments in a very warm "purely personal and private" letter; MacDonald to Borah, Aug. 26, 1929, Reel 6, Borah Scrapbooks.

6. La Follette, Sr., 1923 diary, Box B-1, La Follette Family Papers; Italian ambassador to Borah, July 2, 1927, Box 226, Borah Papers; Belle La Follette and Fola La Follette, *Robert M. La Follette*, 2 vols. (New York: Macmillan, 1953), vol. 2, pp. 1083–84; *La Follette's Magazine*, Aug. 1927. For more on general American attitudes toward the Mussolini government during the 1920s, see John Diggins, *Mussolini and Fascism: The View from America* (Princeton: Princeton University Press, 1972), pp. 23–105.

7. Borah to H. Kamphausen, Sept. 21, 1922; Borah to C. B. Updegraff; both in Box 112, Borah Papers; *Daily Mail*, Oct. 19, 1927, Reel 5, Borah Scrapbooks; Wheeler speech, New York City, Nov. 28, 1923, draft copy in File 4151, Villard Papers; *La Follette's Magazine*, Nov. 1923, Dec. 1923, Jan. 1924, Feb. 1924; *New York Times*, May 5 and June 17, 1923.

8. Borah to John Spargo, June 16, 1921, Box 87, Borah Papers; Borah press release, April 25, 1925, Box 780, ibid.; Borah press release, 1931, Box 782, ibid.; La Follette to Andrew Dzydzan, July 18, 1921, Box B-115, La Follette Family Papers; La Follette diaries and notes on European trip, Boxes B-1 and B-199, ibid.; Wheeler CBS radio speech, Nov. 14, 1931, Box 15,

Wheeler Papers; La Follette and La Follette, *Robert M. La Follette*, vol. 2, p. 1087. For American criticism of Borah's pro-Hungary stance, see Urmanczy Nandor to Borah, Aug. 20, 1928, Box 226, Borah Papers; V. P. Cipra to Borah, Dec. 10, 1931, Box 336, ibid.

9. Borah press releases, Jan. 24 and Nov. 5, 1923; Borah speech, Cleveland, May 9, 1927; both in Box 780, Borah Papers; 65 *CR* 1924, 68th Cong., 1st sess., p. 8081 (Howell); *La Follette's Magazine*, Nov. 1923, March 1924; *New York Times*, Nov. 3, 1923 (Borah), April 28, 1925 (Shipstead). Germans under foreign rule appreciated the peace progressive perspective and appealed to them for help. Three thousand German citizens of South Tyrol (under Italian control) wired Borah, "the noble friend of peace," for assistance in their fight to win freedom from Mussolini's government. Borah doubted that there was anything he could do, since "as long as Imperialism rules, and Imperialism is the program of Mussolini," injustices such as South Tyrol would occur; *The Times* (London), Feb. 25, 1926.

10. Borah to Bishop William Manning, April 5, 1926, Box 252, Borah Papers; 71 *CR* 1929, 71st Cong., 1st sess., p. 1096 (Blaine Resolution); 73 *CR* 1930, 71st Cong., special sess., pp. 214–219 (Blaine); *New York Times*, Aug. 30, 1929 (Borah on Palestine).

11. Shipstead to Norris Huse, May 12, 1923, copy in file 3522, Villard Papers; Brookhart speech, Council on Foreign Relations, Jan. 26, 1923, Box 1, Brookhart Papers; *La Follette's Magazine*, Feb. 1924; Brookhart interview, *Spotlight*, Aug. 1923. Brookhart also argued that an international cooperative exchange agency would stifle revolutionary sentiment, since political unrest would cease "if a cure can be found for economic evils and inefficiency"; Brookhart speech, Council on Foreign Relations, Jan. 26, 1923, Box 1, Brookhart Papers. Blaine speech, Minneapolis, May 17, 1923, Box 71, Blaine Papers; La Follette speech, May 17, 1922, Box B-225, La Follette Family Papers. A recent survey of U.S.-Norwegian relations is Wayne Cole, *Norway and the United States, 1905–1955: Two Democracies in Peace and War* (Ames: Iowa State University Press, 1991), although Cole does not deal with the attitudes of the peace progressives toward Norway.

12. For administration views, see Hogan, *Informal Entente*, pp. 50–56; and Melvyn Leffler, "The Origins of the Republican War Debt Policy," *Journal of American History* 59 (1972):585–603.

13. *La Follette's Magazine*, Oct. 1922, Feb. 1923. For a perceptive contemporary analysis of the peace progressive convictions and political strength on this issue, see *The Times* (London), Sept. 17, 1925. The American correspondent remarked that the dissenters, with "very pronounced views" that Western European financial difficulty came from their international policies, were the leaders "of that section of the American people—stronger in political influence than in numbers—which holds that, properly used, the debts of foreign nations may be the most powerful instrument for peace now existing."

14. Howell to Byron Burbank, May 5, 1926, Box 35, Howell Papers; Borah to W. J. Hubbard, Feb. 6, 1922; Borah to F. H. Hagenbarth, Sept. 22, 1922; both in Box 112, Borah Papers; Borah to Charles Ertz, Jan. 17, 1923; Borah to W. W. Norton, March 3, 1923; both in Box 132, ibid.; Borah press release, Jan. 7, 1923, Box 780, ibid.; 62 *CR* 1922, 67th Cong., 2d sess., p. 1685; 64 *CR* 1923, 67th Cong., 4th sess., pp. 3618–20; *New York Times*, July 26, 1921. When asked what policy he would recommend if forced to choose between economic progress and moral soundness, Borah responded that the United States should choose the option that allowed it to preserve its ideals. He conceded that European economic turbulence, even though harmful to American economic well-being, could continue if the United States refused to renegotiate the debts, but "if we disown and denounce this ruinous program [the Versailles Treaty and its aftermath], we will at least have been no part of a political crime." 62 *CR* 1922, 67th Cong., 2d sess., pp. 1682–84; Borah to Charles Ertz, Jan. 17, 1923, Box 132, Borah Papers.

15. *La Follette's Magazine*, Feb. 1923; 64 *CR* 1923, 67th Cong., 4th sess., pp. 3610–13 (Ladd), 3742–47 (La Follette).

16. *New York Times*, March 16, July 25, Aug. 12, 1926. The London *Morning Post* dismissed Borah's idea of debt cancellation in exchange for reparations cancellation, scoffing that "Senator Borah's contribution to the international problem" was to have the Allies forgo the "meagre installments" coming from Germany; quoted in *New York Times*, March 17 and Aug. 12, 1926. Churchill himself responded to the Gallipoli crack, leading the London *Times* to lament that since the exchange had "degenerate[d] into a bandying of epithets, a fusillade of mutual recrimination . . . it is really necessary to call a halt"; *The Times*, July 27, 1926.

17. Shipstead pamphlet, "War," 1924, Box 1, Shipstead Papers; *Wall Street Journal*, Sept. 8, 1924, copy in Box 16, ibid.; Shipstead article, *Los Angeles Examiner*, Nov. 9, 1924, copy in Box 24, ibid.; *New York Times*, March 13, 1924, Sept. 5, 1924, (Shipstead), April 5, 1924 (La Follette); *La Follette's Magazine*, April 1924; Mary Lorentz, "Henrik Shipstead: Minnesota Independent, 1923–1946" (Ph.D. diss., Catholic University, 1963), p. 177. Borah declined to oppose the Dawes Plan outright but termed it insufficient to meet Germany's needs. He called for the Allies to set a firm lump-sum figure on the amount that Germany would owe, and then give Weimar a reparations holiday of sufficient length to allow the regime time to recover economically. The senator argued that it was "eminently proper to have the experts there but there were certain fundamental propositions which had to be settled before the expert program would be effective." Borah to Walter Lippmann, Dec. 31, 1924, Box 4, Lippmann Papers; *The Times* (London), Jan. 3, 1925.

18. Shipstead quoted in *Chicago Tribune*, Feb. 24, 1925; New York *Journal of Commerce*, Feb. 27, 1925, copy in Box 29, Shipstead Papers.

19. Howell to S. O. Levinson, Dec. 24, 1925, Box 34, Howell Papers; 67 *CR* 1926, 69th Cong., 1st sess., pp. 6676–81 (Dill), 6682–86 (Howell), 6682 (Shipstead), 6692–6701 (Borah); *La Follette's Magazine*, May 1926, June 1927. The senators' preoccupation with forcing sizable repayments from the Western European countries led them to oppose all the debt agreements, even with those countries less threatening than the Western states. The American correspondent for the London *Times* correctly noted that peace progressive opposition to these settlements flowed from a fear that support for them "would weaken the force" of their "contention that similar concessions should not be made to France." For more on the opinions of the peace progressives on debts owed by nations other than England, France, or Italy, see Howell to S. O. Levinson, Dec. 24, 1925, Box 34, Howell Papers; Frazier to Herbert Hoover, May 22, 1924, Box 545, Herbert Hoover Commerce Files, Herbert Hoover Presidential Library, West Branch, Iowa; 67 *CR* 1926, 69th Cong., 1st sess., pp. 8175 (Howell on Belgian debt), 8199 (Frazier and Norris on Belgian debt), 8218 (Howell, Shipstead on Latvian debt); 71 *CR* 1929, 71st Cong., 2d sess., p. 718 (Howell on Rumanian Debt); *The Times* (London), Sept. 17, 1925.

20. *La Follette's Magazine*, Nov. 1923. See also Norris to H. N. Jewett, May 22, 1925, Box 46, Norris Papers; Borah to Murray Brookman, Aug. 25, 1925; Borah to N. A Jacobsen, Sept. 24, 1925; both in Box 174, Borah Papers; 67 *CR* 1926, 69th Cong., 1st sess., pp. 8499–8500 (Borah). Borah called for the State Department to oppose publicly any new American loans to France until the war debt issue had been settled; the peace progressives bitterly criticized this kind of policy when the Department attempted to practice it in Latin America. *New York Times*, Sept. 5, 1927.

21. Hoover speech, Toledo, Oct. 16, 1922, Bible no. 263, Hoover Presidential Library.

22. *New York Times*, Jan. 25, 1922, Jan. 1, 1923; *Collier's*, Jan. 10, 1923; Robert James Maddox, *William E. Borah and American Foreign Policy* (Baton Rouge: Louisiana State University Press, 1969), pp. 131–135; Marian McKenna, *Borah* (Ann Arbor: University of Michigan Press, 1961), p. 188. Maddox argues that the plan was unrealistic and represented part of a continuing Borah effort to refute the charge that he had no constructive program; although both of those charges may be true, the plan should also be viewed as one of many attempts by the peace progressives to aid Germany in the 1920s.

23. 65 *CR* 1924, 68th Cong., 1st sess., pp. 10984–85.

24. 69 *CR* 1928, 70th Cong., 1st sess., pp. 9321–22; *New York Times*, June 22, 1930. After Shipstead, Blaine and Borah backed the resolution the most strongly. Blaine to Ben Baumgartner, Jan. 31, 1929, Box 61, Blaine Papers; *Capital Times* (Madison), Jan. 4, 1927.

25. Borah to Edward von Adeling, Dec. 21, 1934; Borah to Hiram Johnson, Dec. 24, 1934; both in Box 376, Borah Papers; U.S. Senate, Committee

on Foreign Relations, 69th Cong., 1st sess., *Treaty on International Trade in Arms*, pp. 1–6.

26. Borah to A. J. Dunn, n.d., Box 206, Borah Papers; Borah, "The Ghosts of Versailles at the Conference," *The Nation*, Nov. 9, 1921; 61 *CR* 1921, 67th Cong., 1st sess., pp. 6435–36 (La Follette); Maddox, *William E. Borah*, pp. 121–123.

27. For the Washington Conference, see Akira Iriye, *After Imperialism: The Search for a New Order in the Far East, 1921–1931* (Cambridge, Mass.: Harvard University Press, 1965), pp. 1–24. For Senate debate, see John Chalmers Vinson, *The Parchment Peace: The United States Senate and the Washington Conference, 1921–1922* (Athens: University of Georgia Press, 1955), pp. 1–158.

28. Borah to J. C. Saltzman, Dec. 18, 1921, Box 112, Borah Papers; Borah speech, Carnegie Hall, Nov. 13, 1921, Box 779, ibid.; 62 *CR* 1922, 67th Cong., 2d sess., pp. 3776–81, 4316–28 (Borah), 3783 (Johnson), 4075 (Borah); *La Follette's Magazine*, Nov. 1921, April 1922; Richard Coke Lower, *A Bloc of One: The Political Career of Hiram W. Johnson* (Stanford: Stanford University Press, 1993), p. 169. Much more so than the other peace progressives, Johnson articulated an isolationist vision for opposing the treaties, indicative of a drift away from the movement, which became much clearer after 1923. See Johnson draft speech, n.d.; Johnson editorial, *Washington Times*, Aug. 31, 1921; both in Carton 3, Johnson Papers.

29. 62 *CR* 1922, 67th Cong., 2d sess., pp. 3052–53, 3194, 4486–97 (Norris), 3093–97 (Johnson), 3142–43 (Borah).

30. *New York Times*, April 24 and 26, 1925.

31. Norris to Walter Locke, Jan. 6, 1924, Box 3, Norris Papers (Nebraska); *La Follette's Magazine*, May 1923. Both Shipstead and Dill had opposed the World Court publicly during their 1922 campaigns. *Seattle Post-Intelligencer*, Oct. and Nov. 1922; Shipstead campaign pamphlet, 1922, Box 1, Shipstead Papers.

32. Borah to John Greer Hibben, Nov. 3, 1925; Borah speech, Idaho Bar, Jan. 13, 1926; both in Box 219, Borah Papers; 67 *CR* 1926, 69th Cong., 1st sess., pp. 2284–89, 2555–61. On Borah's concerns about the imperialistic nature of the World Court, see Borah to Dana Hawthorne, Dec. 4, 1925, Box 219, Borah Papers.

33. Shipstead press releases, n.d.[1925–1926], Box 22, Shipstead Papers; Shipstead speech, n.d.[early 1926], Box 23, ibid.; 67 *CR* 1926, 69th Cong., 1st sess., pp. 2575–87 (La Follette); *New York Times*, Jan. 14, 1926 (Shipstead). For Nye on the World Court, see Nye to Mrs. V. E. Stemersen, Jan. 22, 1926, Box 50, Nye Papers.

34. 67 *CR* 1926, 69th Cong., 1st sess., pp. 2037 (Borah), 2643–46 (Nye), 2749–50 (Frazier); *New York Times*, Jan. 17, 1926; Nye quoted in *Portland Evening Express*, Jan. 15, 1926, Box 50, Nye Papers. For more on Borah's concern about U.S. involvement in traditional power politics, see *Chicago*

Tribune, April 5, 1925, *Denver Post*, June 29, 1927, Reel 5, Borah Scrapbooks.

35. Shipstead to Villard, Feb. 27, 1925, file 3522, Villard Papers; Shipstead press release, n.d., Box 22, Shipstead Papers; Nye to Mrs. V. E. Stemersen, Jan. 22, 1926, Box 50, Nye Papers; 67 *CR* 1926, 69th Cong., 1st sess., pp. 2118–19 (Brookhart), 2749 (Frazier); *Washington Post*, Jan. 5, 1926; *Chicago American*, March 17, 1926; copies of both in Box 29, Shipstead Papers.

36. Norris to "Boys," March 20, 1926, Box 79, Norris Papers; *New York Times*, Dec. 28 and 29, 1925 (Norris); *Philadelphia Public Ledger*, Dec. 29, 1925 (McMaster), copy in Box 544, Norris Papers; Richard Lowitt, *George W. Norris: The Persistence of a Progressive, 1913–1933* (Urbana: University of Illinois Press, 1971), pp. 367–368.

37. Blaine speeches, Clintonville, Wis., June 22, 1926, Cashton, Wis., July 19, 1926, Box 70, Blaine Papers; *Capital Times* (Madison), July 15, 16, and 22, 1926. For changes in the opinions of the pro–World Court senators during the late 1920s, see Howell to J. E. Taylor, April 28, 1928, Box 128, Howell Papers; Norris to E. W. Yowell, Nov. 30, 1928; Norris to Rev. Frank Smith, Nov. 28, 1930; both in Box 79, Norris Papers.

38. Shipstead to William Hard, May 31, 1923, copy in Box 20, Levinson Papers; Borah speeches, July 25 and Dec. 17, 1924, Box 780, Borah Papers; Borah, "Toward the Outlawry of War," *New Republic*, July 9, 1924; Borah, "Public Opinion Outlaws War," *The Independent*, Sept. 13, 1924; Maddox, *William E. Borah*, pp. 135–149. Hard wrote Levinson that Shipstead was "just built to take up your cause in Minnesota. He knows nothing about it at present but he is absolutely against the League and all its works and he is looking for a way of answering the Leaguers who want to know whether he is for peace or war"; Hard to Levinson, June 12, 1923, Box 20, Levinson Papers.

39. Frazier quoted in Women's Peace Union (WPU) pamphlet, "No More War," May 1926; Frazier quoted in WPU pamphlet, "Making War Legally Impossible," July 1927; both in Box 50, Emily Balch Papers, Swarthmore College Peace Collection (SCPC); Frazier to Esther Van Slyke, Jan. 30, 1926; Frazier statement, May 31, 1928; both in Reel 88.5, Women's Peace Union (WPU) Papers, SCPC; *New York Times*, April 24, April 26, and Aug. 30, 1926; U.S. Senate, Committee on the Judiciary, 69th Cong., 2d sess., *Constitutional Amendment Making War Legally Impossible*, pp. 1–44; U.S. Senate, Committee on the Judiciary, 71st Cong., 2d sess., *Constitutional Amendment Making War Impossible*, pp. 4–5. On the Frazier Amendment and U.S. peace groups, see Charles Chatfield, *For Peace and Justice: Pacifism in America, 1914–1941* (Boston: Beacon Press, 1973), pp. 143–145. The *New York Times* denounced the amendment as representative of the "perverted pacifism" that had led to the "unhealthy condition when army and navy officers who know and abhor war . . . are finding it difficult to

get a hearing for preparedness and national security." Frazier's North Dakota foe, the *Fargo Forum*, ridiculed the idea as "so fanatically absurd as to need no comment"; *Fargo Forum*, Jan. 6, 1928, Box 80, Nye Papers.

40. 69 *CR* 1928, 70th Cong., 1st sess., pp. 6922–26.

41. Blaine speech, Tomahawk, Wis., June 24, 1926, Box 70, Blaine Papers; Dill speech, June 18, 1928, Box 3, Dill Papers; *New York Times*, Feb. 13, 1926 (Dill).

42. Borah to Levinson, July 26, 1927, Box 5, Levinson Papers; 69 *CR* 1928, 70th Cong., 1st sess., p. 2011; 70 *CR* 1929, 70th Cong., 2d sess., pp. 1064–66, 1120–31; *New York Times*, Feb. 5 and Nov. 22, 1928. See also Robert Ferrell, *Peace in Their Time: The Origins of the Kellogg-Briand Pact* (New Haven: Yale University Press, 1952). Howell was not as sure that the League could reconcile itself to Kellogg-Briand, writing that the League, "a political-military alliance, . . . aimed to obviate war by providing for an all enveloping war in the case of hostilities." Howell saw outlawry as something that could replace the failed League rather than transform it. Howell draft speech, Box 10, Howell Papers.

43. Norris to F. W. Kelsey, Dec. 31, 1928, Box 80, Norris Papers; Borah to Levinson, Nov. 10, 1927, Box 5, Levinson Papers; Blaine press release, Jan. 1929, Box 61, Blaine Papers; 70 *CR* 1929, 70th Cong., 2d sess., pp. 1619–20 (Blaine). La Follette also articulated this theme, contending that as the treaty's "benefits are largely psychological, it is my hope that in the future, the ratification of the pact will serve as a means of strengthening the position of groups in various countries who believe that international controversies should be settled peaceably"; La Follette to William Evjue, Jan. 21, 1929, Box 69, William Evjue Papers, Wisconsin State Historical Society, Madison. The senators' conservative opponents recognized the link between the peace progressive support of outlawry and the cruisers bill; the *New York Herald-Tribune* scoffed that the "pacifistic element in the Senate" pretended "to misunderstand the treaty and upon the basis of that misunderstanding . . . oppose[d] the cruiser bill." *New York Herald-Tribune*, Jan. 8, 1929; also *Christian Science Monitor*, Jan. 11, 1929; both in Reel 6, Borah Scrapbooks.

44. Borah to Walter Lippmann, July 26, 1929, Box 4, Lippmann Papers; 70 *CR* 1929, 70th Cong., 2d sess., pp. 1570–79, 1731 (Brookhart), 2511–12 (Borah); *New York Times*, Feb. 5, 1928 (Borah). By this time Brookhart's opinion of the USSR was considerably more favorable than that of any other peace progressive.

45. Hiram Bingham, who feared that the treaty was more powerful than Borah had contended, called on the Senate to acknowledge that "we are surrounded by more or less envious peoples," and accordingly to clarify the treaty before approval. He wished that more senators had done business in foreign countries; if they had, he had no doubt that they would support an interpretation holding that the treaty did not "in the slightest degree

interfere with our right to defend the lives and property of our citizens anywhere in the world." Without such a reservation, "we may well be ashamed of being Americans"; 70 *CR* 1929, 70th Cong., 2d sess., pp. 1467–80.

46. 70 *CR* 1929, 70th Cong., 2d sess., pp. 1044–45, 1123–28.

47. 70 *CR* 1929, 70th Cong., 2d sess., pp. 1400–07. Although Frazier ultimately voted for Kellogg-Briand, he too questioned its effectiveness, noting that since no nation had ever admitted to being an aggressor, permitting wars to be waged for self-defense constituted a severe loophole. He repeated his earlier argument that amending the Constitution was the only effective way to outlaw war, and he quoted Anti-Federalist George Mason on the lack of a need for a standing army; 69 *CR* 1928, 70th Cong., 1st sess., pp. 3324, 6921–22.

48. Blaine to Halbert Hoard, Feb. 4, 1929, Box 7, Halbert Hoard Papers, Wisconsin State Historical Society, Madison; Frazier statement, May 31, 1928; Frazier to Elinor Byrns, Dec. 10, 1928, Jan. 24, 1930; Frazier to Jeanette Rankin, Oct. 9, 1929; Frazier to Freda Lazame, May 24, 1930; Dill to Clayton Helmich, March 17, 1930; all in Reel 88.5, WPU Papers; Dill to Isabel Helmich, Aug. 31, 1929, Reel 88.13, ibid. On Frazier's optimism concerning adoption of the amendment, see Frazier to Sophia Dulles, July 2, 1932, Reel 81.10, Pennsylvania Committee for Total Disarmament Papers, SCPC.

49. Borah press release, Feb. 11, 1930; Borah NBC radio address, March 1, 1930; both in Box 782, Borah Papers; 72 *CR* 1930, 71st Cong., 2d sess., pp. 581–582, 5147–48 (Borah); 73 *CR* 1930, 71st Cong., special sess., pp. 298–300 (Blaine); U.S. Senate, Committee on Foreign Relations, 71st Cong., 2d sess., *Treaty on the Limitation of Naval Armaments*, pp. 1–315.

50. Norris to Ernest Gruening, March 17, 1930, Box 79, Norris Papers; Norris to W. J. Atkinson, June 16, 1930, Box 34, ibid.; 73 *CR* 1930, 71st Cong., special sess., pp. 44–54 (Norris), 55–57, 69–77 (Shipstead). Shipstead said that Stimson's "gratuitous" policy implied that "the Senate is not a component part of the coordinate treaty-making power"; given such logic, the day could come when formal treaties were eliminated altogether and international agreements became binding only through an exchange of notes. The Minnesota senator criticized the U.S. negotiators in London for making too many concessions to the French and Italians without using "an ace in the hole which they had in the reduction which the Congress . . . made in the debts owed by France and Italy." This diplomatic failure only confirmed the peace progressive prophecy that canceling the debts would lead to increased European armaments. When challenged by former peace progressive Hiram Johnson that such a policy would constitute "meddling" and therefore violated traditional U.S. isolationism, Shipstead replied that the United States had a right to show interest in the rest of the world because U.S. policy directly related to the financing of European govern-

ments. Although the United States traditionally had not meddled, and yet still was "considered a haven of refuge for oppressed people from all over the world," it now had no choice but to do so in the name of peace. Shipstead report 1080, Foreign Relations Committee, copy in Box 118, Howell Papers; 73 *CR* 1930, 71st Cong., special sess., pp. 76–77, 300–301.

51. Norris emerged as the most persistent Senate critic of the Wilson administration's handling of conscientious objectors, writing that reports to which he had access indicated "that we are more barbarous in the treatment of these unfortunate men than were the men of the Dark Ages in the treatment of their prisoners." In the early 1920s Borah joined the crusade as part of his broader campaign for spiritual disarmament. The two senators also opposed any continuation of universal military training; Borah feared that placing young men "into military camps under the harsh and sometimes brutal dominance" of the professional military constituted "the taproots of militarism." Finally, the senators believed, as had earlier dissenters, that high military expenditures (in La Follette's words) "go to PROVOKE war, not to 'provide for the common defense.'" Norris to Newton Baker, June 25, 1919; Norris to A. T. Seashore, Dec. 27, 1919; both in Box 46, Norris Papers; Borah press release, April 5, 1922, Box 779, Borah Papers; *La Follette's Magazine*, Jan. 1923; *New York Times*, Feb. 2, 1920, Aug. 6, 1921 (Borah).

52. Borah press release, March 3, 1925, Box 780, Borah Papers; Norris to John Maher, April 12, 1927, Box 46, Norris Papers; Norris to H. T. Davis, Jan. 4, 1927, Box 23, ibid.; 61 *CR* 1921, 67th Cong., 1st sess., pp. 2187 (La Follette), 4694, 4705–10 (Borah); 64 *CR* 1923, 67th Cong., 4th sess., pp. 855–858 (Borah); 70 CR 1929, p. 2417 (Brookhart); *La Follette's Magazine*, Jan. 1923; U.S. Senate, Committee on Military Affairs, 70th Cong., 1st sess., *Promotion and Recruitment in the Army*, pp. 14–98.

53. Norris to Rev. John Little, Jan. 20, 1926; Norris to H. T. Davis, Jan. 4, 1927; both in Box 23, Norris Papers; Norris quoted in *Baltimore Sun*, Dec. 15, 1925, Box 547, ibid.; Blaine speech, Camp Douglas, Wis., July 24, 1924, Box 71, Blaine Papers; Borah press release, April 29, 1921, Box 779, Borah Papers; Borah to M. G. McConnell, Oct. 3, 1925, Box 174, ibid.; 70 *CR* 1929, 70th Cong., 2d sess., p. 1828–31 (Brookhart); La Follette and La Follette, *Robert M. La Follette*, vol. 2, p. 1164; Michael Sherry, *The Rise of American Air Power: The Creation of Armageddon* (New Haven: Yale University Press, 1987), p. 37.

54. La Follette notes on 1921 naval bill, Box B-185, La Follette Family Papers; 60 *CR* 1921, 66th Cong., 3d sess., pp. 2983–86, 4169 (Borah); 61 *CR* 1921, 67th Cong., 1st sess., pp. 1406–09, 4709–10 (Borah), 1732–54 (La Follette); *New York Times*, March 28 and May 14, 1921. Ironically, Borah and Ladd wound up voting for the 1921 bill, justifying their actions on the grounds that the plan for Borah's international conference was attached to the bill as a rider.

55. *New York Times*, Jan. 23, Nov. 12, and Nov. 13, 1928.

56. Blaine speech, Wausau, Wis., March 16, 1928, Box 70, Blaine Papers; Borah press release, Jan. 22, 1928, Box 781, Borah Papers; Norris to H. H. Ruhge, March 31, 1928, Box 34, Norris Papers; *New York Times*, Jan. 22, 1928. In the Wausau address, Blaine defined imperialism as "denying to other governments the right of self-government." He noted that the Shipstead Committee had exposed the "whole rotten mess."

57. *New York Times*, Jan. 31, 1929.

58. Nye speech, Jan. 8, 1929, Box 81, Nye Papers; Frazier to Elinor Byrns, Dec. 10, 1928, Reel 88.5, WPU Papers; 70 *CR* 1929, 70th Cong., 2d sess., pp. 2409 (Frazier), 2413 (Brookhart), 2599 (Nye), 2756 (Blaine). Borah agreed that the naval situation constituted a "dangerous challenge" to the peace pact, and he worried that some countries would conclude that "we are masquerading in the name of peace"; Borah press release, July 24, 1929, Box 782, Borah Papers.

59. 70 *CR* 1929, 70th Cong., 2d sess., pp. 2407–08, 2754–56; 72 *CR* 1930, 71st Cong., 2d sess., pp. 1115–16 (Dill); U.S. Senate, Committee on Military Affairs, 69th Cong., 1st sess., *To Provide for National Defense*, pp. 22–81. The text for the Dill Amendment is at 72 *CR* 1930, 71st Cong., 2d sess., p. 2357.

60. 70 *CR* 1929, 70th Cong., 2d sess., pp. 2180 (Borah), 2840–54 (Norris Amendment).

61. Nye speech, Dinner and Conference on Cruisers, Jan. 8, 1929, Box 81, Nye Papers; Norris to Caroline Pratt, Nov. 22, 1928, Box 79, Norris Papers; 70 *CR* 1929, 70th Cong., 2d sess., pp. 2345, 2409, 2417–18 (Brookhart), 2419–21 (Wheeler), 2596–97, 2602–03 (Nye), 2836 (Shipstead); *New York Times*, Jan. 31 and July 28, 1929.

62. Howell to Captain L. M. Overstreet, Jan. 20, 1930, Box 69, Howell Papers; Borah to Frederick Lynch, Feb. 16, 1928, Box 256, Borah Papers; 70 *CR* 1929, 70th Cong., 2d sess., pp. 2180, 2837 (Borah), 2415 (Brookhart). For Blaine on this point, see 70 *CR* 1929, 70th Cong., 2d sess., p. 4033.

63. Borah press release, 1928, Box 781, Borah Papers; Shipstead quoted in *Hibbing* (Minn.) *Independent*, Aug. 12, 1927, Box 29, Shipstead Papers; 70 *CR* 1929, 70th Cong., 2d sess., pp. 2182–83 (Borah), 2187, 2835–36 (Shipstead).

64. Norris to Caroline Pratt, Nov. 22, 1928; Norris to Franklin Bomersox, Jan. 8, 1929; both in Box 79, Norris Papers; 70 *CR* 1929, 70th Cong., 2d sess., pp. 2594–2604 (Nye), 2619–22 (Norris), 2746 (Frazier).

65. Ernest Bolt, Jr., *Ballots before Bullets: The War Referendum Approach to Peace in America, 1914–1941* (Charlottesville: University Press of Virginia, 1977), pp. 132–152; *New York Times*, May 7, 1924.

66. Shipstead speech, Emergency Foreign Policy Conference, April 30, 1924, Box 21, Shipstead Papers; Borah to Walter Lippmann, Oct. 3, 1925, Box 4, Lippmann Papers; *San Diego Sun*, May 1927, Reel 5, Borah Scrapbooks.

67. Florence Luscombe to Emily Balch, June 6, 1930, Box 8, Balch Papers, SCPC.

68. See especially James Holt, *Congressional Insurgents and the Party System, 1909–1916* (Cambridge, Mass.: Harvard University Press, 1967); David Thelen, *Robert La Follette and the Insurgent Spirit* (Boston: Little, Brown, 1976); and John Wiseman, *Dilemmas of a Party Out of Power: The Democrats, 1904–1912* (New York: Garland, 1988).

69. Norris draft article, 1913, Box 266, Norris Papers; Joseph Smith, *Unequal Giants: The United States and Brazil, 1889–1930* (Pittsburgh: University of Pittsburgh Press, 1991), pp. 91–95.

70. 62 *CR* 1922, 67th Cong., 2d sess., pp. 6967–69, 10123 (Ladd), 10054–86 (La Follette); *New York Times*, Dec. 13, 1921, July 8, 1922, Sept. 9, 1922, July 20, 1923; James Shideler, *Farm Crisis, 1919–1923* (Berkeley: University of California Press, 1957), p. 183.

71. Borah to W. G. Warwick, Dec. 10, 1928; Borah to C. N. Walters, Dec. 21, 1928; Borah to Kinney-Whole Company, Jan. 26, 1929; all in Box 284, Borah Papers; *New York Times*, July 13 and Dec. 12, 1926. Like McMaster, Borah advocated duties "which will give the American market exclusively to the American farmer to the full extent of his ability to supply it"; *Boise Statesman*, Aug. 23, 1928, Reel 6, Borah Scrapbooks.

72. For complete information, see the Appendix.

73. Blaine speech, Stratford, Wis., July 29, 1926; Blaine radio address, Nov. 2, 1928; both in Box 70, Blaine Papers; Norris speech, Omaha, Oct. 20, 1928, Box 7, Norris Papers (Nebraska); Norris, "Tariff and the Farmer," *The Nation*, Sept. 1, 1926; Borah to Southern Idaho Bean Growers' Association, Jan. 26, 1929, Box 284, Borah Papers; Borah to Thomas Stanford, March 16, 1929; Borah to A. D. Bulman, April 20, 1929; Borah to Samuel Dale, May 13, 1929; all in Box 285, Borah Papers; *New York Times*, June 18, June 21, and Sept. 4, 1929; 72 *CR* 1930, 71st Cong., 2d sess., pp. 3975, 5161 (Frazier), 3975, 3980 (Brookhart). A disappointed Blaine wrote that "as good a fellow as Senator Howell . . . is, he fell for the propaganda on farm tariff rates, notwithstanding the fact that he knew full well that most of them were nothing but gold bricks handed to the farmer"; Blaine to William Evjue, Oct. 7, 1930, Box 14, Evjue Papers.

74. Norris to Judson Welliver, June 22, 1929, Box 181, Norris Papers; Villard to Dill, March 6 and 25, 1930; Dill to Villard, March 7, March 20, and April 30, 1930, File 900; all in Villard Papers; Dill press release, n.d., Box 1, Dill Papers; 72 *CR* 1930, 71st Cong., 2d sess., pp. 4409–10.

75. Wheeler fell somewhere between the two blocs, supporting higher agricultural rates less often than the Borah group but also asserting that "tariff revision should be limited to those rates which would be of genuine benefit to the farmer." Wheeler speech, NBC radio, Jan. 11, 1930, Box 15, Wheeler Papers.

76. Blaine press release, Aug. 21, 1929, Box 61, Blaine Papers; Blaine to

Weyenberg Shoe Manufacturing Company, March 19, 1930, Box 62, ibid.; La Follette speech for McMaster reelection campaign (1930), Box C-555, La Follette Family Papers; Norris to Judson Welliver, June 22, 1929, Box 181, Norris Papers; 72 *CR* 1930, 71st Cong., 2d sess., pp. 216–224, 2560 (Blaine), 5976–77 (La Follette).

77. Borah to Harry Curtis, Feb. 11, 1929, Box 284, Borah Papers; Borah to John Robertson, July 8, 1929, Box 285, ibid.; Howell to Will Atkinson, Aug. 28, 1929, Box 110, Howell Papers; 72 *CR* 1930, 71st Cong., 2d sess., p. 5983 (Wheeler); *New York Times*, March 25, 1930.

78. Borah to George Hickok, Feb. 20, 1923, Box 83, Borah Papers; Norris to E. Brosins, April 5, 1929, Box 46, Norris Papers; 61 *CR* 1921, 67th Cong., 1st sess., pp. 961, 965 (Johnson); 65 *CR* 1924, 68th Cong., 1st sess., pp. 6307–15 (Dill and Shipstead); 72 *CR* 1930, 71st Cong., 2d sess., pp. 7323–25 (Borah), 7419–20 (Wheeler).

6. Anti-Imperialism and the Peace Movement

1. LEP pamphlet, 1915; LEP form letter, Nov. 3, 1916; both in Collective Documents Group A, File 85a, SCPC; Sondra Herman, *Eleven against War: American Internationalist Thought, 1898–1921* (Stanford: Hoover Institution Press, 1969), pp. 22–85; C. Roland Marchand, *The American Peace Movement and Social Reform, 1898–1918* (Princeton: Princeton University Press, 1972), pp. 39–73, 151–170.

2. Herman, *Eleven against War*, pp. 114–149; Marchand, *The American Peace Movement*, pp. 183–265; Charles Chatfield, *For Peace and Justice: Pacifism in America, 1919–1941* (Knoxville: University of Tennessee Press, 1971), pp. 13–67.

3. Thomas Karnes, "Hiram Bingham and His Obsolete Shibboleth," *Diplomatic History* 3 (1979):39–58. The vacuum created by Bingham's shift provided an opening for the left, and in the years before 1917 some radicals began turning their attention toward Wilson's Central American and Caribbean policies. The AUAM led a campaign to avoid war with Mexico in 1916, while the first of James Weldon Johnson's articles attacking Wilson's occupation of Haiti appeared in the same year. In general, however, the radicals in the peace movement were too distracted by the European war to be able to present an alternative to Wilsonianism regarding inter-American problems.

4. Hamilton Holt, "The League or Bolshevism?" *The Independent*, April 5, 1919; idem, "The League of Nations: What It Is Doing," *Annals of the American Academy of Political and Social Science*, July 1923, pp. 193–195; George Wickersham, "The Pact of Paris: A Gesture or a Pledge?" *Foreign Affairs*, April 1929, pp. 356–371; Robert Divine, *Second Chance: The Triumph of Internationalism in America during World War II* (New York: Atheneum, 1971), pp. 4–18; Warren Kuehl, *Seeking World Order: The United*

States and International Organization to 1920 (Nashville: Vanderbilt University Press, 1969), pp. 315–330. On LNNPA fundraising success, see memorandum, July 25, 1928, Collective Documents Group A, File 83a, SCPC.

5. *New York Times,* Jan. 13, 1919, Feb. 6, 1919, March 3, 1919, May 21, 1920, June 6, 1920, Oct. 17, 1920, Oct. 18, 1922, Dec. 16, 1922, Jan. 21, 1925, Oct. 3, 1925, May 21, 1926, June 13, 1926, June 29, 1926; Charles DeBenedetti, *Origins of the Modern American Peace Movement, 1915–1929* (Millwood, N.Y.: KTO Press, 1978), pp. 47–54; Albert Marrin, *Nicholas Murray Butler* (Boston: Twayne, 1976), pp. 172–174. (Butler's speeches were regularly printed in the *Times.*)

6. Butler to Sheffield, Nov. 5, 1925, Series 1, Box 5, Sheffield Papers; *New York Times,* April 20, 1925, Aug. 6, 1925, Oct. 21, 1926, April 18, 1927, Sept. 5, 1927, Jan. 1, 1928, Feb. 10, 1928, Jan. 8, 1928, Aug. 20, 1928, Nov. 13, 1928, Dec. 3, 1928, Jan. 7, 1929; Marrin, *Nicholas Murray Butler,* pp. 176–178. Although Butler retained his worldview throughout the 1920s, the decade did erode the middle progressive position that had existed earlier between the Wilsonians under Holt and the legalists under Butler. Harvard President A. Lawrence Lowell, who had emerged in 1919 as a key ideological figure in the LEP, began the period considerably more active on foreign policy issues than Butler, playing an important role in the League of Nations fight by rallying the LEP behind Wilson's plan. After the League of Nations failed to win approval in the Senate, Lowell took a leading role in crusading for American membership in the World Court. He chose, however, not to move beyond these points. Unlike Butler and the LNNPA, he made no arguments against increased military spending, instead generally supporting the military, as he did when pacifists attacked the Reserve Officers Training Corps (ROTC), about which he had "always been very enthusiastic." Nor did Lowell inch toward anti-imperialism. Instead of embracing antimilitarism or anti-imperialism, Lowell championed immigration restriction, serving on the national committee of the Immigration Restriction League, and by the end of the 1920s Lowell and his ilk had gradually drifted away from the established peace movement. Lowell to Jules Jusserand, March 10, 1922, File 232, 1919–1922 series, A. Lawrence Lowell Papers, Harvard University; Lowell to John Weeks, Jan. 12, 1924, File 151, 1922–1925 series, ibid.; Lowell to LeBaron Colt, March 31, 1922, File 1077, 1919–1922 series, ibid.; U.S. Senate, Committee on Foreign Relations, 68th Cong., 1st sess., *Permanent Court of International Justice,* pp. 29–36; *New York Times,* Jan. 11 and March 20, 1919.

7. The group included a host of moderate women's organizations that fitted the American Peace Society mold: the American Association of University Women, the Council of Women for Home Missions, the Federation of Women's Boards of Foreign Missions for North America, the General

Federation of Women's Clubs, the National Board of the YWCA, the National Council of Jewish Women, the National Federation of Business and Professional Women's Clubs, the National League of Women Voters, the National Women's Christian Temperance Union, and the National Women's Trade Union League. List located in Series C, Box 13, File 7, WILPF Papers.

8. Catt to Jane Addams, June 11, 1927, Reel 2, Carrie Chapman Catt Papers, Library of Congress; Carrie Chapman Catt, "National Defense Act," *Woman Citizen*, Dec. 1925; idem, "A Word to General Pershing," ibid., Jan. 1928; idem, "What Has Become of the Court?" ibid., Jan. 12, 1924; idem, "The Monroe Doctrine," ibid., Jan. 26, 1924; idem, "Elements in a Constructive Foreign Policy," *Annals of the American Academy of Political and Social Science*, July 1927, pp. 187–189; *New York Times*, Oct. 21, 1920, Feb. 3, 1922, Feb. 24, 1922, July 19, 1927; DeBenedetti, *Modern American Peace Movement*, pp. 55–56.

9. Borah to A. P. Brown, Nov. 25, 1919; Levinson to Borah, Feb. 14, 1920; both in Box 3, Levinson Papers; Levinson to Borah, Jan. 26, 1923, Box 4, ibid.; Levinson to Villard, Jan. 21, 1922, Box 47, ibid.; Levinson to Robins, Jan. 18, 1923, Box 41, ibid.; Levinson to Shipstead, June 14, 1923, Box 44, ibid.; Levinson to J. Reuben Clark, March 21, 1925, Box 20, Robins Papers; Levinson, "Law to End War," *Forum*, Jan. 1924.

10. Robins to Levinson, Jan. 7, 1923, Box 41, Levinson Papers; Robins to William Thompson, n.d., quoted in Neil Salzman, *Reform and Revolution: The Life and Times of Raymond Robins* (Kent: Kent State University Press, 1991), p. 321; Levinson to Borah, Dec. 22, 1928, Box 5, Levinson Papers; Raymond Robins, "Outlawry of War, the Next Step in Civilization," *Annals of the American Academy of Political and Social Science*, July 1925, pp. 153–156.

11. Robins to Levinson, March 1, 1923, Nov. 3, 1923, Box 41, Levinson Papers; Levinson to Villard, Jan. 2, 1925, Box 47, ibid.; Levinson to Shipstead, Jan. 14, 1926, Box 44, ibid.; Levinson to Robins, March 17 and May 3, 1926, Box 42, ibid.; Robins to Alexander Gumberg, Aug. 5, 1923, Box 3, Gumberg Papers. Although both men devoted the bulk of their attention to outlawry during the 1920s, they also showed some activity on other issues. Levinson emerged as a strong critic of the G.O.P. debt renegotiation schemes, peppering them with public criticism and supplying Howell and Borah with statistical information that both later employed in Senate debates. Levinson to Borah, March 2, March 8, March 31, and Oct. 27, 1926, Box 4, Levinson Papers; Levinson to Howell, April 13, 1926, Box 23, ibid.; Levinson to Borah, May 23, 1928, Box 5, ibid. Robins spent the 1920s continuing his crusade for Russian recognition, activity that brought him closer to the mainstream peace progressive position. Robins, "Universal Peace, a World Challenge," *Annals of the American Academy of Political and Social Science*, July 1926, pp. 158–159.

12. Levinson to Villard, Jan. 28, 1924, Jan. 13, 1927, Aug. 18, 1929, Box 47, Levinson Papers; Robins to Borah, Feb. 2, 1927; Levinson to Borah, Feb. 2, 1929; Levinson to Otis Glenn, Feb. 9, 1929; all in Box 5, Levinson Papers. Levinson did believe that Kellogg-Briand would strengthen the U.S. position in Latin America by assuring the Latin Americans that American relations with their region stood "identically the same" as American-European relations. Levinson to Borah, Jan. 21, Jan. 24, and March 25, 1927, Box 5, Levinson Papers; Levinson to La Follette, Jr., Dec. 13, 1928, Box 26, ibid. On the post-1929 decline in cooperation between Levinson and the peace progressives, see Levinson to G. Harrison Brown, May 19, 1930, Box 9, ibid.; Levinson to Thomas Walsh, March 29, 1930; Levinson to Robins, April 26, 1930; Levinson to F. J. Kelley; all in Box 22, Robins Papers. On the domestic conservatism of the duo, see Robins to Edwin Van Valkenburg, Aug. 28, 1924, File 252, Edwin Van Valkenburg Papers, Houghton Library, Harvard University; Levinson to Borah, June 21, 1926, Box 4, Levinson Papers.

13. Gumberg to Robins, Jan. 12, 1923; Gumberg to Borah, April 20, 1923, Nov. 2, 1924; Gumberg to William Henry Chamberlain, March 15, 1923; all in Box 3, Gumberg Papers; Gumberg clipping from *New York Times*, 1924, copy in Box 4, ibid.; Gumberg to Borah, Dec. 8, 1928, Box 5, ibid.; Peter Filene, *Americans and the Soviet Experiment, 1917–1933* (Cambridge, Mass.: Harvard University Press, 1967), pp. 88–89; James Libbey, *Alexander Gumberg and Soviet-American Relations, 1917–33* (Lexington: University Press of Kentucky, 1977). Gumberg functioned as a staff of one on Soviet affairs for several senators; Wheeler often wrote him seeking statistical information to help "point out the improvements in the present [Soviet] government over the past." Wheeler to Gumberg, June 23, 1923, Aug. 13, 1923, Box 3, Gumberg Papers.

14. *Searchlight on Congress*, Jan. 1922; *Spotlight*, July 1923, Aug. 1923, Dec. 1923 (Haines changed the name of the magazine for the last six months of 1923); *Searchlight on Congress*, Dec. 1925, Jan. 1926.

15. *Searchlight on Congress*, Jan. 1923, Feb. 1923, Dec. 1925, Jan. 1926, March 1926.

16. *Searchlight on Congress*, Feb. 1921, March 1921, Jan. 1922, June 1922, April 1926, May 1926, Jan. 1927, Feb. 1927.

17. Lippmann to Hiram Johnson, Aug. 17, 1919, Box 15, Lippmann Papers; Lippmann to Borah, Dec. 22, 1924, Jan. 1, 1925, Box 4, ibid.; Lippmann to Laura Morgan, Jan. 30, 1929, Box 21, ibid.; Lippmann to Ernest Gruening, Feb. 20, 1930, Box 12, ibid.; Lippmann to Henry Stimson, May 29, 1930, Box 31, ibid.; Ronald Steel, *Walter Lippmann and the American Century* (New York: Vintage Books, 1980), pp. 155–255. On Lippmann, Lamont, and Italy, see Lamont to Lippmann, April 23, 1928, Box 17, Lippmann Papers. Lippmann's relationship with Borah was a curious one. The two cooperated on a host of issues, such as Soviet, Chinese, and Mexican

policies. For examples of flattering comments by Lippmann about Borah, see Lippmann to Borah, Nov. 5, 1924, March 25, 1927, Box 4, ibid. Lippmann nonetheless attempted to maintain a middle course on Borah, too. He wrote the senator that although he believed that Borah was essentially right on foreign policy, he doubted that in the long run "a foreign policy can be properly conducted" with the Secretary of State and the Chair of the Foreign Relations Committee in such constant disagreement; Lippmann to Borah, Sept. 30, 1925, Box 4, ibid.

18. Lippmann to Robert Wagner, Jan. 9, 1929, Box 33, Lippmann Papers; Walter Lippmann, "The Outlawry of War," *Atlantic Monthly*, Aug. 1923; idem, "The Political Equivalent of War," ibid., Aug. 1928.

19. Lippmann to Borah, April 13, 1928, Box 4, Lippmann Papers; Lippmann-Rublee correspondence, Box 29, ibid.; Bingham to Alfred Bingham, Jan. 18, 1927, Series III, Box 14, Bingham Family Papers, Sterling Memorial Library, Yale University; Walter Lippmann, "Vested Rights and Nationalism in Latin America," *Foreign Affairs*, April 1927, pp. 353–363; idem, "Second Thoughts on Havana," ibid., July 1928, pp. 541–544; Sheffield to Chandler Anderson, April 1, 1927, Series 1, Box 5, Sheffield Papers; Steel, *Walter Lippmann*, pp. 326–328.

20. Andrieus Jones (D–New Mexico) was "the pacific sort of Democrat whom Republicans in power like to place on investigating committees"; Jones obliged by asking useless questions. His Ohio Democratic colleague, Atlee Pomerene, was excused by the editors on the grounds that his "limited comprehension make[s] it impossible for him to grasp the Haitian psychology" or the psychology of anyone with a different background from his. Noting that Tasker Oddie (R–Nevada) never seemed to talk, the editors argued that the reason was "less that he is reserved than that he has nothing to say"; while Medill McCormick (R–Illinois), "the saddest spectacle of all," was too lazy to do anything despite his considerable potential; *New Republic*, Feb. 8, 1922.

21. *New Republic*, Dec. 12, 1923, Jan. 23, 1924, Jan. 30, 1924, Jan. 26, 1927, March 14, 1928.

22. *New Republic*, Jan. 31, 1923, Dec. 9, 1925, Jan. 13, 1926, Feb. 3, 1926, Jan. 5, 1927, March 7, 1928, July 10, 1929. The *New Republic* took a mixed attitude toward the European proposals of the leading peace progressives. It praised Borah for "doing more to educate his fellow countrymen about the facts and values of European politics than all the other American political leaders put together," but it also chastised his proposal for an international economic conference for having "shirked" the major issues; *New Republic*, Jan. 3 and Feb. 14, 1923.

23. "War Resisters League," 1925 pamphlet, File 3, War Resisters League Papers, SCPC; "Stop War Now," 1925 WPS pamphlet; "Free Trade and Freedom of Trade Opportunity," 1926 WPS pamphlet; both in Box 1, Women's Peace Society Papers, SCPC; WPU memo on Frazier Resolu-

tion, 1929, Legislative Files, Box 180, Folder 83, Robert Wagner Papers, Lauinger Library, Georgetown University; WPU statement on Frazier resolution, 1929, Box 50, Balch Papers, SCPC. For a more detailed look at the WPU, see Harriet Hyman Alonso, *The Women's Peace Union and the Outlawry of War, 1921–1942* (Knoxville: University of Tennessee Press, 1989).

24. Mary Flahaven to Nevin Sayre, May 9, 1929, Reel 41.50, National Council for the Prevention of War (NCPW) Papers, SCPC; Libby to Dudley Mackenzie, Jan. 21 and Feb. 18, 1927, Reel 41.11, NCPW Papers; Dorothy Detzer to Emily Balch, May 19, 1927, Box 7, Balch Papers; *New York Times*, March 18, 1927; Chatfield, *For Peace and Justice*, p. 109.

25. Frederick Libby, "Do We Need 15 More Cruisers?" Box 50, Balch Papers; Jane Addams, "Feed the World and Save the League," *New Republic*, Nov. 24, 1920; Addams interview with William Hard, 1932, copy in Series A, Box 7a, Folder 1, Women's International League for Peace and Freedom (WILPF) Papers, SCPC; *New York Times*, Dec. 8, 1922, Dec. 30, 1922, Feb. 21, 1928, Feb. 22, 1928, Feb. 26, 1928, April 27, 1928, July 12, 1928, Aug. 15, 1929; *Chicago Tribune*, Dec. 19, 1921. One Republican congressmen called the NCPW a "propaganda factory" spouting "red" doctrines in an effort to hoodwink the American people; *New York Times*, May 6, 1930.

26. Addams presidential speech, 1924 WILPF convention; Addams interview with William Hard, 1932; both in Series A, Box 7a, Folder 1, WILPF Papers; *New York Times*, Dec. 30, 1922, April 16, 1924, Feb. 28, 1926, Dec. 11, 1927. Addams was not the only WILPF member to see the connection between international economic policy and peace that eluded the peace progressives. During the battle over the Hawley-Smoot tariff, Dorothy Detzer wrote Lynn Frazier, by then one of her closest Senate allies, urging him to "continue to make your valiant fight for Peace" by opposing the bill and supporting lower tariffs across-the-board; Detzer to Frazier, May 8, 1930, Series C, Box 15, Folder 35, WILPF Papers.

27. This turn toward anti-imperialism did not come without controversy. See Detzer to Balch, Jan. 29, 1926, Box 7, Balch Papers.

28. Dorothy Detzer, *Appointment on the Hill* (New York: Henry Holt, 1940), pp. 39–40; Detzer to Frederick Libby, March 20, 1925; Series C, Box 13, Folder 8, WILPF Papers; Detzer to Charles Evans Hughes, Jan. 5, 1928, Series C, Box 13, Folder 10, ibid.; Detzer to W. W. Cumberland, Jan. 26, June 8, and Dec. 13, 1928, Series C, Box 13, Folder 26, ibid.; Detzer to Emily Balch, Jan. 3, 1928; Detzer to Mexican Ambassador, March 27, 1929; both in Series C, Box 12, Folder 24, ibid.; Detzer to Balch, March 15, 1926, Box 7, Balch Papers; *The Nation*, Feb. 5, 1931. Detzer also had close ties with the peace progressives, feeding several of them "as much valuable material as possible" on Nicaraguan affairs during the later 1920s; Detzer to Mrs. Richards, Jan. 7, 1927, Box 7, Balch Papers.

29. Balch to Dr. Keppel, Jan. 24, 1929, Box 8, Balch Papers; S. W. Morgan to Paul Douglas, April 7, 1927, SDA 838.00/2306; Balch form letter, Jan. 28, 1930, Series C, Box 15, File 35, WILPF Papers; Emily Balch, ed., *Occupied Haiti* (New York: Writers' Publishing, 1927). Balch originally had proposed investigating Haitian conditions months after the Marines landed, but had found little support for the idea among mainstream peace groups. The differing responses to the aborted 1910s mission and the successful one of the 1920s offers an indication of the increased strength of anti-imperialism in the 1920s American political culture; Balch to Walter Lippmann, Jan. 19, 1916, Box 3, Lippmann Papers.

30. Balch to Maud Stockwell, Nov. 27, 1928, Box 8, Balch Papers; Detzer to Hiram Motherwell, Feb. 28, 1930, Series C, Box 13, Folder 6, WILPF Papers; U.S. Senate, Judiciary Committee, 71st Cong., 2d sess., *Constitutional Amendment Making War Impossible*, pp. 44–49; Detzer, *Appointment on the Hill*, pp. 89–99.

31. FOR to Harding, Feb. 13, 1923, Box 1, Fellowship of Reconciliation (FOR) Papers, SCPC; J. Nevin Sayre, "Pacifism and National Security," 1929; FOR press release, "Reconciliation—East and West," Sept. 13, 1925; FOR pamphlet, "The Near Eastern Problem: Will War Solve It?" 1923; all in Box 22, FOR Papers; *New York Times*, Aug. 1, 1927.

32. Paul Jones to Robins, June 20, 1924, Box 19, Robins Papers; Sayre speech in Nicaragua, n.d.[Jan. 1928]; Sayre press release, Jan. 7, 1928; both in Box E-3, Sayre Papers; Sayre, "A Message on Mexico and Nicaragua," Jan. 15, 1927; Sayre press release, Jan. 25, 1928; both in Box 34, FOR Papers; Sayre memo to Robert Olds, Jan. 28, 1928, SDA 817.00/5353; *New York Times*, Jan. 29, 1928. W. W. Cumberland, the U.S. financial agent to the Managua regime, asked why people like Sayre "insist on racing around the earth and increasing the difficulties for some of us who are trying to bring about peace and fair dealing between nations"; he charged that the actions of Sayre and his group would only encourage Sandino's resistance; W. W. Cumberland to Dorothy Detzer, Dec. 28, 1927, Series C, Box 13, Folder 26, WILPF Papers.

33. Sayre quoted in Detzer to Balch, Oct. 26, 1928, Box 8, Balch Papers; Sayre memo, "FOR Work with Latin America," April 1929; Sayre to Thomson, Oct. 10, 1929, July 8, 1930; Thomson confidential newsletter, 1931; all in Box E-3, Sayre Papers; Thomson newsletter, May 16, 1930, Box 34, FOR Papers; Thomson, "First Annual Report, 1 July 1929–30 June 1930," Box E-11, Sayre Papers. The State Department described Thomson as a "rank idealist . . . certainly doing little to assist in carrying out the policy of the State Department in these countries"; Charles Eberhart to Stimson, Feb. 17, 1931, copy in Box 34, FOR Papers.

34. Lane, "Military Training in Schools and Colleges of the United States," 1925, Box E-3, Sayre Papers; CME editorial, April 29, 1926; Sayre, "Dangers of the ROTC," March 1926; Sayre to Editor, *Barron's*, Feb. 7, 1927;

all in Reel 70.13, Committee on Militarism in Education (CME) Papers, SCPC; CME to Herbert Hoover, Oct. 25, 1929, Box E-11, Sayre Papers; Paul Jones form letter, May 28, 1925; Tucker Smith to Bernice Miller, April 6, 1932; both in Reel 70.33, CME Papers; *New York Times*, April 20, 1926, July 1, 1926, Jan. 16, 1927.

35. Warren Cohen, *The American Revisionists: The Lessons of Intervention in World War I* (Chicago: University of Chicago Press, 1967), pp. 35–90; Frederick Bausman, *Let France Explain* (London: Allen & Unwin, 1922); John Kenneth Turner, *Shall It Be Again?* (New York: B. W. Huebsch, 1922).

36. Gruening to Villard, May 19, 1922, File 1423, Villard Papers.

37. *The Nation* increased its circulation from 7,200 in June 1918 to 24,606 one year later and to 30,294 by the end of 1920. See Villard to Levinson, March 16, 1921, Box 47, Levinson Papers. Levinson was a stockholder of *The Nation*.

38. Villard to Edwin Gay, April 6, 1921; Villard to Gruening, Feb. 10, 1930; Villard to James Kerney, Feb. 10, 1930; Villard to William Allen White, Feb. 11, 1930; Gruening to Villard, March 16, 1930; all in File 1477, Villard Papers; Kerney quoted in Freda Kirchwey to Gruening, n.d., in "Imperialism, 1919–1941" box, Gruening Papers; *The Nation*, July 20, 1921, May 23, 1923, May 30, 1923, July 14, 1926.

39. Villard to Borah, Jan. 20, 1928, File 304, Villard Papers; *The Nation*, Jan. 18, Jan. 25, Feb. 1, and March 21, 1928. Villard had spent most of the 1920s repeatedly urging Borah to run for President, but he wrote Levinson in late 1928 that he found Borah's conduct during that year, which culminated in the senator's endorsement of Herbert Hoover, "nauseating" and "revolting." When Levinson protested, citing Borah's work for outlawry, Villard shot back that the "cause of peace can never be advanced by such hypocrisy." Villard began in mid-1929 urging La Follette to wrest leadership of the progressive camp from Borah. Villard to Levinson, Oct. 12, 1928, Box 47, Levinson papers; Villard to La Follette, Jr., Jan. 5, 1929, File 2159, Villard Papers.

40. Villard to Borah, Feb. 25 and April 12, 1921, File 304, Villard Papers; *The Nation*, Sept. 21, 1921, Dec. 21, 1921, Jan. 11, 1922, Feb. 15, 1922, July 21, 1926, June 29, 1927, Feb. 1, 1928.

41. *The Nation*, Feb. 21, 1923, Oct. 31, 1923, Nov. 3, 1926.

42. Villard to Levinson, Jan. 24, 1922, Box 47, Levinson Papers; *The Nation*, Sept. 14, Sept. 28, and Dec. 14, 1921.

43. Gruening to James Weldon Johnson, Oct. 31, 1921, Box C-326, NAACP Papers, 1909–1939, Library of Congress; Gruening to William Calder, July 11, 1922, 1920s scrapbook, Gruening Papers; Gruening to Joseph France, June 30, 1922, "Imperialism, 1919–1941" box, ibid.; Gruening, "The Senators Visit Haiti and Santo Domingo," *The Nation*, Jan. 4, 1922; idem, "Haiti and Santo Domingo Today–I," *The Nation*, Feb. 8, 1922;

idem, "Haiti and Santo Domingo Today–II," *The Nation*, Feb. 15, 1922; idem, "Monroe versus His Interpreters," *Forum*, Dec. 1923; idem, "Conquest of Haiti and Santo Domingo," *Current History*, March 1922; idem, "Haiti under American Occupation," *Century*, April 1922; U.S. Senate, 67th Cong., 1st and 2d sess., *Hearings before a Select Committee on Haiti and Santo Domingo*, pp. 1199–1220; Hans Schmidt, *The United States Occupation of Haiti* (New Brunswick, N.J.: Rutgers University Press, 1971), pp. 120–122. On Gruening's lobbying for the King Amendment, see Lewis Gannett to Francis Wheeler, Feb. 7, 1922, 1920s scrapbook, Gruening Papers.

44. Gruening to Moorfield Storey, Feb. 13, 1924; Anti-Imperialist League press release, Feb. 13, 1924; both in File 1423, Villard Papers; Gruening campaign press releases, Box B-4, La Follette Family Papers; Gruening to La Follette, Jr., Nov. 1, 1924; Gruening to La Follette, Sr., Nov. 6, 1924; both in Box B-5, ibid.

45. Gruening to La Follette, Jr., March 19, 1926, March 13, 1926 [1927], Box C-4, La Follette Family Papers; Gruening to Villard, Oct. 27, 1928, Series 3, Box 3, Gruening Papers; Gruening to Walter Lippmann, Aug. 25, 1925, Box 12, Lippmann Papers; Sheffield to Kellogg, July 1, 1926; Sheffield to Palmer Pierce, Nov. 21, 1927; both in Series 1, Box 5, Sheffield Papers; Kellogg to Charles Warren, March 5, 1926, Reel 19, Kellogg Papers; Sheffield to Kellogg, April 28, 1926, SDA 812.20211/34; Alexander Weddell to Kellogg, Sept. 14, 1926, SDA 812.20211/39; Joseph Grew to Weddell, Oct. 9, 1926, SDA 812.20211/39; Kellogg to Sheffield, Dec. 10, 1926, SDA 812.20211/44a; Sheffield to Kellogg, Dec. 11, 1926, SDA 812.20211/45; Sheffield to Kellogg, May 19, 1927, SDA 812.20211/68; Sheffield to Kellogg, Dec. 31, 1926, SDA 812.20211/47; Gruening, "Emerging Mexico," *The Nation*, June 10, June 24, and July 1, 1925; John Britton, *Carleton Beals: A Radical Journalist in Latin America* (Albuquerque: University of New Mexico Press, 1987), pp. 56–57.

46. Gruening to Borah, March 9, 1928, Jan. 18, 1929, Series 36, Box 3, Gruening Papers; Gruening to Frederick Libby, Dec. 15, 1928, Series 22, Box 2, ibid.; Gruening to Libby, Feb. 19, 1930, Gruening to Walter Lippmann, Feb. 19, 1930, Series 36, Box 12, ibid.

47. Grew to Alexander Weddell, Oct. 9, 1926, SDA 812.20211/39; Carleton Beals, "Mexico's New Era of Peace," *Current History*, Aug. 1924; idem, "Civil War in Mexico," *New Republic*, July 6, 1927; idem, "New Democracy in Mexico," ibid., Oct. 3, 1928; idem, "Future in Mexico," ibid., Dec. 5, 1928; idem, "Mexico Seeking Central American Leadership," *Current History*, Sept. 1926.

48. Carleton Beals, "With Sandino in Nicaragua," *The Nation*, Feb. 22, Feb. 29, March 14, March 21, March 28, April 4, and April 11, 1928; *New York Times*, July 19, 1927; 69 *CR* 1928, 70th Cong., 1st sess., pp. 1785–90 (Dill),

6968–73 (Norris); Britton, *Carleton Beals*, pp. 68–86; Neill Macaulay, *The Sandino Affair* (Durham: Duke University Press, 1967), pp. 83–84.

49. Gruening to Johnson, Feb. 3, 1922; Johnson to Gruening, Feb. 7, 1922; Johnson memo, Feb. 15, 1922; Johnson to McCormick, July 26, 1922; all in Box C-327, NAACP Papers; James Weldon Johnson, "Self-Determining Haiti," *The Nation*, Aug. 28, Sept. 4, Sept. 11, and Sept. 25, 1920; idem, "Why Latin America Dislikes the United States," *New York Age*, Dec. 31, 1915; William Gibbs, "James Weldon Johnson: A Black Perspective on 'Big Stick' Diplomacy," *Diplomatic History* 8 (1984):329–347. The idea for the Johnson mission actually originated with Oswald Garrison Villard, who served on the NAACP's national board.

50. Barnes to Walter Lippmann, Sept. 16, 1925, Box 3, Lippmann Papers; Moon to Lippmann, Feb. 3, 1927, Box 21, ibid.; Parker Moon, *Imperialism and World Politics* (New York: Macmillan, 1926), pp. 407–456, 513–566; Margaret Alexander Marsh, *The Bankers in Bolivia: A Study in American Foreign Investment* (New York: Vanguard Press, 1928); Leland Jenks, *Our Cuban Colony: A Study in Sugar* (New York: Vanguard Press, 1928); Melvin Knight, *The Americans in Santo Domingo* (New York: Vanguard Press, 1928). On Moon's support for the League of Nations and limited American military intervention in the Russian civil war, see Moon to Walter Lippmann, April 30, 1919, Box 21, Lippmann Papers. For La Follette's use of the Marsh material, see La Follette draft speech, 1928, Box C-554, La Follette Family Papers.

51. For a summary of press opinion on the Nicaraguan occupation, see Lamar Beman, ed., *Selected Articles on Intervention in Latin America* (New York: H. W. Wilson, 1928).

52. Wheeler to Walter Lippmann, March 9, 1927, Box 34, Lippmann Papers. For another of the many examples of this pattern, see Frazier to Laura Morgan, Dec. 17, 1928, Reel 41.61, NCPW Papers.

53. For more on peace progressive assistance to the peace movement, see Dill to Frederick Libby, Feb. 9, 1926; Norris to Laura Morgan, Nov. 19, 1925; both in Reel 41.61, NCPW Papers.

54. Inman report, CCLA, Sept. 8, 1923, Box 13, Samuel Guy Inman Papers, Library of Congress; "Reference material," Columbia University lectures, 1926, Box 50, ibid.; Inman to Walter Lippmann, March 12, 1926, Box 15, Lippmann Papers; Samuel Guy Inman, "Imperialistic America," *Atlantic Monthly*, July 1924; Sheffield to Arthur Schoenfeld, Feb. 21, 1927, Series 1, Box 5, Sheffield Papers; "Rowe Replies to Inman's Attack on American Foreign Policy," n.d., Reel 121, Charles Evans Hughes Papers, Library of Congress; Kenneth Woods, " 'Imperialistic America': A Landmark in the Development of U.S. Policy toward Latin America," *Inter-American Economic Affairs* 21 (1967):55–72.

55. Gruening to José Padin, May 25, 1935, Series 36, Box 8, Gruening Papers; Herring to Walter Lippmann, Oct. 25, 1926, Box 13, Lippmann Papers;

Henry Goddard Leach to Lippmann, Sept. 15, 1930, Box 6, ibid.; CCRLA, "Proceedings of the Seminar of Relations with Mexico, 1–10 Jan. 1927"; CCRLA, "The Seminar in the Caribbean"; E. A. Ross to Alice Blackwell, Nov. 26, 1930; Herring form letter, May 21, 1938; all in CCRLA file, Collective Documents Group A, SCPC; Kellogg to Coolidge, July 11, 1927; Kellogg to William Hard, Aug. 17, 1927; both in Reel 27, Kellogg Papers; Sheffield to William Howard Taft, Feb. 9, 1927, Series 1, Box 5, Sheffield Papers; *New York Times*, Dec. 18, 1926, Dec. 30, 1926, Jan. 9, 1927, Jan. 12, 1927. The Caribbean Seminar attracted the support of the FOR's Charles Thomson, who served on its faculty; FOR newsletter, July 1931, Box 34, FOR Papers.

56. Sheffield to William Lyon Phelps, Feb. 22, 1925; Taft to Sheffield, May 3, 1927; both in Series 1, Box 5, Sheffield Papers; Catt to Alice Stone Blackwell, May 7, 1927, Reel 2, Catt Papers.

7. The Collapse of Wilsonianism

1. *Guide to U.S. Elections* (Washington, D.C.: Congressional Quarterly Publications, 1976), pp. 56–59. This chapter does not include the two Democratic peace progressives (Dill and Wheeler) and analyzes only those Democrats who served in two separate Congresses (or roughly four years) during the decade.

2. Although John Milton Cooper has noted that Wilson proved unable to transform the Democrats to such an extent that they would continue to support his policies after he left the White House, this chapter offers the first detailed analysis of the foreign policy performance of the Senate Democrats during the 1920s. John Milton Cooper, Jr., *The Warrior and the Priest: Woodrow Wilson and Theodore Roosevelt* (Cambridge, Mass.: The Belknap Press of Harvard University Press, 1983), pp. 342–344. For an alternative view on the continuing power of Wilsonianism, see Robert Divine, *Second Chance: The Triumph of Internationalism in America during World War II* (New York: Atheneum, 1971), pp. 3–28.

3. La Follette to Frederick Howe, April 9, 1926, Box C-4, La Follette Family Papers. Political commentator Raymond Clapper added in 1927 that "the Democrats have abandoned the true role of a minority party"; *The Nation*, April 13, 1927.

4. Akira Iriye, *After Imperialism: The Search for a New Order in the Far East, 1921–1931* (Cambridge, Mass.: Harvard University Press, 1965).

5. 67 *CR* 1925, 69th Cong., 1st sess., pp. 2673–74 (Robinson); 68 *CR* 1927, 69th Cong., 2d sess., pp. 3328–29 (Trammell); 69 *CR* 1928, 70th Cong., 1st sess., p. 7511 (Glass); U.S. Senate, Committee on Foreign Relations, 68th Cong., 1st sess., *Permanent Court of International Justice*, pp. 20–168; *New York Times*, Feb. 27, 1923, July 1, 1923, June 1, 1924; Henry Ferrell, Jr., *Claude A. Swanson of Virginia* (Lexington: University Press of Kentucky,

1985), p. 175. As late as 1930, Swanson maintained that he opposed the United States' entering into any political pacts with Europe outside the League of Nations; Swanson to James Ricks, Aug. 1, 1930, Reel 41.61, NCPW Papers. The other members of the bloc included Alben Barkley (Kentucky), Thaddeus Caraway (Arkansas), Duncan Fletcher (Florida), Peter Gerry (Rhode Island), Walter George (Georgia), W. J. Harris (Georgia), Morris Sheppard (Texas), F. M. Simmons (North Carolina), "Cotton Ed" Smith (South Carolina), Augustus Stanley (Kentucky), Hubert Stephens (Mississippi), Park Trammell (Florida), and Robert Wagner (New York). In addition, two other senators, Andrieus Jones (New Mexico) and Henry Ashurst (Arizona), fell in between the identifiable blocs and at best qualified as shaky allies of the leadership.

6. 61 *CR* 1921, 67th Cong., 1st sess., pp. 5006–58 (Sheppard); 64 *CR* 1923, 67th Cong., 4th sess., pp. 1220–21 (Robinson); *New York Times*, April 13, 1923 (Glass), June 29, 1924 (Pittman); Ferrell, *Claude A. Swanson*, p. 172. The centrists also attempted to achieve Wilson's visions by frustrating the chief alternative put forth by the Republican policymakers of the 1920s, the Washington System, and in particular the Four Power Treaty. For representative comments, see 62 *CR* 1922, 67th Cong., 2d sess., pp. 4255–60 (Sheppard), 4325–26 (Glass). Interpreting the vote later in the decade, though, Thomas Walsh said that it "signifies nothing," because all Democrats who opposed the Four Power Treaty acted for different reasons; Walsh to Salmon Levinson, April 4, 1930, Box 47, Levinson Papers.

7. 64 *CR* 1923, 57th Cong., 4th sess., p. 869; 69 *CR* 1928, 70th Cong., 1st sess., p. 1722; 70 *CR* 1929, 70th Cong., 2d sess., pp. 1758–62, 2840–42; Ferrell, *Claude A. Swanson*, pp. 179–183. On Swanson and Mitchell, see Ferrell, p. 172; *New York Times*, Sept. 7, 1925. On Swanson's political influence, see Ferrell, pp. 178–179. Although other centrists did not play the role in 1920s naval policy that Swanson did, they did share his beliefs. Peter Gerry, who joined Swanson in defending the Navy in its battle with Billy Mitchell, also spent the decade backing increased naval funds. The Rhode Island senator believed that American naval supremacy would bring peace, since "the American Navy has always been a great factor in the peace of the world and . . . it should be second to none." Gerry criticized the Washington Conference for imposing too many sacrifices upon the United States, and he opposed all suggestions for more disarmament conferences, reasoning that increasing funding to the point where the United States had the world's largest navy would be "much more likely to be successful in obtaining satisfactory agreements in the future"; 66 *CR* 1925, 68th Cong., 2d sess., pp. 1969–79; *New York Times*, Feb. 11, 1927.

8. 65 *CR* 1924, 68th Cong., 1st sess., p. 10992. The other centrist Democrat to take a prominent role during the German debate was W. J. Harris, who dismissed allegations of German economic distress, contending that he had

seen "just as much suffering in Georgia"; 64 *CR* 1923, 67th Cong., 4th sess., pp. 10962–64.

9. 62 *CR* 1922, 67th Cong., 2d sess., p. 7910 (Fletcher); Key Pittman, "United States and Russia: Obstacles to Recognition of Present Soviet Regime," *Annals of the American Academy of Political and Social Science*, July 1926, pp. 131–133; *The Times* (London), April 25, 1928.

10. 62 *CR* 1922, 67th Cong., 2d sess., p. 1627 (Simmons); 64 *CR* 1923, 67th Cong., 4th sess., pp. 3775–77 (Glass); 67 *CR* 1926, 69th Cong., 1st sess., 26, p. 6487 (Robinson); *New York Times*, Feb. 17, 1923, Sept. 22, 1925; Ferrell, *Claude A. Swanson*, pp. 166–169; Mark Sullivan, "Carter Glass— Sound Democrat," *World's Work*, May 1924. Glass's remarks about the British and Turkey indicated a strong centrist hostility to the Turkish regime, one that they played out by voting as a bloc to kill the Lausanne Treaty. *New York Times*, Nov. 2, 1924 (Swanson), Feb. 8, 1925 (Fletcher); 64 *CR* 1923, 67th Cong., 4th sess., p. 10964 (Harris).

11. Glass to Margaret Crenshaw, Nov. 21, 1928; Glass to Laura Morgan, Dec. 13, 1928; both in Reel 41.61, NCPW Papers; 70 *CR* 1929, 70th Cong., 2d sess., pp. 1454–62 (Barkley), 1728 (Glass); *New York Times*, Nov. 27, 1928. The most positive centrist appraisal of Kellogg-Briand came from the recently elected Robert Wagner, who described the pact as "not a legal document but a popular slogan," which, though not going "far enough," would serve a positive purpose in increasing the spirit of peace. He pointed correspondents to his speech as the key to his ideas on world peace. 70 *CR* 1929, 70th Cong., 2d sess., pp. 1339–41; Wagner to Robert Nicole, Dec. 25, 1928; Wagner to Donald Blaisdell, Jan. 7, 1929; both in Box 121a, Wagner Papers.

12. 62 *CR* 1922, 67th Cong., 2d sess., pp. 5804–05 (Fletcher); 67 *CR* 1926, 69th Cong., 1st sess., p. 5326 (Fletcher); 68 *CR* 1927, 69th Cong., 2d sess., pp. 1844–45, 2200–01 (Robinson); *New York Times*, Nov. 25, 1926 (Swanson); Ferrell, *Claude A. Swanson*, p. 180. Ernest Gruening later recalled that Swanson had "the most fantastic conception of our rights and duties" in Haiti based upon a combination of prejudice and a "fleeting visit" to the country in the mid-1920s; Gruening to William King, Oct. 11, 1932, Series 36, Box 11, Gruening Papers. Meanwhile, Frank Kellogg termed the Virginia senator one of the "most valuable members" of the Foreign Relations Committee, a man never guilty of "playing party politics with foreign affairs"; Kellogg to C. Bascom Slemp, May 15, 1928, Kellogg Papers.

13. 69 *CR* 1928, 70th Cong., 1st sess., pp. 6747–61 (George, Swanson, Caraway), 6990, 7042–43 (Pittman), 7042 (Fletcher), 7244 (Glass); *New York Times*, Jan. 10, 1927, Jan. 24, 1928. The centrist view of the remainder of the world further revealed the group's rather tepid anti-imperialism. Swanson condemned the efforts of Panamanian nationalists to have the League of Nations determine whether the United States or Panama had

sovereignty over the Canal Zone, asserting that the United States would address legitimate Panamanian complaints but would not "tolerate any interference in this matter . . . from any source whatever." He also parted from the peace progressives with his rather vigorous defense of the dispatch of the Marines to China, remarking that American tobacco needed the China market and calling for an "adequate" force of Marines along with a "minimum" of four destroyers to ensure the stability of the situation. Only in the Philippines did the centrists side with the anti-imperialists, expressing support for Filipino independence on the grounds that it would relieve the United States of the "very grave responsibility" of defense of the islands, although like the peace progressives neither the centrists nor any other Democrats raised the issue prominently. 65 *CR* 1924, 68th Cong., 1st sess., p. 3616; *New York Times*, Dec. 24, 1926, Sept. 13, 1927; Ferrell, *Claude A. Swanson*, pp. 174, 183.

14. 62 *CR* 1922, 67th Cong., 2d sess., pp. 434–435 (Harris), 1627 (Simmons), 4259 (Sheppard on Japanese); 64 *CR* 1923, 67th Cong., 4th sess., p. 3775 (Trammell); 65 *CR* 1924, 68th Cong., 1st sess., p. 6537 (Sheppard on immigration); *New York Times*, March 8, 1922 (Harris), Oct. 8, 1922 (Caraway), Dec. 24, 1926 (Swanson).

15. Pittman to W. C. Black, Oct. 7, 1925; Pittman to Harold Hale, Oct. 7, 1925; Pittman to Harold Hale, Dec. 17, 1927; all in Box 14, Key Pittman Papers, Library of Congress; Pittman speech, Fernley, Nev., Oct. 10, 1928; Pittman speech, Sparks, Nev., Sept. 29, 1928; both in Box 120, ibid.; Pittman statement in *New York Times*, July 31, 1928. For the tariff votes, see the Appendix.

16. 61 *CR* 1921, 67th Cong., 1st sess., pp. 1425–26; 64 *CR* 1923, 67th Cong., 4th sess., pp. 3759–62; 65 *CR* 1924, 68th Cong., 1st sess., p. 2574; 68 *CR* 1927, 69th Cong., 2d sess., pp. 1270–71, 1642–43, 2143–44; 69 *CR* 1928, 70th Cong., 1st sess., p. 5424–28; 70 *CR* 1929, 70th Cong., 2d sess., pp. 2846, 3570, 4883–84; *New York Times*, Jan. 5 and 6, 1928; Laurence Hauptman, "To the Good Neighbor: A Study of the Senate's Role in American Foreign Policy" (Ph.D. diss., New York University, 1971), pp. 42–43.

17. 70 *CR* 1929, 70th Cong., 2d sess., pp. 2694–97 (Smith-Wheeler exchange). At the end of Smith's address the senator pleaded with Wheeler that he did not feel well and needed to retire to the cloakroom.

18. A Senate investigating committee eventually cleared Mayfield; *Literary Digest*, Feb. 14, 1925. For Mayfield's obsession with his campaign schedule, see Mayfield to Z. E. Marvin, Dec. 29, 1925, Folder 7a, Box 6, Earle Mayfield Papers, Lauinger Library, Georgetown University.

19. On the idealists and the League, see Walsh to Woodrow Wilson, Dec. 2, 1918; Walsh to J. P. McGuay, Feb. 21, 1919; Walsh to D. W. Lawler, April 14, 1919; Walsh to Fasho Fowa, Dec. 5, 1919; all in Box 185, Thomas Walsh Papers, Library of Congress. For Walsh and Article XI, see Robert

David Johnson, "Article XI in the United States' Decision to Reject the League of Nations," *International History Review* 15 (1993):518–523.

20. Black to Demps Oden, Feb. 14, 1935, Box 211, Hugo Black Papers, Library of Congress; Walsh radio speech, Paris, May 1927; Walsh to Salmon Levinson, Oct. 10, 1927, Jan. 7, 1929; all in Box 47, Levinson Papers; 61 *CR* 1921, 67th Cong., 1st sess., pp. 1847–48 (Walsh); 64 *CR* 1923, 67th Cong., 4th sess., pp. 3954–58 (Owen); 65 *CR* 1924, 68th Cong., 1st sess., pp. 355–399 (Owen), 7006–07 (Neely); 67 *CR* 1926, 69th Cong., 1st sess., pp. 1564, 2679, 2811–13 (Walsh); 70 *CR* 1929, 70th Cong., 2d sess., pp. 1713–19 (Walsh); *New York Times*, Feb. 27, 1923, Sept. 9, 1925, Feb. 14, 1926, March 23, 1926, Dec. 29, 1926, Dec. 18, 1927, June 7, 1928. Mayfield too embraced the idea of moral power's playing the key role in American international affairs, contending that "America's strength [lies] not in vast fleets of standing armies [*sic*]" but in carrying a "message of comfort and healing to the stricken nations of the earth." He failed, however, to offer specifics on how the United States would accomplish this. Mayfield interview, n.d.[1926?], Folder 8, Box 6, Mayfield Papers.

21. 61 *CR* 1921, 67th Cong., 1st sess., pp. 4107–11; Owen quoted in press release, Popular Government League, April 29, 1922, SDA 838.00/1873.

22. In 1919 Walsh warmly praised the work of the rabidly pro-intervention Fall Committee, hoping that Fall's hearings would make it "possible for our Government to take action that will protect the rights of our citizens who have made investments" in Mexico. Later that year the Montana senator speculated that if the United States had joined the League, perhaps the League council would have dealt with Mexican violations of the rights of foreigners by permitting the United States to intervene in Mexico under League counsel and "possibly hold Vera Cruz [*sic*] as a kind of hostage for the good conduct of Carranza." Walsh also backed the Armenian mandate scheme as "an opportunity to do a noble work for civilization without any expense to this country." Walsh to R. W. Peters, Sept. 26, 1919; Walsh to Elizabeth Shepherd, Dec. 18, 1919; both in Box 184, Thomas Walsh Papers; Walsh to E. D. Sisson, Oct. 15, 1919, Box 183, ibid.

23. Walsh to R. R. Purcell, Nov. 20, 1926; Walsh to Walter Schirmer, Jan. 29, 1927; Walsh to L. O. Rothschild, Jan. 31, 1927; Walsh to Anna Luther, Feb. 2, 1927; Walsh to W. H. Poorman, March 2, 1927; Walsh to G. L. Camere, March 24, 1928; all in Box 184, Thomas Walsh Papers; 68 *CR* 1927, 69th Cong., 2d sess., pp. 1565–69 (Walsh); 69 *CR* 1928, 70th Cong., 1st sess., p. 9687 (Walsh); 70 *CR* 1929, 70th Cong., 2d sess., p. 3844 (Black); 72 *CR* 1930, 71st Cong., 2d sess., p. 7512 (Black). Their anti-imperialist sympathies also made the idealists more amenable to peace progressive arguments on debt refinancing, although the idealists played a significant role in debate only on the Italian debt. Harrison launched a nationwide speaking tour in which he advanced the argument that business interests wanted the government to cancel its debt with Italy so that the

Rome regime could repay the debts owed to American private interests more easily. 67 *CR* 1926, 69th Cong., 1st sess., pp. 6621–25; *New York Times*, Feb. 21, 1926.

24. Walsh to Mary Breen, March 10, 1930, Box 183, Thomas Walsh Papers; Black to A. L. Darrow, July 17, 1930; Black to Lyman Ward, July 16, 1930; both in Box 191, Black Papers; 69 *CR* 1928, 70th Cong., 1st sess., pp. 3603–10; 70 *CR* 1929, 70th Cong., 2d sess., pp. 2343–45; 73 *CR* 1930, 71st Cong., special sess., pp. 38–43, 331 (Black); *New York Times*, April 28, 1929. Both Neely and Mayfield wound up voting for the cruisers bill. Mayfield did not offer a reason, while Neely remarked that he could not go against the expressed wishes of his West Virginia constituents, although he called the rhetoric in support of the bill so militaristic as "to indicate that the dove of peace has been exiled." Privately, the senator used even stronger language, conceding that he was going to vote against his political convictions on the cruisers bill largely because of the massive campaign conducted on its behalf in West Virginia. Neely said that he had received more than 2,000 pieces of mail in favor of the bill and only 2 opposing it. Neely quoted in Mary Flahaven to Nevin Sayre, Jan. 28, 1929, Reel 41.50, NCPW Papers; 70 *CR* 1929, 70th Cong., 2d sess., pp. 2182, 2750–51.

25. 67 *CR* 1926, 69th Cong., 1st sess., p. 6625 (Harrison); 72 *CR* 1930, 71st Cong., 2d sess., pp. 224, 5160 (Walsh); *New York Times*, Jan. 19, 1926 (Harrison).

26. The anti-Prohibition issue brought conservatives on both sides of the aisle together; *Outlook* described Bruce, Edwards, and Walter Edge as "the three generals of the Wet Forces"; *Outlook*, March 14, 1926.

27. John Watson to J. W. Hill, Feb. 3, 1922, copy in Box 35, Folder 126, Meredith Papers; Hiram Bingham to Alfred Bingham, Dec. 9, 1926, Series III, Box 14, Bingham Family Papers. Other members of the bloc included Sam Bratton (New Mexico), Nathan Dial (South Carolina), Carl Hayden (Arizona), and John Kendrick (Wyoming). For the paths of Tyson and Copeland to the Senate, see *Outlook*, Sept. 24, 1924; *Review of Reviews*, May 1928.

28. 67 *CR* 1926, 69th Cong., 1st sess., p. 2809; 69 *CR* 1928, 70th Cong., 1st sess., pp. 7509–10; 62 *CR* 1922, 67th Cong., 2d sess., pp. 3710–16 (Underwood), 3906–07 (Ransdell); *New York Times*, Jan. 21, 1922, March 16, 1922, Sept. 22, 1923, April 15, 1923, July 6, 1923; Bruce speech, "America Will Surely Join the League," Baltimore, Armistice Day 1923. Underwood agreed with Ransdell in the limited usefulness of framing international affairs in terms of the League issue, arguing in 1923 that the League had failed and that the major powers therefore needed to look elsewhere for permanent peace.

29. 70 *CR* 1928, 70th Cong., 2d sess., pp. 435, 1129–31, 1279–83, 1332–33. Bayard took a different approach from Bruce, attempting to increase opposition to the treaty by developing the argument that the treaty required

the United States to arbitrate any conceivable dispute that could possibly lead to international war, specifically the question of immigration. Borah retorted that Bruce's "idea of peace is fixed upon the proposition which is now sinking Europe to the bottomless pit"—the belief "that nothing counts in international affairs except sheer, brutal force."

30. 64 *CR* 1923, 67th Cong., 4th sess., pp. 3614–17 (Underwood), 3627–28 (Ransdell); 65 *CR* 1924, 68th Cong., 1st sess., pp. 7015–16 (Dial); 66 *CR* 1925, 68th Cong., 2d sess., p. 3225 (Underwood); 67 *CR* 1926, 69th Cong., 1st sess., pp. 6614–15 (Copeland); *New York Times*, July 21, 1922, Aug. 1, 1923, June 9, 1927, May 5, 1928.

31. 68 *CR* 1927, 69th Cong., 2d sess., pp. 151–152 (Tyson), 363–364 (Ransdell); 70 *CR* 1929, 70th Cong., 2d sess., pp. 2187 (Bruce), 2740–42 (Tyson); *New York Times*, Feb. 1, 1929. On the role of Tyson and Ransdell in blocking the Geneva Convention, see Borah to Hiram Johnson, Dec. 22, 1934, Box 376, Borah Papers. The faction split on the London Naval Treaty, with Ransdell and Steck lukewarm supporters and Copeland and Broussard implacable foes. Copeland was the only conservative to speak during treaty debate, noting that since the United States had an active worldwide trade, it could not act as if "were a little, walled-in country"; 73 *CR* 1930, 71st Cong., special sess., pp. 62–69.

32. Ransdell to Franklin Gunther, May 25, 1926, SDA 812.00/27552; Ransdell to Robert Olds, Dec. 31, 1926, SDA 817.00/4365; 66 *CR* 1925, 68th Cong., 2d sess., p. 2216 (Bruce); 69 *CR* 1928, 70th Cong., 1st sess., pp. 7149–51 (Copeland); 70 *CR* 1929, 70th Cong., 2d sess., pp. 3839, 4028 (Bruce); *New York Times*, Dec. 30, 1926 (Ransdell).

33. 71 *CR* 1929, 71st Cong., 1st sess., pp. 5053–57; 72 *CR* 1930, 71st Cong., 2d sess., pp. 1289, 1297, 1301. Royal Copeland, from a home state with differing needs, took an opposite perspective on the tariff from the three agricultural conservatives; the New York senator regularly voted for low agricultural rates but favored higher rates on most manufacturing products.

34. 61 *CR* 1921, 67th Cong., 1st sess., pp. 1530–33, 6376–79; 62 *CR* 1922, 67th Cong., 2d sess., pp. 436–446; Mark Sullivan, "Jim Reed: Marplot or Able Democrat?" *World's Work*, Aug. 1922. The best coverage of Reed's views on the League comes in Ralph Stone, *The Irreconcilables: The Fight against the League of Nations* (Lexington: University Press of Kentucky, 1970), pp. 77–105; the quote on Reed's racist views is at p. 88. Reed encountered his share of embarrassment during the Washington Treaties debate, though; he spent a good deal of time blasting the Four Power Treaty for not explicitly repudiating the Anglo-Japanese Alliance, only to be humiliated by Irvine Lenroot, who read from the treaty the exact passage that did cancel the alliance. Reed apparently had not read the treaty. *Literary Digest*, Sept. 25, 1926.

35. Reed to Salmon Levinson, April 15, 1922, March 26, 1925, Box 40, Levinson Papers; 64 *CR* 1923, 67th Cong., 4th sess., pp. 3670–74; 67 *CR* 1926,

69th Cong., 1st sess., pp. 1558–66; 70 *CR* 1929, 70th Cong., 2d sess., pp. 1456–62; 2408; *New York Times*, Feb. 15, 1922, Aug. 30, 1925, March 1, 1928.

36. 61 *CR* 1921, 67th Cong., 1st sess., pp. 443–444; 64 *CR* 1923, 67th Cong., 4th sess., pp. 4147–52; *New York Times*, Jan. 22, 1927.

37. 67 *CR* 1926, 69th Cong., 1st sess., pp. 2106–13, 2819–20; 68 *CR* 1927, 69th Cong., 2d sess., pp. 2537–38; 70 *CR* 1929, 70th Cong., 2d sess., pp. 2356, 4885. Blease also wanted to expand the occupation of Haiti; 69 *CR* 1928, 70th Cong., 1st sess., p. 8491.

38. 58 *CR* 1919, 66th Cong., 1st sess., pp. 6618–23; Walsh speech, "Self-Determination for Ireland," David Walsh Papers, Dannin Library, Holy Cross College (no specific file). For Walsh's dissent and contemporary Massachusetts politics, see John Flannagan, "The Disillusionment of a Progressive: U.S. Senator David I. Walsh and the League of Nations Issue," *New England Quarterly* 41 (1968):483–504.

39. *Boston Morning Globe*, Oct. 23, 1924, Scrapbook 33, David Walsh Papers; 72 *CR* 1930, 71st Cong., 2d sess., pp. 220, 224–227, 3976, 3980, 3983, 5158, 5292, 7421, 7514; *New York Times*, July 1, 1922, Aug. 6, 1922, Aug. 7, 1922, June 24, 1923, Jan. 16, 1924, Oct. 31, 1926, Jan. 31, 1930. Walsh's tariff appeal centered more on regional than on ideological lines, so he had little trouble gaining the support of the other Northeastern Democrats—Peter Gerry, Royal Copeland, and Robert Wagner. The Northeasterners thus joined the larger Democratic shift away from the party's traditional low-tariff position, but they still had different priorities from most of their colleagues, who wanted higher rates on agricultural, not manufacturing, products. 62 *CR* 1922, 67th Cong., 2d sess., pp. 11014–20 (Gerry); 72 *CR* 1930, 71st Cong., 2d sess., pp. 219, 222, 2609–10, 2618, 2621 (Copeland).

40. *New York Times*, March 18, 1929; 65 *CR* 1924, 68th Cong., 1st sess., pp. 6533–38.

41. Walsh press release, July 22, 1930, David Walsh Papers (no specific file); 63 *CR* 1922, 67th Cong., 3d sess., p. 65; 65 *CR* 1924, 68th Cong., 1st sess., p. 5137; 68 *CR* 1927, 69th Cong., 2d sess., pp. 1690, 1842; 69 *CR* 1928, 70th Cong., 1st sess., p. 6687; 74 *CR* 1931, 71st Cong., 3d sess., pp. 808–810; *New York Times*, Sept. 22, 1930. For more on Walsh and Cuba, see *Boston Post*, Dec. 17, 1930, Scrapbook 45, David Walsh Papers. Walsh employed many of these sentiments to justify his opposition to the Four Power Treaty, recommending anti-imperialism and open diplomacy as an alternative to the treaty; 62 *CR* 1922, 67th Cong., 2d sess., pp. 4253–55.

42. Walsh to Elizabeth Eastman, Feb. 11, 1929, Reel 41.61, NCPW Papers; *Holyoke Telegram-Transcript*, April 4, 1929, Scrapbook 33, David Walsh Papers; *Boston Post*, Jan. 30, 1931, Scrapbook 45, ibid.; 62 *CR* 1922, 67th Cong., 2d sess., pp. 8919, 8930; 66 *CR* 1925, 68th Cong., 2d sess., p. 1963; 68 *CR* 1927, 69th Cong., 2d sess., pp. 2430–31; 73 *CR* 1930, 71st Cong.,

special sess., pp. 319–322; *New York Times*, April 7, 1922, Jan. 27, 1929, April 28, 1929, June 30, 1929.

43. Some questioned the extent of King's commitment to the League, classifying the senator as only slightly more reliable to Wilson than Reed and David Walsh. See Gus Karger to William Howard Taft, Sept. 5, 1919, Reel 212, Taft Papers. For King on the League, see 58 *CR* 1919, 66th Cong., 1st sess., pp. 8706–17; Laurence Hauptman, "Utah Anti-Imperialist: Senator William H. King and Haiti, 1921–1934," *Utah Historical Quarterly* 41 (1973):116–127.

44. King to Thomas Walsh, Feb. 22, 1930, Box 183, Thomas Walsh Papers; 61 *CR* 1921, 67th Cong., 1st sess., pp. 1497–1503; 65 *CR* 1924, 68th Cong., 1st sess., pp. 7217–18; 70 *CR* 1929, 70th Cong., 2d sess., pp. 2408–09; *New York Times*, Dec. 2, 1925, Dec. 23, 1925, Feb. 17, 1926, Dec. 11, 1928, March 18, 1929.

45. King to Moorfield Storey, Jan. 21, 1922, Box 4, Moorfield Storey Papers, Library of Congress; King to Lewis Gannett, Nov. 5, 1923, Series 36, Box 11, Gruening Papers; Taft to James Sheffield, March 16, 1927, Series 1, Box 5, Sheffield Papers; 62 *CR* 1922, 67th Cong., 2d sess., pp. 8950–55; 64 *CR* 1923, 67th Cong., 4th sess., pp. 1117–31; 67 *CR* 1925, 69th Cong., 1st sess., pp. 493, 7584; *New York Times*, March 13 and 26, 1927. On Russell's opposition to the King visit, see Russell to Kellogg, March 11, 1927, SDA 838.00/2296. The domestic conservative even carried his case to the Communist-front All-America Anti-Imperialist League, which he told in a 1928 address that the Haitians deserved "full and complete freedom"; *New York Times*, May 14, 1928. As a "strong Wilson supporter," though, King would not criticize the origins of the occupation, since he refused to assume "responsibility for openly criticizing the acts of the Woodrow Wilson administration"; King quoted in Ernest Angell to Moorfield Storey, March 11, 1922, Box 4, Storey Papers.

46. King to Thomas Walsh, Feb. 22, 1930, Box 183, Thomas Walsh Papers; 62 *CR* 1922, 67th Cong., 2d sess., pp. 4006, 4714, 6949–6950; 65 *CR* 1924, 68th Cong., 1st sess., pp. 6685–6687; 67 *CR* 1926, 69th Cong., 1st sess., pp. 1567, 2360; *New York Times*, Jan. 8, 1922, Feb. 19, 1922, Feb. 27, 1923, March 4, 1923, April 26, 1927.

47. 57 *CR* 1919, 65th Cong., 3d sess., pp. 3335–37; 61 *CR* 1921, 67th Cong., 1st sess., pp. 4854–55; 62 *CR* 1922, 67th Cong., 2d sess., pp. 690–696; 64 *CR* 1923, 67th Cong., 4th sess., pp. 2489–97; 67 *CR* 1925, 69th Cong., special sess., pp. 291–296; *New York Times*, March 19, 1922, Oct. 16, 1923, Nov. 23, 1923, Aug. 27, 1925.

48. 61 *CR* 1921, 67th Cong., 1st sess., pp. 4989–90; 62 *CR* 1922, 67th Cong., 2d sess., pp. 5795–5809; 68 *CR* 1926, 69th Cong., 2d sess., pp. 2229–30; *New York Times*, Jan. 1, 1924; William King, "Mexico's Policy of Confiscation," *Current History*, June 1926. King praised Ambassador Sheffield as a man "true to American rights and interests" who would have succeeded

in forcing a good settlement had the State Department not "embarrassed" him.

49. David Burner, *Politics of Provincialism: The Democratic Party in Transition, 1918–1932* (New York: Alfred A. Knopf, 1968). For the most recent coverage of the Democrats at this time, see Douglas Craig, *After Wilson: The Struggle for the Democratic Party, 1920–1934* (Chapel Hill: University of North Carolina Press, 1992).

50. See Thomas Knock, *To End All Wars: Woodrow Wilson and the Quest for a New World Order* (New York: Oxford University Press, 1992).

8. The Decline of Anti-Imperialism

1. For information on the economic problems in the Midwest, see *Statistical Abstract of the United States, 1931* (Washington, D.C.: Government Printing Office, 1931), pp. 334–335.

2. Blaine press release, March 1930, Box 62, Blaine Papers; *New York Times*, May 7, May 8, May 18, and Oct. 9, 1930; Sioux Falls *Argus-Leader*, Oct. 27, Oct. 28, and Nov. 1, 1930; Patrick O'Brien, "William H. McMaster: Agrarian Dissenter during 'Normalcy,'" *Emporia State Research Studies* 20 (1972):27–33. The first conservative attempts to use their foreign policy positions against the peace progressives came in the Washington and Montana contests of 1928, which Dill himself conceded were "desperate" fights. *Seattle Post-Intelligencer*, Nov. 1 and 4, 1928; *Helena Independent*, Oct. 30, 1928; Dill to Norris, July 26, 1934, Box 1, Norris Papers.

3. Norris to Henry Field, April 11 and 16, 1932, Box 23, Norris Papers; *New York Times*, May 29 and June 8, 1932; Richard Luthin, "Smith Wildman Brookhart: Insurgent Agrarian Politician," *Agricultural History* 25 (1951):194–195.

4. Blaine press releases, July 28, July 30, Aug. 1, Aug. 4, Aug. 13, Aug. 16, Aug. 26, Aug. 27, Sept. 13, and Sept. 14, 1932; Shipstead speech, Sept. 9, 1932; Chapple press release, Sept. 16, 1932; all in Box 24, Crownhart Family Papers, Wisconsin State Historical Society, Madison; *Milwaukee Journal*, Sept. 9 and 13, 1932; *Wisconsin State Journal*, Sept. 16, 1932; *New York Times*, Sept. 21 and 22, 1922. On expectations that Blaine would win, from differing perspectives, see Charles Crownhart, Jr., form letter, July 31, 1932, Box 23, Crownhart Family Papers; and *Wisconsin State Journal*, Sept. 18, 1932.

5. *Tacoma Times*, July 12, 1934; *Tacoma Ledger*, July 12, 1934; *Seattle Post-Intelligencer*, July 12, 1934; *Washington Post*, July 16, 1934; *Chehalis Bee-Nugget*, July 20, 1934; *Spokane Spokesman-Review*, June 29, 1934; all clippings in Box 3, Dill Papers. For Dill's explanation on why he retired, see Dill, "Why I Quit the Senate," *Saturday Evening Post*, Dec. 15, 1934.

6. Wheeler to Paul Kellogg, Box 1, Wheeler Papers. On the progressives and New Deal liberalism, see Ronald Feinman, *Twilight of Progressivism:*

Western Republican Senators and the New Deal (Baltimore: Johns Hopkins University Press, 1981); and Otis Graham, Jr., *An Encore for Reform: The Old Progressives and the New Deal* (New York: Oxford University Press, 1967).

7. Bone to James Bryan, Feb. 13, 1926, Box 3, Homer Bone Papers, University of Puget Sound Library; Bone to Ralph Benjamin, March 6, 1932; Dill to Bone, May 2, 1932; Bone to Editor, *Grain and Feed Journal*, May 25, 1932; Saul Haas to Bone, May 31, 1932; Bone to Fred Shorter, Oct. 12, 1932; all in Box 9, ibid.; Bone speeches, KMO (Aug. 23, 1932), KHQ (Aug. 29, 1932), n.d.[1932], Box 7, Saul Haas Papers, Allen Library, University of Washington. See also John Wiltz, *In Search of Peace: The Senate Munitions Inquiry, 1934–36* (Baton Rouge: Louisiana State University Press, 1963), pp. 43–45.

8. Borah to William Carlson, Aug. 16, 1929; Borah to Ray McKaig, Sept. 9, 1929; Borah to G. A. Bailey, Nov. 26, 1929; all in Box 285, Borah Papers; 70 *CR* 1929, 70th Cong., 2d sess., p. 3836; 72 *CR* 1930, 71st Cong., 2d sess., pp. 2597, 7525–29 (Dill); 75 *CR* 1932, 72d Cong., 1st sess., pp. 8751 (Nye), 11096–98 (Howell), 11104–05 (Shipstead, Borah).

9. Blaine to Fountain City Cooperative Creamery Association, March 15, 1930, Box 62, Blaine Papers; 71 *CR* 1929, 71st Cong., 1st sess., pp. 4380–81 (Norris, Wheeler); 72 *CR* 1930, 71st Cong., 2d sess., p. 7426 (Norris); 75 *CR* 1932, 72d Cong., 1st sess., pp. 11103–04 (Norris).

10. For the continuing moral arguments, see 70 *CR* 1929, 70th Cong., 2d sess., pp. 3838 (Norris), 3843–44 (Wheeler); 71 *CR* 1929, 71st Cong., 1st sess., pp. 4402 (Norris), 4418–20 (Wheeler); 76 *CR* 1932–33, 72d Cong., 2d sess., pp. 380 (Dill), 1916–19 (Borah), 1923 (La Follette).

11. Howell to Wayland Magee, April 23, 1932, Box 74, Howell Papers; Borah press release, April 16, 1934, Box 782, Borah Papers; 75 *CR* 1932, 72d Cong., 1st sess., p. 11105 (Borah); 76 *CR* 1933, 72d Cong. 2d sess., pp. 379–380 (Dill), 384 (Shipstead), 885 (Howell), 1917–18 (Borah).

12. 78 *CR* 1934, pp. 6314 (Shipstead, Tydings), 6380–81 (Norris). The vote is at p. 6385.

13. Norris to G. G. Douglas, Feb. 3, 1934, Box 41, Norris Papers; Wheeler speech, "The Five Year Plan," 1934, Box 16, Wheeler Papers; 74 *CR* 1931, 71st Cong., 4th sess., pp. 4671–74 (Wheeler), 7038 (Borah); *Chicago Tribune*, March 22, 1932 (Brookhart).

14. Borah to John McKeon, May 11, 1931, Box 326, Borah Papers; Borah to Cane Machine Tool Corporation, Jan. 9, 1932, Box 349, ibid.; Norris to Albert Coyle, June 26, 1933; Norris to George Peek, Jan. 13, 1934; both in Box 41, Norris Papers; 74 *CR* 1931, 71st Cong., 4th sess., pp. 4674 (Wheeler), 7039–40 (Borah); *New York Times*, Sept. 7, 1930 (Wheeler), Aug. 14, 1931 (Borah). Brookhart, who accepted a position as special adviser at the AAA after his 1932 defeat, spent most of his time there working to better the prospects for American-Soviet trade. See Brookhart to Norris,

Aug. 23, 1933, Box 41, Norris Papers; Luthin, "Smith W. Brookhart," p. 195.

15. Wheeler speech, "Silver," n.d.[1934]; Wheeler Chicago speech, "Silver," n.d. [1934]; both in Box 16, Wheeler Papers.

16. Norris to John Simpson, June 30, 1931, Box 34, Norris Papers; Borah to Charles Wood, July 6, 1931; Borah to Alexander Gumberg, July 18, 1931; both in Box 314, Borah Papers; Blaine speech, Oconto, Wis., Aug. 5, 1931, Box 71, Blaine Papers; 75 *CR* 1931–32, 72 Cong., 1st sess., pp. 1097–98 (Shipstead), 1104–05 (Norris), 1111–13 (Blaine); *New York Times*, July 20, 1931 (Shipstead). For Norris' increasingly pessimistic outlook on the European scene, see Norris to Val Peter, June 26, 1931; Norris to John Simpson, June 30, 1931; Norris to Henry Wallace, Jan. 21, 1931; all in Box 34, Norris Papers.

17. Blaine speech, Oconto, Wis., Aug. 5, 1931, Box 71, Blaine Papers; Borah to Herbert Hoover, July 23, 1931, Box 314, Borah Papers; Borah speech, Boise, Aug. 13, 1931, Box 782, ibid.; 75 *CR* 1931–32, 72d Cong., 1st sess., pp. 537 (Wheeler), 1078, 1097–99 (Shipstead), 1114–15 (Blaine); *New York Times*, Oct. 24, 1931 (Borah). Borah had called for linkage between debts and reparations as early as 1927. Borah press release, Sept. 15, 1927, Box 780, Borah Papers. Blaine contended that the Howell Amendment would represent an expression of international goodwill by the United States; *New York Times*, March 29, 1931.

18. Blaine speech, Oconto, Wis., Aug. 5, 1931, Box 71, Blaine Papers (emphasis added); Borah press release, Dec. 24, 1931, Box 782, Borah Papers; Norris to Alex Geist, Dec. 31, 1931, Box 34, Norris Papers; 75 *CR* 1931–32, 72d Cong., 1st sess., pp. 1086–87 (Nye), 1099 (Shipstead).

19. "Memo of Our Conversation with Senator Borah," Oct. 10, 1932, Box 5, Levinson Papers; 75 *CR* 1932, 72d Cong., 1st sess., pp. 8490–94 (Borah); *New York Times*, July 8, 1932 (Shipstead).

20. 76 *CR* 1933, 72d Cong., 2d sess., pp. 1279–90.

21. Borah to A. G. Calvin, Oct. 8, 1932, Box 336, Borah Papers; Borah to H. G. Chase, Nov. 25, 1932, Box 334, ibid.; Blaine speech, New London, Wis., July 28, 1932, Box 71, Blaine Papers; Howell to Roy Hopkins, April 2, 1932; Howell to editor, *Barron's*, April 28, 1932; both in Box 35, Howell Papers; 76 *CR* 1933, 72d Cong., 3d sess., p. 2478 (Frazier).

22. Borah to Thomas Bowles, April 21, 1934, Box 380, Borah Papers. On the Johnson Amendment, see Wayne Cole, *Roosevelt and the Isolationists, 1932–45* (Lincoln: University of Nebraska Press, 1983), pp. 81–94.

23. Bryce Wood, *The Making of the Good Neighbor Policy* (New York: Columbia University Press, 1961), pp. 13–59; Frank Fox, *J. Reuben Clark: The Public Years* (Provo: Brigham Young University Press, 1980), p. 519. For an alternative view of Hoover's policy, see Alexander DeConde, *Herbert Hoover's Latin American Policy* (Stanford: Stanford University Press, 1951).

24. 74 *CR* 1931, 71st Cong., 4th sess., pp. 4221–22 (Borah); 75 *CR* 1932, 72d

Cong., 1st sess., pp. 2243–47 (La Follette, Borah), 13151–55 (Nye, Wheeler). Borah argued that the reservation was needed in the treaty to secure U.S. sovereignty over the Panama Canal Zone; after the vote, Dorothy Detzer criticized the "terrible reservations" and wondered why more progressives had not joined La Follette in his fight; Detzer to Villard, Jan. 29, 1932, Series C, Box 12, File 5, WILPF Papers.

25. Franklin Roosevelt, "Our Foreign Policy," *Foreign Affairs*, July 1928, pp. 573–586. For more on the early Good Neighbor Policy, see "Draft by Sumner Welles of a Statement on Latin American Policy," Feb. 21, 1933, in Edgar Nixon, ed., *Franklin D. Roosevelt and Foreign Affairs*, 3 vols. (Cambridge, Mass.: The Belknap Press of Harvard University Press, 1969), vol. 1, pp. 18–19. For more on Cuban affairs, see *FRUS*, 1933, vol. 5, pp. 278, 355–356, 363–365; Welles to Roosevelt, May 18, 1933, in Nixon, *Franklin D. Roosevelt*, vol. 1, p. 141; Robert Dallek, *Franklin D. Roosevelt and American Foreign Policy, 1932–1945* (New York: Oxford University Press, 1979), p. 61; E. David Cronon, "Interpreting the New Good Neighbor Policy: The Cuban Crisis of 1933," *Hispanic American Historical Review* 39 (1959):538–567. For the administration response to Welles's interventionist tactics, see Wood, *Making of the Good Neighbor Policy*, pp. 61–64. For more on early Roosevelt policy toward Haiti, see *FRUS*, 1933, vol. 5, pp. 733, 747; Roosevelt press conference, Aug. 9, 1933, in Nixon, *Franklin D. Roosevelt*, vol. 1, p. 349.

26. Borah to Gruening, April 14, 1933, Box 357, Borah Papers; Borah to Grau, Oct. 6, 1933; Borah to Harry Ward, Oct. 7, 1933; both in Box 360, ibid.; *New York Times*, Sept. 12 and 18, 1933; *The Nation*, July 25, 1934.

27. *FRUS*, 1933, vol. 4, pp. 17, 55–137, 164, 215–216; Phillips to Roosevelt, Nov. 4, 1933, in Nixon, *Franklin D. Roosevelt*, vol. 1, pp. 459–460; Gruening to Dorothy Detzer, Feb. 9, 1933; Detzer to Hubert Herring, Nov. 1, 1933; both in Series C, Box 13, File 6, WILPF Papers; Roosevelt speech, Woodrow Wilson Foundation Dinner, Dec. 28, 1933, in Nixon, *Franklin D. Roosevelt*, vol. 1, pp. 558–563; Ernest Gruening, *Many Battles: The Autobiography of Ernest Gruening* (New York: Liveright, 1974), pp. 160–165. On the importance of the Montevideo agreements in an international context, see Dorothy Jones, *Code of Peace: Ethics and Security in the World of Warlord States* (Chicago: University of Chicago Press, 1991), pp. 77–80.

28. Roosevelt to House, Feb. 16, 1935, File 222, President's Personal File, Franklin Roosevelt Papers, Franklin Roosevelt Presidential Library, Hyde Park, N.Y.; Cole, *Roosevelt and the Isolationists*, p. 357. On Roosevelt's hope for a national liberal party and his fear of an independent peace progressive ticket, see Arthur Schlesinger, Jr., *The Age of Roosevelt: The Coming of the New Deal* (Boston: Houghton Mifflin, 1958), pp. 504–505; idem, *The Age of Roosevelt: The Politics of Upheaval* (Boston: Houghton Mifflin, 1960), pp. 53, 142. On concessions by the President to the peace progressives on

other issues, see Dallek, *Franklin D. Roosevelt*, pp. 62, 71 (disarmament); Cole, *Roosevelt and the Isolationists*, pp. 137–138; Schlesinger, *Roosevelt: The Politics of Upheaval*, pp. 311–313 (holding company bill).

29. Gruening to Grau, Oct. 3, 1933, Series 27, Box 6, Gruening Papers; Gruening to Col. House, Sept. 5, 1933, Series 36, Box 10, ibid.; Hubert Herring, "Cuba Cleans House," *The Nation*, Aug. 30, 1933; idem, "Haiti's New Deal," ibid., Nov. 22, 1933; idem, "Rebellion in Puerto Rico," ibid., Nov. 29, 1933; *The Nation*, Aug. 23, Aug. 30, Sept. 20, Oct. 11, and Dec. 6, 1933; *New York Times*, July 26, 1933.

30. Gruening to Beals, Sept. 6, 1933, Series 2, Box 1, Gruening Papers; *New Republic*, Sept. 20, 1933, Oct. 4, 1933, Dec. 27, 1933, Jan. 31, 1934; Carleton Beals, "American Diplomacy in Cuba," *The Nation*, Jan. 17, 1934; idem, *The Coming Struggle for Latin America* (New York: Lippincott, 1937), p. 256.

31. Inman to Gruening, March 1, 1937, Series 36, Box 10, Gruening Papers; Samuel Guy Inman, "The New Deal at Montevideo," *The Nation*, Jan. 24, 1934; Ernest Gruening, "Our Era of Imperialism Nears Its End," *New York Times*, June 10, 1934; *The Nation*, Jan. 10, 1934, April 17, 1935; Oswald Garrison Villard, "Issues and Men," *The Nation*, Jan. 10 and Sept. 12, 1934; *New York Times*, Feb. 11, 1934, July 8, 1934, June 9, 1935, June 30, 1935, Aug. 22, 1935 (Inman); *New York Times*, Nov. 4, 1934, Oct. 17, 1935, Oct. 28, 1935, Dec. 15, 1935, Dec. 27, 1935 (Gruening).

32. Borah to Albert Campbell, May 22, 1933, Box 357, Borah Papers; 78 *CR* 1934, 73d Cong., 2d sess., pp. 9007–12, 10375–76 (Borah), 9818 (Bone), 9955 (Norris), 10371, 10384 (Dill); *New York Times*, March 2, 1934 (Borah); the amendment votes are at p. 10363; the final vote is at p. 10385. Dill's action indicated a retreat from 1933, when he argued that reciprocity "would gradually build up a world market for our surplus and would benefit all agriculture"; Dill, "1933 from Progressives' Viewpoint," Jan. 2, 1933, Box 3, Dill Papers.

33. Borah to Jess Hawley, n.d.[Feb. 1935?]; Borah to Edwin Borchard, Feb. 6, 1935; Borah to Joseph Kaschmitter, March 19, 1935; Borah to DeVere Frantz, Feb. 7, 1935; all in Box 421, Borah Papers; *Milwaukee Journal*, Jan. 2, 1935; Portes Gil quoted in *Louisville Courier-Journal*, Feb. 4, 1935, and *Weekly News Sheet*, Feb. 8, 1935; Cole, *Roosevelt and the Isolationists*, pp. 358–359. For administration response to the Borah resolution, see Hull to Pittman, n.d.[Feb. 1935?], Box 421, Borah Papers.

34. 79 *CR* 1935, 74th Cong., 1st sess., pp. 1671, 2571, 2740, 2868–72, 2921.

35. 74 *CR* 1931, 71st Cong., 4th sess., pp. 3460–68, 5587 (Frazier); 75 *CR* 1932, 72d Cong., 1st sess., pp. 12429, 12465 (Frazier), 12445 (Nye).

36. Frazier to Dorothy Detzer, March 28, 1932, Series C, Box 15, Folder 35, WILPF Papers; 75 *CR* 1932, 72d Cong., 1st sess., pp. 9637–39 (Frazier), 9688 (Nye), 12444 (Norris); *New York Times*, Jan. 10, 1932 (Frazier, Norris).

37. Blaine statement, March 1932, Series C, Box 15, File 35, WILPF Papers; Borah speech, Minneapolis, Aug. 3, 1932, Box 782, Borah Papers; 75 *CR* 1932, 72d Cong., 1st sess., pp. 9467 (Shipstead), 9688 (Nye), 13169 (Blaine), 13173–74 (La Follette).

38. Dill said that he liked the bill's provisions for increasing construction of naval vessels at Western shipyards, and he also noted that with Japan "acting more and more belligerent on the Pacific Coast" the United States had to do something. Nonetheless, in the days before the vote he admitted that he was confused about what choice he should make on the bill; Dill to Jeanette Rankin, n.d.[1929], Reel 41.61, NCPW Papers.
   Some of the old arguments about disarmament remained in force as late as the Vinson bill debate. Frazier rebuked the "might makes right" arguments of the preparedness forces for repeating the mistakes that led up to World War I and, interestingly, quoted James Vardaman on the uselessness of military preparedness in the years before it. Nye charged that the bill would permit the Navy "to go the all quarters of the earth, there to make war as we have made war in times past, down in Nicaragua, for example"; 78 *CR* 1934, 73d Cong., 2d sess., pp. 3683–87 (Frazier), 3781 (Nye).

39. 78 *CR* 1934, 73d Cong., 2d sess., pp. 3494–95 (Frazier), 3688–91 (Borah), 3780–85 (Nye), 3794–3800 (Bone); Cole, *Roosevelt and the Isolationists,* p. 78.

40. Cole, *Roosevelt and the Isolationists,* pp. 141–162; Wayne Cole, *Senator Gerald P. Nye and American Foreign Relations* (Minneapolis: University of Minnesota Press, 1962), pp. 60–96. See also John Wiltz, *In Search of Peace: The Senate Munitions Inquiry, 1934–1936* (Baton Rouge: Louisiana State University Press, 1963).

41. Gerald Nye, "Should the Government Exercise Direct Control of Munitions Industries?" *Congressional Digest* 13 (1934):266–270; emphasis added.

42. Nye Committee preliminary report, April 1, 1935, Box 23, Nye Papers; 79 *CR* 1935, 74th Cong., 1st sess., pp. 444–461 (Nye), 477–478 (Bone).

43. *Washington News,* Sept. 12 and 19, 1934; *Washington Herald,* Sept. 12, 1934; *Washington Post,* Sept. 15, 1934.

44. The exception to this pattern was Frazier, who, though hardly disagreeing with his colleague, kept to most of the older arguments; 79 *CR* 1935, 74th Cong., 1st sess., pp. 3097–98, 3101.

45. 79 *CR* 1935, 74th Cong., 1st sess., pp. 7828–35, 7975–90.

46. Norris to B. F. Eberhart, March 8, 1924, Box 1, Norris Papers (Nebraska); Robins to Salmon Levinson, Feb. 13, 1926, Box 42, Levinson Papers; Villard to Borah, Dec. 26, 1922, File 304, Villard Papers; Johnson to Archibald Johnson, June 5, 1926; Johnson to Boys, Dec. 11, 1926; Johnson to Boys, Feb. 2, 1927; Johnson to Archibald Johnson, May 30, 1930; all in *The Diary Letters of Hiram Johnson* (hereafter *Diary Letters*), 5 vols. (New York: Garland, 1983), vol. 5; *The Times* (London), Jan. 19, 1925; Richard

Coke Lower, *A Bloc of One: The Political Career of Hiram W. Johnson* (Stanford: Stanford University Press, 1993), p. 190. Johnson also ridiculed Smith Brookhart, sniffing "personally, he does not amount to much. He is a great, big simpleton, but likable. His economic views are unsound as one can well imagine"; Johnson to Hiram Johnson, Jr., March 29, 1926, *Diary Letters*, vol. 4.

47. *New York Times*, Jan. 4, 1924, March 30, 1926; Johnson to Sons, Jan. 17, 1927; Johnson to Hiram Johnson, Jr., Jan. 7, 1928; both in *Diary Letters*, vol. 4.

48. 66 *CR* 1924, 68th Cong., 2d sess., pp. 2985–93; 67 *CR* 1925, 69th Cong., 1st sess., pp. 2437, 6249, 6568; *New York Times*, Dec. 24, 1922, Jan. 14, 1923, March 9, 1923, July 26, 1923, Nov. 28, 1923, July 26, 1926; Howard DeWitt, "Hiram W. Johnson and American Foreign Policy" (Ph.D. diss., University of Arizona, 1972), pp. 183–203. Johnson dismissed Frank Kellogg as a "weak, timid, and a fearful man" with the "flexibility of a courier and the servility of a sycophant" whose appointment meant that "our foreign affairs in the future will be conducted by Great Britain"; Johnson to Boys, Jan. 13, 1925, *Diary Letters*, vol. 4. Virtually the only European leader of whom Johnson held a positive view was Mussolini, whom he termed the "marvel of modern Italy"; *New York Times*, April 7, 1923.

49. 71 *CR* 1929, 71st Cong., 1st sess., p. 5592; 72 *CR* 1930, 71st Cong., 2d sess., pp. 2593–94, 7126–27, 7151; *New York Times*, May 27, 1924, Oct. 29, 1929; Lower, *A Bloc of One*, p. 165. Unlike many who feared Filipino immigration, Johnson did not advocate independence for the Philippines, pronouncing himself "somewhat vexed" on the question; 72 *CR* 1930, 71st Cong., 2d sess., p. 2594.

50. 68 *CR* 1925–26, 69th Cong., 2d sess., pp. 990–997; Johnson to Hiram Johnson, Jr., Feb. 11, 1927, *Diary Letters*, vol. 4; *New York Times*, July 26, 1926.

51. 70 *CR* 1929, 70th Cong., 2d sess., pp. 1133–36, 2526–33; Johnson to Archibald Johnson, Jan. 19 and 26, 1929, *Diary Letters*, vol. 5; *New York Times*, Dec. 16, 1928, Jan. 4, 1929, Jan. 16, 1929, Feb. 1, 1929.

52. Johnson (for Moses and Robinson), Report of the Minority, *Limitation and Reduction of Naval Armament*, U.S. Senate, Committee on Foreign Relations, 71st Cong., 2d sess., Report 1080, pt. 2; Johnson to Hiram Johnson, Jr., April 19 and May 30, 1930; Johnson to Boys, May 3 and July 21, 1930; all in *Diary Letters*, vol. 5; *New York Times*, April 25, May 15, and May 16, 1930; Lower, *A Bloc of One*, p. 172. Shipstead, the other member of the Foreign Relations Committee to oppose the treaty, did not concur in Johnson's Minority Report and filed one of his own.

53. 74 *CR* 1931, 71st Cong., 1st sess., pp. 1360–61; 78 *CR* 1934, 73d Cong., 2d sess., pp. 9959–64, 10370–71; 79 *CR* 1935, 74th Cong., 1st sess., pp. 2868–74; DeWitt, "Hiram W. Johnson," p. 253.

54. 75 *CR* 1931–32, 72d Cong., 1st sess., pp. 1077–84, 15082–84; 76 *CR* 1933, 72d Cong., 2d sess., pp. 1272–79; Johnson to Boys, Jan. 9, 1932, *Diary Letters*, vol. 5; Lower, *A Bloc of One*, p. 256. The group's nationalistic perspective also appeared in the increasingly close ties between the peace progressives and Bronson Cutting (R–New Mexico), who served as head of the "Bondholder's Committee for Republic of Cuba Bonds," a group that advocated refusing to renew the American commercial treaty with Cuba unless the Cuban government promised to repay American-held bonds in full. For Cutting's distance from the peace progressives in the 1920s, see Cutting speech, Santa Fe, Sept. 12, 1928, Box 82, Bronson Cutting Papers, Library of Congress. For his Cuban activities, see *Boston Transcript*, Sept. 1, 1934, copy in Box 99, ibid.

55. Akira Iriye, *The Origins of the Second World War in Asia and the Pacific* (New York: Longman, 1987), pp. 1–20.

56. Borah to George Anderson, Aug. 30, 1932, Box 336, Borah Papers; Borah to Levinson, March 1, 1933, Box 5, Levinson Papers; *New York Times*, Sept. 25, 1931, Oct. 15, 1931, Nov. 21, 1931, Feb. 23, 1932, March 13, 1932 (Borah), Dec. 6, 1931, Feb. 7, 1932 (Shipstead).

57. 75 *CR* 1932, 72d Cong., 1st sess., p. 2861 (Dill); *New York Times*, Oct. 10, 1931, Feb. 21, 1932 (Brookhart), Feb. 4, 1932 (Dill); Richard Lowitt, *George W. Norris: The Persistence of a Progressive, 1913–1933* (Urbana: University of Illinois Press, 1971), p. 533.

58. Smith to Edith Rogers, Feb. 26, 1932, Reel 70.33, CME Papers; Gruening to Villard, Nov. 18, 1931, File 1477, Villard Papers; Villard to Detzer, Feb. 5, 1932, Series C, Box 19, File 6, WILPF Papers; Levinson to Robins, Feb. 28, 1932; Levinson to Raymond Buell, March 31, 1932; both in Box 24, Robins Papers; Gruening in *Portland Evening News*, Oct. 14, 1931; Levinson, "Disarmament, Manchuria, and the Pact," Feb. 3, 1932, Collective Documents Group A, SCPC; Charles Chatfield, *For Peace and Justice: Pacifism in America, 1914–1941* (Knoxville: University of Tennessee Press, 1971), pp. 223–230; Walter Steel, *Walter Lippmann and the American Century* (New York: Vintage Books, 1980), pp. 328–330.

59. The most extreme example of this came from Nye, who touted the embargo as a way to "cripple those agencies which stand so staunchly in the way of the removal of fears and danger of war," the arms manufacturers. In contrast, Frazier, the peace progressive who most consistently maintained the 1920s perspective on disarmament-related issues, "strongly" supported the arms embargo simply as "one way that we can show our disapproval of wars." Nye to Barbara Wylie, Jan. 31, 1933; Frazier to Barbara Wylie, Feb. 1, 1933; both in Reel 41.61, NCPW Papers.

60. Johnson to Hiram Johnson, Jr., Feb. 13, 1932, *Diary Letters*, vol. 5; *New York Times*, March 6, May 21, and Dec. 1, 1934 (Borah), May 1 and Dec. 20, 1934 (Nye); Cole, *Roosevelt and the Isolationists*, p. 79.

61. Borah speech, Minneapolis, Aug. 3, 1932, Box 782, Borah Papers; *New York Times*, Feb. 16, 1931 (Brookhart).

62. Borah to Levinson, Jan. 15, 1932, Box 5, Levinson Papers; Shipstead interview, *Washington Herald*, Dec. 14, 1932, clipping in Box 16, Shipstead Papers; Blaine speech, New London, Wis., July 28, 1932, Box 71, Blaine Papers; *New York Times*, Feb. 4, 1932 (Dill). Norris also began to espouse sentiments hostile to the Europeans not unlike those of Johnson, condemning the League powers for their relentless "hatred of the American government" because it refused to cancel the debts; Norris to Harley Moorhead, May 4, 1932, quoted in Lowitt, *George W. Norris: Persistence*, pp. 532–533.

63. Borah to Joel Hartman, April 19, 1933; Borah to Ethel Jamison, May 30, 1933; Borah to William Berman, Oct. 9, 1933; all in Box 359, Borah Papers; Borah to Isaac Long, Feb. 24, 1934, Box 380, ibid.; Borah to Louis Birviyi, July 13, 1932; Borah speech, 1932, American-Hungarian delegation; both in Box 338, ibid.; Borah to Protective League for Hungarian Refugees, Dec. 8, 1934, Box 381, ibid. In February 1935 Wheeler argued that the Western Europeans needed to recognize Germany's power and permit some German expansion in Central Europe, but he contended that they had to act that way because German might dictated compromise, not because he sympathized with the Hitler regime. In any case, he called for the United States to stay out of the revision entirely; Cole, *Roosevelt and the Isolationists*, p. 126.

64. Borah speech, Council on Foreign Relations, Jan. 8, 1934, Box 782, Borah Papers; 78 *CR* 1934, 73d Cong., 2d sess., p. 317 (Norris); *New York Times*, June 24, 1933 (Wheeler).

65. 78 *CR* 1934, 73d Cong., 2d sess., pp. 624–625. Dill also retained a vaguely internationalist outlook on economic affairs. See J. M. Perry to Dill, March 21, 1933, copy in Box 10, Bone Papers; Dill to Stephen Chadwick, Feb. 22, 1932, Box 8, Stephen Fowler Chadwick Papers, Allen Library, University of Washington.

66. 79 *CR* 1935, 74th Cong., 1st sess., pp. 479–490 (Johnson), 695–703, 879–884 (Borah), 873–876 (Shipstead); Johnson to Hiram Johnson, Jr., Jan. 13, 1935, *Diary Letters*, vol. 5.

67. Norris to Ray Harmelink, Feb. 5, 1935; Norris to Beatrice White, Dec. 28, 1935; both in Box 136, Norris Papers; 79 *CR* 1935, 74th Cong., 1st sess., pp. 965–966, 1142; Lowitt, *George W. Norris: Persistence*, pp. 73–74. Wheeler, the other pro-Court peace progressive remaining in the Senate, also reversed his position in 1935. Citing explosive situations in the Saar, the Balkans, and Manchuria as examples of the "belligerent propensities of Old World powers," the Montana senator asked his colleagues to take note of "the tenseness of Europe into which the proponents of the World Court adherence would have us cast our lot." He went on to describe the Court as "the meeting place for the political discussions of strictly Euro-

pean national difficulties"; Wheeler speech, NBC radio, Jan. 29, 1935, Box 16, Wheeler Papers.

68. Bone 1935 interview, Box 17, Bone Papers; Norris to Richard Hartley, Oct. 14, 1935, Box 136, Norris Papers; Norris to Jeanette Rankin, Dec. 21, 1935, Reel 41.61, NCPW Papers; 79 *CR* 1935, 74th Cong., 1st sess., pp. 13776–89 (Bone), 13778–79 (Nye), 13955–56 (Borah), 14430–32 (Johnson).

Epilogue

1. 91 *CR* 1945, 79th Cong., 1st sess., pp. 7973–94. For the UN views of the other peace progressives, see 91 *CR* 1945, 79th Cong., 1st sess., pp. 6917–18 (La Follette), 8116–23 (Shipstead).

2. For the peace progressives on the Spanish Civil War, see Wayne Cole, *Roosevelt and the Isolationists, 1932–45* (Lincoln: University of Nebraska Press, 1983), pp. 223–230. The best coverages of the contest between the peace progressives and Roosevelt are Cole, *Roosevelt and the Isolationists*, and Manfred Jonas, *Isolationism in America, 1935–1941* (Ithaca: Cornell University Press, 1966), pp. 32–99, although Robert James Maddox, *William E. Borah and American Foreign Policy* (Baton Rouge: Louisiana State University Press, 1970), also offers some interesting perspectives.

3. See Thomas Knock, *To End All Wars: Woodrow Wilson and the Quest for a New World Order* (New York: Oxford University Press, 1992).

4. Johnson, quoted in Richard Lowitt, *George W. Norris: The Persistence of a Progressive, 1913–1923 (Urbana: University of Illinois Press, 1971)*, p. 1.

Select Bibliography

Manuscript Collections

Emily Greene Balch Papers. Swarthmore College Peace Collection.
Carleton Beals Papers. Mugar Library, Boston University.
Bingham Family Papers. Sterling Memorial Library, Yale University.
Hugo Black Papers. Library of Congress, Washington, D.C.
John Blaine Papers. Wisconsin State Historical Society, Madison.
Homer Bone Papers. University of Puget Sound Library.
William E. Borah Papers. Library of Congress, Washington, D.C.
William E. Borah Scrapbooks (microfilm). Library of Congress, Washington, D.C.
Joseph Bristow Papers. Kansas State Historical Society, Topeka.
Smith Brookhart Papers. Iowa State Historical Society, Des Moines.
William Cabell Bruce Papers. Alderman Library, University of Virginia.
Nicholas Murray Butler Papers. Butler Library, Columbia University.
Carrie Chapman Catt Papers. Library of Congress, Washington, D.C.
Stephen Fowler Chadwick Papers, Allen Library, University of Washington.
Moses Clapp Papers. Minnesota State Historical Society, St. Paul.
Collective Documents Group A. Swarthmore College Peace Collection.
Committee on Militarism in Education Papers. Swarthmore College Peace Collection.
Crownhart Family Papers. Wisconsin State Historical Society, Madison.
Albert Cummins Papers. Iowa State Historical Society, Des Moines.
Bronson Cutting Papers. Library of Congress, Washington, D.C.
C. C. Dill Papers. Eastern Washington Historical Society, Spokane.
Jonathan Dolliver Papers. Iowa State Historical Society, Des Moines.
Roy Empey Papers. Wisconsin State Historical Society, Madison.
William Evjue Papers. Wisconsin State Historical Society, Madison.
Fellowship of Reconciliation Papers. Swarthmore College Peace Collection.
Miller Freeman Papers. Allen Library, University of Washington.
Carter Glass Papers. Alderman Library, University of Virginia.
Ernest Gruening Papers. Rasmuson Library, University of Alaska, Fairbanks.
Alexander Gumberg Papers. Wisconsin State Historical Society, Madison.
Saul Haas Papers. Allen Library, University of Washington.

George Hoar Papers. Massachusetts State Historical Society, Boston.

Halbert Hoard Papers. Wisconsin State Historical Society, Madison.

Herbert Hoover Commerce Files. Herbert Hoover Presidential Library, West Branch, Iowa.

Robert Howell Papers. Nebraska State Historical Society, Lincoln.

Charles Evans Hughes Papers. Library of Congress. Washington, D.C.

Hiram Johnson Papers. Bancroft Library, University of California, Berkeley.

Wesley Jones Papers. Allen Library, University of Washington.

Frank Kellogg Papers. Minnesota State Historical Society, St. Paul.

La Follette Family Papers. Library of Congress, Washington, D.C.

Salmon Levinson Papers. Regenstein Library, University of Chicago.

Walter Lippmann Papers. Sterling Memorial Library, Yale University.

Henry Cabot Lodge Papers. Massachusetts State Historical Society, Boston.

William Logan Papers. University of Iowa Library, Iowa City.

A. Lawrence Lowell Papers. Pusey Library, Harvard University.

Earle Mayfield Papers. Lauinger Library, Georgetown University.

Frank McCoy Papers. Library of Congress, Washington, D.C.

Edmond Meany Papers. Allen Library, University of Washington.

Edwin Thomas Meredith Papers. University of Iowa Library, Iowa City.

NAACP Papers. Library of Congress, Washington D.C.

National Council for the Prevention of War Papers. Swarthmore College Peace Collection.

George Norris Papers. Library of Congress, Washington, D.C.

George Norris Papers. Nebraska State Historical Society, Lincoln.

Gerald Nye Papers. Herbert Hoover Presidential Library, West Branch, Iowa.

Pennsylvania Committee for Total Disarmament Papers. Swarthmore College Peace Collection.

Key Pittman Papers. Library of Congress, Washington, D.C.

Raymond Robins Papers. Wisconsin State Historical Society, Madison.

Franklin Roosevelt Papers. Franklin Roosevelt Presidential Library, Hyde Park, N.Y.

John Nevin Sayre Papers. Swarthmore College Peace Collection.

Henrik Shipstead Papers. Minnesota State Historical Society, St. Paul.

Moorfield Storey Papers. Library of Congress, Washington, D.C.

Henry Suzzallo Papers. Allen Library, University of Washington.

William Howard Taft Papers. Library of Congress, Washington, D.C.

Edwin Van Valkenberg Papers. Houghton Library, Harvard University.

James Vardaman Papers. Mississippi State Historical Society, Jackson.

Oswald Garrison Villard Papers. Houghton Library, Harvard University.

Robert Wagner Papers. Lauinger Library, Georgetown University.

David Walsh Papers. Dannin Library, Holy Cross College.

Thomas Walsh Papers. Library of Congress, Washington, D.C.

War Resisters League Papers. Swarthmore College Peace Collection.

Burton Wheeler Papers. Montana State Historical Society, Helena.

Women's International League for Peace and Freedom Papers. Swarthmore College Peace Collection.

Women's Peace Society Papers. Swarthmore College Peace Collection.

Women's Peace Union Papers. Swarthmore College Peace Collection.

John Downey Works Papers. Bancroft Library, University of California, Berkeley.

Collections of Published Documents

Foot, Solomon. *Miscellaneous Speeches and Addresses.* Washington, D.C., 1866.

Guide to U.S. Elections. Washington, D.C.: Congressional Quarterly Publications, 1976.

Hale, John P. *Speeches, etc., of John Hale, 1846–1865.* Washington, D.C., 1848–1865.

Johnson, Hiram. *Diary Letters of Hiram Johnson.* New York: Garland, 1983.

Link, Arthur S., ed. *Papers of Woodrow Wilson.* 68 vols. Princeton: Princeton University Press, 1966–1993.

Manning, William Ray, ed. *Diplomatic Correspondence of the United States: Inter-American Affairs, 1831–1860.* 12 vols. Washington, D.C.: Carnegie Endowment for International Peace, 1932–1939.

Marburg, Theodore, and Horace Flack, eds. *The Taft Papers on the League of Nations.* New York: Macmillan, 1920.

Morrison, Elting, ed. *The Letters of Theodore Roosevelt.* 8 vols. Cambridge, Mass.: Harvard University Press, 1951.

Nixon, Edgar, ed. *Franklin Roosevelt and Foreign Affairs.* 3 vols. Cambridge, Mass.: The Belknap Press of Harvard University Press, 1969.

Roosevelt, Theodore. *Letters of Theodore Roosevelt and Henry Cabot Lodge.* 2 vols. New York: Scribner's, 1925.

Rutland, Robert, ed. *The Papers of George Mason.* 3 vols. Chapel Hill: University of North Carolina Press, 1970.

Storing, Herbert J., ed. *The Anti-Federalist: Writings by the Opponents of the Constitution.* Chicago: University of Chicago Press, 1985.

Index